Lecture Notes in Computer Science 5967

Commenced Publication in 1973
Founding and Former Series Editors:
Gerhard Goos, Juris Hartmanis, and Jan van Leeuwen

Anna Esposito   Nick Campbell   Carl Vogel
Amir Hussain   Anton Nijholt (Eds.)

Development of Multimodal Interfaces: Active Listening and Synchrony

Second COST 2102 International Training School
Dublin, Ireland, March 23-27, 2009
Revised Selected Papers

 Springer

Volume Editors

Anna Esposito
Second University of Naples, and IIASS
Via Pellegrino 19
84019 Vietri sul Mare (SA), Italy
E-mail: iiass.annaesp@tin.it

Nick Campbell
Carl Vogel
The University of Dublin, Centre for Language and Communication Studies
Trinity College, Dublin 2, Ireland
E-mail: {nick; vogel}@tcd.ie

Amir Hussain
University of Stirling, Department of Computing Science & Mathematics
Stirling, FK9 4LA, Scotland, UK,
E-mail: ahu@cs.stir.ac.uk

Anton Nijholt
University of Twente, Faculty of Electrical Engineering,
Mathematics and Computer Science
P.O. Box 217, 7500 AE, Enschede, The Netherlands
E-mail: anijholt@cs.utwente.nl

Library of Congress Control Number: Applied for

CR Subject Classification (1998): H.5, H.4, H.5.2, H.3, I.4, I.2.10

LNCS Sublibrary: SL 3 – Information Systems and Application,
incl. Internet/Web and HCI

ISSN   0302-9743
ISBN-10   3-642-12396-1 Springer Berlin Heidelberg New York
ISBN-13   978-3-642-12396-2 Springer Berlin Heidelberg New York

springer.com

© Springer-Verlag Berlin Heidelberg 2010
Printed in Germany

Typesetting: Camera-ready by author, data conversion by Scientific Publishing Services, Chennai, India
Printed on acid-free paper   06/3180

This book is dedicated to beauty: we seek beauty in our scientific research, and we find our efforts justified when we catch glimpses during the pursuit

Preface

This volume brings together, through a peer-revision process, the advanced research results obtained by the European COST Action 2102: Cross-Modal Analysis of Verbal and Nonverbal Communication, primarily discussed for the first time at the Second COST 2102 International Training School on *"Development of Multimodal Interfaces: Active Listening and Synchrony"* held in Dublin, Ireland, March 23–27 2009.

The school was sponsored by COST (European Cooperation in the Field of Scientific and Technical Research, www.cost.esf.org) in the domain of Information and Communication Technologies (ICT) for disseminating the advances of the research activities developed within the COST Action 2102: "Cross-Modal Analysis of Verbal and Nonverbal Communication" (cost2102.cs.stir.ac.uk)

COST Action 2102 in its third year of life brought together about 60 European and 6 overseas scientific laboratories whose aim is to develop interactive dialogue systems and intelligent virtual avatars graphically embodied in a 2D and/or 3D interactive virtual world, capable of interacting intelligently with the environment, other avatars, and particularly with human users.

The main focus of the school was the development of multimodal interfaces. Traditional approaches to multimodal interface design tend to assume a "ping-pong" or "push-to-talk" approach to speech interaction wherein either the system or the human interlocutor is active at any one time. This is contrary to many recent findings in conversation and discourse analysis, where the definition of a "turn" or even an "utterance" is found to be very complex. People don't "take turns" to talk in a typical conversational interaction, but they each contribute actively to the joint emergence of a "common understanding." The sub-theme of the school was "Synchrony and Active Listening" selected with the idea to identify contributions that actively give support to the ongoing research into the dynamics of human spoken interaction, to the production of multimodal conversation data and to the subsequent analysis and modelling of interaction dynamics, with the dual goal of appropriately designing multimodal interfaces, as well as providing new approaches and developmental paradigms.

The themes of the papers presented in this book emphasize theoretical and practical issues for modelling human–machine interaction, ranging from the attempt in describing "the spacing and orientation in co-present interaction" to the effort for developing multimodal interfaces, collecting and analyzing interaction data and emergent behavior as well as analyzing the use of nonverbal and pragmatic elements of exchanges, implementing discourse control and virtual agents and using active listening in computer speech processing. The papers included in this book benefited from the live interactions in person among the many participants of the successful meeting in Dublin. Over 100 established and apprenticing researchers converged for the event.

The editors would like to thank the ESF COST- ICT Programme for its support in the realization of the school and the publication of this volume, and in particular the COST Science Officers Gian Mario Maggio, Francesca Boscolo, Bernie O'Neill, and Matteo Razzanelli for their constant help, guidance, and encouragement and

Sietske Zeinstrafor for supporting and guiding the publication effort. That the event was successful owes this partly to more individuals than can be named, but notably: Marcus Furlong, Jean Maypother, Alena Moison. Our special appreciation goes to Gaetano Scarpetta, Dean of the International Institute for Advanced Scientific Studies, who supported and encouraged the editorial process including collecting, reviewing, and improving the manuscripts submitted. The IIASS team, Tina Marcella Nappi, Michele Donnarumma, and Antonio Natale, are acknowledged for their precious technical support in the organization of this volume.

In addition, the editors are grateful to the contributors for making this book a scientifically stimulating compilation of new and original ideas. Finally, the editors would like to express their greatest appreciation to all the members of the COST 2102 International Scientific Committee for their rigorous and invaluable scientific revisions, for their dedication, and their priceless selection process.

Anna Esposito
Nick Campbell
Carl Vogel
Amir Hussain
Anton Nijholt

Organization

International Advisory and Organizing Committee

Anna Esposito   Second University of Naples and IIASS, Italy
Nick Campbell   Trinity College Dublin, Dublin 2, Ireland
Carl Vogel   Trinity College Dublin, Dublin 2, Ireland
Marcos Faundez-Zanuy   Escola Universitaria Politecnica de Mataro, Spain
Amir Hussain   University of Stirling, UK
Anton Nijholt   University of Twente, The Netherlands

International Scientific Committee

Uwe Altmann   Technische Universität Dresden, Germany
Hicham Atassi   Brno University of Technology, Czech Republic
Nikos Avouris   University of Patras, Greece
Ruth Bahr   University of South Florida, USA
Gérard Bailly ICP   Grenoble, France
Marian Bartlett   University of California, San Diego, USA
Štefan Beňuš   Constantine the Philosopher University, Nitra, Slovakia
Niels Ole Bernsen   University of Southern Denmark, Denmark
Jonas Beskow   Royal Institute of Technology, Sweden
Horst Bishof   Technical University Graz, Austria
Peter Birkholz   Aachen University, Germany
Jean-Francois Bonastre   Universitè d'Avignon, France
Nikolaos Bourbakis   ITRI, Wright State University, Dayton, USA
Maja Bratanić   University of Zagreb, Croatia
Antonio Calabrese   Istituto di Cibernetica – CNR, Naples, Italy
Eric Cambria   University of Stirling, Scotland, UK
Paola Campadelli   Università di Milano, Italy
Nick Campbell   Trinity College Dublin, Dublin 2, Ireland
Antonio Castro Fonseca   Universidade de Coimbra, Portugal
Aleksandra Cerekovic   Faculty of Electrical Engineering, Croatia
Josef Chaloupka   Technical University of Liberec, Czech Republic
Mohamed Chetouani   Universitè Pierre et Marie Curie, France
Gerard Chollet   CNRS-LTCI, Paris, France
Muzeyyen Ciyiltepe   Gulhane Askeri Tip Academisi, Ankara, Turkey
Anton Čižmár   Technical University of Košice, Slovakia
Nicholas Costen   Manchester Metropolitan University, UK
Vlado Delic   University of Novi Sad, Serbia
Marion Dohen   ICP, Grenoble, France
Giuseppe Di Maio   Second University of Naples, Italy
Francesca D'Olimpio   Second University of Naples, Italy

Wojciech Majewski	Wroclaw University of Technology, Poland
Pantelis Makris	Neuroscience and Technology Institute, Cyprus
Maria Marinaro	Salerno University and IIASS, Italy
Raffaele Martone	Second University of Naples, Italy
Dominic Massaro	University of California - Santa Cruz, USA
Olimpia Matarazzo	Second University of Naples, Italy
David McNeill	University of Chicago, USA
Nicola Melone	Second University of Naples, Italy
Katya Mihaylova	University of National and World Economy, Sofia, Bulgaria
Michal Mirilovič	Technical University of Košice, Slovakia
Peter Murphy	University of Limerick, Ireland
Antonio Natale	Salerno University and IIASS, Italy
Eva Navas	Escuela Superior de Ingenieros, Bilbao, Spain
Delroy Nelson	University College London, UK
Géza Németh	Budapest University of Technology, Hungary
Friedrich Neubarth	Research Institute for Artificial Intelligence, Austria
Giovanna Nigro	Second University of Naples, Italy
Anton Nijholt	University of Twente, The Netherlands
Jan Nouza	Technical University of Liberec, Czech Republic
Igor Pandzic	Faculty of Electrical Engineering, Croatia
Harris Papageorgiou	Institute for Language and Speech Processing, Greece
Ana Pavia	Spoken Language Systems Laboratory, Portugal
Catherine Pelachaud	Université de Paris 8, France
Paolo Pedone	Second University of Naples, Italy
Bojan Petek	University of Ljubljana, Slovenia
Harmut R. Pfitzinger	University of Munich, Germany
Francesco Piazza	Università Politecnica delle Marche, Italy
Neda Pintaric	University of Zagreb, Croatia
Isabella Poggi	Università di Roma 3, Italy
Ken Prepin	LTCI lab, CNRS, Telecom-ParisTech, France
Jiří Přibil	Academy of Sciences, Czech Republic
Anna Přibilová	Slovak University of Technology, Slovakia
Michael Pucher	Telecommunications Research Center Vienna, Austria
Jurate Puniene	Kaunas University of Technology, Lithuania
Roxanne Raine	University of Twente, The Netherlands
Giuliana Ramella	Istituto di Cibernetica – CNR, Naples, Italy
Kari-Jouko Räihä	University of Tampere, Finland
José Rebelo	Universidade de Coimbra, Portugal
Luigi Maria Ricciardi	Università di Napoli "Federico II", Italy
Maria Teresa Riviello	Second University of Naples, and IIASS, Italy
Matej Rojc	University of Maribor, Slovenia
Algimantas Rudzionis	Kaunas University of Technology, Lithuania
Vytautas Rudzionis	Kaunas University of Technology, Lithuania
Milan Rusko	Slovak Academy of Sciences, Slovak Republic

Sponsors

The following organizations sponsored and supported the International Training
School:

- European COST Action 2102 *"Cross-Modal Analysis of Verbal and Nonverbal
  Communication"* (cost2102.cs.stir.ac.uk)
- Second University of Naples, Faculty and Department of Psychology, Faculty
  of Science, Mathematics, and Physics and Department of Computer
  Engineering & Informatics, Italy
- International Institute for Advanced Scientific Studies "E.R. Caianiello"
  (IIASS), Italy
- Regione Campania (Italy)
- Provincia di Salerno (Italy)
- The School of Computer Science and Statistics, Trinity College Dublin
- Science Foundation Ireland (RFP 05/RF/CMS002)

Table of Contents

Spacing and Orientation in Co-present Interaction 1
  Adam Kendon

Group Cohesion, Cooperation and Synchrony in a Social Model of
Language Evolution 16
  Carl Vogel

Pointing Gestures and Synchronous Communication Management 33
  Kristiina Jokinen

How an Agent Can Detect and Use Synchrony Parameter of Its Own
Interaction with a Human? 50
  Ken Prepin and Philippe Gaussier

Accessible Speech-Based and Multimodal Media Center Interface for
Users with Physical Disabilities 66
  Markku Turunen, Jaakko Hakulinen, Aleksi Melto, Juho Hella,
  Tuuli Laivo, Juha-Pekka Rajaniemi, Erno Mäkinen,
  Hannu Soronen, Mervi Hansen, Santtu Pakarinen, Tomi Heimonen,
  Jussi Rantala, Pellervo Valkama, Toni Miettinen, and
  Roope Raisamo

A Controller-Based Animation System for Synchronizing and Realizing
Human-Like Conversational Behaviors 80
  Aleksandra Čereković, Tomislav Pejša, and Igor S. Pandžić

Generating Simple Conversations 92
  Mark ter Maat and Dirk Heylen

Media Differences in Communication 102
  Roxanne B. Raine

Towards Influencing of the Conversational Agent Mental State in the
Task of Active Listening 113
  Stanislav Ondáš, Elisabetta Bevacqua, Jozef Juhár, and
  Peter Demeter

Integrating Emotions in the TRIPLE ECA Model 122
  Kiril Kiryazov and Maurice Grinberg

Manipulating Stress and Cognitive Load in Conversational Interactions
with a Multimodal System for Crisis Management Support 134
  Andreea Niculescu, Yujia Cao, and Anton Nijholt

Sentic Computing: Exploitation of Common Sense for the Development
of Emotion-Sensitive Systems 148
   Erik Cambria, Amir Hussain, Catherine Havasi, and Chris Eckl

Face-to-Face Interaction and the KTH Cooking Show 157
   *Jonas Beskow, Jens Edlund, Björn Granström,
   Joakim Gustafson, and David House*

Affect Listeners: Acquisition of Affective States by Means of
Conversational Systems 169
   Marcin Skowron

Nonverbal Synchrony or Random Coincidence? How to Tell the
Difference 182
   Fabian Ramseyer and Wolfgang Tschacher

Biometric Database Acquisition Close to "Real World" Conditions 197
   *Marcos Faundez-Zanuy, Joan Fàbregas,
   Miguel Ángel Ferrer-Ballester, Aythami Morales,
   Javier Ortega-Garcia, Guillermo Gonzalez de Rivera, and
   Javier Garrido*

Optimizing Phonetic Encoding for Viennese Unit Selection Speech
Synthesis 207
   Michael Pucher, Friedrich Neubarth, and Volker Strom

Advances on the Use of the Foreign Language Recognizer 217
   Rytis Maskeliunas, Algimantas Rudzionis, and Vytautas Rudzionis

Challenges in Speech Processing of Slavic Languages (Case Studies in
Speech Recognition of Czech and Slovak) 225
   Jan Nouza, Jindrich Zdansky, Petr Cerva, and Jan Silovsky

Multiple Feature Extraction and Hierarchical Classifiers for Emotions
Recognition 242
   Enrique M. Albornoz, Diego H. Milone, and Hugo L. Rufiner

Emotional Vocal Expressions Recognition Using the COST 2102 Italian
Database of Emotional Speech 255
   *Hicham Atassi, Maria Teresa Riviello, Zdeněk Smékal,
   Amir Hussain, and Anna Esposito*

Microintonation Analysis of Emotional Speech 268
   Jiří Přibil and Anna Přibilová

Speech Emotion Modification Using a Cepstral Vocoder 280
   Martin Vondra and Robert Vích

Analysis of Emotional Voice Using Electroglottogram-Based Temporal
Measures of Vocal Fold Opening 286
  Peter J. Murphy and Anne-Maria Laukkanen

Effects of Smiling on Articulation: Lips, Larynx and Acoustics 294
  Sascha Fagel

Neural Basis of Emotion Regulation 304
  Luigi Trojano

Automatic Meeting Participant Role Detection by Dialogue Patterns ... 314
  Jing Su, Bridget Kane, and Saturnino Luz

Linguistic and Non-verbal Cues for the Induction of Silent Feedback 327
  Maria Koutsombogera and Harris Papageorgiou

Audiovisual Tools for Phonetic and Articulatory Visualization in
Computer-Aided Pronunciation Training 337
  Bernd J. Kröger, Peter Birkholz, Rüdiger Hoffmann, and
  Helen Meng

Gesture Duration and Articulator Velocity in
Plosive-Vowel-Transitions 346
  Dominik Bauer, Jim Kannampuzha, Phil Hoole, and Bernd J. Kröger

Stereo Presentation and Binaural Localization in a Memory Game for
the Visually Impaired 354
  Vlado Delić and Nataša Vujnović Sedlar

Pathological Voice Analysis and Classification Based on Empirical
Mode Decomposition 364
  Gastón Schlotthauer, María E. Torres, and Hugo L. Rufiner

Disfluencies and the Perspective of Prosodic Fluency 382
  Helena Moniz, Isabel Trancoso, and Ana Isabel Mata

Subjective Tests and Automatic Sentence Modality Recognition with
Recordings of Speech Impaired Children 397
  David Sztaho, Katalin Nagy, and Klara Vicsi

The New Italian Audio and Video Emotional Database 406
  Anna Esposito and Maria Teresa Riviello

Spoken Dialogue in Virtual Worlds 423
  Gérard Chollet, Asmaa Amehraye, Joseph Razik, Leila Zouari,
  Houssemeddine Khemiri, and Chafic Mokbel

Author Index 445

Spacing and Orientation in Co-present Interaction

Adam Kendon

Philadelphia, Pennsylvania
adamk@dca.net

Abstract. An introduction to the way in which people arrange themselves spatially in various kinds of focused interaction, especially conversation. It is shown how participants may jointly establish and maintain a spatial-orientational system, referred to as an F-formation, which functions as part of the way in which participants in conversation preserve the integrity of their occasion of interaction and jointly manage their attention.

Keywords: Face-to-face interaction, interpersonal spacing, proxemics, posture, orientation.

I begin with a very elementary observation: behaviour of any sort occurs in a three-dimensional world and any activity whatever requires space of some sort. There are three aspects to this requirement: first, any behaving organism requires space within which it can carry out its activities, whatever these may be. If a bird is to build a nest, there must be space available in a tree or bush or hole in the ground where it may do this. If a cat is to take a nap, there must be a space where it can lie down in whatever posture it might choose. Second, the spaces available must have physical properties that will allow the behaving organism to do what it needs to do: A cat seeking somewhere to sleep must at least have firm ground on which to rest – it cannot lie down on water - and it must have space enough in which to repose. Third, however, the space that is required and the possibilities for action it provides for must also somehow be *differentiated* from other spaces. There must be some way in which the behaving organism can distinguish between the space that is presently its *use-space*, and other space, which is irrelevant. This is because any line of activity that an organism engages in involves a highly selective relationship between the acts in which it engages and the information from the environment that, in some way or other, is being used in guiding those acts. Now an organism can actively select out what is relevant from what is irrelevant and so, in terms of where it can be seen to pay attention and in terms of its physical orientations and spatial movements, it can be observed to differentiate its present use-space from irrelevant space. However, whenever possible, it seems, advantage is taken of the differentiated features of the environment that are just about always present to assist it in doing this. Another way to put this is to say that an organism exercises control over what stimulation it deals with partly through selective attention but partly through selecting spaces in the environment that, because of their physical characteristics, shut out some kinds of stimulation, let in others and, within the space itself, make available what is needed.

A. Esposito et al. (Eds.): COST 2102 Int. Training School 2009, LNCS 5967, pp. 1–15, 2010.

Now since different kinds of activity involve different kinds of relationships between space from all these points of view, the nature of the use-space that an organism has varies according to what it is doing. The use space of the cat when sleeping in its basket in the sun in front of its favourite window is quite different from its use-space when it is eating and different again from when it is sitting before a mouse-hole waiting for the mouse to emerge. Likewise, the use-space of someone sitting at a desk before a computer is quite different from the use-space of the same person who gets up from the desk and stands before his bookcase searching for a book.

A further point to bear in mind is that activities are always hierarchically organized. Individual acts, moment to moment behavioural events, are not just concatenated together, one after the other, but are always under the guidance of a larger plan of some sort. Correspondingly, the space selected within which an activity sequence is carried out, is selected in such a way that the various elements within the activity system as a whole can all be accomplished. So, for a given project, a segment of the environment is demarcated and, so to speak, preserved for the duration of the project, notwithstanding the fact that at any given stage of the project not all of this segment

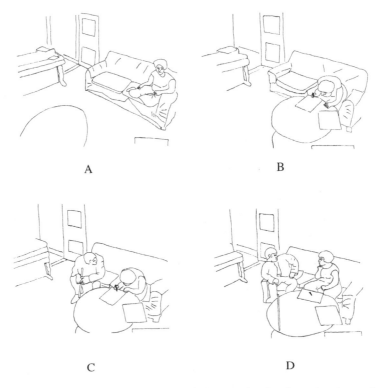

Fig. 1. A: W sits on sofa watching television. B: W at work colouring a drawing on the coffee table. C: H enters and sits beside W, watching her at work. D: H and W orient jointly to one another for conversation. (Drawings after stills from a video-tape made under the direction A. E. Scheflen, Project on Human Communication, Bronx State Hospital, Bronx, New York, c. 1970).

of space may be being used. I will now illustrate these points more specifically, turning from behavin g organisms" in general to human beings.

Consider someone engaged in watching television (Fig. 1 A). In order to do this a situation must be established where the person can remain in some comfort for a relatively extended period of time in such a way that they can have an unobstructed view of the television screen. Hence they claim for themselves, for the duration of this activity, a place where they can put their body and sustain it in comfort, and a space that permits them to maintain an orientation to the television set suited to the requirements of their vision. The result is that, within the wider space within which the television is kept, the television watcher, for the duration of this activity, through his behaviour, defines a segment of the environment which, as one might say, is taken up with, or consumed by the activity of watching television - and this segment of the environment extends from the place of sitting, in a sort of more or less narrow cone, outwards to the television set, possibly a little beyond, and possibly a little wider than would be required if the eyes were only to be focused on the screen.

Now such a space, which I have referred to as a *transactional segment*, comes into existence and is sustained only for the duration of given project. When a person changes his project, the way in which he organizes himself in relation to the space around him and the kind of space that is claimed for the line of activity he is engaged in, changes. Changes in spatial and postural orientation are, for this reason, excellent clues to major junctures in the flow of behaviour. So, as we may note, when the television watcher changes to doing something else (Fig. 1 B) as, in this case, she changes to engage in painting or colouring something on a piece of paper in front of her, we get a different kind of organization and a different kind of transactional segment.

It is of course common in any setting for several individuals to be co-present. How they orient and space themselves in relation to one another directly reflects how they may be involved with one another. Here (Fig. 1 C) someone enters the room and establishes himself in such a way that the activity of the first person becomes the object of his attention, much as television had been for the first person earlier. We see that this is so from the way in which he has positioned his body and oriented its various parts, especially from how he has oriented his face, so that, as far as we can judge, he is focusing his visual attention upon the activities of the hands of the woman who he has sat close to. Here, the second individual's transactional segment encompasses and includes the first individual. Note, however, that the first individual does not change her orientation nor the way her hands are directed toward the paper in front of her. She continues her activity as before and so maintains the transactional segment she had established for this before. Thus although we may say that the second individual has set up a transactional segment that overlaps the transactional segment of the first individual, the first individual does not include the other's transactional segment in her own.

Moments later, however, perhaps when she had come to the end of a particular segment in her painting, she changes her posture and orientation and now she *does* include the other in her transactional segment (Fig. 1 D) The second individual still includes the woman in his transactional segment, but he, too, has changed his posture, mirroring that of the woman. Now they include each other in their transactional segments, however, that they do this in a particular way. They now have a *shared_* transactional segment, a *common* space, within which their *common* activity - in this case exchanging spoken utterances - can be carried on.

Note that, in this case, we may see how the shared space between them is created by a sort of reciprocation of upper body and head orientation, but that this also serves to establish what is *not* in the shared space. The very bodies of the participants, thus, can come to serve in the process of making and maintaining the boundary between the inner world of current engagement, that is between them, and the outer, irrelevant, *disattended* world beyond.

We notice, more generally, then, that when people engage together in talk with one another - what Erving Goffman distinguished as "direct engagement", which is characteristic of "focused interaction" - they very often enter into a distinctive spatial-orientational arrangement (Fig. 2), which is jointly sustained. By the way the participants are oriented in such an arrangement they make available a shared, inner space, which is distinct from an outer space.

Fig. 2. A conversational grouping showing a jointly sustained spatial-orientational arrangement

Note that this spatial-orientational arrangement is sustained through time and its maintenance requires the cooperation of all the participants. They cooperate together to keep up this arrangement and, indeed, if you watch a grouping of this sort over a period of time it is possible to see how, if one participant changes somewhat his spatial position or orientation, the others will adjust their spatial position or orientation to compensate, so that the circular arrangement we see here is maintained. Spatial-orientational arrangements sustained over time in this manner, through the cooperation of the participants, will be referred to as *formations*. There are, in fact, a number of different kinds of formations that people enter into commonly, their spatial-orientational organization differing according to how the participants' attentional involvements are organized. This is governed, of course, by what it is the participants have gathered together to do. Some of the commonly occurring different types of formations will be illustrated briefly later.

The formation that is characteristic of a conversation of the sort we have just introduced in which, as we have seen, the participants organize themselves so that a *shared transactional space* is established and maintained, has been referred to as an *F-formation* and, as may be seen from Fig. 3, we can distinguish various functional spaces within it, functional spaces which are, as one might say, "generated" by the systemic relationships of the behaving individuals.

Fig. 3. An example of a conversational group organized as an F-formation with the main functional spaces indicated. For explanation see text.

The shared, inner space, called here the o-space, which the participants actively cooperate to sustain, is the space reserved for the main activity of the occasion. In conversation this is the exchange of utterances organized around a common theme. This space is surrounded by a narrower one, here called the p-space, which provides for the placement of the participant's bodies and also personal things such as briefcases, handbags, and the like, which are typically treated as in some way a part of a person, even though physically separate. To become a member of a formation of this sort, you have to be in the p-space and, if you come from outside an ongoing formation, and seek to join it, then the participants have to alter their spacing in order to let you into this space. They must adjust their positions to make room for you. There are some interesting observations that can be made about how outsiders sometimes approach existing formations of this type, make a bid for entry, and then gain the permission of the insiders to become members. Only when the newcomer is able to be positioned so that he shares in the p-space is he found to be treated by the others as an equal participant in the proceedings.

Finally, there is the surrounding space, indefinite in extent, which can be identified as serving as a kind of buffer between the F-formation itself and the wider world beyond. This space has been termed the *r-space*. This is the space which, though not used directly by the activities of the interaction, is nevertheless actively monitored by the participants - and also noted by non-participants. This space can be established by considering the way in which different F-formations within the same setting space themselves (Fig. 4), by the way in which participants in the F-formations will take note of what is going on close by, but not beyond; and from the way in which outsiders behave when they enter this zone. For example, if an outsider is making a bid for entry into the ongoing formation, they may often wait within this zone. It thus also functions like a vestibule or visitor's room (Fig. 5). If, on the other hand, an outsider passes an F-formation on his way to somewhere else, and he passes within a certain distance of it, he is likely to display his disattention to the F-formation, for example by looking away or lowering his head as he passes. This also suggests how the F-formation exercises a sort of 'influence' over the space that immediately surrounds it and this is another way in which we can gain clues as to the extent of the so-called r-space.

Fig. 4. Spacing between adjacent F-formations

Fig. 5. An F-formation with three participants and an individual in 'outer position' awaiting an invitation to enter the F-formation. Note the split character of the outsider's orientation to the formation.

Fig. 6. An F-formation at Capodimonte, Naples, Italy. There are four participants and a fifth person that occupies an 'outer position' in the r-space. We have a *grouping* of five persons, but within this grouping there is one F-formation.

Fig. 7. An F-formation with three participants, a solo onlooker and a situation where one person is operating on another for practical purposes. Photo taken in 1978 near Lagaip, Enga Province, Papua New Guinea.

Fig. 8. An F-formation in Osaka, Japan

The circular form of the F-formation that we have illustrated - constructed for a particular kind of interactional activity, talk-mediated jointly focused interaction - is widely seen, from Naples (Fig. 6), to the Highlands of New Guinea (Fig. 7), to Japan (Fig. 8), to mention just a few places at random. But, just as the kind of interactional activity that it contains is not the only kind of interactional activity there is, so, correspondingly, this is not the only kind of spatial-orientational arrangement that people sustain. People come together in gatherings to sustain a variety of different interactional projects and the formations they enter into are structured to match. Note, in the picture from the New Guinea Highlands, the completely different kind of spatial-orientational arrangement that obtains between the two men on the left of this picture in which one is adjusting the wig of the other.

Fig. 9. An L-shaped dyadic F-formation (left) and a Vis-a-vis F-formation (right)

In the circular formation I have been discussing, note that the segment of the world outside the o-space that each participant can attend to if he wishes is *different* for each individual. This commonly arises when what is at issue for the participants is not in that outer world, but between them. Such arrangements are typical for talk about topics which are not related to things in the immediate environment. Where, as here, several participants are involved, the arrangement tends for this sort of talk to be circular. In conversations between just two persons, when the topic is disembodied, the arrangement tends to be "L-shaped". In this case, as you will see, the part of the environment to which each looks if he looks directly in front of him is different for each participant (Fig. 9 left). When, on the other hand, what is at issue between two people is their relationship, we often observe an arrangement where each faces the other directly (Fig. 9 right). This is common when people, in greeting, engage in a close salutation. Typically, when two people greet one another and then continue to talk together on some topic, they can be observed to begin with a face-to-face arrangement and then to shift to an L-arrangement as they move from salutation to talk. This may be seen in the brief sequence illustrated in Fig. 10.

Fig. 10a. GC (far left) announces his intention to greet AF (in striped shirt on right)

Fig. 10b. GC and AF approach one another, preparing to shake hands

Fig. 10c. GC and AF shake hands. Note how their bodies are oriented in a vis-à-vis

Fig. 10d. GC and AF remain in a vis-à-vis arrangement while they continue in a 'greeting' exchange

Fig. 10e. GC and AF talk together about other things. They are now together in a new L-arrangement and occupy a new domain in physical space.

When the participants are jointly concerned about something that *is* in the immediate environment, on the other hand - say looking at an elephant at the zoo or watching a baseball game together (Fig. 11) then, not surprisingly, they arrange themselves so that they can both attend to the same segment of the environment - and we have the so-called "side-by-side" arrangement. Of course, where the parties must also talk with one another, and there are more than two, you may get a kind of compromise between the side-by-side and the circular form, giving rise to a sort of horseshoe shape (Fig. 12).

Fig. 11. Pairs of people in "side-by-side" arrangement watching a baseball game. Note the almost equal spacing between the three pairs here. A further illustration of the way F-formations space themselves differently from one another than the persons that participate in them.

Fig. 12. The 'horseshoe' arrangement that can result when participants in "side-by-side" with more than two members wish to exchange spoken utterances

In the examples shown so far, the participants are potentially equal in status. That is, even if they do not exercise them, when participants are organized in these ways, they have the same right of participation as anyone else. In many encounters, however, this is not so. Some participants have different rights than others. This, too, is reflected in spatial-orientational arrangements. For perhaps obvious reasons, if there is a single party to whom all participants are to give equal attention, but that party's behaviour is different from everyone else's, then a spatial separation between the participants arises which reflects the kind of interaction that obtains as, for example, in the teacher-student interaction so common among us (Fig. 13) or in situations where one person is the performer, the rest constitute the audience (Fig. 14).

Fig. 13. Spatial arrangements typical of occasions when there is an unequal distribution of rights to initiate talk or action

As Goffman showed us long ago, there are many different ways in which people interact, many of which may not involve talk at all. Even so, in such cases, we can see that the spatial arrangements that people enter into derives in a significant way from the kinds of involvements they have with one another. Thus, sometimes people remain together as a distinct gathering, perhaps for no other reason than that they are all

Fig. 14. A 'common-focus' gathering, typical of situations where there is a division of role between performer and audience

simultaneously resting after a meal or waiting for something they are all going to do together, but are not, for the moment, in other ways jointly engaged. This can give rise to an assemblage of people which we might call a 'cluster' in which we can distinguish no formation, in the sense of a common spatial pattern in which all share, maintained through co-operative action (Fig. 15). Another kind of grouping, which does have a distinct arrangement, and one that often exhibits through relative centrality of placement and relative proximity the social relationships of the participants, is the group photograph arrangement (Fig. 16) - a highly specialized kind of human grouping that presumably came into existence only after 1839, after the invention of photography. Yet another type of formation we may recognize is the one that arises

Fig. 15. A 'cluster' where participants are grouped but do not enter into a formation with one another

when all the participants do something in unison. Various forms can be observed here, of which the military marching band (Fig. 17) is one well known type. Then, perhaps, we might usefully contrast the starting line of a race (Fig. 18) with a queue (Fig. 19). In both cases the participants are all intent on the same outcome, an outcome which can only be achieved separately by each individual and is not shared. In the race, everyone wants to win, and is given an equal chance at the start to do so, but winning, unlike buying tickets or boarding a bus is something that only one person can do. The all-or-nothing character of the race outcome, contrasted with the turn-taking organization of the queue, is nicely reflected in the difference in spatial-orientational arrangement that may be observed in these two cases.

Fig. 16. A group photograph

Fig. 17. A military parade band

Fig. 18. The starting line for a cross-country race

Fig. 19. A queue for the bus

In what I have sketched here, I have been dealing with the way in which people organize themselves in the service of their interactional projects when they are in environments which do not limit them in how they can arrange themselves. However, as I mentioned at the beginning, our environment is highly structured - it is full of different surfaces, barriers, furniture, passageways of all kinds. This environmental structuring partly constrains the kinds of formational structures of gatherings that can occur but, of course, the environment is itself structured by people to meet their interactional needs. Furniture arrangements, set up in various ways, provide a kind of permanent scaffolding for interactional occasions and, in some degree, take over the boundary-defining work that is done in unstructured environments by the bodies of the participants. However, often the fixed features of the space cannot be easily changed, interactions of various kinds may have to take place in circumstances that set constraints on its organization and this will have an impact on the nature of the interaction and set limits on what is possible within a given setting. This raises, of course, the issue of the interrelations between the structuring of the environment and the structuring of the interaction. This very complex and fascinating question is one that requires extended discussion. Unfortunately, this cannot be undertaken here.

What I have tried to do is to provide some elementary observations on how people organize themselves spatially in relation to their interactional projects. From this I hope it will be apparent that a development of the observational study of how people employ space, bodily orientation and positioning as a means of organizing the attentional structure of social encounters, might usefully add to our understanding of how interaction is conducted. These observations will also be helpful to those who seek to simulate the spatial aspects of social interaction, along with the simulation of exchanges of speech and gesture and facial expression.

Postscript

This paper is a slightly modified version of a presentation made to the American Anthropological Association in Philadelphia in 1988. The ideas discussed here were first formulated some years before, when I was a colleague of Albert Scheflen with the Project on Human Communication, Bronx State Hospital, Bronx, New York. I have altered it very little from the original text, the reading of which was coordinated with a slide presentation. The photographs inserted in the present text, most of them derived from the slides used in the original presentation, were all taken by myself and I reserve copyright for all of them. As this was a text written for oral presentation, no bibliographical citations have been included. I list below a brief selection of titles which form the background for what is presented here and which will be useful for anyone who wishes suggestions for further reading.

Erving Goffman (1961). "Fun in games" in *Encounters: Two Studies in the Sociology of Interaction*. Indianapolis, IN: Bobbs-Merrill; Erving Goffman (1963). *Behavior in Public Spaces* New York: Free Press of Glencoe; Erving Goffman (1971). Chapters 1 and 2 in *Relations in Public*. New York: Basic Books; Adam Kendon (1990). *Conducting Interaction*. Cambridge: Cambridge University Press; Adam Kendon (1992). The negotiation of context in face-to-face interaction. In Alessandro Duranti and Charles Goodwin, eds., *Rethinking Context: Language as an interactive phenomenon*. Cambridge: Cambridge University Press, pp. 323-334; Albert Scheflen with Norman Ashcraft (1976). *Human Territories: How We Behave in Space-Time*. Englewood Cliffs, NJ: Prentice-Hall, Inc.

Group Cohesion, Cooperation and Synchrony in a Social Model of Language Evolution

Carl Vogel[*]

Computational Linguistics Group, O'Reilly Institute,
Trinity College Dublin, Dublin 2, Ireland
vogel@tcd.ie

Abstract. Experiments conducted in a simulation environment demonstrated that both implicit coordination and explicit cooperation among agents leads to the rapid emergence of systems with key properties of natural languages, even under very pessimistic assumptions about shared information states. In this setting, cooperation is shown to elicit more rapid convergence on greater levels of understanding in populations that do not expand, but which grow more intimate, than in groups that may expand and contract. There is a smaller but significant effect of synchronized segmentation of utterances. The models show distortions in synonymy and homonymy rates that are exhibited by natural languages, but relative conformity with what one would rationally build into an artificial language to achieve successful communication: understanding correlates with synonymy rather than homonymy.

1 Background

Much work that explores models of the evolution of language follows aspects of the methodology utilized to demonstrate the efficacy of the Saussurean bidirectional sign in comparison to alternative strategies for communicating [3]. In that study, communicating agents sampled the behaviors of agents—exploring their utterance patterns in relation to intended meanings—in order to assess what mapping between meanings and expressions to use for interpretation and production. The assumptions of this model include that the agents have omniscience in sampling the mappings in use. That work remains important. However, in one direction, it has been stressed that not all of the pressures on language evolution are genetic, and cultural transmission of features of language must be taken into account [4]. In another direction, others acknowledge that at the outset of language evolution, it is most realistic not to assume that communicating agents share the same perspective on the world or individuation of what there is to talk about [8]. In a larger context of learning of social constructs, others have been exploring the interactions between social transmission and genetic encoding of

---

[*] I am grateful to Khurshid Ahmad and two anonymous reviewers for constructive feedback on an earlier manuscript. This research is supported by Science Foundation Ireland RFP 05/RF/CMS002.

A. Esposito et al. (Eds.): COST 2102 Int. Training School 2009, LNCS 5967, pp. 16–32, 2010.
© Springer-Verlag Berlin Heidelberg 2010

dispositions towards those constructs [2]. Nonetheless, when one wishes to scrutinize the nature of the very first stages in the evolution of natural language, it is necessary to focus on the social dimension, inclusive of the social interaction involving departure of agents from the pool of interlocutors, as well as addition of new agents. This is essential because if language as a communicative system is to persist as something that merits specific genetic encoding, it must first prove to have value in an earlier social context, and it must do so quickly.

The research presented here is in the same spirit as that of other researchers who have sought to work within a simulation framework that allows the experimentation with parameter settings [7]. The system allows the parameters that are not surprising: the number of agents at the outset, the number of discernible phonemes, the duration and number of conversations, memory limitations, fitness conditions, and so on [10]. Distinguishing features are that it assumes an infinite space of possible meanings that agents may comment upon to themselves or to each other, and that success of communication may or may not matter.[1] It is paramaterized to allow sorts of events that may happen to be randomly distributed, or to have more structure through an underlying Zipfian distribution. Although it builds in the assumption that agents witness the same events, it does not assume that they have the same perspective on events. The system was extended to parameterize the removal from the pool of communicating agents those who are not successful within it, and to allow the posing of questions about the denotations of phoneme sequences, but still without incorporating any sense of omniscience in supporting that coordination activity [5]. The alternatives to fitness-based elimination are random elimination and non-elimination. The system was extended further to support the parameterization of agent attunement to rhythm such as would enforce shared segmentation of utterance sequences. The system is put to use to identify parameter settings that lead to simulated communication systems that demonstrate relevant properties of natural languages as they are [6]. Some of those properties that are relevant are the resulting Zipfian distribution in the use of expressions, homonymy tolerance and synonymy avoidance [1]. A key dependent variable monitored is the level of mutual understanding that emerges, even under pessimistic assumptions.

The present work uses this system to explore the relationship between levels of cooperation among agents, the monotonicity of the pool of communicating agents, and synchronization in segmenting the speech signal. Levels of cooperation are modeled with levels of questioning about the meanings of terms. Either there is no questioning at all, and agents are deemed to simply coordinate with each other in a self-organizing fashion, or an agent may inspect its lexicon after a language games in an attempt to coordinate meanings with other interlocutors. This coordination process is fallible. However, it has the effect of creating focus on the individuation of utterance sequences, which does have a strong impact on the likelihood of overall understanding in communications (*a priori*, in order for agents to have the same meanings for words, they must have the same utterances that count as words). Two additional levels of coordination are explored

---

[1] Primal language may have involved bus-stop talk, and not information exchange.

here: questioning after every other language game and questioning after every language game. The initial population size for these experiments involves ten agents. The two conditions involve a monotonic decreasing pool of agents, based on the chances elimination of agents who happen not to be successful in communicating to a requisite threshold, or a non-monotonic pool in which agents may be added or deleted. Thus, the experiments reported here explore whether the level of cooperation interacts with monotonicity in the constitution of the pool of communicating agents. Group cohesion is approximated here by the dynamism of group membership. The most cohesive groups, in the sense used here, are those that are small in size, and may become smaller, but do not add new members. In terms of synchronization, the two levels considered are such that in the lowest level, the only focus on shared segmentation of the speech signal is during any questioning that happens through the corresponding setting of the level of coordination among agents, and in the higher level, agents, regardless of their inability to read each other's minds to determine intended meanings, do have a synchronized determination of the segmentation of utterances into individual units.[2]

1.1   Structure of the Work

Two experiments are described separately, although they differ in the setting of the synchrony parameter. In Section 2 and Section 3 the interactions of group cohesion and levels of cooperation are explored. Group cohesion is represented by two different possibilities, beginning from a small group of agents (ten). In the first condition, the group may lose members who are on average less than ten percent successful in their communications with the others—the group starts small and becomes only more intimate. The second condition is like the first except that new agents may also be admitted. In both cases, removal of agents is conducted at the end of a language game of ten turns. In the second condition, addition of up to one agent at the end of a language game is determined by coin toss. The first group may only contract; the second may expand and contract. The first group is deemed here to represent a greater level of cohesion than the second group. The other factor is in the level of cooperation manifest in the group. All agents behave the same way with respect to the level of cooperation. Cooperation is represented questions posed to the other agents about utterances used. Again, this happens at the end of language games: a random agent is selected, and for each item that the agent has remembered a meaning-phoneme association, the agent asks a random alternative agent if such an association exists for them, as well; if the queried agent has no association for the phoneme

---

[2] The experiments reported here were designed to test the three way interaction described in section 4. The results became available sequentially, with the results of the runs involving asynchronous segmentation of signals among interlocutors (Experiment 1) completing first. The analysis of those results as an experiment involving two interacting factors thus began while the rest of the runs (Experiment 2) were under way, and are described as a stand-alone experiment in a manuscript which is under review and which this paper draws upon.

sequence, then the inquiring agent deletes the association from its own lexicon, and if the queried agent has an association, then the inquiring agent replaces its own with that of the queried agent. This is suggestive of a capitulating implementation of omniscience in the model; however, actually it is acknowledgement of the fact that negotiation of meaning of terms does happen, and although communication of meaning by deixis an ostension is fallible, it does have the effect of urging interlocutors towards common use of terms (if not common understanding). So, the levels of this factor are: no questioning at all, questioning after every second language game and questioning after every language game. In all of the runs of the simulation system for the various other parameters of the system (see Section 1.2) are held constant. In particular, in the first experiment (Section 2) agents are held to be asynchronous in their segmentation of phoneme sequences. The outcome of this experiment is that questioning has a strong impact on improving average overall understanding only in cohesive groups.

The second experiment (Section 3) reconsiders these interactions, but in the context of another factor. Here, agents are further constrained than in the first experiment. In the first experiment, agents perceive and comment on the same events in the world, but potentially have different perspectives on the events and different segmentations of sound patterns in comments. The hypothesis explored in this experiment is that language used for symbolic purposes makes crucial use of prior mechanisms for timing and control of segments. On this view of language, aptitude for "song" in a community is something that may be re-used within a discrete symbol system, and in fact, may make it easier for a discrete symbol system to emerge than if meanings are to be attached to arbitrary sequences of sounds produced. However, in this condition there is not a significant effect of level of cooperation, operationalized in terms of the level of questions entertained.

The data between the two experiments are pooled and the interactions of the factors are addressed in Section 4. Cohesion of the groups is revealed to have a stronger overall effect than synchrony, as it is implemented here as the propensity to share segmentation of signals.

1.2   Background Methods

The Language Evolution Workbench [10] has been extended to support the possibility of agents cooperating after language games by querying whether other agents share vocabulary items [5]. Parameterization associated with the potential for synchronizing the individuation of sound sequences has also been added. Additional tools for assessing the distributions of item use have been provided. Features affecting the size meaning space are parameterized. However, it is an open meaning space. The system is implemented in Prolog. Events are construed as lists of atomic symbols composed of an arbitrary element constituting a relation and arguments. Arguments may, recursively, be events. Although arbitrary in construction (see examples (1)–(7) below), relation names are distinguished from argument types. The list of all partitions of an event into sub-lists provides the space of possible perspectives on any event that might happen. Similarly, utterances are construed as lists of pairs arbitrary atomic symbols where each pair represents a phoneme, and possible segmentations are construed as lists of sub-lists. An event happens (1), and two agents witness it, each from their own perspective, as in (2) and (3), each of which derived from the original event model (1) as an element of the list of all partitions of that original list. One agent comments on the event (4) with a self-understanding of the relationship between that signal and the event commented upon (5)—each segment of the event as construed (2) is mapped to a phoneme sequence in the signal. The other agent interprets the signal as it is heard (6), noiselessly, but potentially with a distinct segmentation of the sounds,[3] and relative to its own perspective on the event, yielding a potentially distinct meaning for the signal for the hearer (7).

For example, the model of the event in (1) involves a list of atoms and place holder argument positions. Relation names are arbitrarily constructed atomic symbols, and relations are designated from among a finite set of relation types distinguished by their argument structure. A Zipfian distribution of events means that events of certain types will accordingly be more likely to recur than other types, and thus models a greater amount of regularity in the world than if events are randomly distributed. The arguments of a relation name may be restricted, according to the type, to be of sort human, animate, inanimate, or relational. Relational arguments correspond to embedding verbs in natural language, and provide for an arbitrarily large space of possible meaning in any run of the system, since events are constructed on the fly. Thus, the event in (1) is objectively an embedding of a one place relation under a two place relation presented as a list that shows no association of arguments. The space of possible subjective perceptions of an event is modeled as the list of all sub-lists of the objective event list, and thus any perception of the objective event is an element of that list of possible partitions.[4] Similarly, utterance are built up out of sequences of list of pairs of atomic symbols, and "words" are construed as lists of pairs.[5]

(1)   [wcflxls,human,wyefxhs,human]
(2)   [[wcflxls],[human],[wyefxhs],[human]]
(3)   [[wcflxls,human],[wyefxhs,human]]
(4)   [[[aa,pp]],[[d,s]],[[ff,t]],[[dd,f]]]
(5)   [[[wcflxls],[[aa,pp]]],
      [[human],[[d,s]]],
      [[wyefxhs],[[ff,t]]],
      [[human],[[dd,f]]]]
(6)   [[[aa,pp],[d,s],[ff,t]], [[dd,f]]]
(7)   [[[wyefxhs,human],[[aa,pp],[d,s],[ff,t]]],
      [[wcflxls,human],[[dd,f]]]]

---

[3] The distinct bracketing in (4) and (6) represent distinct segmentations of the sound.
[4] The best way to make sense of this is by analogy to extensional semantics: given some domain D, the set of all discriminations that one can make in an extensional semantics is given by $\mathcal{P}(D)$, the power set of the domain, and the meaning of any unary relation is an element of $\mathcal{P}(D)$.
[5] In this example, the speaker's utterance in (4) has four "words", and the this signal is segmented by the hearer as (6), which has two "words".

Pragmatic assumptions are built into the system: it is the obligation of the speaker to attach a vocalisation to each component of the event that the speaker has individuated in its perspective on the objective event (as in the speaker's meaning in (5)); it is the obligation of the hearer to find a meaning to associate with each token that it individuates from the speaker's utterance. The hearer has its own perspective on the event and access without noise to the speaker's utterance. If there is no necessary synchronization of utterance segmentation, then the hearer is free to segment the speaker's utterance as it perceives it to be divided. If the synchronization parameter is set, then the hearer will have the same segmentation of the utterance as the speaker; however, this does not predetermine perfect understanding because the hearer must in any case attach meanings to the segments, and they may be lifted from the hearer's perspective on the event or from prior associations of meanings with the perceived utterance segment (cf. hearer's meaning in (7)).

Understanding is measured by the proportion of the utterance-meaning mappings shared by the two interlocutors. This is distinct from measuring the number propositions agreed to—ten percent shared understanding of an utterance is akin to shared understanding of what relation is at stake or who or what is involved in an utterance. Each agent has its own accumulation of propositions attested (each proposition individuated by an underlying meaning and its articulation as a sequence of phonemes), its own lexicon of atomic meanings and their sequence of phoneme labels, and a measure of fitness that various over time, constructed as the average understanding achieved during interpretation turns. In the example above, no common understanding was achieved. Using the parameters of the Language Evolution Workbench as set for the experiments discussed here, there is no immediate ramification for interlocutors if they fail to understand each other in a given turn. Thus, the agents do not obtain feedback on the success of their communication. However, fitness is set to a relevant level that has the effect of eliminating from the pool of communicators those who do not understand their partners up to the small threshold of ten percent of the utterances.

The model provides a discrete speech signal, with no correlate of phonotactic constraints on phoneme co-occurrence; however, by construction, agents may achieve distinct segmentations of any utterance. In an interpretation of synchronization, segmentation is further constrained such that communicating agents will share the same segmentation of uttered signals. For all of the experiments reported here, the initial population has ten agents; entities are modeled as variables (entity types) rather than each being named individually; 100 relation types are discriminated and occur with probabilities guided by a Zipfian distribution; language games each consist of ten events-comment-interpretation cycles; agents are not assumed to be attuned to each other's segmentation rhythm; no level of understanding between the agents is absolutely necessary to be completed; any mapping that does not happen at least twice in a language game is not remembered; at the end of each language game any agent who has not understood at least ten percent of what was attempted to be interpreted exits the pool of communicators. Selection of speakers and hearers is random.

2   Cohesion and Cooperation (without Synchrony)

2.1   Design

Two factors are explored here. The pool dynamic is either monotonically decreasing as a function of "fitness", measured in terms of having at least ten percent success in interpreting, as described above, or non-monotonic, admitting the addition of agents (at most one but not necessarily any), after each language game. The other factor has three levels that has mere coordination at one extreme and a high level of explicit cooperation at the other: no questioning of lexicons; questioning of lexicons after every other language game; questioning after each language game. There were 200 language games (of ten cycles) in each run, and nine runs in each of the six combinations of factors. Each run involves a fresh initialization of agents, and potential meanings and phonemes, etc.

The motive for having the level of cooperation with no explicit cooperation is that explicit negotiation of linguistic terms is relatively rare in dialog within language as it has evolved. The number of language games is kept small at 200, following the intuition that the first users of language would not have the patience to wait thousands of iterations without early rewards. Thus, a system which shows no promise in a relatively small number of games is not a great candidate exemplar of parameter settings that explain human language evolution.

2.2   Results

In this section, graphs of representative runs are shown, and the overall results considered with analysis of variance. In the figures for each of the six combinations of factors, the trajectory of measured values in the overall run are shown. For each combination of factors, the runs that resulted in the lowest and highest overall understanding among agents are shown. The other values plotted over the language games includes: the homonymy rate; synonymy rate; the proportion of meanings lexicalized among all agents; the proportion of phoneme sequences shared among all agents.[6] The size of the pool of agents is also shown. In Figures 1-3, the value plotted is the ratio of the agents remaining to the starting number of agents; and in Figures 4-6 for the runs in which the number of agents can increase, that value is the log (base 10) of that ratio.[7] All of the values plotted, percentages and ratios, are normalized to the same y-axis scale, between 0 and 1 where the communities are parameterized to be non-increasing, and between -0.5 and 2 for parameterization to communities with non-monotonic growth. The results are shown by level of cooperation among agents, first with respect to non-increasing agent pools, and then non-monotonic agent pools.

Non-Increasing Pool of Agents. Figures 1-3 show that where the pool of agents does not increase, levels of understanding can exceed 60%. In general,

---

[6] Homonymy entails that a phoneme sequence point to more than one meaning; "shared phoneme sequences" here refers to sharing by all agents in the pool.

[7] The smallest eventual number of agents reached was 5, and the largest was 55.

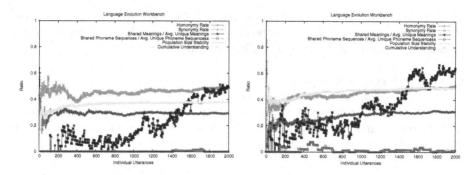

Fig. 1. Fitness based Elimination; No Questions (Left – least understanding; Right – greatest understanding)

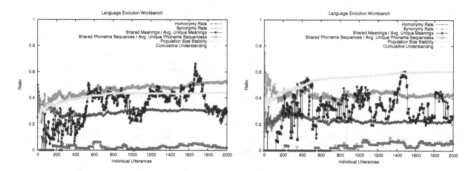

Fig. 2. Fitness based Elimination; Questions after every second language game (Left – least understanding; Right – greatest understanding)

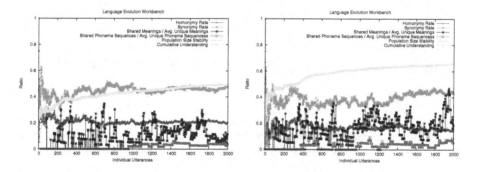

Fig. 3. Fitness based Elimination; Questions after every language game (Left – least understanding; Right – greatest understanding)

understanding hovers around 40%. Overall understanding appears to correlate with the level of shared phoneme sequences, and to be less dependent on the level of shared meanings lexicalized. Contrary to natural language, synonymy rates exceed homonymy rates. Clear impact of the level of cooperation is evident. Cooperation as modeled has the effect of increasing the quantity of shared phoneme sequences, and consequently overall understanding rates.

Agent Pool Increase and Decrease. Figures 4-6 show the worst and best runs for each of the three levels of cooperation in the scenario in which population size may increase or decrease. In fact, the population increases to a maximum of 55 in these runs. The next section discusses the data from the runs pooled within condition, and the resulting analysis of variance.

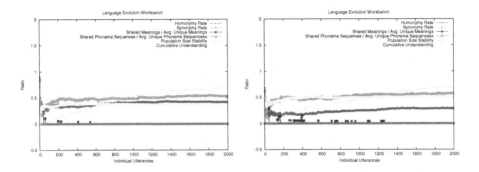

Fig. 4. Fitness based Elimination; New Agents Enter; No Questions (Left – least understanding; Right – greatest understanding)

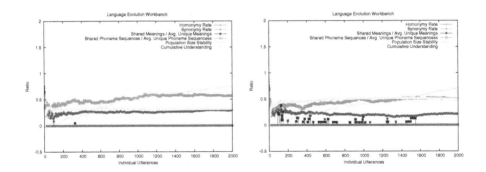

Fig. 5. Fitness based Elimination; New Agents Enter; Questions Every Second Language Game (Left – least understanding; Right – greatest understanding)

2.3 Discussion

Table 1 shows the mean understanding of all runs in each of the six conditions. This involves the level of overall understanding at the end of the runs. Inspection reveals that the greatest systematic impact of level of coordination is within the condition that has a monotonically decreasing pool of agents.

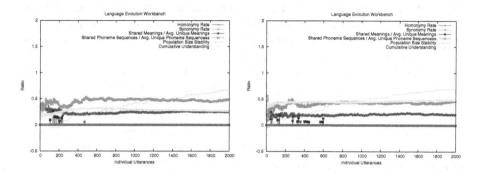

Fig. 6. Fitness based Elimination; New Agents Enter; Questions after each Language Game (Left – least understanding; Right – greatest understanding)

Analysis of variance shows a significant main effect of both factors, monotonicity of the participant pool ($p < .0001$) and level of cooperation ($p < .005$), and the interaction of the two variables ($p < .0002$). Fitting a linear model, there is a significant main effect of monotonicity ($p < .00001$) with a positive coefficient (0.169). Significant interactions appear between the monotonic condition and no questioning (with a negative coefficient (-0.167) and $p < .0001$) as well as the monotonic condition and some questioning (with a negative coefficient (-0.073) and $p < .05$).

3   Cohesion and Cooperation (with Synchrony)

3.1   Design

The design for this section is as before. However, a parameter is set so that when an event happens and an agent comments on it, another agent chosen at random to hear the description, segments the signal in exactly the same way as the first agent. The two agents may ascribe distinct meanings to the segments of the signal. This is the synchrony condition.

3.2   Results

Again, graphs of representative runs are shown, and the overall results considered with analysis of variance. The trajectory of measured values in the overall run are shown, for each of the six combinations of factors within the synchrony condition.

Table 1. Asynchronous: Mean understanding over nine runs, by condition

Cohesion	Level of Cooperation		
	No Questions	Some Questions	Most Questions
Add None	0.425	0.484	0.571
Add Agents	0.423	0.387	0.404

Again, the runs that resulted in the lowest and highest overall understanding among agents are shown. The other values plotted over the language games are as before. In Figures 7-9, the value plotted is the ratio of the agents remaining to the starting number of agents; and in Figures 10-12 for the runs in which the number of agents can increase, that value is the log (base 10) of that ratio.[8] The results are shown by level of cooperation among agents, first with respect to non-increasing agent pools, and then non-monotonic agent pools.

Non-Increasing Pool of Agents. Figures 7-9 show that with a monotonically decreasing pool of agents, understanding levels normally exceed 60%. Overall understanding appears to correlate with the synonymy, rather than homonymy. While this does not coincide with natural language, it is the way that one would build a language if one wanted to give the greatest chance to agents to understand each other. There is no clear difference between having no cooperative effort and a little such effort, but having coordination after each round appears to make a discernible difference.

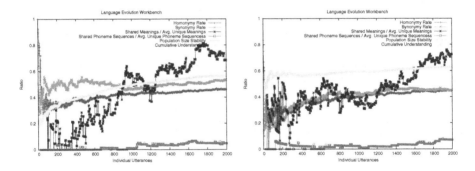

Fig. 7. Fitness based Elimination; No Questions (Left – least understanding; Right – greatest understanding)

Agent Pool Increase and Decrease. Figures 10-12 show the worst and best runs for the three levels of cooperation with a non-monotonic population size: the population increases to a maximum of 64 in these runs. Here, understanding seems to hover at about 50%. The next section discusses the data from the runs pooled within condition, and the resulting analysis of variance.

3.3   Discussion

Table 2 shows the mean understanding of all runs (end of run understanding) in each of the six conditions within this experiment in which agents have synchronized segmentation of the signal. The greatest systematic impact of level of coordination is again within the condition that has a monotonically decreasing pool of agents.

---

[8] The smallest eventual number of agents reached was 6, and the largest was 64.

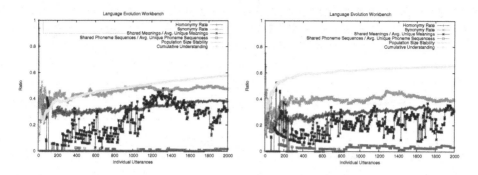

Fig. 8. Fitness based Elimination; Questions after every second language game (Left – least understanding; Right – greatest understanding)

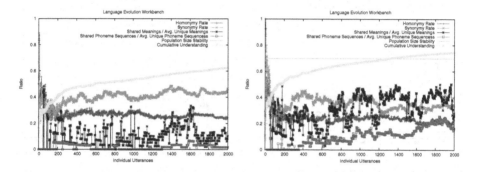

Fig. 9. Fitness based Elimination; Questions after every language game (Left – least understanding; Right – greatest understanding)

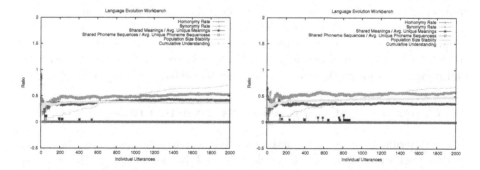

Fig. 10. Fitness based Elimination; New Agents Enter; No Questions (Left – least understanding; Right – greatest understanding)

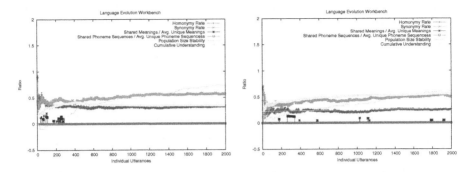

Fig. 11. Fitness based Elimination; New Agents Enter; Questions Every Second Language Game (Left – least understanding; Right – greatest understanding)

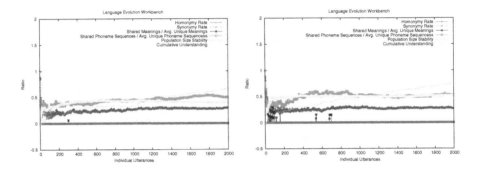

Fig. 12. Fitness based Elimination; New Agents Enter; Questions after each Language Game (Left – least understanding; Right – greatest understanding)

Analysis of variance shows a significant main effect of both factors, monotonicity of the participant pool ($p < .0001$) and level of cooperation ($p < .005$), but not for the interaction of the two variables. Fitting a linear model, there is a significant main effect of monotonicity ($p < .00001$) with a positive coefficient (0.223). Significant interactions appear only between the monotonic condition and no questioning (with a negative coefficient (-0.062) and $p < .05$).

4   Cohesion vs. Cooperation vs. Synchrony

These experiments were constructed to differ exactly with respect to the setting of the synchrony parameter, to explore the interactions of these three factors on overall understanding. Analysis of variance reveals significant main effects of each of the three variables ($p < 0.0001$), with the strongest effect of group cohesion, followed by synchrony. There is also a significant interaction between cohesion and cooperation ($p < 0.0001$), and the interaction between cohesion

Table 2. Synchronous: Mean understanding over nine runs, by condition

Cohesion	Level of Cooperation		
	No Questions	Some Questions	Most Questions
Add None	0.592	0.614	0.670
Add Agents	0.431	0.436	0.448

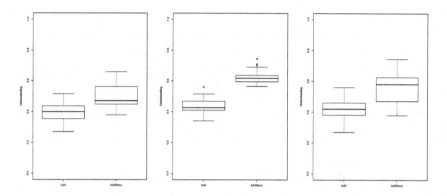

Fig. 13. Understanding as a function of group cohesion: left (Asynchronous), middle (Synchronous), right (Pooled)

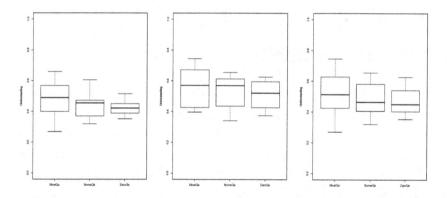

Fig. 14. Understanding as a function of group cooperation: left (Asynchronous), middle (Synchronous), right (Pooled)

and synchrony ($p < 0.0001$). Fitting with a linear model produces a positive coefficient (0.169) for the monotonic level of the cohesion variable with significance ($p < 0.0001$), and for synchronization as in Experiment 2 (0.045, $p \leq 0.05$). Cohesive (monotonic) groups interact with moderate cooperation (-0.073, $p < 0.5$) and with zero cooperation (-0.167, $p < 0.000001$).

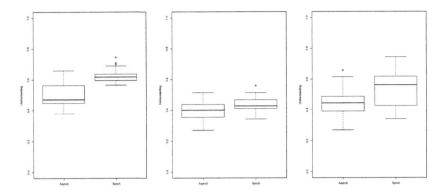

Fig. 15. Understanding as a function of Synchrony: left (AddNone), middle (Add), right (Pooled)

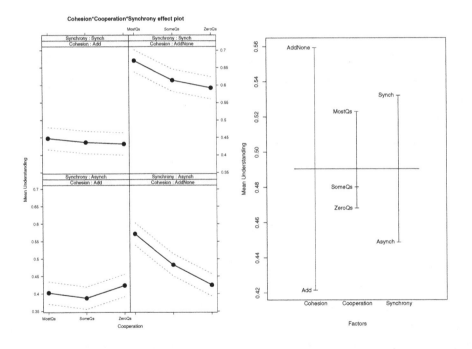

Fig. 16. Interactions of Factors (Left) and Effect Sizes (Right) over Entire Dataset

Figure 13-15 depict the mean understanding at the end of runs in the asynchronous condition (on the left) in comparison to the value for the synchronous condition (in the middle), and with the pooled data. The effect of cohesion is shown in Figure 13; cooperation, in Figure 14; synchrony, in Figure 15. Figure 16 shows the interaction of factors (on the left) and the size of effects (on the right).

5   Conclusion

The experiment presented here considered 216,000 linguistic turns, and interactions among small pools of agents in each. The results depend on the representations used to model the agents, events in the world, perspectives on events, and segmentations of utterances. Nontheless, these representations, although simple, are well motivated. The results also depend on the interpretations supplied to the variables explored relative to these representations. Thus, a result about synchrony as made operational here does not transfer to all implementations of these factors. Further, one has to note that it is an impoverished sense of synchrony to focus on solely the sharing of segmentation. Recent work has suggested that segmentation of the signal is not essential for word detection within a signal, but that word detection supports segmentation [9]. This might be seen as suggesting that shared segmentation propensities are even the wrong places to look for part of the explanation of how convergence on signal-meaning associations may arise. Nonetheless, the results of that work appear to depend on shared individuation of the underlying meanings. In any case, one would expect to be able to replicate these results for closely related implementations of the factors and with respect to alternative underlying representations.

Additionally, the generalizations made here are subject to the caveat that there is no guarantee that the measures shown would have continued on their trajectories at the cut-off point of 200 games in each run—the random elements could make things turn out differently in any extension, and the fluctuations in measures during the first 200 games attest to potential longer-term volatility. The other caveat is that the results provided are relative to the other parameter settings adopted. The intention of the settings for parameters not varied in the experiments was to capture realistic assumptions about the size of the circle of agents involved at the onset of a social innovation like language. The condition allowing enlargement of the agent pool allowed only linear enlargement, and this is perhaps not realistic given contemporary evidence of fads that have taken root. Nonetheless, even with linear growth bounds on the pool of agents, different levels of cooperation did not have a systematic role in explaining the overall level of understanding reached by the end of the runs for that condition. This suggests that level of cooperation enhances the preconditions for understanding in a small pool of agents, but not in an increasing one. The results are compatible with the argument that implicit coordination alone, rather than explicit cooperation, in non-monotonic populations could account for increases of overall understanding. However, in the results here, only the constrained pools demonstrated significant increases in understanding. A reasonable interpretation of the results is that they show that increased collaboration on vocabulary has a greater positive impact within small cohesive groups than in groups with non-monotonic fluctuations in membership.

Where agents demonstrate synchronized segmentation of utterances, there is an enhanced overall rate of understanding. However, a key result of this set of experiments has been that the effect of synchrony is smaller than the effect of group coherence. Yet, the effect of both synchrony and group coherence exceed the effects of cooperation.

References

1. Carstairs-McCarthy, A.: Synonymy avoidance, phonology and the origin of syntax. In: Hurford, J.R., Studdert-Kennedy, M., Knight, C. (eds.) Approaches to the evolution of language. Social and cognitive bases, ch. 17, pp. 279–296. Cambridge University Press, Cambridge (1998)
2. Curran, D., O'Riordan, C.: Increasing population diversity through cultural learning. Adaptive Behavior 14(4) (2006)
3. Hurford, J.: Biological evolution of the saussurean sign as a component of the language acquisition device. Lingua 77, 187–222 (1989)
4. Kirby, S.: Syntax without natural selection: How compositionality emerges from vocabulary in a population of learners. In: Knight, C., Studdert-Kennedy, M., Hurford, J. (eds.) The Evolutionary Emergence of Language, pp. 303–323. Cambridge University Press, Cambridge (2000)
5. Longmore, L.: Talk about talk, population dynamics and agent fitness. MSc in Computational Linguistics, Department of Computer Science, Trinity College, University of Dublin (2008)
6. Oudeyer, P.-Y.: Self-Organization in the Evolution of Speech. Oxford University Press, Oxford (2006) Translated by James Hurford
7. Parisi, D., Cangelosi, A.: A unified simulation scenario for language development, evolution and historical change. In: Cangelosi, A., Parisi, D. (eds.) Simulating the Evolution of Language, pp. 255–275. Springer, Heidelberg (2002)
8. Steels, L., Kaplan, F.: Bootstrapping grounded word semantics. In: Briscoe, T. (ed.) Linguistic evolution through language acquisition: formal and computational models. Cambridge University Press, Cambridge (1999)
9. ten Bosch, L., Van Hamme, H., Boves, L.: Unsupervised detection of words— questioning the relevance of segmentation. In: SCA ITRW, Speech Analysis and Processing for Knowledge Discovery (2008)
10. Vogel, C., Woods, J.: A platform for simulating language evolution. In: Bramer, M., Coenen, F., Tuson, A. (eds.) Research and Development in Intelligent Systems XXIII, pp. 360–373. Springer, London (2006)

Pointing Gestures and Synchronous Communication Management

Kristiina Jokinen

Department of Speech Sciences, University of Helsinki
Siltavuorenpenger 20 A, FIN-00014 University of Helsinki, Finland
Kristiina.Jokinen@helsinki.fi

Abstract. The focus of this paper is on pointing gestures that do not function as deictic pointing to a concrete referent but rather as structuring the flow of information. Examples are given on their use in giving feedback and creating a common ground in natural conversations, and their meaning is described with the help of semantic themes of the Index Finger Extended gesture family. A communication model is also sketched together with an exploration of the simultaneous occurrence of gestures and speech signals, using a two-way approach that combines top-down linguistic-pragmatic and bottom-up signal analysis.

1 Introduction

In the course of conversational interactions, the participants provide verbal and non-verbal feedback that helps them to structure the interaction and to create social rapport. Feedback activity can range from a normal response (e.g. giving an answer to a question) and explicit feedback actions (e.g. asking clarification or informing whether one has understood the partner or not) to providing signals to encourage the speaker to continue speaking (backchannelling). In the widest sense we can say that feedback concerns the speaker's whole reaction towards the new information presented by the partner, and the conversation can be seen as a series of presentation-acceptance cycles which recursively create the common ground and drive the partners interaction forward [1]. Usually, however, feedback is defined in a narrower sense to cover only explicit actions and backchannelling. It is based on the interlocutors' cooperation with each other on a shared task, and related to their grounding strategy that they use to build common ground (e.g. [2]).

In this article, we look at the speakers' non-verbal feedback activity and especially their cooperation with the partner to construct a shared context and mutual understanding of the conversational topic. In verbal communication management, feedback and the construction of common ground have been widely studied. Computational models of grounding provide a means to construct shared context in human computer interactions, and are included as a crucial element in dialogue management strategies in spoken dialogue systems (see discussion in [3]). In cognitive studies, the notion of alignment [4] refers to similar cooperative activity among the participants, i.e. the speakers harmonize their activities and thus provide feedback to the partner, while in conversation analysis, common ground is the shared knowledge that the speakers assume to be known in the conversation yet is also built through the interaction [5].

A. Esposito et al. (Eds.): COST 2102 Int. Training School 2009, LNCS 5967, pp. 33–49, 2010.
© Springer-Verlag Berlin Heidelberg 2010

Non-verbal feedback has been mainly regarded as displaying certain aspects of the speakers' cognitive and emotional state, and to allow the interlocutors to monitor each other's emotions and understanding in a natural way. Its importance is thus related to maintaining fluency of communication rather than providing explicit means to manage the interaction. However, the different non-verbal signals can also function as independent means to coordinate information and manage interaction. For instance, [6] show that gaze is important in signalling the speaker's wish to take a turn, [7] discuss what they call "stand-up" gestures to coordinate the information flow in the dialogues, and the work on Embodied Conversational Agents has shown how these aspects affect the interaction with virtual agents (see an overview e.g. in [8]). The effective use of gestures, facial expressions, and eye-gazing is thus an unobtrusive means to construct shared context in which the conversational interaction takes place.

We will focus on hand gesturing and discuss different gesture functions from the point of view of giving feedback to the partner. We will especially study pointing gestures, i.e. gestures with a particular hand shape, index finger extended, and their use in communication management. The article is structured as follows. In Section 2, we first discuss gestures and gesture families in general, and in Section 3 provide examples of pointing gestures from our multiparty dialogue corpus. In Section 4 we present how conversational interactions are managed and the shared context is constructed in a coordinated and cooperative manner, and in Section 5 we continue by presenting a communication model that takes these aspects into account. Future research on dialogue activity is presented in Section 6, including the two-way approach that combines top-down linguistic-pragmatic analysis with bottom-up signal analysis. Conclusions are drawn in Section 7.

2 Gesture Functions and Gesture Families

As already mentioned feedback giving activity is a conversational strategy that allows interlocutors to coordinate the flow of information and construct common ground within which dialogue topic and joint task can be successfully managed. Giving and receiving feedback contributes to the interlocutors' understanding of the shared context, and it is thus crucial to learn to observe and correctly interpret the feedback signals that indicate the partner's wish to take a turn or to clarify something that was said. Gestures belong to the communicative repertoire that the speakers have in their disposal in order to express meanings and give feedback, and thus it is important to learn how they are used to support smooth communication. Much of the gesturing accompanies speech and gives extra emphasis on the spoken content, but some gestures may function as important signals that are used to manage the dialogue and the information flow.

[9] defines gestures as spontaneous movements of hands and arms, typical for each speaker, while [10] uses the term gesticulation to refer to the gesture as a whole, with a preparatory phase in the beginning of the movement, the stroke, or the peak structure in the middle, and the recovery phase at the end of the movement. According to Kendon, gestures are intentionally communicative actions and they have certain immediately recognizable features which distinguish them from other kinds of activity such as practical actions, postural adjustments, etc. Feedback giving gestures can thus

be distinguished from the speaker's unintentional random hand movements in that they are gestures with a communicative intention: they are interpreted in the context as signalling some crucial aspect of the information that the speaker intends to convey either consciously or unconsciously. It must be emphasised that communicative gestures are also different from gestures used in sign language: the latter are highly conventionalised systems for expressing meanings whereas communicative gestures do not have such conventionalised interpretations but require context in which their meaning can be approximated.

The form of gestures (hand shape, movement, fingers) can provide important information about the meaning of the gesture in a given context. For instance, the form of can vary from rather straightforward picturing of a referent (iconic gestures) to more abstract types of symbolic gestures, up to culturally governed emblems (such as the sign of victory). However, the same gesture form can also have several functions: e.g. an extended index finger may have a descriptive function if it is used as a deictic pointing gesture, a pragmatic function if it emphasizes an important word in an utterance, or interactive function if it points to the next speaker. On the other hand, gestures seem to have several functions on the basis of which they can also be classified. For instance, gestures can complement the speech and single out a certain referent as is the case with typical deictic pointing gestures (*this book*). They can also illustrate the speech like the iconic gestures do (e.g. show a tiny increase with the index finger and thumb while saying *"the increase is very small"*), or give rhythm to the speech as the beats, or batonic gestures do. Beats are usually synchronized with the important concepts in the spoken utterance, i.e. they accompany spoken foci (e.g. when uttering *"and another important point is the amount of tax cuts"*, the beats fall on the words *"another"* and *"amount"*). Gesturing can thus direct the partner's attention to an important aspect of the spoken message without the speaker needing to put their intention in words.

The gesture can also be used to catch the partner's attention, and the speaker can indicate their wish to correct and clarify, provide feedback, or otherwise manage the information flow. These kind of gestures distinguish themselves from the normal flow of verbal information exchange in that they not only accompany or complement the spoken content, but rather, function as independent means for communication management i.e. they are communicative acts or "doing things" in the conversation. [11] refer to this kind of gestures as interactive gestures, while [7] talk about "stand-up" gestures. [10] talks about gestures on meta-discursive level, and also notices that all gesture researchers have recognized the functioning of gestures as an independent utterance, i.e. autonomous of speech.

Although gestures are often culture-specific and their classification is difficult due to multifunctional and overlapping cases, some gesture forms seem to carry meaning that is typical of the particular hand shape itself. For instance, [10] has classified gestures on the basis of their functions in the communicative contexts, and identified different gesture families depending on the general meaning that the gestures express. Such gesture families as Open Hand Supine ("palm up") and Open Hand Prone ("palm down") have their own semantic themes which are related to offering and giving vs. stopping and halting, respectively. For instance, gestures in the "palm up" family generally express offering or giving of ideas, and they accompany speech which aims at presenting, explaining, summarizing, etc. Gestures in the "palm down" family relate to stopping or halting actions, being denied, negated, interrupted or stopped, or considering the situation itself not worthwhile for continuation. Gesture families can also have subgroups that specify the hand form or movement, e.g. gestures in the subgroup Open Hand Supine Vertical are used in relation to cutting, limiting or structuring information, while gestures in the subgroup Open Hand Supine Lateral indicate withdrawal or ignorance, abandoning the task because of not being able or willing to take part in it.

The Index Finger Extended is another gesture family with the distinctive pointing form, the index finger extended. The semantic theme of the Index Finger Extended family appears similar to the Open Hand families, but the main difference is that the Index Finger Extended family refers to precise and explicit actions or objects. A typical pointing gesture has usually been regarded as a deictic pointing act that singles out a concrete object in the physical environment and, with a metaphorical extension also warrants similar pointing to lexical phrases, concepts, ideas, relations, or activities in an abstract dialogue context ("this book, that plan"). As we will see, it also has a wide range of meanings where the pointing to a referent is not really present but rather, the gesture has dialogue management functions. Whether this equals "pointing" in a concrete or abstract sense is something that we do not need to go into here; however, as the correct referent needs to be inferred on the basis of the shared context and the verbal utterance that possibly accompanies the gesture, the gesture seem to direct the partner's attention towards some (contextually salient) object rather than denoting a particular deictic relation. Although deixis is much studied in philosophy and linguistics, it suffices to say that the Index Finger Extended gesture seems to correspond to the speaker's intention to express meanings related to some general aspects or state of the art of some individualized referents.

As will be seen in the examples, individual gestures are also highly multifunctional and the distinctions between gesture families are not clear-cut. This suggests that communicative gestures form a continuum rather than separate categories, and their meanings can only be approximated. However, as suggested in [7], the notion of a gesture family seems to provide a useful starting point for classifying and annotating gestures. If gestures are described in terms of their observable properties (such as the hand form, finger position, movement) and annotated with general communicative functions (as e.g. [12]), it may be possible to define gesture families as distinctive clusters of the features and their functional interpretation in various contexts. Rather than interpreting gestures as single instances, the form and function of the gestures can be related to typical human behaviour, which provides an empirical basis for models of how the interlocutors usually perceive and interpret gestures, and how they naturally produce such gesturing in communicative situations themselves. Moreover, if the features can be automatically recognized, it is possible to do the clustering on the automatically recognized features, and thus produce a bottom-up analysis of possible communicative signalling. This can help us to understand typical human gesturing behaviour and to build more natural interactive systems with interfaces that use gesturing as one of the modalities to natural meaning.

Not many gesture families have been studied in detail, and especially the Index Finger Extended gesture family is not thoroughly identified. Our analyses below aim at shedding some light on this particular gesture family.

3 Data

The data consists of conversations collected in an international setting at the ATR Research Labs in Japan in 2007, and includes videos of four participants engaged in free conversation. The data was recorded with an unobtrusive single 360 degree camera and one microphone as described in [13]. The data was collected on three consecutive days, and it was later transcribed and partially analysed [14]. The dialogues have descriptions of topics and estimations of the emotional level of the speakers, and part of the data is also annotated with gestures, head and facial expressions, and body movement according to the MUMIN annotation scheme [12].

All the speakers speak English but represent different cultural backgrounds. They are familiar with the Japanese culture and most topics deal with issues related to this. The participants did not know each other except one who was familiar with everyone, and thus they talk about various topics and learn to know each other through the interaction. Compared with other multiparty conversation data, our data differs from these in that the participants did not collaborate on a particular task nor did they take part in role playing in a particular scenario either. Our previous experience in conversational data collection with more controlled dialogue situations had revealed that although the participants can become fully engaged in their imaginary roles, they also easily get mixed up with what they think is the expected behaviour of the role, or feel uncomfortable or embarrassed in their adopted role. The data collection thus aimed at supporting participants in natural conversational setting with no other tasks or roles than what they would naturally adopt in similar informal chatting situations.

The data contains several pointing gestures but interestingly enough none of them functions as a prototypical deictic pointing gesture as in *this book, that car*. The lack of concrete deictic reference is apparently due to the conversational activity: the interlocutors are engaged in free flowing chatting with unrestricted topics and not e.g. in navigation or route guidance where pointing to concrete objects is common due to the nature of the task itself. We can of course say that the pointing gestures in our data are metaphorical and they designate referents in the abstract dialogue situation. However, the analysis below shows that the gestures also have other functions that deal with dialogue management and information coordination, so that the metaphorical explanation may not be tenable in all cases. Instead, our analysis strengthens the hypothesis concerning the gesture family Index Finger Extended. All gestures contain an extended index finger, but they are produced with different hand orientation and palm shape. The different functions of the gestures seem to correspond to the form of the hand and give evidence for the semantic themes of the gesture families as discussed in Section 2. Especially, the observations support the general distinction between Index Finger Extended and Open Hand families concerning their general and precise semantics, as the pointing gestures single out the precise new information presented verbally in the utterance. Below we analyse the following functions identified from the data: indicating common ground, acknowledging and creating shared understanding, providing new information, and iconic presentation while acting in synchrony.

3.1 Gesturing to Indicate Common Ground

One of the typical situations is shown in Fig. 1, where the gesture is used to indicate that the new information is common ground and shared knowledge. The topic deals with Japanese comedy and the speaker (lower panel left) has explained what the setting for the special *oubeika* type comedy is. The explanation "usually you have a tall guy and shorter guy", accompanied with an iconic gesture showing the size of the actors (the gesture is still visible in the snapshot), created a moment of shared humour and the partners provide feedback with laughing, smiling, and positive verbal utterances (uttering *I see*). The speaker has a short pause, eliciting more positive feedback, and then tries to continue his turn. However, due to his hesitation to continue, the speaker opposite him (upper panel right) now contributes to the conversation by adding *and a nice guy and ugly one*, while at the same time, the third interlocutor (upper panel left) extends his hand with a pointing gesture and leans forward saying: *it's awful really*. The pointing gesture is notably big, and it is timed accurately with the start of the second speaker's contribution, as if both speakers provide synchronous feedback to the same laughing context. However, while the utterance adds new information to the context, the gesture distinguishes the precise part of the speaker's explanation, "a tall guy and a shorter guy", and provides an evaluative feedback on this particular point.

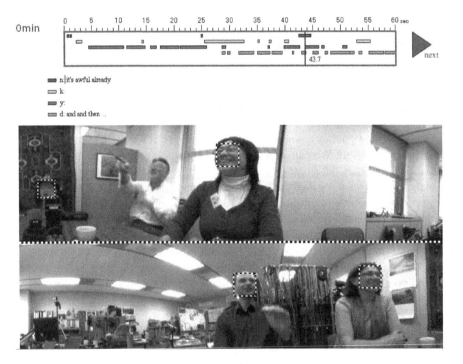

Fig. 1. A pointing gesture *it's awful really* with the timeline showing the speakers' speech activity around the snapshot. The snapshot is marked by the vertical line, and it shows how the original speaker (middle line) continues after the short interruption by the gesturing partner (uppermost line).

The gesture is highly multifunctional and serves the conversation on several levels. Besides pointing out the important aspect of the dialogue topic, without really going into its details verbally, the gesture instantly indicates that the speaker knows the topic and the comedy format, thus confirming that the shared knowledge has been established on his part as well. As the gesture is accompanied with a verbal utterance in which the speaker expresses his evaluation of the format being slightly odd, it also contributes to eliciting feedback from the original speaker so as to further strengthen mutual understanding. In this way the gesture also helps to create a mutual bond between the partners sharing the same evaluation. It is worth noticing that pointing straight to the interlocutor is usually not considered good manners, but as our data exemplifies, this can also be an acceptable means to control the dialogue and even function as a bonding strategy. Finally, the gesture grabs the partner's attention and halts the dialogue for a while. It would be possible for the gesturer to take the turn, but in this case, however, the interruption is just an indication of the shared context, and the original speaker continues his talk.

3.2 Gesturing to Acknowledge and Elicit Shared Understanding

The situation in Fig. 2 is similar to the previous one but now the gesturer is the speaker rather than the listener, and the speaker continues his turn after having created shared context and elicited positive feedback from the partners. The topic concerns visiting a particular temple in Kyoto and seeing all the schoolchildren on their school trips,wanting to talk to foreigners in English. The partner (upper panel left) starts to laugh as if suddenly remembering what it is like there, and this prompts the speaker (lower panel left) to ask a quick question *ever been there?* He accompanies his question with a gesture towards the partner with the index finger extended, thus acknowledging his laugh and the shared knowledge, and simultaneously eliciting explicit feedback from him. The indicated partner immediately replies *yes I've been attacked* (by schoolchildren asking questions in English), which prompts the other partner (lower panel left) also to provide similar positive feedback verbally.

The example shows nicely how the dialogue is managed in an unobtrusive way by gesturing: the main flow of verbal presentation is not disturbed at all, while the participants check and confirm mutual information with each other. The feedback gesture can be counted as a turn of its own, and the speaker seems to have orchestrated the creation of shared context only by a single move of hand. The gesture form itself is not a clear pointing gesture as the other fingers are only partly curled into the palm. The right hand also joins in so that at its peak the gesture opens up towards the other interlocutors so as to include them in the mutual agreement too. Nevertheless the index finger is prominently extended and pointed towards the particular partner who is singled out as the addressee of the shared understanding.

3.3 Gesturing to Provide New Information

In Fig. 3, the topic of the conversation concerns Japanese name conventions and the correct use of the specific suffixes that are added to the name to indicate the addressee's status and relationship towards the speaker. The speaker in the front left proceeds to provide new information about the name convention concerning the name

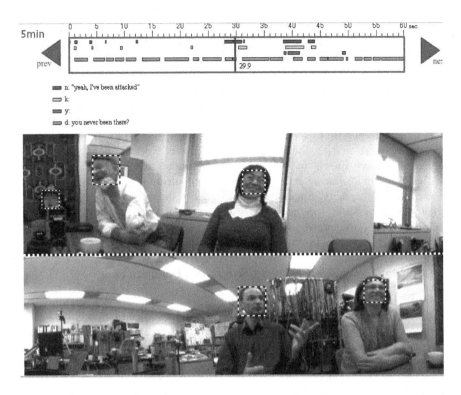

Fig. 2. A pointing gesture which acknowledges the partner's feedback and creates shared understanding, accompanying the utterance *ever been there?* The timeline shows the partner's confirmation in the uppermost line and the second speaker's confirmation as a short speech spurt below this line on the right.

and title in adverts that conference organisers send to people in order to advertise a forthcoming conference: the title Dr or Prof is always used because the name is automatically produced from the database. The speaker starts his utterance with a general pointing gesture with his right hand and continues to use the gesture repeatedly with index finger extended to emphasize the stressed words "doctor", "professor", and "automated". The gesture is a rhythmic beat: it accompanies the speech and gives structure to the presentation. We can also say that it has a metaphorical deictic function as it "points" to the important words and directs the partners' attention to the new information that is being offered. Compared with the previous gesture, the semantics of this one differs in that the speaker does not only acknowledge some established shared context, but provides brand new information that he also knows is new to the other partners (new at least in this dialogue context). The movement and hand shape also seem to support the different semantics. Here the arm is vertical and the hand makes small forward-backward movements punctually while the other fingers are retracted and folded into the palm, whereas in the previous example the movement is rather vague with the arm horizontal, as if offering and eliciting feedback, and the other fingers are also extended leaving the palm open.

Fig. 3. A pointing gesture to provide new information

3.4 Iconic Gesturing and Synchrony

The last example shows two partners' synchronous gesturing as they visually present certain activity explained earlier in words (Figs 4-6). Only one of this kind of clear synchronisation is found in the data, but it is an excellent example of action coordination, and included in the analysis as a special case showing harmony and cooperation, besides also nicely exemplifying the use of iconic pointing gestures.

The speaker in the front left (Figs. 4-6) has started to explain how the university was divided into two institutions, and consequently the university library was divided into two, too. The books were divided between the two new libraries in a meticulous way, and even series were split so that the first volume of a series went into one library, the volume two into the other library, and so on. The addressee, the participant in the back left, seems hesitant about the speaker's abstract explanation *from A to B*, so the partner sitting opposite her (in the back right) starts to clarify this by lifting his right index finger and simultaneously saying *put volume one*. As seen in the snapshot on the left side of Fig. 4, the pointing gesture is small and concerns only the index finger, but it is significant in the conversation. It is also multifunctional, and functions, first of all, as a way to stop the information flow in order to give a short a clarification on what has been presented so far. It is also an attention catcher and the original speaker (front left) immediately responds to it, and to the verbal content of the utterance, by expands his explanation *probably volume one*. Moreover, the gesture halts the dialogue for a split second, and is thus used as a starting point for a combination of verbal and gestural presentation of how the volumes were divided between the two libraries. The extension of the index finger refers to the volume one, and as the hand is moved right, simultaneously with the speaker uttering *volume one,* the gesture iconically presents the moving of this volume to one of the libraries. As the speaker utters *volume two*, left hand moves left with index finger extended as shown in the right snapshot of Fig. 4. The verbal utterances, *volume three, volume four...*are accompanied by right and left hand gestures showing how the volumes went to the different libraries. The original speaker, however, does not give up his turn, but joins the partner with his gestural explanation at this point (Fig.5). He synchronizes his gesturing as well as speaking from the *volume three* onwards, and utters *volume three, volume four* while gesturing in harmony with the partner. As seen in Figs. 6, his right and left hands mirror the partner's left and right hands respectively. This reinforces the iconicity of the gestures as if placing the volumes in the same imaginary "library".

The speakers spontaneously coordinate their gesturing, and create an effective and humorous multimodal show to explain the division of books between the two libraries. It is interesting to notice that the speaker who joins the presentation uses a similar

Fig. 4. The left snapshot shows the right-hand pointing gesture by the speaker in the back right in the beginning of his clarification. The right snapshot depicts the same speaker continuing the explanation with his left hand emphasising *volume two*.

Fig. 5. The speaker in the front left synchronizes his gestures with the speaker in the back. His left hand, with the index finger extended, moves left as the partner's right hand, also with the index finger extended, moves right, and both simultaneously utter *volume three*.

Fig. 6. Synchronized gesturing by the speakers in the front left and in the back right

hand shape, i.e. index finger extended, as his partner, although his previous gesturing has mainly been with an open palm. Although the gesture shape is part of the speakers' alignment and cooperation with the partner, it also exemplifies how a particular hand shape visually supports the semantic content being conveyed. The extended index finger refers to each separate volume, and the gesturing iconically depicts how each book is individually transferred to one or the other library, rather than referring to the moving of the books in general.

4 Constructive Communication Management

The examples show that non-verbal signals can effectively regulate the flow of information in dialogues. Much of the conversational information exchange relies on the assumptions and presuppositions that are not necessarily made verbally explicit but expressed e.g. by gesturing. Such gestures function on the conversational metalevel [10] and they contribute to communication management by directing the partners' attention towards new information, constructing shared knowledge, and creating social bonds. The "meaning" of the gestures correlates with the gesturer's communicative needs on the message level (verbal utterance), but gets its appropriate interpretation within the larger context that does not only include the particular dialogue situation and the activity the participants are involved in, but the interlocutors' own history and ultimately the whole cultural context in which the communicative strategies have developed.

It should be noticed that gestures are often multifunctional and multidimensional (cf. analyses of the gestures in the presented examples), and their interpretation is simultaneously affected by different levels of contextual knowledge. [7] list five levels of communicative context: the linguistic or lexical level, the dialogue level, the social interaction level, the level of the activity the speakers are engaged in, and the level of general cultural context. The contexts influence the way how gestures are used, i.e. how they can be interpreted and produced, but they are not exclusive: gestures can simultaneously have meaning on different communicative contexts. The context levels are meant to set up a systematic framework for the constraints and expectations concerning how contributions, especially gestures are produced and interpreted in a given dialogue situation.

One of the necessary conversational skills is to know how to enable the right type of contextual reasoning. Interlocutors need to observe and monitor each others' reactions so as to draw contextually appropriate inferences about possible changes in emotional and cognitive states. This requires that the speaker is aware of the (verbal and non-verbal) means to coordinate the conversational situation, to catch the partner's attention and to prepare the partner to have a right stance to interpret what will come in the intended way. Although there are individual and cultural differences, the participants seem to coordinate their actions accurately, as part of their general cooperation and alignment with the partners.

If we assume, following [3], that communication is cooperative activity whereby the speakers exchange new information on a shared goal, we can construct a simple model for the example dialogues, with verbal and non-verbal communication integrated as contributions that construct shared context with the new information that they convey. The interlocutors are regarded as rational agents who exchange information following certain conversational principles and obligations, and they constantly monitor their partners and the communicative context so as to take an appropriate action in order to reach the communicative goal. The goal can vary from rather vague "keep the channel open" -type chatting to more specific task-oriented intentions like when the speakers are engaged in planning or instruction giving activities. In our dialogues, communicative goals are rather wide and the goal is basically just to contribute to the conversation with some interesting topics. The speakers are bound by communicative obligations which arise from the particular activity that they are engaged in and from the roles they have in that activity. In our dialogues, the interlocutors have fairly equal roles and they show a high level of cooperative and friendly activity, and the obligations seem to be related to amicable support and attentive companionship.

The construction of the shared context takes place dynamically in the course of the interactive situation. On a general level, the interaction management and the construction of shared context follows a loop that includes the following steps:

1. Observations about the environment

   • Sensory information to higher-level representations

2. Integration of the observations to our knowledge

   • Cognition

3. Manipulation of information

   • Coordinated action

4. Feedback of the success of the action

   • New observations about the environment

Success of interaction depends on the cognitive and emotional impact that the agent's action can produce on the partner, and thus the agents make the new information clearly available for the partner, by presenting it in a way that matches the partner's interests and attention level. Feedback is thus important as it gives the agent information about the partner's attention and understanding while also advances the communicative goals. As already mentioned, an important function of gestures, and non-verbal communication in general, is to supply feedback for the construction of shared context, and they also provide an effective way to lead the conversation and direct the partner towards the intended interpretation without disrupting the verbal activity in conversations.

On the basis of the above sketched communication model, the relevant aspects of the interaction management deal with the monitoring of the conversational environment (effectuated through the agent's attention) and the construction of the shared context (as a result of the agent's deliberation of the next action). In the shared context, gestures are regarded as events which can be related to the accompanying verbal utterance, to the whole dialogue, to the dialogue partners, or to a larger context, and thus the five contextual levels discussed above are also explicitly represented in the shared context.

5   Gestures and Common Ground

[11] hypothesise that the notion of common ground explains the choice of the location and size of the gestures. When a reference is made to the common ground, interlocutors use less explicit, smaller, and peripheral gestures, while in the opposite case, i.e. if reference is not part of the common ground, the gestures become larger and explicit, and they are made in the central place. While this may be true in many cases, the examples presented in this article actually support a different conclusion. The gestures in the two first examples concern shared knowledge but are large and central, while the gestures in the third example and in the beginning of the fourth, synchrony example deal with new information but are smaller and less explicit, yet centrally positioned. The difference may be due to the difference in the dialogue activities in the respective studies, but it is also possible that the size and location of gesturing are not related to the common ground as such, but rather concern the speakers' emotional and cognitive state. For instance, in the first example the large gesture is likely to be caused by the gesturer's excitement and eagerness to contribute to the common ground, whereas in the second example, the gesture is part of the speaker's intention to hold the floor combined with a positive feedback that strengthens togetherness between the partners. The gesture in the example three is rather small as the speaker gives matter-of-fact information, and since the speaker also holds the turn as well as the partners' attention, there is no need to emphasise the speech but with small rhythmical beats. The interrupting gesture in the beginning of example four is also small, but it is visible enough to catch the partner's attention and allow the gesturer to take the turn. The modest gesturing is a sign of politeness towards the partner, i.e. one does not take too much "space", but it also functions as a smooth dialogue strategy that enables the gesturer to indicate his wish to say something, and consequently to take the turn without explicit verbal confrontation or competition for the floor.

There may be big cultural differences in the actual gesturing conventions, but our data motivates the view that in general, the more excited, committed, or agitated the speaker, the larger and more vigorous the gesturing. Smaller, less explicit and less central gesturing indicates that there is no need to catch the partner's attention or fight for the floor in order to convey one's intended message since the speaker already has the turn, or wants to adopt an unobtrusive dialogue management strategy.

As already discussed, the semantic theme of the pointing gesture is related to precision and specificity, and to the construction of shared context either by designating the specific new information that is intended to be part of the mutual knowledge, or by providing and eliciting feedback that consolidates a particular previously presented information as part of the mutual context and agreement. The palm shape and hand orientation that accompanies the extended index finger supports Kendon's semantic theme of the Index Finger Extended gesture family, and is similar to Open Hand families except that with the Index Finger family, the important orientation concerns that of the index finger and not that of the palm.

The palm down position (Index Finger Prone, as in Fig. 1), seems to be related to stopping or halting actions so as to pin down a specific point on the partner's presentation on which feedback is given, while a variation of the gesture in Fig. 3, with the arm lifted (instead of being extended as in the first example) and the palm being 45 degree angle (Index Finger Lateral), has a similar halting effect but only to the effect of keeping the partner's attention on the important pieces of information that the gesturer wishes to say. In Fig. 3, the hand is in lateral position but the shape of the index finger and the other fingers is vague and as described above, the meaning of the gesture is related to a quick acknowledgement of the specific topic. The gesture is akin to the Open Hand Supine Lateral gestures that indicate withdrawal or ignorance. In this case, however, the withdrawal is rather subtle and relates to the acknowledgement of the partner's reaction: since the reaction actually encourages the speaker to continue, there is no need to take further action on it but the intervention can be ignored and the speaker can return back to the central topic. Finally, if the palm is down with the index finger lifted up as in Fig. 4a (Index Finger Vertical), the semantics seems to be related to cutting the action, with an intention to take a turn. It seems like this gesture is related to the subgroup Open Hand Supine Vertical, with the subtle difference that now only one finger is lifted instead of the whole hand, making the gesture less obtrusive, and thus more suitable in smooth cooperative conversations.

The gesture families, associated with general semantic themes, seem a fruitful way to specify the meaning and function of gestures in their various contexts. They enable multilevel communicative interpretation of gestures by guiding the agent towards a general interpretation (based on the semantic theme typical of the particular hand shape such as "I'm offering this information for your consideration and expect you to provide an evaluation of it", or "I think these points are important and expect you to pay attention to them"), and simultaneously allowing the general meaning be unified with a verbally presented message. The interpretation of gestures can thus be specified with the information available through the other information channels as well, and in fact, it is not only the gesture semantics that will be produced but an interpretation of the whole communicative act, i.e. a unification of visual and spoken information into a meaningful message.

6 Future Research with Two-Way Approach

Models of dialogue management and feedback giving processes are relevant in the design and development of natural interactive systems. In this article we have presented some real examples of how certain types of pointing gestures function as a means of communication management and construction of shared knowledge, and future research concerns more detailed analysis of the role and function of gestures in different communicative contexts. For instance, the questions such as how much do the speakers rely on explicit verbal utterances and how much do they also use gesturing and facial expressions in interpreting what the partner says, are still insufficiently understood, and more detailed analysis and quantification is necessary for their modelling for automatic purposes. Future work thus concerns analysis of the form and meaning of gestures and body movement with the help of a suitable annotation scheme, e.g. as suggested in [12], or within the AMI framework, [16]. Also focusing on facial expressions and gazing can provide relevant information about feedback giving processes, and about synchrony of different non-verbal signals in communication.

In order to investigate how non-verbal communication affects interaction management and how the simultaneous activities of giving and eliciting feedback are coordinated by the interlocutors, we study the data using a two-way approach which combines the top-down annotation of dialogues with the bottom-up video and speech analysis (see e.g. [15]). The annotated corpus provides a reference point from the perspective of human perception concerning the recognition and interpretation of the important events in conversations, while the bottom-up approach tries to match the signal-level events with the perceived activity of the interlocutors. The ultimate goal is to relate raw visual and audio stimulus concerning conversational activity to its conscious interpretation in terms of observations of what takes place in the interactive situation.

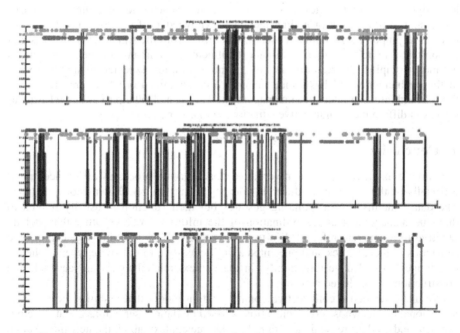

Fig. 7. Dialogue activity of a speaker against the speech of the other interlocutors

Some work in this direction has already started. [15] discusses the two-level method and presents preliminary analysis of the data. For instance, Fig. 7 visualizes the behaviour by two participants: the activity peaks of the speaker's body and gesture movement are shown against the speech activity of all the four interlocutors.[1] The verbal activity of each interlocutor is depicted by the horizontal bars on top of the movement activity, and it includes all vocalizations by the speaker (utterances, laugh, or backchannelling). The vertical peaks show movement activity as detected on the video: gesturing, head turns and nods, as well as body leaning forward and backward.

The uppermost horizontal bar represents the speech spurts by the speaker whose movements are shown in the panel, and when comparing the speech spurts with the occurrence of movements, it can be seen that there are clear movement clusters when the speaker starts to speak. Usually the activity appears shortly after the speaker has started to speak, although in a few cases there is activity immediately before the speech, e.g. in the middle of the uppermost timeline panel, indicating the speaker's excitement or preparation to take the turn. Gesturing and movement activity appears less when the speaker is listening as can be seen in the left side of the upper panel, right side of the middle panel, and in the lower panel in general, although the activity also depends on the individual speaker.

Correspondences between gestures and verbal utterances will be further studied so as to specify the particular movement further and to provide accurate measurements for their timing and synchrony. Using the two-level method of comparing top-down annotation with bottom-up signal processing, we expect to learn more about the interplay between verbal and non-verbal communication, and how observations of low-level signals match with relevant linguistic-pragmatic categories and human cognitive processing, especially in providing feedback. Knowledge of the correspondences allows us to pinpoint how human observations differ from the signal level analysis and to construct models for their automatic treatment. As human-computer interactions get more complex, the resulting models of interaction are expected to supply a view of the enablements and basic mechanisms of communication which are crucial for flexible and intuitive interaction management. They can also help to define what naturalness in different communicative situations actually mean.

7   Conclusions

This article has investigated non-verbal feedback giving processes and concentrated especially on the functions of different pointing gesture in free flowing conversations. The data contains several pointing gestures but their function is usually related to dialogue management and coordination of the information flow rather than deictic pointing to a concrete referent. We used the notion of gesture family to capture the semantics of the gestures, and presented a draft classification of some types of the Index Finger Extended gesture family, in the context related to giving feedback and construction of the shared context.

We also sketched a constructive communication model that assumes the speakers are rational agents whose communication is based on their observations about the environment and on their reasoning, within the dialogue context, about the new information that is being exchanged in the contributions. The model takes the observations from the

---

[1] I am indebted to Stefan Scherer for the signal analysis and producing Fig. 7.

environment as input, and then integrates these to the agent's knowledge through cognitive processing and deliberation. The output is a set of coordinated actions (speech, gesturing, physical task-related actions) that manifest the agent's intentions to change the environment and to get the message across. The agent receives feedback of the success of the action through new observations from the environment, and the same process continues. The interaction with other agents requires cooperation, based on shared context which the interlocutors jointly build.

Finally, we presented the two-level method to analyse conversational data, and discussed some preliminary observations concerning this method. Future work deals with more detailed analysis of how the top-down annotation of dialogues coincides with the signal-level analysis of conversational activity, including experiments with linguistic-pragmatic annotations, sound and video analysis, and further data collection.

References

1. Clark, H.H., Schaefer, E.F.: Contributing to Discourse. Cog. Sci. 13, 259–294 (1989)
2. Traum, D.: Computational models of grounding in collaborative systems. In: Working Papers of the AAAI Fall Symposium on Psychological Models of Communication in Collaborative Systems, pp. 124–131. AAAI, Menlo Park (1999)
3. Jokinen, K.: Constructive Dialogue Management: Speech Interaction and Rational Agency. John Wiley, Chichester (2009a)
4. Pickering, M., Garrod, S.: Towards a mechanistic psychology of dialogue. Behavioral and Brain Sciences 27, 169–226 (2004)
5. Goodwin, C.: Gestures as a resource for the organization of mutual orientation. Semiotica 62(1/2), 29–49 (1986)
6. Argyle, M., Cook, M.: Gaze and Mutual Gaze. Cambridge University Press, Cambridge (1976)
7. Jokinen, K., Vanhasalo, M.: Stand-up Gestures – Annotation for Communication Management. In: Proceedings of the Nodalida Workshop on Multimodal Annotation, Tartu. NEALT Series of Language Technology (2009)
8. Cassell, J., Sullivan, J., Prevost, S., Churchill, E. (eds.): Embodied Conversational Agents. MIT Press, Cambridge (2003)
9. McNeill, D.: Gesture and Thought. University of Chicago Press, Chicago (2005)
10. Kendon, A.: Gesture: Visible action as utterance, Cambridge (2004)
11. Bavelas, J., Chovil, N.: Visible acts of meaning. An Integrated Message Model of Language in Face-to-Face Dialogue. J. Lang and Soc. Psy. 19(2), 163–194 (2000)
12. Allwood, J., Cerrato, L., Jokinen, K., Navarretta, C., Paggio, P.: The MUMIN coding scheme for the annotation of feedback, turn management and sequencing phenomena. In: Martin, J.C., Paggio, P., Kuenlein, P., Stiefelhagen, R., Pianesi, F. (eds.) Multimodal corpora for modelling human multimodal behaviour; Special issue of the International Journal of Language Resources and Evaluation 41(3–4), 273–287 (2007)
13. Douglas, C.E., Campbell, N., Cowie, R., Roach, P.: Emotional speech: Towards a new generation of databases. Speech Comm. 40, 33–60 (2003)
14. Jokinen, K., Campbell, N.: Non-verbal Information Sources for Constructive Dialogue Management. Tutorial at LREC-2008. Marrakech, Marocco (2008)
15. Jokinen, K.: Gesturing in Alignment and Conversational Activity. In: Proceedings of the Pacific Linguistic Conference, Sapporo, Japan (2009b)
16. Carletta, J.: Announcing the AMI Meeting Corpus. The ELRA Newsletter 11(1), 3–5 (2006)

How an Agent Can Detect and Use Synchrony Parameter of Its Own Interaction with a Human?

Ken Prepin[1,2] and Philippe Gaussier[2]

[1] LTCI lab, CNRS, Telecom-ParisTech
46 rue Barrault
75013, Paris, France
ken.prepin@telecom-paristech.fr
[2] Neurocybernetic team, ETIS lab
Cergy-Pontoise University
2, avenue Adolphe-Chauvin, Pontoise
95302 Cergy-Pontoise, France

Abstract. Synchrony is claimed by psychology as a crucial parameter of any social interaction: to give to human a feeling of natural interaction, a feeling of agency [17], an agent must be able to synchronise with this human on appropriate time [29] [11] [15] [16] [27]. In the following experiment, we show that synchrony can be more than a state to reach during interaction, it can be a useable cue of the human's satisfaction and level of engagement concerning the ongoing interaction: the better is the interaction, the more synchronous with the agent is the human. We built an architecture that can acquire a human partner's level of synchrony and use this parameter to adapt the agent behavior. This architecture detects temporal relation [1] existing between the actions of the agent and the actions of the human. We used this detected level of synchrony as reinforcement for learning [6]: the more constant the temporal relation between agent and human remains, the more positive is the reinforcement, conversely if the temporal relation varies above a threshold the reinforcement is negative. In a teaching task, this architecture enables naive humans to make the agent learn left-right associations just by the mean of intuitive interactions. The convergence of this learning reinforced by synchrony shows that synchrony conveys current information concerning human satisfaction and that we are able to extract and reuse this information to adapt the agent behavior appropriately.

Index Terms: Social interaction, intuitive social interaction, synchrony, active-listening, reinforcement learning.

1 Introduction

It is now clear that social interaction cannot be reduced to an exchange of explicit information. When an interaction takes place between two partners, it

A. Esposito et al. (Eds.): COST 2102 Int. Training School 2009, LNCS 5967, pp. 50–65, 2010.

comes with many non-verbal behaviours, such as imitations, perceptual crossing, facial expressions, and many para-verbal behaviours, such as phatics, backchannels or prosody. The first studies raising this issue of the form and the role of non-verbal and peri-verbal behaviours came from Condon et al. in 1966 and 1976 [5] [4]. On one hand, these studies have described the non-verbal and peri-verbal behaviours cited just above, within dyads of persons engaged in discussion together. On the other hand, these studies have suggested that there are temporal correlations between the two behaviours of each dyad: micro analysis of videotaped discussions conduced Condon to define in 1976 the notions of auto-synchrony (synchrony between the different modalities of an individual) and hetero-synchrony (synchrony between partners). Synchrony does not necessarily mean perfect co-occurence but constant temporal relation: just as described by Pikovsky et al., synchronisation can for instance be in *anti-phase* or with a *phase shift* [21].

The form of synchronisation between partners is even now investigated, by studying either behaviour [26] [25] [10] or cerebral activity [22] [28] [19] [20]. All these studies tend to show that when two persons interact together, they synchronise with each other or synchrony emerges between them. Synchrony is a dyadic parameter of the interaction between people, that means this parameter represents and accounts for the mutual coupling between them [12].

Synchrony does not only emerges from interaction, with this status of dyadic parameter, it can also be used by agents to modulate their interaction: it should participate to maintain contact between participants, facilitate verbal exchange and may also convey information. Psychological studies of dyadic interactions between mother and infant showed that very early in life (since two months and certainly earlier) synchrony between partners is a necessary condition to enable interaction: the infant stops interacting and imitating her mother when the mother stops being synchronous with her, all other parameters staying equal [29] [11] [15] [16] [18] [14] [27]. To explain this early effect of synchrony, Gergely and Watson postulate an innate Contingency Detection Module (CDM)[7] [8]. This detection of synchrony will enable the infant to detect the reactivity of her mother; when her mother is contingent, the infant is able to detect relations between her own actions and the actions she perceives from her mother: the action of her mother become a biofeedback of the infant's own actions. To detect the synchrony of the other is not only to detect the reactivity of the other, it is also to detect her/his engagement within the ongoing interaction and moreover it is also to detect her/his agency [17]. In that way, synchrony has been shown to be a premise of the interaction: in Nadel's Still Face experiment [13], the experimenter faces an autistic child which first ignores her. She then forces the synchrony with the child by imitating him, and the child enters in interaction with the experimenter. Child and experimenter finish taking turns and imitating each other. In that case forced synchrony made the child with autism detect the experimenter as a social partner.

This literature contributes to show that some of the signals created by the social interaction, such as synchrony between partners' behaviours, are signals which both enable to bootstrap, regulate and maintain social interaction and also signals which enable to develop a sense of agency and which contain information concerning the ongoing interaction.

How can we build a human-robot interaction which could take advantage of the signals emerging from this interaction so as to self-regulate? And how can we evaluate if the robot involved within this interaction does extract and use these signals?

A dyadic parameter of the interaction such as synchrony is a global parameter of the dyad, which makes sense only when we speak about several systems, but which is also perceivable by each individu of the dyad. That is the interesting point of this parameter, it carries dyadic information, concerning the quality of the ongoing interaction, and at the same time it can be retrieved by each partner of the interaction.

Andry et al. [1] used the rhythm of human actions on a keyboard as a reinforcement signal for learning. They assumed that when a human is satisfied with the computer answers, her/his actions are regular and will give positive reinforcement, and conversly, a break of the rhythm will produce an error signal. In the present paper, we also propose to learn some simple associations being only guided by an implicit reinforcement. In our case, the human and the agent will interact, not through a keyboard and a screen, but in the real world, through action and mutual perception: the agent will be a robot. The reinforcement will not be given by the individual parameter of actions rhythm (of either a human [2] or an agent [1]) but by the dyadic parameter of synchrony, which links the behaviour of both partners and which should be naturally modulated by their mutual engagement. The convergence of the learning reinforced by synchrony will show two things: First, that the dyadic parameters of the interaction emerging from the coupling between agents carry information available for each individual taking part within the interaction. Second, that these signals can be obtained and re-used by the robot and enable it to benefit from the interaction, for instance by learning a rule linked to the partner.

We have built a robot, ADRIANA (ADaptable Robotics for Interaction ANAlysis, [23]), capable to get the information of synchrony of its interaction with a human. We present first the principle of the experiment and of the associated architecture. Then we present in detail the architecture, from the synchrony detection to the use of this synchrony as a reinforcement signal. In section four we present our results on live experimentations with naive human subjects: seven naive subjects enable to improve the robot and architecture kinematics, and then three naive subjects were presented to the fully functionning robot to test its ability to detect and use synchrony. Finally we discuss these results which annonce a step toward intuitive interaction between human and robot, where human has not any knowledge of the robot functionning and only interacts with the implicit rules of every dyad in interaction.

2   How to Extract Relevant Cues of Ongoing Interaction and Proove That?

The aim of this robotic architecture and of its associated experiment is dual. On one hand the architecture should enable the robot to extract synchrony information during an interaction. On the other hand the experiment should prove that the extracted synchrony is relevant for social interactions, that means that synchrony is naturally modulated by human during an interaction.

To prove that, we will use the extracted synchrony to reinforce a learning: if the learning converges, then the synchrony we used is relevant, if the learning does not converge, then the signal we extracted is not appropriate.

2.1   Experimental Procedure

Each naive human subject faces the robot ADRIANA. ADRIANA is equiped with two arms with one degree of freedom and a camera (see fig.1). When the human subject, raises or pulls down one of her arms, the robot, respectively, raises or pulls down one of its arms, randomly the left or the right: the robot imitates the up or down position but not the left and right.

Photographer : RAGUET, Hubert / © CNRS Photothèque

Fig. 1. A naive human subject faces the robot, ADRIANA [23] (right picture), which is equiped with two arms with one degree of freedom and a camera. When the human raises or pulls down one of her arms, the robot respectively raises or pulls down one of its arms. The subject is asked to make the robot learn to imitate "in mirror" (to move the arm on the same side as the one moved by the human).

The instruction given to the naive subject is to "make the robot learn to move the arm which is on the same side as the one you move (in mirror)". The subject does not know how the robot learns and does not know how she/he can influence it. The only way is to try to interact with the robot. If the learning converges in these conditions, that will prove that the cues detected by the architecture are relevant cues of human communication: they are modulated by the human naturally, without having been asked to do so; these intuitive modulations carry information concerning the ongoing interaction, they have enable the convergence of learning. If, furthermore, these cues detected by the architecture are the synchrony variations, that will also prove that synchrony is a parameter naturally modulated depending on the ongoing interaction.

2.2   Architecture Principle

The idea of this architecture is to retrieve the information of synchrony between partners and to use it to reinforce associations between left/right visual field and left/right arms. We assume that synchrony is an indice of partner satisfaction concerning the ongoing interaction.

Synchrony is a dyadic parameter which characterises the reciprocal engagement of two partners. From the whole two partners system (the dyad), synchrony is accessible measuring the temporal relation existing between the actions of one partner and the ones of the other. But from the individual point of view of each partner, this information is also accessible, by comparing the time of her/his own action (ideally using proprioception) and the time of the successive activation within her/his visual field, generated by answer of the other partner.

To enable ADRIANA to compare its actions to the human's actions and to detect synchrony, there are two ways in the architecture, one from its perception and another from its action. If the delay between activation of the action way and activation of the perception way remains constant, that means that human and robot are synchronised: the interaction goes as human expects. In that case the reinforcement of previously used associations will be positive. If the delay predicted between perception and action varies above a threshold, that mean that there is no synchrony between human and robot: the interaction is temporarily disrupted, accounting for unsatisfied human's expectations. In that case, the reinforcement of previously used associations will be negative.

Finally, the convergence of learning will show that the reinforcement signal (the synchrony extracted) is correctly built by the architecture and that the synchrony modulated by the human interacting with the robot is an indice of the satisfaction of human's expectations.

3   Detailed Architecture

Figure 2 shows the full architecture, from visual detection of movement to motor commands sent to the arms. The pathway between perception and action is modulated by the detection of synchrony. In the remaining of this section, we detail the different part of this architecture.

3.1   Synchrony Detection: The Delay Prediction

To detect synchrony with the interaction partner, the architecture predicts the delay between its own actions and the detected actions of the partner. To predict

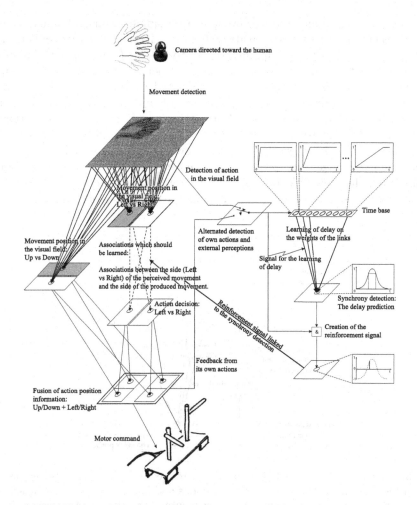

Fig. 2. ADRIANA's architecture. This architecture enable the robot, when it is interacting with a human, to detect the social signal naturally modulated by the human, here the synchrony, and to use this signal to reinforce a learning.

delay between action and perception we used a modified version of the architecture proposed by Andry et al. in 2001 which enables one to learn on the fly complex temporal sequences [1]. The original architecture enables a one shot learning of a temporal sequence of signals thanks to two formal neurons groups, connected together by modifiable links.

The first group of neurons is a *time base*[1]: every neuron is activated by a unique entry but each one has a different activation dynamic, from very quick

---

[1] See the works of Grossberg and Merryl 1996, and Banquet et al 1997, for a more neurobiologically plausible implementation of neurons with a time spectrum activity [9] [3].

to very slow. The input activates every neuron simultaneously, for instance at time t_0, each neuron has an activation dynamic $Act_k(t)$ which depends on the neuron position k in the group: $Act_k(t) = \frac{n}{k}\alpha(t - t_0)$ (where n is the number of neurons in the group and α a constant coefficient, see graphics of the upper part of fig.3). As soon as this group is activated by an input, the pattern of activations of its neurons represent the course of time since the input. It is this pattern of activations which will be learned and which will enable prediction of delay. To enable the architecture to predict delay between its own actions and the actions of the other, we have added a switch between signal coming from perceptive pathway and motor pathway. The *time base* is activated by the signal coming from the motor pathway and the pattern of the *time base* activations is learned when a signal coming from the perceptive pathway occurs.

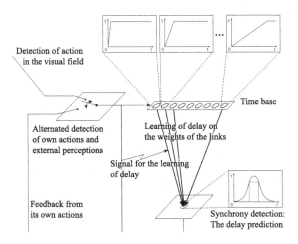

Fig. 3. Synchrony detection. This part of the architecture is dedicated to the prediction of the delay between the robot's own actions and human's actions: i.e. synchrony between human and robot. A first group of neurons, the *time base*, "measures" the course of time as soon as the robot produces an action. Links toward a second group of neurons, the *delay prediction*, have their weights modified when an action of the human is detected. The weights store the delay measured by the *time base*.

The second group is the *delay prediction*. In our case it is a group of one neuron as we have only one delay to predict. This neuron is connected to every neuron of the *time base* group (*one to all* connection). Andry et al. [1] propose a one shot learning of the delay d_i between two successives events ev_i and ev_{i+1} of a sequence. To do so, after ev_i, when the next event ev_{i+1} occurs, the pattern of activations of the *time base* neurons is stored in the weights W_k of the *one to all* links between the two groups: $W_k(t) = Act_k(t)$, and the *time base* is reset. We have modified this *one shot* learning rule to enable a learning of the mean value of the delay according to a Kohonen like learning rule: $W_k(t+1) = W_k(t) + \mu \times (Act_k(t+1) - W_k(t))$, where μ is the learning speed ($\mu = \frac{1}{3}$ in our case, if $\mu = 1$ it becomes a one shot learning). It is necessary to predict a mean delay since this mean delay is representative of the ongoing interaction which takes place between human and robot: when the interaction is satisfying, the human comes back to this "phase shift" when she/he aswers to the robot's actions. When the *time base* is activated once again, by a new motor command of the robot, the neuron of the second group is activated depending on the learned weight, according to the following equation: $\frac{1}{n} \sum_{k=1}^{n} e^{-\frac{1}{2\delta^2}(Act_k - W_k)^2}$ where δ is a coefficient controlling the width of the Gaussian $e^{-\frac{1}{2\delta^2}(x)^2}$ (in our case $\delta = 0.2$, see next section). The prediction of delay is a sum of gaussians: one gaussian for each neuron of the time base, centered on the predicted delay, when $Act_k = W_k$. This signal, also a gaussian centered on the predicted delay, will enable the architecture to built a reinforcement signal (see graph in the lowest right part of fig.3).

3.2 Reinforcement Signal: Synchrony

The prediction of the delay between action and perception is used by the architecture to compute the "level of synchrony" of the human-robot dyad. This level of synchrony is the error between the predicted delay and the real delay: If the predicted delay is close to the real delay, there is constant timing between both partners of the dyad, there is synchrony within the dyad and the interaction might be satisfactory for both partners (in our case for the human, the robot is always engaged in the interaction). If the predicted delay is far from the real delay, timing between partners of the dyad has varied; there is a synchrony break within the dyad; the interaction may have been disrupted by some event (in our case, by the robot which does not satisfy human expectations).

Synchrony between partners of an interaction should account for the quality of the interaction. In our experiment, we use this synchrony as reinforcement signal, assuming that the more satisfied will be the human expectation, the more synchronous the human will be with the robot: the more predictible the delay between robot's actions and human's actions will be.

To build this reinforcement signal, the robot can use two things: on one hand it has the delay it is currently predicting, a gaussian centered on the learned delay (see section 3.1), and on the other hand it has the real current delay, instantaneous signal issuing from the perception of an action in the visual field (see fig.4).

The reinforcement signal *Renf* is the value of the gaussian when an action is perceived in the visual field, i.e. when a signal comes from the movement detection. This reinforcement signal is computed at the level of the & operator in figure 4.

This reinforcement signal which varies between 0 and 1 will then be projected between -1 and 1 to enable positive or negative reinforcements (see the lower graph of figure 4). The width δ of the gaussian must be chosen carefully: it must be large enough to tolerate small variations in the synchrony between human and robot, but also narrow enough to enable detection of synchrony breaks associated to human subject unsatisfaction. We have chosen $\delta = 0.2$

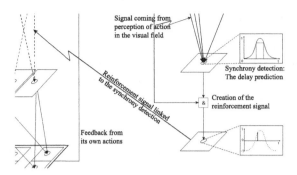

Fig. 4. From synchrony to reinforcement signal. The reinforcement signal is built depending on the quality of the interaction, i.e. depending if the expectations of the human subject are satisfied or not. The more satisfied is the human, the more regular will be her/his productions after the robot actions, thus, the more accurate the predicted delay will be. When the human's action is detected, the current value of the predicted delay, a gaussian centered on the predicted delay, is taken. This value is between 0 and 1, maximum when the prediction is exact and which lower when the real delay moves away (advanced or delayed) from the prediction.

which corresponds to a tolerance of about $0.4sec$ in the delay prediction, before sending a negative reinforcement.

Finally, better is the predicted delay compared to the real delay, better is the reinforcement signal, thus better is the reinforcement, better is the synchrony between human and robot behaviours.

3.3   Learning Based on a Delayed Reinforcement

In order to test the relevance of this "level of synchrony" we used it as a reinforcement signal for the learning of associations: the relevance of this computing will be validated if the "level of synchrony" computed by the architecture enables learning to converge. The learning modulates associations between the side of perception of the robot (left or right visual hemi-field according to the arm moved by the human) and the side of action of the robot (left or right arm of the robot).

The reinforcement signal (the level of synchrony) is generated by the human (who ignores that) and we do not know *a priori* when this signal will vary after an error of the robot. That raises two issues: first the reinforcement signal occurs later than the trials it concerns; second the perceptions-actions associations aimed by the reinforcement signal are not specified. The PCR (Probabilistic Conditioning Rule) of Gaussier and Revel et al. [6,24] solve the first issue: it enables associations between groups of formal neurons to be modified according to a reinforcement signal, even if the reinforcement occurs later than the trials it concerns. The second issue remains since the original PCR was built for a reinforcement signal aiming at a well defined set of associations: the associations used since the previous reinforcement. By contrast, the reinforcement signal linked to the level of synchrony is computed at every trial and we do not know exactly how many associations it concerns. To solve this second issue, we assume that humans naturally make synchrony vary according to her/his satisfaction and we assume that this synchrony modification detected by the architecture (see section 3.2) concerns the actions performed by the robot an a time window of length τ ($\tau = 3$ seems a good length for this window, see section 4). We modified the PCR so that the reinforcement signal at time t concerns the associations used during the time window $[t - \tau, t]$.

The learning rule is a local rule, i.e. it applies to one link between an input neuron and an output neuron and depends only on the activation of these two neurons and on its own weight. Given a link $I_i \rightarrow O_j$, at each time step, the activation rate $ActE_i$ of its input E_i is updated. $ActE_i$ is the percentage of activation times during a window of τ time steps: $ActE_i(t + 1) = \frac{\tau \times ActE_i(t) + 5 \times E_i(t)}{\tau + 5}$ where $E_i = 0$ or 1.

When a reinforcement signal is produced by the synchrony detection (section 3.2), $Renf \neq 0$, two additional variables are updated:

- First the confidence C_{ij} in the weight of the link. It depends for one part on the reinforcement signal (common to every link) and for another part on the impact of this specific link on the reinforcement signal, i.e. the activation rate $ActE_i$ of the entry of the link:

$$C_{ij}(t + 1) = C_{ij}(t) + \alpha \times Renf(t) \times ActE_i(t) \text{ where } \alpha = 0.5$$

    To compute the variation of the confidence in the weight of the link, the reinforcement signal is first projected from $[0; 1]$ to $[-1; 1]$ and then multiplied by the activation rate $ActE_i$ of the entry and a coefficient α. This variation is added to the previous confidence C_{ij}.
- After that, the weight W_{ij} of the link is updated depending on C_{ij}. The confidence C_{ij} is used as a probability to maintain the weight value unchanged: If a random draw is greater than or equal to C_{ij}, then $W_{ij}(t+1) = 1 - W_{ij}(t)$ and $C_{ij}(t + 1) = 1 - C_{ij}(t)$.
    Else, the weight is unchanged.
    When the random draw is greater than the confidence C_{ij} in the weight, the weight is drastically modified (symetrically to 0.5), and thus the confidence in this new weight is also modified (symetrically to 0.5).

These different parts of the architecture, when put together and correctly parametrised, enable the robot to use the synchrony of its interaction with a human as a reinforcement signal.

4   Results

ADRIANA equiped with two arms, a camera and the previously described architecture, has been first parametrised on seven naive subjects and then tested on three other naive subjects.

The first seven subjects enabled us to improve the timing of the different parts of the architecture of the robot:

- Our system does not modulate its rhythm of interaction in live, the arms velocity and the speed of answers to visual stimulation, have been adjusted along these first experiments: To enable human interaction rhythm to be intuitive for the subject, the human needs to feel reciprocal interaction. The reaction of the robot to human's movements must be systematic and almost instantaneous to be trusted to be imitation. It must also be predictible by the human, not in its form but in the fact that particular movement of the human will systematically lead to an answer of the robot. The human must be sure that both she/he is influencing the robot and she/he has the attention of the robot. Otherwise, the human is rapidly discouraged.
- The kinematics of the robot's movement must fit the kinematics perceivable by the robot: the human adapts the kinematics of his actions to the robot kinematics, systematically and with no instruction. It is one facet of the expertise of human in social interaction. For our robot, a good compromise between speed and detection is full movements (raising or pulling down an arm) which last around 1 second: human-robot reciprocal answers are fluid, human actions are systematically detected by the robot, and time delay from an action to the next (between 1 and 2.5 seconds) are also correctly predicted by the robot.
- The kinematics of the robot, kinematics of human induced by the robot and kinematics perceivable by the robot taken as a whole, must be what is intuitively modulated by human when socially interacting, i.e. the inter-individual synchrony. In our case, for actions lasting 1 second, the mean delay of human reactions to the robot actions is $1.5sec$, between $1.4sec$ and $1.7sec$ when the interaction is going well, and modified by more than $0.5sec$ when perturbations such as robot's mistakes occur (the width of gaussian $\delta = 0.2$ which corresponds to a tolerance of $0.4sec$).
- The reinforcement signal comes around 4 seconds (equivalent to about 3 actions) after the corresponding actions of the robot: the reinforcement must concern a time window with a length of at least 3 steps ($\tau = 3$).
- These points contribute to make the robot's production of action to enable synchrony to emerge between human and robot.

The last three subjects have been presented to the whole experimental protocol (without anymore adaptation of the robotic setup). They could interact naturally and robustly with the robot and made the learning converge. A second task was added due to the quick and good results of the first teaching task:

The first instruction given to the subject was to make the robot learn to imitate "in mirror" (for an example see *http://ken.prepin.free.fr/spip.php?article20*, first video "The robot which uses natural cues of social interaction. Part 1").

Then, when the robot did not make anymore mistake (learning has converged and the subject has the feeling of stabilised behaviour), subject have been asked to make the robot imitate "on the opposite side". There was no break in the experiment, the robot had to unlearn previous association and learn new ones, on the fly (for an example see *http://ken.prepin.free.fr/spip.php?article20*, second video "The robot which uses natural cues of social interaction. Part 2").

The results obtained in these three experiments are similar (see fig.5 for an example):

- Learning converged: in our three experiments, an average of 10 reinforcement signals was necessary to enable learning to converge, 30 signals to unlearn and relearn associations. This learning convergence was faster than learning by chance: let N be the number of possible associations (4 in our case: two possibilities for each of the two possible inputs), let τ be the size of

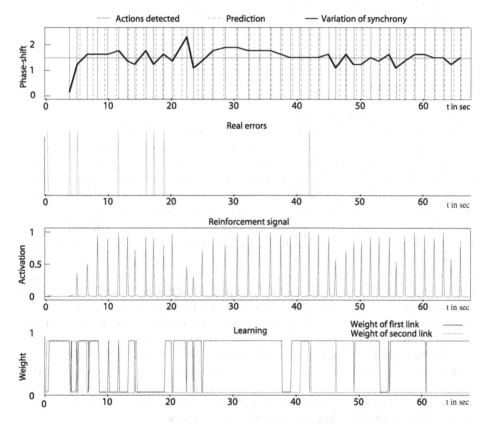

Fig. 5. Results obtained with one subject. The first graph represents together the real (continuous line) and predicted (dotted line) actions of the human and the associated phase-shift between robot and human (bold line). The second curve represents the real mistakes of the robot (according to the instructions: "make the robot imitate in mirror"). The third curve is the reinforcement signal computed using synchrony information: a negative reinforcement is lower than 0.5 and a positive reinforcement is higher than 0.5. This reinforcement depends on the accuracy of the predicted delay compared to the real one. The fourth graph is the evolution of the weight of the links between perception and action. It enable to see if these weights stabilise and if they are opposite (as needed). Let us notice that learning stabilises and moreover that reinforcement signal is clearly linked to the real mistakes of the robot.

the time window concerned by the reinforcement signal (3 in our case: the reinforcement signal depends on the three previous detections of synchrony) and let us assume that the reinforcement can be either positive or negative. In the same conditions (delayed positive or negative reinforcement), a random reinforcement would have $\frac{1}{N} \times \frac{1}{\tau} \times \frac{1}{2} = \frac{1}{24}$ chances to be correct.

- Learning converged in reasonnable time: learning converged in less than half a minute, unlearning and relearning took $1min30sec$.
- At the end of the experiment, while "debriefing", the three subjects spontaneously declared to have enjoyed the experiment.
- The three subjects spontaneously declared they had the feeling of having influenced the robot.
- The three subjects declared they were satisfied with the experiment and were ready for a new one.

5   Discussion

This study leads to two main results.

The most important is that the information of synchrony, naturally given by the naive user, brings relevant sense. Synchrony is not only a phenomenon accompanying every social interaction, it is a parameter which carries information concerning the ongoing interaction. Our results participate to show that this dyadic parameter can be detected and used by each agent involved in the interaction so as to get information on this interaction. In our case, synchrony has conveid information relevant for learning showing that it was directly linked to the satisfaction of naive human subjects' expectations regarding the robot's actions.

The second result is that this architecture enables us to extract and re-use this information. The comparison between actions of the agent and perception is a mean to detect synchrony. The proposed experiment design makes this detection easy: the very simple robot, ADRIANA, and its basic movements lead the human to produce action easily detected by our system, i.e. bounded in time and extractable only by movement detection. The associated learning by a delayed reinforcement enabled us to benefit from this synchrony detection even if we did not known *a priori* its exact relevance and precision over time. This architecture should be an inspiring way to improve HMIs (Human Machine Interfaces) by allowing an intuitive on line learning with naive users.

These two intwinned results, support the idea that an agent's ability to interact with a human and to perceive the relevant signals of this interaction, is not only a matter of technical complexity of its detection system. Both the agent and its behaviours influence the way and the means used by human during interaction: with a simple robot which only raises or pulls down its arms with a specific kinematics, human will interact just raising and pulling down its arms with similar kinematics, easily detectable by the robot. Finally, the agent's own productions influence its possibility of detection and perception.

To investigate synchrony more in details the idea would be to enable the architecture to modify its dynamics depending either on internal states (or motivations) or on the detected synchrony (with for instance synchronisation mechanisms such as dynamical coupling [23]). On one hand, the agent may be able to test the engagement of the human: the agent can modify its production dynamics and measure the subsequent effect of this modification on the human partner; if the human stays synchronous eventhough dynamics have changed, it means she/he is engaged within the interaction, otherwise it means either she/he does not care about the interaction or she/he has expectations not satisfied. On the other hand, the agent may be able to show either its engagement or its un-satisfaction by respectively synchronising or un-synchronising with the human. Such abilities of the social agent would fit the experimental psychology claim that social agents test the engagement of their partner by modifying their production and controlling the reaction of the partner.

Finally, during the interactions enabled by our architecture, knowledge has been exchanged between human and robot. But the form of this exchange contrasts with typical views: Here the knowledge is not directly contained in the transmitted information as it can be when language is used or when a robot imitates a human. Here the robot extracts information from the course of the interaction itself: what is taken into account by the robot is not the transmitted information but the way the interaction evolves through time. The only mean to make this robot learn something is not to show it, to repeat it, to correct it, the only mean to make this robot learn something is to interact with it, to be trully engaged in interaction with it.

Acknowledgements

This work has been mainly financed by a research grant from the DGA and lately supported by the NoE SSPNet (Social Signal Processing Network) European project.

References

1. Andry, P., Gaussier, P., Moga, S., Banquet, J.P., Nadel, J.: Learning and Communication in Imitation: An Autonomous Robot Perspective. IEEE transactions on Systems, Man and Cybernetics, Part A 31(5), 431–444 (2001)
2. Andry, P., Moga, S., Gaussier, P., Revel, A., Nadel, J.: Imitation: learning and communication. In: The Sixth International Conference on Simulation for Adaptive Behavior SAB 2000, Paris, pp. 353–362. MIT Press, Cambridge (2000)
3. Banquet, J.P., Gaussier, P., Dreher, J.C., Joulain, C., Revel, A., Günther, W.: Space-time, order, and hierarchy in fronto-hippocampal system: A neural basis of personality. In: Matthews, G. (ed.) Advances in Psychology, Amsterdam, vol. 124, pp. 123–189. North-Holland, Amsterdam (1997)
4. Condon, W.S.: An analysis of behavioral organisation. Sign Language Studies 13, 285–318 (1976)
5. Condon, W.S., Ogston, W.D.: Sound film analysis of normal and pathological behavior patterns. Journal of Nervous and Mental Disease 143, 338–347 (1966)
6. Gaussier, P., Revel, A., Joulain, C., Zrehen, S.: Living in a partially structured environment: How to bypass the limitation of classical reinforcement techniques. Robotics and Autonomous Systems 20, 225–250 (1997)

7. Gergely, G., Watson, J.: The social biofeedback model of parental affect-mirroring. International Journal of Psycho-Analysis 77, 1181–1212 (1996)

8. Gergely, G., Watson, J.: Early social-emotional development: Contingency perception and the social biofeedback model. In: Early social cognition, pp. 101–136. Erlbaum, Hillsdale (1999)

9. Grossberg, S., Merrill, J.W.L.: The hippocampus and cerebellum in adaptively timed learning, recognition, and movement. Journal of Cognitive Neuroscience 8, 257–277 (1996)

10. Lopresti-Goodman, S.M., Richardson, M.J., Silva, P.L., Schmidt, R.C.: Period basin of entrainment for unintentional visual coordination. Journal of Motor Behavior 40(1), 3–10 (2008)

11. Murray, L., Trevarthen, C.: Emotional regulation of interactions vetween two-month-olds and their mothers. Social perception in infants, 101–125 (1985)

12. Nadel, J.: Imitation et communication entre jeunes enfants. Presse Universitaire de France, Paris (1986)

13. Nadel, J.: The functionnal use of imitation in preverbal infants and nonverbal children with autism. In: Meltzoff, A., Prinz, W. (eds.) The Imitative Mind: Developement, Evolution and Brain Bases. Cambridge University Press, Cambridge (2000)

14. Nadel, J.: Imitation and imitation recognition: their functional role in preverbal infants and nonverbal children with autism, pp. 42–62. Cambridge University Press, UK (2002)

15. Nadel, J., Camaioni, L.: New Perspectives in Early Communicative Development. Routledge, London (1993)

16. Nadel, J., Guerini, C., Peze, A., Rivet, C.: The evolving nature of imitation as a format for communication. In: Nadel, G., Butterworth, J. (eds.) Imitation in Infancy, pp. 209–234. Cambridge University Press, Cambridge (1999)

17. Nadel, J., Prepin, K., Okanda, M.: Experiencing contigency and agency: first step toward self-understanding? In: Hauf, P. (ed.) Making Minds II: Special issue of Interaction Studies 6:3 2005, pp. 447–462. John Benjamins publishing company, Amsterdam (2005)

18. Nadel, J., Tremblay-Leveau, H.: Early social cognition, chapter Early perception of social contingencies and interpersonal intentionality: dyadic and triadic paradigms, pp. 189–212. Lawrence Erlbaum Associates, Mahwah (1999)

19. Oullier, O., de Guzman, G.C., Jantzen, K.J., Lagarde, J., Kelso, J.A.S.: Social coordination dynamics: Measuring human bonding. Social Neuroscience 3(2), 178–192 (2008)

20. Oullier, O., Kelso, J.A.S.: Coordination from the perspective of Social Coordination Dynamics. In: Encyclopedia of Complexity and Systems Science. Springer, Heidelberg (2009)

21. Pikovsky, A., Rosenblum, M., Kurths, J.: Synchronization: A Universal Concept in Nonlinear Sciences. Cambridge University Press, Cambridge (1981)

22. Pineda, J.A.: The functional significance of mu rhythms: Translating "seeing" and "hearing" into "doing". Brain Research Reviews 50, 57–68 (2005)

23. Prepin, K., Revel, A.: Human-machine interaction as a model of machine-machine interaction: how to make machines interact as humans do. Advanced Robotics 21(15), 1709–1723 (2007)

24. Revel, A.: Contrôle d'un robot mobile autonome par approche neuro-mimétique. Doctorat de traitement de l'image et du signal, Université de Cergy-Pontoise (Novembre 1997)

25. Richardson, M.J., Marsh, K.L., Isenhower, R.W., Goodman, J.R.L., Schmidt, R.C.: Rodking together: Dynamics of intentional and unitentional interpersonal coordination. Human Movement Science 26, 867–891 (2007)
26. Richardson, M.J., Marsh, K.L., Schmidt, R.C.: Effects of visual and verbal interaction on unintentional interpersonal coordination. Journal of Experimental Psychology: Human Perception and Performance 31(1), 62–79 (2005)
27. Soussignan, R., Nadel, J., Canet, P., Girardin, P.: Sensitivity to social contingency and positive emotion in 2-month-olds. Infancy 10(2), 123–144 (2006)
28. Tognoli, E., Lagarde, J., DeGuzman, G.C., Kelso, J.A.S.: The phi complex as a neuromarker of human social coordination (2007)
29. Tronick, E., Als, H., Adamson, L., Wise, S., Brazelton, T.B.: The infants' response to entrapment between contradictory messages in face-to-face interactions. Journal of the American Academy of Child Psychiatry (Psychiatrics) 17, 1–13 (1978)

Accessible Speech-Based and Multimodal Media Center Interface for Users with Physical Disabilities

Markku Turunen[1], Jaakko Hakulinen[1], Aleksi Melto[1], Juho Hella[1], Tuuli Laivo[1],
Juha-Pekka Rajaniemi[1], Erno Mäkinen[1], Hannu Soronen[2], Mervi Hansen[2],
Santtu Pakarinen[2], Tomi Heimonen[1], Jussi Rantala[1], Pellervo Valkama[1],
Toni Miettinen[1] and Roope Raisamo[1]

[1] TAUCH, Department of Computer Sciences
[2] IHTE, Department of Software Systems, University of Tampere,
33014 University of Tampere, Finland
mturunen@cs.uta.fi

Abstract. We present a multimodal media center user interface with a hands-free speech recognition input method for users with physical disabilities. In addition to speech input, the application features a zoomable context + focus graphical user interface and several other modalities, including speech output, haptic feedback, and gesture input. These features have been developed in co-operation with representatives from the target user groups. In this article, we focus on the speech input interface and its evaluations. We discuss the user interface design and results from a long-term pilot study taking place in homes of physically disabled users, and compare the results to a public pilot study and laboratory studies carried out with non-disabled users.

1 Introduction

The so-called media center applications, which combine commonly accessed media (e.g., television broadcasts, music, and photographs) under a unified user interface, are becoming increasingly common. Many such systems already exist; both as hardware solutions and as software applications for personal computers and video game consoles. A media center interface can be particularly useful for special user groups, since it facilitates the use of a single, accessible user interface to control a variety of different systems found in digital homes. These systems and applications are typically used with complex remote controllers that make the interaction slow, complicated, or even inaccessible for some. In this context, multimodal interaction can be beneficial for all user groups. For example, Ibrahim and Johansson [6] propose a novel TV program guide system that combines speech interaction and direct manipulation with remote control use. Their results indicate that users prefer the multimodal approach to pure spoken input or pure direct manipulation, as different modalities are better suited for different operations and hence support each other. For special user groups, different modalities provide alternative methods to interact with the system. New solutions may even offer totally revolutionary changes in the lives of people with disabilities by making something previously inaccessible accessible and potentially very useful.

A. Esposito et al. (Eds.): COST 2102 Int. Training School 2009, LNCS 5967, pp. 66–79, 2010.
© Springer-Verlag Berlin Heidelberg 2010

Speech can be utilized to support users with different kinds of impairments. For example, people with motor disabilities, such as paralysis or some neurodegenerative diseases, often have to use input methods that provide very limited means of interaction. With speech recognition some of these users can have much more efficient and richer access to various digital services, including digital television content.

In the context of media center applications, Wittenburg and others [17] have studied unrestricted speech input for TV content search and found retrieval performance to be critical to user experience, indicating that unrestricted speech input is viable only when high recognition rates can be achieved. Error correction can solve some of these problems [4], but errors should be minimized in the first place, in particular for users who cannot use the full scale of input/output modalities. As speech recognition accuracy is dependent greatly on the size of the language model used for recognition, the optimal selection of grammar size is vital. Use of domain specific grammar and vocabulary can be a reasonable choice in order to maximize recognition rates and to avoid negative user experiences. With restricted speech, however, the amount of Out-Of-Vocabulary sentences may become a problem, especially if users do not receive enough guidance on how to speak to the system. Poorly designed grammars may also force users to use unnatural language and thus make speech recognition tedious to use. Speech can provide a powerful input channel if a good balance is found: commands, which would require tedious navigation with current interfaces, can be given with a single utterance. The optimal solution can vary greatly between user groups. Limited grammars, which require learning, may be perfectly acceptable for those users who find current solutions tedious to use. A good example is spoken commands versus navigation with physical keys or buttons: the latter is usually very hard for people with certain physical disabilities. Furthermore, it is possible to personalize the recognition grammars to find the optimal solution for that individual.

When new interface solutions are introduced, in particular to home contexts, special care should be taken to ensure their acceptability. First, new applications and interface techniques create new kinds of styles and contexts of use, so attitudes and expectations towards them may differ greatly. Designing for home environments is particularly challenging, since strong value systems are associated with homes. Some people are keen to try out any new technology to improve their homes, but there are user segments that are reluctant to adopt technical solutions for everyday tasks and who especially appreciate media silence at home [10]. On the other hand, home environments are in many ways suitable for introducing new interaction modalities. Since the use of these technologies is daily and the user population is known, customization, adaptation, and learning techniques can be utilized to make the interaction robust and efficient. For example, recognition-based technologies, such as speech recognition, can be personalized and adapted to specific users by using customized vocabularies and training.

In this article, we present a multimodal user interface for media center applications. The interface contains a zoomable GUI combined with input and output methods including speech input and output, haptic feedback, and gestures. We focus on the speech input functionality, which we combined with voice activity and blow detection to provide an efficient and accessible input method for physically disabled users who cannot operate conventional remote controls. First, we describe the multimodal media center application and its overall user interface. Then, we report the user evaluations that were carried out to study user expectations and experiences, focusing on a long-term in situ evaluation with physically disabled users. We conclude by discussing the implications of our results for the design of multimodal interfaces in similar settings, and directions for future work.

2 Multimodal Media Center

Media center devices and applications are rapidly becoming very popular in homes. It is an application area that provides a lot of opportunities and challenges for the design of user interaction solutions. As a part of the Finnish research project TÄPLÄ [16] we have built a multimodal media center application to study the use of novel interface modalities in home environments. Versions of the system have been developed for different user groups, including two groups with special requirements. Here, we describe the version designed to support physically disabled users.

The media center application offers the functionality to watch and record television broadcasts, listen to music, and view digital photographs. In the first version we have focused on implementing the television broadcast functionality. The application provides full control over digital television content, including a novel electronic program guide (EPG). Next, we present the application from technical and user interface perspectives. A more comprehensive description of the system and its different input and output modalities can be found in [12].

2.1 Technical Setup

The media center application is based on a low-cost PC equipped with a dual terrestrial/cable digital TV receiver. Our aim has been to keep the cost of the required system low so that the potential end users can actually afford to buy one. We have managed to keep the price of the hardware similar to an advanced recording digital TV set top box. Alternatively, users are able to use their existing PC and equip it with a digital TV receiver.

In addition to the computer, a suite of input devices is required. In the default setup for able-bodied users, a Symbian S60 mobile phone is used as a remote control proxy. It provides keypad input, speech input and output, vibration output and accelerometer input. For users who have motor disabilities and who use a wheelchair, a wireless microphone connected to the wheelchair is used for speech input. A wireless access point is used to connect the mobile phone to the computer, or alternatively an audio mixer is used to connect the wireless microphone. A regular high-definition television is used as display. This overall setup is illustrated in Figure 1.

For the long-term pilot study with physically disabled users, as presented here, we used professional wireless lavalier microphones connected to the computer using a regular audio mixer. While these are not unreasonably expensive, a more affordable setup could be achieved by using wireless consumer-level microphones, e.g., cheap Bluetooth headsets.

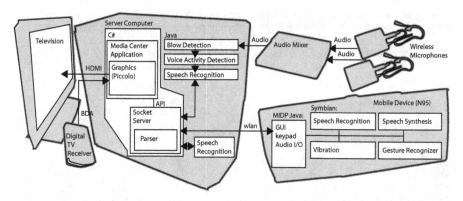

Fig. 1. Multimodal Media Center architecture with two alternative setups including (a) two wireless microphones (upper right) and (b) a mobile phone (lower right). In the evaluation presented here, the wireless microphone setup was used.

The server software implements the media center application functionality in the Microsoft Windows environment. It is written in C# and Java, utilizing the Piccolo graphics toolkit [3]. In this setup, the server also includes the speech recognizer component. A more detailed description of the system architecture is beyond the scope of this article, and is presented elsewhere [12].

2.2 Media Center User Interface

The media center user interface consists of several dedicated views for different media applications (e.g., photographs and music). We focus here on the EPG interface. It consists of a grid view, with columns representing television channels and rows representing time slots. Cells represent individual television programs. The EPG interface is illustrated in Figure 2.

Overlaid animated icons provide guidance and feedback on available user input methods. Speech activation notification is displayed on the screen indicating that the system is listening to the user's speech. This is particularly important when activation is not done with keypad buttons, as is the case for users with motor disabilities. In order to support readability and ease of visual scanning, the user interface implements several focus-plus-context techniques, taking inspiration from such techniques as fisheye menus [1] and the DateLens system [2]. The columns and rows near the center of the display are slightly enlarged and/or highlighted, and a strong enlargement effect is applied to the active cell (program). Partial transparency is used in the active cell to make the content under the enlarged area visible. The display can be zoomed-in from weekly overviews to close-ups of single programs. The aim of this interface is to minimize the need for repetitive low-level navigation tasks by keeping both context and focus information visible at the same time.

Users have full control over the media center via its speech user interface. We have built different speech recognition models for specific use cases, for example, overall navigation in the application (e.g., *"Go to program guide"*), navigation inside the EPG (*"Show Monday afternoon"*) and playing back media (*"Go to documentary*

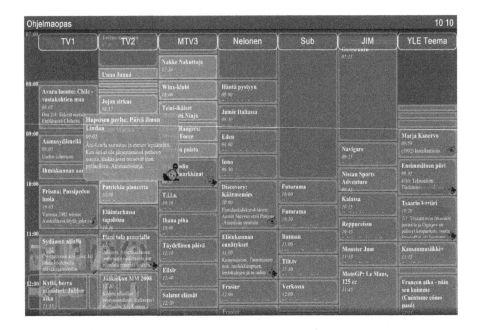

Fig. 2. EPG interface

channel"). It is also possible to record multiple episodes with a single utterance ("*Record all the Tom the Tractor shows this week*"), and to highlight programs based on their genre ("*Show me all the children programs tomorrow morning*"). Speech recognition is implemented with context-free grammars. A grammar containing all program names for seven channels for a week has a vocabulary of about 900 words.

However, there are many challenges in building speech recognition grammars for these kinds of applications, primarily in terms of recognition robustness. Television programs can have unpredictable names, and more importantly, they appear in different languages. Thus, building a grammar automatically can sometimes be problematic. Although we got very promising results with the full grammar (see next section for results), we considered robustness to be the ultimate goal for physically disabled users, who cannot correct recognition errors using other modalities. Because of this, a more simplified grammar was constructed. Navigation between the channels still uses channel names. Program names, however, are indexed with numbers from one to nine. The numbers are displayed next to the program name in the EPG display (Figure 3) and in the listing of recorded programs, and the user can access a specific program by giving its index number as a speech command. In this way the selection of programs is arguably less intuitive, however we were able to eliminate problems associated with inconsistent program names and minimize the number of recognition errors.

The system includes support for two speech recognizers: an embedded recognizer running on a mobile phone, and a server-based recognizer. The choice of the recognizer is a balancing act between speed, vocabulary size and accuracy. Server based recognition was an obvious choice for physically disabled users, since we decided not to include the mobile phone in their setup (for the reasons explained in section 3.1).

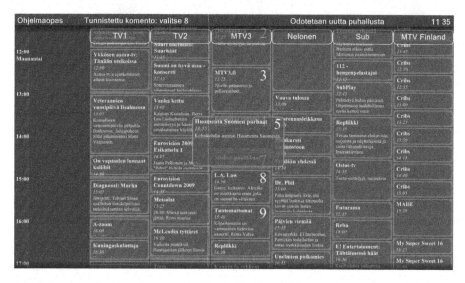

Fig. 3. The accessible user interface for physically disabled users, who cannot use their hands for error correction. For regular use, all program names are included in the language model.

Fig. 4. Wireless microphone installation. Photograph reproduced with permission.

The system uses various mechanisms for activating speech recognition. Continuous listening and voice activity detection are not reliable enough for daily use in the home environment, given that the television itself and other ambient audio sources may already make loud enough noises to cause incorrect speech detection and recognition. In the mobile phone based setups, input is activated either by traditional button pressing ('push-to-talk'), or by a gesture in which the user raises the phone to his/her mouth to start the command, and lowers the phone to end the command and start the recognition [12].

For physically disabled users, who cannot use their hands, neither of the solutions available in the mobile phone interface is a viable option. Instead, we mounted wireless microphones with articulated stands to their wheelchairs in the vicinity of each user's mouth (Figure 4). Additionally, we implemented a detector that activates normal voice activity detection when the user blows into his/her microphone. The voice activity detector records the user utterance and feeds it to the speech recognizer. Even a weak blow directed straight into the microphone registers as a high energy level spike in the audio and can be reliably detected using an absolute energy threshold with an appropriate window size.

3   User Evaluations

The attitudes and expectations people have towards new applications, such as media centers, and novel multimodal interaction techniques, such as speech and gesture input, are not well known in general. Furthermore, designing solutions for home environments is particularly challenging because of the unique values related to them: homes are often regarded as tranquil, esthetic, private, sacred and safe harbors from the busy and stressful outside world. For these reasons, there is an urgent need to know more about user expectations towards and experiences with novel modalities in homes and home-like settings, such as assisted housing and long-term care facilities. It is also very important to find out the expectations and the experiences of people with disabilities towards new technical solutions, as they stand to benefit perhaps the most from them. On the other hand, people with disabilities may have very strong opinions and expectations on user interface issues based on the existing solutions they have relied on for many years. Thus, it is essential to design the systems so that the needs of the specified user groups are supported by taking into account their preferences and habits. In our case, for example, a quadriplegic user needed to have full control over the system by speech alone.

In the beginning of the project, a large consumer survey with more than a thousand respondents showed that people approach speech input with caution [10]. However, our experiences from several applications suggest that the actual experiences with a working speech-based system can result in more positive attitudes [12; 14]. Thus, introducing novel interaction methods into real environments is the key approach in making them widely acceptable and driving adoption.

Next, we present the different evaluations of the media center application we have conducted focusing on speech inputs. First, we introduce the initial experiences from a ten-month living laboratory evaluation carried out in a local media museum. Then, we present the key results from a formal user study carried out in our usability laboratory. Finally, we present findings from a long-term pilot study with two physically disabled users. Findings from evaluations regarding other modalities, such gestures and haptic feedback, have been previously reported elsewhere [13].

3.1 Living Laboratory Evaluation

A Living Lab testing environment was built in Rupriikki Media museum in Tampere. The media center system was available for use to all the guests of the museum, from May 2008 to March 2009. It could be operated by speech and gestures using a mobile phone. In the summer 2008, 21 formative user tests were held in the living lab environment. The main objectives were to elicit the expectations of users towards a smart home environment and its input methods, and specifically the preferred features.

The tests were carried out in three stages; initial expectations were gathered with interviews to assess attitudes and opinions regarding the use of speech and other modalities. Then the participants familiarized themselves with the media center and its input modalities. After approximately ten minutes of free use, the participants were interviewed again to establish how their opinions had changed. The relation between expectations (before the use) and experiences (after the use) was evaluated. The analysis focused on the stated levels of both user expectations and experiences, reported on a 5-point scale, regarding the *pleasantness*, *ease of use* and *convenience* of the application.

At this point the system included a mobile phone display. On the display the user could see the last recognized commands and the state of the system. However, only one user paid any attention to the display and all other users focused on the TV screen instead. We believe that in this context the "flow of use" is strongly related to the interaction with TV screen and adding other displays could unnecessarily complicate the interaction. Based on these findings we decided not to provide a close-proximity display (e.g., on a mobile phone or PDA) for the physically disabled users.

In summary, the participants were overall satisfied with the use of speech but initially approached it with skeptical expectations. This encouraged us to study the use of speech in more controlled settings to further develop the interface towards an accessible version suitable for long-term use in home environment.

3.2 Controlled Laboratory Experiment

We arranged a controlled user experiment in our usability laboratory, in order to study the expectations and user experience of the media center application and its input and output modalities in a formal setting. Towards this end, 26 students from the local university were recruited to participate in the experiment. The SUXES evaluation method [11] was used to collect subjective metrics regarding the use of the media center application. In short, SUXES produces a subjective measure of the gap between the pre-test expectations and the post-test perceptions (experiences). Before the experiment, participants were asked to fill in a questionnaire concerning their expectations with respect to nine different statements about the system. They were asked to mark both an acceptable and desirable level for each statement. Each participant then completed three exercise tasks and 11 evaluation tasks with the application. The tasks reflected typical home usage scenarios, e.g., selecting a recorded program, setting up recordings, and switching channels in the electronic program guide. After completing the tasks, the participants filled in a questionnaire consisting of the same statements they were presented with in the pre-test questionnaire. This time the participants gave only one value to indicate their perceived experience.

The SUXES method makes it possible to estimate what is the current state of the application based on pre-use expectations and post-use experiences. Here, we focus on the following user experience dimensions corresponding to the statements in the questionnaire: *speed, pleasantness, clearness, error-free use, error-free function, learning curve, naturalness, usefulness,* and *future use* of speech input. The expectations and experiences on these statements were asked concerning each multimodal input/output method (speech input, gestures, and haptic feedback). Figure 5 summarizes the main results for each of the dimensions mentioned above for speech input.

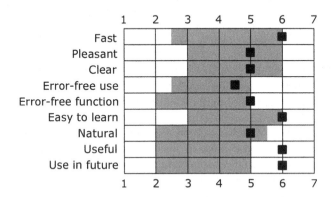

Fig. 5. User expectations and user experience of speech input in the laboratory experiment: the gray areas represent the range of expectations (acceptable – desired) and the black squares represent the perceived experiences.

Application of Friedman's test on the post-use experience values shows that there are significant effects of the input/output modality across all dimensions. Pair-wise comparisons between modalities were carried out by using Wilcoxon signed-rank test with Bonferonni corrected levels of observed significance. When compared to the other modalities, speech was rated significantly higher than gestures in all dimensions ($p < 0.01$). Overall, it was also rated as the most pleasant, clearest, easiest to learn, most useful and likeliest modality to be used in the future. No significant difference was found between speech and haptic feedback in speed, error-free use, error-free function or naturalness.

As the results indicate, our speech interface design was received very positively. Our participants' initial expectations were somewhat conservative, matching the findings of our initial user survey [10] and the local media museum pilot study. Nevertheless, speech input expectations are clearly met, and in some cases even surpassed.

We believe that one reason for the positive feedback was accurate speech recognition. The overall speech recognition rate was 93% (and even 97% when OOV sentences are removed). Still, the most important conclusion is that grammar-based recognition can be efficient in this domain without training. Based on these encouraging results, we were confident that such a speech interface could be robust enough for long-term use. For physically disabled users, however, we wanted the interface to be even more robust, so we introduced the small vocabulary navigation method, as presented in the previous section.

3.3 Long-Term Pilot Study with Physically Disabled Users

Several preliminary interviews were conducted to evaluate candidates for the long term pilot study from a group of physically disabled persons. Two males in their twenties, living in a shared apartment, were chosen as the pilot test users. The media center application was installed in their living room in a way that allowed both users to use it at the same time. This setup is illustrated in Figure 6.

Fig. 6. The system in the home of the two physically disabled pilot users. Photograph reproduced with permission.

The participants were active users of audio-visual media, via both television and computer. For this purpose, they had an existing environment control system attached to their wheelchairs. This old system had a deep hierarchical menu structure and was therefore slow to use and incurred a high cognitive load. It allowed limited control of the living environment such as the front door and intercom, but controlling everything with just one system has its downsides, such as problems with concurrent use.

The participants had an open and eager outlook towards the new speech-based system, and they were willing to accept the incompleteness and development state of the application. Their biggest expectation was that the system should make it easier and faster to control the television compared to their old system. As the new system would function parallel with the old system, the participants were pleased about the idea that they could e.g. open the door while watching the television without having to pause the live stream. As the participants watched television quite a lot, they also expected that as a result of having a separate system for controlling the television, there would be fewer errors while performing different tasks in the apartment.

Both participants were severely physically disabled and were only able to use their hands in a very limited area. Also holding up their heads was limited and therefore both participants had a headrest in their wheelchairs. Wireless lavalier microphones were mounted to their wheelchairs and adjusted into the proximity of the mouth so that the participants were able to activate speech recognition more comfortably, as seen in Figure 4. The system activates speech activity detection as a consequence of a blow directed to the microphone. This feature is essential since the use of an additional push-to-talk button was not a viable option for our participants. The blow-based activation may not, however, be adequate for all users, e.g., for people with severe respiration disabilities.

The pilot study lasted for six weeks and the media center application was used approximately four times a week and two hours at a time. During this time the pilot users filled in a web diary (12 times) containing questions related to the system features and their functionality. Also, the usability of the system was assessed three separate times during the pilot. The usability questionnaire contained 24 claims in four categories: (1) user experience of the speech control, (2) speech control based system introduction and learnability, (3) robustness of the system, and (4) digital television's important functions/services for test users. Both diary and questionnaire were structured because of the physical limitations of the test users. In addition, four face-to-face semi-structured theme interviews were conducted during different phases of the pilot study.

After some initial adjustments and corrections, the pilot users were pleased with the voice commands and used them successfully to choose channels and browse EPG information. Controlling the TV with voice commands was notably quicker compared to using the cumbersome environment control system according to the users. With voice commands, the users were able to change channels much more often than with the previous control system. The ease of control affects positively to the motivation of using TV. The blow activation of the system was accepted and in fact button activation was rejected when it was opted.

The overall experienced success rate of the voice commands was acceptable to the users. Here we have to rely on the users' report since the log data offers no way of identifying exact figures. Users were not bothered by occasional non-recognized commands although it clearly had an effect on the perceived pleasantness of use. Usually the problem was solved by repeating the command with more volume and better articulation. The interviews revealed that the functionality of EPG, recording and changing channels was quite acceptable. Also usefulness of these three functions was acceptable, but the pleasantness was poor. We think that the main reason for poor pleasantness was due to the problems with the robustness of the system and not the speech-based interaction itself.

The users became fluent with operating the system within the first week. In the first interview they reported that they did not need to search for the right commands (using the "Help" command) anymore and that using voice had become easy: no special attention or concentration was required. This improvement was encouraging, since more functionality (recording) was installed for the rest of the pilot study period. We also made minor modifications to the recognition grammars according to their requests, e.g., the command for one channel was first "TV 1" and after the modification "YLE 1", which is the actual Finnish name for the channel, and another channel was first referred as "Sub TV" and later "Sub". After the pilot study, the participants were willing to adopt the system for everyday use and to recommend it to their friends, which has been shown to be a good indicator of positive user experience

[9]. Our test users felt that controlling TV with speech is the best and most natural way for them. They also felt that it was not annoying to hear the other control TV with voice even when oneself was doing something else in the apartment. Whether this is applicable to generic users, remains a question.

3.4 Methodological Lessons Learnt from Evaluations

To date, we have carried out several evaluations to study the feasibility of speech-input and other modalities in the media center context. In the following we will discuss the lessons learnt from conducting these user studies.

One lesson we learned relates to the length of the study. In our long-term experiment in the home environment, it took one week for the pilot users to familiarize themselves with the system and for stable usage patterns to emerge. After the second week, we could not find any new critical issues. This indicates that two weeks is enough to collect data both from the initial phase where the system is being taken into use, as well as data about normal, day-to-day usage. In other contexts, such as in public pilot use, usage patterns are different, and the use of the system may differ dramatically from the patterns found in laboratory studies [15]. The key insight here is that these different methods affect the way the system and speech input is used. Laboratory studies are quite useful for identifying usability problems and comparing different technological solutions, whereas long-term studies are increasingly needed to elicit feedback about real world utility. Public pilots allowed us the chance to deploy the system to a wide audience and increase awareness of speech-based technologies.

Second interesting issue concerns how well we can capture users' experiences with these systems in the home domain. We are essentially dealing with task-based interfaces that are used for entertainment, whereby user experience has multiple dimensions. The question is how can we understand the effects of the different dimensions to the overall experience? We believe that some answers can be gained by broadening our viewpoint. For example, Hassenzahl [5] identifies two independent dimensions of product quality: pragmatic quality and hedonic quality. Jetter and Gerken [7] have further developed this model and introduce the user-product relationship, which includes traditional usability, functionality, hedonic quality and underlying user values. In the studies we have carried out to date, it is obvious that for the most part the users benefit from a system that is functional: they can control the television more fluently and efficiently. Hence, functionality and usability still override hedonic factors. Yet, we have noticed that once the system is stable enough for basic use and more functionality is introduced, the use becomes also hedonically motivated: the speech interface allows people with disabilities to live more independently; it improves their abilities and feelings of equality and creates pleasure through success.

4 Conclusions and Future Work

We presented a multimodal interface for media center applications designed for people with physical disabilities. Speech input combined with a voice activity and blow detection makes the interface usable for users who cannot use their hands. We reported results from several evaluations of the system with different user groups, focusing on long-term deployment carried out in the home of two physically disabled users. In general, the results from the long-term pilot study proved that the system was accessible for physically disabled users. In particular, the test users felt that controlling TV with speech is the best and most natural way for them. They were pleased with the voice commands, and controlling the TV with voice was notably quicker compared to the existing environment control system. After the pilot study, the participants were willing to adopt the system for everyday use and to recommend it to their friends. These are strong indications of good user experience.

In the future, we will carry out two additional studies with the system, one with people with low vision, and second with blind people. The purpose of these studies is to evaluate new interface solutions designed specifically for visually impaired users. After incorporating the findings from these user studies, we will release the speech-based media center application to general public in order to collect feedback and usage statistics from a hopefully large amount of real home users. In terms of additional functionality, the system will include support for other areas such as music, video, photo management, and environmental control. Finally, although the blow activation was the preferred method for activating speech input, we are considering acoustic source localization techniques that utilize multiple microphones embedded in the environment to capture accurate speech input [8] in this rather hostile environment for speech recognition, and in this way facilitate usage based on active listening instead of explicit activation.

Acknowledgements

This work was supported by the Technology Development Agency of Finland (TE-KES) under the Ubicom-programme in the "Ambient Intelligence Based on Sound, Speech and Multisensor Interaction"-project (TÄPLÄ, grant 40223/07).

References

1. Bederson, B.B.: Fisheye menus. In: 13th Annual ACM Symposium on User interface Software and Technology, pp. 217–225. ACM, New York (2000)
2. Bederson, B.B., Clamage, A., Czerwinski, M.P., Robertson, G.G.: DateLens: A fisheye calendar interface for PDAs. ACM Trans. Comput.-Hum. Interact. 11(1), 90–119 (2004)
3. Bederson, B.B., Grosjean, J., Meyer, J.: Toolkit Design for Interactive Structured Graphics. IEEE Trans. Softw. Eng. 30(8), 535–546 (2004)
4. Berglund, A., Qvarfordt, P.: Error Resolution Strategies for Interactive Television Speech Interfaces. In: Rauterberg, M., Menozzi, M., Wesson, J. (eds.) Human-Computer Interaction: INTERACT 2003, pp. 105–112. IOS Press, Amsterdam (2003)
5. Hassenzahl, M.: The thing and I: understanding the relationship between user and product. In: Blythe, M.A., Overbeeke, K., Monk, A.F., Wright, P.C. (eds.) Funology: From Usability To Enjoyment, pp. 31–42. Kluwer Academic Publishers, Norwell (2004)
6. Ibrahim, A., Johansson, P.: Multimodal Dialogue Systems: A Case Study for Interactive TV. In: Carbonell, N., Stephanidis, C. (eds.) UI4ALL 2002. LNCS, vol. 2615, pp. 209–218. Springer, Heidelberg (2003)

7. Jetter, H.-C., Gerken, J.: A Simplified Model of user Experience for Practical Application. In: Second COST294-MAUSE International Open Workshop "User eXperience - Towards a unified view" (2006)

8. Pertilä, P., Korhonen, T., Visa, A.: Measurement Combination for Acoustic Source Localization in a Room Environment. EURASIP Journal on Audio, Speech, and Music Processing 2008, Article ID 278185 (2008)

9. Reichheld, F.F.: The One Number You Need to Grow. Harvard Business Review 81, 47–54 (2003)

10. Soronen, H., Turunen, M., Hakulinen, J.: Voice Commands in Home Environment - a Consumer Survey. In: INTERSPEECH 2008, pp. 2078–2081. ISCA (2008)

11. Turunen, M., Hakulinen, J., Melto, A., Heimonen, T., Laivo, T., Hella, J.: SUXES – User Experience Evaluation Method for Spoken and Multimodal Interaction. In: INTERSPEECH 2009. ISCA (2009)

12. Turunen, M., Hakulinen, J., Melto, A., Hella, J., Rajaniemi, J.-P., Mäkinen, E., Rantala, J., Heimonen, T., Laivo, T., Soronen, H., Hansen, M., Valkama, P., Miettinen, T., Raisamo, R.: Speech-based and Multimodal Media Center for Different User Groups. In: INTERSPEECH 2009. ISCA (2009)

13. Turunen, M., Melto, A., Hello, J., Heimonen, T., Hakulinen, J., Mäkinen, E., Laivo, T., Soronen, H.: User Expectations and User Experience with Different Modalities in a Mobile Phone Controlled Home Entertainment System. In: 11th International Conference on Human-Computer Interaction with Mobile Devices and Services, pp. 1–4. ACM, New York (2009)

14. Turunen, M., Melto, A., Hakulinen, J., Kainulainen, A., Heimonen, T.: User Expectations, User Experiences and Objective Metrics in a Multimodal Mobile Application. In: Third Workshop on Speech in Mobile and Pervasive Environments (2008)

15. Turunen, M., Hakulinen, J., Kainulainen, A.: Evaluation of a Spoken Dialogue System with Usability Tests and Long-term Pilot Studies: Similarities and Differences. In: INTERSPEECH 2006, pp. 1057–1060. ISCA (2006)

16. TÄPLÄ – Ambient Intelligence based on Sound, Speech and Multisensor Interaction, http://tapla.cs.tut.fi

17. Wittenburg, K., Lanning, T., Schwenke, D., Shubin, H., Vetro, A.: The prospects for unrestricted speech input for TV content search. In: Working Conference on Advanced Visual Interfaces, pp. 352–359. ACM, New York (2006)

A Controller-Based Animation System for Synchronizing and Realizing Human-Like Conversational Behaviors

Aleksandra Čereković, Tomislav Pejša, and Igor S. Pandžić

University of Zagreb, Faculty of Electrical Engineering and Computing,
Unska 3, 10000 Zagreb, Croatia
{aleksandra.cerekovic,tomislav.pejsa,igor.pandzic}@fer.hr

Abstract. The Embodied Conversational Agents (ECAs) are an application of virtual characters that is subject of considerable ongoing research. An essential prerequisite for creating believable ECAs is the ability to describe and visually realize multimodal conversational behaviors. The recently developed Behavior Markup Language (BML) seeks to address this requirement by granting a means to specify physical realizations of multimodal behaviors through human-readable scripts. In this paper we present an approach to implement a behavior realizer compatible with BML language. The system's architecture is based on hierarchical controllers which apply preprocessed behaviors to body modalities. Animation database is feasibly extensible and contains behavior examples constructed upon existing lexicons and theory of gestures. Furthermore, we describe a novel solution to the issue of synchronizing gestures with synthesized speech using neural networks and propose improvements to the BML specification.

1 Introduction

Embodied Conversation Agents (ECAs) are graphically embodied virtual characters that can engage in a meaningful conversation with human users [1]. Communication between humans is multimodal and includes speech and non-verbal behaviors, so in order to have believable communication between ECAs and humans, it is necessary to model both types of behavior [2 - 4]. This has posed significant challenge before researchers, as non-verbal behaviors can be exceedingly complex and depend on a multitude of diverse factors, such as gender, emotional state, social relations and cultural background.

Our goal is to develop an animation system for ECA applications that solves the issue of multimodal behaviors and satisfies the following requirements:

- allow modeling of complex communicative utterances, which include verbal and non-verbal behavior
- provide intuitive high-level mechanisms for character motion control
- feasibly extensible with new animations
- applicable to a wide range of domains, such as marketing, virtual tutors, advisors and communicative non-player characters in role-playing games
- open-source and publicly available for the benefit of the research community

A. Esposito et al. (Eds.): COST 2102 Int. Training School 2009, LNCS 5967, pp. 80–91, 2010.
© Springer-Verlag Berlin Heidelberg 2010

To meet these requirements, we base our system on Behavior Markup Language (BML) [5]. BML was developed several years ago as part of the SAIBA framework, an open framework targeted at researchers in the area of ECAs and designed in collaboration with foremost experts in the field of ECAs and human communication, including psychologists, sociologists and linguists. BML is a language for describing physical realizations of multimodal human behaviors. These behaviors are defined in human-readable XML markup, where BML elements represent various primitive actions (e.g. speech, facial and body gestures). BML allows modeling of multimodal behavior by specifying temporal relationships between these elements. The use of BML affords us several distinct advantages:

- BML is intuitive, yet expressive enough to model complex behaviors
- it is fairly simple to implement
- it appears to have been well-received by the research community and is already being used by several research groups [6]

In this paper we present our character animation system based on BML. We describe how motion synchronization and control are achieved using BML, and how character motion is realized at low-level. We also present our solution to the issue of synchronizing non-verbal gestures with speech using neural networks, which is the principal contribution of our paper. Finally, we conclude with a discussion of the current state of our system and future development direction.

2 Related Work

Theoretical background from linguistics, psychology, and anthropology has proven the great importance of non-verbal behaviors in face-to-face communication and its strong relationship with speech. For example, research findings show that eyebrow movements can emphasize words or may occur during word-searching pauses [7], iconic gestures accompany certain lexical units [8], co-expressive gesture and speech are shaped by dialectic between linguistic expressions and spatio-motor representations [8], and synthetic displays are the most frequent facial gestures accompanying speech [9]. This knowledge has been used and incorporated into character animation systems for generating communicative behaviors. Most of the animation systems work on a high planning level; they are based on statistical models which automatically generate multimodal expression from input text [10, 11, 2, 12] or speech [13, 14]. The systems work as black boxes - they use their internal representations of multimodal behaviors and animations which cannot be isolated and used for other purposes. The only exception is the Non-verbal Behavior Generator [2] which has a layered architecture and uses the SmartBody module for behavior synthesis.

Two BML-compliant animation engines have been developed so far - ACE and SmartBody [6]. Articulated Communicator Engine (ACE) developed from an earlier engine based on multimodal utterance representation markup language (MURML) [15]. It provides support for facial expressions, lip synchronization, visual text-to-speech synthesis and hand gestures. It can be integrated with different graphics engines and has been utilized in two different projects - NUMACK and Max.

SmartBody supports facial expressions, speech, body postures, body gestures, gaze, head motions, feedback notifications and interruptions of running behaviors [16]. These elements are implemented as hierarchical motion controllers that act on different body parts. The controller hierarchy also includes special metacontrollers for motion blending, timewarping and scheduling. SmartBody has been utilized in several projects and integrated with a variety of engines, including OGRE, GameBryo, Unreal 2.5 and Source. SmartBody is engine-independent and interacts with the rendering engine via TCP.

Our system is architecturally similar to SmartBody, but with several key differences. Firstly, we introduce a new method of coordinating non-verbal behaviors with speech that employs machine learning techniques to achieve synchrony. Secondly, our system relies on a lexicon of animations which contain metadata necessary for mapping words to appropriate gestures during behavior planning. Finally, our speech synthesis is based on Microsoft Speech API programming interface [17], by far the most popular text-to-speech system that is distributed as part of Microsoft Windows operating system and supported by virtually all commercial TTS engines. In effect, this means that our system is compatible with almost all commercial speech synthesis products in existence.

3   System Features

Realization systems for ECAs address several technical requirements. First, they may control and synchronize different parts of the body in motion, and obtained non-verbal movements are synchronized with speech. The coordination requires descriptions of multimodal human behaviors, which is, in case of our system, provided through BML scripts. In addition to running behaviors the realization system should also respond to world events, especially those of the participating interlocutors. Thus, the body should be interruptible. Finally, realization systems must provide a sufficient illusion of life-like behavior that the human user will be drawn into the social scenario [16].

Our system is implemented as a part of visage|SDK character animation framework [18, 19] and has the following features:

- Specification of character behaviors using BML scripts. In realization phase described behaviors are applied to body parts and scheduled by high-level and low-level controllers.
- Start, stop, schedule or merge behaviors via high-level, BML-compliant API. These are the functions which interrupt behavior execution. They can be used for implementation of responses to the human user and responses to other unexpected events in the environment.
- Extensible database of annotated animations shared between multiple characters. The feature provides extension of non-verbal behaviors applied to various ECAs. Many culture-specific behaviors can be integrated in the system without efforts.
- Visual text-to-speech synthesis (TTS) based on industry-standard Microsoft SAPI [17].
- Lip synchronization.

Similar to the SmartBody, our system relies on a combination of animation approaches to achieve responsive, life-like behaviors. The hierarchical structure of controllers is connected to achieve continuous motion which can be generated using three types of animation: motion capture, keyframe and procedural.

4   Specifying and Realizing Character Behavior

In this section of the paper we describe the realization process. Furthermore, we explain our solution to coordinate non-verbal behaviors with synthesized speech and propose modifications to the BML specification.

4.1   Behavior Realization Process

Behavior realization occurs in three phases (Fig. 1):

- parsing of BML scripts
- behavior preparation and planning
- behavior execution

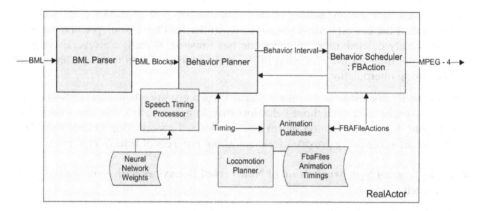

Fig. 1. Architecture of the BML realizer

BML Parser parses BML scripts, generates appropriate BML blocks and adds them to a list.

Behavior Planner reads the list of BML blocks and prepares each block for execution by adding timing information needed for multimodal behavior synchronization. This timing information is retrieved from the animation database, where each primitive animation is annotated with time constraint and type information.

Locomotion Planner is a subcomponent which handles character locomotion. It uses the character's current position and specified destination to compute the duration of the walking action.

Speech can be handled in two ways: using lip-sync or text-to-speech synthesis. If lip-sync is used, speech must be recorded in a preprocessing step and manually annotated in a BML script with necessary timing information. Text-to-speech synthesis is more appropriate, because it does not require a priori annotation. However, most TTS systems (including Microsoft SAPI we use in our system) do not provide a priori phoneme and word timing information necessary for synchronization with non-verbal behavior. To address this issue we employ machine learning and neural networks, as described in the next subsection.

Finally, BML Scheduler is responsible for execution of prepared behaviors. The Scheduler uses timing information to decide which behaviors will execute and when. It is a top-level unit which unifies low-level controllers responsible for realization of primitive behaviors specified as BML elements: locomotion, gaze, speech, gesture, head and face. Low-level controllers run in two different ways:

- Gazing and head controllers run in parallel with the Scheduler. They are implemented in such way that they stop execution of the running gaze/head behaviors if new gaze/head movement occurs. When new gaze direction or head movement occurs, Behavior Scheduler sends those two controllers animation parameter values which correspond to the new movement. Animation is executed depending on the current position of head/eyes, target position and duration. During execution, head and gaze controllers continually notify the Behavior Scheduler about the current state of the executed animation, which is further used for synchrony or progress feedback.
- When new locomotion, gesture or face action occurs, the Scheduler creates a new instance of the corresponding low-level controller for that action. The controller is immediately deleted after the animation has finished. If there are several controllers responsible for the execution of the same action, animation results are calculated using interpolation.

By continually updating the execution phase of each primitive behavior the Scheduler is able to synchronize even those behaviors that do not initially come annotated with timing data, such as IK motion (gaze) and synthesized speech. During execution, the Scheduler also constantly provides feedback about progress of behavior execution.

4.2 Multimodal Synchronization of Non-verbal Behaviors with Synthesized Speech

BML elements correspond to primitive behaviors, e.g. gesture, head, face, speech, gaze, locomotion etc. Synchronization of these different elements is possible because each element has six phases delimited with seven synchronization points - start, ready, stroke-start, stroke, stroke-end, relax, end. Synchronization relationships are specified using references to these points. For example, consider the following BML script:

```
<?BML version="1.0"?>
<act>
<bml id="bml2">
    <gesture id="g1" stroke="s1:tm" type="beat"
    hand="right" handlocation="outward;center;near"/>
    <speech id="s1">
    <text> Trust me, I know what I'm <sync id="tm"/>
    doing. </text>
    </speech>
    <head id="h1" stroke="s1:tm" action="rotation" ro-
tation="nod" amount="1"/>
</bml>
</act>
```

In this example, the speaker utters the sentence "Trust me, I know what I'm doing." (specified in the speech element). As he pronounces the word "doing", the speaker should make a hand gesture (gesture element) and nod his head reassuringly (head element). More specifically, stroke points of the hand gesture and nod need to be aligned with the word "doing". In other words, animations that correspond to these gestures must start playing in advance, so that the onset of their stroke phases corresponds with the uttering of the word "doing".

To achieve this, two approaches can be applied. *Dynamic adaptation* attempts to synthesize necessary synchronization data on the fly [15], whereas *animation planning* requires a priori timing information that needs to be prepared before behavior realization [16, 20, 11, 21].

The latter approach is simpler to implement, but it requires preprocessing and manual annotation of animation clips. We employ it in our system, relying on a database of annotated motion. However, that does not solve the problem of synchronizing non-verbal behaviors with synthesized speech, as most TTS modules do not provide a priori timing information for words and phonemes. Only a few TTS engines are capable of providing this data, such as Mary TTS [22] and Festival [23, 20, 11]. Microsoft SAPI, which we use in the system, only provides viseme, word and sentence boundaries in real-time. Furthermore, the planning approach cannot handle self-interrupting behaviors such as gaze and head motion, nor their synchronization with other behaviors. To address these issues, we use neural networks to determine timing data in real-time.

Designing the Neural Network System. The idea of using machine learning techniques to extract prosodic features from speech is not new. Existing TTS engines often use Bayesian networks, Hidden Markov Models (HMM) and Classification and Regression Trees (CART) to estimate phoneme durations in real-time. However, these approaches are language-dependent due to their reliance on phonemes. Our approach instead relies on *words* as input and is applicable to any language.

In our system backpropagation neural networks (BNNs) [24] are used to estimate word duration and align them with animation in real-time. For that purpose, we had to design the layout of our neural network system and train the BNNs with a database containing word-duration pairs in order to achieve the network configuration which yields optimal synchronization results. We specified the following requirements for our system:

- When determining word duration, TTS does word segmentation on phoneme level. Estimated durations of these phonemes depend on their positions inside the word. Segmentation and duration are language-dependent. Since we aimed to provide a solution applicable to any language, we decided to use simple segmentation of words into letters and train networks to use correlations between letters to estimate word durations.
- As there are many combinations of letters within words and words have different numbers of letters, multiple BNNs would be defined, specializing in words with a specific number of letters.
- BNNs produce output in 0-1 range. Therefore, normalization would be used to scale this output to word durations.
- Letters' ASCII code would be used as BNN input. Letter capitalization would be ignored.

To satisfy these requirements, we experimented with several system layouts. First, we designed a system of six BNNs, each specializing in words of a particular length. The networks were trained with a database containing 1.646 different words. Training was an iterative process, where letters of each word were coded and processed by an NN. The output duration was compared with actual word duration and NN weights subsequently adjusted depending on the estimation error. The process continued until the error dropped below the specified threshold. Once the training was complete, we evaluated the resulting BNN configurations using a set of sample sentences and words. The set contained 359 words, which differed from those used in the training process.

While analyzing the results we observed that considerable estimation error occured for words which were immediately followed by punctuation. This is due to the fact that these words take about 100 ms longer to pronounce than words without punctuation (which we henceforth refer to as *plain words*). To address this issue, we created another experimental layout, which contained 5 pairs of BNNs. Each BNN pair specialized in words of a specific length. However, the first BNN of a pair was trained to handle plain words, while the second one specialized in words followed by punctuation. Upon training and evaluating the BNNs, we found that they were indeed more effective in estimating word durations than the original setup. Therefore, we decided to use the latter approach in our final design (Fig. 2).

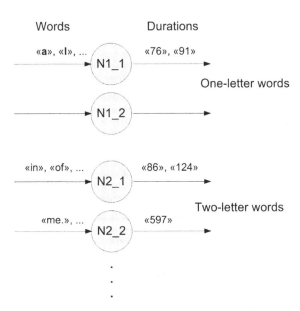

Fig. 2. Determining word durations using neural networks

For our final system we prepared 16 pairs of neural networks (NNs) and trained them to estimate word durations. Each of the 16 pairs was trained to handle words of specific length (1-16), like in our experimental design. The remaining three pairs would handle long words of *varying* lengths (16-20 for the first pair, 20-25 for the second pair, 25-35 for the third pair). The words used for training were extracted from a variety of different contexts, including newspaper articles, film dialogue and literary fiction. The resulting database contained 9.541 words of varying lengths and meanings. The longest word encountered had 16 letters, so in the end we discarded the three pairs of NNs intended to handle long words, leaving a total of 32 BNNs in the system.

Evaluation and results. Once the BNNs were prepared, we evaluated the effectiveness of our method by using the BNNs to estimate the time when an animation should start so that its synchronization point is aligned with a specific word in a sentence. Sample sentences and words used for evaluation differed from those used in the training process. The evaluation was done by summing up the predicted durations of words preceding the synchronization word to compute predicted time interval before synchronization point and comparing it with the correct time interval to determine estimation error. Time intervals used in the evaluation were 500 ms and 1500 ms, corresponding to shortest and longest start-stroke durations for hand gestures, respectively. During evaluation we also took into account the fact that the human eye can tolerate deviations between speech and image of up to 80 ms [25], meaning that multimodal alignment error under 80 ms is unnoticeable to the viewer. The results of the evaluation are presented in Table 1.

Table 1. Evaluation results

Time interval	500 ms	1500 ms
No. of words handled	310	258
No. of precisely aligned words	245	146
Alignment rate (error under 80 ms)	92,26%	73,26%
Alignment rate (no error)	79,03%	56,59%
Largest deviation	329 ms	463 ms
Smallest deviation	1 ms	2 ms
Average deviation	84.37 ms	126.00 ms

As shown in the table, our system was able to align 92,26% of words for the short time interval and 73,26% of words for the long interval with alignment error not exceeding the 80 ms threshold. Furthermore, the system achieved 79,03% and 56,59% alignment rates with no measurable alignment error.

Support for other TTS engines. Though the system uses a text-to-speech engine based on Microsoft SAPI by default, it can be integrated with any TTS engine with minimal effort on the user's part. In order for multimodal synchronization to work correctly, the neural networks need to be retrained with the new TTS engine, which is a largely automatic process that can take from several hours up to a day, depending on the user's system.

4.3 Animation Lexicon

The system can employ three types of animation to visually realize BML behaviors: motion capture, keyframe and procedural. In absence of motion capture equipment, we currently rely mostly on the latter two animation types. Motion clips are organized in a large lexicon of parametrized gestures that should be of great help in modeling highly expressive characters.

Supported BML Behaviors. The system fully implements the following BM behaviors:

- face expressions (joy, sad, angry, fear, surprise)
- eyebrow, mouth and eyelid motion specified by the BML element "face"
- gaze at a specific target
- head nods, shakes, tilts and rotation specified by the BML element "head"
- 52 different types of gestures varying from beats to complex gestures which cannot be described with BML parameters (e.g. scratch head, cross arms)
- walking
- speech – synthesized from text or loaded from an annotated audio file

Procedural animation is used for head motion [26], gaze, facial gestures, facial expressions, several culturally codified gestures [27] and locomotion, whereas almost all gestures are keyframe animations. The lexicon also includes animations for idle behavior to avoid characters standing perfectly still while inactive.

Animation Parametrization. While building the animation lexicon we referred to lexicons proposed in [28] and [29], existing ECA systems [10], literature on human gesturing [30] and even comics such as the popular Asterix which provide an interesting repertoire of gestures. For each gesture type we modeled variations based on dynamics and spatial characteristics (Fig. 3).

Animations are parametrized with corresponding attribute values of BML elements. Our parametrization extends the BML attribute specification based on the parametrization proposed in [28]. We merged BML location attributes into a single vector attribute and added an attribute specifying which part of the head or arm is affected by the gesture. The parametrization also includes emblems, gestures which can be used interchangeably with specific words [7]. In total, our animation parametrization has four dimensions:

- general - gesture type and literal meaning
- space-shape - hand shape and location at stroke-start point
- dynamics - intensity, amplitude, direction and movement trajectory during
- stroke phase
- timing information – specification of synchronization points for the BML scheduling component

The animation lexicon also contains a collection of culturally-codified Japanese and Croatian gestures used in the previously built ECA tour guide system [31].

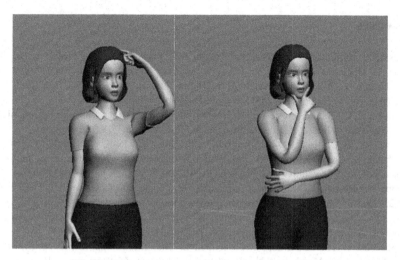

Fig. 3. Variations of the symbolic "thinking" gesture

5 Conclusions and Future Work

In this paper we have presented a character animation and behavior realization system based on Behavior Markup Language (BML) and with support for modeling multi-modal communication. To our knowledge, it is one of only three BML-compliant animation systems in existence. We have developed a universal, language- and engine-independent solution to the issue of synchronizing verbal and non-verbal expression by using neural networks to estimate word durations. The system will serve as a basis for our multi-party tour guide system [31], which will be a true test of its capabilities.

While testing the system, we observed that manual authoring of BML scripts can be a time-consuming and counter-intuitive process that requires a strong understanding of the BML specification and constant animation lexicon look-ups. One idea is to develop a graphical BML tool for more intuitive script authoring, while another is to provide a higher-level component for automatic behavior generation. Considerable research has been done on methods of automatically deriving multimodal behaviors from text and our approach would build upon work presented in [2, 10, 11]. On low level, we plan to introduce a new animation system based on parametric motion graphs. The new system will support example-based parametric motion (achieved by blending multiple motion capture animations with the help of registration curves) [32] and employ parametric motion graphs for transitioning between motions [33]. In addition to this, we must improve our methods of gaze control, as constant gaze shifts play an important role in applications that involve multi-party interaction (such as the aforementioned tour guide system).

Acknowledgements

The work was partly carried out within the research project "Embodied Conversational Agents as interface for networked and mobile services" supported by the Ministry of Science, Education and Sports of the Republic of Croatia.

References

1. Cassell, J.: Embodied Conversational Agents. MIT Press, Cambridge (2000)
2. Lee, J., Marsella, S.: Non-verbal behavior generator for embodied conversational agents. In: Gratch, J., Young, M., Aylett, R.S., Ballin, D., Olivier, P. (eds.) IVA 2006. LNCS (LNAI), vol. 4133, pp. 243–255. Springer, Heidelberg (2006)
3. Pelachaud, C.: Studies on gesture expressivity for a virtual agent. Speech Communication, Special issue in honor of Bjorn Granstrom and Rolf Carlson (2009) (to appear)
4. Stone, M., DeCarlo, D., Oh, I., Rodriguez, C., Stere, A., Lees, A., Bregler, C.: Speaking with hands: Creating animated conversational characters from recordings of human performance. In: Proceedings of ACM SIGGRAPH 2004, vol. 23, pp. 506–513 (2004)
5. Kopp, S., Krenn, B., Marsella, S., Marshall, A., Pelachaud, C., Pirker, H., Thorisson, K., Vilhjalmsson, H.: Towards a common framework for multimodal generation: The behavior markup language. In: Gratch, J., Young, M., Aylett, R.S., Ballin, D., Olivier, P. (eds.) IVA 2006. LNCS (LNAI), vol. 4133, pp. 205–217. Springer, Heidelberg (2006)
6. Vilhjálmsson, H., Cantelmo, N., Cassell, J., E. Chafai, N., Kipp, M., Kopp, S., Mancini, M., Marsella, S., Marshall, A.N., Pelachaud, C., Ruttkay, Z., Thórisson, K.R., van Welbergen, H., van der Werf, R.J.: The behavior markup language: Recent developments and challenges. In: Pelachaud, C., Martin, J.-C., André, E., Chollet, G., Karpouzis, K., Pelé, D. (eds.) IVA 2007. LNCS (LNAI), vol. 4722, pp. 99–111. Springer, Heidelberg (2007)
7. Ekman, P.: About brows: Emotional and conversational signals, pp. 169–202. Cambridge University Press, Cambridge (1979)
8. McNeill, D.: Hand and Mind: What Gestures Reveal about Thought. University of Chicago Press, Chicago (1992)
9. Chovil, N.: Discourse-oriented facial displays in conversation. Research on Language and Social Interaction 25, 163–194 (1991)
10. Neff, M., Kipp, M., Albrecht, I., Seidel, H.P.: Gesture modeling and animation based on a probabilistic re-creation of speaker style. ACM Trans. Graph. 27(1), 1–24 (2008)
11. Cassell, J., Vilhjalmsson, H.H., Bickmore, T.: Beat: the behavior expression animation toolkit. In: SIGGRAPH 2001: Proceedings of the 28th annual conference on Computer graphics and interactive techniques, pp. 477–486. ACM, New York (2001)
12. Smid, K., Zoric, G., Pandzic, I.S.: [HUGE]: Universal architecture for statistically based hUman gEsturing. In: Gratch, J., Young, M., Aylett, R.S., Ballin, D., Olivier, P. (eds.) IVA 2006. LNCS (LNAI), vol. 4133, pp. 256–269. Springer, Heidelberg (2006)
13. Zoric, G., Smid, K., Pandzic, I.S.: Towards facial gestures generation by speech signal analysis using huge architecture. In: Multimodal Signals: Cognitive and Algorithmic Issues: COST Action 2102 and euCognition International School Vietri sul Mare, Italy, April 21-26, Revised Selected and Invited Papers, pp. 112–120. Springer, Heidelberg (2009)
14. Albrecht, I., Haber, J., peter Seidel, H.: Automatic generation of non-verbal facial expressions from speech. In: Proc. Computer Graphics International 2002, pp. 283–293 (2002)
15. Kopp, S., Wachsmuth, I.: Synthesizing multimodal utterances for conversational agents. Computer Animation and Virtual Worlds 15, 39–52 (2004)
16. Thiebaux, M., Marshall, A., Marsella, S., Kallmann, M.: Smartbody: Behavior realization for embodied conversational agents. In: Proceedings of Autonomous Agents and Multi-Agent Systems AAMAS (2008)
17. Microsoft speech API:
http://www.microsoft.com/speech/speech2007/default.mspx

18. Pejsa, T., Pandzic, I.S.: Architecture of an animation system for human characters. In: Proceedings of the 10th International Conference on Telecommunications ConTEL 2009 (2009)
19. Pandzic, I.S., Ahlberg, J., Wzorek, M., Rudol, P., Mosmondor, M.: Faces everywhere: Towards ubiquitous production and delivery of face animation. In: Proceedings of the 2nd International Conference on Mobile and Ubiquitous Multimedia MUM 2003, pp. 49–55 (2003)
20. Hartmann, B., Mancini, M., Pelachaud, C.: Formational parameters and adaptive prototype instantiation for mpeg-4 compliant gesture synthesis. In: Proc. Computer Animation, June 19-21, pp. 111–119 (2002)
21. Van Deemter, K., Krenn, B., Piwek, P., Klesen, M., Schroder, M., Baumann, S.: Fully generated scripted dialogue for embodied agents. Artificial Intelligence 172(10), 1219–1244 (2008)
22. Schröder, M., Trouvain, J.: The German Text-to-Speech Synthesis System MARY: A Tool for Research, Development and Teaching. International Journal of Speech Technology 6, 365–377 (2003)
23. Taylor, P.A., Black, A., Caley, R.: The architecture of the festival speech synthesis system. In: The Third ESCA Workshop in Speech Synthesis, pp. 147–151 (1998)
24. Rojas, R.: Neural Networks - A Systematic Introduction. Springer, Heidelberg (1996)
25. Steinmetz, R.: Human perception of jitter and media synchronization. IEEE Journal on Selected Areas in Communications 14(1) (1996)
26. Brkic, M., Smid, K., Pejsa, T., Pandzic, I.S.: Towards natural head movement of autonomous speaker agent. In: Lovrek, I., Howlett, R.J., Jain, L.C. (eds.) KES 2008, Part II. LNCS (LNAI), vol. 5178, pp. 73–80. Springer, Heidelberg (2008)
27. Huang, H., Cerekovic, A., Pandzic, I.S., Nakano, Y., Nishida, T.: Toward a culture adaptive conversational agent with a modularized approach. In: Proceedings of Workshop on Enculturating Conversational Interfaces by Socio-cultural Aspects of Communication (2008 International Conference on Intelligent User Interfaces, IUI 2008) (2008)
28. Poggi, I.: Mind, hands, face and body: a goal and belief view of multimodal communication. Weidler (2007)
29. Posner, R., Serenari, M.: Blag: Berlin dictionary of everyday gestures
30. Armstrong, N.: Field Guide to Gestures: How to Identify and Interpret Virtually Every Gesture Known to Man. Quirk Books (2003)
31. Cerekovic, A., Huang, H., Pandzic, I.S., Nakano, Y., Nishida, T.: Towards a multicultural ECA tour guide system. In: Pelachaud, C., Martin, J.-C., André, E., Chollet, G., Karpouzis, K., Pelé, D. (eds.) IVA 2007. LNCS (LNAI), vol. 4722, pp. 364–365. Springer, Heidelberg (2007)
32. Kovar, L.: Automated Methods for Data-driven Synthesis of Realistic and Controllable Human Motion. PhD thesis, University of Wisconsin-Madison (2004)
33. Heck, R., Gleicher, M.: Parametric motion graphs. In: Proceedings of the 2007 symposium on Interactive 3D graphics and games, pp. 129–136. ACM, New York (2007)

Generating Simple Conversations

Mark ter Maat and Dirk Heylen

Human Media Interaction, University of Twente
PO Box 217, 7500 AE Enschede, The Netherlands
{maatm,heylen}@ewi.utwente.nl

Abstract. This paper describes the Conversation Simulator, a software program designed to generate simulated conversations. The simulator consists of scriptable agents that can exchange speech acts and conversational signals. The paper illustrates how such a tool can be used to study some effects of seemingly straightforward choices in conversations.

1 Introduction

Even though for humans conversations are routine operations, they are very complex, which is borne out when one tries to build a machine such as an Embodied Conversational Agent (ECA) that has the same conversational skills as humans have. It is not just that interpreting and generating natural language utterances is hard for machines, the interactional skills - involving knowledge such as when to start to talk and when to stop - and the interpersonal skills that are needed in conversation form a daunting challenge for computational linguists and artificial intelligence researchers to accomplish this automatically.

To get an idea of the dimensions involved in conversation, one can look at taxonomies of the kinds of communicative actions that have been suggested by researchers on dialogue. The DIT++ taxonomy developed by Bunt and colleagues (http://dit.uvt.nl) is one of the most elaborate ones. On the highest level, information transfer functions (information seeking and information providing functions) are distinguished from action discussion functions (promises, commands and all the variants), dialogue control functions (dealing with feedback mainly), social obligations management (including salutations, apologizing, etcetera) and interaction management functions. The interaction management functions are further classified into turn, time, contact, communication and discourse structure management functions. The same speech act will typically instantiate different functions at the same time. The challenge for ECA research is to build agents that have skills on all of these dimensions.

In real life conversations, all of these dimensions occur at once. Also changing one parameter in one dimension may have effects on other dimensions. Improving the contact or turn-taking skills of an agent will have an effect on the social/affective level. For instance, an agent that has been programmed not to interrupt the human interlocutor may be perceived as being more polite, or, as the case goes, less interested in the conversation. It thus appears that conversations can only be looked upon holistically. Although we strongly believe this is

A. Esposito et al. (Eds.): COST 2102 Int. Training School 2009, LNCS 5967, pp. 92–101, 2010.

the case, we nevertheless also try to see whether we can tease apart components and get an idea of the possible effects of one particular dimension of conversation on some others. One approach along these lines consist in artificially simulating conversations that abstract away from several dimensions of conversations which allows one to investigate what conversations this leads to and how these conversations are perceived. This approach does not yield final answers (because of decontextualisation and abstraction), but can provide valuable information nevertheless.

In this paper we present a tool that we have built in which we can simulate certain aspects of conversation, in particular turn-taking skills of agents, and test the effects that different parameter settings may have. We focus here on the design of the simulator (Section 3) but will also illustrate it, in Section 4, by briefly summarizing a case study we performed before ([13]) and pointing out other possible employment of the conversation simulator. To motivate the case study and the simulator we first present some background on issues in conversation and their conversation modeling in conversational agents that have to do with turn-taking and some other interaction management functions.

2   Taking Turns

Our research discussed in this paper focusses on the interaction management functions, in particular the turn-management functions, but also time and contact management will be involved. As we discussed in [9], deciding on when to start speaking and when to stop involves a multitude of factors. The desire to say something, the social appropriateness, the context, and many other types of factors are involved. This also means that from a particular decision in a given conversation - A starts speaking while B had not finished his utterance - one might infer many different things. For instance, A was being impolite. In this section we would like to reflect a bit on what is involved in turn-taking processes.

According to Sacks, Schegloff, and Jefferson [11] (SSJ) the basic units of turns are *Turn-Constructional Units* (TCUs). On a syntactic level, these may be sentential, clausal, phrasal or lexical constructions. They have a clear start and end point and accomplish some recognizable social action. (Note that the start and end point may not always be clear to all the participants in the interaction, though). After the production of each such unit the SSJ paper argues that there are three options. First, the speaker can decide not to continue and select another person to continue. This selection may involve a question addressed to a particular interlocutor. Alternatively, (option 2) the speaker can leave it open who he thinks should speak next. But also, the speaker can select himself as the next speaker, continuing the turn (option 3). So, when the end of a TCU is reached, each person involved has to make a choice what to do: wait to be offered the turn from the speaker, wait for the speaker to continue speaking, decide to start speaking when the floor is open or leave it to someone else to take the floor. Of course, besides these choices that fall neatly in the scheme proposed by SSJ (which has been heavily disputed; see [10], for some discussion, for instance), one can also decide to interrupt the current speaker at any given time, or to take the floor even if it was offered to someone else. The various situations that can arise are characterized in Bunt's DIT++ scheme by such actions as: turn-accept, turn-grab, turn-take, turn-assign, turn-keep, and turn-release

Although often the end of a Turn Construction Unit is clear from the content of what is being said, there may also be concomitant prosodic or nonverbal cues (gaze, head movements and gestures) that indicate the end of a turn. Similarly, interlocutors may use paraverbal and nonverbal cues to indicate that they are willing to take the turn. If a person wants to select the next speaker he can give a give-turn cue (e.g. gazing at a person with raised eyebrows), signalling to another person that he or she can now start speaking. If a person wants to speak next (this does not have to be at a point where the current speaker is finished) that person can send a take-turn cue (e.g. audibly breathing in) to the current speaker to signal that he or she will start talking now (see [4], for instance).

The importance of such cues has been investigated in experimental settings by [5] using avatars. In this paper the authors interfered with normal conversation. In the experiment they had two people converse with one another but while they could hear each other, they could not see each other. Instead, each person saw a virtual character that was supposed to represent the other person. They manipulated the characters in such a way that one person would see a very active character, showing a lot of non-verbal turn-taking cues, and the other person would see a very passive character, showing a lot of non-verbal turn-yielding cues. This resulted in conversations in which the person represented by the active character (and viewing the passive character) had longer turns and took the turn a lot faster. For the other person the situation was reversed. This shows that a simple choice of showing more turn-taking or turn-yielding signals is an important feature to take into account in the design of a conversational agent.

When someone decides to take the turn (either because it is open or has been offered) there is still a choice about the exact timing of the utterances. Gerritsen and Claes ([8]) distinguished three cases. A person may wait for the other person to finish speaking, start as soon as possible, even if this means starting before the other person has finished speaking, or add a small pause after the end of the other person's turn. The authors investigated these case across cultures and found interesting differences. Germanic cultures usually start when the other person is finished whereas Roman cultures start as fast as possible and in Japanese culture a small pause is usually added. Such cultural differences were also explored in a paper by Endrass, Rehm and Andrass ([6]) and applied to human-agent interactions. In this study the authors looked at differences in turn-taking behaviors of German and Japanese participants. They found that these differences can be seen in a different usage of pauses and overlapping speech. They also found out that German subjects seemed to prefer a virtual agent that was programmed to their specific (German) culture than one programmed to another one (Japanese).

Overlapping speech, for example when two participants start talking at the same time, happens quite often in conversations. In a paper by Campbell ([2])

recorded conversations are presented which sometimes consist of more than 60% of overlapping speech. However, overlap does not always have to break down a conversation as it includes backchannels, signals of agreement, suggestions for words and phrasings, or even questions during the speech of the other person that are relevant at the given place. These can be all cases where more that one person speaks with only person holding the actual floor and the other contributing without claiming the floor.

This kind of feedback that coincides with speech of others is very important in conversations. In a paper by Bavelas, Johnson and Coates ([1]) it was studied what happened when a listener of a story (told live by a storyteller) was distracted. They found that the listener would give less feedback, and as a result the story-tellers told their story significantly less well, especially the endings. These endings were often abrupt or choppy, or they were retold more than once. Feedback (for example backchannels) or the lack of it can have a huge effect in human-agent conversations as well. For example, in [3], Cassell and Thórisson looked at what happens when a listening agent gives no feedback, gives emotional feedback (show-ing confusion when not understanding and smiling when addressed), or gives what they call envelope feedback (feedback related to the process of the conversation, e.g. gaze behaviour). They found that the agent displaying envelope feedback was seen as more helpful, more lifelike and smoother, and it was also more efficient; the users used less utterances to complete their task.

When overlapping speech arises at occasions where it is not appropriate for one or more of the participants (i.e. one of the participants would prefer to speak and the other to listen) the participants have different choices of what to do. Schegloff [12] discusses three courses of action that are most common. One can stop speaking, continue normally, or start using 'elevated speech', i.e. start speaking louder to indicate that one is not giving up one's claim to the floor. In some cases this behavior might be considered rude, in others it might be borne out of enthusiasm and be perceived more positively. In [13], we looked at the ways people perceive speakers that show different turn-taking strategies. The paper demonstrated that a person who is speaking louder during overlap is often seen as more aroused, unfriendly, disagreeable and rude, while stopping directly at the first sign of overlapping speech is seen as more warm, passive, and submissive. For this we used the conversation simulator that we will describe in the next section. We summarize the main results of the impression management study after that.

3   Conversation Simulator

The previous section shows that what looks like small choices can have a very big impact on a conversation. However, the problem with studying these effects is that conversations are so complex it is hard to create an environment where only the factors that one wants to study are manipulated. It is practically im-possible to video record two conversations in the wild which only differ in their backchannel timings for example. One can get round to this by using simula-tions. By simulating conversations one can decide to keep many factors the same and only change a few. However, for the simulations to provide some ground for making proper inferences about conversations, the conversations should still be true to reality. However, as they abstract from certain elements in the conversation this is more or less impossible. They can be of help though when one is trying to build machines that are able to communicate more or less naturally as the simulation is really a test for the algorithms that one is building and how the agents that communicate using these algorithms are perceived. This is why we build a conversation simulator.

The conversation simulator generates conversations by having two agents communicate with one another by sending each other information about their *communicative actions*. In the current version of the simulator, these actions can be: `being silent`, `speaking normally`, or `speaking louder`, and giving a `backchannel` signal. To simulate that reception and interpretation of a communicative act in real life takes some time, these communicative actions are received with a bit of a delay after an agent has sent them. In the current version this has been set to about 200 ms.

This delay can introduce problems in the interaction (perhaps similar to real life problems). Agents can start at the same time because they notice too late that the other agent has just started; silences can occur, etc. Agents also send their intentions to start or stop speaking to each other by means of certain cues, which correspond to the interaction management cues that occur in natural conversations. These *conversational signals* thus represent non-verbal behaviour in real life, for example gaze behaviour, head movements, audible sighs, etc. In the simulator, the agents can use these signals to signal that the end of their utterance is coming (which may mean that they start another utterance after this), to indicate that the end of their turn is coming, to signal that they will start a turn, and an indication that they want to keep the turn. However, just as in real life people can fail to read these cues, see cues that were not intended. There may also be errors in the transmission of the conversational signals. The program allows one to set a certain error margin, which means that communicative signals that were send by an agent can get lost or can be changed and that some communicative signals may randomly be added.

With this setup it is possible to create different agents with different turn-taking behaviours. The agents can be scripted by a simple xml-like scripting language which defines how it should react to different situations. For example, one can specify that when an agent detects that it is talking while the other agent is talking as well, it will raise its voice. The code required to do this is:

```
<rule name="shout">
    <precondition name="own_state" value="normal_speech" />
    <precondition name="other_state" value="normal_speech" />
    <precondition name="compare" value1="time_in_own_state"
        comparator="greater_than" value2="200" />
    <precondition name="compare" value1="#warning_given"
        comparator="equals" value2="1" />
    <precondition name="compare" value1="#hold_signal_detected"
```

```
        comparator="equals" value2="0" />
    <reaction action="change_mode" mode="elevated" />
</rule>
```

As can been seen in the example, an agent's script consists of a set of rules. Every rule has a name, a set of preconditions (which are required to activate the rule) and a set of reactions (which are fired when the preconditions are met). In the example the agent will raise its voice (`action ... = change_mode ... elevated`) when it detects overlapping speech (both `own_state` and `other_state` have the value `normal_speech`), it is talking for at least 200 ms, and it already gave a warning (a hold signal, this is stored in the parameter #warning_given), and did not detect a hold signal from the other agent (stored in the parameter #hold_signal_detected). The effect of this rule can be seen in Figure 1.

The preconditions can be used to check the current state and the signals received. the system provides the following variables.

- **own state** (silent, speaking normally, speaking loud, backchanneling)
- **other agent state** (same as above)
- **detected signal** (end of utterance, end of turn, start of turn, hold turn)
- **speech time of current utterance left**
- **time in current state**
- **time of other agent in its current state**

The preconditions also support comparisons of numbers, the storage of temporary variables and random numbers. These features make it possible to use additional variables besides the ones defined by the system to keep track of certain states or to make scripts non-deterministic. The reactions can be used to change the behaviour of the agent. It can:

- **start a new utterance**
- **interrupt (stop) an ongoing utterance**
- **change the mode of an ongoing utterance** (switch between speaking normally or loud)
- **change the value of a stored variable**

Conversations are created by having two agents (both with a script) interact with each other, and depending on the scripts and which agents are paired to each other totally different conversations can emerge. These conversations can be made both visible and audible. The visual representation is an image which contains time lines for both agents. On these time lines the communicative actions and signals are displayed. An example of a part of a conversation can be found in Figure 1.

The conversation is also made audible with the use of stored audio files. When an agent decides to speak, in the system it (randomly) chooses a certain audio file it will play, and the chosen audio file also determines the length of that utterance of the agent. The conversation is simulated by playing all the chosen audio files (played real-time while simulating the conversation). During playback

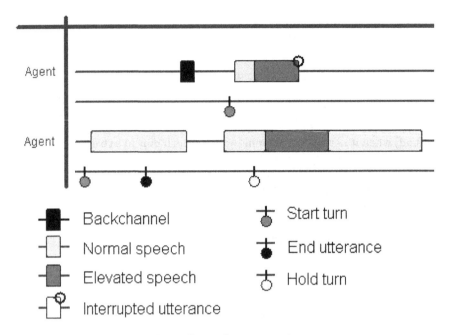

Fig. 1. Example conversation

the audio can be stopped for one agent (when it is interrupted and decides to stop speaking), and the volume can be increased (when an agent starts speaking louder). To make the difference between the agents very clear one agent plays its files through the left loudspeaker and the other through the right loudspeaker, and the pitch of the audio files of one speaker is slightly raised.

For the experiment described in the next section we used audio files that contained utterances from the AMI corpus[1] with a clear start and end point. Next, based on [7] we passed those utterances to a Hann Band Filter (500Hz to 500Hz, with a smoothing of 100Hz). Using this method the audio files were totally incomprehensible but the prosody could still be heard. To generate other types of conversations other audio files can be used.

4   Case study

Now that it is clear what the conversation simulator is and does, the most important question is: what can you do with it? In this section we will give some possible uses of the system and a future direction we want to go in.

One application of the simulator would be to study the effects choices have on the *conversation* itself. For example, one could create different agents with slightly different behaviours and see how this effects the general flow of interaction. What is interesting about these conversations is that the interaction of

---

[1] http://www.amiproject.org

the different agents can be investigated, as the effects of the script of one agent are contingent on what the other agent does - which is governed by its script. Analysis of those conversations, for example on average number of utterances in a turn, average number of finished or interrupted turns, average period of overlapping speech, etc, could give some insight in the kinds of effects choices have.

One could also use this program to study how different audio representations effect the perception of people. For example, one could use very high or low pitched audio, or one could change the speed rate of the participants. Using different audio files, will yield different conversations which could be used to study how people perceive the different conversations.

Another application would be to study how certain behaviours change the way people *perceive* the agents as a persona. We already made a start with this in [13], which we will briefly summarise here. In the study we wanted to learn how different turn taking strategies would change the perception of the conversational participants. More specifically, we looked at *start-up* strategies and *overlap resolution* strategies. The former strategies consist of starting exactly when the other person finishes speaking, starting a little bit early or starting a bit late. The latter strategies are applied when overlapping speech is detected and consists of stopping, continuing normally or raising the voice. These strategies were combined into different agents with different behaviours. The conversations were simulated by pairing the different agents with an agent which randomly chooses a strategy. The resulting conversations were rated by human raters. These raters had to pay attention to the non-random agent (in our case coming from the right loudspeaker) and they had to write down how they perceived that person on different dimensions, using a five-point scale. The dimensions we investigated were the following.

> *unfriendly-friendly, distant-pleasant, passive-active, cold-warm,*
> *negligent-conscientious, disagreeable-agreeable, rude-respectful,*
> *unpredictable-stable, unattentive-attentive, submissive-dominant,*
> *undependable-responsible, negative-positive, not aroused-aroused*

The study showed that the **AtStop** strategy - which means that the agent starts directly when it detects that the other agent finishes its turn and stops when it detects overlapping speech - rated highest on positive traits such as friendliness, agreeability, respect and attentiveness. On the other hand, using the **EarlyRaised** strategy - where the agent starts before the other agent is finished and raises its voice when it detects overlapping speech - received a lot of negative traits such as rude, distant, cold, and unfriendly.

When looking at single strategies, we found that starting before the other agent was finished was seen as more unfriendly, rude, cold and active than the other start-up strategies. The most pleasant start-up was the one where the agent started immediately at the end of the other agent's turn. For overlap resolution strategies people found raising voices more aroused, unfriendly, rude and unpredictable. Stopping on the other hand was seen as warmer, more passive and more negative.

The conversation simulator can also be used in human-agent conversations. We are currently implementing a live version of the system coupled to a microphone so people can talk directly to an agent. One problem with having people rate pre-recorded conversations is that the raters are not really engaged. We think that if they talk to the system directly they will get a much better impression of the agent. The content of the conversation may not be important, but when talking to the system it can actually interrupt you, which probably has a much bigger impact on the perception of the user on that agent.

This live version should be able to detect the same or similar actions and signals as the current agents do in the simulation. This means that the system should recognize silence acts, speech acts and elevated speech acts. But, optimally, this also means that the system should recognise - fairly accurately, but not perfectly - the communicative signals such as start_turn, end_utterance, end_turn and hold_turn.

5   Conclusions

In this paper we described some of the kinds of conversational choices participants have to make during a conversation, including determining what to contribute, when to do it and how to respond on choices of the participants. We also described some effects these choices can have on the conversation itself or on the perception of the participants. To study these effects further and test the algorithms for agents, we proposed a tool in which it is possible to script agents to perform certain conversational behaviour and then simulating a conversation by making the agents communicate with each other. This simulated conversation is then available as a trace with all the actions of the agents graphically present, or as an audio file. In this audio file the agent speech actions are represented by incomprehensible audio fragments in which the prosody can still be heard. We also described some practical uses for the tool, for example using it to study what kind of effects choices have on the conversation itself, or studying how choices effect the perception of participants on each other[2].

Acknowledgement. The research leading to these results has received funding from the European Community's Seventh Framework Programme (FP7/2007-2013) under grant agreement n° 211486 (SEMAINE).

References

1. Bavelas, J.B., Johnson, T., Coates, L.: Listeners as co-narrators. Journal of Personality and Social Psychology 79(6), 941–952 (2000)
2. Campbell, N.: Approaches to conversational speech rhythm: Speech activity in Two-Person telephone dialogues. In: Proc XVIth International Congress of the Phonetic Sciences, Saarbrucken, Germany, pp. 343–348 (2007)

---

[2] A public domain version of the conversation simulator is in preparation.

3. Cassell, J., Thórisson, K.R.: The power of a nod and a glance: Envelope vs emotional feedback in animated conversational agents. Applied Artificial Intelligence 13, 519–538 (1999)
4. Duncan, S., Niederehe, G.: On signalling that it's your turn to speak. Journal of Experimental Social Psychology 10(3), 234–247 (1974)
5. Edlund, J., Beskow, J.: Pushy versus meek - using avatars to influence Turn-Taking behaviour. In: INTERSPEECH 2007, Antwerp, Belgium, pp. 682–685 (2007)
6. Endrass, B., Rehm, M., Andrass, E.: Culture-specific communication management for virtual agents. In: Proceedings of The 8th International Conference on Autonomous Agents and Multiagent Systems, Budapest, Hungary, vol. 1, pp. 281–287. International Foundation for Autonomous Agents and Multiagent Systems (2009)
7. Friend, M., Jeffrey Farrar, M.: A comparison of content-masking procedures for obtaining judgments of discrete affective states. The Journal of the Acoustical Society of America 96(3), 1283–1290 (1994)
8. Gerritsen, M., Claes, M.-T.: Culturele waarden en communicatie in internationaal perspectief. Coutinho (2003)
9. Heylen, D.: Understanding speaker-listener interactions. In: Interspeech 2009 (2009) (page in print)
10. O'Connell, D.C., Kowal, S., Kaltenbacher, E.: Turn-taking: A critical analysis of the research tradition. Journal of Psycholinguistic Research V19(6), 345–373 (1990)
11. Sacks, H., Schegloff, E.A., Jefferson, G.: A simplest systematics for the organization of Turn-Taking for conversation. Language 50(4), 696–735 (1974)
12. Schegloff, E.A.: Overlapping talk and the organization of turn-taking for conversation. Language in Society 29(1), 1–63 (2000)
13. ter Maat, M., Heylen, D.: Turn management or impression management? In: Ruttkay, Z., Kipp, M., Nijholt, A., Vilhjálmsson, H.H. (eds.) IVA 2009. LNCS, vol. 5773, pp. 467–473. Springer, Heidelberg (2009)

Media Differences in Communication

Roxanne B. Raine[1,2]

[1] Universiteit Twente,
Human Media Interaction Group,
Department of Mathematics, Engineering and Computer Science,
7500AE Enschede, The Netherlands
[2] University of Memphis,
Institute for Intelligent Systems,
FedEx Institute of Technology (FIT), rm. 410
365 Innovation Drive,
Memphis, TN 38152, USA
roxi.benoit@gmail.com

Abstract. With the ever-growing ubiquity of computer-mediated communication, the application of language research to computer-mediated environments becomes increasingly relevant. How do overhearer effects, discourse markers, differences for monologues and dialogues, and other verbal findings transmute in the transition from face-to-face to computer-mediated communication (CMC)? Which of these factors have an impact on CMC? Furthermore, how can computer interfaces alleviate these potential shortcomings? When is CMC the preferred communicative medium? These questions are explored in this paper.

Keywords: communication; media differences; computer-mediated communication; face-to-face communication.

1 Introduction

The *bandwith hypothesis* claims that the more analogous to face-to-face (FtF) a communicative medium is, the more effective it should be. However, numerous empirical studies have shown that modes of communication other than FtF can be more useful than FtF depending on environmental constraints, user goals, and measures of success (for discussion see [1] and [2]). The bandwidth hypothesis fails to take into account a number of considerations. First, the availability of conversational tools varies with communicative medium, meaning non-FtF media can be more effective than FtF. Second, exploitation of available resources will vary between and within media depending on goals [3]. Third, different measures of success (e.g., number of items correct in task-oriented conversations or amicability of partner) can yield different results. Finally, whether interlocutors actually use their available resources will also impact performance. In this paper, examples of media similarities and differences will

A. Esposito et al. (Eds.): COST 2102 Int. Training School 2009, LNCS 5967, pp. 102–112, 2010.
© Springer-Verlag Berlin Heidelberg 2010

be explored to elaborate on Whittaker's [1] rejection of the bandwidth hypothesis[1]. It will become evident that sometimes human interaction is enhanced by the use of computer interfaces.

Indeed, there is a vast amount of variability in computer-mediated communication (CMC) environments. For example, email, instant messaging, and message-posting sites have many components that can potentially impact a conversational setting in a variety of ways. Furthermore, these three examples of CMC will not only vary between each other, but also within one framework to another [4]. For example, Google, AOL and Yahoo email accounts differ in communicative tools (such as organization of archives, searchability of messages, and organization of threads) available to users. Skype, AIM and MSN instant messengers differ in verbal or physical feedback allowances. Posting sites can also differ in community membership, interfaces, and levels of interaction available.

2   Interpersonal Judgments

The degree to which interlocutors can relate to each other, the amount they like each other, and how much they allow their interaction to shape their beliefs about each other varies between media. How, to what degree, and in what situations these variations occur remains uncertain. According to Joseph Walther's (1992) *hyperpersonal model* of communication, cue lean media (with fewer communicative tools) promote the belief that someone's interlocutors are like him/herself, and consequently produce higher interlocutor amicability [5]. Walther claims that users of context-scant media perceive each other in high regards because they have fewer disconfirming cues than users of context-rich media.

However, I propose that the hyperpersonal model may be inaccurate on two accounts. First, it presumes that interlocutors enter into communicative settings expecting to like each other or be similar to one another. Second, the assumption that costly communicative media induce higher interpersonal involvement seems unjustified. When interlocutors enter into conversations with agreeable expectations, it is likely that these will be confirmed, and they are [6], [7], [8]. However, negative affectations, prejudices, and stereotypes have also been shown to endure in low-cue media [9], [10]. For example, coworkers were found to band together in IM communications if they were already somewhat close, whereas they distanced themselves further from those who they likely had not viewed as amicably before the IM communications [11]. On such grounds, it seems incorrect to say that low bandwidth correlates with high affiliation.

As an alternative to the hyperpersonal model, I suggest a *preconception hypersensitization*, whereby interlocutors' lack of disconfirming evidence in lower-cue media reinforces *whatever* preconceptions they originally had about each other, whether these preconceptions are positive or negative. According to this view, the less interaction

---

[1] This paper in the COST 2102 Proceedings gives an overview of the current state of CMC research as it relates to this conference. Instead of describing one study in detail, it overviews many studies and relates them to each other. In this process, new theories are introduced to explain the variety of results in the studies overviewed.

conversational partners are allowed, the more likely they are to hold to their initial presuppositions, regardless of affectations or personal experience [12]. Epley and Kruger manipulated participants' beliefs about their interlocutors before a communication by telling the partners false characteristics about each other [9]. The participants either communicated via computer or telephone. In post-test questionnaires, the CMC participants' beliefs about their partners were most similar to the information they were given before the task (as opposed to those who communicated verbally, whose preconceptions had less influence on their post-test opinions). This result complements the proposed preconception hypersensitization hypothesis, but not the hyperpersonal model. Their preconceptions had a stronger influence on their eventual post-test beliefs in lower-cue mediated communications.

3 Costs and Constraints

A number of constraints may affect the grounding process between speakers and addresses in any interaction. These include: copresence, visibility, audibility, cotemporality (one receives messages at roughly the same time as they are produced), simultaneity (partners can send and receive messages simultaneously), sequentiality of turns, and reviewability and revisability of utterances [13], [14].

As different media allow different resources, which medium (or CMC interface) is preferable will depend on the task. If a reviewable, revisable record is desired, interlocutors should use Gmail (an email client that allows large, long-term archives with an easy search feature). Interlocutors who want immediate feedback will prefer FtF or an audio-visual correspondence such as Skype. Hearing-impaired (and other) users benefit from adding avatars to Skype [15], [16], [17]. It has also been shown that in therapy sessions, the degree of synchrony between therapist and client is a good indicator of therapeutic success [18], [19]. Thus, for intimate disclosure, one might prefer higher bandwidth. For these later purposes, it is true that the communicative settings closer to FtF turn out to be the most effective. However, it is also true that this is not always the case.

There are various costs related to media differences: Participants "balance the perceived costs for formulation, production, reception, understanding, start-up, delay, speaker change, display, faults, and repair" [13], (p. 132). Whether a certain medium is effective will depend on how much the participants exploit the particular resources provided, whether these resources are relevant to the purpose of the conversation, and how much cost is associated with using the resources in question. People prefer FtF for reprimanding, but telephone or letter correspondence for refusing unusual requests [20]. It could be argued that one chooses the cue-enriched medium (in this case, FtF) when it is important or desirable to alter a previous perception (here, the behavior that required reprimanding). Again, this can be explained by the proposed presupposition hypersensitization hypothesis.

Self-reported lying rates tended to be higher for telephone than email communication. In contrast, lying rates in FtF and instant messaging interactions are approximately equal [21]. Cotemporality of media seems to be the factor correlated with changes in lying behavior. Perhaps when given enough time to formulate utterances, the participants are more capable of creatively stretching the truth without explicitly lying.

There also tends to be a loss of temporal flexibility (evident in subjects' poor time management strategies over meetings) in video-mediated meetings as compared to FtF [22], which relates to Clark and Brennan's designation of copresence as a factor in communication. It is possible that the loss of physical copresence caused the users to become distracted by the novelty of their audio-visual medium or less capable of detecting each other's physical cues regarding turn-taking structure. The loss of temporal flexibility in the transition to video-mediated communication could be an advantage or disadvantage to the users, depending on their intentions and goals. These are just a few examples of variations within and between media.

4 Discourse Markers

Discourse markers have a profound effect on communicative effectiveness. So much so that they are even used as dependent variables in some conversation studies. In FtF communication, certain types of discourse markers are useful in signaling speaker certainty. Fox Tree and Schrock note that an oh in "prepared text... is likely to be used for some purpose that differs substantially from its use in spontaneous speech" [23].

Some discourse markers, however, retain their functions across media, such as *ok*, which seems to serve the same purpose in FtF, telephone, and CMC [24], [25]. It appears in close proximity to management of and transition between decision-making sequences [24], [25]. *Okay* and *all right* mark a return from a digression in the conversational topic, as a link between different levels of discourse organization, or to start or end interactions [26]. Discourse markers associated with argumentative convergence are also used similarly in instant messaging and FtF conversations [27]. However, 'statements of disagreement-relevant intrusions' are more common in instant messaging than FtF. This finding may be an artifact of IM's lower bandwidth, which requires users to negotiate more than FtF.

Although some discourse markers (like *ok*) prevail in CMC settings, there tends to be a substantial decrease in such devices when transitioning from FtF to CMC [28]. Thus, deficient performance in CMC settings relative to FtF might be due to the differential use of discourse markers. Fox Tree suggests that a loss of discourse markers could cause the discrepancy she found between monologue and dialogue performance (overhearers to verbal monologues performed worse than overhearers to dialogues) [29]. It is possible that this discrepancy could be a handicap for CMC.

However, computer interface designers have a number of options for enhancing CMC environments. It is certainly possible to create an interface that can overcome many, if not all, of these communicative obstacles. For example, the use of discourse markers often provides information about turn relevant transition places in conversations [30], and one can certainly design an interface to facilitate the use of this type of signal between interlocutors.

5 Turn Taking

Many of the differences between CMC and FtF are predicted by Clark and Brennan's costs [13], [31]. First, CMC speakers may try to be more accurate because mistakes tend to be more expensive in CMC (formulation costs, production costs, repair costs). This could possibly cause speakers to provide shorter messages but spend more time planning utterances. Second, a pause in CMC is not as interpretable as in FtF (reception costs, understanding costs, delay costs) [32]. Third, responses to messages will sometimes become scrambled (reception costs, understanding costs, delay costs, asynchrony costs). This may cause confusion in a CMC environment. Looking at Clark and Brennan's constraints on grounding, it is clear that FtF is not always the preferred medium [13].

However, CMC interlocutors also have advantages that are unavailable in FtF. Although CMC settings can lack copresence, visibility, audibility, cotemporality, simultaneity or absolute sequentiality, they also usually have the advantages of reviewability and revisability that typical FtF communication does not. A CMC user does not necessarily have to listen, understand, contemplate, and plan next turns simultaneously with the speaker's utterance delivery due to a leniency in CMC synchronization. This is in sharp contrast to FtF [33]. CMC users have fewer processes to juggle at one time.

Lack of simultaneity and synchronization also decrease one's tendency to use fillers (words strategically placed in pauses, such as *um,* possibly to hold the floor). These types of discourse markers are often helpful to listeners, so their absence could impede listener understanding [34], [35], [36]. Additionally, speakers' turns can become disordered when one party does not know what the other party is doing in real-time [31], [32]. Because these discontinuities are so different between media, it is expected that they will affect comprehension differently in different media, at least to some degree. However, CMC interfaces can be designed to overcome this potential problem.

For example, Garcia and Jacobs used a computer-mediated environment whereby users posted to a message board [38]. This is not entirely asynchronous like email, or completely synchronous like verbal communication, so they call it "quasi-synchronous" (QS-CMC). The location of transition-relevant places was different for QS-CMC than verbal conversations. Participants tended to begin typing messages after they saw a posted message from another participant. Thus, the speaker always determined relevant transition locations. Self-repair of messages in progress were different as well, because in QS-CMC, the 'listener' is not able to observe repairs or definitively interpret speaker pauses. In most CMC settings, pauses can be difficult to interpret. They may be artifacts of computer lag, network problems, the interlocutor's trip to the restroom, or a number of other factors [31]. Thus, the phenomena that arise during pauses are also missing in CMC.

For example, in CMC, a listener would be unlikely to include the continuer *uh huh* during a pause, which establishes he/she understands and the speaker can continue speaking [36]. When users have no tools to indicate that they are done with their turns (e.g., a post to the message board in Garcia and Jacobs' study), task-oriented conversations can suffer. Hancock and Dunham compared two entirely synchronous (What-You-See-Is-What-I-See, or WYSIWIS) interfaces in a study about turn markers [37]. Users who were provided turn taking coordination devices made fewer errors. Thus, even when CMC interlocutors have information about speaker pauses (in WYSIWIS), they benefit from having knowledge of their partners' conversational plans and strategies. Clearly, interface modifications can substantially improve the grounding process. Garcia and Jacobs point out that calling QS-CMC a "flawed form of interaction compared to oral conversation" or "impaired" would assume that verbal communication was the standard by which to measure communication. They propose the term "differently-abled" instead, to emphasize the possibility that QS-CMC can provide other advantages not available in verbal communication [32], (p. 361).

In addition to the differences they found, Garcia and Jacobs also found similarities between their QS-CMC environment and FtF communications. Interlocutors rarely responded to two separate postings in one post, as would be expected in FtF communications. Participants tended to treat transitionrelevant places in QS-CMC similarly to verbal communication (except for the difference mentioned above that the speaker was the sole designator of such locations) [31]. Even though CMC interlocutors can deliver utterances simultaneously, they tend to wait for their turns as in FtF.

CMC interlocutors also tend to entrain on turn taking strategies [38]. Participants' turn sizes tend to mirror each other, as in verbal communication [35]. If one person takes long turns, their partner also tends to take long turns, and vice versa. In synchronous CMC, interface constraints can also influence interlocutor turn sizes [38]. Larger message boxes tend to correlate with longer messages. Thus, CMC design can add constraints to communication that are not factors in FtF communication.

6   Coordinating Representations

CMC has a great advantage of design versatility. As exemplified throughout this paper, there are a number of interfaces and tools available to CMC interlocutors [31], [39], [40]. Depending on which of these tools are available and which are used, communicative effectiveness in CMC can vary. In this section, various uses of coordinating representations in CMC will be explored that can augment cognition in computer-based interactions.

Although coordination devices in WYSIWIS increase communicative effectiveness, the fact remains that no matter how helpful a communicative tool could be, it may not be used. Based on post-test questionnaires, participants in one study said they did not think it would be worth the trouble to use the coordination devices featured in their interfaces [41]. Interestingly, these unused devices would have helped with the exact problems the participants had on the task.

Again, this reiterates Clark and Brennan's costs and constraints on grounding [13]. Apparently, users thought the tool would require too much effort for too little payoff. In the same vein, some CMC modifications may provide little benefit to users, thus proving to be superfluous efforts to programmers. Although the use of avatars is often an advantageous addition to communicative software [15], [16], [17], [42], this is not always the case. Adding pedagogical agents to intelligent tutoring systems does not always improve student performance, even with knowledge of the avatar's facial expressions, gaze and gestures [43]. This could be due to the artificiality of the computational agent, or may indicate that the simulated expressions are unnecessary for certain tasks.

Eye gaze awareness varies drastically between FtF and CMC settings [44], [45], [46]. In their "A look is worth a thousand words" paper, Monk and Gale found that a look actually was worth (almost) a thousand words (949 words, to be exact) [45]. Full gaze awareness drastically reduces the number of words needed to complete a task (as compared to verbal-only communications). When users had information about their interlocutors' eye gaze, turns were reduced by 55% and accuracy was increased by 80%. Moreover, Richardson and Dale [46] found that overhearers to prior conversations did better on comprehension tests of the conversational material if their eye gaze positions were manipulated to match the speakers' eye movements.

CMC can enhance communication with copresence and covisibility. Intelligibility and word-duration are the same for FtF and CMC when CMC environments include verbal and visual copresence [48]. Math students retain more information if instructors use visual gestures [49]. Alone, this result would support the bandwidth hypothesis. However, there is also evidence that interface design could overcome the handicap caused by CMC environments' lack of gesture. When people communicate in a virtual environment, they prefer virtual gesture, even if they share physical copresence [50]. Only when deprived of parallel action in the virtual environment will they revert to physical gesturing. design can add constraints to communication that are not factors in FtF communication.

7 Overhearer Effects

Overhearer effects do occur in CMC environments, but they are not as strong as in verbal communications [51], [52]. Overhearers might perform better in CMC because CMC communication is more public. Speakers may try to be better at communicating in their initial utterances to avoid miscommunications (which are more costly in CMC). Thus, their initial messages are easier to understand, and this is reflected in overhearers' performance and understanding.

There are a number of other differences Čech and I found depending on exactly how overhearers are presented information. We found that matchers, who were allowed to provide the director feedback performed better than other groups of listeners who were not allowed to communicate with their directors. Overhearers who read messages from the matcher and director were next in rank (if they were *not* allowed to communicate with fellow overhearers), and the overhearers who could chat with each other performed worst. This is likely due to attention limitations [53].

We added two more conditions with a new group of participants to investigate the chatters' poor performance compared to the matchers and regular overhearers. In one of these, the chatters communicated with each other over the computer (as before), but were allowed to go through the director and matcher messages at their own leisure, to alleviate the time constraint. These chatters did better than the earlier chatters, but no better than the original overhearers. The additional perspectives in a conversation are not necessarily advantageous, as Fox Tree [29] had suggested might be possible.

In the second replication of the chatter condition, chatterers sat side-by-side and exchanged their opinions and ideas about the original director/matcher dialogues. Like the other chatters, they read the director/matcher messages over the computer and performed the task over the computer. However, they conversed with each other verbally. This caused a large positive effect in their performance. Additional post-tests showed that this result was not solely due to the change of medium (the effect diminished when they faced separate screens). Thus, copresence and covisibility were important factors for engaging the participants in this picture-placing task.

8 Conclusions

CMC offers a number of tools such as reviewability and revisability that are not available in FtF. Some discourse markers are the same in CMC and FtF (such as *okay* and *alright*), but most are not (e.g., *oh*, *umm*, and *uh-huh*). Although the lack of some of these discourse markers may decrease the listener's understanding, computer interfaces are capable of compensating for this discrepancy between media. This will not only require knowledge about which discourse markers would be needed in CMC interfaces, but it would also require knowledge about how to get users to take advantage of such tools provided in the interface design. Whether the cuerichness of FtF offers interlocutors an advantage depends on whether they utilize the tools provided. It also depends on the particular task being performed.

Acknowledgments. Many thanks are owed to Anton Nijholt of the University of Twente, Claude G. Čech of the University of Louisiana at Lafayette, and Danielle McNamara at the University of Memphis, as well as the AMIDA traineeship program. Each of these mentors and this program helped me continue to learn about mediated communication.

References

1. Whittaker, S.: Theories and methods in mediated communication. In: Graesser, A., Gernsbacher, M., Goldman, S. (eds.) The Handbook of Discourse Processes, Erlbaum, NJ (2003)
2. Fox Tree, J., Mayer, S., Betts, T.: At the crossroads of speaking and writing. Presented at the Society for Text and Discourse annual meeting, Rotterdam, the Netherlands (July 2009)
3. Walker, M., Whittaker, S.: Mixed initiative in dialogue: An investigation into discourse segmentation. In: Proceedings of the Association of Computational Linguistics ACL (1990)
4. Herring, S.C.: Introduction. In: Herring, S.C. (ed.) Computer-Mediated Communication: Linguisitc, social, and crosscultural perspectives, pp. 1–10. John Benjamins Publishing Company, Amsterdam (1996)
5. Walther, J.B.: Interpersonal effects in computer-mediated interaction: A relational perspective. Communication Research 19, 52–90 (1992)
6. Rabby, M.K., Walther, J.B.: Computer-mediated communication effects in relationship formation and maintenance. In: Canary, D.J., Dainton, M. (eds.) Maintaining relationships through communication, pp. 141–162. Lawrence Erlbaum and Associates, Mahwah (2003)
7. Rodgers, S., Chen, Q.: Internet community group participation: Psychosocial benefits for women with breast cancer. Journal of Computer-Mediated Communication 10(4) (2005)
8. Walther, J.B., Boyd, S.: Attraction to computer-mediated social support. In: Lin, C.A., Atkin, D. (eds.) Communication technology and society: Audience adoption and uses, pp. 153–188. Hampton Press, Cresskill (2002)
9. Epley, N., Kruger, J.: When what you type isn't what they read: The perseverance of stereotypes and expectancies over email. Journal of Experimental Social Psychology 41, 414–422 (2005)
10. Mensink, M., Rapp, D.: Evil geniuses: Inferences from mismatches between trait descriptions and reader preferences. Presented at the Society for Text and Discourse annual meeting, Rotterdam, the Netherlands (July 2009)

11. Quan-Haase, A., Cothrel, J., Wellman, B.: Instant messaging for collaboration: A case study of a high-tech firm. Journal of Computer-Mediated Communication 10(4) (2005) Article 13
12. Raine, R.: Who dat and where y'at? Acadians and their conventions for consideration of intercultural interlocutors: Towards a disambiguation of perspective taking in communication research. PhD dissertation, the University of Louisiana at Lafayette (2008)
13. Clark, H.H., Brennan, S.A.: Grounding in communication. In: Resnick, L.B., Levine, J.M., Teasley, S.D. (eds.) Perspectives on socially shared cognition, pp. 127–149. APA Books, Washington (1991)
14. Clark, H.H.: Using language. Cambridge University Press, Cambridge (1996)
15. Granstrom, B.: Modelling Listener Reactions to a Conversation – practical exercises. Paper presented at COST conference and winter school in Dublin, Ireland (March 2009)
16. Al Moubayed, S., Beskow, J., Öster, A.-M., Salvi, G., Granström, B., van Son, N., Ormel, E., Herzke, T.: Studies on Using the SynFace Talking Head for the Hearing Impaired. In: Proceedings of Fonetik 2009. Dept. of Linguistics, Stockholm University, Sweden (2009)
17. Al Moubayed, S., Beskow, J.: Effects of Visual Prominence Cues on Speech Intelligibility. To be published in Proceedings of Auditory-Visual Speech Processing AVSP 2009, Norwich, England (2009) (in press)
18. Ramseyer, F., Tschacher, W.: Synchrony: A Core Concept for a Constructivist Approach to Psychotherapy. Constructivism in the Human Sciences 11(1-2), 150–171 (2006)
19. Ramseyer, F., Tschacher, W.: Synchrony in Dyadic Psychotherapy Sessions. In: Vrobel, S., Rössler, O.E., Marks-Tarlow, T. (eds.) Simultaneity: Temporal Structures and Observer Perspectives, pp. 329–347. World Scientific, Singapore (2008)
20. Furnham, A.: The message the context and the medium. Language and Communication 2, 33–47 (1982)
21. Hancock, J.T., Thom-Santelli, J., Ritchie, T.: Deception and design: The impact of communication technology on lying behavior. In: Proceedings of the SIGCHI conference on human factors in computing systems, pp. 129–134. Addison Wesley, Vienna (2004)
22. Kane, B.: What can vocalization patterns tell us about the content of meetings? Paper presented at COST conference and winter school in Dublin, Ireland (March 2009)
23. Fox Tree, J.E., Schrock, J.C.: Discourse markers in spontaneous speech: Oh what a difference an "oh" makes. Journal of Memory and Language 40, 294 (1999)
24. Bangerter, A., Clark, H.H., Katz, A.R.: Navigating joint projects in telephone conversations. Discourse Processes 37(1), 1–23 (2004)
25. Condon, S.L., Čech, C.G.: Ok, next one: Discourse markers of common ground. In: Fetzer, A., Fischer, K. (eds.) Lexical markers of common ground, pp. 17–45. Elsevier, Oxford (2007)
26. Bangerter, A., Clark, H.H.: Navigating joint projects with dialogue. Cognitive Science 27, 195–225 (2003)
27. Stewart, C.O., Setlock, L.D., Fusselll, S.R.: Conversational argumentation in decision making: Chinese and U.S. participants in face-to-face and instantmessaging interactions. Discourse Processes 44, 113–139 (2004)
28. Wilkes-Gibbs, D., Clark, H.H.: Coordinating beliefs in conversation. Journal of Memory and Language 31(2), 183–194 (1992)
29. Fox Tree, J.E.: Listening in on monologues and dialogues. Discourse Processes 27, 35–53 (1999)
30. Schiffrin, D.: Discourse markers. Cambridge University Press, NY (1996) (original work published 1987)

31. Davis, B.H., Brewer, J.P.: Electronic discourse: Linguistic individuals in virtual space. State University Press, Albany (1997)

32. Garcia, A.C., Jacobs, J.B.: The eyes of the beholder: understanding the turn taking system in quasi-synchronous computermediated communication. Research on Language and Social Interaction 32, 337–367 (1999)

33. Clark, H.H., Wilkes-Gibbs, D.: Referring as a collaborative process. Cognition 22, 1–39 (1996)

34. Clark, H.H., Wasow, T.: Repeating words in spontaneous speech. Cognitive Psychology 37, 201–242 (1998)

35. Sacks, H., Schegloff, E., Jefferson, G.: A simplest systematics for the organization of turn taking in conversation. Language 50, 696–735 (1974)

36. Schegloff, E.A.: Discourse as an interactional achievement: Some uses of 'uh huh' and other things that come between sentences. In: Tannen, D. (ed.) Georgetown University roundtable on languages and linguistics 1981: Analyzing discourse: Text and talk, pp. 71–93. Georgetown University Press, Washington (1982)

37. Hancock, J.T., Dunham, P.J.: Language use in computer-mediated communication: The role of coordination devices. Discourse Processes 31, 91–110 (2001)

38. Čech, C.G., Condon, S.L.: Message size constraints on discourse planning in synchronous computer-mediated communication. Behavior Research Methods, Instruments, & Computers 30, 255–263 (1998)

39. Brugnoli, M.C., Morabito, F., Walker, R., Davide, F.: The PASION project: Psychologically augmented social interaction over networks. Psychology Journal 4(1), 103–116 (2006)

40. Rosenberg, D., Foley, S., Lievonen, M., Kammas, S., Crisp, M.J.: Interaction spaces in computer-mediated communication. AI &. AI & Society 19, 22–33 (2005)

41. Alterman, R., Feinman, A., Introne, J., Landsman, S.: Coordinating representations in computer-mediated joint activities. In: Moore, J.D., Stenning, K. (eds.) Proceedings of 23rd Annual Conference of the Cognitive Science Society, pp. 15–20. Lawrence Erlbaum Associates, Inc., Mahwah (2001)

42. Karlsson, I., Faulkner, A., Salvi, G.: SYNFACE—A talking face telephone. In: Eurospeech 2003, pp. 1297–3000 (2003)

43. Craig, S.D., Driscoll, D.M., Gholson, B.: Constructing knowledge from dialogue in an intelligent tutoring system: Interactive learning, vicarious learning, and pedagogical agents. Journal of Educational Multimedia and Hypermedia 13, 163–183 (2004)

44. Hanna, J.E., Brennan, S.E.: Speakers' eye gaze disambiguates referring expressions early during face-to-face conversation. Journal of Memory and Language 57, 596–615 (2007)

45. Monk, A.F., Gale, C.: A look is worth a thousand words: Full gaze awareness in video-mediated conversation. Discourse Processes 33, 257–278 (2002)

46. Richardson, D.C., Dale, R.: Looking to understand: The coupling between speakers' and listeners' eye movements and its relationship to discourse comprehension. Cognitive Science 29, 1045–1060 (2005)

47. Tanenhaus, M., Spivey-Knowlton, M., Eberhard, K., Sedivy, J.: The interaction of visual and linguistic information in spoken language comprehension. Science 268, 1632–1634 (1995)

48. Anderson, A.H., Howarth, B.: Referential form and word duration in videomediated and face-to-face dialogues. In: Bos, J., Foster, M., Matheson, C. (eds.) Proceedings of the sixth workshop on the semantics and pragmatics of dialogue, vol. 13, pp. 13–20. University of Edinburgh Press, Edinburgh (2002)

49. Goldin-Meadow, S., Nusbaum, H., Kelly, S., Wagner, S.: Explaining math: Gesturing lightens the load. Psychological Science 12, 516–522 (2001)
50. Gill, S.P., Sethi, R., Martin, S.: The engagement space and gesteral coordination. In: Cave, C., Guaitella, I., Santi, S. (eds.) Oralite et Gestualite: Interactions et Comportements Multimodaux dans la Communication (Proceedings of ORAGE 2001, International Conference on Speech and Gesture). L'Harmattan, Paris (2001)
51. Čech, C.G., Benoit, R.B.: Are two heads better than one (Listening in on overhearer collaboration). Paper presented at the 44th annual meeting of the Psychonomic Society, Vancouver (November 2003)
52. Raine, R.B., Čech, C.G.: Overhearers in CMC: Deficient or advantageous? Paper presented at COST conference and winter school in Dublin, Ireland (March 2009)
53. Clark, H.H.: How do real people communicate with virtual partners? Paper presented at AAAI Fall Symposium: Psychological Models of Communication in Collaborative Systemsm North Falmouth, MA (November 1999)

Towards Influencing of the Conversational Agent Mental State in the Task of Active Listening

Stanislav Ondáš[1], Elisabetta Bevacqua[2], Jozef Juhár[1], and Peter Demeter[1]

[1] Technical University of Košice, Faculty of Electrical Engineering and Informatics,
Laboratory of speech technologies, Letná 9, Košice, Slovakia
[2] CNRS - Telecom ParisTech, 37/39 rue Dareau,
75014 Paris, France
{stanislav.ondas,jozef.juhar}@tuke.sk,
elisabetta.bevacqua@telecom-paristech.fr, demeter.peto@gmail.com

Abstract. The proposed paper describes an approach that was used to influence conversational agent Greta's mental state. The beginning this paper introduces the problem of conversational agents, especially in the listener role. The listener's backchannels also influence its mental state. The simple agent state manager was developed to impact Greta's internal state. After describing this manager, we present an overview of evaluation experiments carried out to obtain information about agent state manager functionality, as well as the impact of the mental state changes on the overall interaction.

Keywords: Embodied conversational agent, listener, mental state, backchannel.

1 Introduction

Researches have shown that people tend to interact with computers characterized by human-like attributes as if they were really humans [1], [24]. Consequently, the more humane-machine interfaces are consistent with human style of communication, the more their use becomes easy and accessible [2]. Such level of consistency could be reached using Embodied Conversational Agents (ECAs): computer-generated animated characters that are able to carry on natural, human-like communication with users [3]. In this work, to perform our tests, we use the Embodied Conversational Agent Greta [4] developed at the Telecom ParisTech Research Centre, see Section 3.

Human interlocutors in the dialog take the roles of the speaker and the listener. Each of these roles has their own behavioral properties. There is also an effort to give these properties to the virtual humans. Earlier projects usually deal with the behavior of the speaker. Presented work is focused on the modeling of the behavior of virtual listener. Active listening is an important dimension of the conversational agent behavior. Backchannel produced by agents in this role relates to three main factors – what was seen, what was heard and the internal mental state of the listener. Producing of backchannel signals require an understanding of interlocutor's speech. Thus the key limitation relates to the unavailability of partial interpretation of speaker's utterance until he is finished and consecutively to the problems with the synchronization [5].

A. Esposito et al. (Eds.): COST 2102 Int. Training School 2009, LNCS 5967, pp. 113–121, 2010.

The proposed work has their background in the Project 7: "Multimodal Feedback from Robots and Agents in a Storytelling Experiment", which was solved on eNTER-FACE'08 Summer School [6]. This project lies at the intersection between Human-Computer Interaction (HCI) and Human-Robot Interaction (HRI) and was especially focused on active listening and generating feedback during storytelling task. [7].One of the goals of this project was to give the properties of active listener to the both the embodied conversational agent Greta [4] and the robotic dog Aibo.

The proposed paper mainly presents an approach, which was used for influencing of the internal mental state of the listener. For this purpose was developed a simple Agent State Manager (ASM), which uses speech recognition for obtaining information about what was spoken. The second part of the paper deals with the evaluation experiment, which was carried out with 50 students, who told a story to the ECA Greta. Then they filled out the questionnaires about their impression from the interaction.

2 Background – Listener's Behavior

During a conversation the listener is called to provide information on the successfulness of the communication. Through verbal and non verbal signals, called "backchannels" [8], [26], a listener can show his level of engagement in the conversation, providing information about the basic communicative functions, as perception, attention, interest, understanding, attitude (e.g., belief, liking and so on) and acceptance towards what the speaker is saying [9], [23]. Backchannels can be the result of two evaluation stages of the reception of the speaker's message [10]: at the first stage, a non-conscious appraisal of the perceived information can generate automatic behavior, for example to show lack of contact or perception. At a second stage, the more aware evaluation, involving memory, understanding and other cognitive processes, can generate signals to show understanding and other attitudinal reactions, like acceptance or rejection, belief or disbelief and so on. We call *reactive* the behavior derived from perception processing and response the more aware behavior generated by cognitive processing. Another particular form of backchannel is the *mimicry* [12] of the speaker's behavior. By mimicry we mean the behavior displayed by an individual who does what another person does [11]. This type of behavior has been proven to play quite an important role during conversations. When present, it makes the conversation run more smoothly [12], and helps to regulate the conversational flow. For example, listeners often mirror speaker's postural shifts at the end of a discourse segment and this helps the exchange of speaking turns [13].

3 GRETA: An Embodied Conversational Agent

Greta is an Embodied Conversational Agent that communicates through several modalities (like head, face, gaze, gesture and torso) while interacting with a user. The agent architecture follows the design methodology proposed in [14] and is compatible with the standard SAIBA framework (Situation, Agent, Intention, Behavior, Animation) [15].

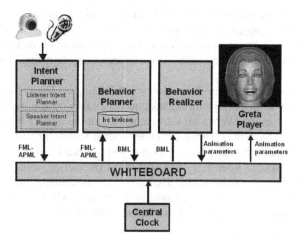

Fig. 1. Greta's Architecture

The architecture of the agent Greta (Figure 2) is modular and distributed. Each module exchanges information and data through a central message system. We use the concept of whiteboard [14] that allows internal modules and external software to be integrated easily. The Intent Planner module is divided into two sub-modules, the Listener Intent Planner and the Speaker Intent Planner that decide of the agent's communicative intentions respectively in the role of the listener and in the role of the speaker. The Intent Planner encodes the agent's communicative intentions into the FML-APML language (Function Markup Language - Affective Presentation Markup Language), a first approach to the FML language (Function Markup Language). The Behavior Planner module receives as input the agent's communicative intentions written in FML-APML and, to convey them, it schedules a number of communicative signals (e.g., speech, facial expressions, gestures) which are encoded with the Behavior Markup Language (BML). Such a language specifies the verbal and non-verbal behaviors of ECAs [15]. The task of the Behavior Realizer is to realize the behaviors scheduled by the Behavior Planner. Finally, the animation is played in the Greta Player. The synchronization of all modules in the distributed environment is ensured by the Central Clock.

3.1 Generation of the Listener's Behavior

The Listener Intent Planner module is in charge of the computation of the agent's behaviors while being a listener when conversing with a user. This component encompasses two modules called response/reactive backchannel and mimicry. Research has shown that there is a strong correlation between backchannel signals and the verbal and non-verbal behaviors performed by the speaker [5], [17]. From the literature [5], [17] we have fixed some probabilistic rules to decide when a backchannel signal should be triggered. Our system analyzes speaker's behaviors looking for those that could prompt an agent's signal; for example, a head nod or a variation in the pitch of the user's voice will trigger a backchannel with a certain probability. Then, the response/reactive backchannel, and mimicry modules compute which type of backchannel should be displayed. The response/reactive backchannel module uses information about the agent's beliefs towards the speaker's speech to calculate the response backchannel signal. We use Allwood's and Poggi's taxonomies of communicative functions of backchannels [9]: understanding and attitudinal reactions (liking, accepting, agreeing, believing, being interested).

A lexicon of backchannels has been elaborated [18], [23]. The response module selects which signals to display from the lexicon depending on the agent's reaction towards the speaker's speech. When no information about the agent's beliefs towards the speaker's speech is given, the response/reactive module selects a pre-defined backchannel among those signals that have been proven to show contact and perception, like head nod and raise eyebrows. When fully engaged in an interaction, mimicry of behaviors between interactants may happen [19]. The mimicry module determines which signals would mimic the agent. A selection algorithm determines which backchannels to display among all the potential signals that are outputted by the two modules.

4 Agent's Mental State Influencing

As was said above the response/reactive backchannel module requires information about *agent's beliefs* and such information can be given predominantly from speaker's speech. Mentioned communicative functions of backchannels relate to agent's belief and we can say that these functions represent the internal agent mental state.

The mental state of the agent Greta determines how the agent reacts to the user's speech and it is represented through mentioned functions: agreement, disagreement, acceptance, refusal, belief, disbelief, liking, disliking, interest, no interest, understanding, no understanding [20]. In the ECA Greta, the agent's mental state has been static and tied together with the agent's baseline. The agent's baseline is defined in [21] as a set of numeric parameters that represents the agent's behavior tendencies.

It is clear, that the mental state of the human interlocutors in the interaction is changing. These changes relates to large range of various factors as are the relationship of the interlocutors, the initial communication intentions and feelings, earlier interactions, the common knowledge, and so on. But the main (direct) impact on the mental state of participants in the interaction has the content of the interaction. Therefore, we need some degree of content understanding, if we want to change the agent's mental state during the interaction. For these purposes the agent state manager (ASM) was developed.

4.1 Agent State Manager (ASM)

The key functionality of the ASM is to change agent's mental state according to the speaker's speech. It is necessary to extract partial meaning before the speaker stops speaking. The question was how can we do this? At the beginning we have selected the simplest way – to process speaker's utterances over the words, because the words are the smallest meaningful parts of the utterance. The designed ASM is shown on Fig. 2.

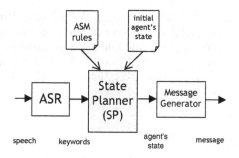

Fig. 2. Architecture of the agent state manager

It consists of three main parts – Automatic Speech Recognition engine (ASR), State planner (SP) and Message generator. The ASM takes words, which are spoken by the speaker and it impacts the mental state of the agent according to the set of rules. At the beginning the initial agent state is loaded from an XML file. The message generator produces the messages, which informs Greta about the new mental state.

The speech recognition engine we have used is based on ATK/HTK [25]. It supports Slovak language and it works in keyword-spotting mode. The ASR engine uses triphone acoustic models, which were trained on Slovak SpeechDat-E database [21], [22]. As a language model we have used a speech grammar which enables the recognition of keywords in phrases. Other words are modeled as "filler words".

The State Planner is the main part of the agent state manager. Its task is to modify the state of the agent according to spoken input (keywords). For this purpose it uses a rule-based approach. This component is initialized with the initial agent state as well as with a set of rules loaded from the file. Each rule consists of the following items: *feature*, *keyword*, *step*, *max_value*, *opposite_feature*, *action*. The items *opposite_feature* and *action* are optional. When the speech recognizer recognizes a keyword, the State Planner looks for an appropriate rule. If ASM finds such rule, it increases the value of the related feature by a given *step* value, while *max_value* is not reached. If some *opposite_feature* is defined in the rule, it is decreased by the same *step*. The State Planner can also create a requirement for some action as are headnod, smile or headshake, if in appropriate rule is defined the parameter *action*.

The last part of the ASM is the Message Generator, which is responsible for preparing an XML file containing the values (features), which represent the new mental state of the agent. It sends the XML file through a TCP socket to the ECA Greta.

5 The Storytelling Experiment

The main goal of the storytelling experiment, which we carried out, was to assess the functionality of the developed agent state manager and to observe the impact of the agent's mental state changes on the human speaker during his storytelling to the agent. The cartoon about Silvester and Tweety was selected as the scenario of this storytelling. We assumed that after such funny story, levels of liking, interest, understanding and acceptance will increase and the agent will produce appropriate (richer) backchannel signals. The backchannel produced by Greta depended only on the speaker's speech. Thus means that other factors did not influenced the interaction.

There were more than 50 speakers, who told the story to the ECA Greta. Before the experiment were necessary to define the keywords for ASR engine, to create profiles (agent's baseline and a set of rules for ASM), to design evaluation questionnaires and to establish the place of the experiment. For the purpose of evaluation were used both the questionnaires and the log files produced by ASM.

5.1 Setup of the Experiment

At the beginning we needed to select keywords for speech recognition. Therefore ten storytelling of mentioned cartoon were recorded. Then the recordings were analyzed in terms of word counts. After eliminating conjunctions and pronouns, which were naturally the most frequent words, we identified a group of keywords: vtáčik (bird), kocúr (tomcat), Silvester, babka (grandmother), kufre (baggages), klietka (cage), pani (lady), poslíček (callboy), dáždnik (umbrella), hlava (head).

We wanted also to compare different profiles of the agent and to assess speaker's impression from the interaction with them. These profiles determine how the agent generates backchannel during the storytelling. Three kinds of profiles – Spike, Poppy and Ann were created, which consist of different rule files for configuration of ASM, different initial mental states and different agent's baselines (adopted from [20]). Accordingly, speakers were divided in to three groups, in such manner that each group told the story to the one of the ECA's profile.

The storytelling experiment was carried out in our laboratory. The ECA ran on the PC with soundcard and the speaker sat in the front of the monitor and told the story in to the headset with microphone. After his storytelling, he filled out the questionnaire about his impression of realized interaction.

5.2 The Results of the Subjective Evaluation

The subjective evaluation was based on questionnaires fulfilling. For this purpose the questionnaire with five questions was designed. The first question was:

1. *"Did you have the feeling that Agent's mood was changing during your storytelling?"* - 90% respondents, who told the story to the Poppy said "yes". The same response was selected also by speakers who communicated with Ann (about 83%) and Spike (about 67%). It means that changing of agent's state influenced the perception of listener's mood by speaker, what relates to the fact, that ECA showed more liking and interest (see also Fig.3).

2. *"Did you have the feeling, that Agent understood you?"* - The most of the speakers (about 92%) who told the story to Ann and 70% of speakers who told the story to Poppy, had that feeling. In the Spike profile, it was 50% of speakers. These results matched also to the level of understanding on Fig. 3. We can say that the internal state of the agent was communicated appropriately to the speaker during the backchannel.

3. *"How did Agent like your storytelling?"* – It was Ann who liked the stories the most. (58.3%) Spike disliked the stories the most (66.7%) and Poppy disliked the stories as well (50%). The lower values of "liking" in the case of Spike and Poppy do

not match the "liking" level. There are two factors, which could cause this situation – the zero initial value of "liking" parameter and not good rules for ASM, which impact "liking" parameter.

4. *"Was Agent interested in your storytelling?"* - The most interested "person" was Ann (the answer "mostly yes" – 50%). On the contrary, agents Spike and Poppy were "mostly not" interested in the storytelling (33.3% and 50%). This is the similar situation as was in the previous question.

5. *"How much did Agent behave like a human being?"* - All speakers who were communicating with Spike labeled "mostly not" answer. In the profile Poppy the answers "mostly not" and "mostly yes" were equal (40%). The respondents had the feeling that the agent in the profile Ann mostly behaves like a human being (58.3%). We supposed such results, because the profile Ann has higher initial values of "acceptance", "belief" and "liking" parameters as well as different set of ASM rules, which allow rapid increasing of mental state parameters.

5.3   The Results of the Objective Evaluation

The objective part of the evaluation experiment was focused on comparing initial agent state and the mental state after the storytelling. Figure 3 brings a comparison of those values for all profiles. We have used log files produced by ASM for obtaining these values.

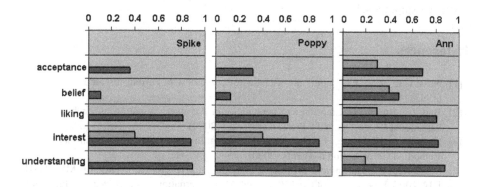

Fig. 3. The initial (blue) and final (violet) ECA's mental state

The first important fact, which we were observed is, that the ASM really impact the agent mental state. The second observation is that the values, which represent the degree of acceptance, belief, liking, interest and understanding, were increased. We have anticipated such situation because the story that was told was positive and funny. The highest values were reached in profile Ann. This results matches also to the results obtained from questionnaires. Speakers, who told the story to the ECA in profile Ann had the feeling, that ECA understood them (about 92%), that she was interested in this storytelling (50%) and she liked the story (about 58%).

6 Conclusions

Presented system is the first step towards the system for maintaining of agent's mental state during the conversation with human. Realized experiment shows that such approach is able to change mental state of the ECA in the role of the listener, but it is necessary to set up the initial agent's state and the rules for ASM carefully. The experiment also brings a need of some internal logic, which for example automatically decreases the value of interest in the case, when long interval of silence occurs. The next problem is that the value of "understanding" increases very quickly when a lot of keywords occur in the speaker's utterance.

Such system should integrate information from several modalities and it also should deliberate overall perception as well as information from memory. The statistical modeling is one of the possible ways.

In the future we want to include other inputs (modalities) in to the ASM – the beginning and the end of speech detection, a type of sentence recognition (question, statement...) based on prosody, and so on.

Acknowledgments. The work presented in this paper was supported by the Slovak Research and Development Agency under research project APVV-0369-07 and Ministry of Education of Slovak Republic under research projects AV 4/0006/07 and VEGA 1/4054/07. We would like to say special thanks to people from project No.7: "Multimodal Communication with Robots and Virtual Agents" of the eNTER-FACE'08 summer school.

References

[1] Nass, C.I., et al.: Computers are social actors: a review of current research, pp. 137–162 (1997)

[2] Ball, G., Breese, J.: Emotion and personality in a conversational agent. Embodied Conversational Characters. MIT Press, Cambridge (2000)

[3] Cassell, J., Bickmcre, T., Campbell, L.: Designing Embodied Conversational Agents. Embodied Conversational Agents (2000)

[4] Pelachaud, C.: Multimodal expressive embodied conversational agents. In: MULTIMEDIA 2005: Proceedings of the 13th annual ACM international conference on Multimedia, pp. 683–689. ACM, New York (2005)

[5] Maatman, R.M., Gratch, J., Marsella, S.: Natural behavior of a listening agent. In: 5th International Conference on Interactive Virtual Agents, Kos, Greece (2005)

[6] eNTERFACE Summer School web page, http://enterface08.limsi.fr/ (June 10, 2009)

[7] Al Moubayed, S., et al.: Multimodal Feedback from Robots and Agents in a Storytelling Experiment. In: Project 7: Final Project Report, eNTERFACE 2008, Paris, France, August 4-29 (2008)

[8] Yngve, V.: On getting a word in edgewise. Papers from the Sixth Regional Meeting of the Chicago Linguistic Society, pp. 567–577 (1970)

[9] Allwood, J., et al.: On the semantics and pragmatics of linguistic feedback. Semantics (1993)

[10] Kopp, S., et al.: Modeling embodied feedback with virtual humans. In: Wachsmuth, I., Knoblich, G. (eds.) ZiF Research Group International Workshop. LNCS (LNAI), vol. 4930, pp. 18–37. Springer, Heidelberg (2008)

[11] Van baaren, R.B. (ed.): Mimicry: a social perspective (February 10, 2003), http://webdoc.ubn.kun.nl/mono/b/baarenrvan/mimi.pdf

[12] Chartrand, T., Bargh, J.: The Chameleon Effect: The Perception-Behavior Link and Social Interaction. Personality and Social Psychology 76, 893–910 (1999)

[13] Cassell, J., et al.: Non-verbal cues for discourse structure. In: Proceedings of the 39th Annual Meeting on Association for Computational Linguistics, Association for Computational Linguistics Morristown, NJ, USA, pp. 114–123 (2001)

[14] Thórisson, K.R., et al.: Whiteboards: Scheduling blackboards for semantic routing of messages & streams. In: AAAI 2005 Workshop on Modular Construction of Human-Like Intelligence, pp. 8–15 (2005)

[15] Vilhjálmsson, H.H., et al.: The Behavior Markup Language: Recent developments and challenges. In: Pelachaud, C., Martin, J.-C., André, E., Chollet, G., Karpouzis, K., Pelé, D. (eds.) IVA 2007. LNCS (LNAI), vol. 4722, pp. 99–111. Springer, Heidelberg (2007)

[16] Heylen, D., et al.: Why conversational agents do what they do? Functional representations for generating conversational agent behavior. In: The first Functional Markup Language workshop. The Seventh International Conference on Autonomous Agents and Multiagent Systems Estoril, Portugal (2008)

[17] Ward, N., Tsukahara, W.: Prosodic features which cue back-channel responses in english and japanese. Journal of Pragmatics 23, 1177–1207 (2000)

[18] Bevacqua, E., et al.: Facial feedback signals for ECAs. In: AISB 2007 Annual convention, workshop "Mindful Environments", Newcastle upon Tyne, UK, pp. 147–153 (2007)

[19] Lakin, J.L., et al.: Chameleon effect as social glue: Evidence for the evolutionary significance of nonconsious mimicry. Nonverbal Behavior 27(3), 145–162 (2003)

[20] Bevacqua, et al: A listening agent exhibiting variable behaviour. In: IVA 2008. LNCS (LNAI), vol. IVA 2008, pp. 262–269. Springer, Heidelberg (2008)

[21] Pollak, P., Cernocky, J., Boudy, J., Choukri, K., Rusko, M., Trnka, M., et al.: Speech-Dat(E) Eastern European Telephone Speech Databases. In: Proc. LREC 2000 Satellite workshop XLDB - Very large Telephone Speech Databases, Athens, Greece, May 2000, pp. 20–25 (2000)

[22] Lindberg, B., Johansen, F.T., Warakagoda, N., Lehtinen, G., Kačič, Z., Žgank, A., Elenius, K., Salvi, G.: A noise robust multilingual reference recognizer based on SpeechDat (II). In: Proc. ICSLP 2000, Beijing, China (2000)

[23] Heylen, D., et al.: Searching for prototypical facial feedback signals. In: Pelachaud, C., Martin, J.-C., André, E., Chollet, G., Karpouzis, K., Pelé, D. (eds.) IVA 2007. LNCS (LNAI), vol. 4722, pp. 147–153. Springer, Heidelberg (2007)

[24] Reeves, B., Nass, C.: The media equation: How people treat computers, television and new media like real people and places (1996)

[25] Young, S.: ATK: An application Toolkit for HTK, version 1.6. Cambridge University, Cambridge (2007)

[26] Sacks, H., Schegloff, E.A., Jefferson, G.: A simplest systematics for the organization of turn taking for conversation. Language 50(4), 696–735 (1974)

Integrating Emotions in the TRIPLE ECA Model

Kiril Kiryazov and Maurice Grinberg

Central and Eastern European Center for Cognitive Science, New Bulgarian University,
Montevideo 21, 1618 Sofia, Bulgaria
kiryazov@cogs.nbu.bg, mgrinberg@nbu.bg

Abstract. This paper presents the introduction of emotion-based mechanisms in
the TRIPLE ECA model. TRIPLE is a hybrid cognitive model consisting of
three interacting modules – the reasoning, the connectionist, and the emotion
engines – running in parallel. The interplay between these three modules is discussed in the paper with a focus on the role and implementation of the emotion
engine which is based on the FAtiMA agent architecture. The influence of emotions in TRIPLE is related to the volume of the working memory, the speed of
the inference mechanisms, the interaction between the reasoning and the connectionist engine, and the connectionist engine itself. Emotions will increase the
most important cognitive aspects of the model like context sensitivity, rich ex-
periential episodic knowledge and anticipatory mechanisms.

1 Introduction

Virtual environments, like the Internet, constantly evolve with respect to the amount
of information and its complexity. In such environments, although increasingly
needed, human level of performance is difficult to achieve, e.g. level of communication, user perception, information selection, etc. This situation stresses the importance
of the design and exploration of cognitively plausible models as 'minds' of the Embodied Conversational Agents (ECA) living in virtual environments. The problems
related to perception and action on the one hand and the interaction with human users
on the other requires context sensitivity, flexibility, believability, and personalization
of the ECA behavior. From a theoretical point of view, analogously to robotics, ac-
complishing tasks in complex environments seems to require novel approaches based
on knowledge about human cognition combined with powerful AI techniques.

The model TRIPLE, introduced for the first time in [1,2], was designed to be a
cognitive architecture for artificial cognitive systems and particularly for ECA platforms. It includes several of the cognitive features mentioned above and at the same
time it tries to achieve maximal computational efficiency in order to allow real time
functioning. These two constraints lie at the basis of this model: using the cognitive
modeling techniques which allow adaptivity, context sensitivity and selectivity of the
agent and at the same time – maximal computational optimization of the code based
on efficient computational and inference methods (e.g. see [3]).

This paper presents the emotional module of TRIPLE and its relations to the other
modules – the Reasoning Engine (RE) and the Similarity Assessment Engine (SAE)
[1,2]. Typically in ECA research [4], the main motive for including emotions is the

A. Esposito et al. (Eds.): COST 2102 Int. Training School 2009, LNCS 5967, pp. 122–133, 2010.

improved interaction with human users (e.g. related to higher believability of the agent).

The second reason is the importance of emotions for the adaptivity and effectiveness of reasoning (see e.g. [5]). For example in [6], the impact of arousal on memory is explored in the framework of ACT-R and arguments are given that any general cognitive architecture should integrate emotions in order to account for a number of psychological findings. In [7], in a framework similar to TRIPLE [8], the effects of emotion on analogical reasoning have been investigated and have been shown to influence retrieval and mapping in a non-trivial manner.

The emotional model in TRIPLE is based on FAtiMA (FearNot! Affective Mind Architecture) which is platform focused on modeling emotions and personality [9,10]. FAtiMA generates emotions from a subjective appraisal of events and is based on the OCC cognitive theory of emotions [11]. The OCC is commonly used in agent architectures for modeling emotional behavior [12]. Moreover, FAtiMA has been successfully applied in various domains [13,14].

The rest of the paper is organized as follows. In Section 2, we give a brief overview of the TRIPLE model. In Section 3, a detailed description of the emotion engine is given and in Section 4, its interaction with the other modules of TRIPLE is described. In Section 5, a sample simulation is described to show the emotional dynamics based on different types of events.

2 The TRIPLE Model

The TRIPLE model is inspired by the DUAL/AMBR model for analogy making [8]. TRIPLE has some important mechanisms adopted from the DUAL/AMBR architecture, but most underlying mechanisms are considerably different. TRIPLE is based on three basic modules which run in parallel and communicate on an event-driven basis (Fig. 1).

The Reasoning Engine (RE), shown in Fig. 1, coordinates and synchronizes the activities of the model and connects the agent with the environment (e.g. the user, other agents, etc.) and with the tools the agent can use (e.g. tools to communicate with the user, access knowledge and data bases, search the Internet, etc.) [1]. RE is also responsible for instance learning – storing of useful episodes in LTM after evaluation. It operates serially on a small amount of knowledge selected by the connectionist mechanisms of the Similarity Assessment Engine (SAE) and influenced by the emotion engine.

The SAE is designed to be a connectionist engine, based on fast matrix operations and is supposed to run continuously as an independent parallel process [2]. The main mechanism is activation spreading in combination with similarity or correspondence assessment mechanisms which allow retrieving knowledge relevant to the task at hand.

The emotion engine, similarly to SAE, is supposed to run in parallel and influence various parameters of the model like the volume of WM, the speed of processing, etc. The emotion engine is supposed also to react to external events without much cognitive processing. The next sections consider the role emotion engine in greater detail.

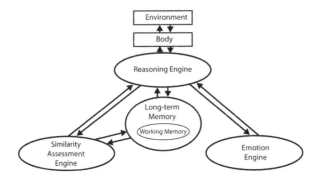

Fig. 1. The basic modules in TRIPLE

3 The Emotion Engine

The Emotion Engine (EE) of TRIPLE is a separate module which communicates with the 'body' of the agent, i.e. receives symbolically represented information about the environment. At the same time EE communicates with the Reasoning Engine (RE) and through it influence several cognitive mechanisms as discussed below (Fig. 1). In the figure only links with the RE are shown since in the current implementation RE also works as a "dispatcher" and handles all communications between the modules.

The structure of EE is given in Fig. 2. It can be formally divided into two parts: 'reactive' and 'deliberative' (see Fig. 2). The reactive part communicates mainly with the environment and provides fast emotional response to some external events. Reactive and deliberative appraisals generate the emotion base potential (when an internal or external event is perceived) which is used to generate a new emotional state. The Emotional State (ES) of the model is based on all emotions related to the mood of the system and on some rules representing the internal emotional dynamics. Considerable changes in the ES result in actions of the avatar to express the strongest emotion. At the same time, the emotions and mood at a given moment influence the reasoning process in a psychologically plausible way.

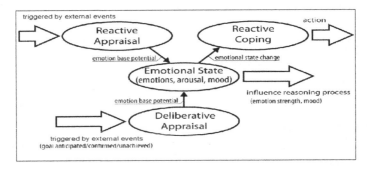

Fig. 2. Structure of the emotion engine and its relation to the other modules of the model

3.1 Reactive Emotional Processing

Following FAtiMA model [9], the reactive process in EE consists of:

- Reactive appraisal: handles specific external events and emotionally appraises them to produce emotions;
- Reactive coping: produces actions based on the strongest current emotion.

Reactive appraisal. The reactive appraisal process is based on a set of predefined emotional reaction rules. They provide a fast appraisal mechanism to generate most types of OCC emotions. When an external event is perceived (an line written by the user for example) it is sent to EE as a specific emotional event. It generates the values of the Appraisal Variables (AV). There are various AV in FAtiMA but the current implementation of TRIPLE EE uses only the 'desirability' AV. EE uses only two emotions generated in a 'reactive' way – 'joy' and 'distress,' which are based on the 'desirability' AV. The other six emotions, which the agent could 'experience', are generated in the 'deliberative' appraisal described below. The 'desirability' AV indicates generally how good or bad the event is for the agent.

External events that are appraised by the reactive module are related to interaction with the agent's user. For example direct feedback from the user or interpretation of some of her feedback can lead to events like 'The user is sad' and 'The user is happy.' Another external event occurs when the system is started and the agent is 'awakened.' This event is appraised as very desirable and thus the ECA begins its activity with 'joy.'

Reactive coping. The reactive coping process is a simplified version of the one implemented in FAtiMA. EE checks continuously for significant changes in the emotional state of the agent. If such a change is intercepted, a corresponding event is triggered and the emotional expression of the agent updated. The current implementation of TRIPLE uses the RASCALLI multiagent platform [15]. In order to facilitate the communication with the user only the strongest emotion of the ES is expressed by the agent's avatar. For each ES, a predefined set of parameters for mouth, eyebrows, body posture, etc. is loaded. These patterns are coded in BML and send to the multimodal generation tool which generates the animation expressed by the 3D avatar. The avatar can also verbally utter some expression of its emotion.

Reactive coping stands for the character's impulsive actions performed by the agent without reasoning (action tendencies). In other words, action tendencies are similar to the innate biological impulses of the humans. The matching process is triggered only when a considerable change in the emotional state occurs. Screen shots of the male and female agent expressing emotions are given in Fig. 3.

3.2 Deliberative Emotional Processing

The deliberative emotional processing is inspired by the deliberative part of FAtiMA model. In TRIPLE, the same prospect-based emotions like in FAtiMA are used and a similar appraisal process. But there are some major differences. The main reason is that the deliberative appraisal in Fatima deals with action plans typical for BDI models. TRIPLE does not implement such BDI type of planning mechanisms but retrieves

Fig. 3. RASCALLO expressing disappointment and RASCALLA expressing joy

action plans and respective outcomes from memory based on analogy-like mechanisms. Moreover, TRIPLE knowledge is represented in a relatively distributed way and uses connectionist mechanisms, in contrast to the pure symbolic implementation of FAtiMA.

As in FAtiMA, the deliberative appraisal consists of emotional appraisal of expected future events related to the agent's goals and has basically two parts:

- Appraisal of goal achievement anticipation;
- Appraisal of goal achievement success/failure.

Appraisal of goal achievement probability. TRIPLE EE uses internal heuristics to generate the emotions 'hope' and 'fear' related to a desired future event. Once generated, these emotions are added to the emotional state and start participating in the emotional dynamics.

These heuristics allow specifying:

- the importance of the agent's goal (value in the interval [0,1], '0' meaning completely unimportant event and '1' a very important one);
- the probability of successfully achieving the goal (value in the interval [0,1]).

The success probability is continuously recalculated as hope and fear for the expected event change over time. The goal achievement success probability is calculated as follows. When an expectation of a future desired event is triggered, it receives a basic probability of success based on the formula:

$$P_{basic}(success) = \frac{\sum_i success\_rating_i}{N} \tag{1}$$

where N is the number of past episodes in which this goal has been anticipated; *success_rating$_i$* is the rating for successful achievement of the goal in episode i. It is a value in the interval [0,1] and shows to what extent the result met the agent's expectation − '0' meaning a complete failure and '1' meaning a complete success. Intermediate values are assigned when the achievement of the goal is not complete.

The basic probability is continuously updated during the run of the system until TRIPLE receives information about the goal achievement success or failure. That update is based on the equation:

$$P(success) = \alpha P_{basic}(success) + (1 - \alpha)P_{current}(success) \qquad (2)$$

where the parameter α stands for the reliance of the agent on its past experience relative to the current one. This parameter could depend on the specific agent as well as on the current emotional state. In the current implementation only predefined values are used. The quantity $P_{current}(success)$ is the current probability of success and is an estimate of how the current events are related to the expectation for the anticipated event. This estimate is obtained by using a heuristic assessment of some internal processes (e.g the time needed by a searching tool to get the information) leading to the achievment of the anticipated goal.

Using the probability of success and the importance of the event, fear and hope emotions are generated using the equations:

$$BaseHopePotential = P(success)Importance(success) \qquad (3)$$

$$BaseFearPotential = (1 - P(success))Importance(failure). \qquad (4)$$

In the current implementation of TRIPLE, the only goal which is emotionally relevant is 'The user is satisfied'. The importance of this goal is a fixed value in any session. The base probability of success is calculated when the agent receives a new task from the user. This probability is updated during the reasoning process when events such as retrieval and transfer of knowledge or the results of a search are obtained. For example, if the search tool returns no answer to a query, the corresponding event will decrease the base probability of success and the agent may start feeling 'fear'.

Appraisal of goal achievement success/failure. The success rating of the goal achievement is calculated based on user's evaluation. In the current ECA implementation, this can be done by pressing two buttons − the 'praise' and the 'scold' buttons. If the user presses the 'praise' button, this means for the agent complete success. Pressing the 'scold' button means the opposite − zero success rating. In the "no feedback" condition, the success rating is set to 0.7, assuming that in this case, it is more likely that the user is satisfied.

If TRIPLE receives information that an expected event had occurred, based on the dominant emotion at this moment, the following prospect-based emotions can be generated: 'satisfaction', 'relief', 'disappointment', and 'fear confirmed' (see Table 1). For example, disappointment is generated if the agent was very hopeful that the user will be satisfied but it is scolded instead.

Table 1. Prospect based emotions

Outcome/ Anticipation	Anticipated Hope	Anticipated Fear
Goal Success	Satisfaction	Relief
Goal Failure	Disappointment	Fears confirmed

The emotions elicited are added to the emotional state and expressed by the agent character. At the same time, this result of the event is used to determine the success_rating, used in future appraisal of the same event.

3.3 Emotional State

OCC theory specifies for each emotion type an emotional threshold and decay rate. An emotional threshold specifies a character's resistance towards an emotion type, and the decay rate assesses how fast the emotion decays over time. When an event is appraised, the emotions created are not necessarily 'experienced' by the character. The appraisal process described so far determines the potential of emotions. Such emotions are added to the character's emotional state (ES only if their potential exceeds the defined threshold specific for each emotion. And even if they do overcome the threshold, the final emotion intensity is given by the difference between the threshold and the initial potential.

Every emotion has an associated quantity called *Intensity* which is related to its strength. Each emotional event can change the emotion intensity. When nothing happens the emotion intensity decays toward zero. The model uses a decay function proposed in [16] which characterizes intensity as a function of time. At any time *t*, the value for the emotion intensity is given by the formula:

$$Intensity(t) = Intensity(t_0)e^{-bt} \qquad (5)$$

where he parameter *b* determines how fast the intensity of this particular emotion will decrease over time. The value $Intensity(t_0)$ refers to the value of the intensity parameter of the emotion when it was generated. When the value of $Intensity(t)$ reaches a predefined threshold, the emotion must be removed from the ES.

The emotions created by the reactive and deliberative appraisals are sent to the ES to be processed. When the ES receives an emotion (even if later it is not added to the ES), its mood level will change according to the emotion potential multiplied by a constant:

$$Potential = Potential + kMood, 0 < k < 1 \qquad (6)$$

for positive emotions and

$$Potential = Potential - kMood, 0 < k < 1 \qquad (7)$$

for negative emotions.

A negative mood increases the potential of every negative emotion and decreases the potential of positive emotions. A positive mood acts in the opposite way. But on the other hand, emotions also influence mood. Positive emotions raise the agent's mood and negative emotions lower it. Depending on the emotion potential, this change will be larger or smaller according to the equations:

$$Mood = Mood + 0.1Potential \qquad (8)$$

for positive emotions and

$$Mood = Mood - 0.1Potential \qquad (9)$$

for negative emotions. Agents tend to maintain their mood for relatively large periods of time.

Finally an emotion is added to the agent's ES only if the emotion potential becomes lareger than the defined threshold ('*EmotionaTheshold*') for that emotion. The final intensity of the emotion is:

$$Intensity = Potential - EmotionalTreshold. \qquad (10)$$

3.4 Impact of Emotions on the Reasoning Process

Some additional mechanisms have been implemented in TRIPLE, which complement the ones taken from FAtiMA. They are based on the integration of emotions in the DUAL/ABMR model for robotic applications and the simulations reported in [7]. The new mechanisms could be formally divided into two basic types:

- Adding emotional nodes to long term memory;
- Modifying internal parameters in RE and SAE based on the current emotional state.

Adding emotion nodes to LTM. Adding emotional nodes in the memory of the agent is related to the explicit representation of emotions in TRIPLE's LTM. First of all, emotion concept nodes for each of the implemented emotions have been added to LTM. Instances of the emotion concepts are then used in the episodic part of LTM so that each episode has an emotion node attached to it. This emoiton node is related to the dominant emotion felt by the agent in that episode and is encoded during the learning process (storing of relevant episodes) by using the most active emotion in the emotional state.

Composition of emotions is an option to be considered in the future, as the episode (or parts of it) may point to a number of emotions with different intensity. The simulation results for analogy making, reported in [7], show that past episodes experienced with congruent to the current emotion will be more likely to be retrieved and used for the analogy-making which could lead to different action plans and outcomes. This is consistent with psychological research which shows that people tend to retrieve memories related to a mood similar to their current mood [17].

Emotion influence on the internal parameters of the model. It is well known that emotions influence reasoning in various ways. Most of the important mechanisms in TRIPLE are influenced by the emotional state of the system. Some of the parameters affected are the following:

- The type of similarity which will be preferred in SAE in the analogy making process – structural or taxonomical;
- The time of waiting for the searching tools before producing an 'I don't know' answer;
- The parameters of the constraint satisfaction mechanism.

This influence of the parameters of TRIPLE based on the current emotional state is based on psychological plausibility as well as pragmatic reasons. The latter could be the interaction between a human user and the agent or the effectiveness and efficiency of the model.

Table 2. External and internal events' effect on the EE

Event	Emotional processing	Example
An emotionally significant external event is processed.	Reactive appraisal is called. It updates the ES based on the appraisal rules and the current value of the mood variable.	The user gave a positive feedback which is appraised as desirable by the agent and reactive appraisal adds 'joy' to ES
A goal is set or a new evaluation of the probability of success is made.	'Hope' and 'fear' are added to the ES, based on heuristics for the *Importance* of the event and its failure/success probability.	When TRIPLE receives a new task 'hope' and 'fear' for the goal – 'The user is satisfied' – are generated.
A goal is achieved or not achieved.	New prospect based emotion is generated based on the dominant emotion	The user 'praises' the agent which was fearful about the outcome and the agent experiences 'relief'.
The emotional state changes considerably.	Reactive coping is triggered and the agent expresses the emotion.	The emotion 'joy' is added to the emotional state with an intensity above threshold. The agent smiles and displays a happy face.
	If the strongest emotion in the ES changes then a new node corresponding to that emotion is added to the description of the target episode.	The node 'Joy-t' is created and is linked to the concept 'Joy' in LTM.

4 Communication of EE with the other TRIPLE Modules

The connection of the emotion module and the other modules of the architecture is event based (see Table 2). In Table 2, various external and internal events are shows (column 1), together with the corresponding emotional processing (column 2) and an example from the simulations (column 3).

5 Simulations

A series of simulations was performed. The emotional dynamics based on one typical simulation session with the ECA is shown in Table 3. The time when each event happens is noted in the first column (in seconds after the start of the system). For each prospect based event in the third column stays its importance (I) for the agent and the estimated probability of success (P). The results are collected based on the human interaction with the system using its graphic interface and monitoring the emotional state.

Table 3. External events and their effect on the system

t [s]	Event	I, P	Emotions / Intensity	Mood	Comment
0	RASCALLO/A ECA is ON		Joy / 6.0	1.80	The agent starts its activity with a smile
5	The user gives RAS-CALLO/A a task	$I=1.0$ $P=0.9$	Hope / 8.51 Joy / 2.59	4.27	For this task, it is hopeful due to the predominant success in previous trials for the same task
7	The search in a DB is over	$I=1.0$ $P=0.95$	Hope / 9.76 Joy / 2.26	4.20	The answer obtained increased the estimated success probability and leads to increased hope potential
15	The user presses the 'SCOLD' button	$I=1.0$ result= failure	Disappoint-ment / 1.19 Joy / 0.73	3.52	After reading the agent answer, the user pressed the 'SCOLD' button expressing that she is not satisfied with the results. The character shows disappointment.

6 Discussion and Conclusion

In this paper, the implementation of the emotion engine of TRIPLE, based on FAtiMA model, was presented and discussed. EE allows for the generation of emotional states and moods based on the OCC model and makes possible the encoding of emotions in LTM and episodic memory. The latter makes retrieval from memory emotion dependent and can influence and diversify the agent behavior. Moreover, the agent based on TRIPLE can 'feel' emotions and be in a specific mood which can be reflected by the expression of the virtual character and be changed by external and internal events. Conversely, the emotional state can influence the cognitive processing of the agent, making it more adaptable and believable.

The simple simulation, reported in the paper shows the potential of emotions in a cognitively inspired ECA architecture. However, in order to fully assess the advantages and disadvantages of such an architecture further exploration using realistic agent-user interactions are needed. Such a work is in progress and the results will be reported in a future publication.

Acknowledgements

This research was supported financially by the project RASCALLI (IST program, contract 27596), funded by the EC.

We would like to gratefully acknowledge the collaboration with Ana Paiva and Joao Dias from Instituto Superior Tecnico (Lisbon) related to the FAtiMA model. We would like to thank the two anonymous reviewers who helped us to considerably improve this paper and Marina Hristova who read the manuscript and gave us useful suggestions.

References

1. Grinberg, M., Kostadinov, S.: The TRIPLE Model: Combining Cutting-Edge Web Technologies with a Cognitive Model in a ECA. In: Proc. International Workshop on Agent Based Computing V(ABC 2008), Wisla, Poland (2008)
2. Grinberg, M., Haltakov, V.: Analogy making in the TRIPLE model. In: New Frontiers of Analogy Research, Analogy 2009. NBU press (2009)
3. Kiryakov, A., Ognyanov, D., Manov, D.: OWLIM – A pragmatic semantic repository for OWL. In: Dean, M., Guo, Y., Jun, W., Kaschek, R., Krishnaswamy, S., Pan, Z., Sheng, Q.Z. (eds.) WISE 2005 Workshops. LNCS, vol. 3807, pp. 182–192. Springer, Heidelberg (2005)
4. Bates, J.: The Role of Emotion in Believable Agents. Communications of the ACM 37(7), 122–125 (1994)
5. Damásio, A.: Descartes' error – Emotion, Reason and Human Brain. Picador, London (1994)
6. Cochran, R.E., Lee, F.J.: Modeling Emotion: Arousal's Impact on memory. In: Proc. of the 28th Annual Conference of the Cognitive Science Society, Vancouver, British Columbia, Canada, pp. 1133–1138 (2006)

7. Vankov, I., Kiryazov, K., Grinberg, M.: Impact of emotions on an analogy-making robot. Poster presented at the 30th Annual Meeting of the Cognitive Science Society, Washington, DC (2008)
8. Kokinov, B.: The DUAL cognitive architecture: A hybrid multi-agent approach. In: Proc. of the Eleventh European Conference of Artificial Intelligence (ECAI 1994), John Wiley & Sons, Ltd, London (1994)
9. Dias, J., Paiva, A.: Feeling and Reasoning: a Computational Model for Emotional Agents. In: Bento, C., Cardoso, A., Dias, G. (eds.) EPIA 2005. LNCS (LNAI), vol. 3808, pp. 127–140. Springer, Heidelberg (2005)
10. Dias, J.: Fearnot!: Creating emotional autonomous synthetic characters for emphatic interactions. Masters thesis, Instituto Superior Tecnico, Lisboa, Portugal (2005)
11. Ortony, A., Clore, G., Collins, A.: The Cognitive Structure of Emotions. Cambridge University Press, Cambridge (1988)
12. Bartneck, C.: Integrating the OCC Model of Emotions in Embodied Characters. In: Proc. of the Workshop on Workshop on Virtual Conversational Characters: Applications, Methods, and Research Challenges, Melbourne (2002)
13. Zoll, C., Enz, S., Schaub, H., Aylett, R., Paiva, A.: Fighting Bullying with the Help of Autonomous Agents in a Virtual School Environment. In: Proc. 7th International Conference on Cognitive Modelling (ICCM 2006). Lawrence Erlbaum, Trieste (2006)
14. Brisson, A., Paiva, A.: Are we Telling the Same Story? In: AAAI Fall Symposium on Narrative Intelligence Technologies, Westin Arlington Gateway, Arlington, Virginia, November 9-11 (2007)
15. Krenn, B.: RASCALLI - Responsive Artificial Situated Cognitive Agents Living and Learning on the Internet. In: Proc. of the International Conference on Cognitive Systems, University of Karlsruhe, Karlsruhe, Germany, April 2-4 (2008)
16. Picard, R.: Affective computing, ch. 5. MIT Press, Cambridge (1997)
17. Teasdale, J.D., Fogarty, S.J.: Differential effects of induced mood on retrieval of pleasant and unpleasant events from episodic memory. Journal Abnormal Psychology 88(3), 248–257 (1979)

Manipulating Stress and Cognitive Load in Conversational Interactions with a Multimodal System for Crisis Management Support

Andreea Niculescu, Yujia Cao, and Anton Nijholt

Human Media Interaction, University of Twente
P.O. Box 217, 7500 AE, Enschede, The Netherlands
{niculescuai,y.cao,a.nijholt}@utwente.nl

Abstract. The quality assessment of multimodal conversational interfaces is influenced by many factors. Stress and cognitive load are two of most important. In the literature, these two factors are considered as being related and accordingly summarized under the single concept of 'cognitive demand'. However, our assumption is that even if they are related, these two factors can still occur independently. Therefore, it is essential to control their levels during the interaction in order to determine the impact that each factor has on the perceived conversational quality. In this paper we present preliminary experiments in which we tried to achieve a factor separation by inducing alternating low/high levels of both stress and cognitive load. The stress/cognitive load levels were manipulated by varying task difficulty, information presentation and time pressure. Physiological measurements, performance metrics, as well as subjective reports were deployed to validate the induced stress and cognitive load levels. Results showed that our manipulations were successful for the cognitive load and partly for the stress. The levels of both factors were better indicated by subjective reports and performance metrics than by physiological measurements.

Keywords: Multimodal interfaces, verbal communication, stress, cognitive load, physiological measurements, qualitative evaluations.

1 Introduction

Nowadays, multimodal conversational interfaces enable users to communicate with computer systems using a wide range of input/output modalities, such as speech, text, touch, etc. Therefore, there is a growing need not only to find reliable evaluation methods for such interfaces but also to determine which factors have the highest impact on their quality assessment. The literature in the field mentions the stress and cognitive load experienced by users while interacting with an interface among the most important influence factors [1].

Cognitive load is often described as the degree of concentration required for a person to solve problems or to complete tasks in a given time [2]. The term, referred in the literature as 'cognitive load'[2], 'cognitive or mental effort' [3], 'cognitive factor' [4] is often associated with the factor 'stress'. Stress represents a psychological response

A. Esposito et al. (Eds.): COST 2102 Int. Training School 2009, LNCS 5967, pp. 134–147, 2010.
© Springer-Verlag Berlin Heidelberg 2010

state to a perceived threat or task demand and is in general signalized by specific emotions such as frustration, anxiety and tenseness [5]. Stress is caused by an existing stress-causing agent that can be a physical-environmental stressor (e.g. noisy environment) or psychological stressor (e.g. work overload). In the literature, both factors are often summarized and measured under the global concept of 'cognitive demand' [6].

There are no doubts that cognitive load and stress are related. When the load reaches a certain level of demand - people unconsciously appraise their abilities to meet the challenge: only if the situation is considered as exceeding the available resources then stress would appear. This appraisal theory was formulated by Lazarus et al. [7] and explains why a tense situation might be perceived as stressful by one person, but not by another.

Based on this theory, our assumption is that, even if related, these two factors can occur independently, i.e. there is no compulsory relationship between them. Also, the stress might be produced by other variables that do not directly relate to cognitive load, such as background noise, frequent misunderstandings, or increased interaction speed. Thus, these two factors might have a different impact on the perceived conversational quality and consequently, they should be identified and measured separately.

Hence, we propose an experiment intended to determine the circumstances in which low/high levels of both stress and cognitive load are alternatively achieved while interacting with a multimodal conversational system for crisis management support. Once such circumstances are identified they will be incorporated in the design of a further study, investigating the impact of stress and cognitive load on the perceived conversational quality.

2 Experiment Set-Up

2.1 Scenario and Trials Design

Crises are situations in which people experience high levels of stress and cognitive load. Therefore, they offer a perfect test environment for our experiments. Accordingly we designed four scenario trials based on a common typical crisis situation: an explosion occurred in a chemical research lab setting an entire floor on fire; a crisis manager in charged of the situation has to take essential, life-critical decisions based on the information received from the system.

Each trial consists of three stages: at first, a virtual assistant, representing the system, presents the current crisis situation using narrative, assisting photos, maps and text; next the crisis manager has to find, using an interactive map, addresses to which rescue workers, fire fighters will be sent or wounded victims will be delivered; alternatively he has to memorize important event facts and insert them in a crisis report; finally, the crisis manager gets chemical description sheets to identify dangerous chemicals that have to be immediately removed by firemen in order to avoid further damages.

2.2 System Design

A first multimodal system prototype was developed using the CSLU toolkit[1]. The prototype, currently under development, provides detailed information about the crisis

---

[1] The toolkit can be downloaded at: http://cslu.cse.ogi.edu/toolkit/

event, such as event description, geographical maps, available rescue resources and estimated number of victims. The system has attached an embodied conversational agent with text-to-speech and speech recognition capabilities. Test users can interact with the system using speech or mouse clicking and receive information in the form of text, speech, images or videos.

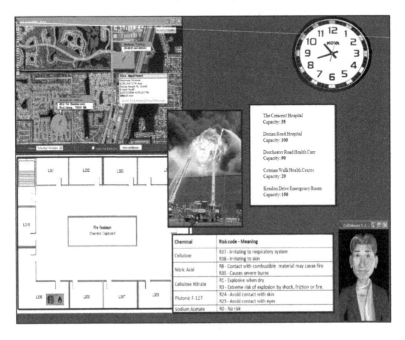

Fig. 1. System screen shot

2.3 Factor Manipulation

The trials were similar but aiming to realize different combinations of low/high stress and low/high cognitive load conditions in a 2x2 factor matrix.

In order to manipulate the stress level we used a combination of six different parameters such as background noise, speech speed, speech length, time limitation, simulated recognition mistakes and dramatic event description. In the low stress conditions, the virtual assistant presents calmly the crisis event using a clear voice with normal speed. He describes the situation as being under control; users are not urged to speed up their performance. In the high stress conditions however, noises (e.g. white noise, ambulance sound) are played in the background in order to induce stress [8]. The agent talks faster, using short sentences and an urgent tone. The crisis situation is described to be dramatic; users are put under time stress by being constantly reminded to make quick decisions; a simulated speech recognition mistake was also built into one of the scenarios.

For the cognitive load manipulation we used two parameters: task complexity and presentation format. Task complexity variations were put into effect for address identification: in the scenarios with low cognitive load the users had to locate given addresses on a map by clicking on the street names; in the scenarios with higher load the users were required not only to identify but also to select the optimal address, according to several factors that needed careful analysis (e.g. hospital capacity, distance to the chemical lab, number of victims). Variations in the presentation format were chosen for the chemical selection task. 'Well'-designed and 'badly'-designed information sheets were applied to achieve low and high cognitive load conditions respectively. Both sheets use a table to present the chemicals and their risk descriptions. The difference between the 'well'- and 'badly'-designed sheet lie in the way the information is spatially organized: the 'well'-designed sheet provides integrated chemicals and risk descriptions in a natural 'row-by-row' sequence facilitating the users 'scan'-reading; in contrast, the 'badly'-designed sheets provide numerical codes that links the chemicals to their corresponding risk descriptions summarized outside the table. As a consequence, the 'badly'-designed sheet requires additional mental effort, causing a split-resource effect and an increase of cognitive load [9].

Chemical	Risk code - Meaning
Cellulose	R36 - Irritating eyes R37 - Irritating to respiratory system R38 - Irritating to skin
Chlorine	R23 - Toxic by inhalation R50 - Very toxic to aquatic organism
Toulene	R11 - Highly flammable in heat R63 - Possible risk of harm to the unborn child R65 - May cause lung damage if swallowed
Alumina	R0 - No risk
Barium chloride	R20 - Harmful by inhalation R25 - Toxic if swallowed

Chemical	Risk code
Benzyl phthalate	R50 R53 R62
Nitric Acid	R8 R35
Dimethyl formamide	R61 R24 R43 R21
Ammonia	R14 R23 R45
Benzyl peroxide	R2 R36 R6

R36 Irritating to eyes
R14 Reacts violently with water
R23 Toxic by inhalation
R45 May cause cancer
R2   Risk of explosion by fire or other sources of ignition
R61 May cause harm to the unborn child
R24 Toxic in contact with skin
R50 Very toxic to aquatic organisms
R6   Explosive with or without contact with air
R43 May cause sensitization by skin contact
R21 Harmful by inhalation and in contact with skin
R8   Contact with combustible material may cause fire
R53 May cause adverse effects in the aquatic environment
R62 Possible risk of impaired fertility
R35 Causes severe burns

a)   b)

Fig. 2. "Well" designed (a) vs. "badly" (b) information sheets

The following table presents a summarization of the factor manipulations in the four trials.

Table 1. Cognitive load and stress manipulation per trial

Trial nr.	Trial description	Cognitive load (CL)	Stress level (S)
1.	T00= low CL/ low S	address identification=1 address decision task=no memory retrieval task=no presentation format= 'well' designed	background noise=no speech speed=normal speech length=normal time limitation= no recog. mistake=no dramatic event description=no
2.	T01= low CL/ high S	address identification=5 addresses decision task=no memory retrieval=no presentation format = 'well' designed	background noise=yes speech speed=high speech length=short time limitation= no recog. mistake=no dramatic event description=yes
3.	T11= high CL/ high S	address identification=1 addresses decision task= yes memory retrieval=no presentation format='badly' designed	background noise=yes speech speed=high speech length=short time limitation= no recog. mistake=yes dramatic event description=yes
4.	T10= high CL/ low S	address identification=no decision task= no memory retrieval=yes presentation format='badly' designed	background noise=yes speech speed=high speech length=short time limitation= no recog. mistake=yes dramatic event description=yes

3   Methods

3.1   Measurements

For our experiment we used a combination of several assessment methods such as subjective rating, physiological measurements and performance metrics.

The subjective ratings were collected after each trial using the NASA task load index (TLX) questionnaire. NASA-TLX contains six workload-related parameters: mental, physical and temporal demands, own performance, effort and frustration. The level of frustration is measured by NASA-TLX with the help of a single question addressing simultaneously five different parameters: feeling insecure, discouraged, irritated, annoyed, and stressed. We considered appropriate to split the question in five separate statements (one for each parameter) in order to get more precise results. We also replaced the term "stressed" – a key concept in our study - with the semantically related word "tense". In our analysis, we treated the concept of "tenseness" apart from frustration, since we consider that these two categories may not always be related.

We added four additional statements to the TLX questionnaire regarding the users' concentration and tiredness level, the system's easy of use, the degree of understanding between users and system.

We relate the frustration, tenseness and temporal demands (work pace) parameters as direct indicators for the stress factor and considered the other parameters as direct indicators for the cognitive load [10]. A 20 level scale was used for ratings.

As physiological measurements, we used the heart rate variability (HRV) and the galvanic skin response (GSR). According to previous studies, certain components of HVR exhibit systematic and reliable relationships with the mental demands of the task. Higher levels of cognitive work load have been associated in the frequency domain with decreased power in the 0.10 Hz band (LF – low frequency band) [11, 12]. Skin conductance response (SCR) is traditionally associated with workload and especially with arousal states accompanied by mental effort and emotions. Higher workload normally yields higher number of responses (or longer SCR intervals) [13, 14].

All trials were recorded with a video camera in order to allow the retrieval of performance metrics.

3.2 Experiment Setup

Four male test users, aged between 24 and 30, all having technical background, participated in the experiment.

After entering the lab and taking a seat, each user was asked to stay relaxed while the physiological sensors were applied. When finished, a physiological baseline was recorded for 5 minutes. Afterwards, the user received a brief introduction of the experiment and performed the trials. A short break was placed after each trial to allow test users to fill in the questionnaire and have a rest.

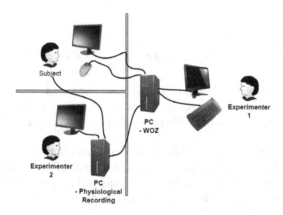

Fig. 3. Experiment set-up

The experiments were performed using the Wizard-of-Oz technique: the speech recognition module was replaced by a human operator in order to ensure a controlled interaction.

Two experimenters were involved in conducting the trials: one was in charged of the physiological measurements, the other one was performing the WOZ simulation. The experiment setup was synchronized as illustrated above (see fig.3).

4   Results

4.1   Subjective Questionnaires

The first two trials – 1 and 2 (T00, T01) - were designed to have a lower cognitive load level compared with the last two trials - 3 and 4 (T11, T10). The results[2] gathered from

---

[2] All results have discrete values; they are presented on a connected line only to facilitate the view.

the questionnaires confirmed that test users perceived the last two trials as being more mentally demanding (see fig.4), harder to accomplish and in general requiring a higher degree of concentration compared with the first two trials. Only user 3 indicated a low level of concentration for trial 4 (see fig.7), a fact that corresponds to his indeed low performance during this trial - the user had extremely long response times and frequent input errors.

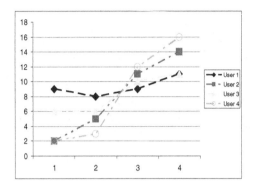

Fig. 4. Mental demand perception

The statements that the system delivered were perceived as less clear during the last two trials, and users perceived their own performance as being the worst mostly during the 3rd trial. On the other side they judged the system as being the easiest to use during 2nd trial.

Concerning the physical demand, the values were quite similar for all trials (only one user indicated higher values of physical demand for the cognitive loaded high trials).

The 4th trial was considered as being the most tiring among all trials. This trial lasted the longest as shown in the figure below (fig.5).

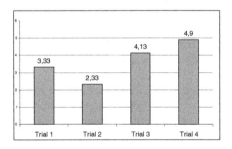

Fig. 5. Trial average completion time in minutes

Interestingly there are not many similarities between the graphs representing the users' tiredness level on one side and their concentration level on the other side (see fig. 6 and 7). We were in fact expecting users to feel more tired after completing a task requiring a high level of concentration.

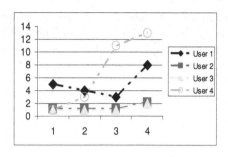

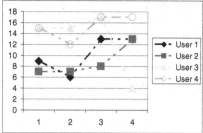

Fig. 6. Tiredness   **Fig. 7.** Level of concentration

Regarding the stress factor, we tried to induce a lower level of stress in trials 1 and 4 (T00, T10) compared with a higher level in trials 2 and 3 (T01, T11).

The perception of temporal demand (work pace rush) was, as expected higher for trials 2 and 3.

However, the same trend could not be observed for the users' degree of frustration: participants felt more frustrated - i.e. more insecure, discouraged, irritated and annoyed - mostly during trials 1 and 3 (especially trial 3, which had the highest negative values). The fact that trial 1 achieved a higher level of frustration than expected, might be explained by 'first impression' effect: during the first trial, users were dealing with an unfamiliar situation that apparently caused frustration; afterwards, they must have felt more confident with the system, and accordingly ranked trial 2 much lower in terms of frustration. There was a general up and down in the participants feeling of being insecure as shown in fig. 8.

Comparing trial 4 with trial 3 - both highly cognitive loaded - we observed that trial 4 apparently caused a much lower frustration level; this fact might confirm our assumption that a highly mentally demanding task is not necessarily accompanied by stress.

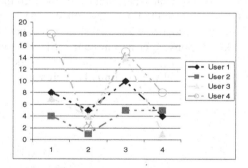

Fig. 8. Feeling insecure

The ranking of the last parameter, the feeling of being tense, showed how different the test participants perceived the trials (see fig. 9): users 1 and 2 indeed felt tenser during trial 2 compared with trial 1 and during trial 3 compared with trial 4. User 3 and 4 felt tenser only during the trial 3; trial 2 was perceived by both users as much more relaxed.

Interestingly, trial 1 was perceived as much tenser for users 3 and 4 compared with user 1 and 2. We compared the trend for this particular trial with the users' perception of being successful and we observed a certain similarity between the graphs; unfortunately, the similarity was not confirmed for the other trials, therefore we cannot make a sustainable association between tenseness and the perceived performance success.

Trial 4 was perceived by all users, except one (user 4), as being less tense when compared with trial 3.

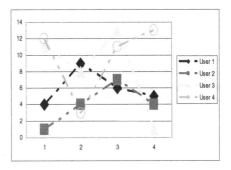

Fig. 9. Feeling tense

Clearly, despite some similarities among participants, the graphic above doesn't show a common trend. Apparently users had similar opinions about cognitively high loaded tasks, but quite different perceptions about the stress level produced while performing these tasks.

4.2 Physiological Measurements

The physiological measurements mainly showed a learning effect: the value of HR (heart rate) decreased and LF (the HRV in the frequency domain) increased trial by trial, both indicating a gradually decreasing cognitive load and stress throughout the experiment.

GSRN (number of skin responses per minute) and GSL (the tonic level of the skin conductance) showed the same effect for two of the users (users 2 and 4), as shown in fig. 10 – indicating their stress level was continually decreasing.

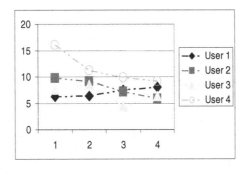

Fig. 10. GSRN values

One user's (1) stress level seemed to be caused by the cognitive load level rather than by the planed manipulation: the values showed that the user was more stressed when the task was more difficult (trial 3 and 4). The values for the last user (3) did not deliver any explainable results.

4.3 Users' Performance Metrics

We extracted from the videos the following users' performance metrics relating to cognitive loaded: the response competition time, reaction time and number of errors. For the stress metric we counted the number of words, verbal hesitations, breaks and mispronunciations.

Each trial was composed of one, two or three tasks, such as **chemical removing tasks** (in trial 1,2,3,4), **address identification tasks** (in trial 1,2,3), **decision tasks** (in trial 2), and **memory retrieval tasks** (in trial 4).

The chemical removing task consisted of three subsequent subtasks, users had to:

- 1) ask for a floor map (using speech)
- 2) localize the room with dangerous chemicals on the map (using mouse click)
- 3) find, based on the "well/badly" designed description sheets, which chemical to remove (using mouse click).

The first and the second subtasks showed a clear learning effect: test users needed on average 2.1 sec. less to ask the question and 1.2 sec. less to localize the room. The 3rd subtask concerning the information presentation format delivered more interesting results: the graphic shows that users 1, 2 and 3 took considerably more time to identify and remove the chemicals when the information sheet was badly designed. Trial 1, even if it had a well-designed sheet, achieved a much higher value than expected due to the same "first impression" effect (see fig. 11).

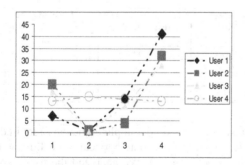

Fig. 11. Competition time for identifying dangerous chemicals

The results achieved by user 4 need to be considered separately, since the user has professional chemical expertise. His completion times are in contrast with those obtained by the other participants. Therefore, we have reasons to believe that the performance time was indeed influenced by the information presentation format and not by other parameter such as tiredness, concentration level or interaction speed.

The address identification task had two subtasks. The participants were required to

- 1) ask for a street map (using speech)
- 2) localize an address on each time different map (using mouse click).

Results showed again a clear learning effect for both subtasks, with users spending an average 16.78 sec. less each time solving the task (see fig.12). The graph is not complete for user 1, who didn't complete this task during trial 3, due to a wizard error.

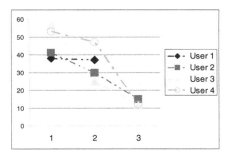

Fig. 12. Completion time for the address identification task

The performance time for the decision and memory retrieval tasks showed quite large differences among users (see tab.2). The differences seem to be related to the perceived concentration level – except for user 3, who indicated a very low concentration level despite the time he spent to solve the task. The reason was, as explained previously, the obvious lack of concentration during the trial (see fig.7).

Table 2. Decision and memory retrieval task times vs. level of concentration values

User	Decision task -trial 3-	Memory retrieval –trial 4-	Level of concentration on 20 point scale	
			-trial 3-	-trial 4-
1	36 sec.	105 sec.	13	13
2	9 sec.	90 sec.	7	13
3	52 sec.	134 sec.	17	4
4	62.s	322 sec.	17	17

According to the tasks users have to complete, they are required to interact with the system differently. Hence, we differentiate between speech responses to speech input and clicking responses to visual input. We analyzed the users' speech response time (time slot between system input and first user's reaction) and observed that the values for speech responses were higher in the first trial (in average 4.1 sec.), decreasing in the following trials 2 and 3 (1.24 sec. and respectively 0.83 sec.) before increasing again in the last trial (2.41 sec.). The decreasing trend for trial 2 and 3 might be an indication that users tried to adapt their verbal behavior to the system's speech rhythm increase.

The response time to visual tasks was higher compared with the verbal responses and did not differ much across the trials: users needed an average of 27.29 sec. for identifying an address on the map and 16.5 sec. for finding the room with chemicals.

Looking at the error distribution (see fig. 13) most of the errors were committed during the 3rd and 2nd trial – the most rushed trials. We identified 4 different types of errors such as speech errors, visual errors (clicking on a wrong target), decisions errors (making a wrong choice) and memory retrieval errors. Most of the errors were memory retrieval and decision making errors, as shown in the figure 11. The values for the error type were normalized to the corresponding number of task types (there were in total 8 speech-based tasks, 6 visual-based tasks, 4 decision making tasks and 1 memory retrieval task).

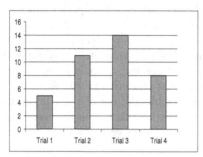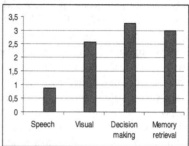

Fig. 13. Error distribution and types

An interesting observation concerns the user's speech behavior during the trials: the total amount of words and verbal breaks were on average higher during trial 1 and 4 (12.6 respectively 4.75) compared with trial 2 and 3 (8.79. 2.5). This behavior demonstrated again the users' unconscious adaptive behavior to the speech rhythm imposed by the system, reacting faster and with shorter statements during the rushed trials 2 and 3. Also other speech disfluecies, such as mispronunciations, occurred only during trial 2 and 3 which indicates a possible increase of stress during these trials.

5 Conclusion

The results showed that our cognitive load manipulation was successful: users perceived trial 3 and 4, as mentally more demanding, harder to accomplish and requiring a higher degree of concentration compared with trials 1 and 2. During trial 3 and 4, the system's statements appeared to be harder to understand and participants perceived the interaction as more difficult. Their tiredness degree was the highest mostly during the last trial - the one having the longest competition time. The information format presentation as well as the decision task complexity seemed to contribute successfully to the proposed manipulation.

The success of the stress manipulation was disturbed by 'first impression' effects: test users indeed perceived trials 2 and 3 as being more rushed, but they felt more frustrated during trials 1 and 3. The frustration degree for the mentally demanding trials 3 and 4 was in general perceived differently: trial 3 was considered as being more frustrating compared with trial 4, a fact that might support our assumption that stress does not necessarily accompany high cognitive high loaded tasks. Thus, the planed stress manipulation was successful only for trial 3. Due to an unplanned high stress level achievement during trial 1 it seems rather difficult to make assumptions about which other (planed) stressor particularly contributed to this manipulation.

Generally, the stress manipulation appeared to be relatively difficult to induce compared with the cognitive load manipulation. One reason might be the fact that stress is a highly complex phenomenon, including aspects that we did not consider in our experiment such as "first impression" effects. Another possible explanation could be that people perceive the stress very differently according to own individual dispositions [7]. These dispositions are not always influenced by people's performance success, as we might have expected: for instance our results did not show a clear relationship between the amount of errors and the perception of own performance success on one side and the users' feelings of frustration and tenseness on the other side.

Also, a less sharp stress perception on participants' side might have weakened the planned stress manipulation: the users' verbal behavior indicated more relaxed feelings during trials 1 and 4 and more stressed reactions during trials 2 and 3; these observations were not confirmed by subjective reports concerning the tenseness.

The lack of reliable objective measurement results did not help the understanding of the stress phenomenon in the experiment context. In fact, both factors – cognitive load and stress - could be better determined by subjective reports and performance metrics than by physiological measurements.

In conclusion, we consider the current experiment a good starting point for forthcoming investigations concerning the effects of stress and cognitive load on the conversational quality assessment. In the future we plan to perform similar experiments with a larger number of users, in order to gain statistical evidence for our findings. "First impression" effects will be avoided by using training sessions before starting the experiment. Also, the interpretation of physiological data can be improved by measuring particular tasks inside each trial, rather than using the whole trial (as performed in this experiment). Further, enlarging the variance in cognitive load and stress between trials might also enhance the effectiveness of physiological measurement since their sensitivity is limited to minor variations.

Acknowledgments

This research is done in the framework of the Interactive Collaborative Information System (ICIS) Project, sponsored by the Dutch Ministry of Economic Affairs, under grant nr: BSIK03024. We thank all test participants for their effort and time. A special thank to Dr. David Salamon for his help with the design of the chemical information sheets.

References

1. Moeller, S.: Quality of telephone-based spoken dialogue systems. Springer, New York (2005)
2. Oviatt, S.: Human-centered design meets cognitive load theory: designing interfaces that help people think. In: Proc. of the 14th annual ACM international conference on Multimedia, Santa Barbara (2006)

3. Love, S., Dutton, R.T., Foster, J.C., Jack, M.A., Stentiford, F.W.: Identifying salient us- ability attributes for automated telephone services. In: Proc. of the 3rd Conf. on Spoken Language (ICSLP), Yokohama, Japan (1994)
4. Jack, M.A., Foster, J.C., Stentiford, F.W.M.: Intelligent dialogues in automated telephone services. In: Proc. 2nd Int. Conf. on Spoken Language Processing (ICSLP), Banff, Canada (1992)
5. Patil, S.A., Hansen, J.H.L.: Speech Under Stress: Analysis, Modeling and Recognition. In: Müller, C. (ed.) Speaker Classification I: Fundamentals, Features, and Methods, pp. 108– 137. Springer, Heidelberg (2007)
6. Hone, K.S., Graham, R.: Towards a tool for the subjective assessment of speech and Sys- tem Interfaces (SASSI). Natural Language Engineering 6(3-4), 287–303 (2000)
7. Lazarus, R.S.: Theory based stress measurement. Psychological Inquiry 1, 3–13 (1990)
8. Kryter, K.D.: The handbook of hearing and the effects of noise: Physiology, psychology, and public health. Academic Press, New York (1994)
9. Chandler, P., Sweller, J.: Cognitive Load Theory and the Format of Instruction. Cognition and Instruction 8, 293–332 (1991)
10. Schell, K.L., Grasha, A.F.: State anxiety, performance accuracy, and work pace in a simu- lated pharmacy dispensing task. In: Perceptual and Motor Skills, vol. 90, pp. 547–561 (2000)
11. Scerbo, M.W., Freeman, F.G., Mikulka, P.J., Parasuraman, R., Di Nocero, F.: The efficacy of psychophysiological measures for implementing adaptive technology. TP-2001-211018 (2001)
12. Wilson, G.F., Eggemeier, F.T.: Psychophysiological assessment of workload in multi-task environments. In: Damos, D.L. (ed.) Multiple-task performance. CRC Press, Boca Raton (1991)
13. Verwey, W.B., Veltman, H.: Detecting short periods of elevated workload. A comparison of nine workload assessment techniques. Applied Experimental Psychology 2, 270–285 (1996)
14. Boucsein, W., Haarmann, A., Schaefer, F.: Combining skin conductance and heart rate variability for adaptive automation during simulated IFR flight. In: Harris, D. (ed.) HCII 2007 and EPCE 2007. LNCS (LNAI), vol. 4562, pp. 639–647. Springer, Heidelberg (2007)

Sentic Computing:
Exploitation of Common Sense for the
Development of Emotion-Sensitive Systems

Erik Cambria[1], Amir Hussain[1], Catherine Havasi[2], and Chris Eckl[3]

[1] Dept. of Computing Science and Maths, University of Stirling, Scotland, UK
[2] MIT Media Lab, MIT, Massachusetts, USA
[3] Sitekit Labs, Sitekit Solutions Ltd, Scotland, UK
{eca,ahu}@cs.stir.ac.uk, havasi@media.mit.edu, chris.eckl@sitekit.net
http://cs.stir.ac.uk/~eca/sentics

Abstract. Emotions are a fundamental component in human experience, cognition, perception, learning and communication. In this paper we explore how the use of Common Sense Computing can significantly enhance computers' emotional intelligence i.e. their capability of perceiving and expressing emotions, to allow machines to make more human-like decisions and improve the human-computer interaction.

Keywords: Common Sense Computing, AI, Semantic Networks, NLP, Analogies, Knowledge Base Management, Emotion and Affective UI.

1 Introduction

Today text is one of the most important modalities for affective analysis and generation because the bulk of computer user interfaces are still text-based. But the inference of emotions from text has always been a difficult task since people usually use non-verbal cues, such as facial expression, vocal inflections and body movement, to reveal, either intentionally or unintentionally, the emotional information. Previous attempts to perform this task mainly relied on statistical methods which have shown to have strong limitations.

We introduce a new paradigm, which we call Sentic Computing, in which we use a novel emotion representation and a Common Sense [1] based approach to infer affective states from short texts over the web.

2 The Importance of Emotions

In normal human cognition, thinking and feeling are mutually present: our emotions are often the product of our thoughts and our reflections are frequently the product of our sentiments. Emotions in fact are intrinsically part of our mental activity and play a key role in decision-making processes: they are special states shaped by natural selection to balance the reaction of our organism to particular situations e.g. anger evolved for reaction, fear evolved for protection and affection evolved for reproduction.

A. Esposito et al. (Eds.): COST 2102 Int. Training School 2009, LNCS 5967, pp. 148–156, 2010.

For these reasons we can't prescind from emotions in the development of intelligent systems: if we want computers to be really intelligent, not just have the veneer of intelligence, we need to give them the ability to recognize, understand and express emotions.

3   The Emotional Web Era

Differently from early web development, retroactively labeled Web 1.0, today Internet is a dynamic being in which information is no more the core – the user is now at the center of it.

This sort of Copernican revolution brought us to the Web 2.0 era, in which the first simple websites evolved to become more and more interactive, from static to dynamically generated, from handcrafted to CMS-driven, from purely informative to more and more social. The passage from a read-only to a read-write web in fact made web users more inclined to express their emotions through blogs, fora, wikis, feeds and chats.

The efforts to understand this new cultural and social phenomenon gave birth to Web Science [2], a new discipline which brings computer scientists and social scientists together across the disciplinary divide, to explore the development of the Web across different areas of everyday life and technological development.

4   Sentic Computing

Within the field of Web Science we introduce a new paradigm, which we call Sentic Computing, whose aim is to use Common Sense to better recognize, interpret and process human emotions in webposts i.e. short texts over the web such as blog posts, forum entries, RSS feeds, tweets and instant messages. The term 'sentic' derives from the Latin 'sentire', the root of words like sentiment and sensation, and it was first adopted in 1977 by Manfred Clynes [3], who discovered that when people have emotional experience, their nervous system always responds in a characteristic way which is measurable.

Sentic Computing is part of the efforts in the fields of computer science, psychology, linguistics, sociology and cognitive science, to develop a kind of computing that relates to, arises from, or influences emotions [4].

In the past, emotion extraction from text witnessed the implementation of different techniques: hand-crafted models [5], keyword spotting e.g. ANEW [6] or LIWC [7] which rely on an often-used source of affect words, lexical affinity [8] and statistical methods e.g. LSA (Latent Semantic Analysis) which has been frequently used by researchers on projects such as Webmind [9]. The problem with these kinds of methods consists in the fact that they mainly rely on parts of text in which emotional states are explicitly expressed: the so called 'attitudinal inscriptions' of the appraisal theory [10].

They are verbs of emotion e.g. to love/to hate, to frighten/to reassure, to interest/to bore, to enrage/to placate, adverbs of emotion e.g. happily/sadly and adjectives of emotion e.g. happy/sad, worried/confident, angry/pleased, keen/uninterested. But more often emotions are expressed implicitly through concepts with an affective valence such as 'playing a game', 'being laid off' or 'going on a first date'. To extract from text these latent emotional states, termed 'attitudinal tokens' within the appraisal framework, we exploit the recent developments in the field of Common Sense Computing.

4.1   A Common Sense Based Approach

Statistical affective classification using statistical learning models generally requires large inputs and thus cannot appraise texts with satisfactory granularity. Our approach allows to affectively classify webposts not only on the page or paragraph-level but even on sentence-level.

Sentic Computing develops an approach previously adopted by Hugo Liu et al. [11] in which a Common Sense knowledge base was exploited to try to extract affective information from emails using the standard notion of basic emotions provided by Ekman. We now use a much richer semantic network, ConceptNet [12] version 4, with almost 10,000 concepts and a set of 72,000+ features extracted from the Open Mind corpus, and the power of cumulative analogy provided by AnalogySpace [13], a process which reveals large-scale patterns in the data, smooths over noise, and predicts new knowledge.

4.2   A Novel Emotion Representation

Our aim is to develop emotion-sensitive systems in fields such as e-health, software agents, e-games, customer care, e-learning and e-tourism.

For this reason, instead of trying to categorize webposts into basic emotional categories, we are interested in understanding how much:

1. the user is happy with the service provided
2. the user is interested in the information supplied
3. the user is comfortable with the interface
4. the user is keen on using the application

Thus we adopt a new emotion representation where the user's affective states are organized around four independent dimensions: Pleasantness, Attention, Sensitivity and Aptitude. This model is a variant of Plutchik's wheel of emotions [14] and constitutes an attempt to emulate Marvin Minsky's conception of emotions.

Minsky sees the mind as made of thousands of different resources and believes that our emotional states result from turning some set of these resources on and turning another set of them off [15]. Each such selection changes how we think by changing our brain's activities: the state of anger, for example, appears to select a set of resources that help us react with more speed and strength while also suppressing some other resources that usually make us act prudently.

To emulate this process we organize the different mental resources around four affective dimensions, each of them representing an independent emotional sphere, whose different levels of activation, which we call 'sentic levels', give the total emotional state of the mind (see Table 1).

Table 1. The four affective dimensions and their sentic levels

	Pleasantness	Attention	Sensitivity	Aptitude
+3	ecstasy	vigilance	rage	admiration
+2	joy	anticipation	anger	trust
+1	serenity	interest	annoyance	acceptance
0	limbo	limbo	limbo	limbo
-1	pensiveness	distraction	apprehension	boredom
-2	sadness	surprise	fear	disgust
-3	grief	amazement	terror	loathing

5 The Sentics Extraction Process

The Sentics Extraction Process goes through a Natural Language Processing module, which performs a first skim of the webpost, a Semantic Parser, whose aim is to extract concepts from the processed text, and eventually the Sentic Converter, a module for analyzing concepts' affective valence.

Fig. 1. The Sentics Extraction Process

5.1 The NLP Module

The module interprets all the affective valence indicators usually contained in webposts such as special punctuation e.g. suspension points to express impatience, question marks to convey doubt or exclamation marks to express irony, complete upper-case words, onomatopoeic repetitions e.g. repetition of letters to emulate a shout or a sensation of surprise and ditto syllables to reproduce a laughter or a moan, exclamation words, and emoticons.

Emoticons in particular are a very good indicator of a webpost's affective valence: they can convey information about the user's affective state either directly e.g. ':-)' = 'joy' or indirectly e.g. '|-o' = 'yawning' which implies the state of boredom. We currently use a database of 300+ smileys, either in Western and East Asian style, which covers almost the totality of the emoticons used today. The module also detects negations and degree adverbs, to let the Semantic Parser correctly weigh the expressed concepts, and finally stems the text i.e. removes function words, pronouns and inflections.

5.2   The Semantic Parser

The aim of this module is to deconstruct text into concepts. This is not an easy task since the semantic analysis of a text is far more difficult than the lexical one and it's still an open problem in many fields e.g. the semantic web, where the task is currently being tackled by using dereferenceable URIs, RDF statements and web ontologies.

To scan the processed text coming out of the NLP module, the Semantic Parser looks for matches in the Common Sense knowledge base combining the closer stemmed words: this way the parser is able to collect not just the atomic concepts such as 'fun' or 'hug' but also compound concepts e.g. 'eat spaghetti', 'play hockey', 'say hello' or 'blow out candle'.

The output of the Semantic Parser is the set of concepts retrieved in the web-post with their relative frequency, valence and status i.e. the concept's occurrence in the text, its positive or negative connotation, and the degree of intensity with which the concept is expressed.

5.3   The Sentic Converter

This module converts the set of concepts given by the Semantic Parser into a list of four-dimensional vectors, which we call 'sentic vectors'.

The 'sentic vector' of a concept is the tuple [Pleasantness, Attention, Sensitivity, Aptitude] whose values are floating point numbers in the range (-3,+3). To build it we rely on an Affective Similarity Map containing all the relevant 'affective concepts' mapped into the four affective dimensions. By 'affective concepts' we mean the concepts which, in AnalogySpace, are neighbours to the 'sentic centroids' i.e. the concepts representing the 24 sentic levels such as joy, surprise and anger (see Table 1).

AnalogySpace is a vector space representation of Common Sense knowledge describing the analogical closure of a semantic network: by selecting the closest vectors to the 24 centroids we practically clusterize the vector space using a K-means approach. These clusters represent groups of concepts semantically related to the concepts embodying the sentic levels, while the rest of the space is labeled as 'limbo' i.e. absence of affective valence.

This way we obtain an Affective Similarity Map whose rows represent the 'affective concepts', whose columns stand for the 'sentic centroids' and whose entries are the distances, i.e. the dot products, between them. For each concept provided by the Semantic Parser, we look up in this map and, whenever a match is found, we extract the relative information, a 'raw sentic vector' containing 24 values, and encode it.

The codification process goes through a normalization step, the identification of the maximum affective similarity value for each affective dimension, and the addition of the corresponding sentic level value (see Table 1).

Depending on the corresponding concept's status, the sentic vector's magnitude is then increased or decreased of 20% and, in case the concept has a negative valence, the vector is switched with its opposite.

6   Interpreting the Sentic Vectors

The sentic vectors represent a webpost's affective valence rating in terms of Pleasantness, Attention, Sensitivity and Aptitude: depending on our needs we can use this information to quantify user's emotive load or visualize it by plotting the vectors in the space specified by the four affective dimensions.

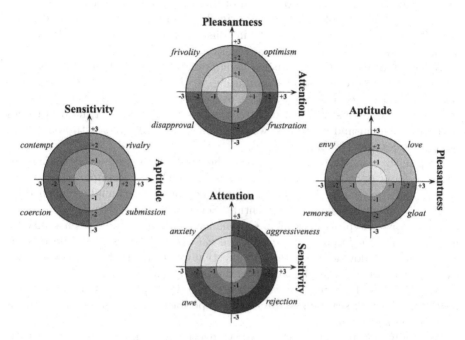

Fig. 2. Particular planes in the sentic vector space

By setting equal to zero the affective dimensions pairwise we can also individuate particular planes representing advanced emotions: the projection of the sentic vectors onto these particular planes gives the webpost's affective valence in terms of compound emotional states such as aggressiveness, which is given by the sum of positive values of Attention and Sensitivity, or remorse, which is given by the sum of negative values of Aptitude and Pleasantness (see Fig. 2).

By averaging the sentic vectors of a sentence we can then summarize its affective valence in a single vector and perform a study of the user's emotional state over time for example in a chat room or in a microblogging application.

This process can be iterated to affectively classify more complex webposts such as blog posts, RSS feeds or forum entries, and evaluate the user's changes of attitudes within a specific web application.

At a higher level we can even perform a user categorization by representing each user with a sentic vector, built with the information gathered from all his/her webposts we have at our disposal, and by plotting it in the vector space to make comparisons with other users and try to affectively classify them.

7   Evaluation

To make a first approximate evaluation of our system we considered a corpus of blogposts from the LiveJournal community, annotated with happy and sad moods. Since the indication of the mood is optional when posting on LiveJournal, the posts we used are likely to reflect the true mood of the authors, and hence form a good test set for the evaluation of the Sentics Extraction Process.

However, since the blogposts are classified just in terms of positive and negative affective valence, we had to take in consideration only the first entry of the sentic vectors i.e. the Pleasantness dimension.

We selected 500 blogposts labeled as happy and as many labeled as sad and processed them through Sentic Computing. To be able to reliably classify the posts, we considered just the absolute average values of Pleasantness superior to 5% and left the rest unlabeled. After running the Sentics Extraction Process over the one thousand blogposts, we obtained almost 70% hits with about 20% false positives and 10% false negatives.

Despite the non-specificity of the test, the results were quite encouraging and left the doors open for future evaluations in which, for example, the Sentics Extraction Process may be tested with a bunch of posts manually classified by users in terms of Pleasantness, Attention, Sensitivity and Aptitude.

To improve the process we plan to enhance the NLP Module's sensibility by making it able to intepret more affective valence indicators in webposts such as superlatives, double negatives and affectively relevant rhetorical devices e.g. climax, anaphora, epistrophe, commoratio, palilogy, aposiopesis.

We also want to refine the Semantic Parser by exploring different Python procedures for text scanning and retrieval to perform a faster and more accurate webpost semantic analysis.

We finally plan to improve the Sentic Converter by blending ConceptNet with a linguistic resource for the lexical representation of affective knowledge.

8   Future Work

General Common Sense knowledge is very useful to discover how concepts are affectively related but we need more specific information to improve the Sentics Extraction Process. To this end we plan to start soon the implementation of a new web interface for the affective Common Sense knowledge acquisition from general public: Open Mind Common Sentics.

The idea is to develop a GUI in which users are asked to give an affective interpretation to random assertions extracted from the Open Mind corpus. After selecting a topic, the user would be given an assertion and asked to type the kind of sensations it arises or simply select one of the available emoticons to intuitively classify the assertion from an emotional point of view.

Open Mind Common Sentics will be complementary to Open Mind Commons, the current interface for collecting Common Sense knowledge from users over the web. In ConceptNet concepts are linked by 24 relations such as 'IsA', 'AtLocation' and 'MadeOf' which respectively answer the questions 'What kind of thing

Fig. 3. Open Mind Common Sentics logo

is it?', 'Where would you find it?' and 'What is it made of?'. We plan to add to ConceptNet the information gathered through Open Mind Common Sentics by inserting a new relation, 'ArisesEmotion', which answer the question 'What kind of emotion it arises?'.

Recruiting new customers is often more expensive than retaining the existing ones. For this reason it's very important to have tools to measure how much your clients are happy with your product or service.

We plan to design a customer care tool which exploits Sentic Computing to evaluate users' level of satisfaction for enterprise 2.0 or e-tourism content management systems. The tool will also be embedded in a health care expert system for clinical decision support to gather patients' attitudes and thus provide better prescriptions.

Today instant messaging clients, which are increasingly used for interpersonal communication, lack the richness of face-to-face conversations. We plan the development of a MSN or Skype add-on in which the chat background or the style font and color change according to the current emotional state of the user and in which a cartoon avatar instantly changes its expression according to the last emotion detected.

A similar approach will be finally employed in fields such as software agents, e-games and e-learning for the development of embodied conversational agents: the sentic vectors will be used as inputs for a facial action coding system to better respond to the user's emotional changes.

9   Conclusions

In this paper we showed how Sentic Computing can help the development of emotion-sensitive systems in fields such as e-health, software agents, e-games, customer care, e-learning and e-tourism.

The approach hereby described is very flexible and lends itself to be used for various purposes: we opted for a four-dimensional vector representation because we were interested in four particular affective dimensions but, depending on the kind of analysis performed and on the emotion representation used, the technique can be easily extended.

The importance of Sentic Computing, anyway, consists not only in introducing a new method for affectively analyze text but also in highlighting the importance of emotions for the development of next-generation systems because, as Marvin Minsky would say, the question is not whether intelligent machines can have emotions, but whether machines can be intelligent without any emotions.

References

1. Cambria, E., Hussain, A., Havasi, C., Eckl, C.: Common Sense computing: From the society of mind to digital intuition and beyond. In: Fierrez, J., Ortega-Garcia, J., Esposito, A., Drygajlo, A., Faundez-Zanuy, M. (eds.) Biometric ID Management and Multimodal Communication. LNCS, vol. 5707, pp. 252–259. Springer, Heidelberg (2009), http://cs.stir.ac.uk/~eca/commansense

2. Hendler, J., Shadbolt, N., Hall, W., Berners-Lee, T., Weitzner, D.: Web Science: an Interdisciplinary Approach to Understanding the World Wide Web. Communications of the ACM 51(7), 60–69 (2008)

3. Clynes, M.: Sentics: The Touch of the Emotions, Doubleday, New York (1977)

4. Picard, R.: Affective Computing. MIT Press, Cambridge (1997)

5. Dyer, M.: Emotions and Their Computations: Three Computer Models. Cognition and Emotion 1(3), 323–347 (1987)

6. Bradley, M., Lang, P.: Affective Norms for English Words (ANEW): Instruction manual and affective ratings. Technical Report C-1, University of Florida (1999)

7. Pennebaker, J., Francis, M., Booth, R.: Linguistic Inquiry and Word Count (LIWC). Erlbaum Publishers, Mahwah (2001)

8. Valitutti, A., Strapparava, C., Stock, O.: Developing Affective Lexical Resources. PsychNology Journal 2(1), 61–83 (2004)

9. Goertzel, B., Silverman, K., Hartley, C., Bugaj, S., Ross, M.: The Baby Webmind Project. In: AISB 2000 (2000)

10. Martin, J., White, P.: The Language of Evaluation: Appraisal in English. Palgrave Macmillan, Basingstoke (2005)

11. Liu, H., Lieberman, H., Selker, T.: A Model of Textual Affect Sensing using Real-World Knowledge. In: IUI 2003 (2003)

12. Havasi, C., Speer, R., Alonso, J.: ConceptNet 3: a Flexible, Multilingual Semantic Network for Common Sense Knowledge. In: RANLP 2007 (2007)

13. Speer, R., Havasi, C., Lieberman, H.: Analogy Space: Reducing the Dimensionality of Common Sense Knowledge. In: AAAI 2008 (2008)

14. Plutchik, R.: The Nature of Emotions. American Scientist 89(4), 344–350 (2001)

15. Minsky, M.: The Emotion Machine. Simon and Schuster, New York (2006)

Face-to-Face Interaction and the KTH Cooking Show

Jonas Beskow, Jens Edlund, Björn Granström,
Joakim Gustafson, and David House

KTH Speech Music and Hearing/Centre for Speech Technology, Lindstedtsvägen 24,
SE-100 44 Stockholm, Sweden
{beskow,edlund,bjorn,jocke,davidh}@speech.kth.se

Abstract. We share our experiences with integrating motion capture recordings in speech and dialogue research by describing (1) Spontal, a large project collecting 60 hours of video, audio and motion capture spontaneous dialogues, is described with special attention to motion capture and its pitfalls; (2) a tutorial where we use motion capture, speech synthesis and an animated talking head to allow students to create an active listener; and (3) brief preliminary results in the form of visualizations of motion capture data over time in a Spontal dialogue. We hope that given the lack of writings on the use of motion capture for speech research, these accounts will prove inspirational and informative.

Keywords: Face-to-face interaction, synchrony/convergence, motion capture.

1 Introduction

Human face-to-face interaction sets the ultimate example for spoken dialogue systems created to draw on a human metaphor [1]. As we are unlikely to generate flawless human behaviour within a foreseeable future, the target is often mitigated: "human enough that we respond to it as we respond to another human" [2]. Still, a number of aspects of face-to-face interaction – for example the temporal dynamics in the interactions and the relations between modalities – are largely unexplored. As an example, consider the well-known phenomenon that interlocutors are more similar to each other than to people they are not currently interacting with. It has been pointed out that this similarity may be better described as a dynamic process that develops throughout the interaction creating synchrony (e.g. [3, 4]). We may, using standard dictionary meanings of the words, distinguish between *synchrony* (i.e. things that happen at the same time or work at the same speed) and *convergence* (i.e. things that come from different directions and meet), as illustrated in Figure 2.

Whereas most studies of interlocutor similarity have focused on only a few data points per conversation (e.g. first half/second half) or even one data point per speaker, a much finer temporal resolution is needed to capture these dynamics. An understanding of these dynamics is crucial for our understanding of human communication. And for face-to-face interaction, all modalities must be taken into account. Many interactional signals, for example feedback and emphasis, seem to be expressed equally well in for example gestures, words, facial expressions or by prosodic means.

Although methods involving the analysis of large amounts of data have yielded unrivalled progress in other areas of speech technology, few data collections to date capture in full the multimodal nature of human face-to-face interaction. Motion capture

A. Esposito et al. (Eds.): COST 2102 Int. Training School 2009, LNCS 5967, pp. 157–168, 2010.
© Springer-Verlag Berlin Heidelberg 2010

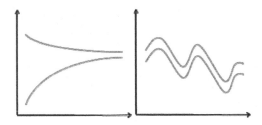

Fig. 1. Schematic illustrations of convergence (left pane) and synchrony (right pane)

has been used extensively by the entertainment business, and today the industry records scene specific motion capture data routinely. Motion capture has also been used to model animated agents in spoken dialogue systems, and some research data of acted dialogues have been recorded (e.g. CMU Graphics Lab Motion Capture Database). However, to our knowledge there is no sizeable database of unrestricted face-to-face conversations including motion capture data and high resolution video available for research. Nor have motion capture techniques been used to any significant extent in speech research. We are hoping that by gathering our experiences of working with motion capture in speech technology and dialogue research in this book chapter, we might inspire some to use the techniques and help others avoid pitfalls.

This book chapter presents a data collection effort, the Spontal project, in which 60 hours of unrestricted conversations between pairs of speakers is being recorded, with recordings capturing audio, hi-resolution video, and motion capture data (the latter is made possible in part because motion capture equipment has recently become considerably more available as well as affordable). Upon completion, the Spontal database will be the largest such data set to date. As the use of motion capture recordings as a means to study conversational behaviour is fairly new, this paper is an attempt to collect and share our experiences so far.

Following the presentation of the Spontal project, we show how the data collection techniques used in Spontal can be used to create small demonstrations and exercises. The motion capture equipment used in the project is quite portable, which has given us the opportunity to bring it to various locations and run tutorials and hands-on exercises on a number of occasions. On these occasions, part of the process is normally prepared in advance, be it for technical reasons, for expedience or simply to save participants some of the nitty-gritty. As this bears similarity with the format commonly used in televised cooking shows, we refer to these events as *cooking shows*. The exercises share several combined goals: (1) to showcase motion capture technology in a spoken dialogue context, as there is a great interest for this, (2) to teach how motion capture data can be used to investigate and to model face-to-face dialogue, especially since some of the experiences involved are hard-earned and many of the mistakes need not be repeated, and (3) to actually research face-to-face dialogue – the data collected during the exercises is valuable for hypothesis generation, as are comments and insights provided by students. Here, we describe exercises aimed at modelling *active listeners and listening speakers*, which were held at VISPP in 2008 and in part at the COST Spring School in Dublin in 2009.

We conclude this overview – or *cook book*, as we half jokingly call it – by presenting preliminary analyses investigating synchrony of movement to serve as an illustration of how motion capture data can provide support for theories and intuitions regarding the dynamics of spoken dialogue.

2 Animated Talking Heads

Before moving on to motion capture, we will describe in brief the setting in which multimodal conversation is modelled at KTH Speech, Music and Hearing and the Centre for Speech Technology using in animated talking heads. The talking head developed at KTH is based on text-to-speech synthesis. Acoustic speech synthesis is generated from a text representation in synchrony with visual articulator movements of the lips, tongue and jaw. Linguistic information in the text is used to generate visual cues for relevant prosodic categories such as prominence, phrasing and emphasis. These cues generally take the form of eyebrow and head movements. Facial gestures can also be used as conversational gestures to signal such things as positive or negative feedback, control of the dialogue flow, and the internal state of a dialogue system (for a summary of spoken dialogue systems at KTH utilizing audiovisual synthesis, see [5]). More recently, we have been exploring data-driven methods to model articulation and facial parameters of major importance for conveying social signals and emotions [6].

Animated synthetic talking faces and characters have been developed using a number of different techniques and for a variety of purposes for more than two decades. Historically, our approach is based on parameterised, deformable 3D facial models, controlled by rules within a text-to-speech framework [7]. The rules generate the parameter tracks for the face from a representation of the text, taking coarticulation into account [8]. Several face models have been developed for different applications, some of them can be seen in Figure 1. All can be parametrically controlled by the same articulation rules.

Fig. 2. Different versions of the KTH talking head

3 Spontal

Spontal: Multimodal database of spontaneous speech in dialog is an ongoing Swedish speech database project which began in 2007 and will be concluded in 2010. It is funded by the Swedish Research Council, KFI - Grant for large databases (VR

2006-7482). The goal of the project is to create a Swedish multimodal spontaneous speech database rich enough to capture important variations among speakers and speaking styles to meet the demands of current research of conversational speech.

60 hours of dialog consisting of 120 half-hour sessions will be recorded in the project. Each session consists of three consecutive 10 minute blocks. The subjects are all native speakers of Swedish and balanced (1) for gender, (2) as to whether the interlocutors are of opposing gender and (3) as to whether they know each other or not. This balance will result in 15 dialogs of each configuration: 15x2x2x2 for a total of 120 dialogs. Currently (November, 2009), about 75% of the database has been recorded. The remainder is scheduled for recording during 2010. All subjects permit, in writing (1) that the recordings be used for scientific analysis, (2) that the analyses be published in scientific writings and (3) that the recordings can be replayed in front of audiences at scientific meetings for demonstration and illustration purposes.

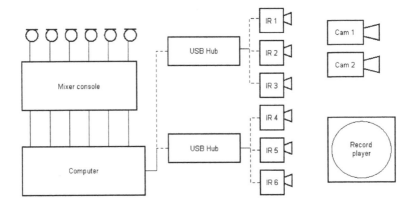

Fig. 3. Schematic over the recording setup used in Spontal

In the base configuration, the recordings are comprised of high-quality audio and high-definition video, with about 5% of the recordings also making use of a motion capture system using infra-red cameras and reflective markers for recording facial gestures in 3D. In addition, the motion capture system is used on virtually all recordings to capture body and head gestures, although resources to treat and annotate this data have yet to be allocated.

Subjects are told that they are allowed to talk about absolutely anything they want at any point in the session, including meta-comments on the recording environment and suchlike, with the intention to relieve subjects from feeling forced to behave in any particular manner.

The recordings are formally divided into three 10 minute blocks, although the conversation is allowed to continue seamlessly over the blocks, with the exception that subjects are informed, briefly, about the time after each 10 minute block. After 20 minutes, they are also asked to open a wooden box which has been placed on the floor beneath them prior to the recording. The box contains objects whose identity or function is not immediately obvious. The subjects may then hold, examine and discuss the objects taken from the box, but they may also chose to continue whatever discussion they were engaged in or talk about something entirely different.

Audio is recorded on four channels using two omni-directional microphones for high audio quality, and two head-set microphones to enable subject separation for transcription and dialog analysis. Video is recorded on two high definition video cameras placed to obtain a good view of each subject from a height that is approximately the same as the heads of both of the participating subjects. To ensure audio, video and motion capture synchronization during post processing, a record player is included in the setup. The turntable is placed between the subjects and a bit to the side, in full view of the motion capture cameras. A marker placed near the edge on the turntable rotates with a constant speed (33 rpm), enabling high-accuracy synchronization and validation of the frame rate in post processing. The recording setup is illustrated in Figure 3.

Motion capture data is recorded on six NaturalPoint Optitrack FLEX:V100 cameras connected to the same computer over two externally powered USB hubs. The recording software is created in-house specifically for the purpose. Each subject is rigged with 12 reflective markers as seen in Fig 4.

1.   Head – Center
2.   Head – Left
3.   Head – Right
4.   Chest
5.   Shoulder – Left
6.   Shoulder – Right
7.   Elbow – Left
8.   Elbow – Right
9.   Wrist – Left
10. Wrist – Right
11. Hand – Left
12. Hand – Right

Fig. 4. A Spontal subject rigged with 12 reflective markers

Markers 1-3 are mounted on 1.25" (3.175 cm) tall marker bases onto a plastic diadem (tiara) and fitted on the head of each subject, directed upwards. Marker 4 is placed in the center of the sternum, between 3 and 10 cm below the suprasternal (jugular) notch, depending on the clothing and any facial hair. Markers 5 and 6 are placed on the outermost parts of the shoulders, as close to the acromion (bone in the shoulder above the deltoid muscle) as possible. Markers 7 and 8 are placed as close to the center of the elbow as possible. Markers 9 and 10 are placed just above the center of the wrist to avoid interference with movements of the hand. Markers 11 and 12 are placed close to the knuckles of the index finger and middle finger. Markers 4-12 are attached using adhesive pads. Finally one marker is placed on the turntable, making for a total of 25 markers. All markers are passive reflective markers with a diameter of 1.111 cm (7/16").

The motion capture data is saved directly to disk with no data manipulation or management at all during the recording session. There is no indexing or tracking of the recorded markers, so each frame contains 25 markers but there is no information as to which marker is placed where on the subject, nor which markers were or were not present in the previous frame. Markers may also be obscured from the cameras by the subject herself causing the marker to disappear for some number of frames. Ghost-markers can also appear in one or more frames – these are not actual markers but reflections on shiny objects that the cameras interpret as a marker. Another issue is that the system is not constantly running at 100 FPS. The frame rate varies between 99,8 and 100,2 FPS, and occasionally it varies around 64 FPS. If left alone, this problem causes significant synchronization issues rendering the motion capture data useless. However, the steady rotation of the turntable included in the setup can be used to control post process re-sampling.

Figure 5 shows a frame from each of the two video cameras aligned next to each other, so that the two dialog partners are both visible. The opposing video camera can be seen in the centre of the image, and a number of tripods holding the motion capture cameras are visible. The synchronization turntable is visible in the left part of the left pane and the right part of the right pane. As in Figure 4, we see the reflective markers for the motion capture system on the hands, arms, shoulders, trunk and head of the subject.

Note that the table between the subjects is covered in textiles, a necessary precaution as the motion capture system is sensitive to reflecting surfaces. For the same reason, subjects are asked to remove any jewellery, and other shiny objects are masked with masking tape.

Fig. 5. A single frame from the video recording

The Spontal database is currently being transcribed orthographically. Basic gesture and dialogue-level annotation will also be added (e.g. turn-taking and feedback). Additionally, automatic annotation and validation methods are being developed and tested within the project. The transcription activities are being performed in parallel with the recording phase of the project with special annotation tools written for the project facilitating this process.

Specifically, the project aims at annotation that is both efficient, coherent, and to the largest extent possible objective. To achieve this, automatic methods are used wherever possible. The orthographic transcription, for example, follows a strict method: (1) automatic speech/non-speech segmentation, (2) orthographic transcription of resulting speech segments, (3) validation by a second transcriber, (4) automatic phone segmentation based on the orthographic transcriptions. Pronunciation variability is not annotated by the transcribers, but is left for the automatic segmentation stage (4), which uses a pronunciation lexicon capturing most standard variation.

Our recording experience so far have presented us with a number of more or less unexpected technical challenges which have been overcome. These include selection and installation of a light source for the video recordings which does not interfere with the motion capture cameras; shiny objects, eyes and eyeglasses which create spurious reflections interfering with the motion capture data; problems with USB power for the motion capture system; and synchronization problems finally solved by the use of the turntable. Fortunately, we have encountered far less obstacles related to our human subjects. Engaging in spontaneous and unstructured dialogues have presented no problems at all, nor have we seen any hesitation regarding coming up with topics of discussion during the interactions. Dividing the half-hour sessions into 10 minute sections and informing the subjects about the elapsed time after each section may reassure the subjects that all is proceeding well, and the introduction of the box after 20 minutes creates diversity in the conversational topics. Our transcribers' general impression so far is that all dialogues are spontaneous and unforced. It seems that the subjects quickly become rather unaware of the audio, video and motion capture equipment and busily proceed with their dialogues. The same observation has also been offered freely, albeit with some surprise, by many subjects after participating in a recording.

4 Modelling an Active Listener

The following section describes, in some detail, a three-session cooking show first held at the VISPP Summer School 2008 in Kuressaare, Estonia. VISPP in general focuses on speech variation in perception and production, and the summer school had talk-in-interaction, expressive speech and multimodal communication as its theme. Our intention in including it here is to show how motion capture data can be used not only to efficiently model aspects of face-to-face interaction, but also to illustrate as well as test intuitions and theories of such interaction.

The summer school attracted in excess of 30 participants, all PhD students, but of varied background. For this reason, we opted to investigate a behaviour that is recognized by everyone: the responses a listener provides to a narrative, often in the form of grunts and head-nods. The goal of the exercise was to increase the students' awareness of this mechanism by creating a rudimentary multimodal automatic active listener, using the KTH talking together with analyses and syntheses the students themselves created.

4.1 Data Recording

The students were initially divided in three groups, each of which did a recording. As the exercise aims to model an active listener, subjects are instructed to take different roles. One subject is the speaker (S) and is instructed to tell a story. Each group was asked to pick a member who enjoys narrating to take the role of S. The second subject is the active listener (AL). AL's role is to listen to S and provide feedback whenever she deems it suitable. Each group were asked to pick an attentive person for the role of AL.

A blacked-out hotel room served as the recording set. With the specific goal of this exercise, it is sufficient to record the motions of AL alone, but the audio from both subjects is required, and it needs to be reasonably well separated. Both subjects were rigged with close talking microphones, and AL was equipped with reflectors on the upper and lower lip and on each eyebrow – enough to model head pose, mouth opening and eyebrow movements. Limiting motion capture to one of the subjects allows us to use four cameras only (strictly speaking, three would suffice, but an extra camera improves results notably), which is a great relief in the confined space provided by a hotel room filled with spectators. In order to minimize the pressure on the subjects, no video equipment was used.

S was asked to think of a topic in advance, and be prepared to speak on it for five minutes. This presented no problems for the S in any of the three groups, although the groups occasionally found it hard not to giggle or become otherwise involved in the interaction.

The actual recordings took place sequentially over a 90 minute session, allowing each group 30 minutes. Each group was taken in to the recording set and given a full demonstration of the system, including a full calibration session, for the first ten minutes. The subjects were then rigged with reflectors and microphones and seated opposite each other, and S proceeded to narrate for five minutes. The last ten minutes were spent storing the recorded data and removing the equipment from the subjects while the group asked questions.

4.2 Analysis

In the next 90 minute session, students were divided into groups of two or three. Each group had students that had belonged to the same group on the recording session.

It is widely held that feedback responses occur more frequently after certain prosodic patterns – a notable example is Ward's description of how to decide where to insert feedback in a conversation automatically using pitch extraction (Ward, 1996). The analysis session was intended to give the students a feel for how pitch movements may be related to the occurrence of feedback from a listener. Since a considerable proportion of the students had no experience in phonetics, a graphical method of drawing templates to match pitch was used.

Students created pitch templates by (1) looking at pitch contours from S in Wavesurfer [9], and (2) selecting examples of contours preceding feedback (AL's audio track was included, as was a 3D rendition of the motion captured head movements) they felt were typical. Using a custom designed add-on to Wavesurfer, (3) these contours were extracted to a standard black/white image. They then (4) edited the image in a standard image editing programme, making the contour wider in order to make it trigger more readily when applied to unseen curves (5). The end product of the analysis exercise was a number of templates – black/white images which were used to match a pitch contour segment. Pitch values inside the white area of the image scored positive and those inside the black areas scored negative, and a threshold on the total value was used to trigger feedback.

4.3 Resynthesis

The resynthesis session aimed at selecting audiovisual sequences for reproduction as canned speech and synchronised 3D-animated head pose, eyebrow and lip movement. Students were placed in the same groups as in the second session and were asked to select typical examples of feedback – auditory, visual and audiovisual. The audio was then replayed with gestures reproduced in an animated talking head. Students reported having no trouble finding good examples.

4.4 Final Session

On the plenary session of the final day, we applied one set of trigger templates and one set of audiovisual feedback segments to one of the narrations, resulting in an automated active listener that – according to the highly subjective views of the audience – did well. The take-home message is that given support and tools, it is possible for laymen to create a multimodal listener providing automatic feedback in less than a day's work, and hopefully gain some insights along the way.

5 A Glimpse at Synchrony in Motion Capture Data

As mentioned above, similarity between interlocutors is a process that can be established and that can develop during a dialogue. 3 employ an automatic approach to the analysis of video to quantify coincidental head movements (synchrony) between therapist and patient during psychotherapeutic sessions. Their approach employs Motion Energy Analysis (MEA) which is based on an image differencing algorithm that takes into consideration differences in the grey-scale distribution changes between subsequent video frames. By using motion capture data collected in the Spontal project, we are able to perform a similar automatic analysis of movement synchrony and produce a number of interesting and useful measurements which can contribute to new ways of analyzing dialogue behaviour.

As an illustration of how motion capture data can be used – even with very little processing – we picked a Spontal dialogue at random and prepared the motion capture data as follows. Note that we present no numerical evidence here. Such analyses would be moot, as the Spontal data needs to be validated and possibly resynchronized before it can be used as scientific evidence proper, as mentioned above.

For each frame, any data point whose position was within 0.5 metres from a point between the participants was discarded, creating a blind area of one metre width right between the speakers. This was done as a precaution to exclude the possibility that a motion capture track gets confused with another between the speakers. This precaution is well motivated for this type of study, as mixing tracks between speakers would instantly create artificial synchrony. This treatment has a relatively small effect on the data, since the speakers are seated further apart than one metre, and the only frames that are lost are those where a speaker leans heavily forward. In the dialogue we used, it is less than 3% of the frames, divided in two continuous sequences.

For each sequence of two frames, the Euclidean distance between the points in each track was calculated. Tracks situated on one side of the blind area (thus belonging to the same speaker) were averaged, as were the tracks belonging to the other speaker. The result is a measure of *average marker movement* in the time between the two adjacent frames, per speaker. As mentioned before, the motion capture equipment aims at 100Hz, but this varies somewhat. However, as the synchronization between the cameras is highly accurate, we do not need to worry – each frame contains data sampled at the same time, which is all we need know for a rough investigation of synchrony.

Next, the two resulting time series of speaker average marker movement were down-sampled and smoothed using a 3000 frames (30s) long median filter with a step-length of 100 frames, resulting in heavily smoothed 1Hz data.

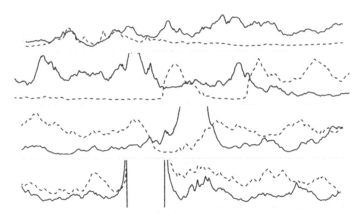

Fig. 6. Plot of Z-normalized average marker movement per speaker over time for the entire dialogue. Speaker A is represented by a solid line, speaker B by a dashed line. Finally, the data in both graphs is Z-normalized over speaker to make the plots easier to read and to facilitate comparison.

We note in Figure 6 that A and B show synchrony over a couple of segments, for example the first few minutes and in the bottom panel. When comparing to the video and audio, we note that the higher activity for A between 3 to 10 minutes into the dialogue, approximately, corresponds to a segment where she narrates a connected story, after which B takes over the narration, which corresponds to the higher activity of B at the end of the second and beginning of third panel. The gap in the final panel is caused by the Spontal setup: about 20 minutes into each recording, the subjects are asked to bend down and pick up a box that sits on the floor beneath them, place it on the table between them, and open it. While they do this, and while they are investigating the contents of the box, they lean into the blind area.

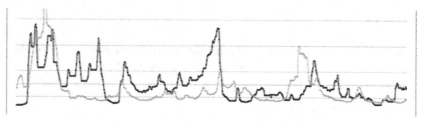

Fig. 7. Plot of Z-normalized average marker movement per speaker over time for the one minute of the dialogue. Speaker A is represented by a black line, speaker B by a grey line.

We also looked at this dialogue with a a 20 frames (200ms) long 20th percentile filter with a step-length of 10 frames, resulting in 10Hz data with very brief peaks removed. In this view, considerably more synchrony is visible on the micro-level, but the graph is too detailed and messy to reproduce here in its entirety. Figure 7 shows a small (1 min, starting at 11.5 minutes into the dialogue) section of that graph.

6 Summary

Studies of face-to-face human interaction are fundamental to basic research on speech in use, as it is arguably the most common and the oldest type of language use. They are equally important to speech technology development, at least to the extent that we aim to create human-like spoken dialogue systems – for example systems aiming to capitalize on the fact that humans already know how to communicate with each other. Face-to-face interaction is by its very nature multimodal, and we feel that there is a lack of substantial multimodal datasets. In particular, audio and video alone may not be sufficient to allow us to investigate in detail the relations between gesture, speech, and facial expressions. Adding motion capture provides precision data in three dimensions that we think will prove valuable in this respect.

As the use of motion capture in speech research is as of yet uncommon, we have presented here some of our experiences in recording face-to-face interactions with audio, video and motion capture. The technical setup for an ongoing large Swedish multimodal database project (Spontal) provided insights into the possibilities and pitfalls of large-scale dialogue recordings involving motion capture. The report on a tutorial in which students created an automated active listener using audio and motion-capture analysis from dyads engaged in narrations showed that current motion capture equipment is relatively portable and can be used for demonstrations, teaching and exploratory research in smaller, ad hoc settings. Finally, our very preliminary data visualizations exemplified how motion capture data may be used to produce interesting and useful measurements which can contribute to new ways of analyzing dialogue behaviour.

We note, naturally, that the tutorial recording settings do not meet research requirements – it is more than likely that the situation produced both subjective biases and artefacts of the extraordinary dialogue situation. Similarly, the analyses of synchrony presented last do not include statistics. The data is preliminary and not yet validated, which would make any statistical significance found void. In spite of this, we hope that given the lack of writing on the use of motion capture for speech research, our early accounts will be found inspirational and worthwhile.

References

[1] Edlund, J., Gustafson, J., Heldner, M., Hjalmarsson, A.: Towards human-like spoken dialogue systems. Speech Communication 50(8-9), 630–645 (2008)

[2] Cassell, J.: Body language: lessons from the near-human. In: Riskin, J. (ed.) Genesis Redux: Essays on the history and philosophy of artificial life, pp. 346–374. University of Chicago Press, Chicago (2007)

[3] Keller, E., Tschacher, W.: Prosodic and gestural expression of interactional agreement. In: Esposito, A., Faundez-Zauny, M., Keller, E., Marinaro, M. (eds.) Verbal and nonverbal communication behaviours, pp. 85–98. Springer, Berlin (2007)

[4] Edlund, J., Heldner, M., Hirschberg, J.: Pause and gap length in face-to-face interaction. In: Proc. of Interspeech 2009, Brighton, UK (2009)

[5] Gustafson, J.: Developing multimodal spoken dialogue systems. Empirical studies of spoken human-computer interaction. Doctoral dissertation, KTH, Department of Speech, Music and Hearing, Stockholm (2002)

[6] Beskow, J., Granström, B., House, D.: Analysis and synthesis of multimodal verbal and non-verbal interaction for animated interface agents. In: Esposito, A., Faundez-Zanuy, M., Keller, E., Marinaro, M. (eds.) Verbal and Nonverbal Communication Behaviours, pp. 250–263. Springer, Berlin (2007)

[7] Carlson, R., Granström, B.: Speech synthesis. In: Hardcastle, W.J., Laver, J. (eds.) The Handbook of Phonetic Science, pp. 768–788. Blackwell Publ. Ltd., Oxford (1997)

[8] Beskow, J.: Rule-based visual speech synthesis. In: Pardo, J. (ed.) Proc of the 4th European Conference on Speech Communication and Technology (EUROSPEECH 1995), Madrid, pp. 299–302 (1995)

[9] Sjölander, K., Beskow, J.: WaveSurfer - an open source speech tool. In: Yuan, B., Huang, T., Tang, X. (eds.) Proceedings of ICSLP 2000, 6th Intl Conf on Spoken Language Processing, pp. 464–467. China Military Friendship Publish, Beijing (2000)

Affect Listeners: Acquisition of Affective States by Means of Conversational Systems

Marcin Skowron

Austrian Research Institute for Artificial Intelligence,
Freyung 6, 1010 Vienna, Austria
marcin.skowron@ofai.at
http://www.ofai.at

Abstract. We present the concept and motivations for the development of Affect Listeners, conversational systems aiming to detect and adapt to affective states of users, and meaningfully respond to users' utterances both at the content- and affect-related level. In this paper, we describe the system architecture and the initial set of core components and mechanisms applied, and discuss the application and evaluation scenarios of Affect Listener systems.

1 Introduction

Emotional factors play an important role in intelligent behaviour; they influence perceptive, cognitive and communicative processes. In interactions between humans and artificial agents, the capability to detect signs of human emotions and suitably react to them can enrich interactions and improve their naturalness. Currently, interactive computer systems do not take into account the emotional dimension which humans expect to find in interaction, and this is a recurrent source of frustration [23]. Recently, there has been considerable interest in the development of artificial systems capable to detect and appropriately react to the users' behavior and emotional states. The recently started project SEMAINE [24] aims to develop Sensitive Artificial Listeners – conversational agents designed to sustain an interaction with a human user despite limited verbal skills, through robust recognition and generation of non-verbal behavior in real time. Other strands of research stress the importance of textual affect sensing, either motivated by the fact that current user interfaces in the human-computer interaction field are mainly text-based [9]; or by considering textual sentiment sensing as key for analyzing the users' sentiment towards specific products, news or movies as expressed e.g., in online postings [25].

The project CyberEmotions[1] deals with modelling and understanding of the role of *collective emotions* in creating, forming and breaking-up of online-communities. In the field of social psychology, collective emotions have been defined as emotions that are shared by a large number of individuals in a certain society [29]. These emotions, experienced by individuals as reactions to societal

---

[1] http://www.cyberemotions.eu (all URLs last accessed 2009-11-15).

A. Esposito et al. (Eds.): COST 2102 Int. Training School 2009, LNCS 5967, pp. 169–181, 2010.
© Springer-Verlag Berlin Heidelberg 2010

and collective experiences, are shared between members of a group for a number of different reasons and are not limited to emotions which are felt by individuals as a result of their membership in a certain group (group-based emotions). Our research in the project focuses on the development of conversational systems that interact with members of various groups to probe for affective states and background knowledge related to those states for a large number of Internet users. We call this sort of systems *Affect Listeners*, which are not monolithic programs, but a family of systems with various constitutions, sharing the following characteristics: These systems communicate with users, rely on integrated affective components for detecting textual expressions of the users' affective states, and use the acquired information to aid selection and generation of responses. Affect Listeners monitor events and processes that draw attention of Internet users, by analysing a number of Internet websites (e.g., volksonomy-driven sites, automatic and semi-automatic news aggregators). These systems interact with users via a range of communication channels and interfaces (e.g., Internet Relay Chat (IRC), Jabber, online chat-site interface).

We aim at systems capable to adapt to the users' affective states, and to suitably respond to users' utterances both on the content- and the affect-related level. The foreseen evaluation scenario of the systems includes also their application in a laboratory for measuring physiological correlates of emotional responses occurring during interaction in experimental settings [7].

The rest of the paper is structured as follows: first, related work in the areas of affect computing, affect sensing from text, and dialog management is presented. Then, the Affect Listeners system architecture is introduced, along with a presentation of the components used in the initial realization of the system. Next a description of the core components related to affect detection and interaction management is provided. Finally the Affect Listeners testing and evaluation scenarios are presented.

2   Related Work

In recent years, we witnessed a growing interest in the development of human-agent interfaces that incorporate emotional behavior [18,15]. Current research concentrates on the advances in embodied conversational agents [16] and speech-enabled animated characters. Research in this field included the creation of a framework to enrich human-agent interactions with an affective dimension and to verify under which conditions emotions can improve general intelligent behaviour of the synthetic characters, leading to more natural interactions between humans and computers [2]. The growth of academic research in affective computing resulted in the establishment of the EU-funded Network of Excellence "Human-Machine Interaction Network on Emotion" - HUMAINE[2] aiming to contribute to "the development of systems that can register, model and/or influence human emotional and emotion-related states and processes". Since 2004, the network and the subsequently established association have been providing a

---

[2] http://emotion-research.net

valuable basis for understanding the role of natural language processing with an emphasis on the modelling of affect in artificial systems.

A body of research relevant for work in Affect Listeners originates from works on affect sensing from text: a study on the extraction of affective components from texts and their application in dialog systems [30], analysis of blogposts [13], or assessing affect qualities of natural language text using large scale real-world knowledge [9]. The main strands of research on dialog management include finite state-based and frame-based approaches [3], plan based approaches [12], information state-based and probabilistic approaches [34]. Linguistic and psychological aspects have been studied in numerous works in the field of psycholinguistics. In [17] the authors, based on computer-aided text analysis, present evidence on links between word use and personality, social and situational fluctuations, and psychological interventions. [10] provides experimental results for the recognition of personality traits, on the basis of text conversations, utilizing both self and observer ratings of personality.

3   System Architecture

3.1   Preconditions

Application scenarios for Affect Listeners include online interactions with Internet users and the interaction with users in a laboratory environment as introduced above. The system-user communication is text-based, real-time and oriented at the detection and acquisition of users' affective states. The initial realization is an open-domain system, i.e., communication is not limited to a specific domain, topic or ICT-mediated community. The main requirements related to the foreseen application scenarios include:

- robust natural language-based communication,
- detection and classification of affective states based on text analysis,
- dialog and affective dialog management,
- modelling system-user interaction to facilitate the acquisition of affective states,
- system acceptance and usage by Internet users.

The system environment contains user utterances and textual data originating from websites. Considering the characteristics of the system environment and the requirements of the foreseen application scenarios, we adopted an interactive and incremental development approach to support redesign at later stages of development and flexibility in the addition of new tasks, components and mechanisms. Moreover, the testing and integration of existing components is prefered to reimplementation, in particular in the initial realizations of the system.

3.2   Initial Realization of the System

The general system architecture includes 3 core layers: perception, control and actuator-communication. Here, we present an overview of the layers' functionalities and introduce the components and software tools which compose them; see sections 4 and 5 for a more detailed description of the core system components and mechanisms such as affect detection and classification related resources, Affect Listener Dialog Scripting commands (ALDS) or User Adaptation Mechanism.

The aim of the initial system realization was to create a sandbox for the integration and testing of components, and to develop the first version of the action selection and response generation components. Figure 1 presents the layers of the system architecture and the interaction loop with the environment.

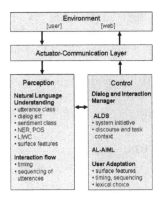

Fig. 1. Layers of the system architecture

Perception Layer: The perception layer integrates a number of natural language processing tools and machine learning-based classifiers for the analysis of both the input from the system's environment and the output of tools in the actuator layer, including the response candidates. The initial implementation includes the following components: maximum entropy based dialog act (DA) classifier[3], maximum entropy and string similarity based utterance classifier [28] (UC)[4], SVM-based question classifier (QC)[5], surface features detector (letter capitalization, punctuation, emoticons), fine-grained answer candidate extraction [26] (NI)[6], utterance focus and utterance interest detector[28], sentiment and affective states related classifiers and resources – Sentiment Classifier (SC)[7],

---

[3] Dialog act classes follow annotation schema used in NPS Chat Corpus [5]: Accept, Bye, Clarify, Continuer, Emotion, Emphasis, Greet, No Answer, Other, Reject, Statement, System, Wh-Question, Yes Answer, Yes/No Question. The 10-fold cross validation accuracy is 71.2%.

[4] 6 utterance classes: greeting, question, rejection, agreement, goodbye, other.

[5] Classification scheme is based on the taxonomy proposed in [8], which consists of 6 coarse-grained and 50 fine-grained question classes. The classification accuracy of the component is 85.5% [27].

[6] The system integrates Named Entity Recognition (NER) component with extraction rules and gazetteers for 50 distinctive answer type classes, that match the question classification taxonomy presented above.

[7] The classifier provides the following annotations: sentiment class (SC), positive sentiment value (PS), negative sentiment value (NS).

Linguistic Inquiry and Word Count (LC), (see section 4 for a more detailed overview of these affect detection and classification resources).

Table 1. Example annotation from the Perception Layer (excerpt)

Utterance: hello George :) good to see you again. how are you doing
- Annotation: UC-GREETING DA-whQuestion QC-DESCdef
LC-Social:CogMech:You:Time: SC-1 NS--1 PS-3 NI-PERSON-George

Control Layer: The control layer manages interaction with the user by analyzing information obtained from the perception layer e.g., timing of message exchanges, dialog act interpretation, utterance classes, sentiment valance and arousal. Furthermore, it monitors the dialog progression based on the system goals, observed dialog states, specific information contained in user utterance and system response candidates. The control layer is also responsible for selecting a system response from the number of response candidates (e.g., parallel response candidates from AL-AIML set), based on their annotation in the system's perception layer and a set of response selection rules. Finally, the control layer makes decisions on postprocessing of a final response and the timing of its dispatch, depending on the user profile and regularities discovered in his/her communicative style.

The Dialog and Interaction Manager is a central component in the Affect Listener system control layer. It is responsible for directing the system-user interaction to achieve the system goals. The component integrates the rule-based action selection, Affect Listener Dialog Scripting (ALDS), command interpreters for Artificial Intelligence Markup Language (AIML) and User Adaptation Mechanism (see section 5 for a detailed description of these components).

Actuator-Communicator Layer: The actuator-communication layer includes a number of software tools, that provide information required for generating system responses, as well as for accepting/decoding a user input and for formating/dispatching system responses. The system communicates with users relying on a range of communication channels, mediated by the interface component. The initial realization of the Affect Listener system includes tools for accessing and processing collaborative tagging driven sites (Digg) and automatic news aggregators (Google News, Bing News), WordNet [4], User Adaptation Mechanism based system response postprocessing tool and communication interfaces (IRC, RPC, interface to online chat-websites).

4   Affect Detection and Classification

The capability to detect and classify textual expressions of users affective states based on the analysis of their utterances is a core prerequisite for the Affect Listener systems. Recently, sentiment analysis of text and lexical affect sensing became a prominent and active research field [14] [19]. In the current realization of the Affect Listener system we use two affect detection and classification resources: Sentiment Classifier [31] and Linguistic Inquiry and Word Count (LIWC) dictionary [17]. In Affect Listener systems these resources are applied for processing both user utterances and the selected system responses (i.e., system responses generated based on text snippets retrieved from the Internet, for which no sentiment score can be calculated beforehand).

Sentiment Classifier. The system is implemented based on three classical classifiers: Naive Bayes, k-Nearest Neighbor and Centroid Document, and provides sentiment classes to text snippets. It is optimized for short textual messages (i.e., blog posts and comments) and detects and takes into consideration negation, exclamation marks, emoticons, intensifiers (i.e., "very" pleased), diminishers (i.e., "somewhat" agree) and text written in capital letters. The system provides positive/neutral/negative classification for a text snippet, and estimates its intensity on the scale between [-5, 5] and 0 for the neutral states. The average precision for the best result is 74% [31].

Linguistic Inquiry and Word Count (LIWC). The LIWC dictionary provides, among others, 32 word categories tapping psychological processes (e.g., social such as family, friends and human; affective such as positive and negative emotions; cognitive such as insight, causation, tentative), 22 linguistic processes (e.g., negations, adverbs, swear words), 3 paralinguistic dimensions (assents, fillers, nonfluencies), 7 personal concern categories (e.g., home, religion, work, leisure) for almost 4500 words and word stems [17]. The Affect Listeners' perception layer uses LIWC dictionary to annotate utterances according to those categories, thus allowing for generating representations of an individual utterance in terms of LIWC categories and, based on the aggregated input from a single agent (user or system), providing insights about its profile.

5   Dialog and Interaction Management

5.1   Affect Listeners Dialog Scripting

Affect Listeners Dialog Scripting (ALDS) commands facilitate the development of dialog scenarios, which require extended[8] system-user message exchanges or fine-grained capabilities to detect cues in user utterances and system responses (natural language processing based analysis, affective states analysis) that cannot be captured by keyword or textual pattern-based matching mechanisms. The ALDS commands take advantage of perception capabilities of the system, including the textual affect sensing, classification of the dialog acts and extended parsing of the text.

Dialog scenarios defined in ALDS are provided to the system in the form of text files, which describe the flow of a foreseen dialog scenario by specifying a set

---

[8] Measured in the number of exchanges and the scope of control over interaction.

of conditional statements, perception channels and applicable actions required
to generate system responses and to monitor the flow of the system-user message
exchanges. A particular scenario is chosen based on the match between the current dialog state with the triggering conditions of a particular scenario. If found,
the system enters the selected dialog scenario and attempts to progress the dialog according to a set of ALDS commands. Otherwise, the control layer manages
the interaction based on other mechanism, i.e., rule based action selection or
AL-AIML described below. The current version of ALDS includes:

- manipulation rules
  - coarse grained processing commands: say, extract, verify if statement,
    use,
  - fine grained processing commands: e.g., extract-dialogAct, extract-entity,
    if-dialogAct, if-sentimentClass use-tool, use-store,
- symbols
  - targets - (intended object of the processing): user utterance, system re-
    sponse, tool output, url,
  - values - (object of the manipulation rules): sentimentClass-positive,
    dialogAct-agree, entity-locationCountry, tool-bingNews, etc.

ALDS scripts are e.g., used for realizing dialog scenarios focused on the acquisition of the user's attitudes and affective states in relation to the set of topics
of interest of the user (detecting high positive (Tab. 2) or negative sentiment
(Tab. 3) in a user's utterance, detecting topic of interest and affective states
associate with it (Tab. 4)).

Table 2. Example of the dialog scenario, triggered by a high positive arousal detected
in the user utterance

User: I am sooooo happy that I could see them live!!
- Annotation: DA-Statement SC-1 NS--1 PS-3
- ALDS matching condition: if-utterance-highArousalPos (3)
System: good to hear it :)
System: what was so special about it?

ALDS scenarios are also used for gaining insights on the attitudes towards
topics which are in the focus of attention of whole Internet communities (i.e.,
information on 'hot topics', which are automatically acquired through a set of
tools from the system actuator layer from news aggregator websites such as
http://news.google.com) and to strengthen communication cooperation with a
user by providing the feeling of participation in joint activities [1] (e.g., initial
message exchanges to introduce the system, if the user interacts with it for the
first time).

Table 3. Example of the dialog scenario, aiming at acquisition of user's topics of interest and the affective states related to it

```
...
System: Tom, any topics you are especially passionate about?
System: What would you like to talk about?
- ALDS matching cond.: SR-'what would you like to talk about?'
User: maybe something about champions league
- Annotation: DA-Statement UI-champions_league NS--1 PS-2
- ALDS scenario matching condition: if-utterance-UI
(champions league)
System: champions league you say ...Did you see this article?
"CONCACAF Champions League important for MLS - Garber"
(http://tinyurl.com/yfe4ej9) Does it sound like anything
of interest for you?
User: no, not really...
- Annotation: DA-Reject LC-Negate:Funct:CogMech:Excl:
- ALDS scenario matching cond.: Dialog act class = Reject
System: i see...
System: but can you tell me what do you find so interesting
about champions league? :)
...
```

Table 4. Example of the dialog scenario, triggered by a high negative arousal detected in the user utterance

```
User: for example the government in my country disturbs me
very much
- Annotation: DA-Statement SC--1 NS--4 PS-1
- ALDS matching condition: if-utterance-highArousalNeg (-4)
System: really??
System: what makes you feel this way?
```

The dialog scenario file consists of a number of command lines. Each command line describes a single user-system message exchange. The command line might further include an arbitrary number of sub-commands specifying the intermediate steps, actions applicable and if-then-else type statements, conditioning the realization of a consecutive sub-command based on true-false values returned for a particular statement. The final sub-command provides a system response generation instruction that incorporates symbols detected by the system in the ongoing dialog scenario. The ALDS commands are processed in a sequence until the exit condition is reached. The ALDS commands are extensible, i.e., new perception capabilities can be defined to add novel scenario triggers or conditioning parameters, without affecting the previously defined ones. Similarly, a new actuator tool can be used to specify and realize new dialog scenarios.

5.2   Affect Listener AIML

In the current realization of Affect Listener systems, the Affect Listener AIML[9] set of response patterns (AL-AIML), provids a robust fall-back mechanism capable to generate system responses for a range of inputs which do not match activation cues of the ALDS scenarios or the rule-based action selection mechanism used by the Dialog and Interaction Management. As presented above, the tasks of Affect Listener systems differ from tasks of domain specific dialog systems (e.g., ticket reservation, guidance systems). The requirements for Affect Listener applications include their capability to acquire users' affective states, while engaging in an open-domain, real-time communication with Internet users. While detection and acquisition of affective states is mediated by the system's perception layer, and mostly realized by specific affect state acquisition scenarios implemented in ALDS scripts, the capability to respond to a wide range of utterances is provided via an adapted AIML set. Response candidates generated based on AL-AIML are annotated in the perception layer and analysed by Dialog and Interaction Management component. System response is selected based on the dialog context and a set of response selection rules implemented in the control layer. The AL-AIML adaptation is based on the standard ALICE set [32], which was modified to provide character traits associated with active listening. The hypothesis is that such system characteristics will facilitate the acquisition of affective states. The AL-AIML set was created, aiming at encouragement of users to share information about their attitude, affective states and motivations, focusing on a user by mirroring questions and demonstrating the system's curiosity and interest; refraining from sounding too elaborate or providing extensive factoid knowledge about chatbot technology. This version of the AL-AIML set contains 14465 patterns, 15550 response instructions and 6918 srai substitution rules.

5.3   User Adaptation Mechanism

The User Adaptation Mechanism was introduced to facilitate establishing rapport with a user. Rapport can be defined as a feeling of connectedness that seems to arise from rapid and contingent positive feedback between partners and is often associated with socio-emotional processes. In [21], Reeves and Nass demonstrate that users prefer systems that become more like themselves over time over those which maintain a consistent level of similarity, even when the resultant similarity is the same. Gill et al. state that emphasizing commonalities and de-emphasizing differences is associated with increased solidarity and building rapport [6] and furthermore that this can also be achieved indirectly through the process of mirroring in which one person adopts some aspects of the behaviour of the other one. Our hypothesis is that establishing rapport with users via textual communication can be partially achieved by synchronizing with or mimicking the user's communication style as well as by providing textual back-channeling and signs of attention. This hypothesis, as well as the one, which postulates

---

[9] Artificial Intelligence Markup Language [32].

that adaptation to the user's communication style facilitates the acquisition of affective states will be tested in the experimental settings.

The described mechanism relies on the detection of user-specific textual communication features (perception layer), on monitoring a set of thresholds defined for deciding on the usage of selected synchronization and mimicking functionalities and the scope of their application (control layer), and on the postprocessing of system responses (actuator layer). The examples of mimicking and synchronization mechanisms include adaptation to a user regarding system response times, surface features of a user's communication style (e.g., usage of punctuation marks, capitalized or small letters), usage of emoticons or lexical choice. The decision on the application of a particular synchronization or mimicking functionality is made after the Dialog and Interaction Management component registers a consistency in a user's communicative style (e.g., a user uses emoticons more frequently than a predefined threshold). After a suitable postprocessing is chosen (e.g., usage of emoticons in the system responses based on the detection of strong valence in system responses [31]), the mechanism alters system responses as long as a particular aspect of a user's communication style remains constant.

6   Evaluation Settings

The evaluation scenario foreseen for Affect Listener systems include testing their performance in two tasks: realizing natural language-based communication and acquiring affective states from the users. System evaluation scenarios include tests with Internet users and tests with users in experimental laboratory settings capable to measure users' physiological emotional responses. The assessment of the system will be conducted by human assessors, and in an applicable scope, based on the automatic analysis of logs of system-user interactions.

Evaluation of the system by human assessors will provide data on users' subjective experiences from interactions with the system and the overall system performance in achieving its goals in the foreseen task (i.e., acquiring affective states of the users). For the Affect Listeners evaluation scenario we plan to perform the following types of human assessor-based tests:

– tests with users of a selected discussion group, followed by an online questionnaire where test participants will be asked to report their individual experience from interactions with the system in quantitative and qualitative ways,
– tests with Internet users, where user-system message exchanges will be accompanied by an input field through which users can select a numerical rating that represent their subjective feeling on the system's capability to preserve the dialog coherence, or users interest and satisfaction from the ongoing communication.

Manual evaluation of the system performance and the analysis of the system-user message exchange logs is a resource- and time-consuming process. On the other hand, automatic and complete evaluation of the conversational system performance extends beyond the state of the art. This does not, however, rule out the applicability of automatic and semi-automatic tests to assess selected system capabilities. The acquired data assists the ongoing iterative system development process, by supporting evaluation of the introduced mechanisms, and various realizations of the systems, including evaluation of a range of approaches for the natural language generation and dialog management.

Examples for measurements which can be automatically derived include the number of messages exchanged, the timing of the messages submitted by a user and the system, sentiment polarity associated with utterances. We are also investigating the scope of application of automatic methods for measuring dialog coherence, described in the literature [20]. Further, we perform automatic analysis of the system-user interaction logs based on the LIWC dictionary to (among others) gain insights on the quantity and types of expressions related to affective states that appear in the system-user interactions logs. In the context of the laboratory scenario presented in the introductory section, we plan to focus on measuring the emotional responses of users to the messages generated by the system and test the effectiveness of dialog scenarios and affect-related (i.e., detection, control and generation) mechanisms implemented in the system.

7   Conclusions

In this paper, we introduced the concept and the constitution of Affect Listeners. The presented set of implemented core components for the detection of textual expressions of users' affective states and for managing the progression of the dialog was integrated in the initial realization of the system. This version demonstrated the system's capabilities to detect and classify a user's textual expression of affective states and to direct a dialog in a way that facilates recognition of the user's topics of interest and the acquisition of background knowledge related to these topics.

The modularity and extensibility of the described system architecture allows for a flexible creation of different realizations of the Affect Listener systems. The development of these task-oriented conversational systems creates an opportunity for an extensive testing of various approaches for modelling system-user interactions in an open domain system that communicates with a wide range of users and via various communication platforms. This includes testing of the applicability of a range of dialog management and natural language generation components.

The system application scenarios include its usage for querying individual users about their affective states in relation to various entities, events and processes, including those automatically detected by the system based on the analysis of online resources and those discovered during the communication with a user. With the introduction of the real-time human-system interaction capabilities we focus on the detection of the current affective states of a large number of the individuals and create a platform, which allows for a selective acquisition of those states. The aggregated data shall provide a basis for extending our understanding of the affective states of individuals, groups of people, relations between the occurrence of external events and collective group feelings, and how those form and spontaneously evolve over time.

Acknowledgments. The work was supported by a European Union grant in the 7th Framework Programme, Theme 3: Science of complex systems for socially intelligent ICT. It is part of the CyberEmotions project (contract 231323). Additional supported has been provided by the Austrian Federal Ministry for Transport, Innovation and Technology and the Austrian Federal Ministry for Science and Research.

References

1. Allwood, J.: The Structure of Dialog. In: The Structure of Multimodal Dialogue II, pp. 3–24. Benjamins, Amsterdam (1999)
2. Arafa, Y., et al.: Affective Interactions for Real-time Applications: the SAFIRA Project. KI 18(1), 30 (2004)
3. Bohus, D., Rudnicky, A.: RavenClaw: Dialog Management Using Hierarchical Task, Decomposition and an Expectation Agenda. In: Proc. of the Eurospech 2003, pp. 597–600 (2003)
4. Fellbaum, C.: WordNet: An Electronic Lexical Database. Bradford Books (1998)
5. Forsyth, E., Martell, C.: Lexical and Discourse Analysis of Online Chat Dialog. In: Proc. of the First IEEE Int. Conf. on Semantic Computing, pp. 19–26 (2007)
6. Gill, D., Christensen, A., Fincham., F.: Predicting marital satisfaction from behavior: Do all roads really lead to Rome? Personal Relationships 6, 369–387 (1999)
7. Kappas, A., Pecchinenda, A.: Don't wait for the monsters to get you: A video game task to manipulate appraisals in real time. Cognition and Emotion 13, 119–124 (1999)
8. Li, X., Roth, D.: Learning Question Classifiers. In: Proc. of the 19th Int. Conf. on Computational Linguistics, pp. 556–562 (2002)
9. Liu, H., Lieberman, H., Selker, T.: A model of textual affect sensing using real-world knowledge. In: Proceedings Int. Conf. on Intelligent User Interfaces (2003)
10. Mairesse, F., Walker, M., Mehl, M., Moore, R.: Using linguistic cues for the automatic recognition of personality in conversation and text. Journal of Artificial Intelligence Research 30, 457–500 (2007)
11. Mann, W., Thompson, S.: Rhetorical structure theory: Rhetorical structure theory: Toward a functional theory of text organization. Text 8(3), 243–281 (1988)
12. McGlashan, S.: Towards multimodal dialogue management. In: Proceedings of Twente Workshop on Language Technology 11, The Netherlands (1996)
13. Mihalcea, R., Liu, H.: A corpus-based approach to finding happiness. In: The AAAI Spring Symposium on Computational Approaches to Weblogs (2006)
14. Neviarouskaya, A., Prendinger, I.M.: Textual Affect Sensing for Social and Expressive Online Communication. In: Paiva, A.C.R., Prada, R., Picard, R.W. (eds.) ACII 2007. LNCS, vol. 4738, pp. 218–229. Springer, Heidelberg (2007)
15. Paiva, A., Prada, R., Picard, R.W.: Affective Computing and Intelligent Interaction. In: Paiva, A.C.R., Prada, R., Picard, R.W. (eds.) ACII 2007. LNCS, vol. 4738. Springer, Heidelberg (2007)

16. Pelachaud, C., Poggi, I.: Towards believable interactive embodied agents. In: Fifth Int. Conf. on Autonomous Agents workshop on Multimodal Communication and Context in Embodied Agents (2001)
17. Pennebaker, J.W., Mehl, M.R., Niederhoffer, K.G.: Psychological aspects of natural language use: our words, our selves. Annual Review of Psychology 54, 547–577 (2003)
18. Picard, R.: Affective Computing. MIT Press, Cambridge (1997)
19. Prabowo, R., Thelwall, M.: Sentiment Analysis: A Combined Approach. Accepted for publication in Journal of Informetrics (2009)
20. Purandare, A., Litman, D.: Analyzing Dialog Coherence using Transition Patterns in Lexical and Semantic Features (2008)
21. Reeves, B., Nass, C.: The Media Equation. Cambridge University Press, Cambridge (1996)
22. Schank, R.C., Abelson, R.: Scripts, Plans, Goals and Understanding (1977)
23. Schröder, M., Cowie, R.: Developing a consistent view on emotion-oriented computing. In: Machine Learning for Multimodal Interaction, pp. 194–205 (2006)
24. Schröder, M., Cowie, R., Heylen, D., Pantic, M., Pelachaud, C., Schuller, B.: Towards responsive Sensitive Artificial Listeners. In: Fourth International Workshop on Human-Computer Conversation (2008)
25. Shaikh, M.A., Prendinger, H., Ishizuka, M.: Sentiment Assessment of Text by Analyzing Linguistic Features and Contextual Valence Assignment. Appl. Artificial Intelligence 22(6) (2008)
26. Skowron, M.: A Web Based Approach to Factoid and Commonsense Knowledge Retrieval, Doctoral Dissertation, Hokkaido University (2005)
27. Skowron, M., Araki, K.: Effectiveness of Combined Features for Machine Learning Based Question Classification. Special Issue on Question Answering and Text Summarization, Journal of Natural Language Processing 6, 63–83 (2005)
28. Skowron, M., Irran, J., Krenn, B.: Computational Framework for and the Realization of Cognitive Agents Providing Intelligent Assistance Capabilities. In: The 6th Int. Cognitive Robotics Workshop (ECAI 2008), pp. 88–96 (2008)
29. Stephan, W.G., Stephan, C.W.: An integrated threat theory of prejudice. In: Oskamp, S. (ed.) Reducing prejudice and discrimination, pp. 225–246. Erlbaum, Hillsdale (2000)
30. Tatai, G., Laufer, L.: Extraction of Affective Components from Texts and Their Use in Natural Language Dialogue Systems. Acta Cybernetica 16, 625–642 (2004)
31. Thelwall, M., Buckley, K., Cai, D., Paltoglou, G.: CyberEmotions project: Internal Report, September 2009, University of Wolverhampton (2009)
32. Wallace, R.: Don't Read Me - A.L.I.C.E. and AIML Documentation (2001), http://www.alicebot.com/dont.html
33. Weischedel, R., Brunstein, A.B.: Pronoun Coreference and Entity Type Corpus, Linguistic Data Consortium, Philadelphia (2005)
34. Williams, J.D., Poupart, P., Young, S.: Partially Observable Markov Decision Processes with Continuous Observations for Dialogue Management. In: Proceedings of the 6th SigDial Workshop on Discourse and Dialogue (2005)
35. Valitutti, A., Strapparava, C., Stock, O.: Developing Affective Lexical Resources. Psychology Journal 2(1), 61–83 (2004)

Nonverbal Synchrony or Random Coincidence? How to Tell the Difference

Fabian Ramseyer and Wolfgang Tschacher

University Hospital of Psychiatry, Department of Psychotherapy, Laupenstrasse 49,
3010 Bern, Switzerland
ramseyer@spk.unibe.ch, tschacher@spk.unibe.ch

Abstract. Nonverbal synchrony in face-to-face interaction has been studied in numerous empirical investigations focusing on various communication channels. Furthermore, the pervasiveness of synchrony in physics, chemistry and biology adds to its face-validity. This paper is focused on establishing criteria for a statistical evaluation of synchrony in human interaction. When assessing synchrony in any communication context, it is necessary to distinguish genuine synchrony from pseudosynchrony, which may arise due to random coincidence. By using a bootstrap approach, we demonstrate a way to quantify the amount of synchrony that goes beyond random coincidence, thus establishing an objective measure for the phenomenon. Applying this technique to psychotherapy data, we develop a hypothesis-driven empirical evaluation of nonverbal synchrony. The method of surrogate testing in order to control for chance is suitable to any corpus of empirical data and lends itself to better empirically informed inference.

Keywords: Nonverbal synchrony, psychotherapy, control for chance, surrogate testing, random sampling, permutation testing, research methodology.

1 Introduction

The phenomenon of synchronized interaction patterns has long been a focus of interest in nonverbal behavior research. Since Condon and Ogston [1] first described interactional synchrony more than 40 years ago, this phenomenon and variants thereof have been investigated in a broad range of contexts. Synchrony has been described in different areas encompassing, among others, mother-infant interaction [2-4], emotion [5], facial imitation [6], teacher-student interaction [7,8], social psychology [9,10], clinical interviews [11] and psychotherapy [12-14]. This diversity has led to numerous definitions and an overwhelming number of terms relating to similar, yet distinguishable phenomena (e.g. synchrony, mirroring, mimicry, imitation, congruence, convergence, coordination, attunement, matching, reciprocity). One important distinction between these terms can be based upon the dynamics of the nonverbal behavior displayed: while some researchers focused on static features (e.g. posture [14]), others tried to capture dynamic features of synchrony (e.g. movement [15,16]). A further distinction concerns the contextual cues (e.g. same posture, facial expression, emotion, movement) and general characteristics of movement (e.g. movement onset,

A. Esposito et al. (Eds.): COST 2102 Int. Training School 2009, LNCS 5967, pp. 182–196, 2010.
© Springer-Verlag Berlin Heidelberg 2010

speed, duration, complexity). In this paper, we will uniquely focus on dynamic features of synchrony: the coordination of patients' and therapists' body-movements during psychotherapy sessions.

For illustrative purposes, a recent study [17] will serve as an example of how to apply statistical tools that help distinguish genuine nonverbal synchrony from 'pseudosynchrony', i.e. the amount of synchrony one would expect to occur due to coincidental coupling between two interaction partners.

2 Comparing Genuine Synchrony with Pseudosynchrony

Synchrony as a global phenomenon in human interaction has been repeatedly reviewed (e.g. [18-20]) and its significance for interaction research seems obvious. Nevertheless, its empirical foundation has been challenged. The major criticism put forward was the lack of a control for coincidental synchrony [18-21] – synchrony that is caused by random coincidence. The problem is that 'genuine synchrony' may be indistinguishable from synchrony that would occur by chance (e.g. between two persons in the same room yet without visual and acoustical contact and currently not engaged in the same face-to-face conversation).

A first attempt at distinguishing genuine synchrony from synchrony expected by chance was McDowall's [21]. His investigation was initiated in response to studies published by Condon & Ogston [1] and Kendon [22]. He concluded that "... only one dyad out of 57 comparisons showed significantly more synchrony than expected by chance." (p. 963). His critical approach to synchrony, however, did not much influence further research. Ten years after McDowall's work, Bernieri and colleagues [23] took this idea to a higher level of sophistication: they worked with pseudointeractions "... by isolating the video image of each interactant and then pairing them with the video images of other interactants recorded in other interactions." (p. 245 [23]). Pseudointeractions thus generate datasets of 'face-to-face interactions' of persons who did not actually interact with each other. The rationale behind this approach is this: if synchrony is a genuine phenomenon that occurs in real interactions, it should be more pronounced in real interactions as compared to pseudointeractions. This was in fact true, as Bernieri et al. were able to show for interactions between mother and child [23]. In another study, disguised displays of movement [15] were used to attain the same effect while simultaneously controlling for artifacts that might be due to visual cues in pseudointeractions (e.g. both persons speaking at the same time). The paradigm of pseudointeractions has been applied to recent research [24] and appears to be well-suited as an empirical control condition for nonverbal synchrony.

Drawing from this approach, we have implemented a novel technique that uses the basic idea of pseudointeractions, which can be applied to a single face-to-face interaction [17]. Our pseudointeractions were generated on short time-scales by using automated surrogate testing algorithms.

Before moving to the technical details of our surrogate data approach, we wish to review a few considerations regarding study-design and methodology that generally apply to research on nonverbal synchrony. After each paragraph, we provide examples of applications to the domain of nonverbal behavior research, putting a main focus on a recent study [17] that will be described in more detail in paragraph 5.

3 Research Methodology

3.1 Hypothesis-Testing vs. Hypothesis-Generating Studies

As a general starting point, the specific type of research question determines which research approach can answer that question. Research questions may target the following domains [25]:

- definition (nature/definition of X)
- description (existence, appearance or history of X)
- quantification (amount/frequency/intensity of X)
- covariation (relationship between X and Y)
- comparison (quantified difference between X and Y)
- measurement (reliability, objectivity, validity of measure X)

In psychology – and related fields as well – an important distinction is made between studies that test specific hypotheses (hypothesis testing) and studies that are used to generate new hypotheses. Depending on the present state of knowledge in a field, one may observe a dominance of hypothesis-testing research with a sound and broad empirical foundation, many replicated, independent findings and good theoretical foundation (e.g. the association between patient-therapist relationship quality and outcome of psychotherapy [26,27]). In research areas still new and less established, and with less solid backing from empirical studies (e.g. the association between therapist age and treatment outcome [28]), the generation of hypotheses may be more dominant. In a simplifying way, one can state that within established fields, hypothesis-testing studies predominate, whereas in less developed fields, hypothesis-generating strategies will be in the foreground.

Examples of applications in nonverbal behavior research in psychotherapy:

Some of the first – and to date now classical – studies on nonverbal synchrony did not use hypothesis-driven strategies: The seminal work of Condon & Ogston [1], for example, was rather an anecdotic, explorative account of what kind of associations these researchers found in dyadic interaction. The same holds true for work done by Scheflen [14,29], who reported instances of synchronous nonverbal behavior from single exemplary cases of psychotherapy sessions. Newer studies by e.g. Geerts et al. [11,30] base their hypotheses on previous studies and established findings.

3.2 Sample versus Convenience Sample

When conducting an experiment, interviewing people, observing interaction, or using any other form of data collection, a researcher is often interested in drawing a representative sample of data from which generalizable conclusions can be drawn. Usually such generalizability is of importance, thus the selection of subjects is crucial to attain this goal. One convenient way to obtain data would be to interview, assess or measure those subjects that are closest at hand and easiest to access: this strategy is called convenience sampling or opportunity sampling (e.g. recruiting all the members of one's laboratory). While such data may yield interesting results per se, their generalizability is questionable because convenience samples tend to be very selective, i.e. the results may not be valid for other groups. The generalizability depends primarily on the heterogeneity or homogeneity of the convenience sample, which would have to be assessed or guessed by comparing the convenience sample with the general population.

A much stronger scientific case can be made by drawing a random sample from a given population. In a truly randomized sampling process, each element/member of a population will have an equal probability to be included in the sample. Within the bounds of the chosen population, a random sampling process yields good generalizability.

Examples of applications in nonverbal behavior research:

The often-cited study by Charny [12] used one single therapy session where nonverbal imitation and progress within the session were investigated. This session pertains to the category of convenience samples; it was recorded from an ongoing therapy. Another prominent study by McDowall [21] used three minutes of one single group-discussion to analyze nonverbal synchrony. Further studies, e.g. LaFrance [8], do not specify how the sample was drawn.

3.3 Experimenter Effect

An important source of bias originates from the investigator conducting the experiment: whether this person is directly involved in the process of data-acquisition or not can be crucial, because his/her hypotheses and preconceptions tend to consciously (or subconsciously) influence subjects, measurements and judgements. The dangers of this so-called experimenter effect have been first extensively described by Rosenthal [31]. The easiest way to circumvent such influences is to separate data acquisition from data analysis. This is especially important when direct social interactions between investigators and subjects constitute a part of the data-acquisition process (such as in interviewing the subjects).

Examples of applications in nonverbal behavior research:

If an investigator interested in nonverbal synchrony were to analyze psychotherapies conducted by him- or herself, the investigator's own nonverbal behavior would either consciously or subconsciously be influenced by his or her hypotheses. Therefore, data generated by the investigator would have to be excluded from analysis. This potential bias was inherent in e.g. the study by Navarre [32], who himself formulated hypotheses on nonverbal behavior and later on conducted psychotherapies for this research. A clear distinction between the person conducting therapy and the person doing the analysis was implemented in the fine-grained analysis of one therapy session (30 minutes duration) by Scheflen [29].

3.4 Blinding of Subjects, Experimenters, Raters, Statisticians

The same principles that hold for investigators also apply to subjects and further persons involved in an experiment (e.g. raters, experts): to rule out bias, subjects must be blind with respect to the hypotheses tested.

Examples of applications in nonverbal behavior research:

Many studies on the so-called chameleon effect [9] implemented investigators' secret confederates who either mimicked subjects or not. In these studies, subjects were unobtrusively debriefed afterwards to check whether they had become aware of unusual behavior of the confederate. However, the standard double-blind paradigm of medical studies is not feasible in psychotherapy research or when working with confederates. Most studies that used raters (e.g. the study on the effect of postural congruence on client's perception of empathy [33]) had their raters blinded to the hypothesis under investigation or to the categories of interactions used. Raters who analyze recorded interactions of such studies should thus not be aware of the individual experimental conditions (e.g. mimicry vs. anti-mimicry). Additionally, raters were unaware of whether confederates were present or not.

4 Statistical Considerations

Controlling possible biases on the part of data acquisition is one important step in order to achieve sound empirical data. Further crucial considerations are mandatory when it comes to statistical evaluation. Depending on the nature of the hypotheses formulated beforehand, statistical analysis can either be descriptive (e.g. for hypotheses of definition or description), or inferential (using tests in order to confirm or disconfirm hypotheses). The scaling properties of the data define which statistical tests are applicable. Current statistical software packages offer a wide range of preprogrammed tests and analyses suitable for the most common cases (e.g. interval-scaled data, ordinal-scaled data).

Before these tests are applied to raw data, several caveats have to be taken into account. Especially in the domain of probabilistic testing (e.g. t-test, ANOVA, etc.), the number of possible comparisons has to be factored into the probabilities applied. The most common form of correction for this inflation of probability is the Bonferroni-correction [34,35]. This correction accounts for the increasing chance of accidentally finding a significant result only because of the number of performed tests or comparisons (out of 100 tests, 5 are bound to be significant by chance when the significance criterion is set at $p < .05$).

Surrogate testing is an elegant way to control for chance findings. Variants of this method are known under different terms: bootstrap, jackknife, randomization test, permutation test. All these approaches rely on the original data itself and produce new, surrogate datasets by rearranging the original data [36]. The term bootstrapping has its origin in the tales of Baron Münchhausen, who pulled himself out of a swamp on his own bootstraps. This is the basic idea in all surrogate data methods: producing 'new' data by utilizing an already available original dataset. Such approaches are primarily used for the estimation of confidence intervals and statistical testing. Usually, numerous surrogate samples are produced (hundreds to millions of datasets). These new, rearranged samples can be distinguished on two dimensions: sample size and sampling method. Fig. 2 shows the different methods used for this process.

Sample Size (for 1 dataset)

		Subsample	Full Sample
Sampling Method	Without Replacement	Jackknife	Randomization Permutation Shuffling
	With Replacement		Bootstrap

Fig. 1. A 2 x 2 classification of resampling strategies (adapted from [35]). The multiple generated new datasets can use any of the strategies shown.

The bootstrapped, 'new' datasets can be compiled either by consecutively taking random items, values, etc. from the original data (without replacement) or by using one item of the original data and leaving this item in the available data (with replacement). The different methods can be described in terms of drawing numbers from a hat:

- Jackknife: systematically recomputing the statistical estimates while leaving out one observation at a time from the sample set. From this new set of "observations" new estimates are computed. Mainly used to detect outliers.
  Drawing from a hat; after each draw calculating statistics for the remaining items inside the hat.
- Randomization, Permutation, Shuffling: Altering the sequence- and/or time structure of data.
  Drawing from a hat; keeping the drawn item until a new set has been assembled.
- Bootstrap: randomly drawing items from the pool of all observations.
  Drawing from a hat; noting the item number and putting back the item after each draw (one number may be drawn multiple times).

The choice between the three methods depends mainly on theoretical and logical considerations. Sampling with replacement would make no sense when e.g. assigning individuals to (surrogate) teams, because by using the replacement sampling method, a bootstrapped team could be theoretically made up of identical individuals, while such a situation is impossible in the method without replacement (where each team member is assigned only once). For applications with few items/samples and where original and bootstrap data should be identical in terms of distribution and data characteristics, sampling without replacement produces better results.

Examples of applications in nonverbal behavior research:

To date, bootstrapping and other resampling methods have been rarely applied in the nonverbal behavioral domain. This lack would not be unassailable because the application of these strategies would be feasible in many studies where observations of behavior have been filmed, transcribed or otherwise recorded on media. This would even apply to some of the examples described above.

5 Calculation of Nonverbal Synchrony in Psychotherapy Sessions

In this section we describe a study on nonverbal sychrony [17] that was conducted with an awareness of the problems discussed above.

Hypotheses

As mentioned in the introduction, nonverbal synchrony has hitherto been studied under various conditions and in different fields of face-to-face interaction. Therefore – in contrast to previous explorative accounts – in our empirical study on nonverbal synchrony in psychotherapy [17], specific hypotheses were formulated that encompassed previous results reported in the literature. One result that had been repeatedly found concerned the association between nonverbal synchrony and the relationship quality of the persons engaged in the interaction.

Hypothesis 1: A positive correlation exists between the amount of nonverbal synchrony and the quality of the therapeutic relationship rated by patient and therapist.

A related association concerns the relation between nonverbal synchrony and the success of the therapeutic intervention. This entails the following hypothesis:

Hypothesis 2: Nonverbal synchrony predicts global success of therapy. There is a positive correlation between nonverbal synchrony and success of therapy at the end of treatment.

Given the specificity of these hypotheses, we were able to refute or confirm these hypotheses using statistical inference. Confirmation of a hypothesis depends on the probability of achieving a similar result by pure chance. This probability is traditionally at $p < .05$, i.e. a probability of 5 percent.

Sample versus Convenience Sample

The population for our investigation on nonverbal synchrony consisted of therapies conducted at the psychotherapeutic outpatient clinic of the University of Bern [37]. Over 300 individual therapies were available, which had been recorded during the time period considered for this study (1996 to 2004). Based on previous findings that reported less synchrony in mixed dyads [38,39], only same-sex dyads were considered. Furthermore, technical necessities (VHS-quality, visibility of both interactants, restriction to verbal exchange without external constraints such as e.g. the use of a pinboard or similar device) limited the total number of therapy sessions available for random sampling. Figure 1 details the randomization process and shows remaining sessions after each step. Taken together, these conditions restrict generalizations to a certain degree: the results obtained apply primarily to (pure) verbal interaction of same-sex patient–therapist dyads in ambulatory therapy settings. In general, however, the random sampling procedure assures that every potentially usable therapy session has the same probability of being drawn for the study. This individual probability can be modified with stratified sampling: characteristics (strata) are defined and further

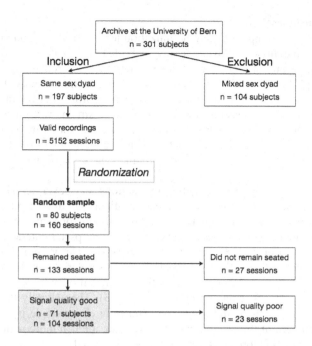

Fig. 2. Flowchart of random sampling procedure and exclusion criteria [17]

control the sampling process. In the nonverbal synchrony study, sex of dyads and phase of therapy (initial vs. final phase) were defined. Sampling 160 sessions out of 5152 sessions results in a probability of $p = .03$ for any individual session to be included in the study. Stratified sampling assigns different probabilities (depending on strata), but helps achieving a balanced random sample.

Experimenter Effect
The requirement of independence between investigator and therapist was met in our study by analyzing only those therapies that had been recorded years before the formulation of the research hypotheses, and that had been conducted by therapists other than the investigators involved. Owing to the comprehensive archive at the University of Bern, a retrospective analysis of nonverbal synchrony was feasible avoiding any experimenter effect.

Blinding of Subjects, Experimenters, Raters, Statisticians
Subjects (therapists and patients) in our nonverbal synchrony study had conducted therapies (in the years 1996 to 2004) independently of the research question (formulated in 2006). Thus they were unaware of their nonverbal movement behavior being subjected to an analysis of nonverbal synchrony later (ethical issues and data privacy had been considered here, of course). Because synchrony was calculated objectively using computer-vision algorithms, there was no need for blinding of investigators.

Statistical Considerations

Figure 3 details an example of the randomization test used in the study on nonverbal synchrony. As mentioned above, the original idea of permutation of interaction sequences as a means of chance control in synchrony research was put forward by Bernieri et al. [23], who produced video clips with pseudointeractions. These pseudo-interactions were generated by dividing split-screen recordings of interaction partners into two separate video streams. Each single video stream was then assigned an arbitrary different interaction partner, thus generating a surrogate video stream of partners who had never actually interacted. This pseudointeraction provided a base-level of pseudosynchrony, with which the genuine synchrony of interactions could be compared.

Starting from this idea of constructing interactions that never actually took place, we generated pseudointeractions within each patient–therapist dyad on a smaller scale: The entire interaction sequence was divided into one-minute segments that were then permuted segment-wise to generate the same pseudointeractions as in the example of Bernieri et al. [23], just at a smaller time scale. Permutation of original data was done with one-minute segments because this assured that the original structure of data was altered only in relation to the dimension of time, whereas the structure of movement bursts remained intact (see Fig. 3). Theoretically the permutation could be performed with smaller units (e.g. shuffling every single point of data). In keeping the structure of the original movement intact, a much more realistic comparison – i.e. a statistically more conservative test – is achieved.

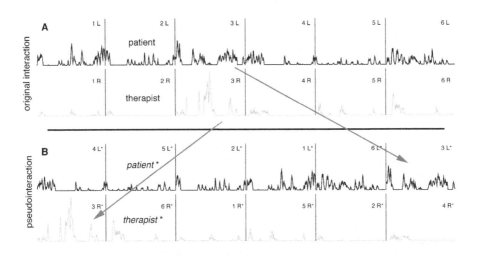

Fig. 3. Bootstrapping of interaction sequences (6 segments with 1min duration each).

Upper panel A: amount of movement of patient (L) and therapist (R), 6 segments (1 to 6) of 1 minute duration; $r = .36$ (correlation whole interaction).

Lower panel B: one (of $N = 100$) exemplary permutation of original data from panel A. The structure of 1-minute segments remains intact while the time-order of the interaction is shuffled (arrows, randomization without replacement); $r = -.19$ (correlation whole interaction).

Thus, for the movement data, interaction partner A's minute 4 may be paired with interaction partner B's minute 9 and so forth (see Fig. 3). Such a permutation of time-segments was done repeatedly ($N = 100$) in order to arrive at a large sample of pseudointeractions (i.e., a surrogate sample) with which the genuine interaction was then statistically compared.

A simple, two-sided z-test is used to compare the genuine synchrony value with the distribution of the 100 pseudosynchrony values. If genuine synchrony is two standard deviations above or below pseudosynchronies, then the deviation from randomness or chance level is deemed significant. Such a comparison can either be done directly at the level of single therapy sessions (one genuine synchrony vs. 100 pseudosynchronies, Fig. 4). Alternatively, a similar comparison may be performed at the level of various therapy sessions: for this group comparison, the 100 pseudosynchronies are averaged to one mean pseudosynchrony value. The comparison is then assessed using a two-sided dependent t-test.

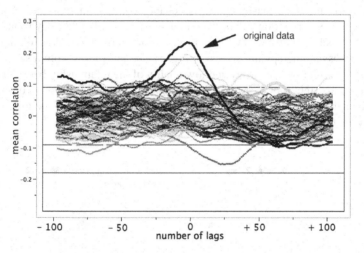

Fig. 4. Genuine cross-correlation coefficients at different lags (*bold black*) among ($N = 100$) bootstrapped pseudo cross-correlations

Technical Considerations

In order to perform these surrogate tests, a considerable amount of recursive computation is needed. These computations are automated because they would otherwise require too many manual steps. As described by Fan [36], until recently there existed no straight and easy ways to implement bootstrapping and related methods. We have used a customizable software environment [40] to program the steps needed. Here we briefly detail which procedures we utilized for our program:

1. generating random sequences for each interactant's windows
2. arranging the original data according to random sequence
3. performing synchrony calculations (cross-correlations of movement data)
4. repeating steps 1 to 3 (e.g. $N = 100$ times) to acquire the necessary distribution of pseudosynchronies.

The movement quantifications shown in Fig. 3 were derived from videotapes of psychotherapies by using a computer-vision algorithm called frame-differencing or motion energy analysis (MEA). This method has first been applied to face-to-face interactions by Grammer and his team at the University of Vienna [10,41]. His methodology was then adapted to the psychotherapy setting by Ramseyer & Tschacher [13,16], and independently by Komori et al. [42], and Nagaoka et al. [43].

The calculation of synchrony described here relies on cross-correlations between the two interactants' time-series by MEA. One suitable method for this calculation was described by Boker et al. [44-46], who also demonstrated a way of visualizing cross-correlation plots in color-coded form. Cross-correlations have further been successfully applied to physiological aspects of behavior movement research [47]. For more details, see the description of methods in Ramseyer & Tschacher [16].

Combination of Methodological Elements

We combined the three basic elements, chance-control, motion-energy analysis (MEA), and cross-correlation calculation, to achieve a novel and highly robust measure of nonverbal synchrony. Two exemplary cross-correlation plots of nonverbal synchrony in psychotherapy are shown in Fig. 5: The left plot is from a session (session # 1 of 40) with low synchrony and low quality of the relationship between patient and therapist, the right plot (session # 26 of 40) represents a later session of the same dyad with high synchrony and good relationship quality. Z-values for low vs. high synchrony are 0.51 and 2.39 respectively.

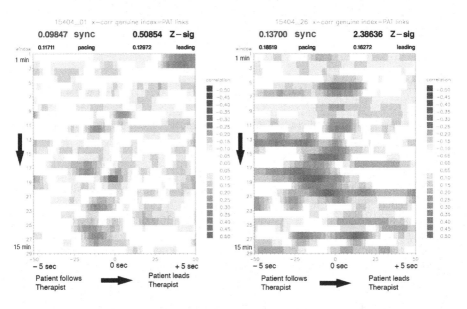

Fig. 5. Color-coded cross-correlation plots of low (left panel) vs. high (right panel) synchrony from one psychotherapy dyad. Gray areas indicate phases of high synchrony.

5.1 Results: Nonverbal Synchrony vs. Pseudosynchrony

Using the statistical methodology described above, we quantified nonverbal synchrony in psychotherapy sessions recorded routinely in an ambulatory psychotherapy setting. The comparison with pseudosynchrony was done at the group-level of all (N = 104) therapy sessions considered. This yielded a significant superiority of genuine synchrony versus pseudosynchrony (T = 5.92; p < .0001) with a moderate effect size [48] (Cohen's d = 0.49). This effect size is similar to results obtained with the original pseudointeraction approach by Bernieri [18,23], recently used in a study by Kimura & Daibo [24] (d = 0.63).

6 Conclusions

Our methodology comparing genuine interactional synchrony with pseudosynchrony yielded a highly significant result. The effect size of this finding was medium, which suggests that the phenomenon is not very easily detected. It was therefore necessary to establish a rigorous reference condition to which the measured phenomenon (nonverbal synchrony) can be compared (pseudosynchrony). We have demonstrated a surrogate testing approach for assessing nonverbal synchrony in psychotherapy. Further applications in established corpora of data are feasible and will help to clarify the highly divergent views in this field, where some researchers claim nonverbal synchrony has been over-evaluated [20] while others view synchrony as the basis of any interaction [18].

The methodology described here is suitable to many different domains. It is conceivable that synchrony found in nonverbal movement might be present in verbal channels as well. Verbal and paraverbal synchrony could thus be similarly assessed and compared to randomness.

The application of the concept of randomness described above has some pitfalls: randomness as conceptualized here depends on the fact that there is not an overarching periodicity that lies beyond the window-size used (if we were to compare two pendulums, i.e. a highly periodic system, with the described method, random synchrony would be as high as genuine synchrony). This implies that before its application, a test on stationarity and especially a check of periodicity should be applied.

Taken together, our findings in psychotherapy sessions support the view that synchrony indeed is a valid marker of relationship quality. One may say that nonverbal synchrony embodies relationship quality. Whether this applies to face-to-face interaction cannot be generalized from psychotherapy sessions alone, but with the methodology available, further research in other domains of interaction, interpersonal or man-machine interaction, will shed more light on the significance of nonverbal synchrony. This methodology can be extended to many other domains and promises to provide more rigorous empirical backing to findings in these fields.

References

1. Condon, W.S., Ogston, W.D.: Sound Film Analysis of Normal and Pathological Behavior Patterns. Journal of Nervous and Mental Diseases 143, 338–457 (1966)
2. Condon, W.S., Sander, L.W.: Synchrony Demonstratet Between Movements of the Neonate and Adult Speech. Child Development 45, 456–462 (1974)

3. Feldman, R.: Parent-Infant Synchrony and the Construction of Shared Timing; Physiological Precursors, Developmental Outcomes, and Risk Conditions. Journal of Child Psychology and Psychiatry 48, 329–354 (2007)
4. Isabella, R.A., Belsky, J.: Interactional Synchrony and the Origins of Infant-Mother Attachment: A Replication Study. Child Development 62, 373–384 (1991)
5. Hatfield, E., Cacioppo, J.T., Rapson, R.L.: Emotional Contagion. Cambridge University Press, Cambridge (1994)
6. Dimberg, U.: Facial Reactions to Facial Expressions. Psychophysiology 19, 643–647 (1982)
7. Bernieri, F.J.: Coordinated Movement and Rapport in Teacher-Student Interactions. Journal of Nonverbal Behavior 12, 120–138 (1988)
8. LaFrance, M., Broadbent, M.: Group Rapport: Posture Sharing As a Nonverbal Indicator. Group-And-Organization-Studies 1, 328–333 (1976)
9. Chartrand, T.L., Bargh, J.A.: The Chameleon Effect: The Perception-Behavior Link and Social Interaction. Journal of Personality and Social Psychology 76, 893–910 (1999)
10. Grammer, K., Honda, R., Schmitt, A., Jütte, A.: Fuzziness of Nonverbal Courtship Communication Unblurred by Motion Energy Detection. Journal of Personality and Social Psychology 77, 487–508 (1999)
11. Geerts, E., van Os, T., Ormel, J., Bouhuys, N.: Nonverbal Behavioral Similarity Between Patients with Depression in Remission and Interviewers in Relation to Satisfaction and Recurrence of Depression. Depression and Anxiety 23, 200–209 (2006)
12. Charny, E.J.: Psychosomatic Manifestations of Rapport in Psychotherapy. Psychosomatic Medicine 28, 305–315 (1966)
13. Ramseyer, F., Tschacher, W.: Synchrony: A Core Concept for a Constructivist Approach to Psychotherapy. Constructivism in the Human Sciences 11, 150–171 (2006)
14. Scheflen, A.E.: The Significance of Posture in Communication Systems. Psychiatry 27, 316–331 (1964)
15. Bernieri, F.J., Davis, J.M., Rosenthal, R., Knee, C.R.: Interactional Synchrony and Rapport: Measuring Synchrony in Displays Devoid of Sound and Facial Affect. Personality and Social Psychology Bulletin 20, 303–311 (1994)
16. Ramseyer, F., Tschacher, W.: Synchrony in Dyadic Psychotherapy Sessions. In: Vrobel, S., Rössler, O.E., Marks-Tarlow, T. (eds.) Simultaneity: Temporal Structures and Observer Perspectives, pp. 329–347. World Scientific, Singapore (2008)
17. Ramseyer, F.: Synchronisation Nonverbaler Interaktion in der Psychotherapie. Synchrony of Nonverbal Interaction in Psychotherapy. Dissertation. Bern (2008)
18. Bernieri, F.J., Rosenthal, R.: Interpersonal Coordination: Behavior Matching and Interactional Synchrony. In: Feldman, R.S., Rime, B. (eds.) Fundamentals of Nonverbal Behavior. Studies in Emotion & Social Interaction, pp. 401–432. Cambridge University Press, New York (1991)
19. Hess, U., Philippot, P., Blairy, S.: Mimicry: Facts and Fiction. In: Philippot, P., Feldman, R.S., Coats, E.J. (eds.) The Social Context of Nonverbal Behavior, pp. 213–241. Cambridge University Press, Cambridge (1999)
20. Rosenfeld, H.M.: Whither Interactional Synchrony? In: Bloom, K. (ed.) Prospective Issues in Infancy Research, pp. 71–97. Lawrence Erlbaum Associates, New York (1981)
21. McDowall, J.J.: Interactional Synchrony: A Reappraisal. Journal of Personality and Social Psychology 36, 963–975 (1978)
22. Kendon, A.: Movement Coordination in Social Interaction: Some Examples Described. Acta Psychologica 32, 101–125 (1970)

23. Bernieri, F.J., Reznick, S., Rosenthal, R.: Synchrony, Pseudosynchrony, and Dissynchrony: Measuring the Entrainment Process in Mother-Infant Interactions. Journal of Personality and Social Psychology 54, 243–253 (1988)
24. Kimura, M., Daibo, I.: Interactional Synchrony in Conversations About Emotional Episodes: A Measurement by The Between-Participants Pseudosynchrony Experimental Paradigm. Journal of Nonverbal Behavior 30, 115–126 (2006)
25. Barker, C., Pistrang, N., Elliott, R.: Research Methods in Clinical and Counselling Psychology. Wiley, Chichester (1998)
26. Horvath, A.O.: The Alliance in Context: Accomplishments, Challenges, and Future Directions. Psychotherapy: Theory, Research, Practice, Training 43, 258–263 (2006)
27. Wampold, B.E.: Psychotherapy: The Humanistic (and Effective) Treatment. American Psychologist 62, 857–873 (2007)
28. Beutler, L.E., Malik, M., Alimohamed, S., Harwood, T.M., Talebi, H., Noble, S., Wong, E.: Therapist Variables. In: Lambert, M.J. (ed.) Handbook of Psychotherapy and Behavior Change, pp. 227–306. Wiley, New York (2004)
29. Scheflen, A.E.: Communicational Structure: Analysis of a Psychotherapy Transaction. Indiana University Press, Bloomington (1973)
30. Geerts, E., van Os, T., Gerlsma, C.: Nonverbal Communication Sets the Conditions for the Relationship Between Parental Bonding and the Short-Term Treatment Response in Depression. Psychiatry Research 165, 120–127 (2009)
31. Rosenthal, R.: On the Social Psychology of the Psychological Experiment: The Experimenter's Hypothesis As Unintended Determinant of Experimental Results. American Scientist 51, 268–283 (1963)
32. Navarre, D.: Posture Sharing in Dyadic Interaction. American Journal of Dance Therapy 5, 28–42 (1982)
33. Maurer, R.E., Tindall, J.H.: Effect of Postural Congruence on Client's Perception of Counselor Empathy. Journal of Counseling Psychology 30, 158–163 (1983)
34. Nickerson, R.S.: Null Hypothesis Significance Testing: A Review of An Old and Continuing Controversy. Psychological Methods 5, 241–301 (2000)
35. Rodgers, J.L.: The Bootstrap, the Jackknife, and the Randomization Test: A Sampling Taxonomy. Multivariate Behavioral Research 34, 441–456 (1999)
36. Fan, X.: Using Commonly Available Software for Bootstrapping in Both Substantive and Measurement Analyses. Educational and Psychological Measurement 63, 24–50 (2003)
37. Grawe, K.: Psychological Therapy. Hogrefe, Seattle, Toronto (2004)
38. Grammer, K.: Strangers Meet: Laughter and Nonverbal Signs of Interest in Opposite-Sex Encounters. Journal of Nonverbal Behavior 14, 209–236 (1990)
39. Grammer, K., Kruck, K.B., Magnusson, M.S.: The Courtship Dance: Patterns of Nonverbal Synchronization in Opposite-Sex Encounters. Journal of Nonverbal Behavior 22, 3–29 (1998)
40. SAS Institute Inc.: SAS/STAT® 9.1 User's Guide SAS Institute Inc., Cary, NC (2004)
41. Grammer, K., Keki, V., Striebel, B., Atzmüller, M., Fink, B.: Bodies in Motion: A Window to the Soul. In: Voland, E., Grammer, K. (eds.) Evolutionary Aesthetics, pp. 295–324. Springer, Heidelberg (2003)
42. Komori, M., Maeda, K., Nagaoka, C.: A Video-Based Quantification Method of Body Movement Synchrony: An Application for Dialogue in Counseling. Japanese Journal of Interpersonal and Social Psychology 7, 41–48 (2007)
43. Nagaoka, C., Komori, M.: Body Movement Synchrony in Psychotherapeutic Counseling: A Study Using the Video-Based Quantification Method. IEICE Transactions on Information and Systems E91-D, 1634–1640 (2008)

44. Boker, S.M., Rotondo, J.L.: Symmetry Building and Symmetry Breaking in Synchronized Movement. In: Stamenov, M.I., Gallese, V. (eds.) Mirror Neurons and the Evolution of Brain and Language, pp. 163–171. John Benjamins Publishing Company, Amsterdam (2002)
45. Boker, S.M., Xu, M., Rotondo, J.L., King, K.: Windowed Cross-Correlation and Peak Picking for the Analysis of Variability in the Association Between Behavioral Time Series. Psychological Methods 7, 338–355 (2002)
46. Rotondo, J.L., Boker, S.M.: Behavioral Synchronization in Human Conversational Interaction. In: Stamenov, M.I., Gallese, V. (eds.) Mirror Neurons and the Evolution of Brain and Language, pp. 151–162. John Benjamins Publishing Company, Amsterdam (2002)
47. Derrick, T.R., Thomas, J.M.: Time Series Analysis: The Cross-Correlation Function. In: Stergiou, N. (ed.) Innovative Analyses of Human Movement, Human Kinetics, Champaign, IL, pp. 189–205 (2004)
48. Cohen, J.: Statistical Power Analysis for the Behavioral Sciences, 2nd edn. Lawrence Erlbaum, Hillsdale (1988)

Biometric Database Acquisition Close to "Real World" Conditions

Marcos Faundez-Zanuy[1], Joan Fàbregas[1], Miguel Ángel Ferrer-Ballester[2],
Aythami Morales[2], Javier Ortega-Garcia[3],
Guillermo Gonzalez de Rivera[3], and Javier Garrido[3]

[1] Escola Universitària Politècnica de Mataró (Adscrita a la UPC)
[2] GPDS Universidad de Las Palmas de Gran Canaria
[3] ATVS, Universidad Autónoma de Madrid
faundez@eupmt.es
http://www.gpds.ulpgc.es/biopassweb/biopass.htm

Abstract. In this paper we present an autonomous biometric device developed in the framework of a national project. This system is able to capture speech, hand-geometry, online signature and face, and can open a door when the user is positively verified. Nevertheless the main purpose is to acquire a database without supervision (normal databases are collected in the presence of a supervisor that tells you what to do in front of the device, which is an unrealistic situation). This system will permit us to explain the main differences between what we call "real conditions" as opposed to "laboratory conditions".

1 Introduction

Biometric system developments are usually achieved by means of experimentation with existing biometric databases, such as the ones described in [1]. System performance is usually measured using the identification rate (percentage of users whose identity is correctly assigned) and verification errors: False Acceptance Rate (FAR, percentage of impostors permitted to enter the system), False Rejection Rate (FRR, percentage of genuine users whose access is denied) and combinations of these two basic ratios, such as Equal Error Rate (EER, or adjusting point where FAR=FRR) and Detection Cost Function (DCF) [2].

A strong problem in system comparison is that most of the times the experimental conditions of different experiments performed by different teams are not straight forward comparable. In order to illustrate this problem, let us see a simple example in the motoring sector. Imagine two cars with the fuel consumption depicted in table 1. According to this table, looking at the distance (which is equal in both cases) and the speed (which is also equal) we could conclude that car number 1 is more efficient. Nevertheless, if we look at figure 1, we realize that the experimental conditions are very different and, in fact, nothing can be concluded. This is an unfair comparison.

It is well known that car makers cannot do that. Slope, wind, etc., must be very controlled and it is not up to the car maker. Nevertheless the situation is not the same in biometrics, because there is no "standard" database to measure performance. Each fabricant can use its own database. This can let to unfair comparisons, as we explain next.

A. Esposito et al. (Eds.): COST 2102 Int. Training School 2009, LNCS 5967, pp. 197–206, 2010.
© Springer-Verlag Berlin Heidelberg 2010

Table 1. Toy example for car fuel consumption comparison

Distance	100 Km	100Km
Speed	100 Km/h	100Km/h
Fuel consumption	8 liters	12 liters

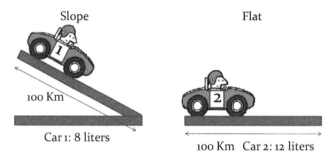

Fig. 1. Experimental conditions corresponding to table 1

We will assume that training and testing of a given biometric system will be done using different training and testing samples, because this is the situation in real operating systems in normal life. Otherwise, this is known as "Testing on the training set": the test scores are obtained using the training data, which is an optimal and unrealistic situation. This is a trivial problem where the system only needs to memorize the samples, and the generalization capability is not evaluated.

The comparison of different biometric systems is quite straight forward: if a given system shows higher identification rate and lower verification error than its competitor, it will be considered better. Nevertheless, there is a set of facts that must be considered, because they can let to reach a wrong conclusion.

Nevertheless, there is a set of facts that must be considered, because they can let to reach a wrong conclusion. We will describe these situations in the next sections.

A. Comparison of results obtained with different databases
When comparing two biometric systems performing over different databases, it must be taken into account that one database can be more trivial than the other one. For instance, it does not have the same difficulty to identify people inside the ORL database [3] (it contains 40 people) than in the FERET database [4] (around 1000 people). For a study of this situation, see [5]. Thus, as a conclusion, a given system *A* performing better on Database *DB1* than another system *B* performing worse on database *DB2*, is not necessarily better, because the comparison can be unfair.

B. Comparison of results obtained with the same database
When comparing two biometric systems performing over the same database, and following the same protocol (same samples for training both competing systems and the remaining samples for testing), it seems that the comparison is fair. In fact it is,

Fig. 2. Car testing in different scenarios. The car must be the same. It does not have too much sense to design a different car for each scenario and to present experimental results in different scenarios for different cars.

but there is a problem: how can you be sure that these results will hold on when using a different database? Certainly you cannot. For this reason, researchers usually test their systems with different databases acquired by different laboratories. In the automobile example, probably, you will get the fuel consumption in several situations (urban, highway, different speeds, etc.) because one car can be more efficient in a particular scenario but it can be worse in a different one. Of course the car must be the same in all the scenarios. It will be unfair to trim the car design before making the test (one design for urban path, one design for rural path, another one for highway, etc. This would be the schematized situation in figure 2, which obviously does not have too much sense).

However, this is the usual situation in biometrics, where a new classifier is designed for each scenario. Instead of this, we propose to design a classifier, to keep it fix, and then to apply it to a different scenario (a different biometric database).The usual approaches for biometric recognition, when moving from one database to another one, imply to fit a new model because different databases contain different users. Thus, there is a risk of fine-tuning on a given database. For instance, in on-line signature recognition, [6] describes the following: "for any given database, perhaps a composite of multiple individual databases, we can always fine tune a signature verification system to provide the best overall error trade-off curve for that database –for the three databases here, I was able to bring my overall equal-error rate down to about 2.5%- but we must always ask ourselves, does this fine tune make common sense in the real world? If the fine tuning does not make common sense, it is in all likelihood exploiting a peculiarity of the database. Then, if we do plan to introduce the system into the market place, we are better off without the fine tuning." This problematic can be illustrated in table 2.

From the example of table 2, if we only look at some results, we obtain the following conclusions:

a) Comparing (A, DB1) with (B, DB1) we conclude that system B is better.
b) Comparing (A, DB2) with (B, DB2) we conclude that both systems perform the same.
c) Looking at the last column we conclude that system A is the best.

Table 2. Comparison of systems *A* and *B* performing on two different laboratory databases and in a real scenario

system	DB1	DB2	"Real" scenario
A	1%	1%	1%
B	0.5%	1%	5%

In which comparison is interested the system seller? Probably in the most favorable one for his/ her product. In which comparison are we (the buyers) interested? Obviously the best characterization of biometric systems is the one that we achieve with a fully operating system, where users interact with the biometric system in a "normal" and "real" way. For instance, in a door opening system, such as the system described in [7-8].

An important point is that the system must store the biometric test samples if we want to be able to repeat the experiments in the future with a different algorithm. Unfortunately, it is not easy to set up this kind of experiments and for this reason most of the research is performed in laboratory conditions. In this case, we have the risk that a well-performing system, such as system B in table 2, may be unable to generalize its good performance in a real application.

A good way to avoid the unfair comparisons represented in figures 1 and 2 is by means of international competitions such as SVC (Signature Verification Competition), FVC (Fingerprint Verification Competition), etc. In this case, all the algorithms are tested using the same evaluation protocol. Even in this case, if we fully re-train a new classifier when moving from one database to another one, we are producing a very time consuming and inefficient mechanism.

In this paper we want to emphasize the main differences between databases collected under "real conditions", as opposed to "laboratory conditions". This is a milestone to produce applications able to work in civilian applications. Next sections summarize the main differences between our proposed approach and classical approaches.

1.1 Classic Design (Step 1)

Biometric system design implies the availability of some biometric data to train the classifiers and test the results. Figure 4 on the left summarizes the flow chart of the procedure, which consists on the following steps:

1. A database is acquired in laboratory conditions. There is a human supervisor that tells the user what to do. Alternatively, in some cases, programs exist for creating synthetic databases, such as SFINGE [9] for fingerprints. Another example would be the software Faces 4.0 [10] for synthetic face generation. Figure 3 shows a synthetic fingerprint and face generated with these programs. Nevertheless, synthetic samples have a limited validity to train classifiers when applied to classify real data.

Usually databases consist of a fixed number of users with a regular number of samples per acquisition session and a concrete number of acquisition sessions. Thus, the number of available samples and the time interval between samples is quite regular and homogeneous for the whole set of users.

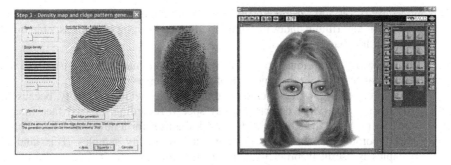

Fig. 3. Examples of synthetic fingerprint and face generation

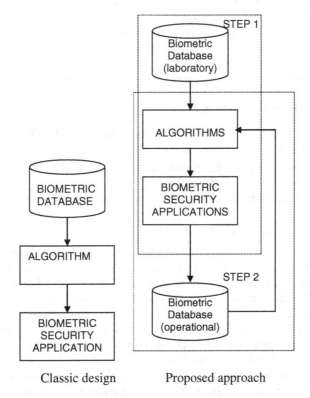

Classic design   Proposed approach

Fig. 4. Classic design (on the left) versus proposed approach (on the right)

2. After Database acquisition, a subset of the available samples is used for training a classifier, user model, etc. The algorithm is tested and trimmed using some other samples of the database (testing subset).

3. The developed system jumps from the laboratory to real world operation (physical access, web access, etc.).

This procedure is certainly useful for developing a biometric system, for comparing several different algorithms under the same training and testing conditions, etc., but it suffers a set of drawbacks, such as:

a) In real world conditions the system will be autonomous and the user will not have chance to obtain the guidance of a human supervisor.

b) Laboratory databases have removed those samples with low quality, because if the human supervisor detects a noisy speech recording, blurred face image, etc., will discard the sample and will ask the user for a new one. This implies that laboratory databases do not contain low quality samples. This kind of samples is useful in order to manage the failure to acquire/ failure to enroll situations.

c) Database acquisition with a human supervisor is a time consuming task. This implies that the time interval between recording sessions and the number of samples acquired in each session tends to be quite modest.

d) Real systems must manage a heterogeneous number of samples per user. Laboratory system developments will probably ignore this situation and thus, will provide a suboptimal performance due to mismatch between the present conditions during development and normal operation.

1.2 Proposed Approach (Step 2)

A more sophisticated approach involves two main steps (see figure 4 on the right). The operation can be summarized in the next steps:

1. Based on algorithms developed under the "classical approach", a physical access control system is operated.

2. Simultaneously to system operation, biometric acquired samples are stored in a database.

This procedure provides the following characteristics:

a) In general, the number of samples per user and the time interval between acquisitions will be different for each user. While this can be seen as a drawback in fact this is a chance to develop algorithms in conditions similar to "real world" where the user's accesses are not necessary regular.

b) While supervised databases contain a limited number of recording sessions, this approach permits to obtain, in an easy way, a long term evolution database.

c) Biometric samples must be checked and labeled a posteriori, while this task is easier in supervised acquisitions.

d) While incorrect (noisy, blurred, etc.) samples are discarded in supervised databases, they exhibit a great interest when trying to program an application able to manage the Failure to Acquire rate. In addition, these bad quality samples are obtained in a realistic situation that hardly can be obtained in laboratory conditions.

2 Multimodal Interface for Biometric Recognition and Database Acquisition

In this section we present a multimodal device specially designed to acquire speech, on-line signature, hand-geometry and face. This system has been developed under the frame of a national coordinated project between four universities, with the next main responsibilities: Universidad de Las Palmas de Gran Canaria (acquisition protocol and contact-less hand-geometry software), Universidad Autónoma de Madrid (box design, speech and on-line signature algorithms) and Escola Universitària Politècnica de Mataró (operational database collection philosophy and face recognition algorithm).

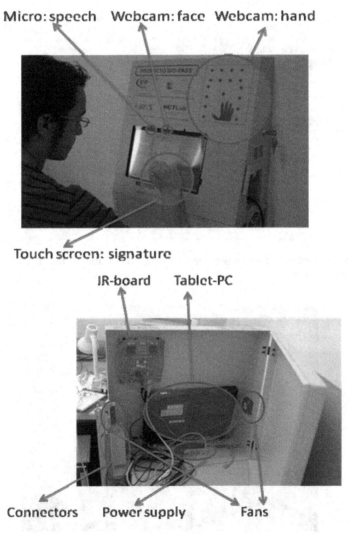

Fig. 5. Multimodal interface for biometric database acquisition (hand-geometry, speech, face and on-line signature). Frontal view (top) and rear view (bottom).

Figure 5 shows the aspect of the multimodal interface. While the system is prepared for four biometric traits, the acquisition protocol asks the user to provide his/her identity and two biometric traits (randomly selected). If both biometric traits are positively identified, the user is declared as "genuine". In case of tilt, a third biometric trait is checked. The core of this system is a hewlett-packard notebook with touch screen (suitable for online signature acquisition). The technological solutions behind each biometric trait are DCT-NN [11] for face recognition, SVM for hand-geometry, HMM for signature and GMM for speaker recognition.

Figure 6 shows some snapshots of the screen and figure 7 shows a physical installation in a wall for door opening system.

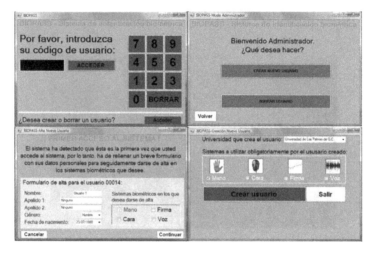

Fig. 6. Some snapshots of the screen: main menu, administrative functions, and enrolment screens (on the bottom)

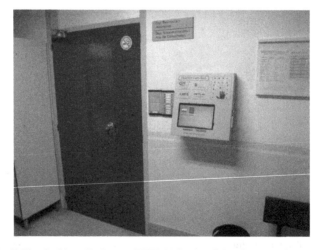

Fig. 7. Physical installation (at EUPMt) in a wall for door opening system

3   Real World: One Step Further from Laboratory Conditions

The goal of research should be to develop applications useful for daily usage. However, nowadays, most of the research is performed in laboratory conditions, which are far from "real world" conditions. While this laboratory conditions are interesting and necessary in the first steps, it is important to jump from laboratory to real world conditions. This implies to find a solution for a large number of problems that never appear inside the laboratory. They can be summarized in the following list:

- The user must face the system without the help of a supervisor.
- The system must be able to manage acquisitions with low quality (Failure to Acquire).
- The algorithms should consider the protocol to remove and to add users in an easy and efficient way (in a reasonable amount of time).
- The system must manage users outside the database ("open world" situation).
- The system must be able to detect coherence between training samples in order to ask for additional samples in case of troubles. In this sense, we have proposed an intelligent enrolment in [6].

In conclusion, the goal is not a fine trimming that provides a very small error in laboratory conditions. The goal is a system able to generalize (manage new samples not seen in the laboratory). It is important to emphasize that the classical Equal Error Rate (EER) for biometric system adjustment implies that the verification threshold is set up a posteriori (after knowing the whole set of test scores). While this is possible in laboratory conditions, this has no sense in a real world operation system. Thus, system performance measured by means of EER offers a limited utility.

Although a large number or different "real world" scenarios exist, and each one will presents its own particularities, most of them will have to deal with the main features described in this section.

4   Conclusions

In this paper we have presented a multimodal interface for biometric database acquisition. This system makes feasible the acquisition of four different biometric traits: hand-geometry, voice, on-line signature and still face image. In this paper we have emphasized the convenience of unsupervised database acquisition.

Acknowledgements

This work has been supported by FEDER and MEC, TEC2006-13141-C03/TCM, and COST-2102.

References

1. Faundez-Zanuy, M., Fierrez-Aguilar, J., Ortega-Garcia, J., Gonzalez-Rodriguez, J.: Multimodal biometric databases: an overview. IEEE Aerospace and electronic systems magazine 21(9), 29–37 (2006)

2. Martin, A., Doddington, G., Kamm, T., Ordowski, M., Przybocki, M.: The DET curve in assessment of detection performance. In: European speech Processing Conference Eurospeech 1997, vol. 4, pp. 1895–1898 (1997)
3. Samaria, F., Harter, A.: Parameterization of a stochastic model for human face identification. In: 2nd IEEE Workshop on Applications of Computer Vision, December 1994, Sarasota, Florida (1994)
4. Color FERET. Facial Image Database, Image Group, Information Access Division, ITL, National Institute of Standards and Technology (October 2003)
5. Roure-Alcobé, J., Faundez-Zanuy, M.: Face recognition with small and large size databases. In: IEEE 39th International Carnahan Conference on Security Technology ICCST 2005 Las Palmas de Gran Canaria, October 2005, pp. 153–156 (2005)
6. Jain, A.K., Bolle, R., Pankanti, S. (eds.): Biometrics, personal identification in networked society. Kluwer academic publishers, Dordrecht (1999)
7. Faundez-Zanuy, M.: Door-opening system using a low-cost fingerprint scanner and a PC. IEEE Aerospace and Electronic Systems Magazine 19(8), 23–26 (2004)
8. Faundez-Zanuy, M., Fabregas, J.: Testing report of a fingerprint-based door-opening system. IEEE Aerospace and Electronic Systems Magazine 20(6), 18–20 (2005)
9. http://biolab.csr.unibo.it/research.asp?organize=Activities&select=&selObj=12&pathSubj=111%7C%7C12&
10. http://www.iqbiometrix.com/products_faces_40.html
11. Faundez-Zanuy, M., Roure-Alcobé, J., Espinosa-Duró, V., Ortega, J.A.: An efficient face verification method in a transformed domain. Pattern recognition letters 28(7), 854–858 (2007)

Optimizing Phonetic Encoding for Viennese Unit Selection Speech Synthesis

Michael Pucher[1], Friedrich Neubarth[2], and Volker Strom[3]

[1] Telecommunications Research Center Vienna (ftw.), Vienna, Austria
pucher@ftw.at
[2] Austrian Research Institute for Artificial Intelligence (OFAI), Vienna, Austria
friedrich.neubarth@ofai.at
[3] Centre for Speech Technology Research (CSTR), University of Edinburgh, UK
vstrom@inf.ed.ac.uk

Abstract. While developing lexical resources for a particular language variety (Viennese), we experimented with a set of 5 different phonetic encodings, termed phone sets, used for unit selection speech synthesis. We started with a very rich phone set based on phonological considerations and covering as much phonetic variability as possible, which was then reduced to smaller sets by applying transformation rules that map or merge phone symbols. The optimal trade-off was found measuring the phone error rates of automatically learnt grapheme-to-phone rules and by a perceptual evaluation of 27 representative synthesized sentences. Further, we describe a method to semi-automatically enlarge the lexical resources for the target language variety using a lexicon base for Standard Austrian German.

Keywords: Speech synthesis, language varieties, phonetic encoding, graphem-to-phone, pronunciation lexicon.

1 Introduction

Data driven methods for speech synthesis, such as unit selection speech synthesis, or more recently HMM-based methods, induced a shift in perspective on various levels of speech processing. One of these levels is phonetic coding which is used as the prime lexical resource. But it has not the status of an independent, linguistically motivated system, anymore. Rather should the resources, specifically the set of symbols used therein, be adapted towards the data itself, reflecting the need to reconcile several conflicting tradeoffs that have to be handled in an optimized way.

The task in speech synthesis is to produce an acoustic output (speech signal) from a string of symbols defined as phonetic (or phonological) units. Such strings are retrieved from a lexicon or derived by grapheme-to-phoneme conversion which can be rule based or based on statistical methods. The set of symbols has usually been taken as given by definition, but as soon as one tries to transcribe actual speech from a certain language variety, the applicability of such a

A. Esposito et al. (Eds.): COST 2102 Int. Training School 2009, LNCS 5967, pp. 207–216, 2010.

set will easily come under scrutiny. A step further, when we attempt to cover varieties further away from a given standard variety (which is generally defining the coding in the linguistic resources), this problem becomes evident very quickly. Within a data-driven approach, however, whatever fine-grained differences there might be, most of the (phonetic) subtleties are covered by the data itself. Here, the task is to retrieve the optimal sequence of sound segments or models more or less directly from the data. An additional dimension emerges when we want to derive the phonetic encoding of language varieties from a standard resource.

The speech synthesis system we developed is based on the Festival Multisyn unit selection synthesis system [1]. Regarding the symbolic encoding used in the pronunciation dictionary there are three tasks with diverging constraints:

1. Automatic segmentation of speech data requires the models to be as distinct and coherent as possible ($\rightarrow$ rich phonetic transcription, many symbols), but prefers many instances of phones for building the models combinations ($\rightarrow$ condensed phonetic transcription, few symbols).
2. Unit selection requires that target segments are unambiguously retrievable ($\rightarrow$ rich phonetic transcription), but also requires high coverage of segment combinations, i.e. the sparsity problem ($\rightarrow$ condensed phonetic transcription).
3. Graphem-to-phone conversion methods (for unknown word handling) prefer less classes in the output, thus having a smaller potential to make errors ($\rightarrow$ condensed phonetic transcription).

Here we are focusing on unit selection synthesis where the optimization of the phone set is vital. In HMM based synthesis there is already a built-in optimization of the phone set by means of context clustering. Only phones, which are relevant according to the data are used in the clustering [2].

It would of course be desirable to have methods for automatically deriving a phone set from a corpus of recordings [3]. Since these methods are not robust enough, yet, we believe that our approach, using multiple phone sets to segment and synthesize speech and evaluating them through subjective listening tests, is justified.

In [4] we already described the methods how to model language varieties (Viennese dialects/sociolects) using a common language resource (Standard Austrian German). Within that project we gained the insight that it is not sufficient to simply define some alternative set of phone symbols and certain rules or methods to obtain the appropriate phonetic transcriptions from the standard resources. The problems are lexical and morphological differences, ambiguous mappings of phones and finally, the target set of phones itself can be disputed, especially in the light of a certain degree of variability regarding the phonetic realization of various phones in a given language variety (including the possibility that speakers do not strictly adhere to only one variety.)

Therefore we decided in a first step to encode a preliminary sample of lexical entries for the Viennese varieties in a phonologically rich form. This means that beyond a mere analysis on a (disputable) phonemic level, we also encoded systematic phonetic or contextually motivated differences, such as intervocalic lenition, final-devoicing of plosives, etc. as well as distinctions with uncertain status, such as open/close mid-vowels. In a next step we designed a set of phonologically motivated rules that operate on these codings, applying various mappings or merges in order to obtain smaller sets of symbols. Five of these sets were used to build synthetic voices which in turn were used to evaluate the qualities of each of these sets.

In the next session we describe the linguistic background of the language varieties (Viennese vs. Standard Austrian German) with special focus on problems occurring during voice building. In section 3 we present the different sets of phonetic symbols and the transformational rules with which we obtain them. Section 4.2 describes the test we performed with these sets in connection with voice building and the results of an evaluation on the resulting unit selection voices, and in section 4.1 we show how these results correlate with the performance of the relevant phone symbol sets within grapheme-to-phone conversion tasks. Finally, we give an outline of the architecture of the methods we use to obtain a large-scale lexicon for each of the language varieties.

2   Linguistic Background

Modeling language varieties for speech synthesis is a challenging task from an engineering viewpoint, but also from a phonological and phonetic perspective there are several questions that demand clarification: i) what is the set of phones in a certain variety, ii) are there clear correspondences between this set of phones and the standard variety, iii) can these correspondences be formulated in terms of phonologically motivated transformations, and iv) how consistent is the variety actually used?

Starting with the last question it turns out that speakers regularly oscillate between various Viennese varieties [5]. This may have to do with the fact that Viennese varieties are rather sociolects than dialects, hence associated with social groups rather than regions. (It seems that regional varieties associated with certain districts in Vienna, as described in the literature, have been lost some time ago.) However, speakers may want to signal a certain amount of affinity to a social group by using a specific language variety or at least displaying certain phonetic aspects of this variety. Nevertheless, from an engineering point of view sociolects and dialects behave alike, they are varieties of a certain language, either defined socially or regionally. Other triggers for one or the other variety are lexical: certain words or word forms (e.g., preterite) do not exist in Viennese, a speaker is automatically forced to perform a certain shift in speaking style. During recording we tried to exercise as much control as possible on these factors.

Regarding the first three questions the answers are positive, with certain provisos: i) some phones still exhibit a high degree of variation (mid vowels, lenis plosives/spirants) such that uncertainties remain, ii) various correspondences between phones contain ambiguities. (Examples: [a] → [ɐ], [ɒ]; [âɛ] → [æː], [a]), and iii) certain transformations have unclear status. The most prominent example for such a transformation is final devoicing, which is clearly operative in Standard Austrian German, but much less obvious in Viennese. It seems that the domain it applies to is the prosodic phrase, not the morpheme/word domain, and for sure it does not apply when a clitic pronoun starting with a vowel follows the consonant.

The strategy to deal with all these factors is to start with a basic lexicon that uses a symbol inventory designed upon phonological considerations. Referring to the last example, final devoicing is coded by a diacritic, intervocalic stops that may or may not have a phonetic realization as spirants are coded specifically as such etc. Of course, for the purpose of defining a symbolic base for a unit selection algorithm, this set is too rich and may lead to sparse data or even inappropriate classifications during voice building and unit selection. However, while building upon such a resource one can think of reintegrating the lexicon with a certain sets of rules in order to obtain phonetic representations of lexical entries and symbol sets that are more sound in number and hopefully more appropriate towards the data. Hope alone is not enough, therefore we designed several sets of transformational rules and a series of tests to be discussed in the remainder of this paper in order to assess the quality of the overall output in relation to the rule sets.

3   Phone Sets

Table 1 contains the description of the transformational rules that were used for defining the relevant phone sets. Most of them merge certain classes of phones, often sensitive to the phonological contexts, only two of them split complex phones (diphthongs, vowel-ɐ combinations) into smaller phone units.

Since it is impossible to test the effect of a single transformation rule applied to the set of phones in isolation, we designed an array of rule sets where each rule has some phonological motivation and chose 5 of these sets for further evaluation.

Table 1. Description of rules defining phone sets

Rule	description
merge_eschwa	merge [ə] with [ɛ]
merge_a_aschwa	merge [aɐ] with [a]
merge_a_aschwa_l	merge [aɐ] with [aː], add length
split_Vaschwa	split V-ɐ diphthongs into separate phones
split_diphthong	split all diphthongs into separate phones
rem_V_nasal	merge nasal vowels with non-nasal
neut_mid_v	merge tense mid vowels w. lax: [e] → [ɛ]
findev	merge final lenis w. fortis (fin. devoicing)
rem_findev	merge final lenis w. lenis (no fin. dev.)
merge_spirants	merge spirants with lenis, nasal or [v]
despirantize	merge spirants w. lenis plosives: [β] → [b]
rem_syllabic	merge syllabic consonants w. non-syllabic
rem_nons_gem	merge long consonants w. short, exc. [s]
rem_length	merge all long phones with short: [aː] → [a]

Table 2. Definition of phone sets by rules

Rule	P1	P4	P6	P7	P9
merge_eschwa	√	×	×	×	×
merge_a_aschwa	√	√	×	×	×
merge_a_aschwa_l	×	×	×	×	√
split_Vaschwa	×	×	×	√	×
split_diphthong	×	×	×	√	×
rem_V_nasal	×	×	√	√	×
neut_mid_v	×	×	×	×	√
findev	√	×	×	×	×
rem_findev	×	√	√	√	√
merge_spirants	×	×	√	√	×
despirantize	×	×	×	×	√
rem_syllabic	×	×	√	√	√
rem_nons_gem	√	√	×	×	√
rem_length	×	×	√	√	×
Number of phones	75	76	47	39	66

Table 2 shows the definitions for the different phone sets where √ stands for applying the respective rule, whereas × means that it is not operative. In the last row the number of symbols within the resulting phone set is shown, but notice that this number applies only to data obtained from Viennese dialect sources (see section 4.1); when data from the 'transformed' Austrian Standard is included, the numbers increase by 3-4 symbols.

The transformation rules only affect the set of symbols, not the lexical representations themselves. The rules do not give ambiguous outputs, so it is possible and easy to generate the corresponding lexical sources. In the following we describe various tests designed in order to evaluate the quality of the overall output with each of the variants of symbolic encoding.

4   Evaluation

4.1   Evaluation of Phone Sets for Automatic G2P Rules

The quality of automatic grapheme-to-phone conversion depends on the coherence or the mapping between graphemic symbols and phone symbols. Therefore we decided to use G2P methods as indirect evidence for the coherence of a given set of phones. For the initial recordings of Viennese dialect/sociolect, we used texts for which an orthography exists that reflects the phonological properties of Viennese dialect at least to a certain degree. These texts were used to automatically learn G2P rules from them. Since the 4 groups of texts obey different standards regarding orthography, we also created different lexica for each of the groups. It has to be mentioned that although the text sources listed below belong to different text genres (poetry, comics, plain text, songs lyrics), they were treated the same way while recording the speech data: each of the texts was split into a set of isolated sentences. The speakers had to read each of these sentences as a separate item, thus minimizing the chance of co-textual influences.

- **artmann.lex:** Isolated sentences from poems by H. C. Artmann [6] ("med ana schwoazzn dintn"). Orthography very close to the actual pronunciation of the dialect and very consistent. (1614 words)
- **asterix.lex:** Sentences from the comic "Asterix" in the Viennese translation by H. C. Artmann. Orthography less coherent due to mimicking of other varieties including the standard variety by orthographic means. (1194 words)
- **wean.lex:** Sentences from various sources, containing typical Viennese words and phrases. Orthography rather inconsistent. (1473 words)
- **ostbahn.lex:** Sentences from songs by Dr. Kurt Ostbahn. Orthography oscillates between orientation towards pronunciation and standard orthography. (391 words)

We were concerned that the standard Festival G2P rule learner is no longer state-of-the-art or inadequate for such small lexica. There was a "Letter-to-Phoneme Conversion Challenge" planned for 2006, but due to illness of the host it was never completed. However, preliminary results suggested [7] that Marelie Davel's and Etienne Barnard's called "Default & Refine" [8] works better for small lexica than "Pronunciation by Analogy" [9]. Marelie Davel kindly provided us her implementation of D&R.

The evaluation described in this section was motivated by the following questions: How consistent are the four sub-lexica? How much consistency do we lose by combining them? And how do the different phonetic encoding schemes fare with the G2P methods?

Since the sizes of our sub-lexica are different and we wanted comparable phone error rates, we evaluated the G2P rules by repeated random sub-sampling validation instead of k-fold cross-validation. This method randomly splits the dataset into training and validation data. For each such split, the classifier is retrained with the training data and validated on the remaining data. The results from each split can then be averaged. The advantage of this method (over k-fold cross validation) is that the proportion of the training / validation split is not dependent on the number of folds, i.e. if we want to compare the consistency of two sub-lexica, we can choose the amount of training data to be equal. The disadvantage of this method is that some observations may never be selected in the validation subsample, whereas others may be selected more than once. However, when the number of repetitions is large enough, our estimates of phone error rates should be reliable enough.

Our assessment of consistency was confirmed: artmann.lex is most consistent, followed by asterix.lex, and wean.lex. Figure 1 shows that for phone set P9 and a subset of 1200 words taken from artmann.lex only for training, the phone error rate in the held-out data is about 17%. Figure 1 also illustrates that artmann.lex is not consistent with asterix.lex. When 1200 words of asterix.lex were used for training, the phone error rate for the held-out data was around 19%, and testing with artmann.lex resulted in about 26% phone error rate.

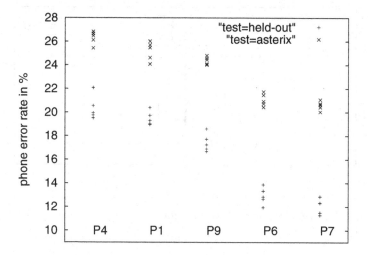

Fig. 1. Phone error rates, shown for 5 random splits of the artmann.lex: 1200 words were used for training, the remaining ones for testing. Each of the 5 phone sets was tested with the held-out data, and also with the entire asterix.lex.

Regarding the coherence of the tested phone sets, the results are a bit disappointing: the smaller the set of phones, the better the performance of the G2P component. One might be surprised that number is the only effective parameter in this experiment. Since the respective phone sets display different context sensitive splits and merges of phone symbols it could be possible that due to a better mapping to orthography one set with a larger number of phones outperforms the others. This is not the case. The conclusion we can draw from this finding is that the claim that a lower number of symbols enhances the performance of G2P methods is correct. This does, however, not tell much about the performance of unit selection speech synthesis, which will be the topic of the next section.

4.2 Evaluation of Phone Sets for Synthesis

For this evaluation we had 8 listeners that had to make pairwise comparisons between 27 prompts synthesized with the respective phone sets (270 comparisons in total). The unit selection voices are built from recordings of our male Viennese speaker. Since we primarily wanted to assess the segmental quality of the synthetic voices (or better: the different phone sets underlying them) relative to the perceived authenticity of the dialect, the subjects definitely had to be acquainted with Viennese dialect, but not to be native speakers of this dialect. The synthesized soundfiles are encoded in 16 bit, 16 kHz sampling rate and were presented to the subjects over a web-based application, the actual setting was that the subjects listened to the synthesized sentences with headphones.

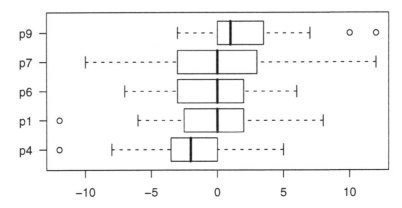

Fig. 2. Box-plots of pairwise comparison score for voice samples generated with different phone sets

Differences between P9 and P1, P9 and P4, and P9 and P6 turned out to be significant ($p < 0.05$) according to a Mann-Whitney-Wilcoxon test. In this evaluation, P9 scored as the best phone set.

Figure 2 shows the results of the pairwise comparisons for the different phone sets. The data for one voice i using a certain phone set consists of scores $s_j = w_{ij} - l_{ij}$, where $j \neq i$ and w_{ij} and l_{ij} are the numbers of comparisons won and lost, respectively, of voice i against voice j per listener.

The good performance of the P9 set can be partly explained by taking into consideration the actual diphone coverage of the 27 test sentences for the different phone sets. This would explain the relative superiority of P9 (only 4 diphones missing) over P6 (26 missing) and P7 (21 missing), but such a line of reasoning would leave unexplained the relatively bad performance of P1 (10 missing) and P4 (12 missing). What is important to note is that missing diphones do not produce gaps in the output, but invoke backoff rules individually defined for each phone set which are much more complex than the backoff rules used in the standard Festival multisyn system (always replacing a missing vowel with schwa). So what we actually evaluated were not the phone sets in isolation, but the phone sets together with their associated backoff rules, taking as implicit parameters segmental quality of the speech synthesis output and dialectal authenticity.

Although the significance of a listening test with only 27 test sentences can be disputed, we take it as the most indicative test for the overall quality of the system. Interestingly, the phone set that turned out as the best among the alternatives (P9) is the one with the most balanced number of phones. P6 and P7 gain their lower numbers mainly by merging nasal vowels with non-nasals and by abandoning length contrasts. P1 and P4 have more phone symbols because they retain spirants and syllabicity of nasals, which can be retrieved by the phonological context. It would be desirable to assess the question which types of processes increase or decrease the overall performance, but due to the large number of possible combinations it seems impossible to investigate the behavior of just one process/transformation rule in isolation.

Regarding the tasks with their intrinsic constraints presented in the introduction, it may be possible to optimize them separately. This would require an objective measure for transcription accuracy for task 1 (automatic segmentation) and an objective or subjective measure for constraint 2 (unit-selection). However, these measures are partly hard to obtain and a combination of the performance for each of the constraints is needed anyway, we decided to do a joint optimization through the subjective listening test described above.

5   Excursus: Conversion Rules for Dialects

To extend the available data for building dialect voices we recorded a large amount of speech data where the speaker had to read a text presented in standard German orthography. The speaker was instructed to "translate" the text into Viennese "on the fly", i.e., to use Viennese pronunciation of the words whenever possible. We tried to control the factors that would force the speaker to switch to the standard variety.

The problem was that while there exist lexical entries for all the words contained in the sentences, the phonetic coding corresponds to the Standard Austrian German variety. Therefore we defined a set of rules, similar to the rules used to obtain the different phonetic encodings, to transform these phonetic strings into Viennese dialect. These rules, however, produce multiple variants for many words: either the rule has ambiguous output per se or it is not predictable whether the rule applies or not.

However, for the automatic phone segmentation of the recorded speech data we generated lattices using all pronunciation variants from the transformed lexicon. During the segmentation process one variant is selected as the best fitting phonetic transcription given the acoustic data. With this kind of feedback loop it is possible to eliminate variants that do not exist or are wrongly predicted.

These transformation rules are primarily intended to obtain a phone segmentation of the recordings. The texts were selected for diphone coverage (with lexical stress, word, and syllable boundaries) by using the standard pronunciation, because at that stage we could not employ a validated Viennese pronunciation lexicon covering these texts. This compromise was based on the assumption that a good coverage of units and combinations of units in Standard Austrian German would coincide with a good coverage in the Viennese dialect/sociolect.

6   Conclusion

By meeting the challenge of creating synthetic voices of language varieties (in our case Viennese sociolect/dialect) by using resources developed for the standard variety, we faced the interesting fact that the optimal phonetic encoding is by no means straightforward. Since the task is neither to obtain maximal phonetic accuracy nor to develop a perfect phonological representation, the optimal encoding has to be decided upon by aspects of engineering, in particular G2P conversion, automatic segmentation, and, most important, unit selection synthesis. Based on our phone set evaluations in Section 4.1 and Section 4.2 one phone set turned out to be the best one for encoding Viennese sociolect/dialect. Still, there was an explicit trade-off: by choosing a set with an average number of phones we accept a higher phone error rate for the G2P rules, but get a better synthesis quality according to the subjective evaluation.

Acknowledgements

The project "Viennese Sociolect and Dialect Synthesis" was funded by the Vienna Science and Technology Fund (WWTF). The Telecommunications Research Center Vienna (ftw.) is supported by the Austrian Government and the City of Vienna within the competence center program COMET. OFAI is supported by the Austrian Federal Ministry for Transport, Innovation, and Technology and by the Austrian Federal Ministry for Science and Research.

References

1. Clark, R., Richmond, K., King, S.: Multisyn voices from ARCTIC data for the Blizzard challenge. In: Proc. Interspeech (2007)
2. Yoshimura, T., Tokuda, K., Masuko, T., Kobayashi, T., Kitamura, T.: Simultaneous modeling of spectrum, pitch and duration in HMM-based speech synthesis. In: Proc. of Eurospeech, September 1999, pp. 2347–2350 (1999)
3. Aylett, M.P., King, S.: Single speaker segmentation and inventory selection using dynamic time warping, self organization, and joint multigram mapping. In: 6th ISCA Speech Synthesis Workshop, Bonn, Germany (2007)
4. Neubarth, F., Pucher, M., Kranzler, C.: Modeling Austrian dialect varieties for TTS. In: Proc. Interspeech 2008, Brisbane, Australia (2008)
5. Moosmüller, S.: Soziophonologische Variation im gegenwärtigen Wiener Deutsch. Franz Steiner Verlag, Stuttgart (1987)
6. Artmann, H.C.: Sämtliche Gedichte. Jung und Jung, Salzburg und Wien (2003)
7. Damper, R.: Personal communication (June 2008)
8. Davel, M., Barnard, E.: Pronunciation prediction with Default & Refine. Computer Speech and Language 22(4) (2008)
9. Damper, R., Stanbridge, C., Marchard, Y.: A Pronunciation-by-Analogy Module for the Festival Text-to-Speech Synthesiser. In: SSW4 (2001)

Advances on the Use of the Foreign Language Recognizer

Rytis Maskeliunas[1], Algimantas Rudzionis[1], and Vytautas Rudzionis[2]

[1] Kaunas University of Technology, Kaunas, Lithuania
[2] Vilnius University Kaunas faculty, Kaunas, Lithuania
rytis.maskeliunas@ktu.lt

Abstract. This paper presents our most recent activities trying to adapt the foreign language based speech recognition engine for the recognition of the Lithuanian speech commands. As presented in our earlier papers the speakers of less popular languages (such as the Lithuanian) have several choices: to develop own speech recognition engines or to try adapting the speech recognition models developed and trained for the foreign languages to the task of recognition of their native spoken language. The second approach can lead to the faster implementation of the Lithuanian speech recognition modules into some practical tasks but the proper adaptation and optimization procedures should be found and investigated. This paper presents our activities trying to improve the recognition of Lithuanian voice commands using multiple transcriptions per command and English recognizer.

Keywords: Lithuanian speech recognition, transcriptions.

1 Introduction

For almost two decades the interest in the development of multilingual speech recognizers continues to be on a rise. It was proven that the multilingual speech recognition models could significantly speed up the development of recognition models for other languages. This is very important for less widely used languages (including the Lithuanian) since available speech corpora usually are not as rich as those for the more widely used languages or even those resources for training are absent. Below we briefly overview some of the experience gained by other researchers that could be valuable for similar studies.

Some basic terms such as the poliphone – phonemic units that could be used in the multilingual recognition and monophone – phonemes that don't have exact analogues in the other language – were discussed in [1]. E.g., there are no analogues for English phonemes DH (as in other), JH (as in jaw), TH (as in fourth) in French language, there are no phoneme SH in Spanish while this phoneme is very important (widely used) in Lithuanian, the Lithuanian R is pronounced entirely different than the sound marked by the same symbol in English, etc. The authors used the data driven approach to find the similarities between the phonemes in one language and the other. Those similarities have been obtained using speech corpora. This method is an alternative for an expert driven method which is more based on the linguistic intuition rather than statistical analysis. This study aimed to build monophone and poliphone

A. Esposito et al. (Eds.): COST 2102 Int. Training School 2009, LNCS 5967, pp. 217–224, 2010.
© Springer-Verlag Berlin Heidelberg 2010

models for 4 languages (British English, Danish, German and Italian). As the number of the phonemes in different languages differs, the experiments showed that it was possible to successfully identify the language, which particular utterance has been pronounced using the monophone data.

IBM researchers [2] performed the investigation of the transfer of the English based speech recognition system for the recognition of French speech. They selected 25 common poliphones for both languages and 24 specific English and 9 specific French monophones. Their tests of the bilingual speech recognition system in the laboratory conditions showed that an error rate for the French vocabulary was twice as high as for the English (14% versus 7%). It should be noted that later closer to real life testing conditions were used and the error rates observed, were higher than presented in this study.

A series of authors [3-11] (specifically the more emphasized studies by T. Schultz and A. Waibel) performed the investigations in the framework of the project GlobalPhone. It was started from the development of monophone and poliphone models for 6 languages [4]. The word error rate for large vocabularies was bigger than 40 % [5, 6]. Other studies were devoted to the development of methods that could improve the recognition accuracy such as the implementation of the articulatory features.

Recent studies performed by the researchers at Microsoft [12] showed that stable procedures for the multilingual speech recognition still aren't found since the same algorithms perform differently using clean speech and noisy speech signals.

Investigation of the possibilities to use the foreign language recognizer for the recognition of Lithuanian speech commands were started several years ago, more recent advances are offered in [13-19]. In the study [19] systematic analysis on how to transcribe Lithuanian diphones for the use in the English speech recognizer was offered. It was observed that the Lithuanian diphones (as well as vowels) are pronounced in a different way than English alternatives. The analysis was performed, in order to test how the English recognizer reacts to the Lithuanian diphthongs and vowels. 4 short Lithuanian words were selected for each of the 3 different possible stress cases. Those words possessed all possible Lithuanian diphthongs. Statistical analysis of the English recognizer reactions to the left and right components of Lithuanian diphthongs was performed. These results enabled to develop possible transcriptions for the analyzed 500 Lithuanian words vocabulary. Several subsets of this list containing 500, 100, 50 and 10 names were formed which enabled to evaluate recognition accuracy when vocabulary size varies. For each name – surname combination in the list, all possible transcriptions were generated and one best transcription has been found for each of the speakers. The search for the best transcription for each speaker enabled to improve the recognition accuracy comparing with the case when statistically best transcriptions were used. This principle could be used for the initialization of possible transcriptions.

The analysis of the research activities enabled us to perform some conclusions. First, it is possible to develop multilingual speech recognition models which could lead to the acceptable recognition results. Second, the multilingual models usually achieve the lower recognition accuracy than the monolingual recognizers. Third, the multilingual models allow to achieve acceptable results for some applications faster and to reduce adaptation expenditures. And finally it should be noted that there are no clear methodology how to adapt the speech recognition model for the particular application.

It should be once more noted that we are trying to implement the foreign language recognition engine for the recognition of the Lithuanian voice commands using the manipulation of the phonetic transcriptions only. The primary reason for this is the "economy": to develop some limited vocabulary practical application as soon as possible and to comply with as many industrial standards as possible. The need to comply with industry standards suggested the use of the Microsoft speech recognition engine. But the use of this recognizer limits the possibilities to manipulate the acoustic models database and leaves only the opportunity to model the transcriptions.

2   The Advances on the Use of Foreign Language Recognizer

In this study we've chosen the same standard Microsoft English speech recognizer for the Lithuanian language applications and deeper analyzed some aspects of the recognition using the same two vocabularies (long and short voice commands) as in our previous works [13-18]. Thus further trying to find out, how the English recognition engine reacts to the Lithuanian voice commands, spoken by the unprofessional Lithuanian speakers and in which way the recognition accuracy could be improved.

2.1   Recognition Methods for the Long Voice Commands Using the Transcription Manipulation

Based on our previous experiences the two stage transcription modeling method for the long Lithuanian words was formed. In the first stage we generated the two transcriptions (specific transcription sets for each word) according to the principles formed in [19]. The recognition accuracy of these transcription sets (long voice commands) was verified using the large enough corpus (more than 30 speakers, different voice characteristics). Poorly recognized words (recognition accuracy less than 95 %) were noted and passed for the improvement in the second stage.

The second stage is the so called "training stage" where we tried to minimize the WER, by generating all possible transcriptions and iteratively choosing the best of them. At first we generated all possible transcriptions using the principles mentioned in the previous works. Typically the number of possible transcriptions for the long voice commands was quite high, e.g. usually more than 500 for each command. This high count transcription set was then passed to the recognizer (using the training corpus, acquired from different speakers, each pronouncing a poorly recognized phrase at least 100 times) and the chosen transcriptions are noted. The experiment was repeated using that chosen transcription set, till few best transcriptions remain. The recognition accuracy was then rechecked for the improvement using the corpus from stage 1. The recognition accuracy improvement task could be viewed as a task of optimization in the space of all possible transcriptions (finding an optimal transcriptions subset for the given task).

We skipped the mathematical formalisms in this paper since they do not form the main value of the presentation. The results (excerpts) from such experiments for the Lithuanian long command ("gudas audrius" in this case) are displayed in the table 1

Table 1. The result comparison, when 22, 10, 4 and 2 optimized transcriptions were used for the Lithuanian voice command "gudas audrius", compared to two original 2 poorly recognized transcriptions (noted as 2 PK)

	The number of transcriptions used				
	22	**10**	**4**	**2**	**2 PK**
Standard deviation	15,72	15,63	18,71	22,49	19,13
Average recognition accuracy, %	**79,79**	78,93	73,79	64,50	24,79

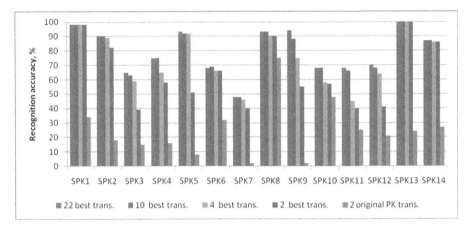

Fig. 1. The recognition accuracy dependence from the transcription number for the different speakers (excerpts)

and the figure 1 (the results for different speakers (unprofessional, age 16 - 65, equal numbers of males and females)). As in the examples offered, in most cases the improvement was quite large, usually more than 50 %, which shows some promise for the further development.

2.2 Recognition Methods for the Short Voice Commands Using the Transcription Manipulation

The recognition of the short voice commands (i.e. digit names) is a much more difficult task than the recognition of the long voice commands. This study tries to define the effective method of generating the transcriptions for such short commands. The method was realized in three stages.

In the first stage we divided each pending word into the simple artificial syllables (consonant - vowel) and generated the all possible transcription sets for each of those syllables. The assumption was made, that if we would have accurately recognized the transcriptions for each syllable we could construct the transcription for the whole word. This simple consonant - vowel structure (CV) also allows the modeling of the most co-articulation peculiarities. The data obtained would also be very useful for the further native Lithuanian language engine development. We haven't analyzed the more advanced CVC structure, as we currently are limited by the corpus we use (not enough high quality data). So in the first stage we generated the all possible CV combinations out of 40 UPS symbols (24 consonants and 16 vowels and diphthongs) compatible with the recognition engine used.

In the second stage we passed the syllable corpus to the recognizer and noted the recognition results for each of the analyzed syllables. The best (most frequently recognized) transcriptions (transcription sets) were selected and used for the whole word transcription forming. 2 criterions were developed for the whole word transcription formation: the syllabic criterion (the most recognized syllables are chosen for further transcription forming) and the phonetic criterion (the most recognized consonants and vowels are chosen). The whole word transcription based on the phonetic criterion proved to be unreliable, as in most cases the WER was quite high.

In the third stage we improved the chosen transcription set recognition accuracy (if necessary) by iteratively maximizing the number of the possible transcriptions (large sets of transcriptions (more than 500 for each word) tend to decrease the overall recognition accuracy for the large vocabularies). The optimization was done as noted the second stage of the long command transcription generation method. Further improvement may be done by utilizing the additional criterions or linguistic expertise.

The excerpts from this group of the experiments are offered in table 2. In this case the recognition accuracy of the word "trys" (three) (which was quite poor (62,5 %) using the old "linguistic" knowledge based transcription generation methods) improved to a practically acceptable 97,5 % by utilizing the 3 stage method. The voices of 40 speakers were used for "training" (generating and iteratively optimizing the transcriptions) and the voices of other 20 speakers were used for the verification.

Table 2. The recognition comparison of the differently obtained transcriptions for the word "trys"

Method used	Transcriptions	Rec. accuracy, %
Two transcriptions generated using the old methods [13-19]	T R IY 1 S T R IH 1 S	62,5
Three stage method	T IY S D IY S F IY S	**97,5**

3 Practical Evaluation

Quite recently we've got the business opportunity to adapt the transcription method to the domain of limited vocabulary Lithuanian recognition - recognize the user's identity number (composed out of 7 digits, 1 was used for the error correction [20]). A limited set of numbers was enough for this practical task and of course in the case of the smaller recognition vocabulary the more accurate recognition results should be achieved, so we've chosen to remove the 3 more poorly recognized digit names. The 3 stage method was used for generating the transcriptions. The transcriptions were adapted to the IVR software used by the customer (commercial telephony English recognizer). The set of 7 digits allowed the achievement of a practically acceptable approximately 99 % recognition accuracy using a headset microphone. In this case 20 unprofessional speakers uttered each phrase 100 times. The results of the experiment are offered in figure 2. We believe that the recognition accuracy of the digits "du" (96,5 %) and "penki" (97,5 %) could be improved, utilizing the more detailed future corpus.

The results were verified utilizing random unprofessional speakers, uttering each word 10 times live via GSM phone. The recognition accuracy of the 7 digit set is displayed in the table 3. In this experiment we have noted three types of the recognized events: the correct answers, the doubts (the recognizer was unable to choose the result) and the insertions (the recognizer recognized the wrong utterance). The overall recognition accuracy achieved was approximately 98 %.

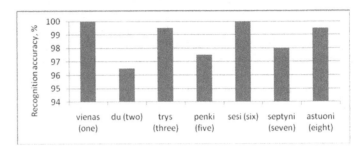

Fig. 2. The results of the recognition accuracy of the chosen 7 digit set

Table 3. The results of a 7 digit set recognition (excerpts: 20 live speakers, each uttering every digit 10 times via GSM phone (200 utterances total))

Voice command	Recognized events:		
	Correct answers	Doubts	Insertions (how many times replaced with)
VIENAS (1)	196	0	4 (4 times 3)
DU (2)	193	1	6 (4 times 1, 2 times 3)
TRYS (3)	198	2	0
PENKI (5)	189	7	2 (3 times 3, 1 time 6)
ŠEŠI (6)	199	1	0
SEPTYNI (7)	194	2	4 (4 times 1)
AŠTUONI (8)	196	1	3 (2 times 1, 1 time 2)
Average	195,0	2,0	3,0
Standard deviation	3,4	2,3	2,2
Average, %	**97,5**	**1,0**	**1,5**

4   Conclusions

1. Utilizing the 2 stage method for the more poorly recognized long voice commands, proved quite successful as in most cases the improvement was quite large, usually more than 50 %, which showed some promise for further development.
2. The 3 stage method for the short voice commands was used successfully for generating the accurately recognized transcriptions of the Lithuanian digits. For example

the word "trys" (three), which was quite poorly recognized (62,5 %) using the old "linguistic" knowledge based transcription generation methods, improved to the practically acceptable 97,5 % by utilizing the 3 stage method.

3. The set of 7 digits used for the real life practical application allowed the achievement of practically acceptable approximately 99 % recognition accuracy using a headset microphone and approximately 98 % using a GSM phone.

References

1. Anderson, O., Dalsgaard, P., Barry, W.: On the use of data-driven clustering technique for identification of poly- and mono-phonemes for four European languages. IEEE Trans. Acoustics, Speech, and Signal Processing i, 121–124 (1994)
2. Cohen, P., et al.: Towards a Universal Speech Recognizer for Multiple Languages. In: Proceedings of Automatic Speech Recognition and Understanding, pp. 591–598 (1997)
3. Schultz, T.: Global Phone: A Multilingual Speech and Text Database developed at Karlsruhe University. In: Proceedings of ICSLP 2002, Denver, Colorado, vol. 1, pp. 345–348 (2002)
4. Schultz, T., Waibel, A.: Multilingual and Crosslingual Speech Recognition. In: Proceedings of the DARPA Broadcast News Transcription and Understanding Workshop, pp. 259–262 (1998)
5. Schultz, T., Waibel, A.: Fast Bootstrapping of LVCSR Systems with Multilingual Phoneme Sets. In: Proceedings of Eurospeech 1997, Rhodes, pp. 371–374 (1997)
6. Schultz, T., Waibel, A.: Experiments on Cross-language Acoustic Modeling. In: Proceedings of Eurospeech-2001, Alborg, pp. 2721–2725 (2001)
7. Stuker, S., Schultz, T., Metze, F., Waibel, A.: Multilingual Articulatory Features. In: Proceedings of ICASSP 2003, Hong Kong, vol. 1, pp. I-144–I-147 (2003)
8. Stuker, S., Metze, F., Schultz, T., Waibel, A.: Integrating Multilingual Articulatory Features into Speech Recognition. In: Proceedings of Eurospeech 2003, Geneva, pp. 1033–1036 (2003)
9. Jin, Q., Schultz, T., Waibel, A.: Speaker Identification using Multilingual Phone Strings. In: Proceedings of ICASSP 2002, Orlando, Florida, vol. 1, pp. I-145–I-148 (2002)
10. Schultz, T., et al.: Speaker, Accent, and Language Identification using Multilingual Phone Strings. In: Proceedings of the Human Language Technology Meeting 2002, San Diego, California, pp. 125–131 (2002)
11. Fugen, C., et al.: Efficient Handling of Multilingual Language Models. In: Proceedings of ASRU 2003, ASRU, St. Thomas, pp. 441–446 (2003)
12. Lin, H., et al.: Learning Methods in Multilingual Speech Recognition. In: NIPS Workshop (December 2008),
   http://ssli.ee.washington.edu/people/hlin/papers/
   nips2008WSL1_03.pdf
13. Rudzionis, V., Maskeliunas, R., Rudzionis, A.: On the adaptation of foreign language speech recognition engines for Lithuanian speech recognition. In: Business Information System. LNBIP, vol. 37, pp. 113–118. Springer, Heidelberg (2009)
14. Maskeliunas, R., Rudzionis, A., Rudzionis, V.: Analysis of the possibilities to adapt the foreign language speech recognition engines for the Lithuanian spoken commands recognition. In: Esposito, A., Vích, R. (eds.) Cross-Modal Analysis of Speech, Gestures, Gaze and Facial Expressions. LNCS (LNAI), vol. 5641, pp. 409–422. Springer, Heidelberg (2009)

15. Maskeliunas, R.: Modeling Aspects of Multimodal Lithuanian Human - Machine Interface. In: Esposito, A., Hussain, A., Marinaro, M., Martone, R. (eds.) Multimodal Signals: Cognitive and Algorithmic Issues. LNCS (LNAI), vol. 5398, pp. 75–82. Springer, Heidelberg (2009)
16. Maskeliunas, R., Rudzionis, A., Ratkevicius, K., Rudzionis, V.: User Identification Based on Lithuanian Digits Recognition. In: Proceedings of the 15th International Conference on Information and Software Technologies, pp. 256–262. Kaunas(2009)
17. Maskeliunas, R., Rudzionis, A., Rudzionis, V., Raktevicius, K.: Voice controlled telephony services. In: Proceedings of the 4th Int. Conf. on Electrical And Control Technologies 2009, pp. 48–54. Kaunas (2009)
18. Maskeliunas, R., Rudzionis, A., Ratkevicius, K., Rudzionis, V.: Investigation of Foreign Languages Models for Lithuanian Speech Recognition. Electronics and Electrical Engineering 3(91), 15–21 (2009)
19. Kasparaitis, P.: Lithuanian Speech Recognition Using the English Recognizer. INFORMATICA 2008 19(4), 505–516 (2008)
20. Koppapu, S.K., Rao, P.: Enhancing spoken connected-digit recognition accuracy by error correction codes – A novel scheme. Sadhana 29(5), 559–571 (2004)

Challenges in Speech Processing
of Slavic Languages
(Case Studies in Speech Recognition
of Czech and Slovak)

Jan Nouza, Jindrich Zdansky, Petr Cerva, and Jan Silovsky

Institute of Information Technology and Electronics, Faculty of Mechatronics,
Technical University of Liberec,
Studentska 2, CZ 46117 Liberec, Czech Republic
{jan.nouza,jindrich.zdansky,petr.cerva,jan.silovsky}@tul.cz

Abstract. Slavic languages pose a big challenge for researchers dealing with speech technology. They exhibit a large degree of inflection, namely declension of nouns, pronouns and adjectives, and conjugation of verbs. This has a large impact on the size of lexical inventories in these languages, and significantly complicates the design of text-to-speech and, in particular, speech-to-text systems. In the paper, we demonstrate some of the typical features of the Slavic languages and show how they can be handled in the development of practical speech processing systems. We present our solutions we applied in the design of voice dictation and broadcast speech transcription systems developed for Czech. Furthermore, we demonstrate how these systems can be converted to another similar Slavic language, in our case Slovak. All the presented systems operate in real time with very large vocabularies (350K words in Czech, 170K words in Slovak) and some of them have been already deployed in practice.

Keywords: Speech recognition, voice dictation, spoken document transcription, Slavic languages, inflective languages.

1 Introduction

During the last decade, speech technology has become a well established platform for human-computer interaction. It has been successfully deployed in voice dictation programs (IBM ViaVoice being one of the first in 1997, [1]), spoken document transcription systems [2], dialogue based information services [3], mobile device interfaces [4], or assistive tools for handicapped people [5]. The earliest systems were produced for major languages, like English, German, French or Japanese. Later some other tongues spoken in Europe and Asia have been covered, too.

Yet, there are groups of languages that still wait for more intensive deployment of modern voice technologies, and the family of Slavic languages is one of them.

A. Esposito et al. (Eds.): COST 2102 Int. Training School 2009, LNCS 5967, pp. 225–241, 2010.
© Springer-Verlag Berlin Heidelberg 2010

Research focused on developing functional text-to-speech (TTS) and speech-to-text (STT) services has existed in many Slavic countries, however, it is mainly the former that have been already applied in broader scale while the latter - automatic speech recognition (ASR) systems - have not reached such a mature level, so far. One of the reasons is the complex nature of Slavic languages. They are inflective, which means that words can get many different forms according to context. Moreover, they have very complex grammar, they allow for rather free word order in sentences, and last but not least, a large set of acoustically and phonetically similar prefixes and suffixes makes the traditional speech recognition algorithms less successful.

In this paper, we want to explain where the main problems and challenges are and how they can be solved. Most of the features that are typical for Slavic languages are demonstrated on Czech because it is the language we have been working on for more than 15 years. For Czech we can also present the solutions that proved to be successful and led to the development of practical systems, both commercial and non-commercial ones. In the last part of the paper we show how the experience gained during the long-term research can be re-used for another similar language, in our case Slovak.

2   Slavic Languages

Slavic (sometimes called also Slavonic) languages are spoken by almost 300 million people living in central, southern and eastern Europe, and in Asian part of Russia. This family of languages consists of three main branches, with the following main representatives:

- West Slavic - Polish, Czech and Slovak,
- South Slavic - Serbian, Croatian, Bulgarian, Slovene and Macedonian,
- East Slavic - Russian, Ukrainian and Belarusian.

The name of the branches highly correlates with geographic distribution of the countries where these languages are used as it is shown in Fig. 1. All the West Slavic languages as well as Slovene and Croatian use Latin alphabet while the other South Slavic and all East Slavic nations use Cyrillic characters.

3   Major Challenges in Machine Processing of Slavic Languages

3.1   Inflective Nature of Slavic Languages

All Slavic languages exhibit very large degree of inflection. This means that the vast majority of lexical items (except of adverbs, prepositions and conjunctions) modify its basic form (lemma) according to grammatical, morphological and contextual relations. Nouns, pronouns, adjectives and numerals change their orthographic and phonetic forms with respect to grammatical case, number and gender. For examples, see Tables 1 and 2. Verbs are subjects to conjugation controlled by grammatical categories, like person, number, gender, tense, aspect, etc. An example is in Table 3.

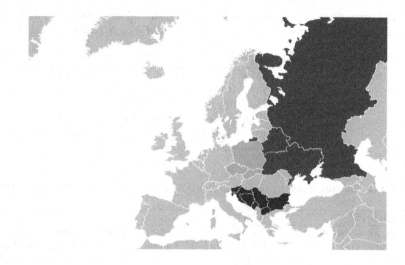

Fig. 1. Three groups of Slavic languages spoken in Europe (source Wikipedia)

Table 1. Comparison of an adjective *(nice)* in English and its inflected equivalents in Czech

English (1)	Czech (12)
nice	krásný, krásného, krásnému, krásném, krásným, krásná, krásné, krásnou, krásní, krásných, krásnými, krásnýma

3.2   Rich Morphology Results in Extremely Large Lexicons

Three examples presented in Tables 1, 2 and 3 show just the most straightforward type of inflection when a lemma is modified by endings attached to a word stem. However, morphology of Slavic languages is even more complex. New words with more or less similar meaning can be created by adding (single or multiple) prefixes, suffixes and endings to a stem, or also by modifying the stem itself. An example of some of these word production patterns, from simple to very complex ones, is shown in Table 4. One can notice, that in Czech (and in the other Slavic languages as well) even a negative form of a verb is a new lexical item (e.g. "neučit") unlike in English were the negative form is expressed by separate particle "not". In a similar way, the grading of adjectives and adverbs is done entirely by adding special suffixes and prefixes, not by separate words, like "more" and "most" in English. Last but not least, Slavic languages often use special words for male and female surnames ("Navratil" vs. "Navratilova") and names of professions (as shown in Table 2).

All these specific features result in very large number of word-forms. This number often exceeds one million distinct items, which have to be covered and managed by automatic speech processing systems. This is a big difference if we compare it to ASR systems designed e.g. for English where the inventory of 50

Table 2. Comparison of a noun *(student)* in English and its inflected equivalents in Czech (notice distinct forms used for *male student* and *female student* in Czech)

English (2)	Czech (20)
student, students	**Masculine:** student, studenta, studentu, studentovi, studente, studentem, studenti, studentů, studentům, studenty, studentech **Feminine:** studentka, studentky, studentce, studentku, studentkou, studentek, studentkám, studentkách, studentkami

Table 3. Comparison of a verb *(break)* in English and its inflected equivalents in Czech

English (5)	Czech (19)
break, breaks, broke, broken, breaking	zlomit, zlomím, zlomíš, zlomí, zlomíme, zlomíte, zlom, zlomme, zlomte, zlomil, zlomila, zlomilo, zlomili, zlomily, zlomen, zlomena, zlomeno, zlomeny, zlomeni

Table 4. Several examples of word production patterns applied to Czech word *učit (teach)*

Pattern type	Czech word	English equivalent *(approximated)*
basic form (verb)	učit	teach
stem + suffix	učit-*el*	teacher
stem + sufix + ending	učit-*el-ovi*	to teacher
prefix + stem	*do*-učit	to have taught
(negative) prefix + stem	*ne*-učit	not to teach
prefix + prefix+ stem + sufix+ suffix + ending	*ne-po*-učit-*el-ný-m*	unteachable

thousands most frequent words yields the coverage rate about 99 %. In general, Slavic languages require ASR vocabularies that are 10 to 20 times larger.

3.3 Free Word Order, But Strong Grammatical Agreement

Another serious complication for automatic speech and text processing is relatively free word order in sentences. A subject of a sentence can occur at an almost arbitrary place, i.e. at the beginning, in the middle as well as at the end of the sentence. The same applies also to a verb or to an adjective. This freedom is possible due to the previously mentioned rich morphology, as the role of the word in the sentence is determined by its inflected form. On the other side, this phenomenon significantly complicates automatic decoding of speech because the decoder cannot rely on any standard word sequence.

Table 5. Fixed word order in English vs. free word order in Czech. All the shown Czech word sequences have the same meaning as the English one.

English	Czech
I love Peter.	Mám rád Petra.
	Rád mám Petra.
	Petra mám rád.

Table 6. Grammatical agreement in Czech demonstrated on a sentence translated from English (The first translation corresponds to *male students*, the second one to *female ones*.)

English	Czech
Two young Czech students were successful in the competition.	**Masculine:** Dva mladí čeští studenti byli úspěšní v soutěži. **Feminine:** Dvě mladé české studentky byly úspěšné v soutěži.

In contrast to the free word order, there is strong grammatical agreement between parts of a sentence in Slavic languages [6]. The inflected form of the sentence subject must agree in gender, person, case and number with the verb and with all the related adjectives, pronouns and numerals. Unlike in English, the agreement is much stronger, as shown in the example in Table 6 where Czech translation of an English sentence significantly differs if the subject, *students*, is of masculine or feminine gender.

4 Solutions Applied to Speech Recognition of Czech

In this section we describe several alternative solutions we investigated during the long term work on ASR systems for Czech language. After explaining them, we present and evaluate some of the developed systems.

4.1 Lexicon

When preparing lexicons for inflected languages, we have to solve one crucial problem: Which words and how many of them should we include in the lexicon. We know that we cannot take all the existing ones, because a) inflected languages allow for producing virtually unlimited number of words, b) even 1 or 2 million words is still a too large inventory to be processed in real time by recent computers. Hence, we have to find a good balance between the lexicon size and the ASR system performance.

During the design of our systems we considered the following strategies:

Lexicon based on most frequent lemmas. The idea was to identify the most frequent basic forms of words (so called lemmas) and to use them for the derivation of all their possible inflected forms. In this approach we utilized the morphologic analyzer and generator developed at Charles University in Prague [6] and the details of the procedure are described in [7]. A set of 74,867 roots (stems + prefixes) together with 5,729 tails (suffixes + ending) produced 972,915 distinct word-forms. On an independent text corpus we found that the coverage rate achieved by this word set was 95.82 %. In other words 4.18 % words in this corpus were out of vocabulary (OOV).

Lexicon based on most frequent word-forms. In this approach we created the lexicon simply from those word-forms that occurred in the training text corpus at least N-times. In our case, the corpus size was 55 million words, N was equal to 3, and the resulting lexicon contained 644,635 items. In spite of its smaller size, the lexicon yielded larger coverage on the independent corpus - 97,07 % [7]. This and the previously mentioned experiments were performed in 2003. Later, we collected much larger training and testing corpora and evaluated the word coverage rate for both the printed (mixture of newspaper and novel text) and spoken documents. The results are shown in Fig. 2. The diagram tells us that if we want to achieve the OOV rate below 2 %, the lexicon should contain at least 300 thousand words.

Lexicon based on morphemes. The very high degree of inflection occurs also in some non-Indo-European languages, e.g. in Finnish, Hungarian, Estonian or Turkish. Linguists and speech researchers from these countries investigated another approach to the lexicon building task. It consisted in the decomposition of words into smaller, morphologically oriented units, morphemes. They should have served as the basic units in the first stage of speech decoding and next, in the second stage, for re-composition of the true words (see e.g. [9]). In this way, even a very large lexical inventory with several million words could be covered by several tens of thousands of morphemes. This approach was tested also for Czech [10], however, the results did not offer any relevant benefit for practical usage. The morpheme based lexicon had three serious drawbacks: 1) it required N-gram language models with $N > 4$ (which complicated fast implementation of the speech decoder), 2) it sometimes produced non-existing words, and 3) it

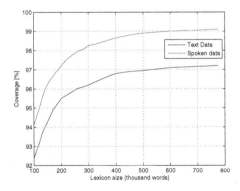

Fig. 2. Coverage rate (for spoken and printed Czech documents) as function of lexicon size (lexicon is made from words ordered by their frequency in the 360M-word corpus)

Table 7. Word error rate and out-of-vocabulary rate as function of lexicon size in Czech broadcast news transcription task

Lexicon size	Min. word frequency	WER[%]	OOV[%]
Lex64K	300	31.5	5.2
Lex100K	140	28.8	3.3
Lex149K	70	26.9	1.9
Lex195K	40	25.9	1.3
Lex257K	20	25.0	1.0
Lex310K	10	24.5	0.8
Lex310K + 1708 multi-word entries	10	23.2	0.8

was based on the assumption that the morphemes are unique and distinctive also from the phonetic point of view, which was not always true for languages like Czech.

Lexicon with added frequent multi-words. The ultimate goal in Slavic language ASR is to find the optimal balance between the lexicon size and ASR system performance. Therefore, we primarily search for the minimal lexicon size that meets the two main performance criteria - recognition accuracy and computation time. However, we found out that the accuracy could be further improved if the vocabulary is enhanced by adding a small number of the most frequently occurring multi-word sequences. This is done also in ASR systems designed for other languages where such collocations, like e.g. "New York" or "Rio de Janeiro" are handled in the same way as single words. We experimented with this strategy and defined several criteria to search automatically for the multi-word candidates [11]. As we show in Table 7, even a small number (1708) of very frequent multi-word entries improves the ASR performance by more than 1 %.

The impact of increasing the size of the lexicon and thus reducing the word error rate (WER) and out-of-vocabulary (OOV) rate is demonstrated in Table 7. The results come from the experiments conducted in a broadcast news transcription project [8].

4.2   Acoustic Modeling and Phonetic Issues

In contrast to English, Slavic languages have an advantage in much more straightforward correspondence between orthography and pronunciation. In general, grapheme-to-phoneme (G2P) transcription can be based on rules, with exceptions applying mainly to the words of foreign origin.

For Czech, we use the phonetic alphabet defined in [12]. It contains 41 phonemes. Non-speech sounds are represented by 7 types of noise. All these 48 elementary acoustic units are modeled by 3-state hidden Markov models (HMM) with distribution functions in form of mixture of Gaussians. During the long-term development process we conducted many experiments to find out the optimal settings of the acoustic model. Our conclusion was that context-independent HMMs (monophones) perform almost as well as the context-dependent ones (triphones), if we use a large number of Gaussian components (at least 100) in each model state. This rather surprising result was achieved under the following conditions: a) using gender-dependent models, b) each trained on approx. 40 hours of carefully annotated training recordings, and c) taking into account the language model. Therefore, in most our systems we employ monophone models (with 100 and more components) and we benefit from much faster and significantly simpler decoding procedure.

All our systems use 39 Mel-frequency based cepstral coefficients (MFCC) computed from 16 kHz sampled signal, parameterized every 10 ms within 25 ms long Hamming window.

Another important issue is accurate phonetic representation of lexicon items. Each word in the lexicon has at least one basic pronunciation form that was either derived automatically by employing a G2P transcriptor or (in case of foreign words) created manually. Many lexicon entries have multiple pronunciations. This applies namely to the words that start with a vowel (then an optional glottal stop is added), those that end with any of the pair consonant (then both voiced and unvoiced final consonants are included), or those that contain a cluster of consonants (in this case also a more colloquial pronunciation form is added). The recent version of the lexicon contains 1.2 pronunciations per word. It is shown (e.g. in [8]) that these additional phonetic variants contribute to almost 10 % relative reduction of the WER.

Another improvement in ASR performance can be achieved if a speaker-fitted acoustic model is used. This is possible namely in dictation applications where the same user is assumed. In other tasks where speakers often change, like in broadcast news transcription, a speaker recognition module can be applied. When speaker's identity is known, the ASR system uses his or her model. In general, a speaker adapted model reduces the WER by 20-25 % relatively.

4.3   Language Model

Nowadays, probabilistic language models (LM) in form of N-grams have become almost a standard in continuous speech recognition. Many ASR systems utilize bigrams (because of their easy implementation), some use also trigrams - either within the decoding procedure itself or for rescoring the hypotheses obtained with bigrams.

For Czech (and for the other Slavic languages as well), an N-gram LM constitutes at least three crucial problems. The first one is the size of the model. When the lexicon size is 10 times larger than in English, the N-gram matrix should be 10^N larger. Even in case of bigrams, it means 100 times more values to be estimated. And this is the second problem. To estimate that huge number of bigram values, one should have much more text data than it is used for an English LM (it means much more than 100 GB of texts). This is impossible simply because such huge corpora do not exist for most languages. The third problem is related to the free word order mentioned in section 3.3. Due to this freedom, an N-gram model built for Czech will never be as reliable as in the languages with a firmer sentence structure.

To cope with the above problems, we investigated several approaches.

Smoothed N-grams. Smoothing is very important because only a small portion of linguistically and semantically possible word sequences is seen in a LM training corpus. The unseen ones must be assigned a small, non-zero probability to give them a chance to be recognized. We experimented with several smoothing techniques, and found the Witten-Bell formula was optimal for the performance as well as well for the implementation of the decoder - for details, see [14] and [15].

Bigrams and multi-words. From the reasons mentioned above we use bigrams in our real-time systems. The bigrams are estimated on a large text corpus. Recently, the corpus contains almost 20 GB of data published in period 1990 - 2009. It is mainly electronic versions of Czech newspaper, further a small portion of professional texts from various fields, some novels available on internet, and transcriptions of broadcast programs (news, debates, talk-shows, parliament sessions, etc.) Even if we utilize the bigrams only, their context span is often longer than just two words. It is because some very frequent multi-word sequences (2 to 3 word long) are included in the lexicon as mentioned in section 4.1. Therefore, quite a lot of bigrams actually cover sequences of 3, 4, 5 and even 6 words. This contributes up to 10 % relative WER reduction [16].

Class based bigrams. In section 3.3 we demonstrated that Czech exhibit quite strong grammatical agreement between the parts of a sentence. Unfortunately, this agreement has very complex nature to be captured by rules that could be applied automatically by a computer. Moreover, some of the rules do not fit to the common left-to-right direction of speech processing. In [15] we proposed a simpler approach. We defined a limited number (less than 500) of classes based on linguistic and morphological categories like nouns, adjectives and pronouns (all in corresponding genders, cases and numbers), further verbs, adverbs, prepositions (classified according to their valences), conjunctions and others. For each lexicon item, we found a mapping between the word and one or more classes - see Table 8. After that we converted the LM training corpus into its class representation and computed class-based bigrams. Their values do not need to be smoothed because a) each class has a lot of its members occurring in the corpus and b) the bigram matrix is much smaller than the classic word-based one. In this way we received information that can be further employed [15], e.g. for conditional smoothing of word bigrams, for searching of possibly grammatically wrong sequences of words or for the fast identification of the words that play a key role in a sentence (a subject, a verb, etc.) Recently, this concept is still under investigation.

4.4   LVCSR Decoder

When developing the decoder for continuous speech recognition of Czech (or any other inflected language), the most challenging task is to manage very large

Table 8. Illustration of a lexicon enriched by additional linguistic class information (It contains examples of a conjunction, a preposition and 2 nouns of different gender, case and number.)

Word	Pronunciation	Linguistic class	Lemma (Basic form)
a	a, á	ConjA	a
⋮	⋮	⋮	⋮
s	s, z, sE, zE	Prep4, Prep7	s
studenta	studenta	NounMasc2S	student
studentek	studentek, studenteg	NounFem2P	studentka

lexicons - with respect to memory, computation speed and efficient usage of language model.

In our case, the decoder was designed for the lexicons that may contain up to 500 thousand recognition items. These items are the phonetic forms of the words and because we employ multiple pronunciations (as explained in section 4.2), the actual lexicon size can go up to 400 thousand lexical entries.

The recent version of the decoder has the following parameters: 1) it can process on-line as well as off-line input data, 2) it is able to manage large lexicons in real-time on currently available PCs and notebooks (a Dual Core CPU running at 2.5+ GHz is required), and 3) it can produce text output in continual way. These features allow for employing the same engine for various tasks: from voice dictation to transcription of on-line captured or previously recorded speech data.

The decoder has been extensively optimized for the lexicons of the desired size. Special effort has been made to speed up computation of Gaussian likelihoods and their efficient caching, to predict the most promising hypotheses at one side and to prune off the non-promising ones at several levels, or to handle bigram matrices effectively. Some of the techniques are mentioned in [14].

4.5   Practical Applications - Czech Voice Dictation Systems

During the last five years, we have developed two types of voice dictation programs for Czech language. Their prototypes were presented already in 2005 [17] but it took us three more years to make them available as commercial products.

The first program, called **MyDictate**, was developed for a special target group: people whose motor handicap prevents them from using computer keyboard and mouse. Therefore, the whole program environment had to be designed as hands-free. In order to simplify all voice typing, correcting, editing and formatting actions, the program uses a discrete speech input [18]. This means that words and phrases are dictated with short pauses between them. At one side, the dictation is slower and less natural, but on the other side, the user can correct - entirely by voice - misrecognized or mispronounced words immediately after they occur. Moreover, because the discrete speech decoder requires significantly less computation, the lexicon can be larger (currently 570K words) and the program runs even on a mid-level PC or notebook.

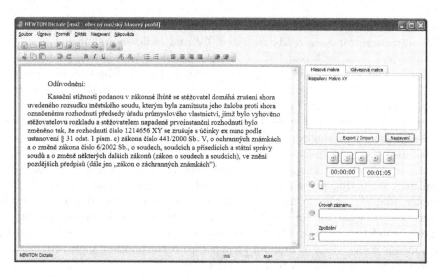

Fig. 3. A snapshot showing NewtonDictate with dictated juristic text

Table 9. Czech dictation in 4 different domains. (All the texts were read in quiet conditions)

Domain	#words in test	WER[%]
Newspaper articles	15492	4.53
Medical text - radiology	7304	2.26
Medical text - pathology	17107	3.16
Juristic text	6612	1.44

The second program is named **NewtonDictate** and it allows for fluent speech input. Its commercial version was developed in collaboration with Czech company Newton Technologies. The layout of the program is shown in Fig. 3. Currently, the software is distributed in three versions. One comes with a general purpose lexicon, the other two are domain specific. The first one contains 350K words and its language model has been trained mainly on newspaper text, which means that it can be used for most common situations. The second one is juristic and it was designed for judges and lawyers. Since summer 2008 it has been tested in Czech courts. The third domain is medicine and recently there exist two fields where the program is used: radiology and pathology.

The performance of the NewtonDictate program was measured on a large set of recordings provided by several tens of test subjects. The results from these evaluations are presented in Table 9.

4.6   Practical Applications - Broadcast Speech Transcription System

The second application of the voice technology is a broadcast speech transcription system. It is a complex modular platform that can be configured for several operational modes, such as a server producing sub-titles for TV programs, an off-line transcriptor for already recorded TV and radio shows, or a system that provides text data for broadcast monitoring, indexing and search services.

The system is composed of modules shown in Fig. 4. The first module processes acoustic track of the broadcast data and converts it into signal parameters (MFCC feature vectors). The second module searches for significant changes in audio characteristics and splits the stream into non-speech segments and segments spoken by a single person. (For the transcription of TV shows we can utilize also the video part of the signal [21].) The next module tries to determine the identity of the speakers. If he or she is in the database (of some 300 frequently occurring persons) and is correctly recognized and verified, his/her speaker adapted acoustic model is used in the speech recognition module. In other cases, at least the speaker's gender is identified and the proper gender dependent model is applied. The last module provides final text post-processing. This means conversions of number strings into corresponding digit strings, capitalization of proper names, text formatting, etc.

In Table 10 we show some relevant results from performance evaluation tests, conducted in 2007. In these tests, always the whole shows were processed and transcribed. In case of TV news, for example, it means that not only studio

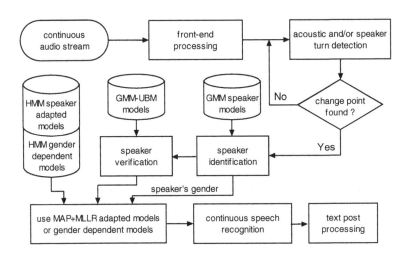

Fig. 4. Modular architecture of the broadcast speech transcription system

Table 10. Results from automatic transcription of several types of broadcast programs

Program Type	Time[min]	#Words	WER[%]	OOV[%]
TV News	62	9760	21.5	1.1
Weather news	10	1745	9.4	0.4
Talk shows	118	13624	33.8	0.6
Parliament sessions	52	6395	20.8	1.1

speech, but also news headlines with music played in background and shots recorded in noisy environments are included in the total WER values.

5 Voice Technology Transfer to Slovak Language

In the situation where we have programs, systems and modules that work for one language it is natural to ask if the same approach could be applied for another language. We have already had one positive experience with porting voice controlled software to other languages. It was program MyVoice that we had developed originally for Czech handicapped users and later modified for Slovak and also for Spanish [22]. In that small project we have verified procedures that seem to be applicable for larger systems, too. In the following sections we present our recent experience with transferring voice technology from Czech to Slovak, i.e. between two rather closely related Slavic languages.

5.1 Lexicon

Czech and Slovak belong to the same West-Slavic branch of languages. They are considered very similar and closely related because in the past they were official languages used within one state (former Czechoslovakia). In order to quantify their similarity on the lexical level we have analyzed a large amount of parallel corpora, in our case documents of the European Union published in both the languages. We have found that about 25 % of lexical items are same in Czech and Slovak. Among the remaining ones there is still a large group of words that are very similar (differing in 1 or 2 letters only).

For creating a representative lexicon of contemporary Slovak and for comput-ing the corresponding language model we were provided by a corpus of newspa-per articles and broadcast news transcriptions from the 2005 - 2007 period. Its

Table 11. Slovak-specific phonemes (with corresponding orthography) mapped onto acoustically closest Czech ones (SAMPA notation is used in this table)

SK letter(s)	SK phoneme	CZ phoneme(s)
ä	{	e
ĺ	L	l
ĺ	l=:	l
ŕ	r=:	r
v	U_^	u
v	w	v
h	G	h
j	I_^	j
ô	u_^o	uo
ia	I_^a	ja
ie	I_^e	je
iu	I_^U\	ju

size was 1.9 GB. After cleaning it (which included also detecting and removing Czech texts frequently occurring in Slovak media), we compiled the first version of the Slovak lexicon. It was made of the 166,535 most frequent words and word-forms. To get pronunciations for them, we modified our grapheme-to-phoneme converter by including Slovak specific phonetic rules described in [23].

Because we knew that the available amount of Slovak acoustic data had not been large enough to train an independent Slovak acoustic model, we had to utilize (and later adapt) the existing Czech AM. Therefore, it was necessary to make conversion from Slovak phonetic inventory to the Czech one. This was done by mapping the Slovak-specific phones and diphthongs into their closest Czech counterparts, either single phonemes or phoneme strings. The mapping rules are summarized in Table 11.

5.2   Acoustic Model

The initial experiment in Slovak speech recognition was done with the Czech acoustic model. The results were surprisingly good - about 25 % WER on the broadcast news task [24]. Anyway, the next natural step was the adaptation of the model. We used 6 hours of annotated Slovak speech and added them to the 61-hour Czech training database. On that data we trained new male and female (i.e. gender dependent) acoustic models. They were used in the experiments whose results are summarized in Tables 12 and 13.

5.3   Language Model

The language model was trained on the 1.9 GB Slovak corpus mentioned in section 5.1. In the corpus we found 234 million occurrences of the 166K-word lexicon items. A bigram LM was computed from 32 million word-pairs seen in the corpus by applying the Witten-Bell smoothing technique. We employed the same tools and the same procedures that had been developed previously for Czech.

5.4   Prototypical Applications - Slovak Voice Dictation System

Because all the Slovak specific modules, i.e. the lexicon, the language model and the acoustic model are fully compatible with the Czech ones, we can use all the voice technology software we developed so far.

In the first series of experiments we tested dictation into the NewtonDictate program. Four Slovak native speakers (two men and two women) were asked to read several articles from Slovak newspapers. The articles were selected to cover various topics (mainly domestic and international news). The results from these initial tests are shown in Table 12. If we compare the values with those in Table 9 (on the first line), we see that the performance of the Slovak version is significantly poorer. There are several reasons for that: 1) the size of the Slovak lexicon is only a half of the Czech one, 2) also the corpus for Slovak language

Table 12. Initial tests of Slovak dictation with NewtonDictate software

Speakers	#words in test	WER[%]
Male speakers	3749	13.45
Female speakers	3811	12.10

model training was much smaller, 3) the Slovak lexicon and language model do not utilize multi-word entries, yet, and 4) the acoustic model for Slovak was trained on the data in which Czech speech prevailed in 10:1 ratio. In future, we will focus on eliminating all these negative factors.

5.5   Prototypical Applications - Slovak Broadcast New Transcription

The second application field where we tested the existing Slovak specific modules was automatic transcription of broadcast news. We used the same system as it is described in section 4.6 with one exception: We could not apply speaker recognition and speaker adaptation modules because we had not had the speaker database that was necessary for their proper function.

The experiments were performed on data collected during March and April 2008. We recorded and annotated a test set consisting of eight complete news shows from three major TV stations and one nation-wide radio. Like in the Czech experiments mentioned in section 4.6, all parts the that contain speech were included in the test set (even headlines with music played in background and shots taken in very noisy conditions). The test data had total duration of 128 minutes and contained 19,021 words in total. Results from the tests are summarized in Table 7. More details about the experiments can be found in [24]. For further improvement, the same issues mentioned in the previous section should be solved.

Table 13. Experiments with Slovak broadcast news transcription

Station	#words	WER[%]	OOV[%]
TV - TA3	5,568	22.85	2.14
TV - STV1	5,318	25.58	2.37
TV - JOJ	5,117	27.81	3.89
Radio - Slovensko	3,018	16.76	2.02
Overall results	19,021	23.95	2.65

6   Conclusions

Slavic languages certainly pose a big challenge for researchers dealing with voice technologies, particularly speech recognition. Their inflected nature and rich morphology result in extremely large vocabularies, whose size (up to several million different word-forms) exceeds the limits of today's common algorithms and available PCs. Therefore, it is necessary to search the methods that can cope with extremely large lexicons or that can choose optimal subsets of those huge lexical inventories. In language modeling, the problem is even more serious. If the classic N-gram approach is used, the LM matrices grow towards extreme sizes, but it also means that they require much more data for reliable estimation. In most languages that size of required amount of training data is not available. Hence, some other methods or modifications of the existing ones must be searched.

In spite of these problems, even on recent computers it is possible to implement solutions that are applicable in practice, e.g. in dictation programs or in systems for automatic transcription of spoken documents. We present the solutions that proved to work for speech recognition of Czech and that seem to be portable also for other Slavic languages. Examples of alternative approaches applied to other languages like, e.g., Slovene, Slovak or Polish can be found in [25,26,27].

Acknowledgement

This work was supported by grants no. 102/08/0707 by the Grant Agency of the Czech Republic and no. OC09066 by the Ministry of Education of the Czech Republic (within EU Action COST 2102).

References

1. http://www.research.ibm.com/hlt/html/body_history.html
2. Gauvain, J.L., Lamel, L., Adda, G., Jardino, M.: The LIMSI 1998 HUB-4E Transcription System. In: Proc. of the DARPA Broadcast News Workshop, Herndon, pp. 99–104 (1999)
3. Os, E., Boves, L., Lamel, L., Baggia, P.: Overview of the ARISE Project. In: Proceedings of Eurospeech 1999, Budapest, pp. 1527–1530 (1999)
4. Tan, Z.-H., Lindberg, B. (eds.): Automatic speech recognition on mobile devices and over communication networks. Springer, London (2008)
5. Tronconi, A., Billi, M.: New technologies for physically disabled individuals. European Transactions on Telecommunications (6), 633–640 (2008)
6. Hajic, J.: Disambiguation of Rich Inflection-Computational Morphology of Czech. Karolinum Charles University Press, Prague (2004)
7. Nejedlova, D., Nouza, J.: Building of a Vocabulary for the Automatic Voice-Dictation System. In: Matoušek, V., Mautner, P. (eds.) TSD 2003. LNCS (LNAI), vol. 2807, pp. 301–308. Springer, Heidelberg (2003)
8. Nouza, J., Zdansky, J., David, P., Cerva, P., Kolorenc, J., Nejedlova, D.: Fully Automated System for Czech Spoken Broadcast Transcription with Very Large (300K+) Lexicon. In: Proc. of Interspeech 2005, Lisbon (September 2005)
9. Hirsimäki, T., Creutz, M., Siivola, V., Kurimo, M., Virpioja, S., Pylkkönen, J.: Unlimited Vocabulary Speech Recognition with Morph Language Models Applied to Finnish. Computer Speech & Language 20(4), 515–541 (2006)
10. Byrne, W., Hajic, J., Ircing, P., Krbec, P., Psutka, J.: Morpheme Based Language Models for Speech Recognition of Czech. In: Sojka, P., Kopeček, I., Pala, K. (eds.) TSD 2000. LNCS (LNAI), vol. 1902, pp. 139–162. Springer, Heidelberg (2000)

11. Kolorenc, J., Nouza, J., Cerva, P.: Multi-words in the Czech TV/radio News Transcription system. In: Proc. of Specom 2006 conference, St. Petersburg, pp. 70–74 (2006)
12. Nouza, J., Psutka, J., Uhlir, J.: Phonetic Alphabet for Speech Recognition of Czech. Radioengineering 6(4), 16–20 (1997)
13. Cerva, P., Nouza, J.: Supervised and unsupervised speaker adaptation in large vocabulary continuous speech recognition of Czech. In: Matoušek, V., Mautner, P., Pavelka, T. (eds.) TSD 2005. LNCS (LNAI), vol. 3658, pp. 203–210. Springer, Heidelberg (2005)
14. Nouza, J.: Strategies for developing a real-time continuous speech recognition system for czech language. In: Sojka, P., Kopeček, I., Pala, K. (eds.) TSD 2002. LNCS (LNAI), vol. 2448, pp. 189–196. Springer, Heidelberg (2002)
15. Nouza, J., Drabkova, J.: Combining Lexical and Morphological knowledge in language model for Inflectional (Czech) Language. In: Proc. of 6th Int. Conference on Spoken Language Processing (ICSLP 2002), Denver, September 2002, pp. 705–708 (2002)
16. Nouza, J., Zdansky, J., Cerva, P., Kolorenc, J.: Continual On-line Monitoring of Czech Spoken Broadcast Programs. In: Proc. of 7th International Conference on Spoken Language Processing (ICSLP 2006), Pittsburgh, September 2006, pp. 1650–1653 (2006)
17. Nouza, J.: Discrete and Fluent Voice Dictation in Czech Language. In: Matoušek, V., Mautner, P., Pavelka, T. (eds.) TSD 2005. LNCS (LNAI), vol. 3658, pp. 273–280. Springer, Heidelberg (2005)
18. Cerva, P., Nouza, J.: Design and Development of Voice Controlled Aids for Motor-Handicapped Persons. In: Proc. of Interspeech, Antwerp, pp. 2521–2524 (2007)
19. http://www.v2t.cz/newton-media.php
20. Nouza, J., Zdansky, J., Cerva, P., Kolorenc, J.: A system for information retrieval from large records of czech spoken data. In: Sojka, P., Kopeček, I., Pala, K. (eds.) TSD 2006. LNCS (LNAI), vol. 4188, pp. 401–408. Springer, Heidelberg (2006)
21. Chaloupka, J.: Visual Speech Segmentation and Speaker Recognition for Transcription of TV News. In: Proc. of Interspeech 2006, Denver, September 2006, pp. 1284–1287 (2006)
22. Callejas, Z., Nouza, J., Cerva, P., López-Cózar, R.: Cost-efficient cross-lingual adaptation of a speech recognition system. In: Advances in Intelligent and Soft Computing. Springer, Heidelberg (2009)
23. Ivanecky, J.: Automatic speech transcription and segmentation. PhD thesis, Kosice (December 2003) (in Slovak)
24. Nouza, J., Silovsky, J., Zdansky, J., Cerva, P., Kroul, M., Chaloupka, J.: Czech-to-Slovak Adapted Broadcast News Transcription System. In: Proc. of Interspeech 2008, Brisbane, September 2008, pp. 2683–2686 (2008)
25. Rotovnik, T., Sepesy Maucec, M., Kacic, Z.: Large vocabulary continuous speech recognition of an inflected language using stems and endings. Speech Communication 49(6), 437–452 (2007)
26. Pleva, M., Cizmar, A., Juhár, J., Ondas, J., Michal, M.: Towards Slovak Broadcast News Automatic Recording and Transcribing Service. In: Esposito, A., Bourbakis, N.G., Avouris, N., Hatzilygeroudis, I. (eds.) HH and HM Interaction. LNCS (LNAI), vol. 5042, pp. 158–168. Springer, Heidelberg (2008)
27. Korzinek, D., Brocki, L.: Grammar Based Automatic Speech Recognition System for the Polish Language. In: Recent Advances in Mechatronics. Springer, Heidelberg (2007)

Multiple Feature Extraction and Hierarchical Classifiers for Emotions Recognition

Enrique M. Albornoz[1,2], Diego H. Milone[1,2], and Hugo L. Rufiner[1,2,3,*]

[1] Centro de I+D en Señales, Sistemas e INteligencia Computacional (SINC(i))
Facultad de Ingeniería y Ciencias Hídricas, Universidad Nacional del Litoral,
Ciudad Universitaria, Paraje El Pozo, S3000 Santa Fe, Argentina
[2] Consejo Nacional de Investigaciones Científicas y Técnicas (CONICET)
[3] Laboratorio de Cibernética, Fac. de Ingeniería, Universidad Nacional de Entre Ríos
lrufiner@fich.unl.edu.ar

Abstract. The recognition of the emotional states of speaker is a multi-disciplinary research area that has received great interest in the last years. One of the most important goals is to improve the voiced-based human-machine interactions. Recent works on this domain use the proso-dic features and the spectrum characteristics of speech signal, with standard classifier methods. Furthermore, for traditional methods the improvement in performance has also found a limit. In this paper, the spectral characteristics of emotional signals are used in order to group emotions. Standard classifiers based on Gaussian Mixture Models, Hidden Markov Models and Multilayer Perceptron are tested. These classifiers have been evaluated in different configurations with different features, in order to design a new hierarchical method for emotions classification. The proposed multiple feature hierarchical method improves the performance in 6.35% over the standard classifiers.

1 Introduction

In the last years, the recognition of emotions has become in a multi-disciplinary research area that has received great interest. This plays an important roll in the improvement of human-machine interaction. For example, security application of the fear emotional manifestation in abnormal situations is studied in [1]; in [2], real-life emotion detection using a corpus of agent-client spoken dialogs from a medical emergency call center is studied; in [3], a framework to support semi-automatic diagnosis of psychiatric diseases is proposed.

The use of biosignals (like ECG, EEG, etc.), face and body images is an interesting alternative to detect emotional states [4,5,6]. However, methods to record and use these signals are more invasive, complex and impossible in some real applications. Therefore, the use of speech signals clearly becomes a feasible option. Most of the previous works in emotion recognition have been based in the analysis of speech prosodic features and spectral information. For the classifier,

* Corresponding author.

A. Esposito et al. (Eds.): COST 2102 Int. Training School 2009, LNCS 5967, pp. 242–254, 2010.

Gaussian Mixture Models (GMM), Hidden Markov Models (HMM) and several other standard techniques have been explored [7,8,9,10].

Very few works have been presented using some combination of standard methods. In [11], two classification methods: stacked generalization and unweighted vote, were applied in emotion recognition. These classifiers improved modestly the performance of traditional classification methods. In [12], a multiple stages classifier with support vector machines (SVM) is presented. Two class decisions are repetitively made until only one class remains, and hardly separable classes are divided at last. Authors build this partition based on expert knowledge or derived it from the confusion matrices of a multiclass SVM approach. A two stages classifier for five emotions is proposed in [13]. In this work, a SVM to classify five emotions into two groups is used. Then, HMMs are used to classify emotions within each group.

In this work, an analysis of spectral features is made in order to define groups of similar emotions. Emotions are grouped based on their properties and a hierarchical classifier is designed. The proposed classifier is evaluated in the same experimental condition than standard classifiers, with important improvements in the recognition rates.

In the next section, the emotional speech data base and an acoustical analysis of emotions are presented. Section 3 describes the feature extraction and classification methods. The method here proposed and the experiments are also explained. Section 4 deals with the classification performance and discussion. Finally, conclusions and future works are presented.

2   Acoustic Analysis of Emotions

2.1   Emotional Speech Corpus

The emotional speech signals used were taken from an emotional speech data base [14], developed by the Communication Science Institute of Berlin Technical University. This corpus had been used in several studies [8,9,15] and allows the development and evaluation of an speaker independent recognizer[1].

The corpus, consisting of 535 utterances, includes sentences performed in 6 ordinary emotions, and sentences in neutral emotional state. These emotions covers the "big six" emotions set except for boredom instead of surprise. Sentences are labeled as: happiness (joy) (71), anger (127), fear (69), boredom (81), sadness (62), disgust (46) and neutral (79).

The same texts were recorded in german by ten professional actors, 5 female and 5 male, which allows studies over the whole group, comparisons between emotions and comparisons between speakers. The corpus consists of 10 utterances for each emotion type, 5 short and 5 longer sentences, from 1 to 7 seconds. To achieve a high audio quality, these sentences were recorded in an anechoic chamber with 48 kHz sample frequency (later downsampled to 16 kHz) and were

---

[1] The corpus is freely accessible from http://pascal.kgw.tu-berlin.de/emodb/

quantized with 16 bits per sample. A perception test with 20 subjects was carried out to ensure the emotional quality and naturalness of the utterances, and those more confused were eliminated.

2.2 Acoustic Analysis

The psychological conceptualization of affects, with two-dimensional and three-dimensional models, is widely known in the categorization of emotions [16,17,18]. These models are often used to group emotions in order to define classes. For example, those associated with low arousal and low pleasure versus those associated with high arousal and high pleasure. In this work the psychological information will be discarded and emotions would be characterized only by spectral information. As the main goal is performance improvement, the focus has been oriented to find discriminative acoustic features. It was studied how to take advantage from this acoustic evidence in the classification, without taking into account information from the phychological level or the taxonomy of human emotions.

For every utterance, the mean of the log-spectrum (MLS) on each frequency band, along the frames, were calculated. Then, the average of the mean log-spectrums (AMLS) over all the utterances with same emotion were computed

$$AMLS_k(f) = \frac{1}{N_k} \sum_{i=1}^{N_k} \frac{1}{T_i} \sum_{t=1}^{T_i} \log \|v(t,f)\|, \qquad (1)$$

where f is a frequency band, N_k is the number of sentences for the emotion class k, T_i is the number of frames in the utterance i and $v(t,f)$ is the discrete Fourier transform of the signal in the frame t.

In Figure 1, the AMLS information is shown for each emotional class. As can be seen in this figure, the most interesting information to discriminate emotion classes was found between 0 and 1200 Hz in the AMLS morphologies. As it can be seen in the figures, some emotions have spectral similarities between them. For example, it can be noticed a similar shape and a maximum between 240 and 280 Hz in Joy, Anger and Fear. A minimum is present close to 75 Hz in Joy, Anger, Fear and Disgust. On the other hand, Boredom, Neutral and Sadness have similar shape and a peak between 115 and 160 Hz.

So, it is possible to define groups using this spectral information. For example, a group could contain Joy, Anger, Fear emotions (JAF) whereas other contains Boredom, Neutral and Sadness emotions (BNS) and finally Disgust emotion alone in a third group. On the other hand, emotion similarities used to propose the groups keep a relationship with accuracies and errors present in confusion matrices [8,9,19]. This relevant knowledge for emotion grouping will be used in the next section to define a hierarchical classifier.

3 Proposed Method

In this section, a new multiple feature hierarchical classification method based on the acoustic analysis described above is presented.

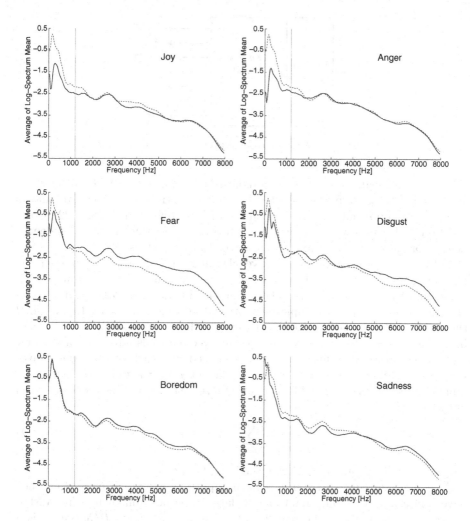

Fig. 1. Average of Mean Log-Spectrum for all emotion classes (both genders). In dash-line the Neutral emotion is presented.

3.1 Features Extraction and Classification Methods

For every emotion utterance, three kinds of characteristics were extracted: MLS, mel frequency cepstral coefficients (MFCCs) and prosodic features. The MLS were computed as defined in Section 2.2. The spectrograms and the MFCC parameterization were calculated by using Hamming windows of 25 ms with a 10 ms frame shift. The first 12 MFCC plus the first and second derivatives were extracted [20].

The use of prosodic features in emotion recognition has been discussed extensively and classic methods to calculate the *Energy* and the F_0 along the signals have been used here [21]. Many parameters can be extracted from them; therefore

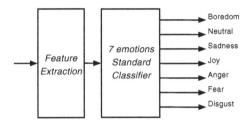

Fig. 2. Structure of standard one-level classifier for 7 emotions

the minimum, mean, maximum and standard deviation, over the whole utterances, were used. This set of parameters has been already studied and the experiments reported an important information gain to distinguish emotions [8,12,22]. Combinations of features were arranged in vectors and every dimension was independently normalized by the maximum from the feature vectors set.

In this work, some standard one-level classifiers (Fig. 2) are used as baselines. Classifiers are based on well known techniques: Multilayer Perceptron (MLP), GMM and HMM. The MLP is a class of artificial neural network and it consists of a set of process units (simple perceptrons) arranged in layers. In the MLP the nodes are fully connected between layers without connections between units in the same layer. The input vector (feature vector) feeds into each of the first layer perceptrons, the outputs of this layer feed into each of the second layer perceptrons, and so on [23]. The input of the neuron is the weighted sum of the inputs plus the bias term, and its activation is some function (linear or nonlinear) of the input:

$$y = \mathcal{F}\left(\sum_{i=1}^{n} \omega_i x_i + \theta\right) \tag{2}$$

where x_i are the inputs and ω_i the weighting factors.

Although Gaussian distributions have important analytical properties, they have limitations to model multimodal data. Superposition of multiple distributions would fit better the real data distribution. *Mixture of Gaussians* is a superposition formed as a finite linear combination of simple Gaussian densities and it is widely used in statistical pattern recognition [24]:

$$p(\mathbf{x}) = \sum_{k=1}^{K} \omega_k \mathcal{N}(\mathbf{x}|\mu_k, \Sigma_k), \tag{3}$$

where $\mathcal{N}$ is a single normal density defined by μ_k and Σ_k. The mixing coefficients verify $\sum_k \omega_k = 1$ and $0 \leq \omega_k \leq 1$ for all k. By using a sufficient number of Gaussians, and by adjusting their means and covariances as well as the coefficients in the linear combination, almost any continuous density can be approximated to arbitrary accuracy [24].

The HMMs are basically statistical models that describe sequence of events and it is a very used technique in speech and emotions recognition. In classification tasks, a model is estimated for every signal class. Thus, it would take into

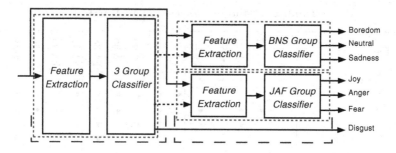

Fig. 3. General structure of the hierarchical classifier for 7 emotions

account as many models as signal classes to recognize. During classification, the probability for each signal given the model is calculated. The classifier output is based on the model with the maximum probability of generating the unknown signal [25]. Here, the problem is presented as:

$$\hat{E} = \arg\max_{E} P(E|A), \qquad (4)$$

where A is the sequence of acoustic features taken from speech signal and E represent the emotion.

Based in previous studies [7], the GMM and a two state HMM were picked. Tests increasing the number of Gaussian components in the mixtures were performed to find the optimal structure. In order to optimize the MLP performance, different numbers of neurons in hidden layer were tested.

3.2   Hierarchical Classifiers

The main motivations for the development of a hierarchical classifier are to take advantage of spectral emotion similarities to improve the emotion recognition rate. We also used the fact that it is more probable that better results for a particular emotion can be achieved when the number of emotions decreases for the same standard classifier. Furthermore, the main differences between specific emotions are more evident with a particular feature vector and the best classification is obtained through a specialized classifier and structure. As can be seen from Fig. 3, the hierarchical classifier is defined in two levels. In a first stage the emotion utterance would be classified in one of 3 groups (BNS, JAF or Disgust), then it would be classified again in its corresponding block group (if it is not Disgust) and finally the emotion label is obtained.

To define the hierarchical model structure in each block, several configurations of MLP and HMM with different parameter vectors, were evaluated. Finally, the model stages were chosen and assembled with classifiers that achieved better results in isolated block tests.

In every MLP block test, 15 feature vectors were tested in 3 different hidden layer configurations (90, 120 and 150 perceptrons). To select the feature vectors

Table 1. Feature vectors used in MLP tests

Parameters	FV12	FV14	FV16	FV18	FV20	FV30	FV32	FV34	FV36	FV38	FV42	FV44	FV46	FV48	FV50
12 MFCC	•	•	•	•	•						•	•	•	•	•
30 Mean Log-Spectrum						•	•	•	•	•	•	•	•	•	•
$\mu(F_0)$, $\mu(E)$		•	•	•	•		•	•	•	•		•	•	•	•
$\sigma(F_0)$, $\sigma(E)$			•		•			•		•			•		•
$Min(F_0)$, $Max(F_0)$				•	•				•	•				•	•
$Min(E)$, $Max(E)$				•	•				•	•				•	•

we considered the most relevant combinations of MLS, MFCC and prosodic parameters. Table 1 shows the number of characteristics for each vector and what kind of features it includes. For example, the feature vector FV14 includes 12 MFCC, the F_0 mean and the Energy mean. On the other hand, a 36 coefficients vector was used for HMM tests (12 MFCCs plus delta and acceleration), like in [7].

In MLP experiments, 60% of data was randomly selected for training, 20% was used for the generalization test and the remaining 20% was left for validation. The MLP training was stopped when the network reached the generalization peak with test data [23]. In HMM cases, the 20% used for test was added to the standard train set.

4   Results and Discussions

In order not to favor one of the emotions over the others, in the experiments the same number of utterances was used for every emotion. This balanced partition has 46 randomly selected utterances for each emotion. Every utterance has one label according to the expressed emotion and represents only one pattern.

A comparative analysis between GMM and HMM for recognition of seven emotions was presented in [7]. Better results were achieved with a two state HMM with mixtures of 30 Gaussians, using a MFCC parameterization including delta and acceleration coefficients. The best result with GMM was with mixtures of 32 Gaussians. Here, the same systems with the balanced partition were tested in order to obtain the baseline reference's to compare results. The classification rates were 63.49% with GMM and 66.67% with HMM. In this work, the number of output nodes in the MLP equals the number of seven emotions and the performance was 68.25% for the network composed by FV46 input neurons and 90 hidden neurons (considered here as the baseline for MLP classification).

For the Stage I in the hierarchical classifier, three different options were evaluated: (a) to re-group HMM baseline outputs into 3 groups (HMM^{7}g^3); (b) to model each group with one HMM (HMM^3); and (c) to use a MLP with 3 output neurons. In HMM cases, the number of Gaussian components in the mixture was set to 30 (as best results in [7]). Table 2 shows the MLP results for each feature vector with train and validation data. Best results obtained for Stage I

Table 2. Results of MLP classification for 3 Groups. Classification rate in [%].

Input	Best Net	Train	Validation
FV12	12+90+3	98.98	85.71
FV14	14+90+3	95.92	87.30
FV16	16+90+3	97.96	87.30
FV18	18+150+3	98.47	79.37
FV20	20+90+3	100.00	77.78
FV30	30+90+3	100.00	87.30
FV32	32+90+3	99.49	85.71
FV34	34+120+3	**98.98**	**88.89**
FV36	36+90+3	99.49	84.13
FV38	38+120+3	100.00	82.54
FV42	42+120+3	92.86	87.30
FV44	44+150+3	96.94	84.13
FV46	46+150+3	94.39	85.71
FV48	48+90+3	100.00	80.95
FV50	50+150+3	100.00	82.54

Table 3. Performance of Stage I classification models

	HMM grouped	HMM	MLP
JAF	88.89	77.78	88.89
BNS	85.19	92.59	100.00
D	66.67	88.89	55.56
average	84.13	85.71	**88.89**

Table 4. Results of JAF with MLP in isolated classification. Classification rate in [%].

Input	Best Net	Train	Validation
FV12	12+150+3	98.81	81.48
FV14	14+150+3	90.48	85.19
FV16	16+150+3	95.24	74.07
FV18	18+90+3	86.90	74.07
FV20	20+120+3	85.71	77.78
FV30	30+90+3	98.81	77.78
FV32	32+120+3	100.00	70.37
FV34	34+90+3	100.00	77.78
FV36	36+120+3	76.19	74.07
FV38	38+90+3	73.81	77.78
FV42	42+90+3	100.00	81.48
FV44	44+90+3	100.00	85.19
FV46	46+90+3	**100.00**	**85.19**
FV48	48+90+3	100.00	85.19
FV50	50+150+3	100.00	85.19

are summarized in Table 3. It can be seen that MLP achieved the best result but it is the worst classifying Disgust. This could be because MLP is not a good classifier when the classes are unbalanced.

For each block in Stage II, HMM and MLP tests were done using the partition data to evaluate the blocks in an isolated form. In HMM case, tests altering the number of Gaussian components in the mixture, increasing by two every time, were performed. A HMM with 26 Gaussians in the mixtures achieved a 74.07% for JAF test, while only 4 Gaussians achieved a 77.78% for the BNS case. The

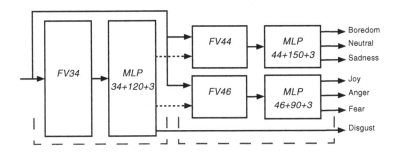

Fig. 4. Best hierarchical classifier for 7 emotions

Table 5. Results of BNS with MLP in isolated classification. Classification rate in [%].

Input	Best Net	Train	Validation
FV12	12+90+3	84.52	66.67
FV14	14+90+3	100.00	74.07
FV16	16+90+3	100.00	66.67
FV18	18+150+3	96.43	48.15
FV20	20+150+3	94.05	51.85
FV30	30+90+3	100.00	74.07
FV32	32+120+3	92.86	74.07
FV34	34+90+3	96.43	66.67
FV36	36+90+3	92.86	62.96
FV38	38+120+3	100.00	59.26
FV42	42+150+3	96.43	70.37
FV44	44+150+3	**97.62**	**81.48**
FV46	46+120+3	100.00	77.78
FV48	48+90+3	95.24	59.26
FV50	50+120+3	97.62	66.67

Table 6. Best results for isolated Stage II classification

Group	Stage II model	Performance
JAF	MLP	85.19
	HMM	74.07
BNS	MLP	81.48
	HMM	77.78

Table 7. Final test of hierarchical model

Stage I		Stage II				Best
Model	Disgust	JAF		BNS		
		HMM	MLP	HMM	MLP	
HMM^{7}g^3	66.67	66.67	**74.07**	62.96	70.37	71.43
HMM^3	**88.89**	55.56	62.96	74.07	77.78	73.02
MLP	55.56	66.67	**74.07**	77.78	**81.48**	**74.60**

Table 8. Results of standard classifiers and hierarchical model.

Model	Performance
GMM	63.49
HMM	66.67
MLP	68.25
Hierarchical	**74.60**

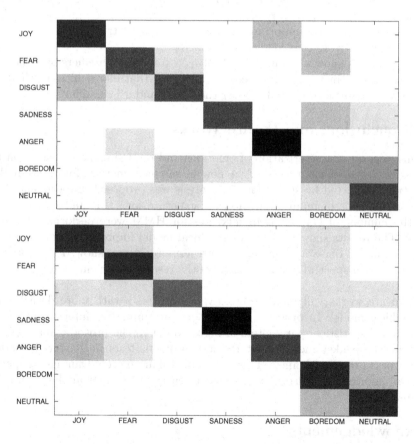

Fig. 5. Confusion matrices from best HMM baseline 66.67% (above) and from hierarchical classifier 74.60% (below)

MLP results for JAF and BNS classification could be seen in Table 4 and Table 5 respectively. Best results for the isolated blocks of Stage II are shown in Table 6.

The best HMM and MLP models for JAF and BNS were extracted. These blocks were evaluated in cascade with each first stage model. In Table 7, the performance for JAF and BNS blocks with both models are shown for each model in Stage I. The performances for the best combination considering each model in Stage I are: 71.43% for HMMs re-grouped (HMM^{7}g^3), 73.02% for 3 HMMs (HMM^3) and 74.60% for MLP.

Finally, the best hierarchical model is formed by a MLP with FV34 and 120 hidden neurons in the Stage I; a MLP with FV46 and 90 hidden neurons for the JAF block and a MLP with FV44 and 150 hidden neurons for the BNS block. Figure 4 shows the best hierarchical model configuration. As can be seen, spectral and some prosodic features (FV34) are the best to classify the 3 groups. However, the MFCC are required to improve the recognition in both blocks of the Stage II. In Figure 5 can be seen the confusion matrix obtained from hierarchical classifier and the confusion matrix obtained from the best HMM baseline. In confusion matrix from hierarchical no emotions have low recognition rate. The main diagonal is more important than in the other matrix which is consistent with the highest rate of recognition obtained.

In Table 8 is shown a comparison between standard classifiers and the best hierarchical classifier here proposed. Results show that hierarchical method improves the performance in 6.35% over the best standard classifier.

5   Conclusions and Future Works

In this paper a characterization of emotions and their similarities based on the acoustical features was presented. A new hierarchical method for emotion classification supported by such acoustic analysis was proposed. Experiments with different number of inputs and internal structure for MLP and tests increasing the number of Gaussians in mixtures for HMM were performed for each block. The results show that the hierarchical model improves recognition rates of the standard one-stage classifiers. Furthermore, it was showed that prosody combined with spectral features improves the results in the emotion recognition task.

In future works will improve cross-validation tests with more data for the hierarchical model. In order to obtain more discriminative information it will be included statistical parameters of higher order in the prosodic analyses. Although the speaker independent results are good, tests in gender dependent frameworks are also planned. This will allow taking more advantage of specific spectral information. Also, it is planned to carry out similar analyses on other languages.

Acknowledgements

The authors wish to thank: the *Agencia Nacional de Promoción Científica y Tecnológica* and *Universidad Nacional de Litoral* (with PAE 37122, PAE-PICT

00052, CAID 012-72), the *Universidad Nacional de Entre Ríos* (with PID 61111-2 and 6107-2), the *Consejo Nacional de Investigaciones Científicas y Técnicas* (CONICET) from Argentina, for their support.

References

1. Clavel, C., Vasilescu, I., Devillers, L., Richard, G., Ehrette, T.: Fear-type emotion recognition for future audio-based surveillance systems. Speech Commun. 50(6), 487–503 (2008)
2. Devillers, L., Vidrascu, L.: Real-Life Emotion Recognition in Speech. In: Müller, C. (ed.) Speaker Classifcation II. LNCS (LNAI), vol. 4441, pp. 34–42. Springer, Heidelberg (2007)
3. Tacconi, D., Mayora, O., Lukowicz, P., Arnrich, B., Setz, C., Troster, G., Haring, C.: Activity and emotion recognition to support early diagnosis of psychiatric diseases. In: Pervasive Computing Technologies for Healthcare, 2008. Second International Conference on Pervasive Health 2008, February 2008, pp. 100–102 (2008)
4. Kim, J., André, E.: Emotion recognition based on physiological changes in music listening. IEEE Transactions on Pattern Analysis and Machine Intelligence 30(12), 2067–2083 (2008)
5. Schindler, K., Gool, L.V., de Gelder, B.: Recognizing emotions expressed by body pose: A biologically inspired neural model. Neural Networks 21(9), 1238–1246 (2008)
6. Vinhas, V., Reis, L.P., Oliveira, E.: Dynamic Multimedia Content Delivery Based on Real-Time User Emotions. Multichannel Online Biosignals Towards Adaptive GUI and Content Delivery. In: BIOSIGNALS 2009 - International Conf. on Bio-inspired Systems and Signal Processing, Porto (Portugal), pp. 299–304 (2009)
7. Albornoz, E.M., Crolla, M.B., Milone, D.H.: Recognition of emotions in speech. In: Proceedings of XXXIV CLEI, Santa Fe Argentina, September 2008, pp. 1120–1129 (2008)
8. Borchert, M., Dusterhoft, A.: Emotions in speech - experiments with prosody and quality features in speech for use in categorical and dimensional emotion recognition environments. In: Proceedings of IEEE International Conference on Natural Language Processing and Knowledge Engineering, IEEE NLP-KE 2005, October 2005, pp. 147–151 (2005)
9. El Ayadi, M., Kamel, M., Karray, F.: Speech Emotion Recognition using Gaussian Mixture Vector Autoregressive Models. In: IEEE International Conference on Acoustics, Speech and Signal Processing. ICASSP 2007, April 2007, vol. 4, pp. 957–960 (2007)
10. Rong, J., Chen, Y.P., Chowdhury, M., Li, G.: Acoustic Features Extraction for Emotion Recognition. In: 6th IEEE/ACIS International Conference on Computer and Information Science, ICIS 2007, July 2007, pp. 419–424 (2007)
11. Morrison, D., Wang, R., Silva, L.C.D.: Ensemble methods for spoken emotion recognition in call-centres. Speech Communication 49(2), 98–112 (2007)
12. Schuller, B., Rigoll, G., Lang, M.: Speech emotion recognition combining acoustic features and linguistic information in a hybrid support vector machine-belief network architecture. In: IEEE International Conference on Acoustics, Speech, and Signal Processing (Proceedings ICASSP 2004), May 2004, vol. 1, pp. I-577–I-580 (2004)

13. Fu, L., Mao, X., Chen, L.: Speaker independent emotion recognition based on SVM/HMMs fusion system. In: International Conf. on Audio, Language and Image Processing, ICALIP 2008, July 2008, pp. 61–65 (2008)
14. Burkhardt, F., Paeschke, A., Rolfes, M., Sendlmeier, W., Weiss, B.: A Database of German Emotional Speech. In: Proc. Interspeech 2005, September 2005, pp. 1517–1520 (2005)
15. Schuller, B., Vlasenko, B., Arsic, D., Rigoll, G., Wendemuth, A.: Combining speech recognition and acoustic word emotion models for robust text-independent emotion recognition. In: IEEE International Conference on Multimedia and Expo, April 2008, pp. 1333–1336 (2008)
16. Cowie, R., Cornelius, R.: Describing the emotional states that are expressed in speech. Speech Communication 40(1), 5–32 (2003)
17. Kim, J.: Bimodal Emotion Recognition using Speech and Physiological Changes. In: Robust Speech Recognition and Understanding, pp. 265–280. I-Tech Education and Publishing, Vienna (2007)
18. Scherer, K.R.: What are emotions? And how can they be measured? Social Science Information 44(4), 695–729 (2005)
19. Noguerias, A., Moreno, A., Bonafonte, A., Mariño, J.: Speech Emotion Recognition Using Hidden Markov Models. In: Eurospeech 2001, pp. 2679–2682 (2001)
20. Young, S., Evermann, G., Kershaw, D., Moore, G., Odell, J., Ollason, D., Valtchev, V., Woodland, P.: The HTK Book (for HTK Version 3.1). Cambridge University Engineering Department, England (2001)
21. Deller, J.R., Proakis, J.G., Hansen, J.H.: Discrete-Time Processing of Speech Signals. Macmillan Publishing, New York (1993)
22. Adell Mercado, J., Bonafonte Cávez, A., Escudero Mancebo, D.: Analysis of prosodic features: towards modelling of emotional and pragmatic attributes of speech. In: Procesamiento del lenguaje natural, September 2005, vol. (35), pp. 277–283 (2005)
23. Haykin, S.: Neural Networks: A Comprehensive Foundation, 2nd edn. Prentice-Hall, Englewood Cliffs (1998)
24. Bishop, C.M.: Pattern Recognition and Machine Learning, 1st edn. Springer, Heidelberg (2006)
25. Rabiner, L.R., Juang, B.H.: Fundamentals of Speech Recognition. Prentice-Hall, Englewood Cliffs (1993)

Emotional Vocal Expressions Recognition Using the COST 2102 Italian Database of Emotional Speech

Hicham Atassi[1,2], Maria Teresa Riviello[3], Zdeněk Smékal[2],
Amir Hussain[1], and Anna Esposito[3]

[1] Department of Computing Science and Mathematics, University of Stirling, UK
[2] Brno University of Technology, Department of Telecommunications, Czech Republic
[3] Second University of Naples, Department of Psychology and IIASS, Italy
atassi@feec.vutbr.cz, iiass.annaesp@tin.it

Abstract. The present paper proposes a new speaker-independent approach to the classification of emotional vocal expressions by using the COST 2102 Italian database of emotional speech. The audio records extracted from video clips of Italian movies possess a certain degree of spontaneity and are either noisy or slightly degraded by an interruption making the collected stimuli more realistic in comparison with available emotional databases containing utterances recorded under studio conditions. The audio stimuli represent 6 basic emotional states: *happiness, sarcasm/irony, fear, anger, surprise,* and *sadness*. For these more realistic conditions, and using a speaker independent approach, the proposed system is able to classify the emotions under examination with 60.7% accuracy by using a hierarchical structure consisting of a Perceptron and fifteen Gaussian Mixture Models (GMM) trained to distinguish within each pair (couple) of emotions under examination. The best features in terms of high discriminative power were selected by using the Sequential Floating Forward Selection (SFFS) algorithm among a large number of spectral, prosodic and voice quality features. The results were compared with the subjective evaluation of the stimuli provided by human subjects.

Keywords: Emotion recognition, speech, Italian database, spectral features, high level features.

1 Introduction

Recently, the classification of emotional vocal expressions has turned out to be a very interesting field of study due to the increasing need for algorithms that can recognize the emotional states of speakers. Such systems can find application in many fields, such as media retrieval and entertainment, as in the robot AIBO equipped by a module for vocal emotion recognition [1, 2] or in call centres [3], where the analysis of users' emotional states could give a fair idea about clients' satisfaction and in remote health monitoring interfaces to identify successful or unsuccessful human-machine interaction, among many others.

A. Esposito et al. (Eds.): COST 2102 Int. Training School 2009, LNCS 5967, pp. 255–267, 2010.
© Springer-Verlag Berlin Heidelberg 2010

The first work dealing with the task of vocal emotion recognition was proposed in 1984 [4], where a relatively simple algorithm was introduced for this purpose. A special interest was then also devoted to those algorithms able to detect stress from speech signals, since stress detection can be very useful in the security domain [5].

The emotion recognition from speech can be either speaker dependent or speaker independent. In the first case, it is allowed to use utterances from the same speaker to validate the classification process. Regarding the classification accuracy, the speaker dependent approach gives much better results than the speaker-independent approach as reported by the excellent results of Navas et al. [6], where about 98% accuracy was achieved by using the Gaussian Mixture Model (GMM) as a classifier and prosodic and voice quality as well as Mel Frequency Cepstral Coefficient (MFCC) as speech features. However, the speaker-dependent approach is not practicable in many applications, since it mostly works with a very large number of possible users (speakers). To our knowledge, for speaker independent applications, the best classification accuracy was 81% [7] and was obtained on the Berlin Database of Emotional Speech (BDES) [9] using a two-step classification approach and a unique set of spectral, prosodic and voice features selected through the Sequential Floating Forward Selection (SFFS) algorithm [8].

The Berlin Database of Emotional Speech (BDES) [9] as well as most of the existing emotional audio databases, consist of audio stimuli recorded under studio conditions and therefore do not possess either naturalistic and/or genuine emotional characteristics. The present work instead proposes a speaker-independent algorithm able to recognize more realistic and genuine vocal emotional expressions. To this aim it uses the Italian COST 2102 database of emotional sentences (http://cost2102.cs.stir.ac.uk). Distinct from the existing emotional databases, this database possesses a certain degree of spontaneity since the Italian actors/actresses producing the sentences were acting according to the movie script and their performance had been judged as appropriate to the required emotional context by the movie director (supposed to be an expert). In addition, as audio records extracted from movies, they are either noisy or slightly degraded by an interruption that makes the Italian database more realistic. A detailed description of the database is given in the next section.

We started with a basic one-step approach by using one classifier and a set of commonly chosen features without any kind of fusion and without any coupling of emotional states (the term "coupling" will be described later). The classification accuracy for this setup (we shall refer to it as a baseline) was not satisfactory (about 40% accuracy on the six basic emotions under examination). Consequently the two-step algorithm of Atassi and Esposito [7] successfully validated by using the Berlin Database of Emotional Speech (BDES) [9] was applied. However, since the Italian database is more spontaneous and the selected sentences were produced in a noisy environment, the classification accuracy was extremely low (about 47%).

In the light of the above facts, it appears obvious that there is a need to find a new approach that will be able to make a significant improvement in terms of classification accuracy, which is a challenging issue given the spontaneity and realistic nature of the data considered.

The paper is organized as follows: The first section gives a brief description of the Italian database while the second and third sections are dedicated to describing the feature extraction and classification processes respectively. The next section reports the results and finally some concluding remarks are presented.

2 The Italian Database of Emotional Speech

The collected data are based on extracts from Italian movies whose protagonists were carefully chosen among actors and actresses that are largely acknowledged by the critique and considered capable of giving some very real and careful interpretations. The database consists of audio stimuli representing 6 basic emotional states: *happiness, sarcasm/irony, fear, anger, surprise*, and *sadness* [10].

For each of the above listed emotional states, 36 stimuli were identified, 18 expressed by an actor and 18 expressed by an actress, for a total of 216 audio stimuli. The stimuli were selected short in duration (the average stimulus' length was 2.5s, SD = ± 1s). This was due to two reasons: 1) longer stimuli may produce overlapping of emotional states and confuse the subject's perception; 2) emotional states for definition cannot last more than a few seconds and then other emotional states or moods take place in the interaction [11].

Care was taken in choosing the stimuli such that the semantic meaning of the sentences expressed by the protagonists was not clearly expressing the portrayed emotional state and its intensity level was moderate. For example, we avoided to include in the data, sadness stimuli where the actress/actor were clearly crying or happiness stimuli where the protagonist was strongly laughing. This was because we wanted the subjects to exploit emotional signs that could be less obvious but that were generally employed in every natural and not extreme emotional interaction.

The emotional labels assigned to the stimuli were given first by two expert judges and then by three native judges independently. The expert judges made a decision on the stimuli carefully exploiting emotional information on facial and vocal expressions such as frame by frame analysis of changes in facial muscles, and F_0 contour, rising and falling of intonation contour, etc, as reported by several authors in literature [12, 13, 14, 15, 16] and also exploiting the contextual situation the protagonist was interpreting.

The native judges made their decision after watching the stimuli several times. There were no opinion exchanges between the experts and naïve judges and the final agreement on the labelling between the two groups was 100%.

The stimuli in each set were then randomized and proposed to the Italian subjects with the aim to assess the selected stimuli trough the judgment of native Italian speakers participating at the experiments. To this aim the stimuli were divided into two sets. A first set of 60 audio stimuli, 10 stimuli for each emotion (5 produced by a male and 5 by a female) were assessed by a group a 30 Italian subjects. A second set of 156 stimuli was assessed by a different group of 40 Italian subjects. In both the groups, males and females were equally distributed.

Subjects were required to carefully listen and/or watch the experimental stimuli via headphones in a quiet room. They were instructed to pay attention to each presentation and decide which of the 6 emotional states was expressed in it. Responses were recorded on a matrix paper form (60x8) where the rows listed the stimuli numbers and the columns the 6 possible emotional states plus an option for any other emotion not listed in the form called "*others*", plus the option for a *neutral* state. For each emotional stimulus, both the frequency response distribution among the 8 emotional classes under examination (*happiness, sarcasm/irony, fear, anger, surprise, sadness, others,* and *neutral*) and the percentage of correct recognition were computed. The same procedure was then repeated for the remaining 156 stimuli with the new group of 40 Italian subjects. Details on the procedures and the stimuli assessment are reported in [17-18, 38].

3 Features Extraction

Features usually used to recognize emotional vocal expressions can be divided into three main groups: prosodic features, voice quality features and spectral features. In the present work a combination of them is used. Following below more details on such features are discussed.

3.1 Prosodic and Voice Quality Features

Prosodic and voice quality features are widely employed to recognize emotions from speech [19, 20]. The contours (consisting mostly on smooth averages of variations in time of F_0 and related measurements such as the first and second derivatives [21, 22]) of these features but also, some statistical measures (known as high level features) obtained from these contours are frequently used to train a classifier. A previous work [7] showed the high discriminative power of these high level features in distinguishing within couples of emotions, hence their usage also in the proposed application. In addition, also voice quality features such as harmonicity, frequencies and bandwidths of first three formants and their first and second derivatives [24] were used. In summary a total number of 225 high level features including mean, maximum, minimum, slope, standard deviation and other statistical measurements measured in speech frames 125 ms long with 50% of overlap were considered.

3.2 Spectral Features

These features are derived from the FFT power spectrum of speech segments. In the present work three types of spectral features are taken into account:

MFCCs: Mel Frequency Cepstral Coefficients. These well-known features are adopted, as an encoding method, in many fields of speech and audio signal processing among those musical genre recognition, speaker and speech recognition. And in many dedicated works on the recognition of emotional vocal expressions [6, 25].

PLPs: Perceptual Linear Predictive features were primarily used for speech recognition and showed better results in comparison with the typical MFCC encoding [26]. Some works employed PLPs such as [27] for vocal emotion recognition.

MELBs: Mel Bank Spectrum features are rarely used for emotion recognition, one of the exceptions is the work presented in [28]. MELBs are used in the speech processing domain as features for Voice Activity Detector (VAD) algorithms [29] as well as for speech segmentation [30]. However it should be mentioned here that many proposed papers have employed spectral energies in different frequency bands as features to recognize emotions from speech [21], and analogously, MELBs could be considered as an enhanced alternative for those band energies since it involves the mapping of the power spectrum onto the perceptual MEL frequency scale.

Generally, the classifier training process could be carried out either on frame or utterance level. On the frame level, each frame is considered as a single input training pattern. The classification (decision making) process is then applied on each frame separately. The final decision about the utterance emotion is taken according to the appearance of each class (emotion) in the obtained result. We found out through experiments made that this approach doesn't give satisfying results.

If each utterance is considered as a single input pattern in the classification process, it should be taken into account the different number of segments obtained from each utterance, that yields feature vectors with various lengths after the concatenation of the spectral characteristics (such as MFCC) extracted from the frames of each utterance under examination. A possible solution to this inconvenient is to zero padding in order to have vectors of the same length. However, this solution didn't give satisfying results in terms of classification accuracy. A better way to handle the problem would be to use feature space reduction techniques such as Vector Quantization algorithms like k-means or Principal Component Analysis (PCA) [31]. In the present work a relatively simple space reduction method is proposed based on spectral vector averaging that had provided better results than PCA or k-means on the data under examination. The principle of the proposed space reduction approach is shown in Figure 1 and is applied according to the following steps:

1. The spectral feature vectors are extracted from speech frames 250 ms long with 50% of overlap. The frame length was set through several trial and error processes. It could be surprising that the chosen length (250ms) is significantly longer than that usually used for phoneme-based speech applications as observed by Apolloni et al. [27] "*affective acoustic parameters are characterized by a lower rate of variability in time than linguistic ones*".

2. The spectral feature vectors obtained from the first, second and third part of a given utterance are separately averaged, i.e., the centroids of corresponding spectral feature vectors are computed. All three utterance parts have the same length. The purpose of dividing utterances into parts was to include temporal information in the final feature vector. The centroids are computed as follows:

$$\mathbf{x}_m^j = \frac{\sum_{n=\alpha_1}^{\alpha_2} \mathbf{x}_n^j}{\left\lfloor \frac{N}{3} \right\rfloor}, \qquad j = 1, 2, 3. \tag{1}$$

Where $\mathbf{x}_m^j$ is the j-th mean feature vector (centroid) of j-th utterance's part, N is the number of extracted spectral feature vectors, $\alpha_1 = \left\lfloor \frac{(j-1)N}{3} \right\rfloor$ and $\alpha_2 = \left\lfloor \frac{jN}{3} \right\rfloor - 1$.

The final spectral feature vector $\mathbf{x}_{sp}$ is obtained by concatenating the three centroids:

$$\mathbf{x}_{sp} = [\mathbf{x}_m^1, \mathbf{x}_m^2, \mathbf{x}_m^3]^T \tag{2}$$

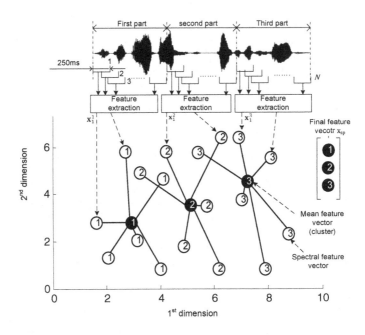

Fig. 1. The spectral features averaging procedure (for a better illustration, only the two-dimensional feature space is displayed)

3.3 Feature Selection

The Sequential Floating Forward Selection (SFFS) algorithm [8] was exploited in order to identify features that showed the maximum capability of discriminating within couples of emotions (we shall refer to this as emotion coupling). The SFFS algorithm was applied separately on the prosodic-voice quality features and the spectral features.

The advantage of the SFFS algorithm is that it identifies the best features according to their classification accuracy by using an arbitrary classifier. In our experiments, a GMM classifier (with one Gaussian per class) was used both for feature selection via the SFFS algorithm and for the overall validation of the proposed vocal emotion recognition algorithm. Thus, it could be stated that the features in our experiment were chosen with a high level of reliability since each GMM classifier used in the final proposed system has already found its optimal features through the SFFS algorithm.

The features that showed the best performance in distinguishing within couples of emotions are described in the Appendix.

4   Classification

Automatic recognition of emotional vocal expressions could be carried out by using different kinds of classifiers, such as Artificial Neural Networks [27, 32], Fuzzy logic systems [33], Hidden Markov Models [19], *k*-Nearest Neighbour [23], Support Vector Machines [34] and Gaussian Mixture Models [7, 21] among many others. Gaussian Mixture Models in combination with other classification schemas (fusion) is a classification strategy widely used in many pattern recognition applications [35, 36]. The proposed classifier uses two classification techniques fused together in two classification steps as illustrated in Figure 2.

The first step (see Figure 3) is used to train each sub-classifier $D^{(i)}$ to distinguish within couples of emotions. The likelihoods output by each classifier are then multiplied by each other. The final decision about the classes scores $\aleph_\omega$, $\aleph_{\omega'}$ is made according to the following formula

$$\aleph_\omega = \begin{cases} 1 & \text{for} \quad P(\omega|\mathbf{x}_{sp})P(\omega|\mathbf{x}_{pv}) > P(\omega'|\mathbf{x}_{sp})P(\omega'|\mathbf{x}_{pv}) \\ 0 & \text{for} \quad P(\omega|\mathbf{x}_{sp})P(\omega|\mathbf{x}_{pv}) < P(\omega'|\mathbf{x}_{sp})P(\omega'|\mathbf{x}_{pv}) \end{cases} \tag{3}$$

Where $P(\omega|\mathbf{x})$ is the posterior density distribution of the emotion category ω and given the feature vector $\mathbf{x}$ and $\mathbf{x}_{sp}$, $\mathbf{x}_{pv}$ are spectral and prosodic-voice quality feature vectors respectively.

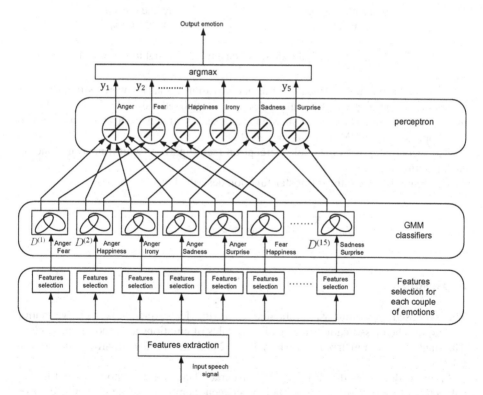

Fig. 2. The proposed classifier

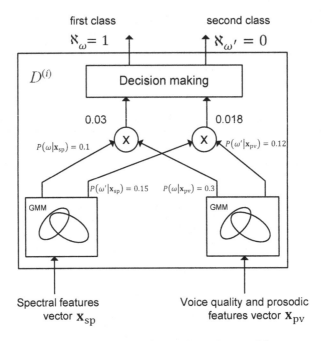

Fig. 3. The fusion of prosodic-voice quality and spectral feature vectors

The GMM parameters (mean vector and covariance matrix) were estimated using Estimation-Maximization (EM) algorithm [31] initialized using the k-means clustering algorithm [31]. Only one Gaussian was used to model each emotion category. This applies to all GMM used in our classifier.

The second step uses a Simple Perceptron (see Figure 2) with 6 neurons (one for each emotion).

The neurons have a linear transfer function described by:

$$ y_\omega = \sum_{i=1}^{N} \aleph_i^\omega, \qquad N = 5 \tag{5} $$

5   Results

The proposed algorithm was validated using the leave-one-speaker-out validation technique. The classification rates within couples of emotions are reported in Table 1. The final confusion matrix is shown in Table 2 and the average classification rate was 60.7%.

Figure 4 illustrates the differences in accuracy between the automatic and human subjective classification. The correlation between them is high (the normalized correlation here is $R=0.79$) even though the proposed system performs better for all the emotions except than for irony.

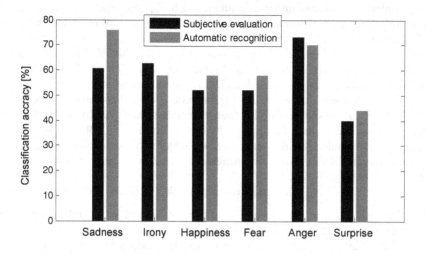

Fig. 4. The classification performance achieved by the proposed system and by human subjects

Table 1. Cross-emotion recognition within couples of emotions (average classification rate: 76.4 %)

	Anger	Fear	Happiness	Irony	Sadness	Surprise	average
Anger	-	73	70	76	84	77	**76**
Fear	71	-	72	87	76	68	**75**
Happiness	73	74	-	76	73	72	**74**
Irony	74	85	78	-	79	84	**80**
Sadness	89	80	77	81	-	85	**83**
Surprise	71	62	66	76	73	-	**70**

Table 2. The final confusion matrix for the six emotions under examination (average classification rate: 60.7 %)

	Anger	Fear	Happiness	Irony	Sadness	Surprise
Anger	**70**	6	6	12	6	0
Fear	9	**58**	9	9	12	3
Happiness	12	6	**58**	3	15	6
Irony	12	0	15	**58**	9	6
Sadness	0	6	12	3	**76**	3
Surprise	12	14	12	3	15	**44**

6 Conclusions and Future Work

This paper proposes a new approach for automatic speaker-independent vocal emotion recognition validated by using the COST 2102 Italian database of emotional speech. The proposed system is mainly based on a new classifier consisting of the fusion of a Simple Perceptron and fifteen GMM classifiers designed to distinguish within couples of emotions under examination. The optimal spectral, prosodic and voice quality features that showed high discriminative power were chosen by using the SFFS algorithm.

The mean classification rate of the presented system is 60.7% with a significant improvement of 20.7% with respect to the baseline result (40%) obtained with an automatic system previously proposed in [7] that , to our knowledge, had provided the best classification results on the BDES [9] database used as benchmark in recent literature. The obtained results are slightly better than those achieved by human subjects (56.5% on average) even though there is a high correlation ($R = 0.79$) among them. In the light of above results, it is difficult to answer why the presented system performed better than human subjects, since the difference in terms of classification accuracy among them is not significant.

Finally, as this work is a pilot study, our next work will aim to investigate:

- New approaches, features and classification algorithms in order to improve the currently obtained classification accuracy.
- The differences, if any, in the set of acoustic speech features that better describe emotional states if different languages are used.
- The influence of the speech quality on the classification performance using the Perceptual Evaluation of Speech Quality (PESQ) method proposed in [37].

Acknowledgments

This work has been funded by: COST 2102 "Cross Modal Analysis of Verbal and Nonverbal Communication", http://cost2102.cs.stir.ac.uk; Regione Campania, L.R. N.5 del 28.03.2002, Project ID N. BRC1293, Bando Feb. 2006; and by Projects OC08057, G1/2701/2009 of the Ministry of Education, Youth and Sports of the Czech Republic. We would also like to thank Mrs. Riana Atassi for her editorial help.

References

1. Christian, J., Deeming, A.: Affective Human-Robotic Interaction. Affect and Emotion in Human-Computer Interaction: From Theory to Applications, Christian Peter, Russell Beale (2008)
2. Sony AIBO Europe, Sony Entertainment,
   http://www.sonydigital-link.com/AIBO/
3. Petrushin, V.: Emotion in Speech: Recognition and Application to Call Centers. In: Proceedings of the Conference on Artificial Neural Networks in Engineering, pp. 7–10 (1999)
4. Van Bezooijen, R.: The Characteristics and Recognisability of Vocal Expression of Emotions. Drodrecht, The Netherlands, Foris (1984)
5. Rahurkar, M., Hansen, J.H.L.: Frequency Band Analysis for Stress Detection Using Teager energy Operator Based Feature. In: Proc. Int. Conf. Spoken Language Processing (ICSLP 2002), vol. 3, pp. 2021–2024 (2002)
6. Navas, E., Hernáez, L.I.: An Objective and Subjective Study of the Role of Semantics and Prosodic Features in Building Corpora for Emotional TTS. IEEE Transactions on Audio, Speech, and Language Processing 14, 1117–1127 (2006)

7. Atassi, H., Esposito, A.: A Speaker Independent Approach to the Classification of Emotional Vocal Expressions. In: Proc. of 20th Int. Conf. Tools with Artificial Intelligence, ICTAI 2008, pp. 147–151. IEEE Computer Society, Dayton (2008)
8. Pudil, P., Ferri, F., Novovicova, J., Kittler, J.: Floating search method for feature selection with non monotonic criterion functions. Pattern Recognition 2, 279–283 (1994)
9. Burkhardt, F., Paeschke, A., Rolfes, M., Sendlmeier, W., Weiss, B.: A Database of German Emotional Speech. In: Proceedings of Interspeech, pp. 1517–1520 (2005)
10. Ekman, P.: Facial expression of emotion: New findings, new questions. Psychological Science 3, 34–38 (1992)
11. Oatley, K., Jenkins, J.M.: Understanding emotions. Blackwell, Oxford (1996)
12. Banse, R., Scherer, K.: Acoustic profiles in vocal emotion expression. Journal of Personality & Social Psychology 70(3), 614–636 (1996)
13. Scherer, K.R.: Vocal communication of emotion: A review of research paradigms. Speech Communication 40, 227–256 (2003)
14. Scherer, K.R., Banse, R., Wallbott, H.G.: Emotion inferences from vocal expression correlate across languages and cultures. Journal of Cross-Cultural Psychology, 76–92 (2001)
15. Scherer, K.R., Banse, R., Wallbott, H.G., Goldbeck, T.: Vocal cues in emotion encoding and decoding. Motivation and Emotion 15, 123–148 (1991)
16. Scherer, K.R.: Vocal correlates of emotional arousal and affective disturbance. In: Wagner, H., Manstead, A. (eds.) Handbook of social Psychophysiology, pp. 165–197. Wiley, New York (1989)
17. Esposito, A., Riviello, M.T., Di Maio, G.: The COST 2102 Italian Audio and Video Emotional Database. In: To be published in Proceedings of WIRN 2009, Vietri sul Mare, May 28-30, IOS press, Amsterdam (2009)
18. Esposito, A., Riviello, M.T., Bourbakis, N.: Cultural Specific Effects on the Recognition of Basic Emotions: A Study on Italian Subjects. In: Holzinger, A. (ed.) USAB 2009. LNCS, vol. 5889, pp. 135–148. Springer, Heidelberg (2009)
19. Schuller, B., Rigoll, G., Lang, M.: Hidden Markov Model-Based Speech Emotion Recognition. In: Proc. of IEEE International Conference on Acoustics, Speech and Signal Processing, ICASSP 2003, Hong Kong, China, vol. 2 (2003)
20. Nogueiras, A., Marino, J.B., Moreno, A., Bonafonte, A.: Speech emotion recognition using hidden Markov models. In: Proc. European Conf. Speech Communication and Technology (Eurospeech 2001), Denmark (2001)
21. Ververidis, D., Kotropoulos, C.: Emotional speech classification using Gaussian mixture models and the sequential floating forward selection algorithm. In: Proc. Int. Conf. Multimedia and Expo, ICME 2005 (2005)
22. Ververidis, D., Kotropoulos, C.: Automatic Speech Classification to five emotional states based on gender information. In: Proc. 12th European Signal Processing Conf., Vienna, pp. 341–344 (2004)
23. Pao, T., Chen, Y., Yeh, J.: Emotion Recognition from Mandarin Speech Signals. In: International Symposium on Spoken Language Processing, Chinese (2004)
24. Lugger, M., Yang, B.: The Relevance of Voice Quality Features in Speaker Independent Emotion Recognition. In: Proceedings of ICASSP, Honolulu, Hawaii (2007)
25. Nwe, T.L., Foo, S.W., De Silva, L.C.: Speech emotion recognition using hidden Markov models. Speech Communication 41, 603–623 (2003)
26. Hermansky, H.: Perceptual Linear Predictive (PLP) Analysis of Speech. Journal of Acoustic Society (4), 1738–1753 (1990)
27. Apolloni, B., Aversano, G., Esposito, A.: Preprocessing and Classification of Emotional Features in Speech Sentences. In: Kosarev, Y. (ed.) Proc. of International Workshop on Speech and Computer, SPIIRAS, pp. 49–52 (2000)

28. Busso, C., Lee, S., Narayanan, S.S.: Using Neutral Speech Models for Emotional Speech Analysis. In: Interspeech- Eurospeech, Antwerp, Belgium, pp. 2225–2228 (2007)
29. Stejskal, V., Smekal, Z., Esposito, A., Bourbakis, N.: The Significance of Empty Speech Pauses: Cognitive and Algorithmic Issues. In: Mele, F., Ramella, G., Santillo, S., Ventriglia, F. (eds.) BVAI 2007. LNCS, vol. 4729, pp. 1–13. Springer, Heidelberg (2007)
30. Esposito, A., Aversano, G.: Text Independent Methods for Speech Segmentation. In: Chollet, G., Esposito, A., Faúndez-Zanuy, M., Marinaro, M. (eds.) Nonlinear Speech Modeling and Applications. LNCS (LNAI), vol. 3445, pp. 261–290. Springer, Heidelberg (2005)
31. Duda, R., Hart, P., Stork, D.: Pattern Classification, 2nd edn. Wiley, Chichester (2003)
32. Scherer, S., Oubbati, M., Schwenker, F., Palm, G.: Real-time emotion recognition using echo state model. In: André, E., Dybkjær, L., Minker, W., Neumann, H., Pieraccini, R., Weber, M. (eds.) PIT 2008. LNCS (LNAI), vol. 5078, pp. 200–204. Springer, Heidelberg (2008)
33. Lee, C., Narayanan, S.: Emotion recognition using a data-driven fuzzy inference system. In: Proceedings of Eurospeech, pp. 157–160 (2003)
34. Schuller, B., Rigoll, G., Lang, M.: Speech emotion recognition combining acoustic features and linguistic information in a hybrid support vector machine-belief network architecture. In: Proceedings of International Conference on Acoustics, Speech and Signal Processing (ICASSP 2004), vol. 1, pp. 557–560 (2004)
35. Kuncheva, L.I.: Combining Pattern Classifiers: Methods and Algorithms. Wiley, Hoboken (2004)
36. Faundez-Zanuy, M.: Data Fusion at Different Levels. In: Multimodal Signals: Cognitive and Algorithmic Issues: COST Action 2102 and euCognition International School Vietri sul Mare, Italy, pp. 21–26 (2008)
37. Beerends, J.G., Rix, A.W., Hollier, M.P., Hekstra, A.P.: Perceptual evaluation of speech quality (PESQ) The new ITU standard for end-to-end speech quality assessment, Part I – Time-Delay Compensation. J. Audio Eng. Soc. 50(10), 755–764 (2002)
38. Esposito, A., Riviello, T.: The New Italian Audio and Video Emotional Database. In: Esposito, A., et al. (eds.) Development of Multimodal Interfaces: Active Listening and Synchrony. LNCS, vol. 5967, pp. 255–267. Springer, Heidelberg (2010)

Appendix

The selected prosodic, voice quality and spectral features for all couples of emotional states using the SFFS algorithm.

Emotions couples	prosodic and voice quality features	Spectral features
Anger X fear	energy slope minimum, pitch slope mean, range of pitch second derivative, mean of energy second derivative	ΔMFCC, ΔMELB
Anger X happiness	energy range, second formant mean	MELB, ΔPLP
Anger X irony	mean of pitch second derivative, pitch minimum, pitch standard deviation, second formant bandwidth standard deviation	PLP, ΔPLP
Anger X sadness	pitch range, maximum of energy second derivative, pitch mean, energy median, second formant standard deviation	PLP, MELBS
Anger X surprise	maximum of pitch second derivative, maximum of energy second derivative, pitch slope standard deviation, mean of pitch second derivative, first formant mean, harmonicity mean.	ΔMELBS, ΔPLP
Happiness X fear	jitter, energy slope maximum, harmonicity mean	MFCC,ΔPLP,ΔMELBS
Happiness X irony	Jitter, pitch minimum, mean of pitch second derivative, maximum of pitch first derivative, maximum of pitch second derivative	ΔPLP,MELBS
Happiness X sadness	pitch relative maximum, range of energy second derivative, harmonicity standard deviation	MELBS,ΔMELBS
Happiness X surprise	jitter, standard deviation of energy second derivative, second formant standard deviation, harmonicity maximum	ΔΔPLP,ΔΔMELBS
Irony X fear	mean of energy second derivative, pitch slope maximum, pitch slope minimum, pitch standard deviation, mean of pitch first derivative, jitter, standard deviation of energy second derivative	MFCC,ΔPLP,ΔΔPLP
Sadness X fear	energy slope minimum, pitch median, First formant frequency mean, first formant bandwidth mean	MFCC,PLP,ΔPLP, ΔΔMELBS
Sadness X irony	energy median, Energy slope minimum, energy range	MEBLS, MFCC, ΔPLP
Sadness X surprise	energy slope maximum, pitch relative maximum, minimum of pitch second derivative	PLP,MELBS,ΔMFCC, ΔΔMFCC
Surprise X fear	range of pitch second derivative	MFCC , PLP, ΔPLP
Surprise X irony	mean of pitch second derivative, energy slope standard deviation, relative maximum of energy first derivative, energy slope standard deviation, range of pitch first derivative	ΔPLP, ΔΔPLP, MELBS

Microintonation Analysis of Emotional Speech

Jiří Přibil[1,2] and Anna Přibilová[3]

[1] Institute of Photonics and Electronics, Academy of Sciences CR, v.v.i.,
Chaberská 57, CZ-182 51 Prague 8, Czech Republic
[2] Institute of Measurement Science, SAS,
Dúbravská cesta 9, SK-841 04 Bratislava, Slovakia
Jiri.Pribil@savba.sk
[3] Slovak University of Technology, Faculty of Electrical Engineering & Information
Technology, Dept. of Radio Electronics, Ilkovičova 3, SK-812 19 Bratislava, Slovakia
Anna.Pribilova@stuba.sk

Abstract. The paper addresses reflection of microintonation in male and female acted emotional speech. Microintonation component of speech melody is analyzed regarding its spectral and statistical parameters. Achieved statistical results of microintonation analysis show good correlation comparing male and female voices for four emotional states (joy, sadness, anger, neutral state) portrayed by several professional actors.

Keywords: Speech analysis, emotional speech, jitter, microintonation.

1 Introduction

Emotional speech is characterized by prosodic features (F0, energy, duration) and several voice quality features (e.g. jitter, shimmer, glottal-to-noise excitation ratio, Hammarberg index) [1-4]. The voice quality parameter "jitter" describes pitch perturbations in the context of vocal expression. There exist different approaches to define vocal jitter: majority of authors use definitions resulting from perturbation in pitch period [1, 5-11], some authors define jitter as pitch frequency perturbation [12, 13]. According to [14] jitter is difficult to manipulate for actors and there is only tendency for anger portrayals to show more jitter than sadness portrayals. On the other hand, in [15] an example is reported that a speaker may increase F0 jitter for "happiness" rather than increasing the overall pitch level. For similar perturbations in the context of music performance the term "microintonation" is used [14]. However, phoneticians use also the term "microintonation" or "micromelody" describing local changes in F0 as a part of microprosody [16]. Strictly speaking, "microprosody" comprises pitch, duration, and energy short-term localized changes [17].

In our present work we analyze microintonation of male and female emotional speech representing joy, sadness, anger, and a neutral state. Our approach to microintonation estimation is somewhat similar to that of [18] where jitter related to microvariations of a pitch curve is computed as a relative number of zero crossings of a derivative pitch curve normalized by utterance duration.

A. Esposito et al. (Eds.): COST 2102 Int. Training School 2009, LNCS 5967, pp. 268–279, 2010.
© Springer-Verlag Berlin Heidelberg 2010

Our research aimed at microintonation analysis was motivated by requirement of higher naturalness of synthetic speech with expression of emotions. We want to implement microintonation into a pitch-synchronous cepstral speech synthesizer by superimposing a small random variable to each pitch period. In this way the effect of jitter can be modeled in the voiced parts of the synthesized speech. Randomization will be controlled by statistical results of analyzed emotional speech corresponding to different emotions. This modification can be applied directly to the text-to-speech (TTS) system enabling expressive speech production [19].

On the other hand, we need to remove the microintonation component before creating a database of emotional prosodic prototypes for emotional speaking style conversion using a similar TTS system [20]. When compared with other speech melody components, the microintonation signal is a high-frequency signal and it can be filtered out of the melody contour and processed separately. Microintonation statistical and spectral analysis for several speakers expressing several emotions will be further used to synthesize a FIR filter suppressing the microintonation part of the speech signal.

2 Subject and Method

Microintonation, together with sentence melody and word melody, represents melody of speech given by F0 contour. Microintonation component of speech melody can be supposed to be a random, band-pass signal that can be described by its spectrum and statistical parameters. Fig. 1 shows the block diagram of our speech processing method of microintonation analysis.

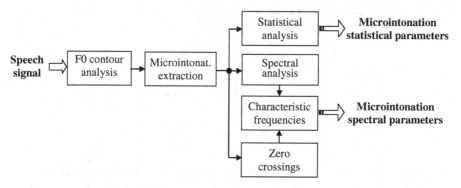

Fig. 1. Block diagram of microintonation statistical and spectral parameters estimation

Speech frames classified as voiced are analyzed separately depending on emotional state (joyous, sad, angry, and neutral) and voice type (male, female). The whole microintonation analysis procedure is divided into four phases:

1. Determination of F0 values, definition of the voiced and unvoiced parts of the processed speech signal.
2. F0 contour analysis, microintonation extraction, calculation of zero crossing parameters, determination of pitch periods and jitter calculation (for comparison with microintonation values) in the voiced parts of the speech signal.

3. Microintonation and zero crossing statistical analysis of the concatenated signal (see Fig. 2 and Fig. 4).
4. Microintonation signal spectral analysis and 3-dB bandwidth (B_3) determination from the concatenated signal (see Fig. 3 and Fig. 5).

The introductory microintonation processing phase consists of the following steps:

1. Determination of the melody contours from the voiced parts of speech smoothed by a median filter.
2. Determination of $F0_{mean}$ values and calculation of the *linear trend* (LT) by the mean square method.
3. Calculation of differential microintonation signal $F0_{DIFF}$ by subtraction of these values from the corresponding F0 contours ($F0_{mean}$ and LT removal)

$$F0_{DIFF}(n) = (F0(n) - F0_{Mean}) - LT(n) \ . \tag{1}$$

4. Calculation of the absolute jitter J_{Abs} values, as the average absolute difference between consecutive pitch periods L measured in samples [10]

$$J_{Abs} = \frac{1}{f_s(N_L - 1)} \sum_{n=1}^{N_L-1} |L_n - L_{n+1}| \, , \tag{2}$$

where f_s is the sampling frequency and N_L is the number of extracted pitch periods.

5. Detection of zero crossings, calculation of zero crossing periods L_Z.

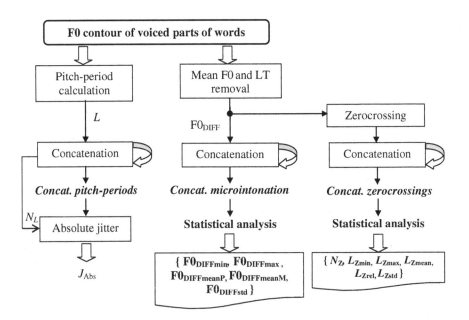

Fig. 2. Block diagrams of microintonation signal analysis: basic and zero crossing statistical analysis, absolute jitter calculation

Basic statistical analysis phase is performed in tree steps:

1. Statistical analysis of microintonation signal: minimum, maximum, and standard deviation (mean value of microintonation signal approaches to zero). For both positive and negative microintonation values the mean parameters are determined.
2. Statistical analysis of zero crossing periods: minimum, maximum, mean values, standard deviation, and a relative value defined as $L_{Zrel} = N_F / N_Z$ - where N_Z is the total number of zero crossings in each of the four emotions, and N_F is the total number of voiced frames.
3. Calculation and building of histograms from zero crossing periods L_Z for each of the emotion groups and both voices. Subjective evaluation by visual comparison of histograms and objective evaluation by hypothesis tests of distributions and analysis of variance (ANOVA) with multiple comparison of groups.

Spectral analysis of concatenated differential microintonation signal is also carried out for all emotions. This analysis phase is divided into three steps (see Fig. 3):

1. Calculation of the frequency parameters from the zero crossing periods $L_{Zx} = \{L_{Zmin}, L_{Zmax}, L_{Zmean}, L_{Zrel}, L_{Zstd}\}$ as $F_{Zxl} = f_F / (2 \cdot L_{Zx})$, where f_F is the frame frequency.
2. Microintonation signal spectral analysis by periodogram averaging using the Welch method.
3. Determination of B_3 values from these spectra for each of the emotion types.

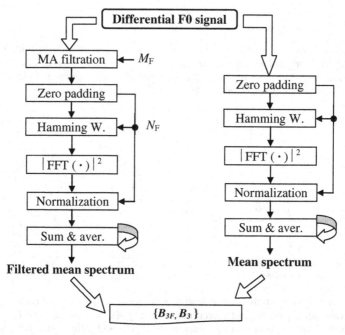

Fig. 3. Block diagrams of microintonation signal spectral analysis

To obtain spectrum of smoothed microintonation signal (see Fig. 5b), the concatenated differential F0 signal is filtered by a moving average filter of the length M_F (Voiced parts shorter than M_F+2 frames are not processed in further analysis).

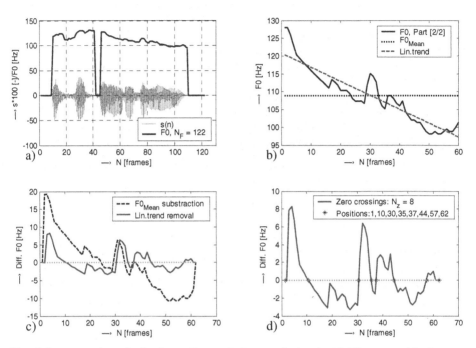

Fig. 4. Demonstration of microintonation analysis: speech signal with F0 contour (a), the second voiced part: original F0, mean F0, and LT (b), differential signal after F0$_{mean}$ and LT subtraction (c), zero crossings of differential F0 signal (d) – the sentence "Řekl Radomil" ("Radomil said") uttered in sad emotional style by a male Czech speaker.

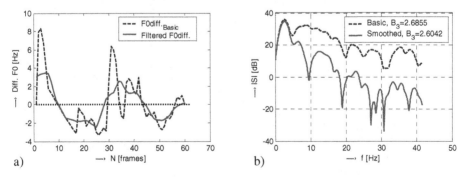

Fig. 5. Demonstration of microintonation smoothing and spectrum determination (obtained from the same sentence's second voiced part as in Fig. 4): basic differential F0 signal and the one filtered by moving average (a), corresponding spectra and their 3-dB bandwidths B3 (b).

3 Material, Experiments, and Results

Speech material for microintonation analysis was collected in two databases (male and female voices – 132 sentences, 8+8 speakers altogether) consisting of neutral and emotional sentences uttered by several speakers (extracted from the Czech and Slovak stories uttered by professional actors). Classification of emotional states was carried out manually, by subjective listening method with the help of distributed listening test program [21]. Each of the extracted sentences was evaluated by a small group of listeners. Every sentence having been evaluated as expressing the same emotional state by all listeners was added to our database.

The frame length depends on the mean pitch period of the processed signal. In our experiment, we had chosen overlapped 24-ms frames in 12-ms intervals for male voice, and 16-ms frames in 8-ms intervals for female voice. It corresponds to the frame frequency $f_F = 83.3$ Hz for males, and $f_F = 125$ Hz for females. The typical mean pitch-period length in samples of neutral emotional style, male voice is $L \approx 140$ which corresponds to 8.75 ms for $f_s = 16$ kHz, in the case of female voice it is $L \approx 80$ samples, corresponding to 5 ms.

Pitch contours were given with the help of the PRAAT [1] program [22]. The minimum length of the processed voiced parts was experimentally set to 10 frames and the corresponding filter length of $M_F = 8$ was chosen. Number of analyzed voiced parts / voiced frames) was:

- neutral: 112/2698, joy: 79/1927, sadness: 128/3642, anger: 104/ 2391 – <u>Male</u>.
- neutral: 86/2333, joy: 87/2541, sadness: 92/2203, anger: 91/2349 – <u>Female</u>.

Results of basic statistical microintonation analysis in comparison with absolute jitter values for all four emotional states are summarized in Tab. 1 (male voice) and Tab. 2 (female voice). Results of performed zero crossing analysis for male / female voices are shown in Tab. 3 / Tab. 4. Summary histograms of zero crossing periods L_Z for different emotions in dependence on the speaker gender are shown in Fig. 7 and Fig. 8.

For objective statistical comparison of zero crossing periods L_Z the Ansari-Bradley test [24] was performed. If is the test of the hypothesis that two independent samples come from the same distribution against the alternative that they come from distributions having the same median and shape but different variances. The result is $h = 0$ if the null hypothesis of identical distributions cannot be rejected at the 5% significance level, or $h = 1$ if the null hypothesis can be rejected at the 5% level. This test also returns the probability of observing the given result, or one more extreme by chance if the null hypothesis is true. Small values of this probability cast doubt on the validity of the null hypothesis.

The results of the hypothesis tests based on comparison of distributions are presented in Tab. 5 for the male voice group, in Tab. 6 for the female voice group, and in Tab. 7 for both voices. The second approach based on ANOVA was applied to zero

---

[1] The PRAAT internal settings for F0 values determination were experimentally chosen by visual comparison of testing sentences (one typical sentence from each of emotions and voice classes) as follows: cross-correlation analysis method [23], pitch-range 35÷250 Hz for male and 105÷350 Hz for female voices.

crossing periods L_Z together with multiple comparison test. Fig. 9 shows the graph with each group mean represented by a symbol and an interval around the symbol. Two means are significantly different if their intervals are disjoint, and are not significantly different if their intervals overlap.

Table 1. Summary results of microintonation basic statistical analysis (differential F0 parameters in [Hz]) together with absolute jitter values (in [ms]) – <u>male voice</u>

Emotion	$F0_{DIFFmin}$	$F0_{DIFFmax}$	$F0_{DIFFmeanP}$ [*]	$F0_{DIFFmeanN}$ [**]	$F0_{DIFFstd}$	J_{Abs}
Neutral	-10.57	13.18	2.66	-3.07	3.92	0.2908
Joy	-31.76	37.62	7.27	-7.22	9.71	0.7057
Sadness	-32.97	25.71	4.02	-3.95	5.57	0.4485
Anger	-46.32	45.17	8.62	-8.89	10.23	0.6014

[*] calculated from positive microintonation values.

[**] calculated from negative microintonation values.

Table 2. Summary results of microintonation basic statistical analysis and jitter values – <u>female voice</u>

Emotion	$F0_{DIFFmin}$	$F0_{DIFFmax}$	$F0_{DIFFmeanP}$ [*]	$F0_{DIFFmeanN}$ [**]	$F0_{DIFFstd}$	J_{Abs}
Neutral	-44.39	38.35	4.11	-5.46	7.06	0.1673
Joy	-40.87	43.55	11.85	-10.78	14.39	0.3329
Sadness	-54.28	50.66	7.05	-7.32	10.29	0.2354
Anger	-44.35	42.95	10.16	-10.16	13.07	0.3450

[*] calculated from positive microintonation values.

[**] calculated from negative microintonation values.

Table 3. Summary results of zero crossing analysis (zero crossing period L_Z parameters in [frames]) – <u>male voice</u>

Emotion	N_Z	L_{Zmax} [*]	L_{Zmean}	L_{Zstd}
Neutral	592	26	6.04	4.19
Joy	403	59	8.26	6.52
Sadness	681	57	6.82	5.69
Anger	521	23	6.74	4.57

[*] $L_{Zmin} = 1$.

Table 4. Summary results of zero crossing analysis – <u>female voice</u>

Emotion	N_Z	L_{Zmax} [*]	L_{Zmean}	L_{Zstd}
Neutral	636	27	4.77	3.79
Joy	448	36	7.68	5.44
Sadness	680	40	5.41	4.81
Anger	381	23	5.83	3.66

[*] $L_{Zmin} = 1$.

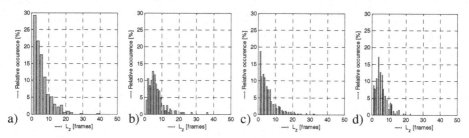

Fig. 7. Histograms of zero crossing periods L_Z calculated from differential F0 signal: "neutral" style (a), and emotions - "joy" (b), "sadness" (c), and "anger" (d) – male voice

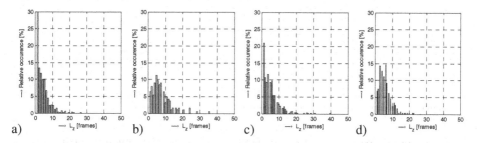

Fig. 8. Histograms of zero crossing periods L_Z calculated from differential F0 signal: "neutral" style (a), and emotions - "joy" (b), "sadness" (c), and "anger" (d) – female voice

Table 5. Partial results of zero crossing periods L_Z Ansari-Bradley hypothesis tests based on comparison of distribution – <u>male</u> voice group

*)	Neutral	Joy	Sadness	Anger
Neutral	**0/1**	$1 / 3.37 \ 10^{-7}$	1 / 0.035	1 / 0.066
Joy		**0/1**	$1 / 8.99 \ 10^{-7}$	1 / 0.006
Sadness			**0/1**	1 / 0.021
Anger				**0/1**

*) null hypothesis / probability values for 5% significance level.

Table 6. Partial results of zero crossing periods L_Z hypothesis tests – <u>female</u> voice group

*)	Neutral	Joy	Sadness	Anger
Neutral	**0/1**	$1 / 4.8810^{-15}$	1 / 0.006	1 / 0.017
Joy		**0/1**	1 / 0.002	$1 / 4.01.10^{-8}$
Sadness			**0/1**	1 / 0.002
Anger				**0/1**

*) null hypothesis / probability values for 5% significance level.

Table 7. Summary results of zero crossing periods L_Z hypothesis tests (comparison <u>male</u> vs. <u>female</u> voice group) between particular emotions

	Neutral	Joy	Sadness	Anger
$h / p^{*)}$	0 / 0.4397	0 / 0.8926	0 / 0.6953	0 / 0. 5773

*) null hypothesis / probability values for 5% significance level.

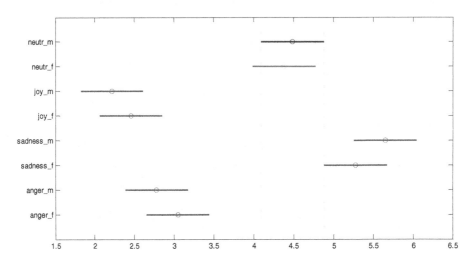

Fig. 9. Graphics results of zero crossing periods L_Z multiple comparison of ANOVA (<u>male</u> and <u>female</u> voice groups) for corresponding emotions

Zero crossing periods were subsequently used to calculate microintonation signal spectral analysis. Obtained results of spectral analysis including the 3-dB bandwidth values are shown in Tab. 8 for male voice, and in Tab. 9 for female voice. The average microintonation spectra (with and without smoothing by moving average) can be seen in Fig. 10 (male voice), and Fig. 11 (female voice).

Table 8. Summary results of spectral analysis (frequency parameters in [Hz] derived from concatenated differential F0 signal) – <u>male voice</u>.

Emotion	F_{Zmin} [*]	F_{Zmean}	F_{Zrel}	F_{Zstd}	B_3	B_{3F} [**]
Neutral	1.60	6.89	8.83	9.93	6.75	4.56
Joy	0.71	5.04	6.45	6.39	4.56	3.82
Sadness	0.73	6.11	7.78	7.23	4.39	2.69
Anger	1.81	6.18	8.00	9.12	5.37	4.07

[*] $L_{Zmin} = 1 \Rightarrow F_{Zmax} = f_F / 2$.
[**] 3-dB bandwidth corresponding to the signal smoothed by moving average filter with $M_F = 8$.

Table 9. Summary results of spectral analysis – <u>female voice</u>

Emotion	F_{Zmin} [*]	F_{Zmean}	F_{Zrel}	F_{Zstd}	B_3	B_{3F} [**]
Neutral	2.23	11.88	14.60	16.52	11.59	6.71
Joy	1.56	9.41	11.94	11.94	9.03	5.61
Sadness	1.56	9.33	11.66	11.52	7.20	3.17
Anger	2.08	9.88	12.59	14.11	10.74	5.86

[*] $L_{Zmin} = 1 \Rightarrow F_{Zmax} = f_F / 2$.
[**] 3-dB bandwidth corresponding to the signal smoothed by moving average filter with $M_F = 8$.

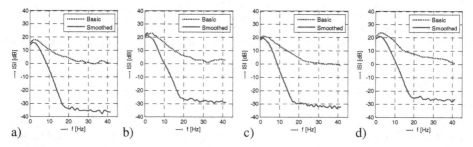

Fig. 10. Spectra of microintonation used for 3-dB bandwidth determination for emotions (with and without smoothing by moving average): "neutral" (a), "joy" (b), "sadness" (c), and "anger" (d) - male voice, $f_F = 83.3$ Hz

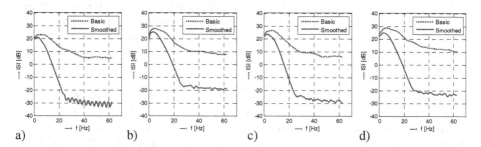

Fig. 11. Spectra of microintonation used for 3-dB bandwidth determination for emotions (with and without smoothing by moving average): "neutral" (a), "joy" (b), "sadness" (c), and "anger" (d) - female voice, $f_F = 125$ Hz

4   Conclusion

Statistical and spectral analysis of microintonation signal component of speech melody for several speakers and four emotional states (joy, sadness, anger, neutral state) was performed. From comparison of basic statistical microintonation analysis stored in Tab. 1 and Tab. 2 follows, that absolute jitter values are in accordance with the human vocal tract properties. Female shorter pitch periods are accompanied with shorter values of the absolute jitters, but higher relative changes in the frequency domain (mean $F0_{DIFF}$ values). The highest values of jitter correspond to "joy" and the lowest ones correspond to "sadness" for both voices. Similar results are shown in [25].

The same tendency can be observed for statistical results of zero crossing analysis. Although different frame lengths were used in microintonation frequency analysis for male and female voices, we can see matched similar values for all corresponding emotions. Visual comparison of histograms of zero crossing periods L_Z is not significant, but higher relative occurrence of low L_Z values can be noticed in "neutral" style for both voices. From objective statistical comparison of zero crossing periods L_Z by Ansari-Bradley hypothesis test follows, that the null hypotheses were rejected at the 5% significance level for each of the emotion types inside the gender group (see Tab. 5 and Tab. 6). On the other hand, the null hypotheses between the corresponding emotions of both types of voices are in all cases fulfilled at the same significance level (see Tab. 7). The result of final multiple comparison of ANOVA also confirms good correlation between particular emotions as shown Fig. 9.

Obtained results of spectral analysis (especially the B_3 and B_F values in Tab. 8 and Tab. 9) will be used to synthesize a digital filter for suppression of microintonation component of a speech signal. For microintonation removal from the F0 contour we can use FIR filters, e.g. an averaging filter or using Hann, Bartlett, or Hamming window. The first zero frequency of the transmission function of the averaging rectangular filter F_1 (approximate 1/2 of the main lobe width) will be given by $F_1 = f_F / M$, where M will the filter length. If we set this frequency F_1 equal to e.g. B_3 value, we obtain the rectangular filter length $M_R = f_F / F_1$. For the other three mentioned filters, the required filter length will be $M_X = 2 . M_R$. As regards visual comparison of average spectra in Fig. 10 and Fig. 11, the applied filtering by moving average was effective, the minimum signal suppression is about 25 dB for all emotions of both voices.

Out next aim will be to construct a special random noise generator for microintonation control and implement it to our TTS system with expressive speech production. This random generator will produce the samples (values for pitch-period length randomization) with different distribution in dependence of chosen type of emotion, as were analyzed in this paper.

Acknowledgments. The work has been done in the framework of the COST 2102 Action. It has also been supported by the Grant Agency of the Czech Republic (GA102/09/0989), by the Grant Agency of the Slovak Academy of Sciences (VEGA 2/0142/08) and the Ministry of Education of the Slovak Republic (VEGA 1/0693/08).

References

1. Iriondo, I., Planet, S., Socoró, J.-C., Martínez, E., Alías, F., Monzo, C.: Automatic Refinement of an Expressive Speech Corpus Assembling Subjective Perception and Automatic Classification. Speech Communication 51, 744–758 (2009)
2. Gobl, C., Ní Chasaide, A.: The Role of Voice Quality in Communicating Emotion, Mood and Attitude. Speech Communication 40, 189–212 (2003)
3. Keller, E.: The Analysis of Voice Quality in Speech Processing. In: Chollet, G., Esposito, A., Faúndez-Zanuy, M., Marinaro, M. (eds.) Nonlinear Speech Modeling and Applications. LNCS (LNAI), vol. 3445, pp. 54–73. Springer, Heidelberg (2005)
4. Campbell, N.: On the Use of Nonverbal Speech Sounds in Human Communication. In: Esposito, A., Faundez-Zanuy, M., Keller, E., Marinaro, M. (eds.) COST Action 2102. LNCS (LNAI), vol. 4775, pp. 117–128. Springer, Heidelberg (2007)
5. d'Alessandro, C., Darsinos, V., Yegnanarayana, B.: Effectiveness of a Periodic and Aperiodic Decomposition Method for Analysis of Voice Sources. IEEE Transactions on Speech and Audio Processing 6, 12–23 (1998)
6. Schoentgen, J.: Decomposition of Vocal Cycle Length Perturbations into Vocal Jitter and Vocal Microtremor, and Comparison of Their Size in Normophonic Speakers. Journal of Voice 17, 114–125 (2003)
7. Rank, E., Kubin, G.: An Oscillator-Plus-Noise Model for Speech Synthesis. Speech Communication 48, 775–801 (2006)
8. Hagmüller, M., Kubin, G.: Poincaré Pitch Marks. Speech Communication 48, 1650–1665 (2006)

9. Shahnaz, C., Zhu, W.-P., Ahmad, M.: A New Technique for the Estimation of Jitter and Shimmer of Voiced Speech Signal. In: Proceedings of the Canadian Conference on Electrical and Computer Engineering, CCECE 2006, Ottawa, Canada, pp. 2112–2115 (2006)
10. Farrús, M., Hernando, J., Ejarque, P.: Jitter and Shimmer Measurements for Speaker Recognition. In: Proceedings of the International Conference Interspeech 2007, Antwerp, Belgium, pp. 778–781 (2007)
11. Vasilakis, M., Stylianou, Y.: Spectral Jitter Modeling and Estimation. Biomedical Signal Processing and Control 4, 183–193 (2009)
12. Perrot, P., Aversano, G., Chollet, G.: Voice disguise and automatic detection: Review and perspectives. In: Stylianou, Y., Faundez-Zanuy, M., Esposito, A. (eds.) COST 277. LNCS, vol. 4391, pp. 101–117. Springer, Heidelberg (2007)
13. Murphy, P.: Source-Filter Comparison of Measurements of Fundamental Frequency Perturbation and Amplitude Perturbation for Synthesized Voice Signals. Journal of Voice 22, 125–137 (2008)
14. Juslin, P.N., Laukka, P.: Communication of Emotions in Vocal Expression and Music Performance: Different Channels, Same Code? Psychological Bulletin 129, 770–814 (2003)
15. Tao, J., Xin, L., Yin, P.: Realistic Visual Speech Synthesis Based on Hybrid Concatenation method. IEEE Transactions on Audio, Speech, and Language Processing 17, 469–477 (2009)
16. Duběda, T., Keller, E.: Microprosodic Aspects of Vowel Dynamics – An Acoustic Study of French, English and Czech. Journal of Phonetics 33, 447–464 (2005)
17. Low, P., Vaseghi, H.: Applying F0, Duration and Power Models with Microprosody Components in Text to Speech (TTS) Synthesis. In: Proceedings of the 47th International Symposium on Multimedia Systems and Applications, ELMAR 2005, Zadar, Croatia, pp. 229–232 (2005)
18. Navas, E., Hernáez, I., Luengo, I.: An Objective and Subjective Study of the Role of Semantics and Prosodic Features in Building Corpora for Emotional TTS. IEEE Transactions on Audio, Speech, and Language Processing 14, 1117–1127 (2006)
19. Přibil, J., Přibilová, A.: Application of Expressive Speech in TTS System with Cepstral Description. In: Esposito, A., Bourbakis, N.G., Avouris, N., Hatzilygeroudis, I. (eds.) HH and HM Interaction. LNCS (LNAI), vol. 5042, pp. 200–212. Springer, Heidelberg (2008)
20. Přibil, J., Přibilová, A.: Emotional Style Conversion in the TTS System with Cepstral Description. In: Esposito, A., Faundez-Zanuy, M., Keller, E., Marinaro, M. (eds.) COST Action 2102. LNCS (LNAI), vol. 4775, pp. 65–73. Springer, Heidelberg (2007)
21. Přibil, J., Přibilová, A.: Distributed Listening Test Program for Synthetic Speech Evaluation. In: Proceedings of the 34 Jahrestagung für Akustik DAGA 2008, Dresden, Germany, pp. 241–242 (2008)
22. Boersma, P., Weenink, D.: Praat: Doing Phonetics by Computer, Version 5.0.32 (Computer Program), http://www.praat.org/ (Retrieved August 12, 2008)
23. Boersma, P., Weenink, D.: Praat - Tutorial, Intro 4. Pitch analysis, September 5, (2007), http://www.fon.hum.uva.nl/praat/manual/Intro_4__Pitch_analys is.html
24. Everitt, B.S.: The Cambridge Dictionary of Statistics, 3rd edn. Cambridge University Press, Cambridge (2006)
25. Tao, J., Kang, Y., Li, A.: Prosody Conversion from Neutral Speech to Emotional Speech. IEEE Transactions on Audio, Speech, and Language Processing 14, 1145–1154 (2006)

Speech Emotion Modification Using a Cepstral Vocoder

Martin Vondra and Robert Vích

Institute of Photonics and Electronics,
Academy of Sciences of the Czech Republic Chaberská 57,
CZ 18251 Prague 8, Czech Republic
{vondra,vich}@ufe.cz

Abstract. This paper deals with speech modification using a cepstral vocoder with the intent to change the emotional content of speech. The cepstral vocoder contains the analysis and synthesis stages. The analysis stage performs the estimation of speech parameters – vocal tract properties, fundamental frequency, intensity, etc. In this parametric domain the segmental and suprasegmental speech modifications may be performed and than the speech can be reconstructed using the parametric source-filter cepstral model. We use the described cepstral vocoder and speech parameter modifications as a tool for research in emotional speech modeling and synthesis. The paper is focused rather on the description of this system and its possibilities than to precise settings of parameter modifications for speech generation with given emotions. The system is still under development. Plans for future research are shortly summarized.

1 Introduction

Today's Text-To-Speech (TTS) systems produce high quality and intelligible speech, but there is still much to do with regard to naturalness. The research is now focusing on enabling the production of various expressive speaking styles.

The first efforts to produce emotional speech begun after the first rule-based TTS system was developed. The well known ones are the Affect Editor [1], HAMLET [2] and EMOSYN [3], which use the commercial DECtalk or KLSYN88 TTS system. These methods are based on the modification of rules for neutral speech synthesis obtained by the analysis of natural emotional speech. The quality of output speech is given mainly by the used TTS system which generates intelligible, but machine-like speech. Now for TTS synthesis concatenation of speech units obtained from natural speech recordings is mainly used. The diphone or triphone units are the most often used. In these systems it is possible to change only the prosody of the produced speech. First experiments to produce emotional speech by prosody modification in this type of TTS system were performed by Burkhardt [4]. For convincing emotional speech we have to include not only prosody or suprasegmental speech parameters, but we must also control the voice quality given by the segmental features. For this purpose spectral modification techniques [5, 6] were used, which were originally developed for voice conversion [7, 8].

A. Esposito et al. (Eds.): COST 2102 Int. Training School 2009, LNCS 5967, pp. 280–285, 2010.

In our institute we have developed voice transformation techniques which are based on a cepstral vocoder [9]. It allows both prosody and spectral modification, but it decreases the quality of speech to some extent because it is based on a parametric source-filter model, where only a binary excitation signal is used. We aspire to improve the quality by better voiced excitation modeling using a prototype excitation obtained by inverse speech filtering.

Section 2 is dedicated to the description of the cepstral vocoder, section 3 describes methods for pitch, duration and excitation signal modification. The last section 4 contains a conclusion and some directions for future research.

2 Cepstral Vocoder

The cepstral vocoder is composed of the analysis and synthesis parts, see Fig. 1. The speech parameters are estimated in the analysis part. For vocal tract modeling with 16 kHz sampling frequency the first 51 real cepstral coefficients are computed and the information about the excitation given by the fundamental frequency is estimated.

The synthesis part consists of the excitation (for voiced speech the excitation signal prototypes, for unvoiced speech white noise is used) and of the cepstral model of the vocal tract. The cepstral vocal tract model is a time varying digital filter with coefficients given by the cepstrum corresponding to the minimum phase speech signal, obtained by appropriate windowing of the real cepstrum [10].

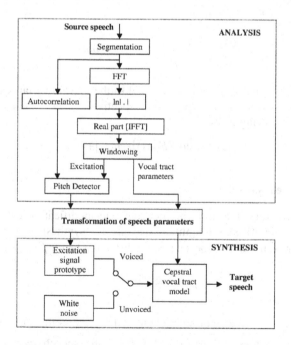

Fig. 1. Cepstral vocoder for voice conversion

3 Speech Modification

In this section the speech parameter modifications are described. These modifications are applied on the parameters of the source speech to reach the target speech by reconstruction of speech from modified source speech parameters in the cepstral vocoder. The source speech can be a sentence in neutral style and the target speech is the same sentence in some emotional speech style pronounced by the same speaker. This allows the comparison between the converted and the target speech and can be easily evaluated by listening tests. The description is focused rather to the demonstration how speech can be modified by the cepstral vocoder than to give precise settings of parameter modifications for reaching speech with prescribed emotion.

3.1 Fundamental Frequency Modification

The fundamental frequency F_0 modification applied in the described speech modification system matches the mean values and standard deviations of the source and target speakers. This approach was inspired by the method used in the voice conversion technique [11]. In order to take into account the nonlinearity of F_0 perception we do not operate directly with F_0 in Hz but we use the natural logarithm of F_0.

$$\log(F_{0T}(t)) = a \log(F_{0S}(t)) + b .\tag{1}$$

$F_{0T}(t)$ denotes the target instantaneous fundamental frequency and $F_{0S}(t)$ is the source instantaneous fundamental frequency,

$$a = \sqrt{\frac{\sigma_{TF}^2}{\sigma_{SF}^2}} = \frac{\sigma_{TF}}{\sigma_{SF}} , \quad b = m_{TF} - a m_{SF} .\tag{2}$$

The values σ_{TF}, σ_{SF} and m_{TF}, m_{SF} correspond to the $\log(F_0)$ variances and mean values for the target and the source speakers, respectively. This expression may be rearranged into the following form

$$\log(F_{0T}(t)) = a[\log(F_{0S}(t)) - m_{SF}] + m_{TF} .\tag{3}$$

3.2 Speech Rate Modification

In the cepstral vocoder the uniform speaking rate modification can be simply performed by choosing different lengths of analysis and synthesis frames for which one set of parameters is used. The speech rate modification factor β can be formulated as

$$\beta = \frac{L_{synthesis}}{L_{analysis}} ,\tag{4}$$

where $L_{synthesis}$ is the synthesis frame length and $L_{analysis}$ is the analysis frame length. The speech rate decreases for $\beta > 1$, for $\beta < 1$ the speech rate increases. In the simplest case the speech rate modification factor β is constant for the whole utterance. This enables linear speech rate modification. In a real situation the speech rate fluctuates during speech according to the speaking style even for the same speaker. Generally, in emotional speech the speech rate is modified. But every phonetic unit can have a different speech rate modification factor β. In accordance with literature [12] we use the approximate duration variations of phones by different modification factors β for voiced speech, for unvoiced speech and for pauses.

3.3 Excitation Signal for Speech Synthesis

Classical speech vocoders use various algorithms to determine the excitation signal for parametric synthesis. The well known ones are RELP (Residual Excited Linear Prediction) and CELP (Code Excited LP). These algorithms are the so called analysis by synthesis approaches. The aim is to reach the most natural excitation signal in the synthesis stage. Because excitation signal carries significant characteristics of the emotional content of speech [14] we cannot use the excitation signal obtained in the analysis stage.

First we want to use the glottal model for excitation of voiced speech where it is possible in order to control some properties of human glottis to obtain tense, falsetto, harsh, creaky, etc. voice characteristics which can relate to speech emotion [15]. In our approach there is a problem with the cepstral representation of speech which estimates the vocal tract spectrum based on the assumption of flat excitation spectrum. Some properties of the excitation are thus included in the cepstral vocal tract model. For this reason, in our vocoder a prototype excitation signal is used. This prototype is obtained by inverse filtering of the steady part of one vowel. For each emotion one excitation pitch pulse (Fig. 2) is created, which is either abbreviated or lengthened by adding zeros to obtain the appropriate pitch. This excitation pitch pulse is continuously repeated for the synthesis of voiced speech.

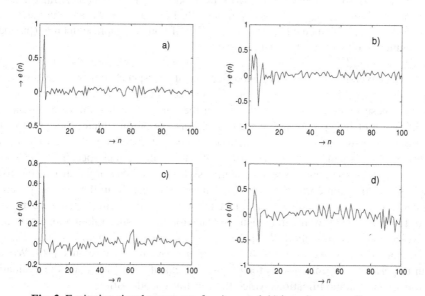

Fig. 2. Excitation signal prototypes for a) neutral, b) joy, c) sorrow, d) anger

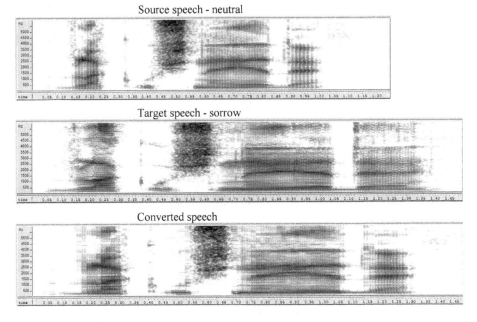

Fig. 3. Spectrograms of source, target and converted speech

4 Conclusion

This paper describes the basic framework for modification of speech characteristics in order to reach emotional expressivity in speech. For this task we use the parametric cepstral vocoder which enables the modification of both the suprasegmental (prosody) and segmental (speech timbre) speech features.

For the modification of the fundamental frequency we use the simple mean-variance conversion method. For modification of the speech rate we use three constant speech rate modification factors for voiced speech, unvoiced speech and for pauses. These factors can be obtained from the analysis of natural speech data. For modification of the speech timbre we use various excitation signal prototypes for the parametric cepstral speech reconstruction. These prototypes are obtained by inverse filtering of the steady part of one vowel of natural emotional speech. Fig. 3 shows spectrograms of the source speech (neutral style) and of the target speech (sorrow). The last spectrogram corresponds to the converted speech from the source speech by the cepstral vocoder (F_0, speech rate and excitation signal modifications were used).

In future we want to integrate also modification of the spectral envelope similar to the voice conversion method [7, 8]. Next, more sophisticated modifications based on a codebook of utterance contours of F_0 would improve the performance [16]. We also plan to perform perception tests for the assessment of our system and the evaluation of various speech modifications which the cepstral vocoder offers.

Acknowledgements

This paper has been supported within the framework of COST2102 by the Ministry of Education, Youth and Sport of the Czech Republic, project number OC08010 and by the National research program "Targeted Research" of the Academy of Sciences of the Czech Republic, project number 1QS108040569.

References

1. Cahn, J.E.: Generating Expression in Synthesized Speech. Master's Thesis, MIT (1989)
2. Murray, I.R., Arnott, J.L.: Implementation and testing of a system for producing emotions-by-rule in synthetic speech. Speech Communication 16, 369–390 (1995)
3. Burkhardt, F., Sendlmeier, W.F.: Verification of Acoustic Correlates of Emotional Speech using Formant-Synthesis. In: Proc. of ISCA Workshop on Speech & Emotions, pp. 151–156 (2000)
4. Burkhardt, F.: Emofilt: the Simulation of Emotional Speech by Prosody-Transformation. In: Proc. of Interspeech 2005, Lisbon, Portugal, September 4-8, pp. 509–512 (2005)
5. Türk, O., Schröder, M.: A Comparison of Voice Conversion Methods for Transforming Voice Quality in Emotional Speech Synthesis. In: Proc. of Interspeech 2008, Brisbane, Australia, September 23-26, pp. 2282–2285 (2008)
6. Inanoglu, Z., Young, S.: Data-driven emotion conversion in spoken English. Speech Communication 5, 268–283 (2009)
7. Stylianou, Y., Cappe, O., Moulines, E.: Continuous probabilistic transform for voice conversion. IEEE Trans. on Speech and Audio Proc. 6(2), 131–142 (1998)
8. Kain, A., Macon, M.: Spectral voice conversion for text-to-speech synthesis. In: Proc. of the IEEE ICASSP, vol. 1, pp. 285–288 (1998)
9. Vích, R., Vondra, M.: Voice Conversion. In: Proc. of the Summer School DATASTAT 2006, pp. 281–293. Masaryk University, Brno, Czech Rep. (2007)
10. Vích, R.: Cepstral Speech Model, Padé Approximation, Excitation and Gain Matching in Cepstral Speech Synthesis. In: Jan, et al. (eds.) EuroConference BIOSIGNAL, Proc. of 15th Biennial International Conference, June 2000, pp. 77–82. Brno University of Technology, Brno (2000)
11. Arslan, L.M.: Speaker Transformation Algorithm using Segmental Codebooks (STASC). Speech Communication 28, 211–226 (1999)
12. Eimas, P.D., Miller, J.L.: Perspectives on the study of speech. Lawrence Erlbaum Associates, Inc., Hillsdale (1981)
13. Vích, R., Vondra, M.: Voice Conversion Based on Nonlinear Spectrum Transformation. In: Proceedings of 14th Czech-German Workshop, Prague, September 13-15, pp. 53–60 (2004)
14. Airas, M., Alku, P.: Emotions in Short Vowel Segments: Effects of the Glottal Flow as Reflected by the Normalized Amplitude Quotient. In: André, E., Dybkjær, L., Minker, W., Heisterkamp, P. (eds.) ADS 2004. LNCS (LNAI), vol. 3068, pp. 13–24. Springer, Heidelberg (2004)
15. Gobl, C., Chasaide, A.N.: The role of voice quality in communicating emotion, mood and attitude. Speech Communication 40, 189–212 (2003)
16. Inanoglu, Z.: Transforming Pitch in a Voice Conversion Framework. Master's Thesis, St. Edmunds College, University of Cambridge (2003)

Analysis of Emotional Voice Using Electroglottogram-Based Temporal Measures of Vocal Fold Opening

Peter J. Murphy[1] and Anne-Maria Laukkanen[2]

[1] Department of Electronic and Computer Engineering,
University of Limerick, Limerick, Ireland
`peter.murphy@ul.ie`
[2] Department of Speech Communication and Voice Research,
University of Tampere, Tampere, Finland
`anne-maria.laukkanen@uta.fi`

Abstract. Descriptions of emotional voice type have typically been provided in terms of fundamental frequency (f0), intensity and duration. Further features, such as measures of laryngeal characteristics, may help to improve recognition of emotional colouring in speech, and, expressiveness in speech synthesis. The present contribution examines three temporal measures of vocal fold opening – as indicated by the time of decreasing contact of the vocal folds estimated from the electroglottogram signal. This initial investigation, using a single female speaker, analyses the sustained vowel [a:], produced when simulating the emotional states anger, joy, neutral, sad and tender. The results indicate discrimination of emotional voice type using two of the measures of vocal fold opening duration.

1 Introduction

The study of emotion as expressed in speech has been examined in terms of fundamental frequency (f0), waveform intensity and syllable duration in a number of studies; an up-to-date overview of the literature is provided in [1]. Speaker-independent automatic recognition of emotion, using four or five emotions, has been reported to be in the range of 50%-60% accuracy [2]. The use of laryngeal cues may allow for improved recognition rates or improved synthesis of emotional attributes. Relatively few studies have focussed on glottal characteristics of emotional voice [1, 3-10]. In the present study three measures of vocal fold opening time are derived from the electroglottogram for the sustained vowel [a:]. In the following section the electroglottogram and the measurements taken from this signal are briefly described.

2 Electroglottography

The electroglottograph consists of two electrodes placed external to the larynx (Fig.1). A high frequency current is passed between the electrodes and the output signal varies depending on the impedance of the substance between the electrodes. As the vocal folds vibrate they move through high impedance (open glottis) to low impedance

A. Esposito et al. (Eds.): COST 2102 Int. Training School 2009, LNCS 5967, pp. 286–293, 2010.
© Springer-Verlag Berlin Heidelberg 2010

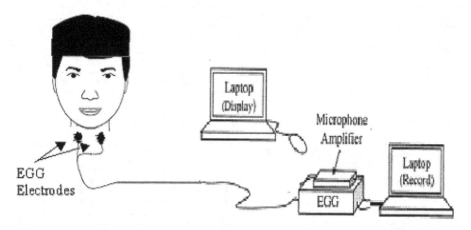

Fig. 1. Illustration of electroglottogram (EGG) recording setup

(closed glottis) values. As the impedance decreases with contact the electroglottogram (EGG) signal provides a measure of vocal fold contact [11-14] (Fig.2 – top row). The electroglottogram provides complimentary information to the glottal flow; the maximum in the electroglottogram occurs when contact is maximum while the maximum in the glottal flow occurs during the open phase. An important aspect of the EGG signal is that it is essentially free of supra-glottal acoustic influences, which can produce source–filter interaction, making glottal flow determination and interpretation challenging.

2.1 Measurements Taken from the EGG Waveform

Fig.2 and Table 1 indicate how the measures amplitude, cycle length (and hence fundamental frequency) and the vocal fold opening times (NTO1, 2 and 3) are estimated. It has been shown (through correlation of vocal fold image and EGG data, cf. [13,14]) that the minimum point in the DEGG signal corresponds with the point of glottal opening. NTO1 is a measure of the time of decreasing contact of the vocal folds from the point of maximum contact to the point where the glottis opens. The final phase of opening corresponds to where the glottis is open but the folds are still in contact in certain places along the length and depth of their structure.

NTO1 is estimated by determining the time between the positive peak of the EGG and the negative peak of the DEGG signals, per cycle and dividing by the cycle duration. NTO2 also uses the EGG positive peak as its starting point and the first zero-crossing after the negative peak in the DEGG signal is taken as the end of the contact phase. NTO3 is estimated as the difference between these times (NTO3=NTO2-NTO1). NTO1 is an indicator of vocal fold opening during the glottal closed phase while NTO3 provides a measure of opening that takes place during the glottal open phase. NTO2 provides a measure of vocal fold opening in its entirety as represented by vocal fold contact via the EGG signal (the EGG signal on its own does not provide detailed information on vocal fold characteristics during the advanced stages of glottal opening – during this region the glottal flow signal or the photoglottogram, which provides an approximation of the projected glottal area, can provide additional information).

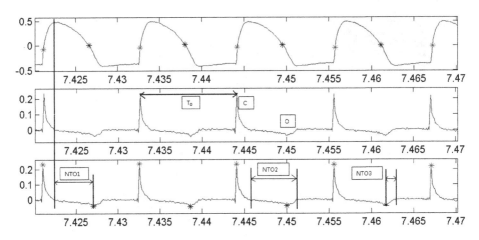

Fig. 2. neutral phonation: Top row: EGG signal (y-axis amplitude – arbitrary units - indicating increasing vocal fold contact, x-axis – sample number – indicating time) EGG with (nearest sample to) zero crossing points indicated (negative to positive – first asterisk – in the glottal cycle, positive to negative – second asterisk – in the glottal cycle), Middle row: DEGG (rate of change of vocal fold contact) indicating peaks at closure (C) and opening (O) and T0 estimation, Bottom row: DEGG (rate of change of vocal fold contact) asterisk at positive peak. Measurement symbols (NTO1,2,3 – normalized - when divided by cycle duration - time of glottal opening 1,2,3, and T0 - cycle duration, are described in Table 1).

The following measures were estimated from the EGG (and derived) signal(s).

Table 1. Measures estimated from the electroglottogram (EGG) and the first derivative of the electroglottogram (DEGG) signals

Measure Symbol	Description	Method of Measurement
T_0	glottal cycle duration	measured between points of glottal closure as determined from the positive peaks in the DEGG signal
f0	fundamental frequency	$1/T_0$
NTO1	normalised vocal fold opening time 1 – vocal fold opening duration during the closed phase	opening time 1 is measured from the peak in the EGG signal to the negative peak in the DEGG signal – dividing by the cycle duration provides the normalised value
NTO2	normalised vocal fold opening time 2 – vocal fold opening duration in its entirety (as estimated from the EGG signal)	opening time 2 is measured from the peak in the EGG signal to the next zero crossing of the DEGG signal – dividing by the cycle duration provides the normalised value
NTO3	normalised vocal fold opening time 3 – vocal fold opening duration (as estimated from the EGG signal) during the open phase	opening time 3 is the difference between NTO2 and NTO1

3 Measurement

The EGG and speech signals were recorded in a sound treated room in the Department of Speech Communication and Voice Research, University of Tampere, Tampere, Finland. The sustained vowel [a:] was phonated while simulating the emotions anger, joy, neutral, sad and tender by a single speaker who was experienced in portrayals of phonatory modes and emotional voice type. One hundred and thirty eight cycles of a steady portion of the vowel were selected for analysis. The five emotions chosen have been analysed in previous studies [1,3,9,10]; they reflect positive and negative valence, and high and low psycho-physiological activation levels. Sadness and tenderness have low activation levels, while joy and anger have a high level of activation. Sadness and anger have negative valence while joy and tenderness represent positive valence. Fig.3 shows the electroglottogram for anger, joy, neutral, sad and tender, respectively. Fig.4 shows the same information for the DEGG signal.

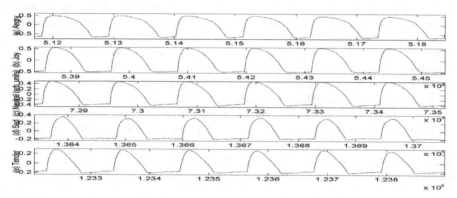

Fig. 3. EGG segments of the emotions (a) anger, (b) joy, (c) neutral, (d) sad and (d) tender: (y-axis amplitude – arbitrary units - indicating increasing vocal fold contact, x-axis – sample number – indicating time)

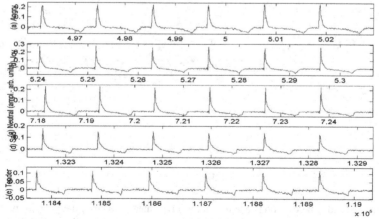

Fig. 4. DEGG segments of the emotions (a) anger, (b) joy, (c) neutral, (d) sad and (d) tender: (y-axis amplitude indicating rate of change of vocal fold contact – arbitrary units - indicating increasing vocal fold contact, x-axis – sample number – indicating time)

NTO1, 2 and 3 are estimated as described in section 2.1 and values are taken for all the emotional portrayals.

4 Results

Figures 5, 6 and 7 shows NTO1, 2 and 3, respectively, versus cycle number for the emotions anger (a), joy (j), neutral (n), sad (s) and tender (t). Average values are provided in Table 2.

From figures 5 and 6 and Table 2 it can be seen that NTO1 and NTO2 are highest for anger and lowest for sad and tender.

5 Discussion

Normalised time of vocal fold opening shows discriminatory ability of emotional voice type along the activation dimension. As stated previously sadness and tenderness are associated with low activation levels, while joy and anger are associated with high activation levels. The NTO2 and NTO3 measures differentiate the data along this activation dimension; the averaged data are ordered as anger and joy>neutral>sad and tender. Higher activation may be associated with increased adductory force or increased loudness for example. When adduction is greater (e.g. as for anger [9,10]) the opening time is greater with the converse being the case for sad and tender. It is not clear why the emotional portrayal for joy has a prolonged final phase of opening (e.g. compare NT01 and NTO2 for joy and neutral in Fig.5 and Fig.6 and in Table 2). One general speculation is that a greater opening time may be advantageous in certain situations for absorbing energy from the airstream supplied from the lungs (this could

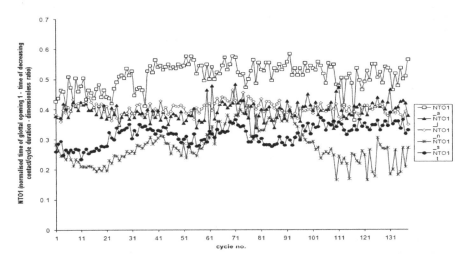

Fig. 5. Normalised time of glottal opening 1 (NTO1 – measured from the positive peak in the EGG signal to the negative peak in the DEGG signal) versus glottal cycle number for the emotional portrayals anger (a), joy (j), neutral (n), sad (s) and tender (t)

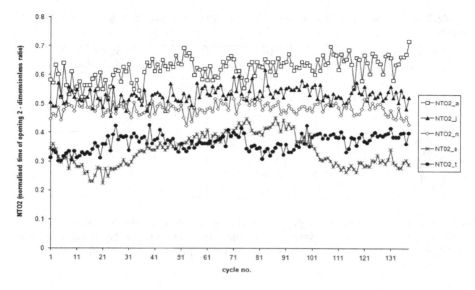

Fig. 6. Normalised time of glottal opening 2 (NTO2 – includes final phase of opening) versus glottal cycle number for the emotional portrayals anger (a), joy (j), neutral (n), sad (s) and tender (t)

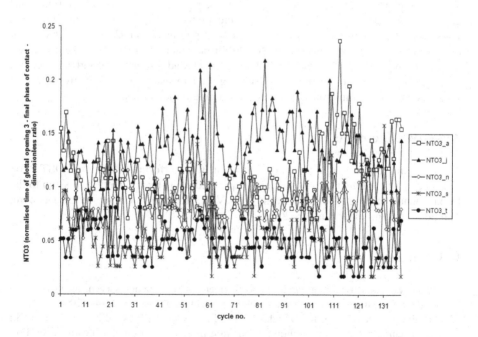

Fig. 7. Normalised time of glottal opening 3 (NTO3 – final phase of opening) versus glottal cycle number for the emotional portrayals anger (a), joy (j), neutral (n), sad (s) and tender (t)

Table 2. Electroglottogram based glottal opening time measures averaged over 138 glottal cycles

Measure /Emotion	Mean Fundamental Frequency (f0)	Mean Normalised Time of Glottal Opening 1 (NTO1)	Mean Normalised Time of Glottal Opening 2 (NTO2)	Mean Normalised Time of Glottal Opening 3 (NTO3)
Anger	180	**0.51**	0.62	**0.11**
Joy	178	**0.40**	0.53	**0.13**
Neutral	177	**0.40**	0.48	**0.8**
Sad	175	**0.28**	0.34	**0.6**
Tender	176	**0.32**	0.37	**0.5**

be due in part, for example, to phasing of the vocal fold motion along the depth of the fold [12,15]). As alluded to previously further information regarding vocal fold opening during the glottal open phase can be supplied using the inverse filtered flow signal or the PGG signal.

6   Conclusion

This preliminary study of a single female speaker portraying different emotions suggests that measures of vocal fold opening time are useful for discriminating emotional voice type. Two of the measures, the entire opening phase (NT02) as measured using EGG and the final phase of opening (NTO3) discriminate the data along the activation dimension with values ordered as follows; anger and joy>neutral>sad and tender. Future work will examine these and other glottal measures with data from several speakers and in combination with other measurement modalities.

Acknowledgements

The recording and initial analysis development was performed during a COST 2103 (Advanced Voice Function Assessment) supported short-term scientific mission to the Department of Speech Communication and Voice Research, University of Tampere, Tampere, Finland in December, 2007.

References

1. Airas, M., Alku, P.: Emotions in vowel segments of continuous speech: analysis of the glottal flow using the normalized amplitude quotient. Phonetica 63, 26–46 (2006)
2. McGilloway, S., Cowie, R., Douglas-Cowie, E., Gielen, S., Westerdijk, M., Stroeve, S.: Approaching automatic recognition of emotion from voice: a rough benchmark. In: Proceedings of the ISCA workshop on Speech and Emotion, Belfast, pp. 207–212 (2000)
3. Toivanen, J., Waaramaa, T., Alku, P., Laukkanen, A.-M., Seppänen, T., Väyrynen, E., Airas, M.: Emotions in [a]: A perceptual and acoustic study. Logopedics Phoniatrics Vocology 31, 43–48 (2006)

4. Gobl, C., Ní Chasaide, A.: The role of voice quality in communicating emotion, mood and attitude. Speech Communication 40, 189–212 (2003)
5. Yanushevskaya, I., Tooher, M., Gobl, C.: Time- and amplitude-based voice source correlates of emotional portrayals. In: Proceedings of Affective Computing and Intelligent Interaction, ACII, Lisbon, pp. 159–170 (2007)
6. Laukkanen, A.-M., Vilkman, E., Alku, P., Oksanen, H.: Physical variations related to stress and emotional state: a preliminary study. J. Phonetics 24, 313–335 (1996)
7. Cummings, K.E., Clements, M.A.: Analysis of the glottal excitation of emotionally styled and stressed speech. J. Acoust. Soc. Am. 98, 88–98 (1995)
8. Rossato, S., Audibert, N., Aubergé, V.: Emotional voice measurement: A comparison of articulatory-EGG and acoustic amplitude parameters. In: Proceedings of the 2nd Int. Conf. on Speech Prosody, Nara, Japan, pp. 749–752 (2004)
9. Murphy, P.J., Laukkanen, A.-M.: Electroglottogram analysis of emotionally styled phonation. In: Esposito, A., Hussain, A., Marinaro, M., Martone, R. (eds.) Multimodal Signals: Cognitive and Algorithmic Issues. LNCS (LNAI), vol. 5398, pp. 264–270. Springer, Heidelberg (2009)
10. Murphy, P., Laukkanen, A.-M.: Investigation of Normalised Time of Increasing Vocal Fold Contact as a Discriminator of Emotional Voice Type. In: Esposito, A., et al. (eds.) Proceedings of the 2nd COST 2102 International Conference on Cross-Modal Analysis of Speech, Gesture, Gaze and Facial Expressions Prague. LNCS (LNAI). Springer, Heidelberg (2009)
11. Rothenberg, M., Mashie, J.: Monitoring vocal fold abduction through vocal fold contact area. J. Speech Hear Res. 31, 338–351 (1988)
12. Titze, I.: Interpretation of the electroglottographic signal. J. Voice 4, 1–9 (1990)
13. Henrich, N., d'Alessandro, C., Castellengo, M., Doval, B.: On the use of the derivative of electroglottographic signals for characterization of nonpathological phonation. J. Acoust. Soc. Am. 115, 1321–1332 (2004)
14. Childers, D.G., Hicks, D.M., Moore, G.P., Eskenazi, L., Lalwani, A.L.: Electroglottography and vocal fold physiology. J. Speech Hear. Res. 33, 245–254 (1990)
15. Titze, I.: Parameterization of the glottal area, glottal flow, and vocal fold contact area J. Acoust. Soc. Am. 75, 570–580 (1984)

Effects of Smiling on Articulation:
Lips, Larynx and Acoustics

Sascha Fagel

Berlin Institute of Technology, Straße des 17. Juni 135
10623 Berlin, Germany
sascha.fagel@tu-berlin.de

Abstract. The present paper reports on results of a study investigating changes of lip features, larynx position and acoustics caused by smiling while speaking. 20 triplets of words containing one of the vowels /aː/, /iː/, /uː/ were spoken and audiovisually recorded. Lip features were extracted manually as well as using a 3D motion capture technique, formants were measured in the acoustic signal, and the vertical larynx position was determined where visible. Results show that during production of /uː/ F1 and F2 are not significantly affected despite of changes of lip features while F3 is increased. For /aː/ F1 and F3 are unchanged where for /iː/ only F3 is not affected. Furthermore, while the effect of smiling on the outer lip features is comparable between vowels, inner lip features are differently affected for different vowels. These differences in the impact on /aː/, /iː/ and /uː/ suggest that the effect of smiling on vowel production is vowel dependent.

Index Terms: Smiled speech, motion capture, vowel production.

1 Introduction

Many aspects of speech are affected when the speaker is smiling compared a neutral expression. The changes in speech production lead to observable differences in the acoustic and optic signals and smiling in speech can also be perceived. This has strong implications for speech recognition and speech synthesis with respect to both acoustic and visual modalities. This section describes previous findings in the production, acoustics and perception of speech produced while smiling ("smiled speech"). The remaining sections of the paper describe method and results of a study on the effect of smiling on the acoustic and facial properties of speech. Previous and current findings are integrated in the conclusions.

1.1 Effects of Smiling on Speech Production

Fant [1] mentioned that lip protrusion in rounded vowels lengthens the vocal tract and hence lowers formant frequencies. The reverse relationship was described by Shor [2] in speech produced while smiling: the mouth widens and the lips retract resulting in a shortened vocal tract. Hence, smiling during speech constitutes a conflicting demand on the lip shape, at least in rounded vowels. Humans need to have a strategy to

A. Esposito et al. (Eds.): COST 2102 Int. Training School 2009, LNCS 5967, pp. 294–303, 2010.

maintain the acoustic properties of the speech signal so that it can still be decoded by a listener.

Riordan [3] found that larynx lowering can compensate for reduced lip rounding due to smiling during speech. However, no compensatory larynx lowering was found in unrounded vowels. Another – presumably the main function – of vertical larynx position is F0 control (e.g. Honda et al. [4]). Savariaux et al. [5] found in a lip tube experiment that the tongue position can compensate for reduced lip rounding. All three articulatory parameters – vertical larynx position, tongue position, and lip spreading – contribute to the effective length of the vocal tract to different degrees. In a study of radiographic and labial films Dusan [6] investigated the vocal tract length during the production of consonants and vowels and found correlations to lip protrusion with $r_{consonant}=0.72$ and $r_{vowel}=0.77$, to the position of tongue dorsum with $r_{consonant}=0.63$ and $r_{vowel}=0.74$, and with the lowest correlation among these three parameters to vertical larynx position with $r_{consonant}=0.63$ and $r_{vowel}=0.65$.

1.2 Acoustic Consequences and Effects of Smiling on Speech Perception

The properties speech produced while smiling and possible compensations and their effect on format frequencies can be analyzed by a simulation using an articulatory speech synthesizer (e.g. Birkholz [7]). Lip protrusion lowers F1 and F2 and only to a marginal degree F3. The reduction of the vertical lip opening mainly decreases F2 but also lowers F1 and F3. Moving the tongue dorsum backwards lowers F2. Larynx lowering has a main effect in lowering F3 and also lowers F2. In a simple model of speech production (Patterson et al. [8]) the cavity in front of the constriction (closer to the lips) mainly accounts for the second formant, the first and third formant are mainly produced by the back cavity, i.e. behind the constriction (closer to the larynx). This simplification describes the formant frequencies better the narrower the constriction between front and back cavities. Furthermore, tongue and larynx are connected with one another through the hyoid bone and hence do not move completely independently.

Not surprisingly, smiling in speech can be identified auditorily (e.g. Tartter [9]). However, an increased amplitude of speech leads to robust identification of that speech as smiled – although speakers do not produce speech with significantly increased amplitude when smiling. It was shown that smiling while speaking leads to increased formant frequencies. Where Tartter [9] found an increased F0 in speech produced while smiling compared to non-smiled speech, in a repetition of that study Tartter & Brown [10] did not find such an effect. The effect on segmental duration was not significant.

Lasarcyk & Trouvain [11] varied several speech production parameters in a study using an articulatory speech synthesizer [7]. The results showed that synthetic speech with raised larynx was identified as more smiled – even if the spreading of the lips was kept constant. In a study by Drahota et al. [12] audio stimuli with higher F0 were perceived as more smiled even though this effect did not occur significantly in speech produced while smiling (whether or not a stimulus was produced with a smile was identified visually). Analogously, stimuli with higher intensity were perceived as more smiled although this parameter was not significantly changed by smiling in the speech production.

In a study on auditory-visual perception of expressive speech [13] Fagel cross-combined the audio and video tracks of utterances that were perceived as *happy, angry, sad,* and *content* when presented in a single modality (audio alone or video alone). However, a *content* voice combined with an *angry* face was perceived as *sad,* and an *angry* voice combined with a *content* face was perceived as *happy.* A possible explanation is that the valence (i.e. positive/negative evaluation) is transmitted predominantly by the face and the activation (i.e. arousal/relaxation) is transmitted predominantly by the speech audio. Hence, cross-modal effects can be expected in the perception of smiling in speech, too.

As a consequence of the abovementioned studies it is necessary not only to investigate the production of speech while smiling but also the perception of smiling in speech. Edmond et al. [14] listed further possible influences on the perception of smiling – lexical, cultural, gender, and speaker effects – which have yet to be investigated.

2 Experimental Setup

2.1 Corpus and Material

A list of 20 word triplets with each word containing one of the vowels /aː/, /iː/, /uː/ was compiled in analogy to minimal pairs. The word triplets were selected among a longer list of possible triplets in order to contain the vowels under investigation in a wide variety of consonantal contexts with respect to differences in place and manner of articulation. The words are

1.	Maß	mies	Mus
2.	Basen	Biesen	Busen
3.	Paar	Pier	pur
4.	fahren	vieren	Fuhren
5.	Saale	Siele	Suhle
6.	Saat	sieht	Sud
7.	nah	nie	Nu
8.	da	die	du
9.	dar	dir	Dur
10.	Stahl	stiehl	Stuhl
11.	lad	Lied	lud
12.	blasen	bliesen	Blusen
13.	Schale	schiele	Schule
14.	Schar	schier	Schur
15.	Schaf	schief	schuf
16.	Gras	Grieß	Gruß
17.	graben	Grieben	Gruben
18.	brat	briet	Brut
19.	Hafen	hieven	Hufen
20.	haben	hieben	huben

The 60 words were spoken in a series of single word utterances – each word triplet in one breath group – by a male speaker with the instruction to speak them once with neutral expression and once with a positive expression that comprises smiling. In case of the speech produced while smiling the speaker tried to keep the smile constant over each entire single word utterance. Four cameras (DragonflyExpress from Point Grey Research) recorded the face of the speaker synchronously at 60 frames per second: three cameras with left center and right view of the face and one camera recording the larynx region against black background. 44 colored markers were attached to the speaker's face. The audio speech was recorded with a head mounted microphone (AKG C 420L + B29L) at a distance of 15cm to the lips. The setup is shown in Figure 1, the four camera views are shown in Figure 2.

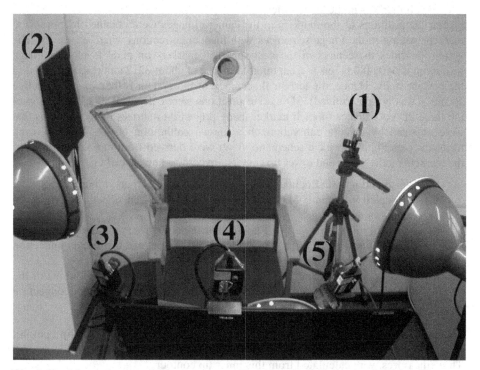

Fig. 1. Experimental setup with larynx camera (1) against black background (2), left (3), center (4) and right (5) camera

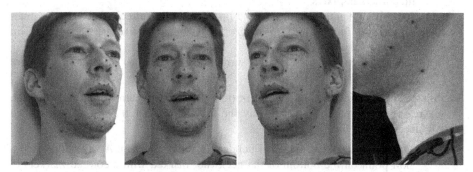

Fig. 2. The four camera views on the subject

2.2 Measurements

12 measures were derived from the recordings.

3D Data. The audio track of the recordings were annotated on phone level in order to obtain the center of the realization of the vowels under investigation. The markers that were glued on the face of the speaker were once registered manually using the web-based CLIC'N'TRAK [15] 3D motion capture software. This is done by clicking once each marker in one reference image from each of the three camera views (left, center, and right). The reference between the three views on one marker were defined by clicking all markers in the same order.

The 2D positions of the markers in the camera images were obtained by automatic marker tracking in the image sequences with manual corrections where necessary. The system provides the centers of the near-spherical markers on pixel level. The image resolution is 640x480 pixels at a captured face area of about 32x24cm (face cameras) in the present study. Hence, the technical accuracy of the system is 0.5mm (the effective accuracy was not determined). 3D marker positions were calculated by triangulation of the three 2D coordinates of each marker using projection matrices of the cameras that were obtained by camera calibration on a known calibration object. The following measures (see Figure 3a for a schematic view) were derived from the 3D positions of the markers on the upper and lower lip centers, lip corners and check bones.

- Lip spreading: 3D Euclidean distance between lip corners in mm
- Vertical lip opening: 3D Euclidean distance between upper and lower lip centers in mm
- Absolute lip protrusion: 3D Euclidean distance between the midpoints of the direct connection of the upper and lower lip centers and the direct connection of the cheek bones in mm
- Relative lip protrusion: 3D Euclidean distance between the midpoints of the direct connection of the upper and lower lip centers and the direct connection of the lip corners in mm

2D Data. As the marker data only provides information about the outer lip contour, the inner lip contour was manually marked by the use of an image editor (Figure 3b). Three measures were calculated from this inner lip contour.

- Inner lip opening width: 2D Euclidean distance between left and right inner lip corners in pixels
- Inner lip opening height: average lip opening height calculated on the inner lip contour normalized to horizontal connection line between inner lip corners in pixels
- Inner lip area: amount of pixels surrounded by the inner lip contour in square pixels

The images of the centers of vowel realization of the fourth camera that recorded the larynx region were marked manually by the use of the CLIC'N'TRAK software. The derived measure was the

- Vertical larynx position: 2D Euclidean distance between Adam's apple and a skin point on the bottom of the neck (not marked with a colored marker) in pixels

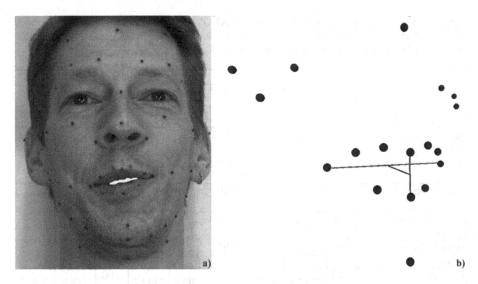

Fig. 3. The area surrounded by the inner lip contour (a) and a schematic view of the 3D measures (b): connection line between lip corners (lip spreading), connection line between upper and lower lip centers (vertical lip opening), and connection line between mid points of these connection lines (relative protrusion).

Acoustic Measures. The fundamental frequency (F0) and the first three formants (F1 – F3) were extracted automatically with praat [16] at the centers of vowel realization. In some /u:/ realizations only one formant at F1/F2 was extracted, so the data were manually checked and corrected where necessary.

3 Results

Table 1 shows the mean values and the significance levels of the measurements in non-smiled versus smiled speech for all three vowels. All mean values whose differences between non-smiled and smiled speech were non-significant are shown in bold face. Vertical larynx position could not be measured for the vowels /a:/ and /i:/ because the larynx disappeared upwards out of the observable range. For /u:/ the larynx was raised in smiled speech compared to non-smiled speech.

3.1 Outer Lip Measures

Lip spreading increased and vertical lip opening decreased from non-smiled to smiled speech for all three vowels with the effect on vertical lip opening being the smallest for /i:/. The between-vowel differences of all mean values are significant with the differences in lip spreading becoming small in speech produced while smiling (56.6mm ± 1.3mm) but still significant (p<.05; not listed in the table).

Table 1. Mean values and the significance levels (ANOVA) of the measurements in non-smiled versus smiled speech for the vowels /a:/, /i:/ and /u:/. Non-significant differences between non-smiled and smiled speech are shown in bold face.

measure	/a:/			/i:/			/u:/		
	sig.	non-smiled	smiled	sig.	non-smiled	smiled	sig.	non-smiled	smiled
lip spreading (mm)	.000	45.1	56.6	.000	49.9	57.8	.000	37.5	55.3
vertical lip opening (mm)	.000	46.9	37.3	.002	29.9	28.0	.000	34.1	23.8
absolute lip protrusion (mm)	.000	96.6	93.0	.000	93.1	91.1	.000	98.1	93.2
relative lip protrusion (mm)	.000	15.6	21.3	.000	16.9	21.9	.000	14.1	20.9
inner lip width (pixels)	.000	87.78	119.9	.000	79.3	114.0	.000	16.6	48.4
inner lip height (pixels)	.000	41.4	30.7	.892	**17.8**	**18.0**	.001	6.0	4.1
inner lip area (sq. pixels)	.607	**3742.9**	**3807.1**	.000	1495.8	2142.7	.000	118.6	250.3
F0 (Hz)	.000	104.0	149.0	.000	124.5	192.2	.000	124.8	213.3
F1 (Hz)	.852	**746.2**	**744.4**	.000	262.8	301.0	.248	**290.4**	**305.6**
F2 (Hz)	.000	1136.6	1245.6	.001	2004.1	2099.6	.736	**767.6**	**777.4**
F3 (Hz)	.874	**2273.9**	**2293.6**	.083	**2829.8**	**2886.8**	.001	2191.3	2299.7
vertical larynx position	--	--	--	--	--	--	.000	43.5	65.3

3.2 Lip Protrusion

Relative lip protrusion increased and absolute lip protrusion decreased from non-smiled to smiled speech for all three vowels at comparable degrees. The absolute lip protrusion decreased more if the vowel itself was more protruded. The between-vowel differences in non-smiled speech are significant (p<.001; not listed in the table). The between-vowel differences in speech produced while smiling are significant at a lower levels (p<.05 to p<.001; not listed in the table) or non-significant for the difference between /a:/ and /u:/, respectively.

3.3 Inner Lip Measures

The inner lip width increased from non-smiled to smiled speech for all vowels with the highest percentual increase for /u:/. The inner lip opening height is decreased for /a:/ and /u:/ but not for /i:/ what is inline with the small change of outer vertical lip opening for /i:/. As a result of these two effects the inner lip area is not significantly increased for /a:/ (increased width, decreased height), is significantly increased for /i:/ (increased width, non-decreased height), and is largely increased for /u:/ (largely increased width not compensated by decreased height).

3.4 F0 and Formants

F0 increased from non-smiled to smiled speech. Vowels can only be limitedly compared with one another as the order of vowels in a sequence of three single word utterances (e.g. "lad – Lied – lud") was not randomized and hence a prosodic effect on "utterance" level cannot be excluded. The increase was least for /a:/, higher for /i:/ and most for /u:/.

For /a:/ and /i:/ F3 does not raise significantly from non-smiled to smiled speech. For /a:/ also F1 is not increased. For /u:/ F3 is significantly increased.

4 Conclusions

As expected smiling results in stretched lips with smaller differences between vowels in smiled compared to non-smiled speech. At the same time the vertical lip opening is reduced. Inner lip measures do not show such a consistent picture: smiling affects inner lip height (/a:/), inner lip area (/i:/), or both (/u:/). The decreasing level of significance of lip spreading and protrusion of between-vowel differences in smiled speech compared to non-smiled speech suggests that the lip spreading reaches a level of saturation. Furthermore, the increase of relative protrusion and the decrease of absolute protrusion indicates that the lip centers reach this level of saturation earlier when they get deformed by contact to the incisors while the lip corners still can move further backwards. It is assumed that the outer lip contour maintains consistent visibility of smiling where the inner lip contour through an adapted lip shape) helps to maintain the acoustics in order to preserve the identification of vowel qualities. A perceptual evaluation study is planned to further investigate this conclusion.

The speech produced while smiling investigated in the present study was produced as read speech with acted smiling. So the external validity of this study is somewhat limited as it cannot be assumed that the way of smiling observed in this study occurs in spontaneous speech. Specifically, it can be assumed that the magnitude of smiling during spontaneous utterances may vary. Hence, the actual intensity of the smile that occurs at each speech segment under investigation has to be taken into account. However, to accurately determine the course of a smile in an utterance is yet an unsolved problem. For the present work the smile was intended to be constant – either present or not present – over the single word utterance resulting in minimal effect of the graded intensity of the smile on the measurements. It is known that real smiles are connected to activation of the orbicularis oculi to produce a so-called Duchenne smile (where the eyes contribute to the smile) and faint smiles – that may occur when acted – might lack such activation resulting in non-Duchenne smile. In the present study it was not determined which type of smile was produced though the measurements did not include the eye region but only the lip region of the face. So the internal validity of the present study can be assumed high.

Assuming that smiling has a major effect on the front cavity, the formant patterns of /a:/ and /i:/ can mostly be explained by the fact that the cavity in front of the constriction mainly accounts for the second formant while the first and third formant are mainly produced by the back cavity. However, the increase in F1 for /i:/ is not supported by this explanation. The increased F0 is assumingly accompanied by a raised larynx (but could not be measured in the present study) which can partly account for the increased F1. It is remarkable that in the case of the rounded vowel /u:/ the vowel quality by F1 and F2 is not significantly affected by smiling where F3 is significantly increased. As the acoustically relevant inner lip area is increased, this indicates a presence of a compensation. This supports the previous finding that compensation occurs predominantly in rounded vowels. Whether this compensation is realized by tongue position adjustment cannot be answered in the present study due to the lack of tongue data. In the case of /u:/ a lowered larynx in speech produced while smiling might have been expected in order to maintain the vocal tract length. This effect could not be found in the experimental results what also suggests the presence of other more relevant compensation strategies.

Smiling accesses in parts physiological mechanisms that are also involved in the production of speech which results in conflicting demand in case of rounded vowels. The effect of smiling on the measures of vowel realization used in the present study is highly significant in most cases. However, the effect appears differently on different vowels. This suggests that smiling combines with articulatory configurations in a vowel-dependent manner. This has strong implications on the visual synthesis of smiled speech. Using a single (linear) parameter that changes a neutral face into a smiling face and superimposing articulatory movements that were measured on a neutral face will not produce satisfactory results. Even adjusting the lip spreading parameter in smiled speech will not suffice due to the vowel dependency of the effect of smiling. Analogously, a phoneme-dependent approach is necessary for audio synthesis of smiled speech (e.g. when applying a voice conversion technique). However, in order to determine in detail the nature of the dependency between vowel production and smiling a study of a more complete set of vowels is required.

Acknowledgements. Many thanks to the members of the EU COST Action 2102 on "Cross-Modal Analysis of Verbal and Non-verbal Communication" for their valuable comments, and to Jürgen Trouvain for the basic idea of the present study and for a number of interesting and relevant references. This work was supported by the German Research Foundation DFG (FA 795/4-1).

References

1. Fant, G.: Acoustic Theory of Speech Production. Mouton, The Hague (1960)
2. Shor, R.E.: The production and judgment of smile magnitude. Journal of General Psychology 98, 79–96 (1978)
3. Riordan, C.J.: Control of vocal-tract length in speech. J. Acoust. Soc. Am. 62, 998–1002 (1977)
4. Honda, K., Hirai, H., Masaki, S., Shimada, Y.: Role of vertical larynx movement and cervical lordosis in F0 control. Language and Speech 4, 401–411 (1999)
5. Savariaux, C., Perrier, P., Orliaguet, J.P.: Compensating for labial perturbation in a rounded vowel: an acoustic and articulatory study. In: Proceedings of EUROSPEECH, pp. 89–92 (1993)
6. Birkholz, P.: 3D-ArtikulatorischeSprachsynthese. PhD dissertation, University of Rostock (2005)
7. Dusan, S.: Vocal Tract Length during Speech Production. In: Proceedings of INTERSPEECH (2007)
8. Patterson, R., Monaghan, J., Walters, T.: A simple, formant-pattern model of speech communication (2009),
http://www.acousticscale.org/wiki/index.php/
A_simple,_formant-pattern_model_of_speech_communication
(retrieved April 26, 2009)

9. Tartter, V.C.: Happy talk: Perceptual and acoustic effects of smiling on speech. Perception and Psychophysics 27(1), 24–27 (1980)
10. Tartter, V.C., Braun, D.: Hearing smiles and frowns in normal and whisper registers. J. Acoust. Soc. Am. 96(4), 2101–2107 (1994)
11. Lasarcyk, E., Trouvain, J.: Spread Lips + Raised Larynx + Higher F0 = Smiled Speech? - An Articulatory Synthesis Approach. In: Proceedings of ISSP (2008)
12. Drahota, A., Costall, A., Reddy, V.: The vocal communication of different kinds of smile. Speech Communication 51(4), 278–287 (2008)
13. Fagel, S.: Emotional McGurk Effect. In: Proceedings of Speech Prosody (2006)
14. Émond, C., Trouvain, J., Ménard, L.: Perception of smiled French speech by native vs. non-native listeners: a pilot study. In: Proceedings of the Interdisciplinary Workshop on Phonetics of Laughter, pp. 27-30 (2007)
15. Fagel, S.: CLIC'N'TRAK – A Web-based 3D Motion Capture System (computer program documentation) http://avspeech.info/clicntrak/ (retrieved April 26, 2009)
16. Boersma, P., Weenink, D.: Praat: doing phonetics by computer Version 4.3.14 (Computer program), http://www.praat.org/ (retrieved May 26, 2005)
17. Duchenne de Boulogne, C.-B.: The Mechanism of Human Facial Expression. Paris: Jules Renard (edited and translated by R. Andrew Cuthbertson). Cambridge Univ Press, Cambridge (1862)

Neural Basis of Emotion Regulation

Luigi Trojano

Dept. of Psychology, Second University of Naples
Via Vivaldi 43, 81100 Caserta, Italy
luigi.trojano@unina2.it

Abstract. From the neurobiological point of view emotions can be defined as complex responses to personally-relevant events; such responses are characterized by peculiar subjective feelings and vegetative and motor reactions. In man the complex neural network subserving emotions has been traditionally studied via clinical observations of brain-damaged patients, but in recent years the development of modern neuroimaging techniques such as Positron Emission Tomography (PET) or functional Magnetic Resonance (fMRI) has allowed to investigate the neural basis of emotions and emotion regulation in normal subjects. The present chapter offers a brief overview of the main neural structures involved in emotion processing, summarizes the role recently ascribed to mirror neurons in empathy, and describes the possible neural basis of integrated emotion regulation typical of our species.

Keywords: Emotions, emotion regulation, empathy, neurobiology.

1 Introduction

From the neurobiological point of view emotions can be defined as complex responses to personally-relevant events; such responses are characterized by peculiar subjective feelings and by vegetative and motor reactions. Most authors agree in describing emotions as intense and "quite brief"; intensity and duration cannot be defined precisely, but the term "quite brief" is intended to distinguish emotions from instantaneous reflex responses, which fade away in a few seconds, and from mood and personality traits, which are long-lasting. Moreover, emotions can be considered as "emergency", automatically-triggered, and quite stereotyped reaction patterns, thus very different from higher cognitive activities which can generate flexible behavioural responses [1].

Basic emotions are triggered by relevant stimuli and include hormonal, vegetative and motor changes, with cognitive and social counterparts typical of each species. The preservation of basic emotional reactions with relatively few changes along phylogenetic evolution is perhaps the best evidence supporting their adaptive value and suggests the existence of "emergency" reaction schemata for dealing with sudden changes in the environment. The activation of such reaction schemata is subserved by several cortical and subcortical brain structures intimately connected with each other in a complex neural network. Single neural structures in the network are activated

A. Esposito et al. (Eds.): COST 2102 Int. Training School 2009, LNCS 5967, pp. 304–313, 2010.

sequentially but in many cases connections among them are bidirectional so that they can mutually influence each other.

In man the complex neural network subserving emotions has been traditionally studied via clinical observations of brain-damaged patients, but recently the development of modern neuroimaging techniques such as the Positron Emission Tomography (PET) or the functional Magnetic Resonance (fMRI) has allowed to investigate the neural basis of emotions and emotion regulation in normal subjects. In the following paragraphs I will offer a brief overview of the main neural structures involved in emotion processing, and consider the emerging role ascribed to mirror neurons in empathy. In addition I will discuss the possible neural basis of integrated emotion regulation typical of our species. A more extensive review of literature can be found elsewhere [2].

2   Neural Structures Involved in Emotion Processing

Most neural structures involved in emotion processing are located in the medial surface of temporal and frontal lobes of both hemispheres (Figure 1); such structures are cumulatively considered as part of the so-called limbic lobe.

The limbic lobe was thought to be implied in olfactory perception, but first Papez in 1937 hypothesised that its neural structures are tightly interconnected to form a circuit with a special role in emotion processing. However, it is well established now that several neural structures not strictly enclosed in the limbic lobe play a role in emotion processing; therefore, nowadays the notion of *limbic system* has prevailed, including the traditional Papez's circuit (and limbic lobe), and other neural structures such as insular cortex and amygdala that are strongly involved in emotion processing. It is important to stress that the limbic system is not a closed network but it has a high degree of interrelations with many other cortical and subcortical areas.

The *amygdala*, the core of the limbic system, is located deep in the medial part of the temporal pole, and is made of several distinct nuclei: cortico-medial nuclei receive input from olfactory pathways, whereas baso-lateral nuclei get sensorial information (from thalamus and sensory cortical areas) and memory traces (from hippocampus). Numerous projections from the amygdalae innervate the hypothalamus and the brainstem, and these fibres are those triggering behavioural and visceral emotional reactions. Actually, hypothalamus controls heartbeat, blood pressure, salivation, sweating, pupils dilation, and all of these physiological parameters change during emotional arousal; the hypothalamus can also induce hormonal changes (with increase of adrenaline and cortisol blood levels). On the other hand, the brainstem controls facial muscles and startle reflex. Neurofunctional studies in man have confirmed previous studies on animals showing that the amygdala is strongly involved in most negative emotions (for instance in recognition of aggressive facial expressions) [3], and more in general in whatever intense emotional reaction, but also in processing salient or ambiguous social information [4]. Epileptic patients with dysfunction of anterior temporal lobes often show intense, disproportionate rage or fear reactions. Surgical excision of amygdalae in severely epileptic patients determines the impaired recognition of fearful facial expressions, and the loss of biological indexes of fear reactions (increase of blood pressure and heart rate, startle reflex) [3].

The *insula*, located deep in the lateral scissure, is part of the brain cortex. Its anterior part projects to the central nuclei of amygdala and receives information about smell, taste sensations, and the inner body state [5]; the posterior part projects to the thalamus and receives information from the auditory, somatosensory and premotor cortical areas. Classical research studies that exploited direct electrical stimulation in patients undergoing brain surgery have shown that the stimulation of the insula induces nausea, vomiting and unpleasant feelings in the throat and the mouth [6]. The insula seems also to be responsible for feeling related to changes of the inner body state [7]. Recent neurofunctional studies have demonstrated that it is strongly activated during perception of disgusting tastes [8], together with the amygdala and the anterior part of the cingulate gyrus which is a cortical area enclosed in the limbic system and crucially involved in the processing of emotion.

The anterior part of the *cingulate gyrus*, in the medial surface of the two hemispheres, is strongly involved in emotion processing, and in particular in the evaluation of emotionally-relevant experience and the consequent elaboration of motivated behaviour [4]. Actually, many fMRI studies demonstrated that the cingulate gyrus is activated during error detection, evaluation of the degree of the errors, the rewards and the losses associated with errors. Therefore, the cingulate is thought to be involved in reward-based decision-making and in determining intentional behaviour. On the other hand the cingulate gyrus is interconnected with the amygdalae and with the inferior (orbital) part of the frontal lobes.

In its turn, the *orbital frontal cortex* is connected with the insula, the amygdalae, and the dorsal thalamus, ensuring the control of the motivation and emotions. The surgical removal of connections to and from the orbital cortex was attempted in the '50s to treat aggressive patients; as a consequence, the patients became apathetic, amnesic and environment-dependent. A theoretical model of emotional reactions and behavioral control, defined as the *"somatic marker hypothesis"* [9], foresees that the process of decision-making is guided by somatic changes related to emotion processing. According to this model, mental representations of previous somatic changes are stored in the orbital and medial cortex of the frontal lobes, and can determine the subjects' behaviour even without being consciously recollected. Therefore, the orbital cortex would be central in connecting the emotional reactions to the overt behaviour. The information coming from the amygdala and the hippocampus are integrated in this part of the brain and are used to select the most adequate behaviour to a given stimulus. Lesions in this part of the frontal lobes dramatically impair decisional processes, emotional reactions and volitional behaviour, as first reported in the late XIX century for the famous patient Phineas Gage, who according to the modern reconstructions had a bilateral lesion of the orbital and medial frontal cortex [10]. These early observations have been subsequently confirmed by modern descriptions of changes in social conduit as consequences of orbito-frontal lesions (see for example in [11] the description of a patient who after a bilateral orbito-frontal lesion drastically changed his lifestyle, abandoned his military career, was fired from many jobs, and divorced many times).

The orbito-frontal cortex is also connected with another important part of the frontal lobe, the dorsolateral prefrontal cortex, that is not part of the limbic system but is crucially involved in the planning, the organization, and the regulation of intellectual function and actions (executive functions) [12,13].

The *hippocampus*, and the cortex surrounding it (parahippocampal cortex) in the medial part of the temporal lobe, has been traditionally considered as a part of the limbic lobe, as recalled above, but it is now well established that the hippocampus has a specific role in episodic memory. However, thanks to its tight interconnections with amygdalae, the anterior cingulate gyrus and the hypothalamus, the hippocampus exerts a crucial role in handling learned emotional reactions, in evaluating the emotional value of memories, and in regulating the processing of emotions in response to context-related stimuli.

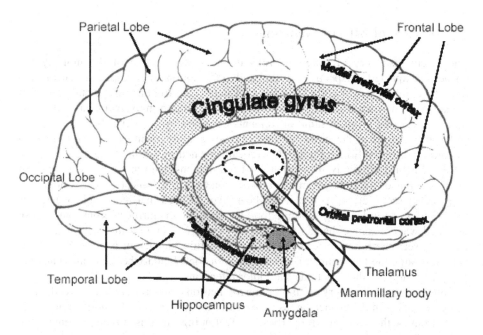

Fig. 1. Outline of the medial surface of the left hemisphere. The neural structures identified by the dashed lines are deep in the hemisphere and are not visible on the surface. The limbic lobe is identified by punctuation. The limbic system encloses several other structures implied in the processing and regulation of emotions (see text).

In concluding this brief overview of the neural structures involved in the processing of emotions, it is important to emphasize that the above cortical structures and nuclei can play their role only thanks to the wide network of their interconnections. In most cases, such interconnections form cortico-subcortical loops, involving deep brain nuclei such as the basal ganglia and the thalamus. Among the basal ganglia, which are located deep in the frontal, parietal and temporal lobes, the caudate nucleus is reciprocally connected with the insula and is involved in the perception of disgust, whereas the striate nucleus is connected with the cingulate gyrus and is part of the reward circuit. The thalamus is another large set of deep nuclei that serve as a relay station within all the sensorial pathways [14]. However, the anterior and dorsal nuclei of the thalamus are so strongly involved in the processing of emotions that they are sometimes defined as limbic thalamus [15]. Limbic nuclei of the thalamus are reciprocally interconnected with the cingulate gyrus, orbital frontal cortex, hippocampus and amygdala, and can thus participate in emotional reactions and empathic processes [16]. Several other structures are part of the limbic system, such as the mamillary bodies, but their specific role is yet to be understood, whereas other neural structures not intimately connected with the limbic system, such as the cerebellum [17] have been recently shown to be implied in the processing of emotions, thanks to the modern neurofunctional studies. A thorough comprehension of the neural structures involved in the processing of emotions will require further extensive studies.

3 The Role of Mirror Neurons

The recent discovery of mirror-neurons in the motor system of the monkey has opened unexpected perspectives to the study of emotions and empathy. Mirror neurons represent a class of cortical neurons located in the frontal and parietal areas that are active both when a subject performs specific voluntary movements and when the same subject observes the same movements executed by another subject [18]. After early observations in the monkey, many studies employing modern neurofunctional techniques have confirmed the existence of mirror neurons in the frontal and parietal cortex of man. Differently from what has been demonstrated in monkeys, in humans the motor mirror neuron system can also respond when a subject observes novel actions, never seen before, so that it has been hypothesised that motor mirror neurons can be involved in learning by imitation [19]. The motor mirror neurons can be also recruited when a subject hears noise specifically related to an action, or when a subject only sees the initial movements of a purposeful sequence of actions. Such findings have suggested that mirror neurons can even contribute to the recognition and the comprehension of others' actions and motor intentions.

Following the discovery of motor mirror neurons, several studies have demonstrated that also in the cortical areas involved in the processing of emotions there can be neurons with analogous properties. Early findings in this direction come from studies of brain damaged patients. For instance, patients have been described who after an insular lesion selectively lose the feeling of disgust (but not that of other emotions), and cannot recognize facial expressions typical of disgust [8, 20].

Such clinical observations have been confirmed and extended by fMRI studies in normal subjects. For instance, Wicker *et al.* [5] presented pleasant or disgusting smells to their subjects, and then showed to them videorecordings of actors exposed to the same stimuli showing the appropriate facial expressions. The results demonstrated the activation of the amygdala (which is connected to the olfactory pathways) in the olfactory perception condition independently from the kind of stimulus, whereas the insula only responded to disgusting stimuli. In addition, the insula was activated, in the absence of olfactory stimuli, when the subjects observed disgusted facial expressions: the anterior part of the insula was activated in the very same way both when subjects perceived disgusting smell, and when observed disgusted facial expressions.

Converging evidence on the existence of emotional mirror neurons come from several studies on the empathy for pain. Singer et al [21] reported a study where normal subjects received small, painful electrical shocks on their fingers, or alternatively, watched videorecordings where the same stimuli were applied to the hands of their own partner. Results demonstrated that both the conditions (experienced or observed pain) activated the same cortical areas in the anterior insula and in the cingulate gyrus.

Even "social" emotions, such as shame or humiliation, seem to be characterised by activation of the same cortical areas both in direct or observed experience. From these data it would be possible to conclude that some cortical areas involved in the processing of emotions are equipped with emotional mirror neurons since they are activated also during the observation of other people whose facial mimicry expresses some emotional content. Mirror neurons can be thus involved in full comprehension of others' emotions and could contribute to the complex human ability of mind-reading, a set of cognitive abilities allowing subjects to think about the mind (e.g, beliefs, desires, emotions) of others [22].

A further support to the above data comes from a recent fMRI study [23] where subjects required to produce a specific emotional expression were interfered by the observation of a facial expression different from the one they were trying to produce. The cortical areas activated in the condition when observed and produced facial expressions conflicted with each other are those involved in the emotion processing, and in particular the inferior frontal gyrus and the right insula. Incidentally the prevalence of activation in the right insula is consistent with the hypothesis that the right hemisphere is particularly involved (is "dominant") in the processing of emotions [1, 24].

4 Neural Basis for Emotion Regulation

The control of emotional reactions is crucial for adaptive behaviour and social mediation. Being able to change our own emotions allows us to produce behavioural responses more adequate to the environment, and this can occur by means of both automatic and strategic cognitive mechanisms [25]. On the basis of what has been briefly summarised in the preceding sections it is possible to sketch a model of the structures and the connections implied in the emotion regulation (Figure 2). The amygdala is the core structure, which receives many kinds of sensorial information and diffusely projects to the hypothalamus and to the brainstem, thus determining the biological phenomena connected to the emotional reactions. While physiological changes are quite stereotypical, in the sense that they are not exclusive from one emotion to another, the subjective interpretation and the affective value of each emotion is often unique and can modulate the behaviour to the purpose of achieving the best adaptive response. In this perspective, too, the amygdala plays a central role, thanks to its connections with the insula, the cingulate gyrus and the orbito-frontal cortex which is in turn connected to the dorsolateral prefrontal cortex. The bidirectional connections between the amygdala and the orbito-frontal cortex, particularly in the right hemisphere, are the basis for the emotion regulation: after having integrated all sensorial information, the amygdala informs the orbito-frontal cortex about the current emotional state, and, in turn the orbito-frontal cortex modulates the activation in the amygdala as a function of the environmental, social, and personal context. The modulation of the activation in the amygdala by the orbito-frontal cortex occurs via a delicate process of response selection, where the cingulate gyrus (that is related to motivational decisions) plays an important role, particularly when it is necessary to solve conflicts between inner and outer states.

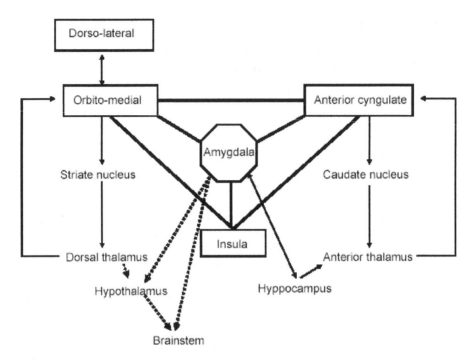

Fig. 2. Outline of a possible model of emotion regulation [2]. The amygdala receives sensorial input from the thalamic nuclei (not shown) and emotionally-relevant memory traces from the hyppocampus. Then, the amygdala projects to the hypothalamus and the brainstem signals that start the physiological changes related to the emotional arousal. Such processes are modulated by a tightly interconnected neural network including the amygdala, the insula, and the cortico-subcortical loops originating from the orbital frontal cortex and the cingulate gyrus. The dorsolateral prefrontal cortex (executive function, cognitive strategies) indirectly controls the emotion regulation.

Such mechanisms take place automatically, in a sort of *habitual emotion regulation* [26], but additional regulatory processes can be put in motion on the basis of the cognitive strategies ("*reappraisal*"), related to activation of other frontal areas. Actually, when normal subjects try to inhibit negative emotions (evoked by sad images) by means of cognitive strategies, a widespread activation is present, particularly in the dorso-lateral prefrontal cortex and in the cingulate gyrus; moreover, the more efficient the reappraisal strategy, the more evident activation in these cortical areas [27].

The tight network between the amygdala and the prefrontal cortex is the kernel for the regulation of positive emotions too, as shown by a recent fMRI study [28] in which prefrontal activation appeared to be even stronger. Since prefrontal activation is likely related to emotional control, from these findings it would be possible to suggest that positive emotions can be modulated more flexibly. Another kind of emotion modulation can occur by means of cognitive strategies aimed at modifying the cognitive value attributed to emotional stimuli [29].

An interesting and stimulating perspective for emotion regulations has been recently provided by the real-time fMRI, a technique by which normal subjects are informed about current status of their own cortical activity in a sort of biological *feedback* [30, 31]. By applying this new method, Caria *et al.* [32] succeeded in training normal subjects to control the activation of their own anterior insular cortex: during the experiment each subject tried to apply cognitive strategies to enhance or reduce insular activation and was continuously informed about efficacy of the strategy. The possibility of controlling the activation of our own cortical areas through a combination of cognitive strategies and *"neuro-feedback"* techniques opens new ways for non-pharmacological treatments of emotional disturbances, anxiety among others.

In this perspective some recent fMRI studies have explored the effect of meditation strategies on the emotional control. Lutz *et al.* [33] required to a group of subjects well experienced in a specific meditation technique (*"loving-kindness-compassion meditation state"*) to listen neutral, emotionally-positive, or emotionally-negative sounds. Results showed the activation of the insula and the cingulate gyrus in both meditation-expert and naïve subjects during listening, but the activation in the meditation-expert was stronger than in the naïve subjects while listening sad sounds, thus suggesting that meditation techniques might enhance, or modulate the emotional control.

5 Conclusions

To afford an ever changing environment successfully, man has developed a flexible control system capable of modulating the quite stereotyped, "emergency", emotion processing system. The wide neural network implied in the emotion regulation demonstrates how behaviour is determined by complex mechanisms, still not completely understood. However, modern neurofunctional techniques seem to open new horizons to comprehend neural basis of psychic activity, as suggested by the studies on the role of mirror neurons in empathy and by the research on the possible application of neuro-feedback to the treatment of disorders in the emotion regulation.

References

1. Gainotti, G.: Disorders of Emotional Behaviour. J. Neurol. 248, 743–749 (2001)
2. Grossi, D., Trojano, L.: I Fondamenti Neurofunzionali della Regolazione delle Emozioni. In: Matarazzo, O., Zammuner, V.L. (eds.) La Regolazione delle Emozioni, pp. 33–56. Il Mulino, Bologna (2009)
3. Hamm, A.O., Weike, A.I.: The Neuropsychology of Fear Learning and Fear Regulation. Int. J. Psychophysiol. 57, 5–14 (2005)
4. Phan, K.L., Wager, T.D., Taylor, S.F., Liberzon, I.: Functional Neuroimaging Studies of Human Emotions. CNS Spectra 9, 258–266 (2004)
5. Wicker, B., Keysers, C., Plailly, J., Royet, J.P., Gallese, V., Rizzolatti, G.: Both of Us Disgusted in My Insula: The Common Neural Basis of Seeing and Feeling Disgust. Neuron 40, 655–664 (2003)
6. Penfield, W., Faulk Jr., M.E.: The Insula; Further Observations on its Function. Brain 78, 445–470 (1955)

7. Wiens, S.: Interoception in Emotional Experience. Curr. Opin. Neurol. 18, 442–447 (2005)
8. Calder, A.J., Keane, J., Manes, F., Antoun, N., Young, A.W.: Impaired Recognition and Experience of Disgust Following Brain Injury. Nat. Neurosci. 3, 1077–1078 (2004)
9. Damasio, A.R.: The Somatic Marker Hypothesis and the Possible Functions of the Prefrontal Cortex. Philos. T. R. Soc. B. 351, 1413–1420 (1996)
10. Damasio, A.R.: Descartes' Error: Emotion, Reason, and the Human Brain. Grosset/Putnam, New York (1994)
11. Cato, M.A., Delis, D.C., Abildskov, T.J., Bigler, E.: Assessing the Elusive Cognitive Deficits Associated with Ventromedial Prefrontal Damage: A Case of a Modern-day Phineas Gage. J. Int. Neuropsychol. Soc. 10, 453–465 (2004)
12. Grossi, D., Trojano, L.: Lineamenti di Neuropsicologia Clinica. Carocci, Roma (2002)
13. Grossi, D., Trojano, L.: Neuropsicologia dei Lobi Frontali. Il Mulino Editore, Bologna (2005)
14. Carrera, E., Bogousslavsky, J.: The Thalamus and Behaviour: Effects of Anatomically Distinct Strokes. Neurology 66, 1817–1823 (2006)
15. Schmahmann, J.D., Pandya, D.N.: Disconnection Syndromes of Basal Ganglia, Thalamus, and Cerebrocerebellar Systems. Cortex 44, 1037–1066 (2008)
16. Nummenmaa, L., Hirvonen, J., Parkkola, R., Hietanen, J.K.: Is Emotional Contagion Special? An fMRI Study on Neural Systems for Affective and Cognitive Empathy. NeuroImage 43, 571–580 (2008)
17. Schutter, D.J., van Honk, J.: The Cerebellum in Emotion Regulation: a Repetitive Transcranial Magnetic Stimulation Study. Cerebellum (2009)
18. Rizzolatti, G., Fadiga, L., Gallese, V., Fogassi, L.: Premotor Cortex and the Recognition of Motor Actions. Brain Res. Cog. Brain Res. 3, 131–141 (1996)
19. Rizzolatti, G., Craighero, L.: The Mirror-Neuron System. Ann. Rev. Neurosci. 27, 169–192 (2004)
20. Adolphs, R., Tranel, D., Damasio, A.R.: Dissociable Neural Systems for Recognizing Emotions. Brain Cog. 52, 61–69 (2003)
21. Singer, T., Seymour, B., O'Doherty, J., Kaube, H., Dolan, R.J., Frith, C.D.: Empathy for Pain Involves the Affective but not Sensory Components of Pain. Science 303, 1157–1162 (2004)
22. Frith, C.D., Frith, U.: Interacting Minds - a Biological Basis. Science 286, 1692–1695 (1999)
23. Lee, T.W., Dolan, R.J., Critchley, H.D.: Controlling Emotional Expression: Behavioral and Neural Correlates of Nonimitative Emotional Responses. Cereb. Cortex 18, 104–113 (2008)
24. Gainotti, G.: Neuropsicologia delle Emozioni. In: Denes, G., Pizzamiglio, L. (eds.) Manuale di Neuropsicologia: Normalità e Patologia dei Processi Cognitivi, pp. 810–836. Zanichelli, Bologna (1996)
25. Gross, J.J.: Antecedent- and Response-Focused Emotion Regulation: Divergent Consequences for Experience, Expression and Physiology. J. Personal. Soc. Psychol. 74, 224–237 (1998)
26. Abler, B., Hofer, C., Viviani, R.: Habitual Emotion Regulation Strategies and Baseline Brain Perfusion. Neuroreport 19, 21–24 (2008)
27. Banks, S.J., Eddy, K.T., Angstadt, M., Nathan, P.J., Phan, K.L.: Amygdala-frontal Connectivity during Emotion Regulation. Soc. Cog. Affect. Neurosci. 2, 303–312 (2007)
28. Kim, S.H., Hamann, S.: Neural Correlates of Positive and Negative Emotion Regulation. J. Cog. Neurosci. 19, 776–798 (2007)

29. Ochsner, K.N., Gross, J.J.: The Cognitive Control of Emotion. Trends Cog. Sci. 9, 242–249 (2005)
30. Weiskopf, N., Veit, R., Erb, M., Mathiak, K., Grodd, W., Goebel, R., Birbaumer, N.: Physiological Self-regulation of Regional Brain Activity using Real-time Functional Magnetic Resonance Imaging (fMRI): methodology and exemplary data. NeuroImage 19, 577–586 (2003)
31. Weiskopf, N., Sitaram, R., Josephs, O., Veit, R., Scharnowski, F., Goebel, R., Birbaumer, N., Deichmann, R., Mathiak, K.: Real-time Functional Magnetic Resonance Imaging: Methods and Applications. Magn. Reson. Imaging 25, 989–1003 (2007)
32. Caria, A., Veit, R., Sitaram, R., Lotze, M., Weiskopf, N., Grodd, W., Birbaumer, N.: Regulation of Anterior Insular Cortex Activity using Real-time fMRI. NeuroImage 35, 1238–1246 (2007)
33. Lutz, A., Brefczynski-Lewis, J., Johnstone, T., Davidson, R.J.: Regulation of the Neural Circuitry of Emotion by Compassion Meditation: Effects of Meditative Expertise. PLoS ONE 3, e1897 (2008)

Automatic Meeting Participant Role Detection by Dialogue Patterns

Jing Su, Bridget Kane, and Saturnino Luz

Department of Computer Science,
O'Reilly Institute
Trinity College Dublin
Dublin 2, Ireland
`sujing@cs.tcd.ie, kaneb@tcd.ie, luzs@cs.tcd.ie`

Abstract. We introduce a new concept of 'Vocalization Horizon' for automatic speaker role detection in general meeting recordings. We demonstrate that classification accuracy reaches 38.5% when Vocalization Horizon and other features (i.e. vocalization duration and start time) are available. With another type of Horizon, the Pause - Overlap Horizon, the classification accuracy reaches 39.5%. Pauses and overlaps are also useful vocalization features for meeting structure analysis. In our experiments, the Bayesian Network classifier outperforms other classifiers, and is proposed for similar applications.

Keywords: Content-free meeting analysis, speaker role detection, meeting segmentation, multimedia information retrieval.

1 Introduction

Multiparty meeting browsing and retrieval is an active research topic. High quality audio and video records facilitate people in reviewing meetings. However, it is time consuming to listen to the whole length of meeting and locate the material of interest. In order to access audio recordings in an effective way, it would be useful to find a structure in the audio, especially a structure related to the content of an audio recording.

Although text-based approaches have been employed in the analysis of meeting data [4], we prefer to develop a content-free approach for meeting structure analysis, which avoids speech recognition errors and is more acceptable when dealing with confidential material. In this study we analyze to which extent content-free analysis can capture certain regularities of meetings (such as the role structure) which are commonly seen as intimately related to content. Participant role definitions may be not unique for general meetings. However, the AMI corpus [11] offers unique definitions for each meeting participant (detailed in Section 3), which facilitates our research.

Many contributions have been made on audio structure analysis. For the task of speech/ non-speech segmentation, Maganti [10] compared the performance of four methods: (i) energy based method, (ii) energy combined with zero-crossing,

A. Esposito et al. (Eds.): COST 2102 Int. Training School 2009, LNCS 5967, pp. 314–326, 2010.

(iii) modulation spectrum based segmentation and (iv) multi-layer perceptron. Results show that modulation spectrum based approach is accurate and close to manual segmentation for all the channels.

Speaker segmentation achieves promising accuracy with Bayesian Information Criterion (BIC) [2]. BIC based algorithm detects speaker change in continuous speech and achieves speaker segmentation. Gaussian Mixture Models (GMM) demonstrates high performance in labelling all vocalizations from the same speaker, and helps speaker clustering (or speaker identification) [12].

Advances in audio structure analysis [10,12] generally use acoustic features and segment audio recordings to the level of speaker identity. More demands on audio structure understanding emerge, and are hardly satisfied by techniques that are only based on acoustic features. In multi-party meeting recordings, users would like to locate audio materials with topic reference, or collect talk from different speakers with the same role. In order to retrieve more content related audio structures, supervised learning techniques are applied. In this paper, we discuss our approaches to classify the vocalization events according to speaker role using content-free measures for analysis. Acoustic features and conversational features are involved, and meeting transcription is not utilized.

In Section 2 we review recent progress of meeting structure analysis with vocalization features. Based on these works we propose our feature set and the hypothesis of its utility in Section 3. In Section 4 we test the hypothesis with supervised learning methods, and the evaluation of feature set is presented in Section 5.

2   Background

The importance of different types of features, content-free and content-dependent, has been investigated for some meeting analysis tasks. Hsueh and Moore [5], for instance, examined the effectiveness of multimodal features on the task of dialogue segmentation within a Maximum Entropy framework. They found that lexical features (i.e. cue words) are the most essential feature class to be combined into the segmentation model. However, lexical features must be combined with other features, in particular conversational features (i.e. lexical cohesion, overlap, pause, speaker change), to train well-performing models. On the other hand, many non-lexical feature classes (e.g. prosody), are not beneficial for recognizing boundaries when used in isolation. Esposito [3] indicated that pauses are not only generated by psychological motivations but they are also used as a linguistic means for discourse segmentation. Pauses are used by children and adults to mark the clause and paragraph boundaries. Following the research above, we are prompted to investigate conversational features (e.g. pauses and overlaps) are useful for detecting a specific discourse structure, speaker role.

Banerjee and Rudnicky [1] conducted fundamental research on meeting state detection and meeting participants role detection, with only speech-based features. They trained a decision tree classifier that learns to detect these states and roles from simple speech-based features that are easy to compute automatically. This classifier detects meeting states 18% more accurately than a random classifier, and detects participant roles 10% more accurately than a majority classifier. The results imply that simple and easy to compute features, e.g. the frequency of speaker change, can be used for this purpose.

In Banerjee and Rudnicky's work, the classifier's input is from a sliding window along a time sequence. They designed a taxonomy of *meeting states*. For the task of meeting states detection, four features are extracted from audio material in the window: (i) the frequency of speaker change, (ii) the number of participants who have spoken within the window, (iii) the number of overlaps in speech, (iv) the average length of the overlaps. For participant's role detection, more features are included, i.e. the total amount of speech from one speaker in the window, and the amount of overlap speech. To obtain the features above in an automatic way, speaker segmentation and clustering techniques can be used [12]. Thus Banerjee's method is a convenient approach for automatic meeting structure detection, compared with meeting transcription or manual annotation of features. Theoretically, it may be troublesome to detect *overlap* in continuous speech. *Voiced unclassified speech* can be used instead of *overlap*, and then these Voiced unclassified speech events can be labelled with corresponding speakers. The corresponding speakers are the identified speakers of the previous and following vocalizations.

Laskowski [8] applied new features to the task of role classification (by content-free methods): (i) talkspurt initiation, (ii) talkspurt continuation, for (iii) single-participant vocalization, or (iv) vocalization overlap. Talkspurt initiation for vocalization overlap leads to 53% single-feature-type 4-way classification rate on the AMI corpus.

We are using similar features as those used by Banerjee and Rudnicky, but in different format and to a more general meeting corpus. A widely accepted multi-party meeting database, the AMI corpus, is the target of our research (Section 3). Details of our experiment are given in Section 4.

3   Data Preparation

The AMI corpus contains a large quantity of meeting audio recordings. These meetings share common scenarios in an electronics company, where employees discuss the development of a new type of remote control device. With the consideration of budget and confidentiality, the meeting records are only simulations of true meetings in a company. Meeting participants are from three institutes: IDIAP in Switzerland, University of Edinburgh in UK, and TNO in Holland. In almost all the AMI meetings, there are four roles: the project manager (PM), the industrial designer (ID), the user interface designer (UI), and the marketing expert (ME). These roles are fixed. Participants in a simulated meeting may be lacking the necessary specific knowledge and experience, so they are trained before meetings.

With the benefit of fixed roles in the AMI corpus, we want to know if different participants in the same role behave with similar characters. In each AMI meeting, the project manager (PM), the industrial designer (ID), the user interface designer (UI), and the marketing expert (ME) are always named as speaker A, B, C and D respectively. If a method can always successfully categorize the talks as labelled from each individual speaker, then speaker roles are detected.

3.1 Feature Set

We wish to apply classification methods to identify speaker roles. Features available from the AMI corpus are: speaker ID, empty pauses, filled pauses, overlaps and referring start/end time. For general meeting recordings, if no annotations are available, we can obtain these features with speaker identification techniques, speech/ non-speech segmentation procedure. Since speech recognition is not being used, and we can avoid speech recognition errors. While speaker identification techniques (diarisation) are not perfect, diarisation error rates are typically lower than speech recognition error.

Features such as pauses and overlaps are distributed with variable frequency and length, and they are not naturally following each vocalization event. Banerjee and Rudnicky [1] extracted features based on a sliding window with fixed length. All features from one window were treated as one sample. But a fixed length window with fixed step length will break many continuous vocalizations. We adopt a more natural representation, by collecting features on each vocalization event. That is, vocalization duration, vocalization starting time, following pause length and following overlap length. For simplicity, here the pause only refers to an empty pause. A vocalization event is defined as a piece of continuous speech from one speaker, without an empty pause longer than 0.5 second. Features (vocalization duration, etc.) will serve as input to several classification schemes.

Conventionally, features on vocalizations are highly emphasized in the research of dialogue patterns. On the other hand, pauses are only regarded as natural connections of vocalizations, with no important influence on dialogue patterns. This perspective is misleading. For example, long and short pauses could have different meanings, even if the same words are pronounced on each side of the pause. If we only collect the textual features from vocalizations (words), we cannot distinguish the different meanings. Based on this consideration, we especially study pauses and overlaps, and use them as features for speaker role detection.

3.2 Vocalization Horizon

In most experiments, the vocalization event or a moving window is treated as an independent sample. Classification accuracy is only about 10% higher than random assignment, which is not of practical use. It is desirable to use an alternative way of feature extraction from meeting recordings. We postulate that the features from previous and following vocalization events can be influential factors on the present vocalization event. We designed two ways to implement the influential factors. The first approach is to use the duration of previous and following vocalization events, as a feature of the present event. We define this feature as *Vocalization Horizon*. The level of Vocalization Horizon is the number

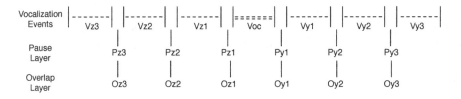

Fig. 1. Schematic Diagram for Vocalization Horizon, Pause Horizon and Overlap Horizon (Horizon = 3). **Voc** is the current vocalization, **Vy1** to **Vy3** are vocalizations after **Voc**, **Vz1** to **Vz3** are vocalizations before **Voc**. All 6 instances of vocalizations form the Vocalization Horizon. In Pause Layer and Overlap Layer, each instance labels the position of possible pause or overlap. Between two consecutive vocalizations, there is either a pause or an overlap, or neither, but cannot be both. All 6 instances of pauses form the Pause Horizon, and all 6 instances of overlaps form the Overlap Horizon.

of Vocalizations involved as features on either side of the current vocalization. For example, level 1 means that only the nearest one vocalization before and after current vocalization is used in the Vocalization Horizon feature.

The second approach is to use the duration of nearby pauses and overlaps as features. We define these features as Pause Horizon and Overlap Horizon (Figure 1). We assume there is either empty pause or overlap between any two consecutive vocalization events. When there is no pause or overlap, the corresponding duration is labeled zero. So GAP_Horizon (Table 1) can combine Pause Horizon and Overlap Horizon. The effectiveness of feature sets is checked through supervised learning algorithms.

3.3   Hypotheses

Based on the features available from the AMI corpus, we hypothesize on meeting structure and role detection. These hypotheses are tested by machine learning methods, detailed in Section 4.

Hypothesis 1: The patterns of vocalization, pause and overlaps not only relate to personal habit, but also relate to the structure of meetings, such as discussion, presentation and briefing. These patterns of vocalization can reveal meeting structures.

Hypothesis 2: consecutive vocalization events influence each other and are not independent. Vocalization Horizon is an influential factor in the meeting structure, e.g. speaker role. The degree of influence decreases as the distance increases between the current vocalization and the horizon vocalization.

3.4   Statistics

In Section 4.2 and Section 4.3 we compare the classification accuracy of two feature sets. In the experiment described, it is possible to compare the Mean accuracy difference of two feature sets. When the difference is statistically significant, we can use one feature set with more confidence.

In our classification tests, each feature set will be tested upon the same data sets. To exclude the possibility that the Mean accuracy difference is due to chance, the paired t-test [7] is used as a statistical criterion. Since AMI meeting data are independent from each other, the classification accuracy values are also independent. The paired t-test is based on assumption that all samples are normally distributed. The normality of accuracy values can be tested upon Shapiro-Wilk test [13].

4   Experiments

4.1   Effect of Different Feature Sets

We use 8 meetings from the AMI corpus. In each meeting there are four participants. The project manager (PM), the industrial designer (ID), the user interface designer (UI), and the marketing expert (ME) are labeled as speaker A, B, C and D respectively. For each meeting the feature set holds 990 instances of vocalizations on average. The number of vocalizations in each AMI meeting ranges from 172 to 2014. For each meeting the classification outcome is based on 10-fold cross-validation. Since the target variable Speaker Role is categorical, C4.5, Naive Bayes and Bayesian Network algorithms are chosen as classifiers. For feature sets, we choose three ways to combine the features, these are VOC_Horizon, GAP_Horizon, and SUM_Horizon, as shown in Table 1. VOC_Horizon contains only features related to the present vocalization event and adjacent conversation events. GAP_Horizon contains only features related to the present vocalization event and adjacent pauses and overlaps. SUM_Horizon contains all of the features in these two sets (VOC_Horizon and GAP_Horizon).

Table 1 shows three feature sets from one meeting (see Table 5 for a description of the variables). By comparing the performance of classifiers operating on each of these sets we can distinguish which feature sets are more powerful for speaker

Table 1. Three feature set combinations

Feature Set	Features
VOC_Horizon	voc_start, voc_dur, z1_dur, z2_dur, z3_dur, y1_dur, y2_dur, y3_dur
GAP_Horizon	voc_start, voc_dur, PO_z1_dur, PO_z2_dur, PO_z3_dur, PO_y1_dur, PO_y2_dur, PO_y3_dur, PO
SUM_Horizon	voc_start, voc_dur, z1_dur, z2_dur, z3_dur, y1_dur, y2_dur, y3_dur, PO_z1_dur, PO_z2_dur, PO_z3_dur, PO_y1_dur, PO_y2_dur, PO_y3_dur, PO

Table 2. Classification accuracy from three feature sets and three classifiers

	VOC_Horizon	GAP_Horizon	SUM_Horizon
C4.5	37.59%	37.30%	37.29%
NaiveBayes	27.44%	29.47%	28.03%
BayesNet	38.50%	39.54%	39.43%

role classification. Table 2 shows that the Bayes Network classifier performs best for any of the feature sets. The classification accuracy of 39.54% is approximately 15% higher than the baseline[1]. This result is also higher than the 10% gain reported in [1]. It should be noted, however, that the data sets used in [1] are different from ours, as are the definitions of 'roles'. In [1], there are only 3 roles: presenter, information provider and information consumer, and the speakers for each role vary as the meeting progresses. In our data set, AMI corpus, there are 4 roles, and each participant's role is fixed throughout the meeting.

Performance details of each classifier are shown in Figure 3 and Figure 4 (in Appendix C). The three feature sets perform differently with each classifier, as shown in Table 2. C4.5 classifier generates the highest accuracy with VOC_Horizon features, and two Bayesian classifiers generate the highest accuracy with GAP_Horizon features. There is little advantage in using SUM_Horizon even the best performance (39.43%) is less than that achieved by Bayesian Network classifier with GAP_Horizon. We see that, when the classifier is chosen, the performance of different feature sets does not differ much. The choice of classifier appears to be important and in our experiment the Bayesian Network classifier performed best.

4.2 Effect of Vocalization Horizon

In Section 3.3 we hypothesize that: consecutive vocalization events influence each other and are not independent. The degree of influence decreases as the distance increases between the current vocalization and the horizon vocalization. In this Section, we describe our test to investigate if Vocalization Horizon is useful for role detection in meeting recordings, and to which extent the levels of Vocalization Horizon can influence classification accuracy.

VOC_Horizon feature set is built upon 8 meeting recordings. C4.5 and Bayesian Network classifiers are used for classification. The Bayesian Network classifier obtains the highest accuracy in Table 2, so we also test it on Vocalization Horizon features.

The first row of Table 3 show that accuracy values of Horizon levels 1, 2, 3 are quite close to each other. The paired t-test shows $p = 0.0805$ between Horizon = 0 and Horizon = 3. For other Horizon levels, the p values are similar. Although statistical significance (at the $p < 0.05$ level) for the effect of VOC_Horizon features

---

[1] In the AMI corpus, only 4 participants are involved in each meeting. Each participant holds a unique role. There are only 4 classes in our study. If all vocalizations are allocated to a random class, the accuracy value is 25%.

Table 3. Vocalization Horizon effect with VOC_Horizon feature sets on BayesNet and C4.5 classifiers.

	Horizon = 3	Horizon = 2	Horizon = 1	Horizon = 0
BayesNet	38.50%	38.40%	38.48%	37.50%
C4.5	37.59%	38.39%	39.28%	36.70%

on accuracy could not be demonstrated with the Bayesian Network classifier, some influence influence on is still observable. For decision trees (Table 3, row 2) we see that the highest mean classification accuracy emerges when Horizon = 1. We find that the accuracy does not improve when we add more vocalization features. The effect of Horizon varies with different data sets. Figure 2 shows that in a single meeting the best accuracy may emerge for Horizon = 2. Therefore we do not recommend adopting a fixed optimal Horizon. On the other hand, from Figure 2, we see the fact that in most feature sets the classification accuracy is higher for Horizon = 1 than for Horizon = 0. The paired t-test shows $p = 0.023$ between Horizon = 0 and Horizon = 1. The effect of Vocalization Horizon is statistically significant[2].

The results of C4.5 and Bayesian Network classifier show that Vocalization Horizon features improve classification accuracy in general. The improvement from C4.5 is statistically significant, and Hypothesis 2 in Section 3.3 is supported. We can apply Vocalization Horizon to speaker role detection with confidence.

4.3   Effect of Pauses and Overlap Horizon

We use the Bayesian Network classifier to test the effect of Pause Horizon and Overlap Horizon. As before, the paired t-test is used to evaluate the significance of accuracy difference.

Table 4. Effect of Vocalization Horizon on a BayesNet with GAP_Horizon feature sets

MeetingID	Horizon = 3	Horizon = 2	Horizon = 1	Horizon = 0
2002a	37.39%	39.56%	39.38%	39.93%
2002b	40.77%	41.31%	39.51%	38.42%
2002c	41.08%	39.60%	38.34%	37.37%
2002d	40.67%	38.83%	36.69%	34.56%
2003a	37.79%	37.21%	40.70%	41.28%
2003b	44.04%	44.04%	44.77%	42.75%
2003c	39.90%	38.55%	40.57%	34.34%
2003d	34.66%	34.32%	35.80%	33.41%
Mean	39.54%	39.18%	39.47%	37.76%
p-value	0.19	0.185	0.059	

---

[2] Normality is satisfied for both data sets used in this section.

In Table 4, Horizon = 3 gives the highest mean accuracy , but the accuracy difference with Horizon = 0 is not significant. For Horizon = 3, most accuracy values are higher than the ones in Horizon = 0, but in meeting 2002a and 2003a, accuracy decreases. This phenomenon illustrates that classification accuracy does not favour greater Horizon level in all cases, and a fixed Horizon level for all data sets is not recommended. Again in Table 4, we find that $p = 0.059$ with Horizon = 1, approaching the 5% significance criterion. We regard this as evidence of the effectiveness of Pause and Overlap Horizon for role classification, though further study is necessary to settle this question conclusively.

5   Conclusions

Our aim in this study was to assess the usefulness of content-free Vocalisation Horizon features in automatically detecting speaker roles. The automatic detection of speech from a particular role is a problem of practical significance in that role-annotation would potentially facilitate a review of a meeting according to the speech contribution of any particular role involved in a discussion, as well as support higher-level tasks such as segmentation in meetings for which the participant role structures are well defined [9].

We have shown that, for the AMI corpus meeting recordings, speaker role detection can be achieved with nearly 40% accuracy. Vocalization Horizon, Pause Horizon and Overlap Horizon are demonstrated to be useful concepts and are found to be significant factors for role detection. We suggest that different levels of Vocalization Horizon need to be tested on a variety of data sets. In classification tests, we found that Bayesian Network classifier outperforms the Naive Bayes classifier and C4.5 decision trees on three feature sets. This result may be explained by the fact that there is independence among features but not among vocalization events. Bayesian Network classifier are therefore recommended for other speaker role detection tasks with similar features.

Although from an information retrieval perspective the results reported above are of limited practical significance, they do show that simple features such as the duration of talk spurts, pauses and overlapping speech can reveal higher-level regularities in meeting data. Speaker role is one of the important aspects of meeting structure, such as in routine workplace meetings described in [6]. We expect that progress in speaker role detection will be helpful for meeting structure analysis, and eventually lead to ease of retrieval of elements from meeting recordings.

Acknowledgments

This research was supported by Science Foundation Ireland Research Frontiers grant under the National Development Plan.

References

1. Banerjee, S., Rudnicky, A.: Using simple speech-based features to detect the state of a meeting and the roles of the meeting participants. In: INTERSPEECH 2004, pp. 2189–2192 (2004)
2. Chen, S.S., Gopalakrishnan, P.S.: Speaker, environment and channel change detection and clustering via the bayesian information criterion. In: DARPA Broadcast News Transcription and Understanding Workshop (1998)
3. Esposito, A., Stejskal, V., Smekal, Z., Bourbakis, N.: The significance of empty speech pauses: Cognitive and algorithmic issues. In: Mele, F., Ramella, G., Santillo, S., Ventriglia, F. (eds.) BVAI 2007. LNCS, vol. 4729, pp. 542–554. Springer, Heidelberg (2007)
4. Galley, M., McKeown, K., Fosler-Lussier, E., Jing, H.: Discourse segmentation of multi-party conversation. In: ACL 2003: Proceedings of the 41st Annual Meeting on Association for Computational Linguistics, Morristown, NJ, USA, pp. 562–569. Association for Computational Linguistics (2003)
5. Hsueh, P.-Y., Moore, J.D.: Combining multiple knowledge sources for dialogue segmentation in multimedia archives. In: Proceedings of the 45th Annual Meeting of the ACL. Association for Computational Linguistics (2007)
6. Kane, B., Luz, S.: Achieving diagnosis by consensus. Computer Supported Cooperative Work (CSCW) 18(4), 357–392 (2009)
7. Kutner, M.H., Nachtsheim, C.J., Neter, J., Li, W.: Applied Linear Statistical Models, 5th edn. McGraw Hill, New York (2005)
8. Laskowski, K., Ostendorf, M., Schultz, T.: Modeling vocal interaction for text independent participant characterization in multi-party conversation. In: SIGDIAL 2008 (2008)
9. Luz, S.: Locating case discussion segments in recorded medical team meetings. In: SSCS 2009: Proceedings of the ACM Multimedia Workshop on Searching Spontaneous Conversational Speech, Beijing, China, October 2009. ACM Press, New York (2009)
10. Maganti, H.K., Motlicek, P., Gatica-Perez, D.: Unsupervised speech/non-speech detection for automatic speech recognition in meeting rooms. IDIAP-RR 57, IDIAP, Martigny, Switzerland (2006)
11. Renals, S., Hain, T., Bourlard, H.: Recognition and interpretation of meetings: The AMI and AMIDA projects. In: Proc. IEEE Workshop on Automatic Speech Recognition and Understanding, ASRU 2007 (2007)
12. Reynolds, D., Rose, R.: Robust text-independent speaker identification using gaussian mixture speaker models. IEEE Transactions on Speech and Audio Processing 3(1), 72–83 (1995)
13. Shapiro, S.S., Wilk, M.B.: An analysis of variance test for normality (complete samples). Biometrika 52(3/4), 591–611 (1965)

A   The Notations in the Feature Set

Table 5. notations in Table 1

Feature ID	Description
voc_start	start time of present vocalization
voc_dur	duration of present vocalization
z1_dur	duration of previous vocalization
z2_dur	duration of the 2nd previous vocalization
z3_dur	duration of the 3rd previous vocalization
y1_dur	duration of next vocalization
y2_dur	duration of the 2nd next vocalization
y3_dur	duration of the 3rd next vocalization
PO_z1_dur	duration of the following pause or overlap
PO_z2_dur	duration of the 2nd following pause or overlap
PO_z3_dur	duration of the 3rd following pause or overlap
PO_y1_dur	duration of the nearest pause or overlap before present vocalization
PO_y2_dur	duration of the 2nd nearest pause or overlap before present vocalization
PO_y3_dur	duration of the 3rd nearest pause or overlap before present vocalization
PO	norminal variable for pause, overlap and null

B   Effect of Vocalization Horizon

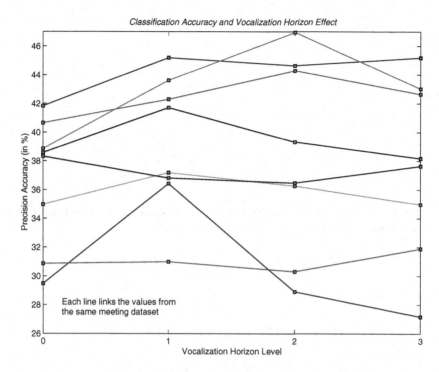

Note: Each line links the values from same meeting data set. The meetings here are labeled from ES2002a to ES2003d in the AMI corpus.

Fig. 2. Speaker Role Classification Accuracy and Vocalization Horizon Effect

C   Performance of Classifiers

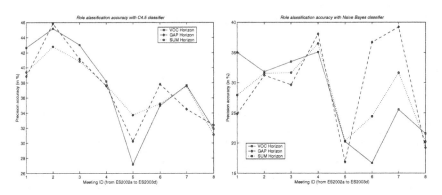

Fig. 3. C4.5 classifier accuracy on Speaker Role Classification (left) and Naive Bayes classifier accuracy on Speaker Role Classification (right)

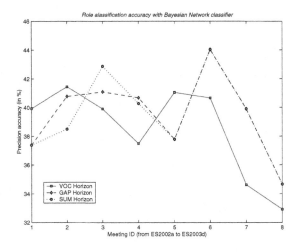

Fig. 4. Bayesian Network classifier accuracy on Speaker Role Classification

Linguistic and Non-verbal Cues for the Induction of Silent Feedback

Maria Koutsombogera[1,2] and Harris Papageorgiou[1]

[1] Institute for Language & Speech Processing, Artemidos 6&Epidavrou, 15125 Athens, Greece
[2] University of Athens, Department of Linguistics, University Campus, 15784 Athens, Greece
{mkouts,xaris}@ilsp.gr

Abstract. The aim of this study is to analyze certain linguistic (dialogue acts, morphosyntactic units, semantics) and non-verbal cues (face, hand and body gestures) that may induce the silent feedback of a participant in face-to-face discussions. We analyze the typology and functions of the feedback expressions as attested in a corpus of TV interviews and then we move on to the investigation of the immediately preceding context to find systematic evidence related to the production of feedback. Our motivation is to look into the case of active listening by processing data from real dialogues based on the discourse and lexical content that induces the listener's reactions.

Keywords: Silent feedback, multimodal dialogues, non-verbal expressions, dialogue acts, morphosyntactic structures, semantics.

1 Introduction

This paper is an analysis of non-verbal feedback in two-party dialogues. Specifically, in a corpus of TV interviews we examine the silent responses of the dialogue participant who holds the role of the listener in any given time. In that sense, listener's feedback gives evidence of the collaborative nature of dialogue; the listeners communicate to the speakers via non-verbal signs that they follow the flow of the discussion; they perceive, understand, agree or not with the message conveyed; they might express the willingness to take the turn or give support to the speakers to go on with their turn, as well as other attitudes or emotions [1]. Our study focuses on the following points:

- the actual expression of feedback; the modalities the listener employs and the communicative functions of feedback (e.g. agreement, understanding, interruption etc.)
- non-verbal and linguistic events that induce the hearer's feedback and can be located in the speaker's immediately preceding utterance.

Non-verbal cues include accompanying or reinforcing movements performed by the speaker that may induce similar synchronized feedback responses by the listener.

As a discourse element, feedback has strong context dependence with the previous dialogue act; thus, we study the correlation of dialogue acts with feedback instances in order to find the most preferred acts that induce a feedback response. Moreover, we

A. Esposito et al. (Eds.): COST 2102 Int. Training School 2009, LNCS 5967, pp. 327–336, 2010.
© Springer-Verlag Berlin Heidelberg 2010

investigate whether feedback is synchronized to certain morphosyntactic structures of the speaker's turn by looking into the relation of feedback instantiations and phrase unit boundaries (verb, noun, adjective and adverbial phrases). Finally, we assume that in most of the cases, there is a trigger word that induces a feedback response. Trigger words are usually the heads of the aforementioned chunks and can be grouped to an extent according to their semantic content.

In the context of human interaction, communicative feedback has been thoroughly studied in its linguistic dimension through a robust theoretical framework [1] and from a multimodal point of view with an emphasis on its distributional, functional, typological and acoustic aspects [2] or the investigation of the effect that a combination of cues (e.g. morphological categories, prosody, gaze) might have on the production of feedback [3]. Moreover, there are attempts to describe feedback in different social activities or other contexts [4] or model it for purposes of behavior simulation [5]. Interactional synchrony was first described by Condon and Ogston [6] who looked into speech and body motion coordination between the speaker and the hearer, and was further pursued among others by Kendon [7], who elaborated on patterns of movement coordination.

In this study we do not take into account any features related to speech analysis (e.g. prosody). Our motivation is to look into the case of active listening by processing data from real dialogues and find evidence about its systematicity based on linguistic cues that induce hearer's feedback, i.e. (a) the discourse structure as described by dialogue acts and (b) the lexical content in terms of morphosyntactic structures and semantic properties of the feedback context.

2 Corpus

The corpus we analyzed consists of face-to-face interactions between an interviewer and an interviewee as attested in 6 hours of overall 11 Greek TV interviews (8 political, 2 cultural and 1 scientific). Some interviews are hosted by the same person, thus the corpus includes 19 different speakers, 11 interviewees and 8 interviewers.

The first part of our dataset contains approximately 3 hours of interviews that are analyzed and annotated at multiple levels such as speech transcription, dialogue act labeling, video annotation of non-verbal modalities and their respective semantic/pragmatic functions based on the MUMIN coding scheme [8]. A more detailed description about the creation and content of this corpus is provided in [9]. For the purposes of the present study we focus on all the information concerning silent feedback (by either the interviewer or the interviewee), i.e. the segments where feedback behavior of the participant that does not hold the floor is observed and all annotations that are aligned with it. The annotations of interest include the labeling of the modality[1] through which feedback is expressed, its semiotic type and the respective feedback function (in terms of perception, understanding, acceptance and expression of emotions and attitudes).

Moreover, in order to explore the linguistic content that is synchronized or precedes the expressions of interest, the transcript of the speaker's utterance where the

---

[1] Movements of the head as a whole and parts of it (eyebrows, gaze direction etc.), handedness and trajectory of gestures and torso movements.

hearer's feedback takes place as well as its dialogue act tag are included in the analysis. The context threshold is set to 5 content words preceding feedback, plus the word(s) that is/are synchronized with it. Consequently, if feedback occurs at the beginning of an utterance, we also take into account the last words of the previous utterance and its respective dialogue act value as well. In order to enrich our data we included a second 3-hour subset of interviews. For this subset, we annotated only the parts where a silent feedback expression was observed, we transcribed the speaker's utterance that is synchronized with it and labeled its dialogue act.

3 Data Analysis

The interviews do not present uniformity with regards to the participants shown on screen. That is, depending on the setting and the restrictions imposed by editing, in half of the cases the camera focuses either on the speaker or the listener, while in the other half both speakers are included in the scene. The features of typology and function of non-verbal feedback as well as the linguistic cues that precede it were observed on the whole corpus. However, in order to study hearer's feedback in relation to the speaker's non-verbal behavior, we used those interviews where both participants are simultaneously visible (cf. Table 1).

Table 1. Corpus distribution according to participants visible on screen

participants on screen	duration of videos (min.)	silent feedback instances
1	179.12	272
2	161.50	253
total	**340.62**	**525**

Our data pertain to a typical interview setting, where speakers have unequal speaking rights; the interview host suggests the topics of discussion and the guest occupies most of the interview time to express his/her opinions and elaborate on the topics discussed. Thus, the host as a listener produces more feedback (77.4%) than the guest (22.6%). This distribution is calculated on half of the videos where both speakers are visible on camera. We cannot provide safe figures for the other half (1 person visible), as the participants may express feedback that in any case is not shown on screen.

3.1 Feedback Typology

The listeners employ various non-verbal modalities in order to give feedback. Head-nodding is the most popular among them (68.51%), followed by smiling (10.82%). Generally, there is a preference for moving the head (nod, tilt, jerk, shake, turn sideways) or parts of it (smiling, eyebrows raising or frowning, gazing down, away or towards the speaker, protruding lips etc.). The use of hand gestures is quite rare and is restricted mainly to metaphoric types such as shoulder raising or opening hands with palms up i.e. to denote ignorance. A small number of torso movements (back and forth, leaning sideways or bending slightly forward) was also attested. Some of the feedback movements are complex, i.e. the listener nods and smiles at the same time or raises the shoulders and eyebrows simultaneously. The distribution of feedback modalities is depicted in Table 2a.

3.2 Feedback Functions

Feedback is a reaction to a communicated content. In that sense, all feedback attestations have specific communicative functions as they may show perception and/or understanding of the preceding message, agreement, refusal, desire for more information or clarification as well as a lot of attitudinal reactions that denote the listener's state of mind.

In our data, most of the silent feedback instances, specifically head-nodding, have an acknowledgement function [10] by providing support to the speakers that their contribution has been perceived and that the conversation may proceed. Furthermore, the listeners' silent reactions may be more or less marked with: (a) the degree of perception of the message; nodding or blinking (understanding), eyebrows frowning (not understanding), (b) The degree of acceptance; smiling and making deep nods to show agreement, shake head for disagreement, eyebrows frowning and raising shoulders when doubting, (c) Willingness to interrupt (move torso forward and raise hand) and (d) personal involvement in the discussion; eyes semi-closed to show attention, raising eyebrows when interested, gazing away while thinking. Finally, attitudinal or emotional reactions such as surprise (eyes wide open), irritation (frowning) or satisfaction (smile and nod) were also attested (see table 2b).

Table 2. a. Modalities employed for feedback by the listener, b. Functions of listener's feedback

a.

modality	%
nod	45.43
repeated nods	23.08
smile	10.82
eyebrow raise	4.32
eyebrow frown	1.93
head side turn	1.92
hands open	1.20
torso forward	1.20
other	10.10

b.

function	%
perception	51.31
accept	24.73
understanding	8.42
attention/interest	3.95
disagree	2.63
surprise	1.32
non-understanding	1.06
interruption	1.05
other	5.53

3.3 Non-verbal Cues in the Speaker's Behavior

In the interviews where both participants are visible, 67% of the hearer's feedback is related to the speaker's non-verbal behavior. That is, most of the feedback instances either co-occur with the stroke of the speaker's gestures (Ex. 1) or happen shortly after them (Ex. 2).

Ex.1[2]: speaker: S, hearer: H

S:	An mas diskolevi o idios o tropos litourgias mas in akoma pio diskolo leme poli apla
	If us is difficult proper way function our is even harder we say very simply
	| **index**[3] | | **hand**[4] |
	na paroume tis sostes apofasis
	to take the right decisions
	| **hand** |
H:	| **nod** | | **nod** |
	| **nod** |
[**Translation**: If we are having difficulty with the proper way we function, it's even harder, so we simply say, to make the right decisions]	

Ex. 2: speaker: S, hearer: H

S:	Akrivos ego ime sidagmatologos opos leme diladi eho asholithi me to dimosio dikeo
	Exactly I am constitutionalist as we say thus have dealt with public law
	| **gaze tow**[5] | | **gaze tow** |
H:	| **nod** | | **nod** |
[**Translation**: Exactly, I am a so-called constitutionalist, thus I am dealing with public law]	

We have examined this temporal coordination of movements focused on visual criteria, even though it is attested in the literature [7] that it's sufficient for the listener to hear the speech of his/her co-participant so that interactional synchrony takes place.

The hearer uses mostly visual input so as to organize his/her movements which follow the non-verbal behavior of the speaker. In our data, when this type of synchrony takes place, there always exists visual contact between the participants. Thus, this is considered as a case of mimicking with regard to the choice of the non-verbal modality through which feedback is expressed.

The form of the listener's movements is not necessarily a mirror image of the speaker's movements. In fact, movement mirroring exists in only 10.2% of the cases observed. Those cases are movements of nodding/head tilting or brow-raising by the speaker followed by analogous movements by the hearer. In the rest of the cases the listener employs different modalities or forms of movement as a response to those of the speaker. The most preferred movement of the hearers is nodding, which coincides with the stroke of speakers' hand beats, their forward movement of the torso, and their gazing towards the hearers. In any case, the speakers' non-verbal expressions which are related to feedback are richer in quantity, modalities employed and forms of movement than those of the hearers.

3.4 Linguistic Cues in the Speaker's Utterance

So far we have examined the typology and functions of the feedback movements, as well as their possible relation with the non-verbal expressions of the speaker that are more or less coordinated with them. We now move on to examine the relation of the

---

[2] Greek examples are transliterated and then translated to English.

[3] Index finger pointing.

[4] Hand (palm) open.

[5] Gaze towards interlocutor.

silent feedback with regard to the linguistic analysis of the utterance in which it takes place in terms of dialogue acts, morphosyntactic structures and semantic content.

Dialogue act of preceding utterance. Each utterance in our interview corpus that is synchronized with the hearer's feedback is annotated with information about its communicative act. The coding scheme employed is based on a multidimensional taxonomy of dialogue acts [11]. Our goal is to study the role of the communicative context in which silent feedback takes place. The dialogue acts dimensions to which the speaker utterances of interest pertain are the following:

– Information-seeking functions: direct questions, indirect questions or prefatory statements that are used as an introduction to questions.
– Information-providing functions: pure answers, informs (statements), elaboration by means of explanation or exemplification, justification (argumentation of the speaker with regards to a point of discussion). We also include in this category the third party statements that the speaker might quote or read to the listener, as well as the narration discourse type.
– Directive functions: suggestions to the listener.
– Allo-feedback: evaluation of the addressee's utterances; it is usually related to negative judgment, as the speaker may attack the listener or accuse him/her of something.
– Social obligations: welcome and farewell greetings, interviewee presentation.
– Topic management: negotiation of the discussion agenda, such as opening, shifting to or closing a topic.
– Own-communication management: self-correction or rephrasing.
– Time management: pausing or producing fillers.

The distribution of the most prevalent subtypes of the above dimensions is shown in Fig. 1.

The listener produces feedback as a reaction to the aforementioned communicative contexts. The majority of feedback movements is induced by the elaboration and

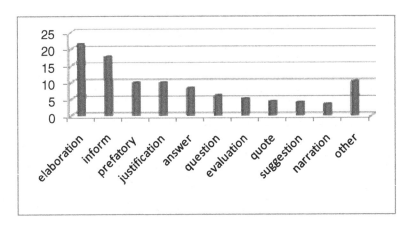

Fig. 1. Distribution of dialogue act labels of the speaker's utterance that is synchronized with listener's feedback

inform features, as the listener shows signs of perception and understanding of the message, and provides the speaker with support to go on. Moreover, when an information-seeking act is performed, the listener usually gives signs of understanding and willingness to answer even if the question is not formulated yet. This is the case of prefatory statements, where the hearer seems to be able to predict that a question is about to follow. Finally, when the listeners suspect that the evaluations that the speakers express about them are hostile, they tend to react in terms of disagreement, disappointment, doubt, or willingness to interrupt.

Morphosyntactic structures. Our starting point is the hypothesis that silent feedback might happen as a reaction to the speaker's words which are localized just before the feedback expression. Those words form parts of larger syntactic chunks. We thus try to find possible correlations between chunk boundaries and feedback instances. The basis for this idea is analogous to the syntactic criteria for the transition relevance place as described in Ford and Thompson [12], according to which the listener projects when the speaker is going to finish a turn and this time point might coincide with the completion of a syntactic unit.

In order to check this assumption, we took into account a window of 5 content words that immediately precede the feedback instance; these parts of the utterances were parsed and the output syntactic structures were analyzed. The decision on this window is based on gesture and speech coexpressiveness as defined in the semantic synchrony rule [13], i.e. if gesture and speech co-occur, they cover the same idea unit at the same time. We believe that this rule applies not only within the same speaker, but between a speaker who uses the verbal channel and a listener who reacts non-verbally as well. This assumption is further corroborated by the observation in our data that, in most of the cases, one of the last three words before the listener's feedback carries the content to which the listener reacts. We extended this context to five words in order to cater for an approx. 5% of exceptional cases. This context has proved to be sufficient and any extension of it to more than 5 words does not provide any significant evidence.

The data distribution shows that feedback happens preferentially after specific structures, namely verb (vp), noun (np), adjective (adjp), adverbial phrases (advp) and a small percentage of prepositional phrases (pp) (cf. Fig. 2). A 6.4% of feedback takes

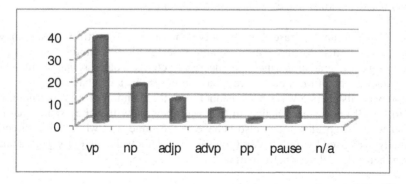

Fig. 2. Distribution of syntactic structures in the phrases that precede feedback

place during pauses, perhaps used as a filler, while 20% of the instances could not be classified according to the specified morphosyntactic criteria (n/a).

A quite interesting point is the fact that out of the n/a instances that could not follow the morphosyntactic unit completion criteria, 73% of them is attributed to cases where the feedback is synchronized to the speaker's movements, as described in paragraph 3.3. In that case feedback induction is not related to the verbal content, but could be linked to the non-verbal behavior of the speaker. The remaining 17% of the n/a instances obviously follows other criteria or phenomena, most probably prosodic or other paralinguistic features.

Semantics. The aforementioned phrase units contain lexical elements that function as trigger words, in the sense that they are marked with specific semantic content which is related to feedback induction. In the examples[6] that follow we make an attempt to describe some semantic features of words or structures preceding or coinciding with the silent feedback expressions as observed in our corpus. The cases that follow are spread throughout the corpus and are not restricted to specific topics or interview types; they are rather word or structure-dependent.

Verbs. Feedback responses are very common after verbs of deontic modality, i.e. verbs that express necessity of performing what is being said: must, need to, ought to, etc. The same behavior was also attested after verbs that lack neutrality, either in terms of judgment (deplore, accuse), statement (admit, insinuate) or other semantically marked verb forms (won, opposed to, etc).

Verb phrases that are found in correlative conjunctions such as "not only/but also", "either/or", "neither/nor" are followed by a feedback expression just before the realization of the second correlative element.

Pronouns that initiate a verb phrase seem to be important; Greek is a pro-drop language, as it allows for null subject constructions. However, when first singular person types of the personal pronoun are phonologically realized- for reasons of focus- they are followed by a feedback response by the listener: I'm saying that, let me explain, I am interested. Moreover, the use of the first plural person types of the personal pronoun seems to evoke the same behavior: we will discuss this, let's go to the next topic, etc. We believe that this type of pronoun marks the collaboration of the participants and their mutual commitment to the discussion, which is something that the listener usually acknowledges with a feedback response.

Nouns. Heads of noun phrases with negative polarity (thief, hostility, lies, pathogeny, repugnance, confusion, implication, vampire, resignation), denoting influence (impact, instigator), gradation (increase, decrease, etc.) or other semantically marked nouns (declaration of love, blaze) are usually followed by a feedback response.

Moreover, listeners always backchannel after the mention of a proper noun referring to a well-known personality; in that way they show that they share a common ground with the speaker. They also behave in the same way while being directly or indirectly addressed by the speaker (you said that, let's welcome our guest), acknowledging their role and their participation in the discussion.

---

[6] All examples are translated from Greek to English.

Adjectives. Some of the attested feedback instances follow adjectives which identify qualities that someone or something has (excellent, correct, weird, responsible, fluid etc.). Qualitative adjectives might be gradable when followed by submodifiers such as "very", "rather" etc. It's worth mentioning that most of the qualitative adjectives have negative polarity (painful, difficult, unhappy, melancholic, impossible, sparing). Other adjective types related to feedback are ranking/ordering (first, second, top-level, descending, higher) and emphasizing (absolute, complete).

Adverbs. The most common type of adverbs[7] that induce feedback responses are sentential adjuncts that, in general, indicate the speaker's opinion or reaction to what is being said, such as: anyway, of course, at least, etc. Further subdivisions of this class were attested in the data; adverbs that speakers use to indicate reality or possibility (actually, probably, definitely), to generalize (basically), to denote the ordering of their arguments (first, second, to sum up), to provide justification for a statement based on the common ground (apparently, obviously). Moreover, the listeners tend to produce feedback after emphasizing (indeed, by all means) or focusing adverbs (mostly, especially) that stress the truth or the seriousness of a statement and generally after adverbs of degree (well, badly, terribly) which inform about the extent of an action or an attitude that the speaker is expressing.

Finally, feedback expressions are very common after linking adjuncts such as: also, as well (indicating addition), equally, likewise (indicating parallel), instead, however (indicating contrast).

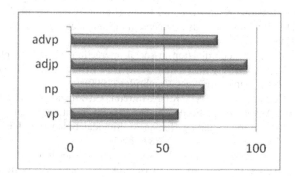

Fig. 3. Percentage of phrase units containing feedback trigger words which comply with semantic criteria

4 Conclusions

We have attempted to present a description of events that induce silent feedback based on the non-verbal behavior of the speaker and the linguistic content of his/her utterance. We believe that although speech analysis provides a very rich set of informative features for feedback induction, it could be combined with non-verbal and linguistic cues which are of equal importance not only to the analysis of this behavior, but to its modeling and simulation as well.

---

[7] The classification followed is described in Collins COBUILD English Grammar [14].

Since the majority of our data are political interviews, we plan to explore possible quantitative or qualitative variations in a more balanced –in terms of discourse genres- corpus (e.g. cultural, casual, etc.). Moreover, our goal is to define a more detailed scheme of morphosyntactic and semantic criteria according to which the linguistic content is classified. Finally, it's important to study the correlation of all the aforementioned multimodal features in an attempt to discover more about the sequence of events that lead to silent feedback responses.

References

1. Allwood, J., Nivre, J., Ahlsén, E.: On the semantics and pragmatics of linguistic feedback. Journal of Semantics 9(1), 1–29 (1993)
2. Allwood, J., Cerrato, L.: A Study of Gestural Feedback Expressions. In: Paggio, P., Jokinen, K., Jönsson, A. (eds.) First Nordic Symposium on Multimodal Communication, Copenhagen, pp. 7–22 (2003)
3. Bertrand, R., Ferré, G., Blache, P., Espesser, R., Rauzy, S.: Backchannels revisited from a multimodal perspective. In: Proceedings of International Conference on Auditory-Visual Speech Processing (AVSP 2007), pp. 1–17 (2007b)
4. Ahlsén, E., Allwood, J., Nivre, J.: Feedback in different social activities. In: Juel-Henrichsen, P. (ed.) Nordic Research on Relations Between Utterances. Copenhagen Working Papers in LSP 3, pp. 9–37 (2003)
5. Allwood, J., Kopp, S., Grammer, K., Ahlsén, E., Oberzaucher, E., Koppensteiner, M.: The analysis of embodied communicative feedback in multimodal corpora: a prerequisite for behavior simulation. Journal on Language Resources and Evaluation 41(3-4), 255–272 (2007)
6. Condon, W.S., Ogston, W.: Speech and Body Motion Synchrony of the Speaker-Hearer. In: Horton, D.L., Jenkins, J.J. (eds.) Perception of Language, Merrill, Columbus, Ohio, pp. 150–173 (1971)
7. Kendon, A.: Movement coordination in social interaction: some examples described. In: Kendon, A. (ed.) Conducting Interaction: Patterns of Behavior in Focused Encounters, pp. 91–116. Cambridge University Press, Cambridge (1990)
8. Allwood, J., Cerrato, L., Jokinen, K., Navarretta, C., Paggio, P.: The MUMIN Coding Scheme for the Annotation of Feedback, Turn Management and Sequencing Phenomena. Multimodal Corpora for Modeling Human Multimodal Behaviour. Journal on Language Resources and Evaluation 41(3-4), 273–287 (2007)
9. Koutsombogera, M., Papageorgiou, H.: Multimodality Issues in Conversation Analysis of Greek TV Interviews. In: Esposito, A., Hussain, A., Marinaro, M., Martone, R. (eds.) Multimodal Signals: Cognitive and Algorithmic Issues. LNCS, vol. 5398, pp. 40–46. Springer, Heidelberg (2009)
10. Clark, H.H., Schaefer, E.F.: Contributing to discourse. Cognitive Science 13, 259–294 (1989)
11. Bunt, H.C.: Dimensions in Dialogue Act Annotation. In: Proceedings of Fifth International Conference on Language Resources and Evaluation, pp. 1444–1448. ELRA, Paris (2006)
12. Ford, C.E., Thompson, S.A.: Interactional Units in Conversation: Syntactic, Intonational, and Pragmatic Resources for the Management of Turns. In: Ochs, E., Schegloff, E.A., Thompson, S.A. (eds.) Interaction and Grammar, pp. 134–184. Cambridge University Press, Cambridge (1996)
13. McNeill, D.: Hand and Mind: What Gestures Reveal About Thought. University of Chicago Press, Chicago (1992)
14. Sinclair, J. (Editor-in-Chief): Collins COBUILD English Grammar. Collins, London (1990)

Audiovisual Tools for Phonetic and Articulatory Visualization in Computer-Aided Pronunciation Training

Bernd J. Kröger[1], Peter Birkholz[1], Rüdiger Hoffmann[2], and Helen Meng[3]

[1] Department of Phoniatrics, Pedaudiology, and Communication Disorders,
University Hospital Aachen and RWTH Aachen University, Aachen, Germany
bkroeger@ukaachen.de, pbirkholz@ukaachen.de
[2] Department of Acoustics and Speech Communication,
Dresden University of Technology, Dresden, Germany
ruediger.hoffmann@ias.et.tu-dresden.de
[3] Department of Systems Engineering and Engineering Management,
The Chinese University of Hong Kong (CUHK), Shatin, NT, Hong Kong SAR of China
hmmeng@se.cuhk.edu.hk

Abstract. This paper reviews interactive methods for improving the phonetic competence of subjects in the case of second language learning as well as in the case of speech therapy for subjects suffering from hearing-impairments or articulation disorders. As an example our audiovisual feedback software "Speech-Trainer" for improving the pronunciation quality of Standard German by visually highlighting acoustics-related and articulation-related sound features will be introduced here. Results from literature on training methods as well as the results concerning our own software indicate that audiovisual tools for phonetic and articulatory visualization are beneficial for computer-aided pronunciation training environments.

Keywords: Audiovisual speech tools, pronunciation training, second language learning, speech therapy.

1 Introduction

Second language learners often show severe problems in learning phonetic segmental features of speech sounds as well as prosodic features of target languages since learning is influenced by the phonetic segmental and prosodic knowledge concerning their native language [1, 2]. Since the vocabulary and the grammar of a foreign language can be acquired by using mainly cognitive learning strategies, i.e. processing abstract and discrete linguistic items by grammatical rules, the learner is easily aware of problems at the *linguistic level*. But this is not necessarily the case at the *phonetic level*. Moreover second language learners try to adapt the phonetic segmental and prosodic systems of their first language or mother tongue (L1) to the trained second language (L2). The resulting L2 foreign accent is easily detectable for speakers which are familiar with the target language (e.g. native speakers of the target language), while second language learners often are not even aware of their phonetic faults with respect to L2 [1, 2].

A. Esposito et al. (Eds.): COST 2102 Int. Training School 2009, LNCS 5967, pp. 337–345, 2010.
© Springer-Verlag Berlin Heidelberg 2010

Phonetic learning is also a problem for hearing-impaired children in the case of first language acquisition, if their hearing-impairment is innate or if it occurred in the first months after birth [3]. Since the auditory perception as well as the auditory feedback loop of these children is impaired, they are not able to learn the phonetic features of sounds or of the prosodic patterns of L1 as easy as normal hearing children. Speech produced by these children may be intelligible but often sounds strange. However, the linguistic capabilities of these children are often completely unaffected, since these children are capable of learning lexical items and grammatical rules, for example, of sign languages [4]. Phonetic problems also occur for acquired hearing impairments, e.g. in adults or the elderly due to a defective auditory feedback control loop. These people may lose control concerning the exact pronunciation of some phonetically difficult sounds of their mother tongue. Problems on the phonetic level of language acquisition also occur for children suffering from articulation or speech sound disorders. Here a common phenomenon is that these children shift posterior plosives (e.g. /g/ and /k/ are realized as /d/ and /t/), or they show a misarticulation of fricatives [5, 6, 7]. Other complex articulatory and coarticulatory problems occur for people suffering from motor speech disorders like apraxia of speech or dysarthria [8].

Thus in both cases (second language learning and phonetic oriented speech therapy) learners need intensive *phonetic treatment* with regard to the target language. Since phonetic treatment requires a lot of interaction between teacher and learner in order (i) to detect phonetic errors of learners (ii) to make the learner aware of his phonetic problems with respect to the target language and (iii) to advice the learner to do corrections of his articulations in direction towards the sound system and towards the prosodic system of the target language, it is not trivial to design phonetic treatment in terms of human-computer interaction.

This paper focuses on the problem of *computer-aided pronunciation training (CAPT)* and addresses three important research issues: (i) Can phonetic errors be detected by machine, for example by using speech recognition algorithms? (ii) Can learners become aware of their phonetic errors by using a human-machine interface exclusively? (iii) Is it possible to develop computer-aided self-learning environments for advising the learner an efficient way to overcome phonetic problems with respect to the target language? It will be argued in this paper that *audiovisual tools* as part of computer-aided self-learning environments are effective in enhancing the phonetic competence of learners with respect to a target language.

2 Auditory Tools

Acoustic speech signals of communication partners as well as the auditory feedback signals of learners provide the most important cues for improving the phonetic competence concerning a target language. In L1 acquisition infants process acoustic speech signals comprising words, phrases, or complete sentences produced by communication partners (e.g. caregivers). They also process the acoustic self-productions of their words and sentences and compare the auditory percept of their self-productions with the temporarily or permanently stored auditory percepts already learned [9]. In addition, visual information of lip and lower jaw movements, which occur during speech, may be helpful, but even if this visual information is not available, as is the case for blind children, speech acquisition proceeds as fast as for normal children [10]. But if children are suffering from severe hearing impairments, speech acquisition can strongly be delayed [11]. Thus many computer-aided language learning environments use acoustic tools that allow learners to listen to words and/or sentences, produced by native speakers of the target language [12]. The next step is to allow speech recordings within the computer-aided language learning environment, in order to enable learners to become aware of their own word and sentence productions [13].

If the improvement of the phonetic competence and thus the elimination of a foreign accent is the primary goal, more specific auditory and acoustic tools should be integrated into the computer-aided language or pronunciation learning environment. In this case tools for pronunciation training should be capable of detecting phonetic errors of learners automatically. Normal speech recognition software does not cater especially for detecting phonetic pronunciation errors, for example in the case of L2 learning or in the case of specific speech errors occurring in different types of speech disorders. For detecting these kinds of pronunciation errors it is necessary to access comprehensive speech data bases comprising knowledge concerning typical errors resulting from a specific L2-L1 interference. Consequently it is necessary to implement knowledge, how L2 learners with a specific L1 background produce sounds, words, and prosodic features in the L2 target language [14, 15, 16, 17].

3 Visual and Audiovisual Tools

Acoustics-related visual aids display relevant auditory features of the acoustic speech signal. This can be the oscillogram, the spectrogram, the F0- and intensity-contour of a speech item (i.e. syllable, word, or sentence), or the spectrum, F0-, and intensity value of a specific point in time within a speech item. Oscillogram, spectrogram, F0-, and intensity-contour of a whole speech item can be displayed synchronously for self-productions of learners and for pre-recorded correct sample productions done by native speakers of the target language. The visual comparison of both productions allows learners to detect mispronunciations. In the case of prosodic features, i.e. intonation and stress pattern, as well as sound duration (e.g. vowel or consonant productions that are too long or too short), oscillogram, F0-, and intensity contour are helpful not only to detect pronunciation errors but in addition to indicate the direction how the learner can produce the speech item in a more correct way. The comparison of oscillograms indicates how sound durations should be changed. The comparison of intensity-contours indicates how stress patterns should be changed and the comparison of F0-contours indicates how intonation patterns should be changed [18]. The ⬜ompareison of formant trajectories (given in spectrograms) indicates how vocalic and consonantal articulation targets should be changed. In the case of fricatives, the comparison of the spectral energy distribution indicates how fricative production can be changed [19]. The display of these acoustics-related parameters can be *stylized* (e.g. in CoKo for spectra and spectrograms, see [20], in SpeechViewer for intonation contours, see [21]) in order to enable learners to process this visual information easily and in order not to discourage learners without any technical or scientific background to use this training software.

Articulation-related visual aids can be used for training a correct articulation of static targets for vowels and consonants as well as a correct coarticulation within syllables and words. These aids display vocal tract organs or articulators (e.g. lips, tongue, velum, larynx with glottis) and their functioning in speech production, i.e. the positioning and movement of articulators in sound, word, or sentence production. Articulation-related visual aids are already used in some pronunciation training environments. Badin et al. [22, 23] and Bailly et al. [24] developed a realistic 3D virtual talking head comprising a 3D-model of speech articulators (i.e. lips, lower jaw, tongue, velum) on the basis of a comprehensive MRI, CT, EMA, and video database of several speakers. This model is capable of displaying the complete face or a cut-away view of the head including lips, tongue, and velum (Grenoble talking head). Badin et al. [23] were able to show that humans have the capability of "tongue reading" (i.e. interpreting the normally non-visible parts of the tongue) especially in the case of a strongly degraded or in the case of an absent acoustic signal. Engwall et al. [25, 26] developed a data based 3D-virtual tutor (Stockholm talking head, called "Artur"). The Stockholm talking head is embedded in a complex pronunciation training environment capable of detecting mispronunciations in the visual and acoustic domain and capable of giving a set of instructions how to improve the articulation with respect to the target language (Swedish). Kröger et al. [27] developed a 2-D virtual model for the sagittal view of a talker of Standard German (Aachen model, called "Bernie") and developed a 3D-virtual model of the speech articulators [28]. Both models were tested in therapy of developmental speech disorders [29. 30] indicating that even preschoolers can acquire the ability to understand (i.e. to "read") lip, tongue and velum speech movements. In accordance with Badin et al. [23] the results of Kröger et al. [30] indicate that lip reading is predominant and easier than tongue and velum reading. The virtual talking head of Massaro et al. [31, 32, 33, 34, 35] called "Baldi", has been applied already for many languages (i.e. multilingual talking head [33]) and "Baldi" has been used as a tutor in computer-aided environments for spoken and written language training as well as for articulation training.

4   A Preliminary Articulation-Related Audiovisual Tool for Improving Sound Quality in Standard German

As a prototype for an articulation-related audiovisual tool, the 2D-articulatory model "Bernie" (Fig. 1a and Fig. 1b, right side) has been integrated in our pronunciation training environment "SpeechTrainer" for improving the quality of speech sounds in the case of therapy of articulation disorders ([s]-misarticulation) as well as in the case of second language learning with Standard German as L2.

With respect to learners pronunciation problems a target sound can be chosen from the list of German long vowels, nasals, fricatives or laterals (see Fig. 1a and Fig. 1b, middle). The appropriate reference spectral envelope and reference zero crossing rate is displayed (Fig. 1a and Fig. 1b, left side, bold light curve and bold light vertical line below; here for /a:/). Then the learner tries to adapt the spectral envelope and the zero crossing rate of his sound production (Fig. 1a and Fig. 1b, left side, dark curve and dark vertical line below) towards the visually displayed target spectral envelope and

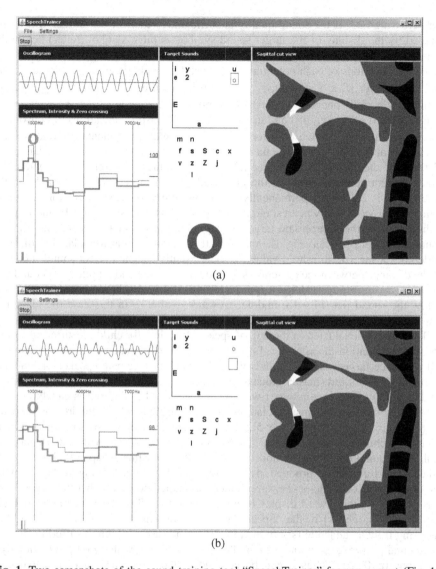

Fig. 1. Two screenshots of the sound training tool "SpeechTrainer" for non-correct (Fig. 1a) and for correct production (Fig. 1b) of Standard German long vowel [o:]. Left side in (a) and (b): Oscillogram of current sound produced by the learner (on top); 14 step bark scaled spectral envelope from 0 to 8 kHz (curves below oscillogram); amplitude including db-value (right side adjacent to spectral envelope); zero crossing rate (vertical lines below spectral envelope on the bottom) for current sound produced by the learner (black thin curve or line) and for the selected target sound (bold grey curve or line). Middle in (a) and (b): Vowel space (on top) including Standard German long vowels; consonant list (below). The selected target sound is marked by gray color. The gray rectangle indicates the sound quality currently produced by the learner. The "reward sound symbol" for correct sound production is displayed at the bottom (only in b). Right side in (a) and (b): Midsagittal view corresponding to the current sound quality produced by the learner.

zero crossing rate. If the sound quality is sufficiently reached, the learner will be rewarded by the display of the target sound symbol as huge symbol (letter) below the target sound list (Fig. 1b middle, "reward symbol").

Five realizations of each potential target sound (vowels [iː, eː, ɛː, aː, oː, uː, yː, øː] and consonants [f, s, ʃ, ç, x, v, z, ʒ, j, l]) were recorded by a native Speaker of Standard German (phonetic expert). In addition IPA sounds filling the gaps in the vowel space (i.e. [ɔː, œː, əː]) and in addition typical mispronunciations of consonants (in this preliminary version only for [s], i.e. interdental and addental [s]-realizations) were recorded by the same speaker and stored as "gap sounds". The Mahalanobis distance of the 14 bark-scaled spectral envelope values plus zero crossing rate between current acoustic input on the one hand and all target and gap sounds on the other hand is calculated permanently in 50 ms intervals. The articulatory configuration of the acoustically nearest target or gap sound is displayed (Fig. 1a and Fig. 1b, right side) and the appropriate target or gap sound is marked by a rectangle in the sound table (Fig. 1a and Fig 1b, middle). If in addition this Mahalanobis distance undergoes a specific threshold value for the currently selected target sound (i.e. 30% of the distance between the currently selected target sound and all other target and gap sounds), the currently selected target sound symbol is displayed in an extra region below the sound list (Fig. 1b, middle. "reward symbol"). In this case the learner is rewarded for his correct target sound production.

The tool was evaluated in therapy of speech disorders for children suffering from a specific articulation disorder, i.e. [s]-misarticulation ("sigmatism", a sort of lisping). All reference target and gap sounds were recorded by a female speaker of Standard German, 22 years old (master student of speech therapy). Two tests were performed. (i) The goal of the *sensitivity test* was to evaluate whether the tool is capable of discriminating different [s]-misarticulations on the acoustic level. 11 children participated in this test (6 male, 5 female; age: 5,2 to 6,9). Logopaedic diagnostics resulted in identifying 4 children with addental [s]-realisation, 4 children with interdental [s]-realization and 3 children with normal [s]-production for this group. All children were asked to perform 40 [s]-productions each (40 trials) without looking at the computer monitor. The test conductor (i.e. speech therapist) noted down whether the target sound was reached by the reward display or not for each trial. The resulting rate of initially reaching the target [s] in the "SpeechTrainer"-tool was 0% in the case of children suffering from an addental [s]-production, 2% in the case of children suffering from an interdental [s]-production, and 58% in the case of children with no [s]-production dysfunctions ($p < 0.001$). Thus it can be concluded that "SpeechTrainer" is capable of differentiating normal and disordered [s]-production. (ii) The goal of the *learning test* was to evaluate whether the patient is capable of correcting his [s]-articulation by using the "SpeechTrainer"-tool. One subject (male, 5,9 years old) suffering from a [s]-misarticulation problem ([s]-interdentalis) used the "SpeechTrainer"-tool for 5 minutes feedback computer training (FCT) within each of 10 therapy sessions over a time period of 10 weeks. 12 [s]-realizations of this subject produced before and after each FCT were checked as described in the sensitivity test. A significant increase of correct [s]-realizations (before to after FCT) occurred for each FCT (towards 42% at the beginning and towards 67% at the end of the 10 week therapy period, $p < 0.01$). Moreover a baseline increase of correct [s]-realizations before FCT over the 10 weeks of speech therapy from 0% to 33% occurred as well ($p < 0.01$).

Furthermore the tool was evaluated for second language learning (two Czech L2 learners of Standard German, male, 24 and 26 years old). Here, all reference target and gap sounds were recorded by a male speaker of Standard German, 50 years old (phonetician). The *learning test* was performed by both subjects in order to evaluate whether subjects are capable of correcting their L2-[oː]-articulation towards a more closed vowel quality by using the "SpeechTrainer"-tool. Both subjects used the "SpeechTrainer"-tool for 5 minutes FCT in 5 learning sessions over a time period of 2 weeks. The [oː]-realizations were evaluated before and after each FCT within each learning sessions by performing 12 [oː]-realizations. A significant increase of correct L2-[oː]-realizations (before to after FCT) occurred within each learning session from 27% to 48% (speaker 1, p<0.01) and from 35% to 56% (speaker 2, p<0.05) while a significant increase of correct produced realizations before FCT was found over the two weeks of training (i.e. over these 5 sessions) only for speaker 1 (from 22% to 32%, p<0.05).

5 Discussion

This paper stresses the need of audiovisual tools in computer-aided pronunciation training environments. Beside typical acoustics-related audiovisual tools such as those for comparing oscillograms, sonograms, F0-contours, and intensity-contours between teacher and learner pronunciations of words or sentences, articulation-related audiovisual tools are introduced. An articulation-related audiovisual tool for isolated sound pronunciation developed in the Aachen Lab has been evaluated. Results indicate that this tool can be used successful in therapy of [s]-articulation disorders as well as in second language learning for strengthening vowel quality. Instantaneous and continuous learning benefits (i.e. learning benefits within one training session and over the whole time period of training) were verified for the subject suffering from [s]-articulation disorder and for one of the two second language learners. It was not possible to evaluate to what degree the visualization of the articulatory information (i.e. mid-sagittal view of speech sounds) contributes to these learning outcomes. But all learners reported that they used the visual articulatory information as an additional cue beside the spectral envelope matching in order to correct their articulation.

Acknowledgments. This work was supported in part by the German Research Council DFG grant Kr 1439/13-1 and grant Kr 1439/15-1.

References

[1] Flege, J.E.: Phonetic approximation in second language acquisition. Language Learning 30, 117–134 (1980)

[2] Munro, M.J., Derwing, T.M.: Foreign accent, comprehensibility, and intelligibility in the speech of second language learners. Language Learning 49, 285–310 (1999)

[3] Geers, A.E., Moog, J.S.: Predicting spoken language acquisition of profundly hearing impaired children. Journal of Speech and Hearing Disorders 52, 84–94 (1987)

[4] Strong, M. (ed.): Language Learning and Deafness. Cambridge University Press, Cambridge (1988)

[5] Gibbon, F.E.: Undifferentiated lingual gestures in children with articulation/phonological disorders. Journal of Speech, Language, and Hearing Research 42, 382–397 (1999)

[6] Rvachew, S., Jamieson, D.G.: Perception of voiceless fricatives by children with a functional articulation disorder. Journal of Speech and Hearing Disorders 54, 193–208 (1989)

[7] Rvachew, S., Grawburg, M.: Correlates of phonological awareness in preschoolers with speech sound disorders. Journal of Speech, Language, and Hearing Research 49, 74–87 (2006)

[8] Kent, R.D.: Research on speech motor control and its disorders: A review and prospective. Journal of Communication Disorders 33, 391–428 (2000)

[9] Kröger, B.J., Kannampuzha, J., Neuschaefer-Rube, C.: Towards a neurocomputational model of speech production and perception. Speech Communication 51, 793–809 (2009)

[10] Perez-Pereira, M., Castro, J.: Language acquisition and the compensation of visual deficit: New comparative data on a controversial topic. British Journal of Developmental Psychology 15, 439–459 (1997)

[11] Yoshinaga-Itano, C., Sedey, A.: Early Speech Development in Children Who Are Deaf or Hard of Hearing: Interrelationships with Language and Hearing. Volta Review 100, 181–211 (1999)

[12] Accent School (2008), http://www.accentschool.com/

[13] Pronunciation Power (2006), http://www.englishlearning.com/

[14] Jokisch, O., Koloska, U., Hirschfeld, D., Hoffmann, R.: Pronunciation learning and foreign accent reduction by an audiovisual feedback system. In: Tao, J., Tan, T., Picard, R.W. (eds.) ACII 2005. LNCS, vol. 3784, pp. 419–425. Springer, Heidelberg (2005)

[15] Harrison, A.M., Lau, W.Y., Meng, H., Wang, L.: Improving mispronunciation detection and diagnosis of learners' speech with context-sensitive phonological rules based on language transfer. In: Proceedings of Interspeech, Brisbane, Australia, pp. 2787–2790 (2008)

[16] Meng, H., Lo, Y., Wang, L., Lau, W.: Deriving salient learners' mispronunciations form cross-language phonological comparisons. In: Proceedings of the IEEE Workshop in Automatic Speech Recognition and Understanding, ASRU, Kyoto, Japan, pp. 437–442 (2007)

[17] Wang, L.X., Feng, X., Meng, H.: Mispronunciation detection based on cross-language phonological comparisons. In: Proceedings of the IEEE IET International Conference on Audio, Language and Image Processing, Shanghai, China, pp. 307–311 (2008)

[18] Better Accent Tutor (2009), http://www.betteraccent.com/

[19] Vicsi, K., Csatari, F., Bakcsi, Z.s., Tantos, A.: Distance score evaluation of the visualised speech spectra at audio-visual articulation training. In: Proceedings of EUROSPEECH 1999, Budapest, Hungary, pp. 1911–1914 (1999)

[20] Vicsi, K., Hacki, T.: CoKo - Computergestützter Sprechkorrektor mit audiovisueller Selbstkontrolle für artikulationsgestörte und hörbehinderte Kinder. Sprache-Stimme-Gehör 20, 141–149 (1996)

[21] Öster, A.M.: Teaching speech skills to deaf children by computer-based speech training. STL-Quarterly Progress and Status Report 36(4), 67–75 (1995)

[22] Badin, P., Bailly, G., Boë, L.J.: Towards the Use of a Virtual Talking Head and of Speech Mapping tools for pronunciation training. In: Proceedings of the ESCA Tutorial and Research Workshop on Speech Technology in Language Learning (STiLL 1998), pp. 167–170 (1998)

[23] Badin, P., Tarabalka, Y., Elisei, F., Bailly, G.: Can you "read tongue movements"? In: Proceedings of Interspeech 2008, Brisbane, Queensland, Australia, pp. 2635–2638 (2008)

[24] Bailly, G., Bérar, M., Elisei, F., Odisio, M.: Audiovisual speech synthesis. International Journal of Speech Technology 6, 331–346 (2003)

[25] Engwall, O., Bälter, O., Öster, A.M., Kjellström, H.: Designing the user interface of the computer-based speech training system ARTUR based on early user tests. Journal of Behaviour and Information Technology 25, 353–365 (2006)

[26] Engwall, O., Bälter, O.: Pronunciation feedback from real and virtual language teachers. Journal of Computer Assisted Language Learning 20, 235–262 (2007)

[27] Kröger, B.J., Hoole, P., Sader, R., Geng, C., Pompino-Marschall, B., Neuschaefer-Rube, C.: MRT-Sequenzen als Datenbasis eines visuellen Artikulationsmodells. HNO 52, 837–843 (2004)

[28] Kröger, B.J., Birkholz, P.: A gesture-based concept for speech movement control in articulatory speech synthesis. In: Esposito, A., Faundez-Zanuy, M., Keller, E., Marinaro, M. (eds.) COST Action 2102. LNCS (LNAI), vol. 4775, pp. 174–189. Springer, Heidelberg (2007)

[29] Kröger, B.J., Gotto, J., Albert, S., Neuschaefer-Rube, C.: A visual articulatory model and its application to therapy of speech disorders: a pilot study. In: Fuchs, S., Perrier, P., Pompino-Marschall, B. (Hrsg.) Speech production and perception: Experimental analyses and models. ZAS Papers in Linguistics, vol. 40, pp. 79–94 (2005)

[30] Kröger, B.J., Graf-Bortscheller, V., Lowit, A.: Two- and three-dimensional visual articulatory models for pronunciation training and for treatment of speech disorders. In: Proceedings of Interspeech 2008, Brisbane, Queensland, Australia, pp. 2639–2642 (2008)

[31] Massaro, D.W.: Perceiving Talking Faces: From Speech Perception to a Behavioral Principle. MIT Press, Cambridge (1998)

[32] Massaro, D.W.: A computer-animated tutor for spoken and written language learning. In: Proceedings of the 5th International Conference on Multimodal Interfaces, Vancouver, British Columbia, Canada, pp. 172–175 (2003)

[33] Massaro, D.W.: The psychology and technology of talking heads: Applications in language learning. In: van Kuppevelt, J.C.J., Dybkjær, L., Bernsen, N.O. (eds.) Advances in Natural Multimodal Dialogue Systems, vol. 30, pp. 183–214. Springer, Heidelberg (2005)

[34] Massaro, D.W., Liu, Y., Chen, T.H., Perfetti, C.: A multilingual embodied conversational agent for tutoring speech and language learning. In: Proceedings of Interspeech 2006, Pittsburgh, PA, USA, pp. 825–828 (2006)

[35] Massaro, D.W., Bigler, S., Chen, T., Perlman, M., Ouni, S.: Pronunciation training: the role of eye and ear. In: Proceedings of Interspeech 2008, Brisbane, Queensland, Australia, pp. 2623–2626 (2008)

Gesture Duration and Articulator Velocity in Plosive-Vowel-Transitions

Dominik Bauer[1], Jim Kannampuzha[1], Phil Hoole[2], and Bernd J. Kröger[1]

[1] Department of Phoniatrics, Pedaudiology and Communication Disorders,
University Hospital Aachen and RWTH Aachen University, Aachen, Germany
[2] Institut für Phonetik und Sprachverarbeitung, Ludwig-Maximilians-Universität,
Munich, Germany
dobauer@ukaachen.de, jkannampuzha@ukaachen.de,
hoole@phonetik.uni-muenchen.de, bkroeger@ukaachen.de

Abstract. In this study the gesture duration and articulator velocity in consonant-vowel-transitions has been analysed using electromagnetic articulography (EMA). The receiver coils where placed on the tongue, lips and teeth. We found onset and offset durations which are statistically significant for a special articulator. The duration of the offset is affected by the degree of opening of the following vowel. The acquired data is intended to tune the control model of an articulatory speech synthesizer to improve the acoustic quality of plosive-vowel-transitions.

Keywords: Speech, articulatory speech synthesis, articulation, electromagnetic articulography, EMA.

1 Introduction

The articulators in a human vocal tract are physically affected by inertia, which causes a transitional phase between two successive articulatory constellations. All these movements are coded in the acoustical signal. In a digital model of the vocal tract, velocity and acceleration of articulators must be modelled somehow to provide natural transitions from one phone to another. One method to deal with this problem is to capture the articulator velocity and the gesture durations in different phone contexts from a human speaker. The gesture-based control of an articulatory speech synthesizer requires detailed knowledge of the synchronization and the speed of articulatory action units [1], [2]. In our recent work, we analysed the synchronization of action units based on acoustic observations [3]. Since some articulatory events like the begin of a consonantal movement (before the articulator really forms a constriction) are hard to estimate from an acoustic representation of the signal, we decided to perform an EMA-study to measure the articulator speed in consonantal stops.

The control model of Kröger and Birkholz divides the articulatory movement into an onset and offset interval [4], [2]. These intervals can also be found in the EMA representation of articulatory movements. (For a detailed description of electromagnetic articulography see [5].) In Figure 1, the onset and offset of an apico-alveolar

A. Esposito et al. (Eds.): COST 2102 Int. Training School 2009, LNCS 5967, pp. 346–353, 2010.

stop movement in the utterance "ich habe [de:] gesagt" are highlighted. The upper two tiers show the oscillogram and spectrogram, the lower two trajectories show tongue tip position and tongue tip speed.

In the onset interval, the tongue tip height is strictly increasing (velocity > 0). After a short (quasi-) stationary phase, where the tongue is in contact with the palate (velocity = 0) the constriction is released. During this offset phase, the tongue height is strictly decreasing (velocity < 0). It is easy to see that the onset transition already starts when the preceding vowel becomes audible. Similarly, the offset reaches into the following vowel. In this study we measured the duration of these intervals in different vowel-contexts to obtain information on consonantal timing for use in articulatory speech synthesis control. From our results we expect an advantage in naturalness and intelligibility in plosive-vowel transitions in articulatory speech synthesis.

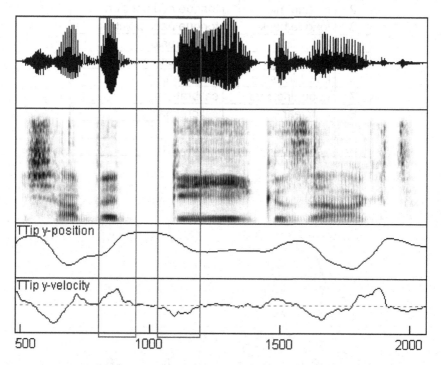

Fig. 1. The German sentence "Ich habe [de:] gesagt." in an oscillogram, spectrogram and two different EMA representations of the tongue tip movements. The upper EMA trajectory represents the y-position of the corresponding coil, (i.e. the tongue tip height) the lower trajectory shows the velocity in y-direction. The onset interval (left box) and the offset interval (right box) are marked. X-axis is time in milliseconds.

2 Method

The EMA session took place at the EMA lab of the Institute of Phonetics at the Ludwig-Maximilians-University Munich using the Carstens AG 500 articulograph with one subject. A total of ten receiver coils were used, four of them for the purpose of correcting for head movement. Three coils were glued on the tongue to capture the oral constrictions performed by the tongue. To observe labial stops, both lips were also equipped with sensor coils. The sensor on the lower incisors was used to observe the jaw opening, while the sensor at the upper incisors as well as the sensors behind the ears and at the nasal bone are used as fixed points to remove the overlaid head movements from the articulator signals. See Table 1 for a list of coil locations and Fig 2 for a schematic view.

Table 1. List of EMA-receiver-coils used in this study, with their location and function

No.	coil location	function
1	tongue tip	tongue tip position
2	tongue mid	tongue mid position
3	tongue back	tongue back position
4	lower lip	lip protrusion
5	upper lip	lip protrusion/position
6	lower incisors	jaw opening
7	upper incisors	calibration
8	right ear	calibration
9	left ear	calibration
10	nasal bone	calibration

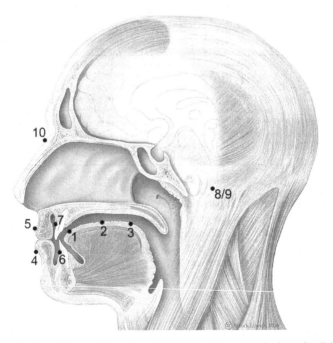

Fig. 2. Schematic view of the coil locations. See Table 1 for a description of coil locations and functions. (Drawing with permission of Patrick Lynch).

During the session we recorded a set of 90 plosive-vowel-syllables. Each syllable has been produced in the carrier sentence "Ich habe [xxx] gesagt." The plosives were [p],[b],[t],[d],[k],[g] the vowels were [i],[e],[a],[o],[u]. The 30 different syllables were recorded three times in total. The syllables were presented randomly to the speaker on a video-screen.

After normalization for head movement we identified the closure gesture in the articulatory trajectories and determined the duration of the onset and the offset using the software MVIEW [6].

3 Results

A. Onset Interval
The descriptive analysis of the consonantal onset showed that the duration ranges between 97ms to 166ms for apical plosives, 104ms to 197ms for dorsal plosives and 95ms to 157ms for labial plosives. Mean onset duration was 165ms for apical plosives, 132ms for dorsal plosives and 118ms for labial plosives (see Fig. 3). In the inferential analysis we tested if the factors 'place', 'voicing' and 'vowel' cause significant changes in onset and offset durations. 'Place' is divided into the specifications 'labial', 'apical' and 'dorsal', 'voice' is divided into "voiced and 'voiceless' and 'vowel' can be [i], [e], [a], [o] and [u].

The ANOVA showed a significant influence of the main factor 'place' and the interaction factor 'place+vowel' (see Table 2). A post-hoc Tukey-Kramer analysis indicated a highly significant difference in onset durations for labial and apical movements $p<0.0001$) and between apical and dorsal onsets ($p<0.0001$). There was a significant difference between dorsal and labial movements ($p<0.05$). Post hoc tests were performed for main effects only. The main factors 'vowel' and 'voice' were not significant in the ANOVA (Table 3).

Table 2. Results of the ANOVA for onset durations. (Significance levels: 0<***<0,001<**< 0,01<*<0,05<.<0,1)

ONSET	Df	F	Pr(>F)	
place	2	39,0265	0,0000	***
voice	1	3,1214	0,0824	.
vowel	4	2,0219	0,1027	
place:voice	2	0,1629	0,8500	
place:vowel	8	2,8809	0,0088	**
voice:vowel	4	2,3249	0,0667	.
place:voice:vowel	8	2,1082	0,0488	*

B. Offset Interval
There is a strong variation in the offset duration. For the offset interval we observed durations between 110 and 285ms. The duration range for the plosive offset was 157ms to 285ms for apical plosives, 142ms to 265ms for dorsal plosives and 112ms to 227ms for labial plosives. The mean offset duration was 215ms for apical plosives, 198ms for dorsal plosives and 184ms for labial plosives (see Fig.4).

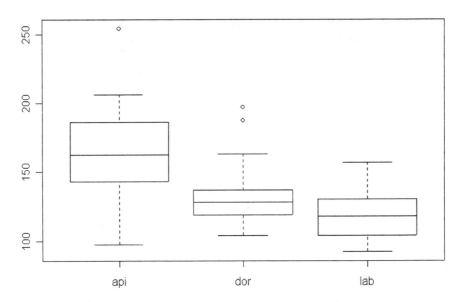

Fig. 3. Onset durations (in milliseconds) grouped by the factor 'place'. The dashed lines connect minimum and maximum values, the boxes represent the interquartile ranges and the horizontal lines inside the boxes represent mean values. Outliers are marked with rings.

Table 3. Results of the ANOVA for offset durations. (Significance levels: 0<***<0,001<**< 0,01<*<0,05<.<0,1)

OFFSET	Df	F	Pr(>F)	
place	2	15,3654	0,0000	***
voice	1	0,5189	0,4741	
vowel	4	3,6006	0,0107	*
place:voice	2	7,9165	0,0009	***
place:vowel	8	2,9107	0,0082	**
voice:vowel	4	2,7922	0,0341	*
place:voice:vowel	8	1,5559	0,1576	

The ANOVA of offset durations showed a significant influence of the main factors 'place' and 'vowel' and the interaction factors 'place+vowel', 'place+vowel' and 'voice+vowel' (see Table 3). A post-hoc Tukey-Kramer analysis indicated a highly significant difference in onset durations for labial and apical movements p<0.0001). The post hoc analysis also showed statistically significant differences for [a] vs. [i] (p<0.01), [a] vs. [e] (p<0.01), [a] vs. [o] (p<0.05) and [a] vs. [u] (p<0.05). All these vowel combinations have a highly different degree of opening (see Fig. 5). The post hoc tests were performed for main effects only. The main factor 'voice' was not significant in the ANOVA.

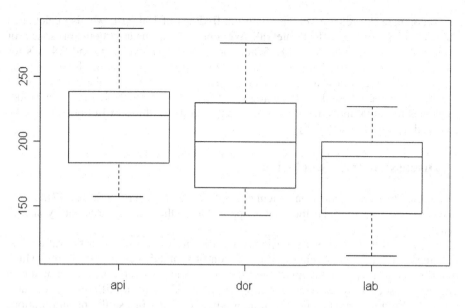

Fig. 4. Offset durations (in milliseconds) grouped by the factor 'place'. The dashed lines connect minimum and maximum values, the boxes represent interquartile ranges and the horizontal lines inside the boxes represent mean values.

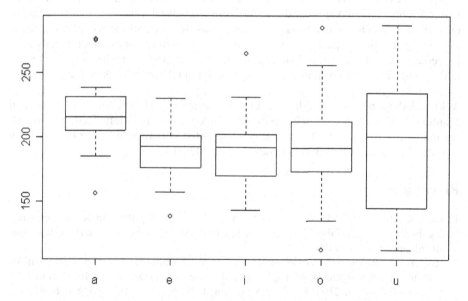

Fig. 5. Offset durations of consonantal stops in different vowel contexts. The dashed lines connect the minimum and the maximum values, the boxes represent the interquartile range and the horizontal lines inside the boxes represent the mean value. Outliers are marked with rings.

To compare the release velocity with the findings of Löfqvist, we also calculated the velocities for the offset interval. We observed a mean articulator speed of 11,8cm/s for labial movements, 12,5cm/s for tongue tip movements and 8,4cm/s for tongue body movements. The fastest labial release that we found was 18,6cm/s in the syllable [be:], the fastest tongue tip movement was 24,8cm/s in the release of the syllable [da:], the fastest dorsal opening was 18,5cm/s in the syllable [ga:]. The velocity values for labial movements are consistent with the findings of Löfqvist, where he analysed the lip kinematics [7].

4 Discussion and Conclusion

In contrast to other studies on articulator velocity and gesture durations [7],[8] our main interest was to make the values applicable in the field of articulatory speech synthesis.

We showed that there is a statistically significant difference in onset durations depending on the active articulator. The creation of synthetic action unit scores, which describe the articulatory movements in the vocal tract and serve as the input for an articulatory speech synthesizer, can now be enhanced by using different onset durations for different articulators. As an approximation we will use the mean durations we found in this study. The offset duration was also affected by the vowel [a] that increased the duration. This may be a result of the high degree of opening of the vowel [a].

The values of articulator velocity can be used to establish a plausibility check of the gestural scores to avoid speed values which are not natural. Since the speaking rate of the analysed speech was in a modal rate, we cannot determine if the articulator speed is affected by the global speaking rate. It is planned to perform an evaluation study after implementation of the results found in this study. We expect a higher degree of naturalness in the plosive burst and the aspiration noise in CV and CVC syllables.

Acknowledgments. We would like to thank Elizabeth Heller, Susanne Waltl and Manfred Pastaetter for their help during the EMA-Session and Mark Tiede for providing the software MVIEW. This work was supported in part by the German Research Council DFG grant KR 1439/13-1 and grant Kr 1439/15-1.

References

1. Birkholz, P., Kröger, B.J.: Vocal Tract Model Adaptation Using Magnetic Resonance Imaging. In: Proceedings of the 7th International Seminar on Speech Production, Belo Horizonte, Brazil, pp. 493–500 (2006)
2. Kröger, B.J., Birkholz, P.: A Gesture-Based Concept for Speech Movement Control in Articulatory Speech Synthesis. In: Esposito, A., Faundez-Zanuy, M., Keller, E., Marinaro, M. (eds.) COST Action 2102. LNCS (LNAI), vol. 4775, pp. 174–189. Springer, Heidelberg (2007)
3. Bauer, D., Kannampuzha, J., Kröger, B.J.: Articulatory speech re-synthesis: Profiting from natural acoustic speech data. In: Esposito, A., Vích, R. (eds.) Cross-Modal Analysis of Speech, Gestures, Gaze and Facial Expressions. LNCS, vol. 5641, pp. 344–355. Springer, Heidelberg (2009)

4. Kröger, B.J., Schröder, G., Opgen-Rhein, C.: A Gesture-Based Dynamic Model Describing Articulatory Movement Data. J. Acoust. Soc. Am. 98(4), 1878–1889 (1995)
5. Hoole, P., Nguyen, N.: Electromagnetic Articulography. In: Hardcastle, W.J., Hewlett, N. (eds.) Coarticulation – Theory, Data and Techniques, Cambridge Studies in Speech Science and Communication, pp. 260–269. Cambridge University Press, Cambridge (2000)
6. Tiede, M.: MVIEW: software for visualization and analysis of concurrently recorded movement data (2005)
7. Löfqvist, A.: Lip Kinematics in Long and Short Stop and Fricative Consonants. J. Acoust. Soc. A. 117(2), 858–878 (2005)
8. Adams, S.G., Weismer, G., Kent, R.D.: Speaking Rate and Speech Movement Velocity Profiles. Journal of Speech and Hearing Research 36, 41–54 (1993)

Stereo Presentation and Binaural Localization in a Memory Game for the Visually Impaired

Vlado Delić and Nataša Vujnović Sedlar

Faculty of Technical Sciences, University of Novi Sad, Serbia
vdelic@uns.ac.rs, natasav@uns.ac.rs

Abstract. Socialization of the visually impaired represents a challenge for the society and science today. The aim of this research is to investigate the possibility of using binaural perception of sound for two-dimensional source localization in interactive games for the visually impaired. Such an additional source of information would contribute to more equal participation of the visually impaired in online gaming. The paper presents a concept of an online memory game accessible both by the sighted and the blind, with a multimodal user interface enabled with speech technologies. The final chapter discusses the effects of its initial application and testing, as well as perspectives for further development.

Keywords: Speech technologies, visually impaired, games, binaural localization, stereo presentation.

1 Introduction

Socialization of the visually impaired, especially young people faced with this handicap, represents a challenge for modern society and science. Apart from education, the aspect of entertainment is as important for the sighted people as it is for the blind.

The technology of today allows the making of applications intended for education and entertainment of the visually impaired. Unfortunately, little is being done in that direction. The team working on text-to-speech synthesis (TTS) and automatic speech recognition (ASR) at the Faculty of technical sciences in Serbia has for the last few years focused on improving education of the visually impaired and their access to information. The results of their work are the speech synthesizer *anReader*, which has become an official aid for the visually impaired in Serbia [1], as well as a specialized audio library for the visually impaired [2], a voice portal based on both ASR and TTS [3] which can be accessed either via phones or personal computers, enabling the visually impaired to listen to the news or obtain information about their rights. This paper presents an attempt to make a step forward in the socialization of the visually impaired in Serbia by enabling them to play at least certain types of computer games more equally as people who possess sight.

Computer games are a part of everyday life for children and the young, and therefore the communities of the visually impaired are leaning towards the development of computer games suited for all children, including the handicapped ones, in order to make their inclusion into the society less difficult. These communities deem that: "To

A. Esposito et al. (Eds.): COST 2102 Int. Training School 2009, LNCS 5967, pp. 354–363, 2010.

give people with visual disabilities the chance to have access to multimedia games should be seen as an important issue for better inclusion and participation in society" [4]. Sadly, the making of these games world-wide has been financed mostly by non-government organizations with very limited funds.

The core of the problem of developing or adapting video games to the visually impaired is the graphic user interface (GUI). The GUI that is being used in multimedia games is not suitable for the visually disabled, and furthermore, it differs from game to game. International Game Developers Association (IGDA) in their study "Accessibility in Games: Motivations and Approaches" in 2004, debated availability of games to every person with a handicap including the visually impaired [5]. The study presents speech synthesizers, screen readers and speech recognition as assistive technologies which can contribute to greater availability of games for the visually impaired. Unfortunately, the application of these new technologies which would allow adaptation of the user interface to the ergonomics of the visually impaired is not a primary concern for the game industry. On the other hand, a connection between the visually impaired children and these technologies is of crucial importance for their inclusion into the society.

Throughout the cooperation with the blind instructors who teach the visually impaired to use computers we have noticed that, in Serbia, no serious work is being done with children until the time they get to a special boarding school for children with such a disability. Until that time, they spend too little time interacting with other children, their motor skills do not develop as much as they should, and they are not as familiarized with computers as children of their age who are not visually impaired. This project represents an attempt to help create interactive multimedia games in which visually impaired children could play on a more level ground with other children of the same age who are not handicapped in such a manner.

In the second chapter four classes of computer games are described and their audio and video interfaces are discussed. Speech technologies in computer games are presented in the third chapter, as well as their particular function related to the visually impaired players. Audio presentation and binaural localization in computer games are presented in the fourth chapter. Realization and testing of the first memory game intended for the visually impaired, equipped with speech technologies in Serbian, are described in the fifth section. The summary and certain directions for future work are given in the sixth chapter.

2 Computer Games for the Visually Impaired

For a game player, regardless of whether he or she is or is not visually impaired, the most important aspect of a game is its playability [6]. Playability of a game for people with a handicap is achieved by a high-level adaptation to their ergonomics. The visually impaired, in accordance with their handicap, can play so-called audio and tactile multimedia games. Audio computer games are games whose user interface is presented by using audio effects, while in tactile computer games user interface is based on a set of specialized touch-sensitive panels. Communities of the visually impaired tend to favor audio computer games, because there is a number of their members (particularly those who were not born blind, but have acquired their blindness later in life) who are not familiar with tactile interfaces.

As stated in the introduction, user interfaces differ from game to game, and consequently, the ability to be adapted to the visually impaired, as well as the adaptation itself, also differs from game to game. Literature usually separates video games into four classes: action games, adventure games, strategy games and puzzle games. Action games are the games where the point of the greatest importance is a right-timed response to audio and visual information that the player receives. Audio signals are the key factor of these games when adapted to visually impaired people. These audio signals have to differ from each other so that the player could easily identify them and respond at the right moment and in a right manner. The characteristics of adventure games are an interesting scenario, investigation of new areas and resolving mysteries. Riddles and the scenario are not as important as the motion of the avatar – a figure in the virtual world controlled by the player. Because of such characteristics, almost no games of this type were developed for the visually impaired. Strategy games usually require the player to control armies, vast territories and resources by using maps. The player must manipulate numerous parameters to allow the survival and growth of the population. Unfortunately the sense of sight is vital for the use of maps, and thus only games which are principally oriented to management and simulation are possible to adapt to the visually impaired. Puzzle games are the only games which are based on the same principles regardless of whether they are audio or tactile.

Furthermore, the accessibility of multimedia games to the visually impaired does not rest solely on their ability to be presented in audio or tactile formats, but the language of the game is important as well [7]. Most audio games have very extensive user manuals about the way they interact with players. For individuals who do not speak English playing video games is virtually impossible as only a small number of them are translated and adapted to other languages. This is an enormous problem for the visually impaired, especially for children born in areas where speech technologies are not developed.

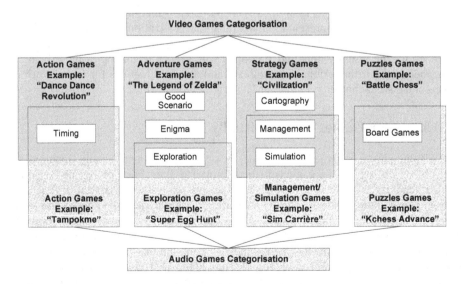

Fig. 1. Video and Audio Games Categorisation

3 Speech Technologies in Computer Games

Sight and hearing are the two primary senses which people employ in their interaction with computers, so using just visual or auditory interfaces have their limitations, and it is not possible to present every situation in its authentic form by using either one of these interfaces. In different papers we can find different approaches and methods of presenting a user interface using sound, all these papers together are important steps towards the union between the visually impaired and the virtual world.

Generally speaking, the audio interface of a game consists of speech, music and various sorts of audio effects [8]. They must be presented to a visually impaired user in such a manner that allows him/her a suitable, timely reaction.

Speech is mostly used to introduce the user to the guidelines and rules of the game, and for this purpose synthesized speech is most commonly used. Synthesized speech can be used in the game itself more or less depending on the type of the game. If greater authenticity of the situation is to be achieved, or in order to ensure that the right reaction will be made, synthesized speech can be replaced by recorded, live speech. It should be noted that the papers emphasize speech technologies as those contributing the most to adaptation of video games to the visually impaired.

By using audio effects we attempt to illustrate situations or various objects in the game [9]. For the visually impaired it is of particular importance to have certain audio effects which tell them whether their reaction was suitable or not.

Music can also be a good element for depicting states and situations a player could find himself/herself in, or it can be used just as a background.

3.1 ASR in the Computer Games

Due to the lack of sight, the blind rely on other senses heavily, especially on the senses of touch and hearing, making them more advanced [10], and allowing them to easily learn to use keyboards very skillfully for communicating with computers (attempts have been made to add sound to the motion of the mouse pointer). The alternative to using keyboards is automatic speech recognition (ASR). Because of intra- and interpersonal differences in the speakers' voice, different setups and qualities of microphones and communication channels, as well as different levels of ambient noise, ASR is a very demanding task for the computer and is not well developed for all languages. Studies usually mention using ASR for issuing certain (already standardised) voice commands, but unrestricted human-to-computer speech communication is less commonly applied.

3.2 TTS in the Computer Games

A computer that can synthesize speech from any text in a familiar (preferably native) language enables a visually impaired person to independently read books, magazines, browse the Internet and access news, newspapers and every other kind of written information. It enables the intimacy of written communication – the visually impaired now have their own e-mail groups and fora, they write to each other, as well as to everyone else completely equally. All this allows them to broaden their education and be trained for a number of professions which, without the aid of a computer that can synthesize speech in their native language, they could not possibly practice.

Psychophysical and material effects of professional training leading to a greater possibility of finding employment are evident.

Apart from TTS (in a familiar language) another necessity is a screen reader. Furthermore, the visually impaired have to be trained to use the computer via speech technologies. As screen readers are already available, being implemented into any newer version of the operating system, the most important thing for a visually impaired person is to have high-quality TTS software in their native language [11]. Unfortunately, because of language dependence of this technology, a quality synthesizer must be developed individually for every language. Put simply, a synthesizer developed for one language cannot be successfully utilized for speech synthesis in any other language, as is the case with human incapability of reading texts in unfamiliar languages – we are not able to properly articulate many sounds, words or sentences. To be able to recognize certain words and grasp the meaning from a continuous speech flow, proper intonation of every syllable, word, and sentence is of major importance. The primary problem for TTS is that the text it is supposed to read contains no tags which would denote how long any speech unit should last, or how to intonate that unit during that period, or whether a syllable should be accented. All these problems are far from being solved for most languages.

Quality and naturalness of synthesized speech reached so far are not on a satisfactory level for many applications. However, sufficient quality has been reached for some languages, leading to significant changes in the way of life of the visually impaired. In Serbia, the development of *anReader* in the last few years has certainly contributed to a rapid increase in the number of visually impaired computer users (nearly tenfold in the last 7 years, since the software was first introduced).

4 Audio Presentation and Binaural Localization in Computer Games

In the process of creation of audio games attention is paid to presenting information in audio form, because that sound presentation must carry all relevant information that allows the player to react in a timely and adequate way [12]. The GUI of a video game carries most of the information, which gives particular broadness and freedom while developing such games as opposed to audio games.

Portraying all relevant information in audio form presents an interesting challenge because presentation of audio information to the user is limited. In sound-based games the player gets a mental picture of all present objects and persons by listening to the sounds which characterize them. Stereo positioning is used to spatially distinguish the sounds of objects. It allows the sound to traverse from left to right, and vice versa. These sounds are critical for the player and his understanding of the game. Yet stereo positioning only gives the player one dimension, which is a constraint having in mind two dimensions of a monitor.

On the other hand, binaural localization with four or five channels produces a feeling of being surrounded by a unique sound field. This occurs because every channel distributes different information, a different form of sound, so the user has a sensation of sound coming from one direction. Although this form of audio spatial presentation is paramount, it is most commonly not acceptable for visually impaired users because of financial or other reasons.

5   Realization of the First Memory Game Intended for the Visually Impaired, with Speech Technologies in Serbian

On demand from a non-government organization "Iskrica" from Novi Sad, a team from the Faculty of technical sciences working on development and application of speech technologies has ventured into making the first memory game, in Serbian, intended for the visually impaired.

It is a simple and well-known memory game with sixteen fields hiding eight pairs of objects. The goal of the game is to locate the pairs, with a speech synthesizer naming every object in such a way that determining its position on a four-by-four board is facilitated by way of binaural localization. The user has two options – to select the square by giving verbal commands (ASR) by pronouncing the coordinates of the square, or simply to use the keyboard. For recognition of verbal commands the speech recognition software developed on FTS, whose accuracy on such a small set of commands exceeds 99%, is used.

The basic problem while developing the game was the binaural two-dimensional localization of objects, one that would allow visually impaired players a quick, suitable response. The problem would be solved more easily if the solution employed more than two sound channels, but as most visually impaired users only have ordinary headphones, a two channel solution was to be found. Based on characteristics of binaural hearing [13] we have decided that the horizontal position of the field be presented by simple stereo presentations – different interaural levels between ears, while the vertical position of the field is indicated by using different audio frequencies (pitch of the synthesized speech).

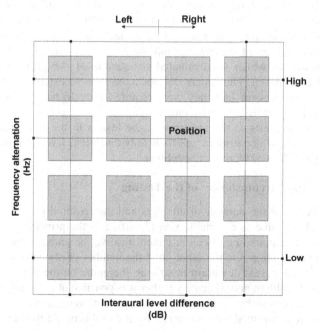

Fig. 2. Audio presentation of the object position

Different interaural levels of sound produced in the left and the right channel of stereo presentation define four horizontal positions: furthermost left (L=1, R=0), left (L=2/3, R=1/3), right (L=1/3, R=2/3), furthermost right (L=0, R=1). Difference in volume of two neighbor fields presented in one ear equals 33.3%. Vertical positions of objects are represented by using different pitch, namely the f0 frequency. Four f0 frequency levels are adopted in this particular case, with the objects in the uppermost level being named using synthesized speech with the highest chosen frequency, and the ones in the lowermost level being named using synthesized speech with the lowest chosen frequency.

5.1 Testing

After making the game a test was carried out. The goal of the test was to investigate the possibility of using binaural perception of sound for two-dimensional source localization in interactive games for the visually impaired. Such an additional source of information would contribute to more equal participation of the visually impaired in online gaming.

5.2 Population Studied

For the needs of testing two groups composed of nine testers (aged from nine to twelve) were designated. The children were split equally, based on their age, between the groups, the care was taken not to create a distinct difference in the average age of the two groups that would affect the results. One group consisted of the visually impaired testers from the „School for visually impaired children" in Zemun. The testers from this group were selected according to their knowledge regarding speech technologies and computers, because visually impaired children in Serbia are introduced to computers as means of aid only in the fifth grade, which is relatively late especially because speech technologies for the Serbian language are indeed of sufficient quality. Testers of the other group were sighted children, and this was the group in reference to which we evaluated the results of the group composed of visually impaired children. The testers did not have to have extensive experience in working with computers, in fact they were required only to have basic knowledge such as turning it on and using at least one program.

According to the needs of the experiment, the testers in the first group were selected so that the visual impairment was their only disability, having in mind that this handicap is often followed by other disabilities.

5.3 Variables and Circumstances of the Testing

During the experiment the number of attempts and the required time for solving the game were tracked. Time as a variable was identified as the principal indicator as to whether a visually impaired child can or cannot resolve the game in the same period of time as sighted children. On the other hand the number of attempts as a parameter could point towards a great deviation in solving the game on the part of sighted and visually impaired children and indicate whether it is possible at all to create this game in such a way that both sighted and visually impaired children could play it together.

All testers were confronted with this game for the first time. At the beginning of the experiment all testers were obliged to read the rules of the game, where the visually impaired children did it by using their speech synthesizers. All testers were allowed to play the game only five times before the official testing took place. During the test phase every player played the game three times.

While testing, the visually impaired testers used ordinary headphones similar to the ones they use at home. By employing these procedures a most realistic situation was to be created.

Although the game was designed so that it can be played by giving verbal commands, testing was done strictly by using keyboards.

5.4 Results

Whilst performing the experiment all testers have accomplished the given tasks, while doing so the group of visually impaired children have achieved times ranging from 42.3s to 87.7s and the group of sighted children from 28.0s to 42.3s. In spite of a somewhat longer time needed by visually impaired testers to complete the game, the number of attempts lies, in both groups, within quite similar boundaries. The visually impaired testers have resolved their games in 16.0-21.0 attempts, while the sighted children have done so in 15.3-21.7 attempts. Two individuals from the first group stood out by solving their games in 42.3 and 43.0 seconds respectively.

The visually impaired testers had to wait to hear the name of the object being named. Although all testers adjusted the speed of pronunciation during the preparatory phase, it stands as one of the main parameters affecting the speed of solving the game, and is dependent on the user. On the other hand, the sighted children have said that the aggravating circumstance was that the objects were presented by words, rather than a picture.

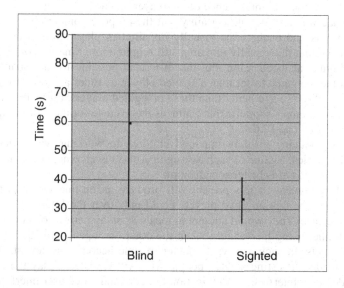

Fig. 3. Time needed by testers to solve the game. Average time for the blind is very close to 60s and standard deviation is about 14s, on the other hand for the sighted average time is 33s and standard deviation is about 4s.

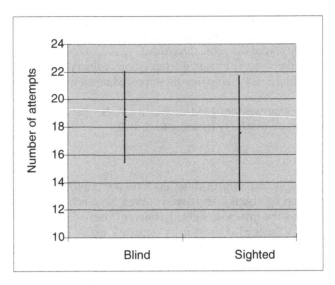

Fig. 4. Number of attempts at solving the game. Average number of attempts for the blind is 18.7 and standard deviation is 1.6 and for the sighted average number of attempts is 17.6 and standard deviation is 2.1.

6 Conclusion

The influence of the testers on the results is substantial, as the achieved results depend on the concentration and intelligence of the player, his/hers experience etc. Despite of their influence we can say with certainty that the proposed binaural two-dimensional localization aids and enables the visually impaired to play multimedia games. The results indicate that the visually impaired still require more time for solving the game in spite of binaural localization, but that it is also possible for a visually impaired player to solve the game faster than a sighted player, as times achieved by some visually impaired players were better than those of sighted players. Furthermore, the average number of attempts supports this claim, as the average for the first group was 18.7 and for the second one 17.6.

Besides introducing visually impaired children to working with computers and speech technologies, a game of such a design permits development of motor skills and represents a step towards better socialization.

Future development of this project will produce an on-line version of the same memory game, one that any two players could play over the Internet, each with his own user interface. They would attempt to locate as many pairs of objects on the same board, each one taking his/her turn when the other one opens two squares with mismatching objects. In such a way, the factor of time becomes irrelevant. Also, plans have been made for testing sighted people who will repeatedly play the game using just the video user interface, a combination of audio and video user interfaces, as well as just the audio user interface (with the monitor turned off). These tests are to measure the contribution of stereo presentation to two-dimensional positioning of objects.

The proposed concept of spatial localization of sound sources and positioning participants in the game enables the development of other games with similar goals.

Acknowledgments. The work described in this paper was supported in part by the Ministry for Science and Technological Development of the Republic of Serbia, within the project TR1101.

References

1. Sečujski, M., Obradović, R., Pekar, D.: AlfaNum System for Speech Synthesis in Serbian Language. In: Sojka, P., Kopeček, I., Pala, K. (eds.) TSD 2002. LNCS (LNAI), vol. 2448, pp. 237–244. Springer, Heidelberg (2002)
2. Mišković, D., Vujnović, N., Sečujski, M., Delić, V.: Audio library for the visually impaired as an application of text-to-speech synthesis (in Serbian). In: Proc. 49th ETRAN, Budva, S&M, vol. II, pp. 400–402 (2005)
3. Ronto, R., Pekar, D., Đurić, N.: Realization of a speech-enabled telephone portal based on TTS and ASR (in Serbian). In: Proc. 49th ETRAN, Budva, S&M, vol. II, pp. 392–395 (2005)
4. Archambault, D., Ossmann, R., Gaudy, T., Miesenberger, K.: Computer Games and Visually Impaired People (2009), http://cedric.cnam.fr/PUBLIS/RC1204.pdf
5. International Game Developers Association: Accessibility in Games: Motivations and Approaches (2009),
   http://www.igda.org/accessibility/
   IGDA_Accessibility_WhitePaper.pdf
6. Cunningham, S., Grout, V., Hebblewhite, R.: Computer Game Audio: The Unappreciated Scholar of the Half-Life Generation. In: Audio Mosty Conference – a Conference on Sound in Games, Piteå, Sweden, October 11-12 (2006)
7. Gaudy, T., Natkin, S., Archambault, D.: Pyvox 2: an audio game accessible to visually impaired people playable without visual nor verbal instructions. In: 3rd International Conference on E-learning and Games, Nanjing, June 25-27 (2008)
8. Gaver, W.: Auditory Interfaces. In: Helander, M., Landauer, T.K., Prabhu, P. (eds.) Handbook of Human-Computer Interaction, 2nd edn. Elsevier, Amsterdam (1997)
9. Ratanasit, D., Moore, M.M.: Representing Graphical User Interfaces with Sound: A Review of Approaches. Journal of Visual Impairment and Blindness 99(2), 69–84 (2005)
10. Doucet, M.-E., Guillemot, J.-P., Lassonde, M., Gagné, J.-P., Leclerc, C., Lepore, F.: Blind subjects process auditory spectral cues more efficiently than sighted individuals. Exp. Brain Res. 160, 194–202 (2005)
11. Delić, V.: A Review of R&D of Speech Technologies in Serbian and their Applications in Western Balkan Countries. In: Proc.12th Int. Conf. "Speech and Computer" (SPECOM), Moscow, pp. 64–83 (2007)
12. Röber, N., Masuch, M.: Playing Audio-Only Games a Compendium of Interacting with Virtual, Auditory Worlds. In: Proceedings of DiGRA Conference: Changing Views – Worlds in Play (2005)
13. Jovičić, S.T.: Binaural Perception (in Serbian). A Chapter in Speech Communication, physiology, psychoacoustics and perception (in Serbian), Nauka, Belgrade, Serbia, pp. 294–366 (1999) ISBN 86-7621-096-9

Pathological Voice Analysis and Classification Based on Empirical Mode Decomposition

Gastón Schlotthauer[1,4], María E. Torres[1,3,4], and Hugo L. Rufiner[2,3,4]

[1] Lab. de Señales y Dinámicas no Lineales, Fac. de Ingeniería
Universidad Nacional de Entre Ríos, Oro Verde, Entre Ríos, Argentina
metorres@santafe-conicet.gov.ar
[2] Lab. de Cibernética, Fac. de Ingeniería, UNER, Oro Verde, Entre Ríos, Argentina
[3] $SINC(i)$, Fac. de Ing. y Cs. Hs., Univ. Nac. del Litoral, Santa Fe, Argentina
[4] Consejo Nacional de Investigaciones Científicas y Técnicas (CONICET), Argentina

Abstract. Empirical mode decomposition (EMD) is an algorithm for signal analysis recently introduced by Huang. It is a completely data-driven non-linear method for the decomposition of a signal into AM - FM components. In this paper two new EMD-based methods for the analysis and classification of pathological voices are presented. They are applied to speech signals corresponding to real and simulated sustained vowels. We first introduce a method that allows the robust extraction of the fundamental frequency of sustained vowels. Its determination is crucial for pathological voice analysis and diagnosis. This new method is based on the ensemble empirical mode decomposition (EEMD) algorithm and its performance is compared with others from the state of the art. As a second EMD-based tool, we explore spectral properties of the intrinsic mode functions and apply them to the classification of normal and pathological sustained vowels. We show that just using a basic pattern classification algorithm, the selected spectral features of only three modes are enough to discriminate between normal and pathological voices.

1 Introduction

Empirical Mode Decomposition (EMD) has been recently proposed by Huang et al. [1] to adaptively decompose nonlinear and non stationary signals in a sum of well-behaved AM-FM components, called Intrinsic Mode Functions (IMFs). This new technique has received the attention of the scientific community, both in applications [2,3] and in its interpretation [4,5]. The method consists in a local and fully data-driven splitting of a signal, in fast and slow oscillations. The advantage of an AM-FM resonance model of speech was previously discussed in [6], where using a Gabor filter bank with six fixed band pass filters, non-linear features were extracted for instantaneous frequency estimation, phoneme classification, and automatic speech recognition. In this work, we propose two new methods based on EMD (and its variants) with focus in two pathological voice applications: differential diagnosis and fundamental frequency extraction. Preliminary versions of these algorithms were presented in [7,8,9].

A. Esposito et al. (Eds.): COST 2102 Int. Training School 2009, LNCS 5967, pp. 364–381, 2010.

The fundamental period T_0 of a voiced speech signal can be defined as the elapsed time between two successive laryngeal pulses, and the fundamental frequency or pitch is $F_0 = 1/T_0$ [10]. Even if F_0 is useful for a wide range of applications, its reliable estimation is still considered one of the most difficult tasks. In speech, F_0 variations contribute to prosody, and in tonal languages, they also help to distinguish segmental categories. Current applications are related with speech and speaker recognition, speech based emotions classifications, voice morphing and the analysis of pathological voices.

In the clinical evaluation of disordered voices, the analysis of F_0 perturbation is a standard procedure in order to assess the severity of pathologies and in monitoring the patient progress [11]. A reliable and accurate estimation of F_0 is essential for this application. Conventional F_0 extraction algorithms assume that speech is produced by a linear system and that speech signals are locally stationary [10]. However, in the case of pathological voices, these assumptions are over-simplifications.

In voice pathology assessment, several parameters extracted from pitch estimation are commonly used. It is therefore important to have a good and reliable F_0 estimation. Unfortunately, no previous method for F_0 extraction operates consistently in the case of pathological voices. This is due to the fact that the vocal folds vibrations of pathological voices present more serious and complex irregularities than the case of normal voices. Some of the difficulties that arise in F_0 estimation, especially when pathological voices are analyzed, include period-doubling and period-halving.

A few EMD based algorithms have been proposed for F_0 extraction [12,13], however they suffer the "mode mixing" problem. Wu and Huang [14] proposed a modification of the EMD algorithm, called Ensemble EMD (EEMD), which largely alleviates this effect, but at the price of a very high computational cost. Taking advantage of its benefits, here we present a new method based on EEMD which is able to extract the F_0 in normal and pathological sustained vowels, improving the behavior of the previous estimators.

In the present paper, we also explore some spectral properties of the IMFs. The comparison of real data IMFs spectra allows us to present preliminary results of an application of this method to the analysis and discrimination between normal and pathological speech signals.

We study a couple of dysphonias with different etiology [15], frequently confused and not easily identified by local clinicians: Adductor Spasmodic Dysphonia (AdSD) and Muscular Tension Dysphonia (MTD).

In recent years, the use of acoustical measures, in combination with pattern recognition techniques, has motivated the appearance of several works concerning the automatic discrimination between pathological and normal voices. In [16], a database with 89 records of the sustained vowel /a/ corresponding to normal and pathological (MTD and AdSD) cases were separated into three classes with a 93.26 % of correct classifications, and into two classes (normal and pathological) reaching a 98.94 %, overcoming the best reported results in the literature. The authors used a pattern recognition scheme with eight acoustical parameters and neural networks. In this paper we show that the spectral properties of the IMFs could be useful to discriminate between normal and pathological voices. These preliminary results suggest that they might provide also clues in order to differentiate between AdSD and MTD.

The paper is organized as follows. In Sec. 2 the data used for the experiments and basic concepts to be used are described. In Sec. 3 the EEMD based F_0 extraction method is presented. In Sec. 4 the pathological voice classification problem is stated and a method based on EMD is described. In Sec. 5 the results for both methods are shown. Finally, in Sec. 6 the discussion and conclusions are presented.

2   Materials and Methods

2.1   Artificial Data

In order to explore the performances of the proposed techniques, experiments were performed with synthetic normal and pathological voices. These signals have been generated using a phonation model that incorporates the perturbations involved in normal voices and in common laryngeal pathologies. This allowed us to maintain controlled experimental conditions, making possible the discussion of the technique and the selection of the appropriate parameters.

The speech signal $y[n]$ was modeled using the classical linear prediction model $y[n] = -\sum_{p=1}^{P} y[n-p]a[p] + x[n]$, where $a[p]$ are the linear predictor coefficients, and $x[n]$ is the input representing the glottal pulses. The input is modeled by a train of pulses, with variable period and amplitude:

$$x[n] = \sum_{k=1}^{K} G[k]\, \delta\left[n - \sum_{i=1}^{k} P[i]\right],$$

where $G[k]$ are the corresponding gain coefficients and P the periods' values. Different stochastic models for jitter and shimmer have been proposed in the literature. In this work we assume, for a pulse train with a jitter $jitt\%$, a normal probability distribution for each period P:

$$pdf\,(P[k]) = \frac{1}{\sigma_P \sqrt{2\pi}} \exp\left(-\frac{(P[k] - P_0)^2}{2\sigma_P^2}\right),$$

where P_0 is the mean period and $\sigma_P = \frac{P_0\, jitt\,\%}{200}$. In order to avoid period approximation problems, a uniform randomized roundness function and a sampling frequency of 50 KHz have been used.

In a similar way, the gain coefficients distribution is given by:

$$pdf\,(G[k]) = \frac{1}{\sigma_G \sqrt{2\pi}} \exp\left(-\frac{(G[k] - 1)^2}{2\sigma_G^2}\right).$$

Four hundred signals were synthesized, 100 corresponding to male and 100 to female, for each group of normal and pathological voices. For each situation, the model parameters were obtained from the statistics of real signals, adopting a fundamental frequency with a distribution $\mathcal{N}(144, 22.5)$ for male voices and $\mathcal{N}(245, 24.5)$ for female voices; a $\mathcal{N}(0.4, 0.1)$ jitter distribution for normal voices and $\mathcal{N}(5, 1)$ for pathological voices; and a shimmer with distribution $\mathcal{N}(1, 0.2)$ and $\mathcal{N}(8, 1)$ respectively.

2.2   Real Data

The implementation of the method proposed for estimation of F_0 was analyzed using a database of vowel signals from 710 persons of both genders [17]. It includes sustained phonation of the vowel /a/ of 53 healthy individuals and patients with a wide variety of voice disorders (organic, neurological, traumatic and psychogenic). The healthy voices belong to 21 males and 32 females, with mean ages 38.81 ± 8.49 and 34.16 ± 7.87 years, respectively. The set of 657 pathological voices contains samples of 169 male speakers, 238 female speakers and 247 without data about gender. The average ages are 49.80 ± 17.46 years for males and 46.83 ± 17.41 years for females. Some of the present disorders are adductor and abductor spasmodic dysphonia, A-P squeezing, cysts, erythema, gastric reflux, granulation tissue, hyperfunction, interaytenoid hyperplasia, keratosis / leukoplakia, paralysis, polypoid degeneration, scarring, ventricular compression, vocal fold edema, vocal fold polyp, vocal tremor, and others. In this database, the average fundamental frequency of normal voices is between 120.39 and 316.50 Hz.

For voice classification experiments a corpus of sustained vowels /a/ was used. The speech utterances from this corpus were registered in an anechoic room (global reverberation time < 30 ms). Each subject was requested to phonate the sustained vowels as steadily as possible toward an electrodynamic unidirectional microphone Shure SM58 at a distance of about 15 cm from the mouth. Each vowel had a duration of 1 to 5 sec. The data was digitized with a professional Turtle Beach Multisound FIJI sound card, at 44 KHz, 16 bits and no compression was used. Later, the data was low-pass filtered and down-sampled to 22 KHz. All the voices were classified by an experienced voice pathologist. It was considered a first set of 106 voices (half normal and half of diverse pathologies, randomly selected from a larger database), here named database DB1, and a second one of 14 normal voices, 13 of AdSD, and 6 of MTD, here named database DB2.

Here it is important to point out that patients affected with AdSD may attempt to prevent their symptoms by increasing the tension in their laryngeal muscles in an effort to compensate their disease signs. The consequence is the appearance of additional physical disturbances similar to MTD along with AdSD. The over-riding symptoms of MTD can escalate over time making difficult to discern the underlying symptoms of AdSD [18].

2.3   EMD and EEMD

As it was stated in Sec. 1, EMD decomposes a signal $x(t)$ into a (usually) small number of IMFs. IMFs must satisfy two conditions: (i) the number of extrema and the number of zero crossings must either be equal or differ at most by one; and (ii) at any point, the mean value of the upper and lower envelopes is zero.

Given a signal $x(t)$, the non-linear EMD algorithm, as proposed in [1], is described by the following algorithm:

1. find all extrema of $x(t)$,
2. interpolate between minima (maxima), obtaining the envelope $e_{min}(t)$ $(e_{max}(t))$,
3. compute the local mean $m(t) = (e_{min}(t) + e_{max}(t))/2$,
4. extract the IMF candidate $d(t) = x(t) - m(t)$,
5. check the properties of $d(t)$:
   - if $d(t)$ is not an IMF, replace $x(t)$ with $d(t)$ and go to step 1,
   - if $d(t)$ is an IMF, evaluate $r(t) = x(t) - d(t)$,
6. repeat the steps 1 to 5 by *sifting* the residual signal $r(t)$. The sifting process ends when the residue satisfies a predefined stopping criterion [4].

As already pointed out, one of the most significant EMD drawbacks for some applications is the so called mode mixing. It is illustrated in the left column of Fig. 1, where 60 ms of a sustained vowel /a/ are analyzed by EMD. The four IMFs with higher energy are shown. The appearance of oscillations of notoriously disparate scales in IMF 2 is clear. Another example can be seen in IMF 5, where oscillations are marked with circles. These oscillations are very similar to those marked on IMF 4.

EEMD[1], is an extension of the previously described EMD. It defines the true IMF components as the mean of certain ensemble of trials, each obtained by adding white noise of finite variance to the original signal. This method alleviates the mode mixing of the EMD algorithm [14]. An example of the EEMD abilities can be seen in the right column of Fig. 1. An ensemble size of $N_e = 5000$ was used, and the added white noise in each ensemble member had a standard deviation of $\epsilon = 0.2$. In general a few hundred of ensemble members provide good results [14]. The remaining noise, defined as the difference between the original signal and the sum of the IMFs obtained by EEMD, has a standard deviation $\epsilon_r = \epsilon/N_e$. For a complete discussion about the number of ensemble members and noise standard deviation, we refer to [14]. The IMFs 2 to 5 are shown in the right column of Fig. 1, below the sustained vowel /a/. The IMFs obtained by EEMD seem to be much more regular than the EMD version and, additionally, we can appreciate that in IMF 5 the oscillations capture the fundamental period of the sustained /a/.

This fact is remarked in Fig. 2.a, where the sustained vowel /a/ is pictured and the EEMD related IMF 5 is superimposed in a red line. In Fig. 2.b the power spectral densities (PSD) of /a/ and IMF 5 are plotted. The PSD of IMF 5 has

---

[1] Matlab software available at http://rcada.ncu.edu.tw/

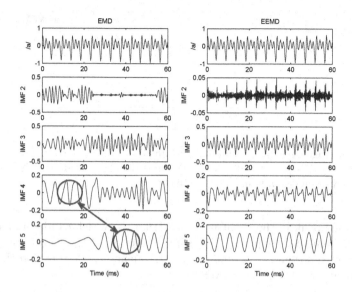

Fig. 1. A sustained real vowel /a/ corresponding to a normal subject, analyzed by EMD (left column) and EEMD (right column). The corresponding IMFs 2 to 5 are shown. In IMFs 4 and 5 corresponding to EMD two segments where "mode mixing" occurs, are marked with circles.

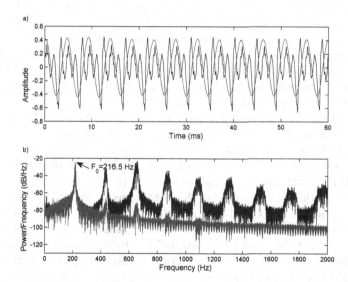

Fig. 2. a) A sustained real vowel /a/ corresponding to a normal subject (blue) and IMF 5, obtained by EEMD (red). b) PSD estimates of the sustained vowel /a/ (blue) and its EEMD based IMF 5 (red). The peak of the spectrum of the IMF 5 is marked as $F_0 = 216.5$ Hz.

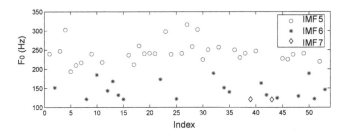

Fig. 3. F_0 average over the 53 analyzed sustained real vowels corresponding to normal subjects. Circles (red), stars (blue) and diamonds (black) indicate the signals in which F_0 was found in modes 5, 6 and 7 respectively

a well defined peak in the frequency $F = 216.5$ Hz, which can be understood as a mean fundamental frequency. A visual inspection of the waveform (Fig. 2.a) allows the estimation of the fundamental frequency as close to 200 Hz, what is in agreement with the PSD of IMF 5.

3   Instantaneous Frequency Extraction

In this section we present and discuss the main ideas of the algorithm, based on EEMD, for the extraction of F_0.

Once the EEMD is computed, we want to identify the mode in which F_0 stands almost alone. With this in mind, a visual inspection of the decomposition of the normal voices in our database, allows to identify the candidate mode, as can be appreciated observing the second column in Fig. 1 and Fig. 2.a. Clearly F_0 is present in modes 3, 4 and 5. In the two first ones it is mixed with other components of the original signal, but it appears alone in the last one. This fact is reinforced by the sinusoidal like waveform of IMF5.

In our 53 samples of normal voices, F_0 was found in the IMFs 5, 6 and 7. Only in two cases it has been found in IMF 7, with average values of 120.394 Hz and 121.102 Hz, while in nineteen cases it was found in IMF 6, with average values in between 121.652 Hz and 189.295 Hz. In the remaining 32 voice, F_0 was found in IMF 5 with average values in between 193.934 Hz and 316.504 Hz.

Fig. 3 shows the average values of the instantaneous frequencies obtained from the modes identified by visual inspection in each normal voice in our database. In red circles are indicated those voices whose F_0 was identified at mode 5, while the blue stars and the black diamonds indicate those cases corresponding to an identification in modes 6 and 7 respectively. It can be appreciated that it exists a relationship between the F_0 average value and the mode in which F_0 has been identified. This is consistent with the results of Flandrin *et al.*[19]. They showed that, when applied to white noise, the EMD acts as an adaptive dyadic filter bank.

In order to obtain an automatic method to select the mode in which F_0 is hidden, we explore the discrimination abilities of the Shannon entropy in the

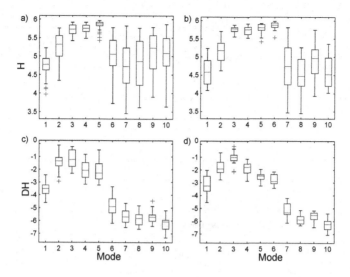

Fig. 4. a, b) Discrete entropies of modes 1 to 10 for the sustained real normal vowels /a/ at which F_0 was found in modes 5 and 6, respectively. c, d) Differential entropies of modes 1 to 10 for the sustained real normal vowels /a/ for which F_0 was found in modes 5 and 6, respectively.

present context. In the discrete case, it is defined as: $H(x) = -\sum_{i=1}^{M} p_i \log(p_i)$, with the understanding that $p \log(p) = 0$ if $p = 0$, where p_i is the probability that the signal x belongs to a considered interval and M is the partitions number [20].

Fig. 4.a displays the boxplots of the Shannon discrete entropy (H) corresponding to the ten first modes of the sustained normal vowels for which F_0 was found in mode 5.

In Fig. 4.b are shown those voices for which F_0 was found in mode 6. The histogram-based discrete entropy was estimated with 500 bins. It can be appreciated that the first mode has average entropy lower than for the other four or five modes (Figs. 4.a and 4.b, respectively.) This is consistent with the fact that the first mode mainly contains high frequency noise: the one added to the original voices to perform the EEMD.

It can be observed that, for those voices for which F_0 is in IMF 5, the entropy has a jump after this mode, while a similar jump is observed in the 6th mode for those voices in which the fundamental frequency was found in IMF 6. There is however an overlap, which does not appear if we use an estimate of the differential entropy (DH) [21] instead of the discrete one. DH was estimated using a smoothing Gaussian kernel probability density estimation with 500 equally spaced points that cover the range of each IMF [21].

The results shown in Figs. 4.c and 4.d correspond to the differential entropy of those voices for which the fundamental frequency was found in modes 5 and 6. It should be noted here that in the case of the normal voices, the IMFs obtained through the EEMD have sinusoidal shapes and their probability density

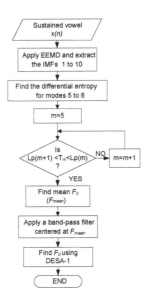

Fig. 5. Flow diagram corresponding to the full F_0 extraction method based on EEMD

functions are also similar to a pdf of a sinusoidal function. Therefore, if we remember that the differential entropy of a sinusoidal of amplitude A is given by $DH = \ln(\pi A/2)$, it would be reasonable to propose the logarithm of the power of the IMFs as an index to find the mode where F_0 is hidden. This idea will be addressed in future works.

Taking into account these results, for modes $m = 5, 6$ and 7, we can propose thresholds T_5, T_6 and T_7 such that: $-3.365 < T_5 < -3.234, -4.224 < T_6 < -3.433$ and $-5.762 < T_7 < -4.172$. In this way, given a voice, if its DH corresponding to mode 5 is higher than T_5 and its DH corresponding to mode 6 is lower than T_5, it could be expected its F_0 would be hidden in mode 5. If this is not the case, the presence of a jump in between modes 6 and 7 should have to be tested using threshold T_6, and afterwards in between modes 7 and 8 by means of threshold T_7. This hypothesis should have to be tested on a larger database, which is right now not available. This would allow setting more accurate thresholds.

Once the mode where it is expected to find F_0 is selected, spurious components must be eliminated. For this task we adopt a type II Chebyshev bandpass filter, with a bandwith of 150 Hz and centered on the frequency corresponding to the maximum of the spectrum of the selected mode. This frequency is a good approximation of the average value of F_0, as shown in Fig. 2.b. At this point, an AM-FM separation algorithm must be applied. The DESA-1 [22] provides us better results than Hilbert-Transform based methods, as reported in [23]. The flow diagram corresponding to the full algorithm is displayed in Fig.5.

4 Pathological Voice Classification

In the last section the ensemble version of EMD was used in order to improve the possibility of finding the F_0 in a unique mode. Here, we will explore the non linear decomposition capabilities of EMD to produce some discriminative information useful for pathological voice classification.

In a previous work we selected eight standard acoustic parameters extracted from sustained vowels, including short-term perturbations of fundamental frequency and intensity (termed *jitter* and *shimmer*, respectively), and glottal noise measures [16]. These feature vectors were used to perform an automatic classification of normal and pathological voices, such as those here considered, improving the best reported results. In [27] we explored different dimensionality reduction techniques to perform the visualization and classification using similar feature vectors. Even if in this work we obtained good results for final vector of dimensions 2 and 3, it must be noticed that the physical meaning of each dimension was lost due to the transformations involved. Therefore in this work we explore a new EEMD based approach that could allow to reduce the dimensionality of the feature vector, retaining certain physical meaning of its components.

In our experiments, the EMD algorithm of sustained real vowels stopped at IMF 12 ± 1. As an example a sustained normal vowel /a/ and the first eight IMFs of its EMD are shown in Fig.6. Inspired by Fig. 7 we propose to consider for our classification and visualization purposes, a new feature vector in $\mathbb{R}^6$, which components are the maximum PSD of the IMFs 2-4 and the corresponding frequencies.

It must be emphasized that the EMD based algorithms act as an adaptive filter bank that is guided by the data [4], meaning that for signals with different

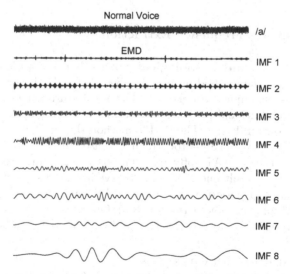

Fig. 6. Sustained real normal vowel /a/ in the first row and IMFs 1-8 of its EMD

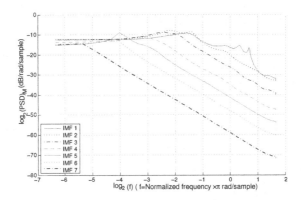

Fig. 7. Log-log power spectrum density, estimated with Burg algorithm, corresponding to each of the IMFs of a Spanish sustained real normal vowel /a/ displayed in the previous figure.

frequency content, a given frequency can be found in different modes. This fact can reinforce the differences between the normal and pathological signals. In this way, the use of the proposed feature vectors could allow to provide new information to improve the discrimination between this kind of data.

Using these new feature vectors, a K-nearest neighbors' classification rule was applied and a K-fold cross validation method, with 20 subsamples, was used in order to estimate the classifier performance.

5   Results

5.1   Instantaneous Frequency Extraction

Simulated Normal and Pathological Voices For illustration purposes, F_0 was extracted with the method proposed in Sec. 3 from both normal and pathological simulated sustained vowels /a/. The results are shown in Fig. 8. For comparison, two additional pitch extraction methods were applied to the same data and also shown in Fig. 8. The RAPT method (black) [24] was implemented using VOICEBOX[2], while an autocorrelation-based method (blue) [25] was implemented using the PRAAT software[3]. The parameters involved in these two algorithms are the default ones. We can observe in Fig. 8 several evident errors in doubling or halving-period events both in RAPT and AC-based methods, specially for the pathological voice case (Fig. 8.b). On the contrary, the EEMD based method here proposed performs smoothly and without errors in both simulation conditions.

---

[2] VOICEBOX Matlab toolkit v. 1.18 (2008),
    http://www.ee.ic.ac.uk/hp/staff/dmb/voicebox/voicebox.html.
[3] PRAAT v.5.0.32, http://www.praat.org.

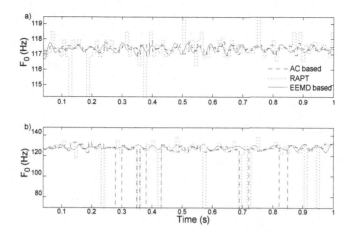

Fig. 8. F_0 of two simulated sustained vowels /a/ (generated as explained in Sec. 2.1) are analyzed: (a) normal simulated voice (b) pathological simulated voice. The results obtained by the autocorrelation based method (blue), RAPT (black) and the proposed EEMD based method (red) are shown.

Real Normal and Pathological Voices. As in the previous example, F_0 was extracted with the method proposed in Sec. 3 and the other two methods, from two sustained real normal vowels /a/. The results are presented in red in Figs. 9.a (EDC1NAL) and 9.b (JTH1NAL). Even if the results look similar, a careful inspection would reveal the above mentioned stair-case nature of the last two methods. This windowing artifact could be a problem for instantaneous frequency estimation.

The Pearson correlation coefficient between the mean F_0 of the 53 healthy sustained vowels /a/ reported in [17] and the averaged instantaneous frequency obtained by our method was $r = 0.999995$.

In Fig. 10 the F_0 corresponding to two pathological voices are presented. In Fig. 10.a the fundamental frequency of a sustained vowel /a/ from a patient suffering muscular tension dysphonia is analyzed with the proposed method. On the other hand, in Fig. 10.b a voice with adductor spasmodic dysphonia is studied. As in Fig. 9, the F_0 obtained with RAPT and auto-correlation based methods are also superposed in black and blue. Even if the autocorrelation based method had been reported to be the best pitch estimation technique for the analysis of pathological sustained vowel /a/ [26], it can be observed in that it fails several times (See Fig. 10). Also does RAPT algorithm, while the method here proposed, exhibits a much better behavior.

In a study with 35 disordered sustained vowels /a/ (15 from patients suffering muscular tension dysphonia and 20 suffering adductor spasmodic dysphonia) we have observed that, in the task of a correct F_0 extraction, while RAPT and auto-correlation based methods both fail in 22 voices (62.86 %), the here proposed algorithm reduced the number of failures to only 10 voices (28.57 %). The F_0 estimation was considered failed when at least one doubling or halving-period

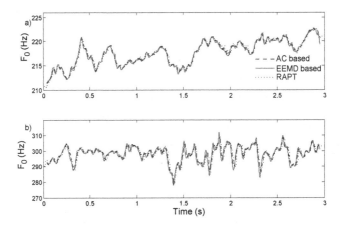

Fig. 9. F_0 of two healthy sustained vowels /a/ from database described in Sec. 2.2 are analyzed (a) EDC1NAL and (b) JTH1NAL. The results obtained by the autocorrelation based method (blue), RAPT (black) and the proposed EEMD based method (red) are shown.

event, or a "spike-like" artifact appears. In the method here proposed, we have observed that these spike-like artifacts were coincident with pathological voice segments of very low energy. In order to detect them and to prevent this kind of mistakes in the F_0 estimation, we consider that a voice-activity detection method could be applied as a pre-processing stage. However, the failures of the other two algorithms were more notorious. It is important to emphasize that the total length of the segments where the RAPT and autocorrelation-based methods fail, largely exceed the total length of all spike-like events related with the here proposed method. For this reason, if another quantifier is used in the algorithms comparison, as for example the percentage of signal length where the F_0 estimations are satisfactory, then the advantage of the EEMD based method would be more pronounced. These improvements will be addressed in future works.

5.2 Pathological Voice Classification

Simulated Normal and Pathological Voices. In order to study the classification capability of the second new tool presented in Sec. 4, for each of the simulated voices we have selected as feature vectors' components the maximum PSD (log2) and the corresponding frequencies, of IMF i, $i = 2, 3, 4$.

With a simple and general-purpose classifier, a K-nearest neighbors' classification rule, the best performance was obtained using $K = 1$, reaching a 99% of correct classifications. In Table 1.a the obtained confusion matrix is presented. This result confirms that the IMFs' spectra provide relevant features that can be used as descriptors for the proposed classification task. The importance of this experiment is based on the fact that both normal and pathological synthetic

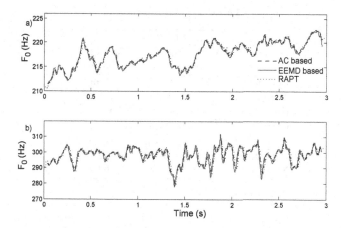

Fig. 10. F_0 of two pathological sustained vowels /a/ with: a) muscular tension dysphonia and b) spasmodic dysphonia. The results obtained by the autocorrelation based method (blue), RAPT (black) and the instantaneous F_0 estimated with the proposed EEMD based method (red) are shown.

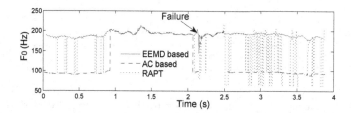

Fig. 11. F_0 of a pathological sustained vowel /a/. Autocorrelation method (blue), RAPT (black) and EEMD based method (red). Although the proposed method fails around $t = 2.1$ s, the other ones fails are more evident (period-doubling and period-halving errors).

voices have been simulated without added noise, and that the difference between them is only due to short-term perturbations of their fundamental frequency and intensity, as imposed in the model. Therefore, the proposed method is able to distinguish between normal and altered voices with very similar Fourier spectra. This a desirable property in the kind of pathologies we are dealing with.

Real Normal and Pathological Voices. Following the same procedure as in the previous section, but with the real voices DB1, we obtained, with $K = 3$ a 93.40% of true positive classifications. In Table 1.b we present the corresponding confusion matrix, were we can appreciate that we obtained a 94.34% of correct classifications of the normal voices and a 92.45% in the pathological case. Taking into account that in Medicine, a pathological case is considered the positive one, these results indicate that the proposed method has a sensitivity of 0.925 and a specificity of 0.926.

Table 1. Confusion matrix

(a)	Simulated voices		
Class	Classifications		Correct
	Pathologic	Normal	Classifications
Pathologic	198	2	99%
Normal	2	198	99%
(b)	Real voices (DB1)		
Class	Classifications		Correct
	Pathologic	Normal	Classifications
Pathologic	49	4	92.45%
Normal	3	50	94.34%

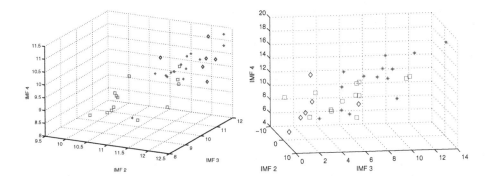

Fig. 12. (a) Frequency (log2) corresponding to the maximum Psd of three IMFs, of normal (stars) and pathological (diamonds – MTD – and squares – ASD) voices (DB2). (b) Maxima Psd (log2) corresponding to three IMFs of normal (stars) and pathological (diamonds – MTD – and squares – ASD) voices (DB2).

In the case of discrimination between MTD and AdSD, we show some preliminary results that suggest that the new tools here presented could also be useful. Unfortunately the amount of data available at the present time is not enough to perform an appropriate statistical study from the point of view of signal analysis, even if from the medical point of view it is encouraging. Plotting for each voice the log2 values of the frequencies at which the maximum value of PSD is obtained for IMFs 2, 3, and 4, we can appreciate in Fig. 12.a) that it seems to be possible to separate AdSD from the normal and MTD. Plotting the maxima of the PSD (in log2), we see in Fig. 12.b) that it is possible to separate most of the MTD from the other pathology and the normal ones. Both plots collaborate to provide a possible separation in three classes. Therefore, these figures suggest that, if a larger set of data would be available, it could be possible to perform a first separation in two classes, class 1: ASD and class 2: normal and MTD, and them continue working on with class 2 to accomplish the final classification. We can appreciate that, for IMFs 2, 3, and 4, those voices in class 1 reach their maximum value of PSD at lower frequencies than the voice belonging to class 2. While MTD and normal voices could be separated just using the maxima of the PSD in IMF 3.

6   Discussion and Conclusions

In this work we have discussed some drawbacks and advantages of both the EMD and the EEMD and how both of these methods can be useful to extract relevant information from voice signals. We have presented the abilities of EEMD for extracting the F_0 from sustained vowels /a/ in combination with an instantaneous frequency estimator algorithm (DESA-1). Additionally, a technique for the automatic selection of the mode from which F_0 can be extracted was here proposed. The new method was successfully tested on normal and pathological sustained voices and compared with other algorithms. The EEMD based method has the advantage to be parameters free, what is an interesting property for non-computational expert operators. As a drawback, the proposed method inherits the high computational cost of the EEMD algorithm. However, its utility in research and clinical applications without the need of on-line F_0 estimation is clear. These preliminary results suggest important advantages of the method here proposed and encourage us to continue the research on these ideas. Although very promising, all the conclusions here presented need to be statistically tested on a larger database. An extension to spontaneous speech and noisy signals will be addressed in future works.

We have also introduced a new method to discriminate between normal and pathological speech signals based on the spectral analysis of the IMFs obtained by means of EMD. We have applied this new tool to the analysis of speech signals corresponding to sustained vowels of different data sets: real and simulated voices. Inspired by the analysis of real data, we have performed an automatic classification of simulated voices (normal and pathologic), with a high accuracy rate (99.00%). In the case of discrimination between normal and pathological real voices we have obtained a performance of 93.40%.

The synthetic stimuli are generated by very simple LPC-synthesis excited by an impulse train. The real excitation spectrum of a voice is more complicated and would probably be a more difficult and realistic test to the proposed methods. This is confirmed by the fact that with the synthetic stimuli, the classifier has an accuracy rate of 99 % compared to 93 % with real voices. In future works we propose to use a more realistic glottal flow waveform as excitation.

We consider that it could be possible to overcome the best reported value by refining the proposed method. These preliminary results strongly suggest that spectral tools based on EMD are useful for the discrimination between normal and pathological voices. Moreover, they suggest that it could be possible to develop an automatic tool for differentiation between pathologies. Future works of this group include the application of these results to a wider database of real signals, in continue collaboration with voice pathologists, and the analysis and discussion of other classification techniques.

Acknowledgments

This works was supported by UNER (Argentina), ANPCyT (Argentina) and CONICET (Argentina). The authors would like to thank Dr. M. C. Jackson-Menaldi of Lakeshore Prof. Voice Center, Lakeshore Ear, Nose and Throat Center, St. Clair Shores (USA) and Depart. of Otolaryng., School of Med., Wayne U., Detroit (USA), for her valuable suggestions. The authors also thank Kay Elemetrics Corp.

References

1. Huang, N., Shen, Z., Long, S., Wu, M., Shih, H., Zheng, Q., Yen, N., Tung, C., Liu, H.: The empirical mode decomposition and the Hilbert spectrum for nonlinear and non-stationary time series analysis. Proc.: Math., Phys. and Eng. Sciences 454, 903–995 (1998)
2. Huang, N.E., Shen, S.S.P. (eds.): Hilbert-Huang transform and its applications. Interdisciplin. Math. Sc., vol. 5. World Sci., Singapore (2005)
3. Schlotthauer, G., Torres, M.E.: Descomposición modal empírica: análisis y disminución de ruido en señales biológicas. In: Proc. XV Congreso Argentino de Bioingeniería SABI, Paraná, E.R. Argentina (2005) File:101PS.pdf
4. Rilling, G., Flandrin, P., Gonçalvès, P.: On empirical mode decomposition and its algorithms. In: Proc IEEE-EURASIP Workshop NSIP-03, Grado, Italia (2003)
5. Rilling, G., Flandrin, P.: On the influence of sampling on the empirical mode decomposition. In: IEEE Int. Conf. On Acoust., Speech and Signal Proc. ICASSP 2006, Toulouse, vol. III, pp. 444–447 (2006)
6. Dimitriadis, D., Maragos, P.: Continuous energy demodulation methods and application to speech analysis. Speech Commun. 48(7), 819–837 (2006)
7. Schlotthauer, G., Torres, M.E., Rufiner, H.: A new algorithm for instantaneous F_0 speech extraction based on ensemble empirical mode decomposition. In: Proc. of 17th Eur. Sign. Proces. Conf. 2009, Glasgow, UK, pp. 2347–2351 (2009)
8. Schlotthauer, G., Torres, M.E., Rufiner, H.: Voice fundamental frequency extraction algorithm based on ensemble empirical mode decomposition and entropies. In: Proc. of 11th Int. Congr. of the IFMBE 2009, Munich, pp. 984–987 (2009)
9. Torres, M.E., Schlotthauer, G., Rufiner, H.L., Jackson-Menaldi, M.C.: Empirical mode decomposition. spectral properties in normal and pathological voices. In: Proc. of the 4th Eur. Conf. of the Inter. Fed. for Med. and Biol. Eng., pp. 252–255 (2009)
10. Hess, W.: Pitch and Voicing Determination of Speech with an Extension Toward Music Signals. In: Springer Handbook of Speech Proc., pp. 181–208. Springer, Heidelberg (2008)
11. Schlotthauer, G., Torres, M.E., Jackson-Menaldi, M.C.: A pattern recognition approach to spasmodic dysphonia and muscle tension dysphonia automatic classification. J. of Voice (2010) (in press)
12. Huang, H., Pan, J.: Speech pitch determination based on Hilbert-Huang transform. Signal Process 86(4), 792–803 (2006)
13. Weiping, H., Xiuxin, W., Yaling, L., Minghui, D.: A Novel Pitch Period Detection Algorithm Bases on HHT with Application to Normal and Pathological Voice. In: 27th Annual Intern. Conf. of the IEEE-EMBS 2005, pp. 4541–4544 (2005)

14. Wu, Z., Huang, N.E.: Ensemble empirical mode decomposition: A noise-assisted data analysis method. Adv. Adapt. Data Anal. 1(1), 1–41 (2009)
15. Verdolini, K., Rosen, C.A., Branski, R.C., Andrews, M.L.: Classification Manual for Voice Disorders-I, 1st edn. Lawrence Erlbaum Assoc., Mahwah (2006)
16. Schlotthauer, G., Torres, M.E., Jackson-Menaldi, C.: Automatic diagnosis of pathological voices. WSEAS Trans. on Signal Proc. 2, 1260–1267 (2006) (And references therein)
17. Kay Elemetrics Corp.: Disordered voice database 1.03. Mass. Eye and Ear Infirmary, Voice and Speech Lab, Boston (1994)
18. Jackson-Menaldi, M.C.: La voz patológica. In: Editorial Médica Panamericana, Buenos Aires (2002)
19. Flandrin, P., Rilling, G., Gonçalvès, P.: Empirical mode decomposition as a filter bank. Signal Proc. Lett., IEEE 11(2), 112–114 (2004)
20. Shannon, C.E.: A mathematical theory of communication. Bell Syst. Tech. J. 27, 379–423, 623–656 (1948)
21. Papoulis, A.: Probability, Random Variables and Stochastic Processes, 3rd edn. McGraw-Hill Companies, New York (1991)
22. Maragos, P., Kaiser, J., Quatieri, T.: Energy separation in signal modulations with application to speech analysis. IEEE Trans. on Signal Proc. 41(10), 3024–3051 (1993)
23. Diaz, M., Esteller, R.: Comparison of the non linear energy operator and the hilbert transform in the estimation of the instantaneous amplitude and frequency. Latin Am. Trans., IEEE (Revista IEEE America Latina) 5(1), 1–8 (2007)
24. Talkin, D.: A robust algorithm for pitch tracking (RAPT). In: Speech Coding and Synth., pp. 121–173. Elsevier Science, Amsterdam (1995)
25. Boersma, P.: Accurate short-term analysis of the fundamental frequency and the harmonics-to-noise ratio of a sampled sound. In: Proc. of the Inst. of Phonetic Sci., vol. 17, pp. 97–110 (1993)
26. Jang, S., Choi, S., Kim, H., Choi, H., Yoon, Y.: Evaluation of performance of several established pitch detection algorithms in pathological voices. In: Proc. 29th Annual Intern. Conf. of the IEEE Eng. in Med. and Biol. Soc., vol. 2007, pp. 620–623 (2007) PMID: 18002032
27. Goddard, J., Schlotthauer, G., Torres, M.E., Rufiner, H.L.: Dimensionality reduction for visualization of normal and pathological speech data. Biomed. Sig. Proc. and Control 4, 194–201 (2009)

Disfluencies and the Perspective
of Prosodic Fluency

Helena Moniz[1,2], Isabel Trancoso[2,3], and Ana Isabel Mata[1]

[1] Faculdade de Letras da Universidade de Lisboa (FLUL), Centro de Linguística da Universidade de Lisboa (CLUL), Alameda da Universidade, 1600-214, Portugal
[2] INESC-ID, Rua Alves Redol, 9, 1000-029, Lisboa, Portugal
[3] Instituto Superior Técnico, Universidade Técnica de Lisboa, Lisboa, Portugal
{helena.moniz,isabel.trancoso}@inesc-id.pt,
aim@fl.ul.pt

Abstract. This work explores prosodic cues of disfluent phenomena. We have conducted a perceptual experiment to test if listeners would rate all disfluencies as disfluent events or if some of them would be rated as fluent devices in specific prosodic contexts. Results pointed out significant differences ($p < 0.05$) between judgments of fluency *vs.* disfluency. Distinct prosodic properties of these events were also significant ($p < 0.05$) in their characterization as fluent devices. In an attempt to discriminate which linguistic features are more salient in the classification of disfluencies, we have also used CART techniques on a corpus of 3.5 hours of spontaneous and prepared non-scripted speech. CART results pointed out 2 splits: break indices and contour shape. The first split indicates that disfluent events uttered at breaks 3 and 4 are considered felicitous. The second one indicates that these events must have plateau or ascending contours to be considered as such; otherwise they are strongly penalized. The results obtained show that there are regular trends in the production of disfluencies, namely, prosodic phrasing and contour shape.

Keywords: Disfluencies, fluency ratings, prosody, perception and production.

1 Introduction

Disfluencies, e.g., filled pauses, prolongations, repetitions, substitutions, deletions, insertions, characterize spontaneous speech and play a major role in speech structuring [1], [2], [3], and [4]. For speech processing, the analysis of the regular patterns of those phenomena is crucial [5] and [6]. In automatic speech recognition (ASR), their identification accounts for more robust language and acoustic models [7] and even in text to speech synthesis (TTS) these phenomena are being modeled to improve the naturalness of synthetic speech [8]. Moreover, when combining ASR and TTS with speech-to-speech translation systems, spontaneous speech translation still needs substantial improvements [9]. Recent studies in psycholinguistics (e.g., [10]) have also targeted the relation of non-verbal communication (gestures) with silent and filled pauses, highlighting the

A. Esposito et al. (Eds.): COST 2102 Int. Training School 2009, LNCS 5967, pp. 382–396, 2010.

pragmatic and semantic similarities between them. The multifaceted analysis of filled pauses can also be accounted for on an emotion oriented perspective, such as in [11].

There are two main perspectives in the literature to describe disfluencies: i) as speech errors that disrupt *the ideal delivery of speech* or ii) as fluent linguistic material used to manage speech. For a survey on these, the study by [12] provides answers to the question raised by the authors: "What are fillers really good for?". As this study highlights, fillers may be used for different purposes related with, e.g., speech structuring [4], introducing new information [13] and producing fluent strategies in second language learning [14]. The fluent component of these phenomena is still rather controversial, even though [15], [2] and [16] have already pointed out the benefits of disfluencies for communicative purposes, and their contribution for on-line planning efforts. Moreover, crosslinguistic studies of filled pauses have pointed out language universal and language specific regularities [2], [17], [18], both segmental and prosodic. As in [2], we concentrate on phenomena which indicate "normal spontaneous management of speech": *"(self-)repairs", "(self-)correction", "hesitation phenomena", "(self-)repetition", "(self-)reformulation", "substitution" and "editing"*.

Taking this into account, can we say that all disfluencies behave alike? What linguistic features (syntactic, prosodic, morphological) play a major role in the production of disfluencies? Are disfluencies really disfluent when they have pragmatic and metalinguistic functions (on-line planning, lexical search, connecting ideas and speech structuring)? Are disfluencies really linguistic material to be deleted in order to obtain the intended message, as in a scripted version of speech, when they may in fact structure spontaneous speech?

In the literature there are clear steps forward in the description of disfluencies as *normal spontaneous management of speech*, but little is said about their linguistic properties, more specifically, their prosodic properties. Our study aims at analysing and contributing to this description.

1.1   Definitions of Fluency

The notion of fluency[1] covers a wide set of different aspects both in a first language (L1) as well as in a second language (L2) - e.g., oral proficiency, adaptation to different communicative contexts, mastering linguistic structures in a target language, *inter alia*. In one of the first studies describing fluency [20], it is described as a satellite concept with four dimensions: i) the temporal dimension, i. e., to keep the speech flowing; ii) the syntactic and semantic dimension, concerning the coherence and logic of speech; iii) the sociopragmatic dimension, that is, the appropriate uses of speech in different communicative contexts; and iv) the creativity one, i. e., to make conscious use of language and to explore a more metaphorical trend in it. We could state, then, that fluency is the effective way we use language, with respect to all modules of grammar. As synthesized by [21], "a working definition of fluency might be *the rapid, smooth,*

---

[1] For a more detailed analysis, *vide* [19] and references therein.

accurate, lucid, and efficient translation of thought or communicative intention into language under the temporal constraints of on-line processing. This concept of fluency is applicable in principle to both monolinguals and multilinguals, to native speakers and learners". To what extent does this *working definition of fluency* includes/excludes disfluencies, is still unclear.

The study by [22] pointed out the importance of prosody for the characteristics of fluent speech. The author analysed informal dialogues between native and non-native speakers of English and concluded that the most fluent strategies are related with phrasing and boundary tones. Therefore, the more fluent speakers do not interrupt their speech on a word by word basis, they respect prosodic constituents cohesion, and use boundary tones that indicate continuation meaning (e.g., plateaus with filled pauses). In line with [22] findings, we aim at analysing the influence of phrasing and contour type on fluency/disfluency distinctions.

1.2   Preliminary Studies on Disfluencies for European Portuguese

Silent and filled pauses in European Portuguese (EP) were first studied by [23]. Its main focus was the temporal organization of discourse and the syntactic distribution of silent and filled pauses. Based on reading and spontaneous speech data, the author pointed out that, as expected, filled pauses were only uttered in spontaneous speech, making them speech style discriminating events. The syntactic distribution of silent and filled pauses was also accounted as a distinctive feature. Filled pauses were mainly uttered within a phrase, while silent pauses had two different patterns: in the reading corpus they were essentially located at syntactically higher positions, i. e., sentences and clauses; and in the spontaneous data at or within phrase boundaries.

In EP the first study to present the relative frequency of different disfluency types, their distribution, the way they may associate with each other, and with different intonational and durational patterns was the one by [24]. Filled pauses and segmental prolongations have also been detailed in [25] and [26].

The definition of filled pauses does not seem to be ambiguous across languages, corresponding to elongated segments (in EP, [ɒː]; [əː]; [iː]; [mː] or one of these vowels with the nasal coda [m], like [ɒːm]).

In EP, as in other languages, final lengthening is a cue for intonational phrase boundaries ([27], [28] and [29]). These are not the elongations accounted for in this work. The prolongations that we have been studying are mainly elongated functional words (e.g., conjunctions and prepositions, such as [iː], *e - and*; [kɨː], *que - that*; [dɨː], *de - of*) that appear in contexts where a strong reduction or a deletion are the expected processes in EP. We also have been analysing lexical/functional words elongated in sequences with self repairs or with additional clarifications. Both of them can be automatically identified by comparing the relative durations of the same words or segments in fluent contexts for the same speaker. Prolongations, thus, seem to also have restructuring and planning functions that should be accounted for.

Different disfluency types tend to occur in different prosodic contexts. Prosodic studies for EP ([30], [27], [28], [29], [31], [32], and [33]) have pointed out the need for at least two levels of phrasing, major and minor intonational phrases (IP). The main distinction is that major IP shows a wider pitch range and bigger final lengthening than the minor IP boundary, indicating (as pointed out by [29] and [32]) that these constituents correspond to boundaries with different strength. These two levels of boundary strength are marked with 3 (minor IP) and 4 (major IP), as in ToBI [34].

In our work we have been using break indices 3 and 4 as well. In spontaneous data, the break index 3 seems crucial to account for sentence internal chunks, advantageous for the description of disfluencies, and the way they relate to adjacent prosodic constituents. Moreover, in the joint attempt to propose a ToBI system for European Portuguese [32], the authors working with professional reading and spontaneous speech data pointed out the importance of having the break index 3 as well. The use of a common system of annotation is also beneficial for comparison with other languages, aiming at a cross-linguistic validation of the behaviour of the so called disfluencies.

Different filled pauses, for instance, tend to occur in different prosodic contexts: (i) *aam* generally occurs at major intonational phrase boundaries, (ii) *aa* is most likely found at minor intonational phrase boundaries; (iii) *mm* occurs mainly in coda position (e.g., [quːm], [ɒːm]). Segmental prolongations are more likely found at internal clause boundaries and at intonational phrase boundaries, behaving as *aa*. Previous studies also pointed out that filled pauses are uttered mainly with plateau contours or with gradual descending contours, whereas segmental prolongations exhibit more complex F0 contours.

Silent pauses are consistently used as a cue to either automatically recognize disfluencies [35] or to analyse their psycholinguistic implications [1], [4]. Our previous study [36] pointed out that more than 80% of prolongations and filled pauses are followed by silent pauses of a reasonable length, supporting the view that their presence may effectively be used by listeners as a cue to an upcoming delay. The absence of such a pause is strongly penalized as misleading information.

1.3   Objectives

The aim of this paper is to validate the assumption that prosodic phrasing is crucial to perform a fluency/disfluency rating task, a view supported both by a perceptual experiment as well as by Classification and Regression Trees techniques (CART) [37]. Our concrete goal in this work is to find out what linguistic features are more salient when we classify all types of disfluencies as either fluent or disfluent phenomena. We want to quantify and progressively find thresholds to differentiate fluency from disfluency, and this task is harder than it seems, since fluency is a complex notion, and not even expert annotators can objectively state that the prosodic behaviour is more salient than the morphosyntactic or semantic ones.

This paper is organized as follows: section 2 is dedicated to the description of the corpora used and to the annotation guidelines. The analysis of the perceptual test and of CART results will be detailed in sections 3 and 4, respectively. Finally, in section 5 we will point out our conclusions and future work.

2 Corpora

This work uses subsets of the CPE-FACES [28] and LECTRA [38] corpora. CPE-FACES stands for Corpus of European Portuguese Spoken by Adolescents in School Context. It includes spontaneous and prepared non-scripted speech at high school (two teachers and twenty five students), totaling 15h, all orthographically transcribed. The prepared non-scripted speech corresponds to oral presentations about a book the students have read, according to specific programmatic guidelines, whereas in the spontaneous ones they were unexpectedly asked to speak about a pleasant personal experience.

The corpus collected within the LECTRA project aimed at transcribing university lectures for e-learning applications, namely, making the transcribed lectures available for hearing impaired students. The corpus has a total of 74.7h and corresponds to 5 different courses[2], of which only 10h were orthographically transcribed.

For the present work, we use subsets of these corpora manually annotated in a more detailed way for disfluencies and fluency ratings: 2h, for the high school corpus, and 1.5h for the university one. The subcorpus of the high school presentations was selected with the purpose of mirroring different levels of proficiency at the end of compulsory schooling (14-15 years old) and it also accounts for the production of one of the high school teachers. The subset of the university lectures was selected with similar criteria in mind.

2.1 Annotation

The multilayer manual annotation comprehends the orthographic transcription, the disfluent description, the prosodic annotation and the syntactic annotation. A full report on this can be found in [24] and [38]. The disfluency tier was annotated accordingly to [6] and [39]. We added the category "prolongation" following the latter study. Procedurally, prolongations can be measured and compared with the same linguistic material in other locations. In EP, prolongations in the sense of management of speech are often related with specific lexical items, e. g., functional words with elongated vowels in a context where we would expect reduction or elision of those vowels. In our previous studies we have found that we may also have lexical words prolongated with two effects: prolongation affecting more than the last syllable of the word and final lengthening corresponding to an interval ≥ than 1 second.

Additional tiers were added with prosodic information (break indices, contour shape and F0 restart), part of speech information (POS of the disfluency and adjacent words) and fluent/disfluent judgments. These judgments were done by the first author of this work and then a randomly selected sample of the first corpus was also annotated by two other expert linguists, in terms of ease of expression, as felicitous or infelicitous. The agreement between the three annotators was of 95%.

---

[2] Two other courses are currently being annotated.

The disfluency rate is 13.2% (1569 disfluencies and 11,851 words) in the high school corpus for the teacher and the four students. If we consider only the teachers from both corpora, the high school teacher has 7.0% of disfluencies, whereas the university teacher has 3.2%. Both values are in line with findings by [40], who reported an interval of 5% to 10% in human-human conversation and also with [41], who reported an average of 6% for other languages.

3   Perceptual Test

We have conducted a perceptual experiment with 40 subjects, regarding fluency/disfluency judgments [24], [25]. We have selected 30 stimuli from the high school subset with different disfluencies in different prosodic contexts and also with baselines for all the speakers. The guidelines given for the task were: *the excerpts you are about to listen were extracted from oral school presentations and uttered by four speakers: a teacher and three students. Listening to the stimuli we can say that there are moments of ease of expression as well as moments without this characteristic. Help us in identifying both moments, scoring the excerpts you are about to listen in the scale presented.* The following five-point scale was used: (1) very bad; (2) infelicitous; (3) acceptable; (4) good or (5) excellent/very good.

Aiming at a more detailed analysis of the experimental results, we have undertaken a statistical analysis. Figure 1 shows the median values scored for each type of disfluency and the standard deviation values.

As figure 1 shows, the events corresponding to values ≥ 3.0 are: filled pauses (FP), prolongations (PRL), substitutions (SUB), and deletions (DEL). Participants scored fragments (FRAG), complex disfluencies (VARIA) and more than two repeated elements (REPs) with scores under the median value of 3.0, the last one being the most penalized. Above a median value of 3.5, only two types of events clearly emerge: single filled pauses and prolongations (PRL and PRLs, for single and two consecutive prolongations, respectively). The implications of such a partition are quite interesting from a psycholinguistic point of view as well as from a generation of natural speech perspective. The events grouped as disfluent pose more comprehension difficulties whereas the most fluent ones do not, e.g., vocalized elongated material. If we cluster them into classes, we would distinguish the disrupting ones from those that behave as sustained supported linguistic material.

We did not predict, however, to have a single REP more penalized than a single DEL based on [41] and also on the validation of the annotator's rates by two expert linguists. In [41], the author pointed out that, in the experiments that she had undertaken, repetitions did not disturb the understanding of the subsequent units while deletions did. We should say, though, that the examples of deletion we have used were uttered after a prosodic break 4, had F0 restart, and a plateau contour (H* H-L%). This plateau contour is the same found in filled pauses considered fluent as well as in prolongations. For the time being, we just want to point out that the participants in the perceptual experiment seem more sensitive to the prosodic properties than to the specific type of disfluency.

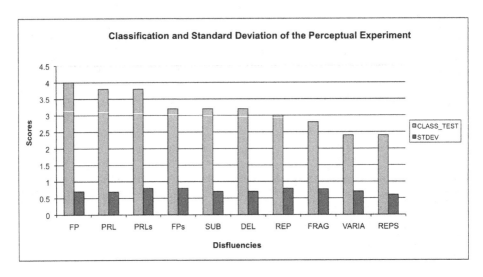

Fig. 1. Median values for disfluencies scores and standard deviation

The difference between the scores considered fluent (above 3) and the scores considered disfluent (below 3) was significant ($p < 0.05$), with Mann-Whitney U-test, so was the difference between distinct types of disfluencies. Distinct prosodic contexts were also significant: i) the difference between disfluent events produced at break indices 4 (scored as fluent) and the ones uttered within an intonational phrase (scored as disfluent); ii) the difference between disfluent events with plateau contours *vs.* events with descending ones. The prosodic conditions with the highest median scores are those that match the following properties: disfluencies uttered at break index 4, with F0 restart and plateau contours.

3.1   Discussion

Filled pauses, prolongations and repetitions have been considered by [42] and [4] as associated to planning efforts. In corpora of school presentations and lectures, which are intrinsically associated with clarifying messages and planning carefully what to say next, these types of disfluencies are thus worth studying in detail. Figure 2 shows a stylization in semitones (ST) for each disfluency, and its prosodic context, in the stimuli used in the perceptual test. For each stimulus, we have plotted the onset, maximum and offset values of the disfluent event (Onset_U, Max_U, Offset_U); the maximum and the offset values of the previous constituent (Max_Prev, Offset_Prev); and the onset and maximum values of the subsequent prosodic constituent (Onset_Next, Max_Next). The F0 measurements are not represented in the real temporal intervals.

As figure 2 shows, prolongations judged felicitous exhibit F0 ascending contours with high sustained boundary tones, typically observed at the end of a

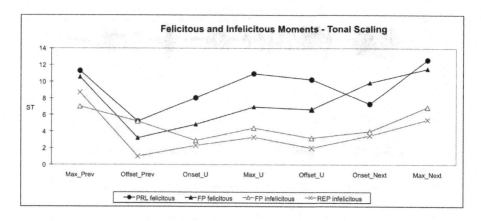

Fig. 2. Tonal scaling of prolongations, filled pauses, and repetitions

prosodic constituent with continuation meaning. Filled pauses also judged fluent are uttered in a tonal space in between the prosodic adjacent constituents, have plateau contours and behave mostly as parentheticals. When filled pauses are considered infelicitous, they are produced in a lower register with descending contours, disrupting tonal scaling. As for repetitions, the examples that we have tested were prosodically ill-formed and considered disfluent (e.g., lexical and function words repeated), we did not include emphatic repetitions. The disfluent repetitions behave mostly as disfluent filled pauses, but were preceded by strong melodic breaks.

Figures 3 and 4 show examples of stimuli of the perceptual test judged felicitous and infelicitous, respectively. The examples were done using Praat [43] and Pauline Welby's scripts [44][3].

Figure 3 represents a felicitous example of a filled pause [ɒː] (*aa*, uh) uttered at a break 4 with a plateau contour. This filled pause introduces a new topic of discussion in the teacher's presentation. The filled pause can be described as a hold while the speaker is planning/structuring her next topic.

An example judged disfluent is illustrated in figure 4, where the verb [s'õw̃] (*são*, are) is repeated. As in the first example, the repetition by itself forms a prosodic constituent, in this specific case with a descending contour. The unit disrupts the F0 global contour, and consequently the scaling between peaks.

The results shown in Figure 2 partially agree with the ones of [45] and [46], in the way that filled pauses have linear and gradual F0 descending contours. However, in our data, they may exhibit ascending or plateau contours as well. As pointed out by [46], filled pauses tend to be uttered between the previous peak and the baseline of the speaker. A result that was also observed in our data is that these events are uttered at a tonal space in between adjacent prosodic constituents.

---

[3] These scripts may draw the F0 contour in unvoiced portions of the signal.

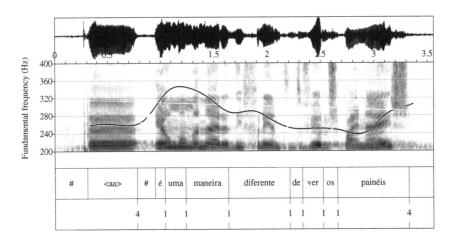

Fig. 3. Felicitous example: "aa é uma maneira diferente de ver os painéis" (uh it is a different way to see the panels)

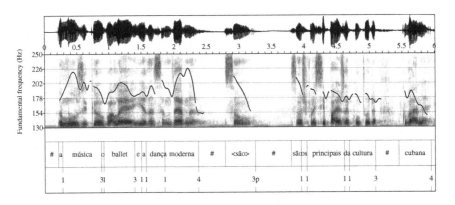

Fig. 4. Infelicitous example: "a música o ballet e a dança moderna são são os principais da cultura cubana" (music, ballet, and modern dance are are the principal [aspects] of cuban culture)

The intonational pattern (H) H+L* L% accounts for neutral declaratives in EP, e.g. [29]. When this pattern is associated with uncommon phrasing options it promotes judgments of disfluency, such as the ones exemplified in figure 4. Non-falling, continuation meaning or plateau contours are, otherwise, the ones most ajustable to managing speech, since they clearly indicate cohesion between units and are therefore more consentaneous with speech structuring as a whole. We could ultimatelly say that they may be judged as felicitously integrated if they are adjusted to the adjacent prosodic units and jointly make a cohesive structure.

The segmental and suprasegmental characteristics of disfluencies, some idiosyncratic and some general, may be seen as contributions for the discussion of their classification as regular words and for the possible delimitation of these phenomena as intonational phrases, when they do not coarticulate with the previous word. These important phonetic and prosodic cues used by speakers to signal managing strategies at different levels of the prosodic structure may be used to identify disfluencies in automatic speech recognition applications.

In previous work [25], we have pointed out that segmental prolongations do not seem to undergo regular external sandhi processes for EP. One of these processes occurs when the first word ends in a consonant /s/, phonetically realized as [z] when the following word starts with a vowel. In connected speech the regular behaviour would be to produce [z] before the vowel, as in [d'uɐz 'al mɐʃ] "duas almas" *two souls* (example extracted from [47]). In prolongations of words ending in /s/, a different behaviour was observed. As an example, take the adversative conjunction "mas" *but*. When the vowel [iː] is appended as a prolongation, it is often pronounced as [mɐʒiː] instead of [mɐziː].

For filled pauses produced within an intonational phrase, these findings seem to hold as well as for our present data. Examples such as "efeitos especiais aa" *special effects uh*, with no silent pause or glottalization interval between the second word and the filled pause, are pronounced as [ʃ] instead of [z] ([if'ɐjtuz iʃpɨsj'ajʃ ɐː]). The regular external sandhi process is applied in the coarticulation of the first two words, but not between the last one and the filled pause [ɐː].

The implications of these processes and their relationship to the prosodic structure are still a matter for further study. For the time being we want to stress that different strategies may be used by speakers: regarding intonational aspects, disfluencies may behave like other prosodic units in similar prosodic contexts, but prolongations and filled pauses have ways to be distinguished from the rest of the segmental material.

4   CART Experiment

Our CART experiment was conducted using the SAS software[4]. We started by dividing the annotated data into training, validation and test data (60%, 20% and 20%, respectively). In our data, 56.4% of disfluencies were manually classified as disfluent and the remaining 43.6% as fluent events. The features used were: judgments of fluency/disfluency (as target feature), break indices, F0 contour, F0 restart, morphosyntactic information of the adjacent words, morphosyntactic information of the disfluency (including whether it corresponds to a sentence internal chunk or a complete sentence), speaker and speech situation (spontaneous and prepared non-scripted speech).

The first split in the tree is on the variable break indices. This variable allows the distinction between disfluencies uttered within a prosodic constituent (classified most often as infelicitous), and at break indices 3 and 4 (classified as felicitous). Within a constituent, 78.3% of these events are infelicitous, and the

---

[4] http://www.sas.com

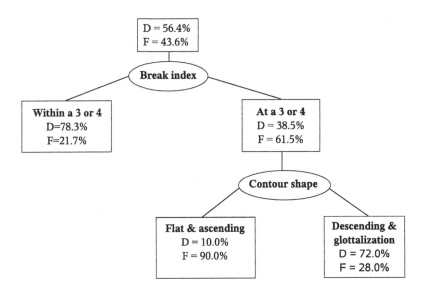

Fig. 5. CART results: D stands for disfluent/infelicitous, and F for fluent/felicitous classification

remaining 21.7% are classified as fluent devices. The latter (21.7%) are uttered either at the onset of an intonational phrase and have F0 restart (10.4%), or at the end of a constituent with boundary tones that signal continuation (break 3) or finality (break 4), as in neutral statements in European Portuguese.

The second split in the tree (F0 contours) shows that events produced at breaks 3 or 4 with plateau or rising contours are mainly considered fluent (90%) *vs.* the ones uttered in similar positions, but with descendent contours or with glottalization effects (72%).

In a second experiment, we withdrew the main feature (break indices) and retrained the tree. This would enable us to use mostly features that are more easily extracted in an automatic way. The retrained decision tree pointed out that if the F0 contour is a plateau or a rising contour and the morphosyntactic information accounts for completed chunks, then 88.7% of the events were considered fluent. If the disfluent sequence has F0 restart, then it is fluent 70.7% of the cases. Without F0 restart and with descending contours, the events are classified as disfluent 95.3%. Moreover, with glotallization effects and also with no F0 restart they are classified as disfluent in 80.0% of the cases.

The test misclassification rate in the first experiment was 29.05% and in the second, 32.9%, when accounting for the six most important leaves. In both experiments the classification of disfluencies is above chance level.

In both experiments we would expect that the duration feature would be selected from the first splits, as it was shown by [48], though this was not the case. Only when we consider 12 leaves then duration does play a role, but the importance of that feature is not above chance level. In future work we intend to discriminate the classification by type of disfluency and check whether this feature may play a more salient role in the classification of disfluencies, as demonstrated by [48].

Summing up, the binary partition of fluent *vs.* disfluent events is discriminated based on prosodic features, specifically prosodic phrasing and F0 contour.

5 Conclusions and Future Work

Previous sections have shown that prosodic phrasing is crucial to perform an evaluation task regarding fluency/disfluency distinctions, but contour shape also plays an important role in this kind of task. Both the perceptual experiments and the CART pointed out that disfluencies may behave and even be rated as fluent devices. Results suggest, in line with findings for other languages, that speakers control different segmental and suprasegmental aspects, and they seem to do it, in many cases, in a *surgical* way - adequately adjusting to the adjacent constituents.

This work may be seen as a rehearsal for a more detailed study, aiming at the discrimination between fluent and disfluent phenomena in spontaneous and prepared non-scripted speech, based on larger corpora for EP.

The fluent component of these communicative devices poses a terminology problem - should we continue to call them disfluencies, a term widely used by the scientific community, when they behave fluently in certain contexts? Our work pointed in the opposite direction, and we would like to extend it, namely with more data. Another research direction is to analyse all the segmental and suprasegmental cues of all types of disfluencies in order to automatically identify them. We also want to analyse the different pragmatic functions they may have. For instance, in our current data, filled pauses often precede new information or computer jargon translations into EP. The communicative devices we have been describing seem, thus, to be uttered at different levels of the prosodic structure, and these levels may be associated with different pragmatic functions.

By bringing empirical evidence supporting regularities at different levels which are crucial to a better understanding of the *grammar of talk* - we aim at contributing to a characterization of the so called disfluencies in EP. Despite the growing interest for such phenomena in recent years, both of the linguistic and of language engineering communities, there is still much work to be done.

Acknowledgments

The authors would like to thank Professor Julia Hirschberg for her scientific generosity and our reviewers for many helpful comments. They would also want to thank Tiago Luís for his technical support and our two colleagues, Vera Cabarrão and Aida Cardoso, who annotated the university lectures. This work was partially supported by COST Action 2102: "Cross Modal Analysis of Verbal and Nonverbal Communication", FCT projects PTDC/PLP/72404/2006, and CMU-PT/HuMach/0039/2008. The PhD thesis of Helena Moniz is supported by FCT grant SFRH/BD/44671/2008.

References

1. Levelt, W.: Speaking. MIT Press, Cambridge (1989)
2. Allwood, J., Nivre, J., Ahlsén, E.: Sppech management - on the non-written life of speech. Nordic Journal of Linguistics 13 (1990)
3. Swerts, M.: Filled pauses as markers of discourse structure. Journal of Pragmatics 30, 485–496 (1998)
4. Clark, H., Fox Tree, J.: Using uh and um in spontaneous speaking. Cognition 84 (2002)
5. Nakatani, C., Hirschberg, J.: A corpus-based study of repair cues in spontaneous speech. Journal of the Acoustical Society of America (JASA) 95, 1603–1616 (1994)
6. Shriberg, E.: Preliminaries to a Theory of Speech Disfluencies. PhD thesis, University of California (1994)
7. Liu, Y., Shriberg, E., Stolcke, A., Hillard, D., Ostendorf, M., Harper, M.: Enriching speech recognition with automatic detection of sentence boundaries and disfluencies. IEEE Transaction on Audio, Speech, and Language Processing 14, 1526–1540 (2006)
8. Adell, J., Bonafonte, A., Escudero-Mancebo, D.: On the generation of synthetic disfluent speech: local prosodic modifications caused by the insertion of editing terms. In: Proc. Interspeech 2008, Brisbane, Australia (September 2008)
9. Tomokiyo, L., Peterson, K., Black, A., Lenzo, K.: Intelligibility of machine translation output in speech synthesis. In: Proc. Interspeech 2006, Pittsburgh, USA (September 2006)
10. Esposito, A., Marinaro, M.: What pauses can tell us about speech and gesture partnership. In: Esposito, A., Bratanic, M., Keller, E., Marinaro, M. (eds.) Fundamentals of Verbal and Nonverbal Communication and the Biometric Issue, pp. 45–57. IOS Press, Amsterdam (2007)
11. Benus, S., Enos, F., Hirschberg, J., Shriberg, E.: Pauses in deceptive speech. In: Speech Prosody Conference (2006)
12. O'Connell, D., Kowal, S.: Communicating with one another - towards a psychology of spontaneous spoken discourse. Springer, New York (2008)
13. Arnold, J., Fagnano, M., Tanenhaus, M.: Disfluencies signal theee, um, new information. Journal of Psycholinguistic Research 32 (2003)
14. Rose, R.: The communicative value of filled pauses in spontaneous speech. PhD thesis, University of Birmingham, UK (1998)
15. Heike, A.: A content-processing view of hesitation phenomena. Language and Speech 24 (1981)
16. O'Connell, D., Kowal, S.: Uh and um revisited: are they interjections for signaling delay? Psycholinguistic Research 34 (2005)
17. Eklund, R., Shriberg, E.: Crosslinguistic disfluency modeling: a comparative analysis of swedish and american english human-human and human-machine dialogs. In: International Conference on Spoken Language Processing, Sydney, Australia (1998)
18. Vasilescu, I., Adda-decker, M.: A cross-language study of acoustic and prosodic characteristics of vocalic hesitations. In: Esposito, A., Bratanic, M., Keller, E., Marinaro, M. (eds.) Fundamentals of Verbal and Nonverbal Communication and the Biometric Issue, pp. 140–148. IOS Press, Amsterdam (2007)
19. Koponen, M., Riggenbach, H.: Perspectives on Fluency. University of Michigan Press, Michigan (2000)

20. Fillmore, C.J.: On fluency. In: Kempler, D., Wang, W. (eds.) Individual Differences in Language Ability and Language Behavior, pp. 85–102. Academic Press, London (1979)

21. Lennon, P.: The lexical element in spoken second language fluency. In: Koponen, M., Riggenbach, H. (eds.) Perspectives on Fluency, pp. 25–42. University of Michigan Press (2000)

22. Wennerstrom, A.: The role of intonation in second language fluency. In: Koponen, M., Riggenbach, H. (eds.) Perspectives on Fluency, pp. 102–127. University of Michigan Press (2000)

23. Freitas, M.J.: Estratégias de organização temporal do discurso. Master's thesis, University of Lisbon (1990)

24. Moniz, H.: Contributo para a caracterização dos mecanismos de (dis)fluência no Português Europeu. Master's thesis, University of Lisbon (2006)

25. Moniz, H., Mata, A.I., Viana, M.C.: On filled pauses and prolongations in European Portuguese. In: Proc. Interspeech 2007, Antwerp, Belgium (September 2007)

26. Moniz, H., Mata, A.I., Viana, M.C.: Mecanismos de (dis)fluência em contexto escolar. In: Frota, S., Santos, A.L. (eds.) XXIII Encontro Nacional da Associação Portuguesa de Línguística, pp. 329–343. Associação Portuguesa de Linguística (2008)

27. Falé, I.: Fragmento da prosódia do português europeu: as estruturas coordenadas. Master's thesis, University of Lisbon (1995)

28. Mata, A.I.: Para o Estudo da Entoação em Fala Espontânea e Preparada no Português Europeu. PhD thesis, University of Lisbon (1999)

29. Frota, S.: Prosody and Focus in European Portuguese. In: Phonological Phrasing and Intonation. Garland Publishing, New York (2000)

30. Viana, M.C.: Para a Síntese da Entoação do Português. PhD thesis, University of Lisbon (1987)

31. Vigário, M.: The prosodic word in European Portuguese. Mouton de Gruyter, Berlin (2003)

32. Viana, M.C., Frota, S., Falé, I., Mascarenhas, I., Mata, A.I., Moniz, H., Vigário, M.: Towards a p_tobi. In: Unpublished Workshop of the Transcription of Intonation in the Ibero-Romance Languages, PaPI 2007 (2007),
    http://www2.ilch.uminho.pt/eventos/PaPI2007/
    Extended-Abstract-P-ToBI.PDF

33. Frota, S.: The intonotional phonology of european portuguese. In: Sun-uh (ed.) Prosodic Typology II. Oxford University Press, Oxford (2009)

34. Silverman, K., Beckman, M., Pitrelli, J., Ostendorf, M., Wightman, C., Price, P., Pierrehumbert, J., Hirschberg, J.: Tobi: a standard for labeling english prosody. In: International Conference on Spoken Language Processing, Banff, Canada (1992)

35. Stolcke, A., Shriberg, E., Bates, T., Ostendorf, M., Hakkani, D., Plauché, M., Tür, G., Lu, Y.: Automatic detection of sentence boundaries and disfluencies based on recognized words. In: International Conference on Spoken Language Processing, pp. 2247–2250 (1998)

36. Moniz, H., Mata, A.I., Trancoso, I., Viana, M.C.: How can we use disfluencies and still sound as a good speaker? In: Proc. Interspeech 2008, Brisbane, Australia (September 2008)

37. Breiman, L., Friedman, J., Olshen, R., Stone, C.: Classification and Regression Trees. Wadsworth and Brooks, Pacific Grove (1984)

38. Trancoso, I., Martins, R., Moniz, H., Mata, A.I., Viana, M.C.: The lectra corpus - classroom lecture transcriptions in european portuguese. In: LREC 2008 - Language Resources and Evaluation Conference, Marrakesh, Morocco (May 2008)

39. Eklund, R.: Disfluency in Swedish Human-Human and Human-Machine Travel Booking Dialogues. PhD thesis, University of Linkopink (2004)

40. Shriberg, E.: To "errrr" is human: ecology and acoustics of speech disfluencies. Journal of the International Phonetic Association 31, 153–169 (2001)

41. Fox Tree, J.: Pronouncing "the" as "thee" to signal problems in speaking. Cognition 62, 151–167 (1995)

42. Clark, H., Wasow, T.: Repeating words in spontaneous speech. Cognitive Psychology 37 (1998)

43. Boersma, P., Weenink, D.: Praat: doing phonetics by computer, version 5.1.20

44. Welby, P.: The slaying of Lady Mondegreen, being a study of French tonal association and alignment and their role in speech segmentation. PhD thesis, Ohio State University (2003)

45. O'Shaughnessy, D.: Recognition of hesitations in spontaneous speech. In: IEEE Conference on Acoustic, Speech, and Signal Processing, pp. 521–524 (1992)

46. Shriberg, E.: Phonetic consequences of speech disfluency. In: International Congress of Phonetic Sciences, San Francisco, pp. 612–622 (1999)

47. Mateus, M.H., d'Andrade, E.: The Phonology of Portuguese. Oxford University Press, Oxford (2000)

48. Shriberg, E.: A prosody-only decision-tree model for disfluency detection. In: Eurospeech 1997, Rhodes, Greece, pp. 2383–2387 (1997)

Subjective Tests and Automatic Sentence Modality Recognition with Recordings of Speech Impaired Children

David Sztaho, Katalin Nagy, and Klara Vicsi

Laboratory of Speech Acoustics, Budapest University of Technology and Economics,
Department of Telecommunications and Media Informatics,
Stoczek u. 2, 1111 Budapest, Hungary
sztaho@tmit.bme.hu, menjus@gmail.com, vicsi@tmit.bme.hu

Abstract. Prosody recognition experiments have been prepared in the Laboratory of Speech Acoustics, in which, among the others, we were searching for the possibilities of the recognition of sentence modalities. Due to our promising results in the sentence modality recognition, we adopted the method for children modality recognition, and looked for the possibility, how it can be used as an automatic feedback in an audio - visual pronunciation teaching and training system. Our goal was to develop a sentence intonation teaching and training system for speech handicapped children, helping them to learn the correct prosodic pronunciation of sentence. HMM models of modality types were built by training the recognizer with a correctly speaking children database. During the present work, a large database was collected from speech impaired children. Subjective tests were carried out with this database of speech impaired children, in order to examine how human listeners are able to categorize the heard recordings of sentence modalities. Then automatic sentence modality recognition experiments were done with the formerly trained HMM models. By the result of the subjective tests, the probability of acceptance of the sentence modality recognizer can be adjusted. Comparing the result of the subjective tests and the results of the automatic sentence modality recognition tests processed on the database of speech impaired children, it is showed that the automatic recognizer classified the recordings more strictly, but not worse. The introduced method could be implemented as a part of a speech teaching system.

Keywords: Speech Prosody Recognition, Automatic Speech Recognition, Prosody Database, Speech Technology, Hidden Markov Models.

1 Introduction

The construction of computer aided systems, that improve the quality of speech learning and teaching, became available due to latest results achieved in computer technology and digital speech processing. Speech training methods are especially useful for persons with different kind of speech or hearing diseases. It is most important in case of hard of hearing or deaf children. These children partially or fully can't learn the way of forming correct pronunciation, including not only the phonemes, but also

A. Esposito et al. (Eds.): COST 2102 Int. Training School 2009, LNCS 5967, pp. 397–405, 2010.

larger segmental features, like prosody because of the distortion of auditory feedback. Recently speech technology has appeared in second language learning too. The capabilities of the technology include measuring and displaying the dynamic characteristics of speech parameters, using auditive, visual and automatic feedback [1]. Experiments have shown, that for example a visual F0 display of supra-segmental features combined with audio feedback is more effective than audio feedback alone [2][3], especially if student's F0 contour is displayed along with a reference model.

Our main goal is to develop a speech teaching system for speech handicapped children through a computer-aided system. This way, we are going to teach the correct pronunciation of the different sentence modalities by visual and automatic feedback.

Until now, two main groups of teaching systems exist. One group of these systems takes advantage of the acoustic similarity between the trainee's acoustic production and a template to measure the correctness of trainee's production. In SPECO [4] and ISTRA [5] similar metric was estimated. In the other phoneme-based Hidden Markov Models are applied as an automatic feedback.

In the first part of the paper we give a short description of the former work and research done in the field of modality recognition so far. We introduce the automatic recognition system and the database of healthy children that was used to train and evaluate it. We describe a possible training method tested by a preliminary database of speech impaired children.

Moreover the description of a subjective test follows in order to examine, how the human listeners make decisions when listening to different type of the intonation curves of sentences, pronounced by different pronunciation quality (in the pronunciation of healthy and speech handicapped children). These results then were compared to the automatic recognition results (made with the prosodic children database of speech handicapped children).

2 Sentence Modality Recognition

For sentence modality recognition a formerly developed automatic prosodic classifier was used [6]. This recognition system is based on prosodic Hidden Markov Models. The features used for the training of these prosodic models, and for the recognition are fundamental frequency and energy values, their derivates and second derivates.

The prosodic HMM models were built using HTK toolkit [8]. For the extraction of fundamental frequency and energy values the Snack toolkit [7] was applied (using an auto-correlation pitch determining algorithm for the extraction of fundamental frequency). The calculation was done with 150 ms window size and 10 ms timestep in order to get a smooth pitch-curve. Fundamental frequency values were corrected by antioctave filtering and median filtering.

In order to train and evaluate the automatic recognition system, a database of prosodic sentences were recorded with correctly speaking healthy children. The recordings were classified manually into five intonation classes according to fundamental frequency curves. After annotating all sentences, the average number of samples per each class was 1600. To every HMM model an intonation class was assigned. The classes of intonation and examples are shown in Table 1. After the segmentation of the recordings, evaluation tests were made in order to prove the usefulness of the automatic recognizer. In order to do this, same sentences were selected from each child for every intonation class to model a future real time use. During the tests 70% of the recordings were used as training samples and 30% as test samples. The results of the evaluation tests are shown in Table 2. The second "Falling and Falling-descending" class were originally two different class, but evaluation tests revealed, that they are hardly distinguishable. Therefore they were closed up into one type.

Table 1. Classes of intonation used during the creation of prosodic HMM models

TYPE OF INTONATION	TYPE OF SENTENCE	EXAMPLE	FORM OF INTONATION
Descending (D)	declarative sentence	"David has the croissant."	
Falling and Falling-descending (F-Fd)	question to be complemented, imperative	"Oh, how glad I am!" and "You must stand there too!"	
Ascending-falling (Af)	yes-no questions	"Does he have got the hat??"	
Floating (Fl)	clauses (not closing)	"Anna is standing at the corridor, ..."	
Rising (R)	one word questions (in Hungarian)	"Want some?"	

Table 2. Recognition results with sentence set 1 for reduced class set

	D	F- Fd	Af	Fl	R	CORR [%]
D	42	1	0	0	0	97.7
F-Fd	1	51	5	4	1	82.3
Af	0	0	27	1	1	93.1
Fl	1	1	1	36	0	92.3
R	0	0	0	0	36	100

Another two sentence sets were selected to examine the recognition performance of a more diverse data set in the same way as the first one. Figure 1 shows, how the more diverse training data affects the performance of the recognition. It shows that the best recognition can be achieved by using less diverse training and testing data. Therefore in the real teaching system, only a specific data set should be used at a time.

After the evaluation tests of the prosodic recognition with correctly speaking children, a preliminary sound material of speech impaired children was recorded with two hearing handicapped children by speaking the same sentences as in the case of correctly speaking children. Automatic recognition tests were made to model the real use of the teaching system with this preliminary database of speech impaired children. In Figure 2, there is an example shown, how the recognition system can be used in a real environment. The first fundamental frequency contour is from a healthy child, the second is from a hard of hearing child, and both of them were classified correctly. The third recording is from a hard of hearing child, and the recognizer did not classify it correctly to the same class as the others. The strictness can be adjusted by modifying the probability of the acceptance.

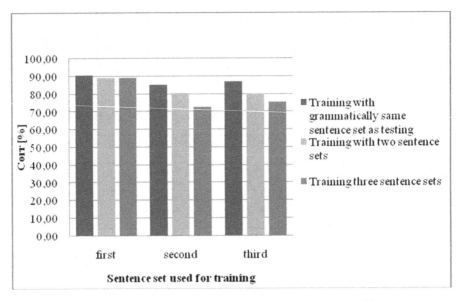

Fig 1. Effect of the diverse training data on automatic recognition

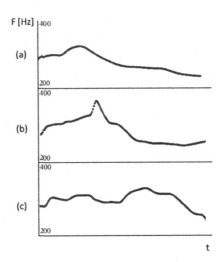

Fig 2. Recognition of the recording of hard of hearing children. (Description: (a) recording from healthy child; (b) a correctly classified recording from hard of hearing child; (c)) a falsely classified recording from hard of hearing child).

3 Subjective tests

In order to carry out subjective tests, a larger database was prepared, which was recorded with 19 speech impaired children with age between 10 and 14. This database of speech impaired children consisted of the same sentences and dialogues as the database of healthy children. But because of the time consuming recording method, due to the pronunciation problems of the hard of hearing children, the sentences of this database were recorded only once.

From the database of the hard of hearing children the sentence sets 1 and 2 were selected as shown in Table 3. This time there was only one representative per child left from each given sentence in the testing set. This resulted about 50 sentences in each sentence set. With these, subjective tests were carried out, in order to examine, how human listeners can classify the recordings. The result of these subjective tests was compared to the recognition result of the above mentioned recognizer.

Table 3. Categories of the subjective tests

Class of the automatic recognition	Sentence set 1	Sentence set 2	Category of the subjective tests
D (Descending - Declarative)	David has got a croissant.	Pete got the hat.	Declarative
F (Falling – Question to be complemented)	Oh, I am so glad!	I wish he was standing there!	Exclamation
Af (Ascending-falling - Yes-no questions)	Does he have the hat?	Did you get a mark in the school today??	Question (complex)
Fd (Falling-descending – Imperative)	You should stand to there, too!	Go here quickly!	Imperative
Fl (Floating - Clause (not closing))	Anne is standing at the corridor, (...)	Anne will go with you, (....)	Clause (not closing)
R (Rising – One word question)	Wants some?	But...?	Question (one word)

For the listening tests a software was used, which was formerly made in the laboratory for subjective tests of earlier research [9] [10]. The user display of the program can be seen in Figure 3. The listening test takes about 15 minutes, therefore the fatigue of the listeners did not disturb the results. The great disadvantage of these tests is that the grammatical information is included in the sentences, which the automatic recognizer did not take into consideration. Therefore there could be some distortion in the results even though every listener was warned to decide clearly by the heard intonation.

21 people carried out the test. Their decisions are shown in Table 4 for all of the recordings, and in Figure 4. The result show that the subjective recognition of declarative and clause (not closing) sentences show divergence from the others. The classification of the clause sentences seemed to be difficult to the listeners. The reason was that to the listeners the difference between a declarative and the clause sentence was not clear. Many clause sentences were identified as declarative. Often the obvious clause sentences (that has rising fundamental frequency at the end) were identified as declarative ones.

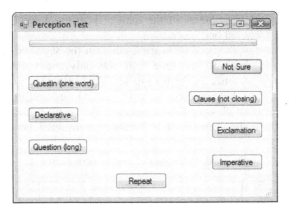

Fig 3. User display of the program used for subjective tests

Table 4. Results of subjective tests in % with both sentence sets 1 and 2

	D	F	Af	Fd	Fl	R	NS (Not Sure)
D	89	1	2	0	6	0	2
F	23	63	1	3	1	0	9
Af	11	1	81	0	0	1	5
Fd	13	5	1	77	0	0	4
Fl	44	1	11	1	35	0	8
R	10	0	0	0	3	80	6

In order to compare the results of subjective tests to the results of automatic recognition, the same classes were also contracted as in the evaluation tests, so the number of classes was the same. The confusion matrices are shown for sentence sets 1 and 2 in the case of human listeners and automatic recognition tests in Table 5 and 6.

In both cases, the human listeners recognized the modalities better. However this does not mean that the automatic recognition is insufficient. As it could be seen during testing the real use of the automatic recognizer, the main goal is not to accept a falsely said sample. Therefore it must be noted, that the automatic recognizer had classified the recordings just more strictly. If we look at only those recordings, that more than 50 percent of the human listeners classified correctly, then only 9 percent of these samples were classified falsely by the automatic recognizer. If this acceptance level is not 50 but 70 percent, the percentage of falsely classified samples by the automatic recognizer is 14 %. It must be added, that more than the half of the falsely classified recordings belong to the clause (not closing) class, which had interpretation problems, as mentioned before. It is also important, that the automatic recognizer does not take the grammatical information into consideration, but the human listeners do.

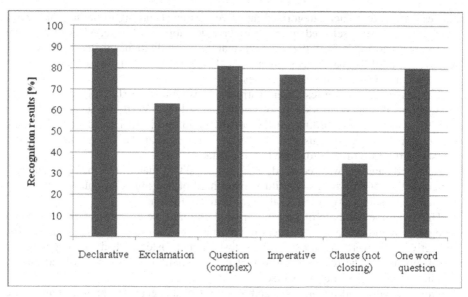

Fig 4. Recognition results of subjective tests

Table 5. Confusion matrix for subjective tests (left) and automatic recognition (right) made with sentence set 1. The results are in %; NS: Not sure.

	D	F-Fd	Af	Fl	R	NS		D	F-Fd	Af	Fl	R
D	90	1	3	3	1	3	D	56	0	0	44	0
F-Fd	17	75	1	1	0	6	F-Fd	5	53	0	42	0
Af	6	1	88	1	2	3	Af	0	14	57	29	0
Fl	44	5	10	32	0	9	Fl	9	27	0	64	0
R	25	2	0	1	64	8	R	0	10	0	20	70

Table 6. Confusion matrix for subjective tests (left) and automatic recognition (right) made with sentence set 2. The results are in %; NS: Not Sure.

	D	F-Fd	Af	Fl	R	NS		D	F-Fd	Af	Fl	R
D	88	1	0	8	0	2	D	10	70	0	20	0
F-Fd	17	75	2	0	0	6	F-Fd	14	71	0	14	0
Af	17	4	72	0	0	7	Af	29	29	43	0	0
Fl	44	2	11	35	0	8	Fl	25	38	0	38	0
R	9	0	1	5	76	9	R	0	10	0	40	50

4 Conclusion

In the paper we presented a method to develop a teaching system for children that are able to be taught sentence modality pronunciation. First, a database was created consisting of recordings from healthy children. The text material of the databases was assembled from two texts. The first consisted sentences of six Hungarian modality classes which were later categorized into five classes according to intonation curves. The sentences were selected from a formerly developed software, SPECO [4]. The second text was made from the first text, making three dialogues using the same sentences. The built database was segmented and annotated marking the sentence modality classes according to intonation curves.

Automatic recognition tests were carried out using a formerly built recognizer for recognition of sentence modality of adults' recordings. Verifying tests were made with the database of recordings of the healthy children in order to adapt and prepare the recognizer to its real usage. The results showed that the recognition ratio decreased in the case of more diverse training data.

A second database was recorded, using the same text material as the first database, but consisting of recordings of children with hard of hearing. This database was segmented in the same way as the database of healthy children.

Then with the database of speech impaired children we examined how the trained recognizer could be used in a therapy environment. In order to verify our results, subjective tests were prepared. In these tests human listeners had to categorize the heard sentences. The results showed that the automatic recognizer classified the recordings more strictly, but not worse.

This method could be implemented as a part of a speech teaching system, while experiments show that sentence modality recognizer can be useful for automatic feedback of a sentence modality tracing tool for speech handicapped children. Moreover the proposed method can be useful for any computer assisted language learning (CALL) system too.

Acknowledgement

We would like to thank to "Dr. Béla Török" Kindergarten, Elementary School and Special School, and Elementary School of Farkasrét making available for us to make recordings with the children.

References

1. Vicsi, K.: Computer-Assisted Pronunciation Teaching and Training Methods Based on the Dynamic Spectro-Temporal Characteristics of Speech. In: Dynamics of Speech Production and Perception, pp. 283–304. IOS Press, Amsterdam (2006)
2. de Bot, K.: Visual feedback of intonation: Effectiveness and induced practice behavior. Lang. Speech 26(4), 331–335 (1983)
3. James, E.: The acquisition of prosodic features of speech using a speech visualizer. IRAL 14(3), 227–243 (1976)
4. Vicsi, K., Csatári, F., Bakcsi, Z., Tantos, A.: Distance score evaluation of the visualized speech spectra at audio-visual articulation training. In: Proc. Eurospeech, pp. 1911–1914 (1999)
5. ISTRA Indiana Speech Training Aid Features. Bloomington, IN: Communication Disorders Technology, Inc. (2003), http://www.comdistec.com/istra_faq.shtml
6. Vicsi, K., Szaszák, Gy.: Using Prosody for the Imporvement of ASR - Sentence Modality Recognition. In: Proc. of Interspeech2008, Bristol, ISCA Archive (2008), http://www.isca-speech.org/archive

7. The Snack Sound Toolkit, http://www.speech.kth.se/snack/
8. HTK Speech Recognition Toolkit, http://htk.eng.cam.ac.uk/
9. Szaszák, Gy., Vicsi, K.: Speech recognition supported by prosodic information for fixed stress languages. In: Proceeding of TSD conference Brno, pp. 262–269 (2000)
10. Szaszák, Gy., Vicsi, K.: Using prosody in fixed stress languages for improvement of speech recognition. In: Esposito, A., Faundez-Zanuy, M., Keller, E., Marinaro, M. (eds.) COST Action 2102. LNCS (LNAI), vol. 4775, pp. 138–149. Springer, Heidelberg (2007)

The New Italian Audio and Video Emotional Database

Anna Esposito[1,2] and Maria Teresa Riviello[1,2]

[1] Second University of Naples, Department of Psychology, Caserta, Italy
[2] International Institute for Advanced Scientific Studies (IIASS), Vietri sul Mare, Italy
iiass.annaesp@tin.it, mteresariviello@libero.it

Abstract. This paper describes the general specifications and characteristics of the New Italian Audio and Video Emotional Database, collected to improve the COST 2102 Italian Audio and Video Emotional Database [28] and to support the research effort of the COST Action 2102: "Cross Modal Analysis of Verbal and Nonverbal Communication" (http://cost2102.cs.stir.ac.uk/). The database should allow the cross-modal analysis of audio and video recordings for defining distinctive, multi-modal emotional features, and identify emotional states from multimodal signals. Emphasis is placed on stimuli selection procedures, theoretical and practical aspects for stimuli identification, characteristics of selected stimuli and progresses in their assessment and validation.

Keywords: Dynamic vocal and facial expressions of emotion, audio and video recordings, perceptual assessment.

1 Introduction

Human emotion recognition can usually be carried out by analyzing either facial expressions [1] or speech [2] or combining both facial and vocal information (Multimodal systems [3]). The task has received much attention in the last few years in the context of Human Computer Interaction (HCI) that involves research aimed to identify methods and procedures capable of automatically identifying human emotional states exploiting the multimodal nature of emotional expressions. This requires investigations on several key aspects of the research field, such as the development and the integration, in automatic systems, of algorithms and procedures for applications in communication, and for the recognition of emotional states from gestures, speech, gaze and facial expressions, in anticipation of the implementation of intelligent avatars and interactive dialog systems that could be exploited to improve the learning and understanding of human emotional behavior and facilitate the user's access to future communication services.

A considerable part of the research approaches the problem of recognizing emotional facial expressions exploiting static images as the ones contained in the *Japanese Female Facial Expression* (JAFFE) database [4] or in the ORL Database of Faces [5]. Many of the processing techniques for emotional feature detection [6, 7, 8, 9, 10, 11] and extraction, such as Principal Component Analysis (PCA)[12,13]), Linear Discriminant Analysis (LDA) [14], and Gabor filters [15], have been proposed and tested for the processing of these kind of databases.

A. Esposito et al. (Eds.): COST 2102 Int. Training School 2009, LNCS 5967, pp. 406–422, 2010.

Research has also been conducted on the extraction of facial expressions from video sequences. Most works in this area develop a video database from subjects making expressions on demand, such as the Cohn-Kanade facial expression database [16] and the eNTERFACE database [17], or extracting sequences from talk show [18, 19], where the presence of cameras and the consciousness to be on the spot surely works as a bias on the protagonist's spontaneous behaviors.

Similarly automatic recognition of emotional vocal expressions has been implemented by exploiting several classifying and encoding procedures (Artificial Neural Networks [20], k-Nearest Neighbor [21], Linear Discriminant Analysis [22], Support Vector Machine [23], Hidden Markov Model [24] and Bayesian classifier based on Gaussian Mixture Model [25] among many others.) for identifying acoustic features relevant to the identification of emotional states (the most popular and widely used is the Mel Frequency Cepstral Coefficients (MFCC) [25, 26]).

However, most of the existing emotional audio databases (such as the Berlin Database of Emotional Speech, BDES [27]) exploited as benchmark by the above mentioned methods, consists of audio stimuli recorded under studio conditions and therefore do not possess either naturalistic and/or genuine emotional characteristics. Likewise, the JAFFE database [20] or the ORL Database of Faces [37] contain static images which usually capture the apex of the emotional expressions, i.e. the instant at which the indicators of the expressed emotion are most marked, neglecting that in daily experience, emotional states are intrinsically dynamic processes and associated facial expressions vary along time. In addition, the recordings extracted from the talk shows, even though dynamic in nature, generally show emotional feelings brought to the extreme, resulting in artificial and extremely stylized emotional expressions.

These recordings can be considered satisfactory to the extent that the intended emotions can be correctly identified by addressees afterwards.

By reading the same sentence or watching the same face with different simulated emotional states it should be possible to allow principled analysis of speech and faces and comparisons of the changing acoustic and visual features. However, it is not obvious whether actors reproduce the genuine emotion or generate a stylized idealization of it in which some features of everyday reality are intensified, and others are disregarded.

Since such emotions are acted or brought to extremes,, it is questionable whether they authentically represent the characteristics of speech and faces made by ordinary people when they spontaneously experience similar emotions. The risk in using such kind of artificial data is that we may be able to produce synthetic data where it is possible to recognize the *intended* emotion, but we may also be aware at the same time that such an emotion is not *felt* or sincere.

In the light of the above considerations, the new Italian Audio and Video Emotional Database, created to enrich the previous COST 2102 Italian audio and video Emotional database [28], was collected and is proposed to provide a set of more realistic and genuine facial and vocal emotional expressions that could help to the improvement of existing methods and the definition of new methodologies and mathematical models for the automatic modeling and implementation of naturally human-like communication interfaces. The general specifications and characteristics of the collected set of stimuli are reported below.

2 Materials

As for the previous COST 2102 Italian Audio and Video Emotional Database [28] the collected data are based on extracts from Italian movies whose protagonists were carefully chosen among actors and actresses that are largely acknowledged by the critique and considered capable of giving some very real and careful interpretations. Differently from all the other existing emotional databases proposed in literature, in this case the actors/actresses had not been asked to produce an emotional expression by the experimenter, rather, they were acting according to a movie script and their performance had been judged as appropriate to the required emotional context by the movie director (supposed to be an expert). Moreover, even though the emotions expressed in the extracted video-clips were simulations under studio conditions (and may not have reproduced a genuine emotion but an idealization of it) they were able to catch up and engage the emotional feeling of the spectators (the addressers) and therefore we are quite confident of their perceptual emotional contents. The final database consists of audio and video stimuli representing 6 basic emotional states: happiness, sarcasm/irony, fear, anger, surprise, and sadness [29].

For each of the above listed emotional states, 26 stimuli were identified, 13 expressed by actors and 13 expressed by actresses, for a total of 156 stimuli. The stimuli were selected short in duration (the average stimulus' length was 2.5s, SD = ± 1s). This was due to two reasons: 1) longer stimuli may produce overlapping of emotional states and confuse the subject's perception; 2) emotional states by definition cannot last more than a few seconds and then change into other emotional states or moods generated by the dynamic of the interaction [30].

Care was taken in choosing video clips where the protagonist's face and the upper part of the body were clearly visible. Care was also taken in choosing the stimuli such that the semantic meaning of the sentences expressed by the protagonists was not clearly expressing the portrayed emotional state and its intensity level was moderate. For example, sadness stimuli where the actress/actor was clearly crying or happiness stimuli where the protagonist was strongly laughing were not included in the data. This was because we wanted the subjects assessing the stimuli to be able to exploit only emotional signs that were generally employed in every natural and not extreme emotional interaction.

From each complete stimulus - audio and video - we extracted the audio and video alone coming up with a total of 468 stimuli (156 stimuli audio alone, 156 video alone, and 156 audio and video combined).

The emotional labels assigned to the stimuli were given by two expert judges independently. A first judge selected the stimuli from the movie by carefully exploiting emotional information on facial and vocal expressions through a frame by frame analysis of changes in facial muscles, F0 contour, rising and falling of intonation contour, etc, as reported by several authors in literature [29, 31 - 43] and also exploiting the contextual situation the protagonist is interpreting. The second judge exploited the same emotional information described above, without knowing the context, and labeled the stimuli independently. A large amount of stimuli was collected, however, in the present database were included only the stimuli that obtained an agreement of 100% by the two judges.

The collected stimuli, being extracted from movie scenes containing environmental noise are also useful for testing realistic computer applications.

The stimuli in each set (audio alone, video alone, and combined audio and video stimuli) were randomized and proposed to three different groups of Italian subjects (aged from 20 to 35 years) in order to assess them without bias.

2.1 Participants

The total number of participants was 120 arranged into three different groups where male and female subjects were equally distributed: 40 subjects were involved in the evaluation of the audio alone, 40 in the evaluation of the video alone, and 40 in the evaluation of the video and audio combined. The assignment of the subjects to the task was random. Subjects were required to carefully listen and/or watch the experimental stimuli via headphones in a quiet room. They were instructed to pay attention to each presentation and decide as quickly as possible at the end of the stimulus presentation, which emotional state was expressed in it. Responses were recorded on a matrix paper form of 156 rows and 8 columns, where the rows listed the stimuli's numbers and the columns the emotional states of *happiness, sarcasm/irony, fear, anger, surprise*, and *sadness*, plus an option for *any other emotion* (where subjects were free to report a different emotional label than the six listed) and the option "*no emotion*" that was suggested when according to the subject's feeling the protagonist did not show any emotional state.

3 Stimuli Assessment

The following Tables (1, 2, 3, 4, 5, 6) report, for each emotional labelled stimulus the percentage of agreement expressed by the subjects participating to the experiments. The data are grouped in male (those portrayed by actors) and female (those portrayed by actresses) stimuli.

For each stimulus and for each actor/actress, the percentage refers to the agreement expressed by the subjects under the three experimental conditions, i.e. Audio and Video combined, Audio alone, and Video alone. For these two last conditions the single channel stimuli were extracted from the combined audio and video stimuli.

Figures 1, 2, 3, 4, 5 and 6 provide the histograms of the same data for a better visualization. The numbers attached to the stimuli served as reference for reading the histograms and are reported on the x-axis of the Figures.

Table 1. Subjects' percentage of agreement on the happiness stimuli under the three experimental conditions. The data are grouped into male (those portrayed by actors) and female (those portrayed by actresses) stimuli.

Happiness

Stimuli Male	Audio &Video	Video	Audio	Stimuli Female	Audio &Video	Video	Audio
1	55	72,5	77,5	14	55	85	40
2	70	55	25	15	67,5	70	40
3	22,5	45	42,5	16	75	92,5	57,5
4	97,5	57,5	72,5	17	90	77,5	70
5	87,5	70	70	18	50	70	42,5
6	72,5	65	67,5	19	62,5	77,5	52,5
7	67,5	22,5	45	20	77,5	92,5	80
8	87,5	90	45	21	82,5	82,5	10
9	70	60	50	22	70	75	77,5
10	40	20	57,5	23	65	70	50
11	52,5	77,5	42,5	24	87,5	100	77,5
12	87,5	82,5	77,5	25	85	95	85
13	72,5	47,5	35	26	82,5	87,5	47,5

Table 2. Subjects' percentage of agreement on the irony stimuli under the three experimental conditions. The data are grouped into male (those portrayed by actors) and female (those portrayed by actresses) stimuli.

Irony

Stimuli Male	Audio &Video	Video	Audio	Stimuli Female	Audio &Video	Video	Audio
1	25	5	17,5	14	40	55	52,5
2	77,5	32,5	70	15	57,5	37,5	47,5
3	62,5	47,5	45	16	72,5	45	55
4	57,5	20	57,5	17	70	5	57,5
5	67,5	15	65	18	72,5	20	60
6	30	30	15	19	85	85	75
7	15	67,5	47,5	20	52,5	57,5	40
8	10	52,5	12,5	21	80	55	72,5
9	60	35	10	22	25	27,5	22,5
10	50	20	65	23	80	47,5	82,5
11	65	62,5	45	24	85	57,5	55
12	62,5	72,5	62,5	25	75	40	82,5
13	52,5	80	55	26	80	77,5	25

Table 3. Subjects' percentage of agreement on the fear stimuli under the three experimental conditions. The data are grouped into male (those portrayed by actors) and female (those portrayed by actresses) stimuli.

Fear

Stimuli Male	Audio &Video	Video	Audio	Stimuli Female	Audio &Video	Video	Audio
1	85	55	37,5	14	72,5	77,5	37,5
2	62,5	85	32,5	15	35	32,5	17,5
3	62,5	85	42,5	16	57,5	27,5	62,5
4	70	80	60	17	42,5	27,5	62,5
5	85	85	62,5	18	70	42,5	37,5
6	50	60	30	19	57,5	62,5	50
7	90	90	67,5	20	45	30	60
8	77,5	45	30	21	72,5	82,5	70
9	60	60	65	22	80	87,5	67,5
10	25	12,5	15	23	40	12,5	25
11	22,5	7,5	10	24	77,5	60	80
12	67,5	60	5	25	15	40	7,5
13	87,5	90	62,5	26	52,5	12,5	45

Table 4. Subjects' percentage of agreement on the anger stimuli under the three experimental conditions. The data are grouped into male (those portrayed by actors) and female (those portrayed by actresses) stimuli.

Anger

Stimuli Male	Audio& Video	Video	Audio	Stimuli Female	Audio& Video	Video	Audio
1	82,5	47,5	77,5	14	47,5	45	42,5
2	42,5	42,5	15	15	87,5	85	82,5
3	92,5	97,5	80	16	80	32,5	57,5
4	92,5	92,5	70	17	82,5	90	55
5	90	97,5	87,5	18	50	62,5	47,5
6	67,5	95	70	19	77,5	67,5	80
7	90	92,5	82,5	20	77,5	97,5	67,5
8	80	65	57,5	21	87,5	75	72,5
9	47,5	57,5	55	22	80	97,5	77,5
10	77,5	97,5	70	23	87,5	92,5	87,5
11	95	15	75	24	90	67,5	80
12	45	65	45	25	95	97,5	82,5
13	95	70	70	26	90	87,5	82,5

Table 5. Subjects' percentage of agreement on the surprise stimuli under the three experimental conditions. The data are grouped into male (those portrayed by actors) and female (those portrayed by actresses) stimuli.

Surprise

Stimuli Male	Audio& Video	Video	Audio	Stimuli Female	Audio& Video	Video	Audio
1	80	77,5	35	14	90	32,5	65
2	80	45	65	15	72,5	40	55
3	57,5	57,5	70	16	77,5	87,5	15
4	7,5	32,5	5	17	55	20	27,5
5	62,5	27,5	32,5	18	65	65	20
6	77,5	52,5	40	19	55	32,5	32,5
7	82,5	35	70	20	25	0	17,5
8	32,5	57,5	55	21	75	55	50
9	40	42,5	5	22	97,5	100	52,5
10	72,5	60	5	23	85	50	85
11	67,5	47,5	42,5	24	42,5	47,5	72,5
12	72,5	35	45	25	75	17,5	25
13	92,5	77,5	85	26	30	57,5	20

Table 6. Subject's percentage of agreement on the sadness stimuli under the three experimental conditions. The data are grouped into male (those portrayed by actors) and female (those portrayed by actresses) stimuli.

Sadness

Stimuli Male	Audio& Video	Video	Audio	Stimuli Female	Audio& Video	Video	Audio
1	80	62,5	47,5	14	80	95	77,5
2	62,5	57,5	27,5	15	77,5	82,5	75
3	75	92,5	70	16	95	90	60
4	50	80	40	17	85	82,5	60
5	77,5	62,5	77,5	18	77,5	90	25
6	40	20	20	19	62,5	65	32,5
7	80	42,5	45	20	92,5	97,5	80
8	77,5	65	77,5	21	75	60	70
9	27,5	47,5	35	22	67,5	12,5	85
10	42,5	72,5	37,5	23	35	57,5	27,5
11	57,5	45	35	24	100	70	75
12	77,5	52,5	55	25	80	67,5	77,5
13	42,5	47,5	40	26	67,5	22,5	65

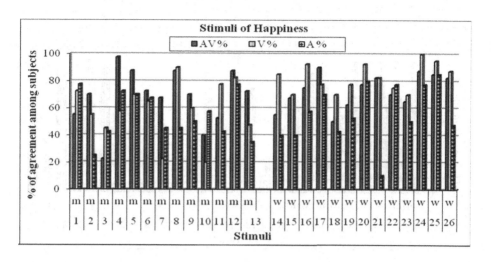

Fig. 1. Subject's percentage of agreement on the happiness stimuli under the three experimental conditions: AV (combined Audio and Video), V (Video alone), A (Audio Alone)

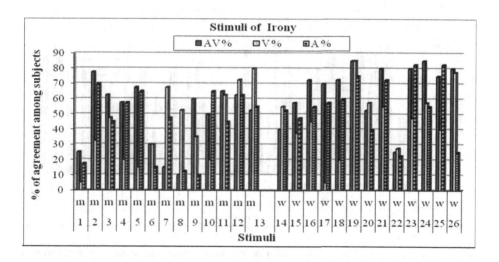

Fig. 2. Subject's percentage of agreement on the irony stimuli under the three experimental conditions: AV (combined Audio and Video), V(Video alone), A (Audio Alone)

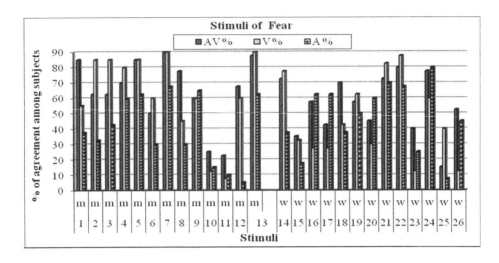

Fig. 3. Subject's percentage of agreement on the fear stimuli under the three experimental conditions: AV (combined Audio and Video), V(Video alone), A (Audio Alone)

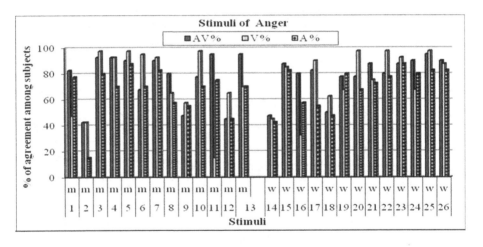

Fig. 4. Subject's percentage of agreement on the anger stimuli under the three experimental conditions. AV (combined Audio and Video), V(Video alone), A (Audio Alone)

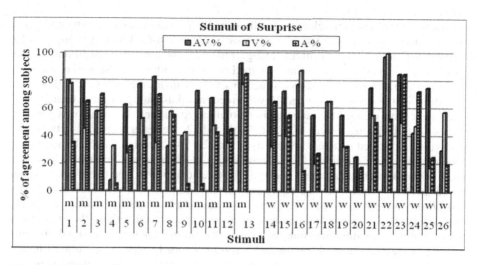

Fig. 5. Subject's percentage of agreement on the surprise stimuli under the three experimental conditions. AV (combined Audio and Video), V(Video alone), A (Audio Alone)

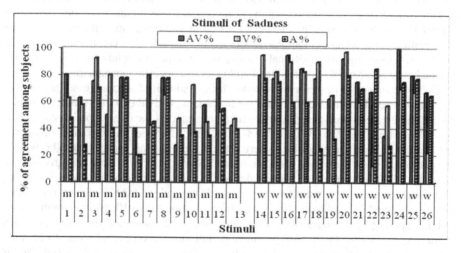

Fig. 6. Subject's percentage of agreement on the sadness stimuli under the three experimental conditions. AV (combined Audio and Video), V(Video alone), A (Audio Alone)

4 Discussions

The reported data show that many of the selected stimuli result informative about the emotional states under examination.

In particular, from Table 1 and Figure 1 it is possible to infer that the happiness stimuli n. 1, 4, 5, 6, 9 12, 16, 17, 19, 20, 22, 23, 24 and 25 meet the agreement of more than 50% of the subjects under all the three different experimental conditions. The stimuli n. 2, 8, 11, 14, 15, 21 and 26 obtained less than 50% of agreement under the audio alone, but were clearly identified under the video alone and the audio and video combined. In particular, the stimulus n. 21 gets just 10% of agreement under the audio alone while it was highly recognized under the other two conditions (82,5% both in the video alone and in the combined audio and video). The stimuli n. 7 and 13 meet more than 50% of the subjects' agreement only under the audio and video combined, while the stimuli n. 10 and 18 were recognized as happy by more than 50% of the subjects only under the audio and video alone conditions. In details it is possible to note that the happy stimuli n. 4, 5, 6, 9, 12 and 17 are better identified in the audio and video combined, whereas stimuli n. 14, 16, 20, 24, 25 and 26 are better identified in the video alone condition. The stimulus n. 3 is the only one that meets less than 50% of the subjects' agreement under all the three conditions, and therefore, it seems to be ineffective in conveying happy emotional information. It is confused with sarcasm/irony both in the video alone and in the audio and video combined, whereas in the audio it has not a specific collocation since it is confused with all the other emotional states. Such stimulus could be excluded from the database if it should be employed for developing applications and algorithms aimed to the recognition of happy facial and vocal expressions. It must be worth to note that for some stimuli the recognition in the video alone, is more than 20% higher than that obtained either in the audio and in the audio and video combined (see for example the stimuli n. 11, 14, 16, 20, 24) , whereas for others it is the opposite (see for example the stimulus n. 13 for the audio and video combined, and the stimuli n. 4, 6 for the audio alone). This phenomenon is also observed for the other classes of emotional stimuli and calls for an explanation more complex than that discussed in [28, 45-47] since it appears that the nonlinear processing of emotional stimuli under dynamic condition cannot be explained only in terms of cognitive load and language specific mechanisms.

The percentages of agreements obtained for the stimuli of sarcasm/irony seem to be generally lower than the ones obtained for happiness . Only the ironic stimuli n. 12, 13, 19, 21 and 24 meet more than 50% of agreement under all the three experimental conditions. The stimuli n. 2, 4, 5, 16, 17, 18, 21, 23 and 25, meet an agreement below the 50% in the video alone condition, whereas the agreement was higher than 50% both in the audio and in the audio and video combined. Some stimuli obtained an agreement of more than 50% of agreement only under one condition, such as the audio and video combined condition for stimuli n. 3, 9 and 15, the video alone condition for stimuli numbered 7 and 8, the audio alone condition for stimulus n. 10, while stimulus n. 11 obtains a percentage of agreement above 50% both in the video and the audio and video combined conditions. In the case of ironic stimuli, the audio channel seems to be more informative than the video alone, probably because irony is an emotional state that is better expressed through prosodic and supra-segmental speech features. Again, some stimuli, as those n. 1, 6, and 22, did not meet a sufficient percentage of subject's agreement, whereas, others, such as the stimuli n. 14 and 20 did not meet an agreement of more that 50% in the audio and in the audio and video combined respectively. Moreover, it is useful to note that the stimulus n. 17 meets only 5% of agreement in the video alone whereas it obtained 70% and 57,5% of agreement in the audio and video combined and the audio respectively. These discrepancies among the three conditions, could be of interest in suggesting which vocal and/or facial emotional features are exploited for decoding a given emotional state as well as which feature interferes making the decoding difficult in one condition with respect to another.

In assessing the stimuli of fear, it was fund that the stimuli n. 1, 8, and 18, received, in the audio and video combined an agreement significantly higher (more than 30%) than that obtained with the audio and the video alone. Furthermore, the stimuli n. 8 and 18, received in these last two conditions an agreement below 50%, and the stimulus n.1 was identified above 50% only under the video alone.

In addition, the visual channel seems to be very effective in conveying features signaling fear since the stimuli n. 2, 3, 4 and 6 obtained in the video alone condition a percentage of agreement higher than that observed in the audio alone and the audio and video combined. Features of fear are maintained in the visual channel since the stimuli n.5, 7, 9, 12, 13, 14, 19 and 22 obtained similar percentage of agreement either in the video alone or in the audio and video combined.

The video alone condition obtained less agreement than the audio alone and the audio and video combined only for the stimuli n.16 and 24. An agreement of more than 50% was obtained by the fear stimuli n. 4, 5, 7, 9, 13, 19 21, 22 and 24 under all the three proposed experimental conditions as well as others, such as the stimuli n. 10, 11, 15, 23, 25 which did not meet an agreement above 50% in all the three experimental conditions.

The stimuli of anger show, in the video alone condition the same trend observed for the stimuli of fear. The combined channels (audio and video combined) obtained an agreement higher than that observed in the video alone, only for the stimuli n.1, 2, 8, 11, 13, and 16 which reached a higher label agreement than the video alone. The stimuli n. 2 and 14 are those that received less than 50% of agreements for the assigned label under the three proposed experimental conditions.

The stimuli of anger n. 1, 11 and 16 received a high percentage of label agreement both in the audio alone and in the audio and video combined, whereas in the video alone they received a label agreement below 50%. In general, the emotional states classified as anger received the higher percentage of agreements with respect to the other emotional states under examination.

The stimuli of surprise n. 3, 13, 21 and 22 obtained a percentage of label agreement under all the three proposed experimental conditions. The higher percentage of agreement was obtained by the combined audio and video stimuli, even though there are cases where the audio alone or the video alone obtained a percentage of agreements similar to those observed in the audio and video combined.

We can speculate that surprise, being so short as expression in itself could not be easily recognized when it is decoded through dynamic stimuli probably because the surprising effect becomes soon coloured by the "kind of surprise" that is expressed: if it is a beautiful surprise it soon turns into happiness, if it is a bad surprise it turns into fear or sadness.

Many of the sad stimuli (n. 3, 5, 7, 12, 14, 15, 16, 17, 20, 21 and 25) appear to be effective in transmitting the information on such emotional state under all the three experimental conditions. As happened for the stimuli of fear, few stimuli (the stimuli n. 1, 7, 12 and 24) received higher label agreements in the combined audio and video condition than in the audio and video alone. The sad stimuli n. 15, 16, 17, 19 and 20 obtained high percentages of label agreements both in the combined audio and video and in the video alone conditions. The stimuli n. 3, 5, 8, 14, 21, 25 and 26 instead, obtained a high percentage of label agreements in the combined audio and video and in the audio alone conditions. In addition, the stimuli n. 3, 4, 10, 14, 18 and 23 were better identified as sad in the video alone. The stimuli n. 6 and 9 obtained a percentage of label agreement less than 50% in all the three proposed experimental conditions.

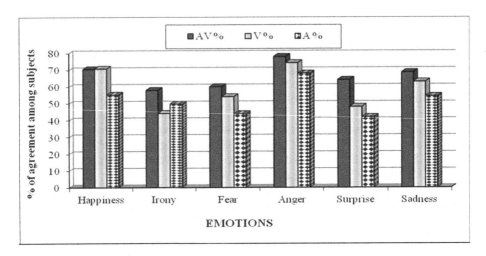

Fig. 7. Summary of the assessment results on the collected stimuli. On the x-axis are the basic emotions under consideration and on the y-axis is reported (for each emotion) the percentage of correct agreement under the three proposed experimental conditions.

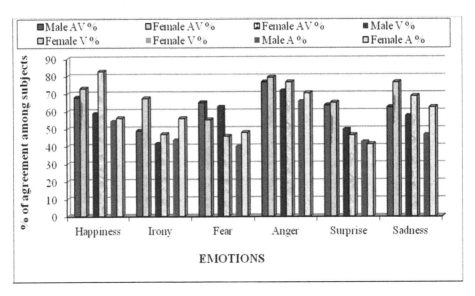

Fig. 8. The histograms refer to the percentage of correct recognition obtained by the three groups, each of 40 subjects, tested separately on the audio, the video, and the audio and video combined, on emotional stimuli portrayed by males (first bar of each block of two) and by females (second bar of each block of two)

The above data and the reported observations seem to suggest that the information on the emotional state is decoded through a nonlinear procedure that does not account f or what is called "emotional redundancy". It seems instead that there are cases when the emotional stimulus is clearly identified in one channel and that the addition of emotional information through the other one (either the visual or the auditory, depending on the stimulus and on the channel that better identify the emotional states under examination) produces a decrease in the amount of features to be exploited and a confusion in the subject's perception.

Which channel is favored seems, according to the data at the hand, to be dependent on the emotional state under examination.

Figure 7 summarizes the assessment results obtained on the collected stimuli showing, the total percentage of agreement among subjects that each emotional label obtained in each of the three proposed experimental conditions.

Finally, Figure 8 displays the percentage of subject's agreement according to the actor's gender. The data seem to suggest that, in general, there are no gender differences in identifying emotional expressions portrayed by females or by males even though, it appears that female faces better encode visual emotional cues of happiness, and female voices better encode auditory emotional cues of irony, and sadness.

5 Conclusions

The stimuli described in the present work, together with those contained in the COST 2102 Italian Audio and Video Emotional Database discussed in [28], constitute a large database of 648 stimuli (216 audio, 216 video and 216 audio and video) which represent the first emotional data for the Italian language. The audio stimuli of this database have already been successfully exploited to test a new speaker-independent approach for the classification of emotional vocal expressions (see [44] in this volume). The database is foreseen to be of great utility for the development of new algorithms for the recognition of vocal and facial emotional expressions and for cross cultural comparing human emotional decoding procedures [28, 44, 45, 46, 47]. A similar database containing audio and video sequences extracted from American movies has been assessed on Italian subject [48]. In progress is the comparison of the decoding procedure used by the American and the Italian subjects on the above database.

Acknowledgements

This work has been partially funded by COST 2102 "Cross Modal Analysis of Verbal and Nonverbal Communication", http://cost2102.cs.stir.ac.uk/ and by Regione Campania, L.R. N.5 del 28.03.2002, Project ID N. BRC1293, Bando Feb. 2006. Acknowledgements go to **Miss Tina Marcella Nappi** for her editorial help.

References

1. Bindu, M., Gupta, P., Tiwary, U.: Cognitive Model-Based Emotion Recognition From Facial Expressions For Live Human Computer Interaction. In: Proceedings of the IEEE Symposium on Computational Intelligence and Signal Processing CIISP (2007)
2. Ververidis, D., Kotropoulos, C.: Emotional Speech Recognition: Resources, Features and Methods. Elsevier Speech Communication 48(9), 1162–1181 (2006)

3. Sebe, N., Cohen, I., Gevers, T., Huang, T.: Emotion Recognition Based on Joint Visual and Audio Cues. In: Proceedings of the 18th International Conference on Pattern Recognition, ICPR 2006 (2006)
4. Kamachi, M., Lyons, M., Gyoba, J.: Japanese Female Facial Expression Database, Psychology Department in Kyushu University, http://www.kasrl.org/jaffe.html
5. Samaria, F., Harter, A.: The ORL Database of Faces. Cambridge University Press, Cambridge, http://www.cl.cam.ac.uk/research/dtg/attarchive/facedatabase.html
6. Roth, D., Yang, M., Ahuja, N.: A SNoW-Based Face Detector. In: Advances in Neural Information Processing Systems, pp. 855–861 (2000)
7. Ryu, H., Chun, S.S., Sull, S.: Multiple Classifiers Approach for Computational Efficiency in Multi-scale Search Based Face Detection. In: Jiao, L., Wang, L., Gao, X.-b., Liu, J., Wu, F. (eds.) ICNC 2006. LNCS, vol. 4221, pp. 483–492. Springer, Heidelberg (2006)
8. Schneiderman, H., Kanade, T.: A Statistical Method for 3D Object Detection Applied to Faces and Cars. In: International Conference on Computer and Pattern Recognition, vol. 1, pp. 746–751 (2000)
9. Esposito, A., Přinosil, J., Smékal, Z.: Combining Features for Recognizing Emotional Facial Expressions in Static Images. In: Esposito, A., Bourbakis, N.G., Avouris, N., Hatzilygeroudis, I. (eds.) HH and HM Interaction. LNCS (LNAI), vol. 5042, pp. 56–69. Springer, Heidelberg (2008)
10. Sung, K., Poggio, T.: Example-Based Learning for View-Based Face Detection. IEEE Transaction on Pattern Analyses and Machine Intelligence 20, 39–51 (1998)
11. Viola, A.P., Jones, M.J.: Robust Real-Time Face Detection. International Journal of Computer Vision 57(2), 137–154 (2004)
12. Turk, M., Pentland, A.: Face Recognition Using Eigenfaces. In: Proceedings of IEEE Conference on Computer Vision and Pattern Recognition, pp. 586–591 (1991)
13. Jollife, I.T.: Principal Component Analysis, 2nd edn. Springer, New York (2002)
14. Fisher, R.A.: The Statistical Utilization of Multiple Measurements. Annali of Eugenics 8, 376–386 (1938)
15. Petkov, N., Wieling, M.B.: Gabor Filtering Augmented with Surround Inhibition for Improved Contour Detection by Texture Suppression. Perception 33, 68c (2004)
16. Kanade, T., Cohn, J.F.: Comprehensive Database for Facial Expression Analysis. In: Proceedings of the Fourth IEEE International Conference on Automatic Face and Gestures Recognition, Grenoble, France (2000)
17. Martin, O., Kotsia, I., Macq, B., Pitas, I.: The eNTERFACE05 Audio-Visual Emotion Database. In: Proceedings of ICDEW (2006)
18. Douglas-Cowie, E., Cowie, R., Schröder, M.: A New Emotion Database: Considerations, Sources and Scope. In: Proceedings of the ISCA Workshop on Speech and Emotion: A Conceptual Framework for Research, Textflow, Belfast, pp. 39–44 (2000)
19. Grimm, M., Kroschel, K., Narayanan, S.: The Vera Am Mittag German Audio-Visual Emotional Speech Database. 978-1-4244-2571-6/08/$25.00 ©2008 IEEE (2008)
20. Davis, S., Mermelstein, P.: Comparison of Parametric Representations for Monosyllabic Word Recognition in Continuously Spoken Sentences. IEEE Transactions, on Acoustic, Speech and Signal Processing 28, 357–366 (1980)
21. Pao, T., Chen, Y., Yeh, J.: Emotion Recognition from Mandarin Speech Signals, Spoken Language Processing. In: International Symposium on Chinese (2004)
22. Lee, C., Narayanan, M.: Toward Detecting Emotions in Spoken Dialogs. IEEE Trans. Speech and Audio Process 13, 293–303 (2005)

23. Schuller, B., Rigoll, G., Lang, M.: Speech emotion recognition combining acoustic features and linguistic information in a hybrid support vector machine-belief network architecture. In: Proceedingss of International Conference on Acoustics, Speech and Signal Processing (ICASSP 2004), pp. 557–560 (2004)

24. Schuller, B., Rigoll, G., Lang, M.: Hidden Markov Model-Based Speech Emotion Recognition. In: Proc. of IEEE International Conference on Acoustics, Speech and Signal Processing, ICASSP 2003, Hong Kong, China, vol. 2 (2003)

25. Hu, H., Xu, M., Wu, W.: GMM Supervector Based SVM with Spectral Features for Speech Emotion Recognition. In: Proc. of IEEE International Conference on Acoustics, Speech and Signal Processing, ICASSP (2007)

26. Navas, E., Hernáez, I.: Luengo: An Objective and Subjective Study of the Role of Semantics and Prosodic Features in Building Corpora for Emotional TTS. IEEE Transactions on Audio, Speech, and Language Processing 14, 1117–1127 (2006)

27. Burkhardt, F., Paeschke, A., Rolfes, M., Sendlmeier, W., Weiss, B.: A Database of German Emotional Speech. In: Proceedings of Interspeech, pp. 1517–1520 (2005)

28. Esposito, A., Riviello, M.T., Di Maio, G.: The COST 2102 Italian Audio and Video Emotional Database. In: Apolloni, B., Bassis, S., Morabito, C.F. (eds.) Neural Nets WIRN 2009, vol. 204, pp. 51–61 (2009)

29. Ekman, P.: Facial Expression of Emotion: New Findings. New Questions. Psychological Science 3, 34–38 (1992)

30. Oatley, K., Jenk, J.M.: Understanding emotions. Blackwell, Oxford (1996)

31. Banse, R., Scherer, K.: Acoustic profiles in vocal emotion expression. Journal of Personality & Social Psychology 70(3), 614–636 (1996)

32. Cacioppo, J.T., Berntson, G.G., Larsen, J.T., Poehlmann, K.M.T.A.: Ito: The Psychophysiology of emotion. In: Lewis, J.M., Haviland-Jones, M. (eds.) Handbook of Emotions, 2nd edn., pp. 173–191. Guilford Press, New York (2000)

33. Ekman, P., Friesen, P., Hager, W.V.,, J.: The facial action coding system, 2nd edn. Research Nexus eBook, Salt Lake City, Weidenfeld & Nicolson, London (2002)

34. Ekman, P., Friesen, W.V.: Facial action coding system: A technique for the measurement of facial movement. Consulting Psychologists Press, Palo Alto (1978)

35. Ekman, P., Friesen, W.V.: Manual for the Facial Action Coding System. Consulting Psychologists Press, Palo Alto (1977)

36. Izard, C.E., Ackerman, B.P.: Motivational, organizational, and regulatory functions of discrete emotions. In: Lewis, J.M., Haviland-Jones, M. (eds.) Handbook of Emotions, 2nd edn., pp. 253–264. Guilford Press, New York (2000)

37. Izard, C.E.: Innate and universal facial expressions: Evidence from developmental and cross-cultural research. Psychological Bulletin 115, 288–299 (1994)

38. Izard, C.E., Dougherty, L.M., Hembree, E.A.: A system for identifying affect expressions by holistic judgments. Unpublished manuscript, Available from Instructional Resource Center, University of Delaware (1983)

39. Izard, C.E.: The maximally discriminative facial movement coding system (MAX). Unpublished manuscript, Available from Instructional Resource Center, University of Delaware (1979)

40. Scherer, K.R.: Vocal communication of emotion: A review of research paradigms. Speech Communication 40, 227–256 (2003)

41. Scherer, K.R., Banse, R., Wallbott, H.G.: Emotion inferences from vocal expression correlate across languages and cultures. Journal of Cross-Cultural Psychology 32, 76–92 (2001)

42. Scherer, K.R., Banse, R., Wallbott, H.G., Goldbeck, T.: Vocal cues in emotion encoding and decoding. Motivation and Emotion 15, 123–148 (1991)

43. Scherer, K.R.: Vocal correlates of emotional arousal and affective disturbance. In: Wagner, H., Manstead, A. (eds.) Handbook of social Psychophysiology, pp. 165–197. Wiley, New York (1989)

44. Atassi, H., Riviello, M.T., Smékal, Z., Hussain, A., Esposito, A.: Emotional Vocal Expressions Recognition using the COST 2102 Italian Database of Emotional Speech. In: Esposito, A., et al. (eds.) Development of Multimodal Interfaces: Active Listening and Synchrony. Lectures Notes in Computer Science, vol. 5967, pp. 406–422. Springer, Heidelberg (2010)

45. Esposito, A.: The Amount of Information on Emotional States Conveyed by the Verbal and Nonverbal Channels: Some Perceptual Data. In: Stylianou, Y., Faundez-Zanuy, M., Esposito, A. (eds.) COST 277. LNCS, vol. 4391, pp. 249–268. Springer, Heidelberg (2007)

46. Esposito, A.: Affect in Multimodal Information. In: Tao, J., Tan, T. (eds.) Affective Information Processing, pp. 211–234. Springer, Heidelberg (2008)

47. Esposito, A.: The Perceptual and Cognitive Role of Visual and Auditory Channels in Conveying Emotional Information. Cognitive Computation Journal 1(2), 268–278 (2009)

48. Esposito, A., Riviello, M.T., Bourbakis, N.: Cultural Specific Effects on the Recognition of Basic Emotions: A Study on Italian Subjects. In: Holzinger, A., Miesenberger, K. (eds.) USAB 2009. LNCS, vol. 5889, pp. 135–148. Springer, Heidelberg (2009)

Spoken Dialogue in Virtual Worlds

Gérard Chollet[1], Asmaa Amehraye[1], Joseph Razik[1], Leila Zouari[2],
Houssemeddine Khemiri[2], and Chafic Mokbel[3]

[1] CNRS-LTCI Télécom-ParisTech, 46 rue Barrault, 75013 Paris - France
[2] TECHTRA-Ecole Supérieure des Communications de Tunis, 2083 Cité
El-Ghazala-Ariana, Tunisia
[3] Mathematics Department, University of Balamand, 100 El-Koura, Lebanon
{chollet,amehraye,razik,khemiri}@telecom-paristech.fr,
beltaifa@yahoo.com, chafic.mokbel@balamand.edu.lb

Abstract. Human-computer conversations have attracted a great deal of interest especially in virtual worlds. In fact, research gave rise to spoken dialogue systems by taking advantage of speech recognition, language understanding and speech synthesis advances. This work surveys the state of the art of speech dialogue systems. Current dialogue system technologies and approaches are first introduced emphasizing differences between them, then, speech recognition and synthesis and language understanding are introduced as complementary and necessary modules. On the other hand, as the development of spoken dialogue systems becomes more complex, it is necessary to define some processes to evaluate their performance. Wizard-of-Oz techniques play an important role to achieve this task. Thanks to this technique is obtained a suitable dialogue corpus necessary to achieve good performance. A description of this technique is given in this work together with perspectives on multimodal dialogue systems in virtual worlds.

1 Introduction

Spoken dialogue systems aim to enable naive users to interact with complex computer applications in a natural way using speech. They range from question-answering systems to conversational ones where the goal is to establish a natural dialogue with the user. They attracted a great deal of interest in the last decades thanks to the spread of virtual reality applications. Thereby, research gave rise to multimodal dialogue systems by taking advantage of speech recognition and visual information processing advances. The main purpose of a spoken dialogue system is to provide an interface between a user and a computer-based application. Architecturally, these systems are designed around five main modules (see figure 1): speech recognition, language understanding, dialogue manager, natural language generation and speech synthesis. The dialogue manager module plays a key control role because it is responsible of determining the system actions. It is also responsible of maintaining coherence, over time, between dialogue elements. Spoken dialogue systems are classified regarding strategies used by the dialogue manager module. There are five main system classes: finite state-based systems

A. Esposito et al. (Eds.): COST 2102 Int. Training School 2009, LNCS 5967, pp. 423–443, 2010.
© Springer-Verlag Berlin Heidelberg 2010

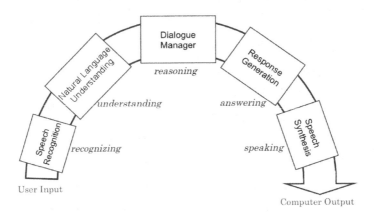

Fig. 1. Dialogue system classical architecture

where the dialogue flow is defined as the transitions between predetermined states [72]; frame-based systems [35], [27] where data slots are filled according to information got from the user; agent-based systems dedicated to more sophisticated dialogue systems where the computer is considered as an intelligent agent designed to take some initiatives and so to be cooperative with the user [53];plan-based systems [52], [23], [46] which aim to divide a specific task into subtasks (called goals or plans), control the dialogue interaction to accomplish them and complete the whole task. This technique requires an adequate structure and an appropriate management strategy to achieve good performance; finally, the stochastic-based systems where the goal is to learn and optimize the dialogue decisions. Recently, combination of more than one technique has been employed, such methods will be also addressed to emphasize their contribution to spoken dialogue systems development. Finally, for evaluation purpose and analysis of multimodal interfaces, wizard-of-Oz strategy based on user observation will be addressed as a way to improve the design of spoken dialogue systems. This strategy is often used as a primary step to collect natural language corpus data to develop systems.

2   Human-Machine Interaction and Virtual Worlds

2.1   Virtual Reality

It is natural for man to escape from the daily reality for different reasons (artistic, cultural or professional). The progression of technical assistance has been able to satisfy this need by visual or sound representations where the user is only behaving as a viewer. Virtual reality provides an additional dimension by providing a virtual environment in which the user became an actor. Virtual reality can only be envisaged recently, thanks to the significant increase of computers power, particularly the possibility of creating real-time images and allowing the real-time interactivity, between the user and the virtual world. Virtual reality is not born spontaneously, mainly, simulators of transportation made it possible for professionals to interact with a partially virtual environment for the last 50 years. Virtual reality involves essentially many areas like the human sciences, life sciences and technology.

In 2003 Arnaldi [3] proposed a technical definition of virtual reality: "Virtual Reality is a scientific and technical area operating on computing and behavioural interfaces to simulate in a virtual world the behaviour of 3D entities, which are real-time interaction among themselves and with one or more users".

So we must create an interactive virtual world and in real time. The creation of a virtual world is a major issue of virtual reality: modeling, digitizing and computer processing of the virtual world are complicated. We can note the particular case involving a real world with a virtual world (techniques of augmented reality) [26].

Real-time interaction is obtained if the user perceives no lag time (latency) between its action in the virtual environment and the response of the latter. This constraint is difficult to satisfy. Otherwise, we may seek not to disturb the subject by this time lag, even if he perceives it.

The user must be in the most effective pseudo-natural immersion in the virtual world. This feeling is a subjective concept which depends on the application and the device (interfaces, software, etc.).

These two conditions (interaction and immersion) are rarely achievable. As against, they must be partly performed, even modestly, to speak of a system based on virtual reality.

2.2   Human-Machine Interaction

Human-machine interaction is getting more attention as more people are confronted with computing systems. The relationship between user and digital signal processing is old, and complex. At the beginning it was just by keyboard and mouse, nowadays, speech recognition, speech synthesis, touch screen and gesture are used.

These services are merging and manipulating different kinds of signal such as text, graphics, images and speech. The ability to provide these services is considered as a challenge for digital signal processing specialists and computer scientists and the need for machines to understand humans becomes increasingly important [29].

The latest scientific findings indicate that emotions play an essential role in rational decision-making, perception, learning, and various cognitive tasks [18] .Therefore, giving machines a degree of emotional intelligence should permit more meaningful and natural human-machine interaction.

A major issue in present day human-machine interaction design is how to deal with communication problems. Since a spoken dialogue system can never be certain that it understood the user correctly, it is in a constant need for verification of its current assumptions.

3   Dialogue System Approaches

The Dialogue manager is one of the most important components of spoken dialogue systems. It controls the interaction by means of dialogue grammar and holds information needed by system modules. One way to classify the dialogue system strategies is to take into account the degree of initiative given to the user in each dialogue step. Three degrees of initiative can be distinguished:

- System-driven: the system asks the user step by step and the user is then supposed to answer those questions and to provide only the required information. The phone service applications are example of those systems.
- User-driven: all progress and initiative come from the user which asks the system for required information. The system is supposed to answer correctly without asking the user for more details.
- Mixed Initiative: allow both the system and the user to control the dialogue interaction. Since the user can take initiative and give over information.

In practice the degree of initiative is not sufficient to discriminate systems since there are some common points between the three degrees presented below. In order to be more specific, dialogue systems are classified according to strategies adopted by the dialogue manager giving rise to five main classes:

3.1   Finite State-Based Systems

This is the first proposed model for human-machine dialogue systems which is known for its simplicity. In this model, the dialogue flow is a sequence of predetermined steps called states [72]. Transitions between states refer to various alternative paths through the dialogue graph. This method is suitable for systems with well defined and structured tasks where the complete dialogue model is defined at the development stage. For this reason finite state-based systems are not flexible and don't allow natural dialogue nor applicability to other domain. In addition they inhibit the user's ability to ask questions and to take initiatives.

3.2   Frame-Based Systems

Frame-based or form filling systems have been proposed in order to overcome state-based system limitations. A frame is a combination of slots containing information elicited from the user when each slot is related to a specific category [35], [27]. The dialogue manager aims at filling the slots with appropriate information in order to be able to generate the next action. In a frame-based approach we do not need to represent the dialogue flow explicitly.

3.3   Agent-Based Systems

Those systems allow complex communication between the systems, the user and the underlying application in order to solve some problem or task [53].

The dialogue is supposed to be between two intelligent agents where computer agent can make some reasoning and takes initiatives. As a consequence, it allows natural dialogue in complex domains. Those systems are very complex and hard to build.

3.4   Plan-Based Systems

In this range of systems, the dialogue is considered as a planning process motivated by the achievement of certain goals.

The dialogue manager must optimize the plan to achieve those goals by taking appropriate actions. As in agent-based systems, the plan-based systems rely on the user cooperativeness in order to get suitable information [52], [23], [46].

3.5   Markovian-Based Systems

Several Markovian based approaches have been proposed in the past decade to learn and optimize dialogue strategies. [6] proposed the use of Hidden Markov Models (HMMs) to model the distribution of possible sentences given a sequence of semantic units. This permits to identify the optimal sequence of semantic units given the sentence at the output of the speech recognition system. Experiments conducted on currency inquiry database and on city bus timetable inquiry have shown satisfactory results. In [43], the Markovian Decision Process (MDP) has been experimented to learn dialogue strategies. The key idea for a given task is to define the problem by:

- State of the dialogue system: this represents the knowledge the system has about internal and external resources it interacts with.
- Action set: It is defined as the possible actions the system can conduct, e.g. requesting information from the user.
- Dialogue strategy: It is defined for each state as the next action to be undertaken by the system.

A dialogue strategy is a path in the state space. Each path has a cost (number of interactions, errors, incomplete values, etc.) and the idea is to determine the optimal strategy leading to the minimal cost. In MDP, the costs are represented by their conditional probability distribution given the state and a possible action. This permits not only to determine, in use, the optimal strategy to conduct but also to learn this strategy from examples. From this point, different approaches have been proposed in the literature. Reinforcement learning for spoken dialogue has been proposed in [63]. [70] used partially observable MDP in their spoken dialogue system.

3.6   Multi-strategy Dialogue Management

Recently, combination of more than one strategy has been employed in order to take advantage of the positive points of each strategy. Several new methods have employed example-based techniques by exploiting the benefits of data-driven approaches to automatic speech recognition and spoken language understanding (SLU) [40], [38], [60]. The example-based technique (called also template-based approach) aims at automatically generate system responses from dialogue corpus when several utterance examples are already annotated. Since the retrieved examples are not unique, the best one is chosen using the utterance similarity. In other words, the next action refers to the next best example. In [55], the authors used data captured from over 11.000 players of *The Restaurant Game* to generate behavior and dialogue in real time. The goal is to automate virtual agents by means of behavior and dialogue coming from human-human interactions. The language understanding employed require no constraints on spontaneous human speech in virtual worlds environment (see [28]). It is based on the notion of perceived affordances which are structured units of interaction that can be used for prediction at certain levels of abstraction.

In [35], the authors use a frame-based state representation and the dialogue examples to generate action hypotheses. First, the system groups the states dynamically using frame-based representation according to user's utterance and its SLU result. Then the system uses an example-based approach to generate only system action hypotheses that are suitable for current states.

In [15], a promising method employed three strategies: finite state-based, frame-based and agent-based. The dialog manager can determine the most suitable dialogue strategy to be used according to circumstances, and change to a different strategy whenever required.

4   Speech Recognition

One important thing to clarify before talking about speech recognition is to mention that speech recognition is not speech comprehension. Recognition is the process that aims to identify the sequence of words pronounced in a sound sample depending on an acoustic and a linguistic modeling. Comprehension/ understanding is a different process that analyzes and tries to interpret this word sequence at a semantic level and to get some information in the framework of reaching a goal. However, these two processes are strongly linked in a dialogue system.

There are almost two ways to define a speech recognition system in order to provide useful information to the dialogue manager: keyword spotting and full sentences spotting.

In the first case, keywords are searched within the word sequence provided by the speech recognition system. In the second case, complete sentences are attended to be recognized. But as the last method is not flexible, the dialogue system based on this technique is very constrained. That is the reason why most of dialogue systems are based on keyword spotting techniques.

Thus, most projects are based on the use of a Large Vocabulary Continuous Speech Recognition (LVCSR) engine as Julius [39] developed by Kyoto Univeristy, Sphinx [36] developed by CMU or HTK [71]developed by Cambridge Univerisity. All of these systems are based on a usual stochastic modeling of the acoustic units by Hidden Markov Models and can use both statistical language model (LM) or grammar-based LM.

Different level of acoustic units modeling can be used: phones, syllables, and words. It depends on the needs of the final application. If the dialogue application is very constrained, a word level choice is possible. But if it is an open-dialogue system, then classical LVCSR techniques should be used and the acoustic unit will be phones.

A second important point concerns the language modeling approach. There are two possible cases: a deterministic and a stochastic way.

4.1 Deterministic Grammar Approach

This kind of approach is based on the definition of a graph describing the grammar, that is to say the allowed word sequences for the task. A deterministic grammar imposes some constraints on the interaction between the user and the system. Such systems are not easy to use for naive people that don't know the rules. Even if filler model must be trained, writing such a grammar is complex, time consumer and must be quite exhaustive.

4.2 Large Vocabulary and Stochastic Approach

In this approach, a LVCSR is used to recognize an open sentence, with no constraints. However, the size of the dictionary defining all the possible words that the system may recognize is limited. Nowadays, usual size is about 120 000 words. Thus the LVCSR system cannot recognize everything and the dictionary should be specialized to the task but must include everyday words. In this case, a classical n-gram stochastic language modeling is used and the keywords are searched within the words sequence provided by the system. The advantage of this approach is that there are fewer constraints on the user who can interact more freely and more spontaneously. However, there are more mistakes and noisy words in the provided sequences.

4.3 Realtime Objective

One important challenge in the use of speech recognition systems in daily life is to have a system that can response without too much delay. The point of obtaining a real-time system is still crucial. Different ways have been studied in order to speed up ASR without impacting too much the recognition rate. The two main directions are: optimization and parallelization.

Process optimization: The process optimization consists in approximating several computing consuming part of the decoding process in order to lower the complexity of the algorithms. For example, in the Julius ASR, several options are available in order to boost the recognition:

- Gaussian pruning: this method consists in computing the acoustic likelihood of a model only with a part of the gaussians representing the model. For example, computation of only the top N-best gaussians is available. Besides some more aggressive methods are implemanted like computing the triphone likelihood only on the gaussians of high monophone likelihood;
- Inter-word triphone approximation for the beginning and the end of words: to limit the computation to a smaller set of possible triphone contexts;
- Beam search width: Julius performs a beam search decoding of the hypotheses for both Viterbi and A^* algorithms used in its first and second pass. To shrink the size of the beams decreases the number of remaining hypotheses and thus decreases the computation cost. Some similar parameters can also be tuned to make recognition faster as the decoding stack size, or the maximum number of hypotheses to be expanded.

Those implemented methods are state-of-the-art ones.

Parallelization and GPU (Graphics Processing Unit): Another possibility to deal with the tradeoffs between time consumption and recognition rate is to distribute the computation cost. These kinds of techniques were investigated in past years by parallelizing the computation through several computers or processors. The availability of multi-core processors made these techniques possible in daily computers and even in notebooks. For example, the state of the Hidden Markov Models can be distributed among processors sharing memory [57], or using a master/slave technique with each processor possessing a copy of models [24]. Noda and al. [54] tried to break loop dependencies by using an iterative process on intermediate values but this method brings some approximation and thus an increasing recognition error rate. In [51], the authors proposed a method to parallelize both training and recognition steps of a ASR on several computers. They also introduced some load-balancing strategies to decrease the average time consuming of the recognition.

Besides this evolution of processor, the increasing performance and programmable capability of modern graphic cards shows a new and greater interest in using GPU to speed up the computation in the ASR.

Before focusing on the GPU capability, several authors started to work in developing specific ASR hardware platforms. For example, Lin and al [44] , [45] compared the software and hardware implementation of a 1000 words speech recognition system. They showed that the FPGA implementation is 7x faster than the software version and thus allows real-time recognition.

As the GPU is more dedicated to intense arithmetic operation, computation is more and more powerful. Researchers try to take advantage of this computation power at different level: features computation [8], likelihood computation [10], [19], [20], and decoding step [14].

Depending on the feasibility to parallelize these costly computation steps, the speed up gain is generally around 5x or more. These kinds of gain let us the possibility to realize a fast and accurate ASR system with a minimum of hard approximations.

5   Speech Synthesis

Recently, a new voice synthesis approach based on HMM has been proposed [66]. The main advantage of this method is that the synthesis process is possible especially with a small corpus and it is easier to vary voice characteristics such as speaking style, emotions, etc, than with usual systems based on selection and concatenation of acoustical units.

The parameterization of the acoustic signal is a source-filter model: Mel Frequency Cepstral Coefficients (MFCC) are used for the spectral representation of the signal, and the pitch for the source excitation. State duration densities are associated to each trained HMM phone in order to model the temporal structure of the speech.

According to an arbitrarily given text, a sequence of HMM is constructed by concatenating context dependent HMM. The state durations of the HMM are computed to maximize the output probability of the state durations. Then the corresponding MFCC and pitch sequence is generated and inverted to synthesize the output voice signal.

By manipulating the different parameters of the HMM sequence (pitch, spectrum, duration), it is directly possible to synthesize the same sentence but with different characteristics without needing to learn specific HMM models.

6   Voice Conversion

An interesting technique regarding voice processing is the automatic voice conversion. It can be included in the framework of a dialogue system in two ways:

- Personalization of the voice of the system,
- Personalization of the user voice in the context of a dialogue in a virtual world between avatars.

In the first case, the user may change the default voice to one more comfortable, for example male to female, or default voice to a well-known voice. For this kind of personalization, the solution can be to train HMM models on the target voice data or to use automatic voice conversion technique. In the second case, the point of view is different. The user wants to personalize his voice in the virtual world. As the user can pronounce any words, it is not possible to use a concatenated model for the transformation. Thus, one solution can be an automatic voice conversion method.

Voice conversion techniques are based on the learning of a conversion function between the two voices. Such a transformation should affect the signal at two levels: segmental and supra-segmental levels. At the segmental level, state of the art techniques usually try to apply a spectral transformation in order to make the signals corresponding to two different voices close enough under an acoustic criterion. A usual method is based on a GMM-joint conversion function [32]. To train this function, a parallel corpus of both voices saying the same text is necessary. After a time alignment of the corpus, both signals are decomposed in a sequence of aligned parameters vectors. To allow analysis and synthesis of both voice signals, a Harmonic plus Noise Model (HNM) is used.

Perrot [56] proposed another technique based on the cascading combination of a GMM based method and an automatic low bit rate coder/decoder system named ALISP [5,12]. ALISP was initially designed as a low bit rate coder/decoder system for voice. This system is based on the construction of a dictionary of acoustic units shared by both the sender and the receiver. The voice signal is analyzed with HNM modeling and the selection of the acoustical units is made through a HMM modeling and classification process. Then corresponding unit index in the dictionary are sent. According to this index sequence, the dictionary units are concatenated and the voice is synthesized.

The aim of the cascading method is to first apply a spectral conversion of the voice by the joint-GMM method then to analyze the converted sound with ALISP and synthesized with a dictionary of the target voice.

In order to overcome the constraint of having the same text pronounced by the same speakers, a new approach has been proposed in [33]. The idea is to estimate the transformation parameters so that the feature vectors of the source speaker become best modelled by the acoustic model, a GMM, of the target speaker.

Besides the segmental transformation, supra-segmental information must also be adjusted in order to have a precise voice transformation. Prosodic information of the target speaker may be extracted and used while synthesizing the transformed source speaker voice. Advanced models of the pitch and the excitation signals may be used [11]. [1] proposes the use of segmental analysis in order to perform voice conversion.

7   Spoken Language Understanding

Spoken language understanding (SLU) aims to interpret the meanings of users utterances to be able to respond to what users have said [30]. We distinguish three applicative frameworks: human-machine dialogue (form filling, call-routing, etc), data mining (speech archives, etc) and speech translation [4]. In the context of human-machine dialogue systems, SLU converts a sequence of words into a semantic representation that can be used by the dialogue manager.

7.1   Architecture

A classical architecture of a SLU system (Fig. 2) consists of a speech recognizer, a semantic parser, and a dialogue act decoder. The speech understanding module is the front end of the dialogue manager. Its role is to analyze the speech recognizer output and to produce a representation of its semantic content. The dialogue manager takes a decision including the context.

The acoustic signal A is first converted into a word sequence W by the speech recognizer. The word sequence is then mapped into a set of semantic concepts C by the semantic parser. The dialogue act decoder infers the user's intention G_u

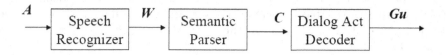

Fig. 2. The SLU system architecture

based on the semantic concepts and the current dialogue context. Finally, the deduced information may be passed to the dialogue manager to decide appropriate actions to take in response to the user's query. [30].

7.2 Approaches

Substantial research has been done in SLU. The techniques used were either:

- Based on knowledge: In this case hand crafted semantic rules are used to extract keywords or phrases to fill slots in semantic frames. The rules are improved progressively as new examples are collected. Some knowledge based SLU are the MIT's TINA [62], the CMU's PHOENIX [69] and the SRI's Gemini [21] [64].
- Data driven: This approach relies on stochastic models which are trained on annotated corpora. Examples of data driven SLU systems are the AT&T Markov model-based CHRONUS [41] and BBN's hierarchical Hidden Understanding Model (HUM) [49].

Both approaches have drawbacks. Therefore, recently mixed approaches have been proposed [30].

Linguistic approach: This approach is based on a syntactic and semantic analysis of the sentence. Among the first studies on language modeling, we count those that Chomsky [13][9] has conducted. He created formal grammars in order to characterize a language by a set of rules. Depending on their descriptive capacity, the grammars are commonly divided into four categories:

- regular grammars
- context-free grammars
- context-sensitive grammars
- un-restricted re-write systems

As spontaneous speech doesn't usually respect any grammar (because of the repetitions, the hesitations, the incomplete sentences..), some semantic and case grammars have been proposed [9]. For the same purpose, converting a syntactic analyser to a semantic one [62] has also been specified.

Stochastic approach: The use of stochastic techniques for SLU modeling offers an alternative to rule-based techniques by reducing the human expertise and development cost [42], [31], [59]. In this case, SLU can be viewed as a pattern recognition problem.

First, the speech recognizer recognizes the word sequence W from each input acoustic signal. Then the recognized word sequence W is mapped into a set of semantic concepts C. A concept is a class of words related to the same subject and having the same semantic properties.

$$C' = argmax P(C/W) \tag{1}$$

Using the Bayes rule, the comprehension problem can be resolved by the following equation :

$$C' = argmax P(W/C) P(C) \tag{2}$$

Here, we distinguish two terms:

- A lexical model represented by $P(W/C)$. It computes the probability of a sequence of words when concepts are known.
- A semantic model represented by $P(C)$ is the probability of a sequence of concepts.

Mixed approach: The linguistic approach relies on semantic grammar rules and requires manual processing. The knowledge based approach needs a fully annotated corpus in order to reliably estimate model parameters. Therefore Young et al [30] have proposed a hierarchical semantic parser that captures the embedded semantic structure in user utterances. It is trained using constrained Expectation-Maximization (EM) directly on annotated data.

7.3   Integration

The integration of the SLU system in a dialogue system can be performed in two manners [4]:

Sequential approach: each of the system components (ASR, SLU and the manager) performs separately. The ASR system produces the transcription (text), the SLU module processes this transcription and the manager exploits the SLU output.

It should be noted that this approach is suboptimal. In fact, the solution of each stage depends on the exact solution of the previous stage.

Integrated approach: In this integrated approach [4], it is possible to output a word lattice or N best word hypotheses instead of the single best hypothesis by the speech recognizer. The semantic parse results may then be incorporated with the output from the speech recognizer to rescore the N best list since it provides additional knowledge [30]. Similarly, it is possible to retain the N best parse results (or an interpretation lattice) from the semantic parser and leave the selection of the best hypothesis until the dialogue act decoding stage. In this case, the decision strategy will be based on multiple hypothesis outputs.

7.4   Evaluation

Metrics : The SLU specific evaluation metric is the Concept Error Rate (Eq. 3). The reference concepts are compared to the concepts found by the SLU system.

$$CER = \frac{(I + D + S)}{reference - concepts} \times 100 \qquad (3)$$

where I, D and S are insertions, deletions and substitutions respectively.

We notice that, the recognition errors are not taken into account. In fact, the concept detection can be useful even the majority of the keywords are recognized [9].

Other measures, employed in information retrieval domain, can also be used. The precision represents the correct concepts found by the system compared to all the concepts output by the SLU system.

$$Precision = \frac{(Correct - found - concepts)}{found - concepts} \times 100 \qquad (4)$$

The recall is the percentage of correct found concepts compared to the concepts to be found.

$$Recall = \frac{(Correct - found - concepts)}{concepts - to - be - found} \times 100 \qquad (5)$$

The F measure combines the precision and the recall in order to define the efficiency of the system:

$$F - mesure = \frac{2 \times Precison \times Recall}{Precision + Recall} \qquad (6)$$

Campaigns: Various projects have built the foundations of evaluation methodologies for spoken dialogue systems [7], such as the ATIS [47] and COMMUNICATOR [68] projects in the USA, and the European project DISC [22].

From 1990 to 1995, DARPA sponsored a spoken language understanding programme to measure the performance of various SLU systems. The utterance understanding error rates ranges from 6.5% to 44.9% for context independent utterances. More recently, the DARPA Communicator project [50] aims to support rapid, cost-effective development of multi-modal speech enabled dialogue systems [30].

In 2003, the French government sponsored the MEDIA project [48] in order to evaluate the understanding capabilities of dialogue systems. The evaluation methodology is based on test sets taken from a corpus of real world dialogs and common evaluation metrics. The understanding capacity of dialogue systems have been evaluated in both literal and contextual mode. The understanding error rate ranges from 29% to 41.3% [7].

8   Towards Multimodal Dialogue Systems

Although the development of speech recognition, this dialogue system module remains the main problem with the systems usability because of the occurring recognition errors. Nowadays, the accent is put on the use of more input channels toward multimodal dialogue system development. Gesture, facial expressions, pen-based, touch screen and keyboard inputs are used with speech to complement each other and create more natural and flexible dialogue with more transparency and using strengths of one mode to compensate for weaknesses of others.

When we use various modalities, it is important to think about how to coordinate or to merge the different inputs information. There are two solutions:

– Feature-level fusion: where the input modality features are first extracted and then merged. This method is especially used for synchronised modalities (speech, lip movements) [16] ,[37] . The disadvantage of this approach is that it requires a large amount of data for training and high computational costs.
– Semantic-level fusion: where recognizers from each single modality are used separately and as a consequence can be trained and integrated individually without training the whole data again. The simplicity is then the main advantage of this approach.

Multimodal dialogue state-of-the-art concerns some industrial or scientific projects, for example: TALK is an adaptive multimodal and multilingual human-computer dialogue system in-home and in-car; SmartKom [67] is one of the most advanced multimodal dialogue system employing mixed-initiative and an embodied conversational agent; ARCHIVUS [2] which allows access to multimedia database of recorded and annotated multimodal meetings; Galatea [34] which is an open-source toolkit for building anthropomorphic spoken dialogue agents; COMIC [25], CommRob, etc.

Our research about multimodal dialogue is related to MyBlog3D project (https://picoforge.int-evry.fr/cgi-bin/twiki/view/Myblog3d/Web/) which aims to foster mutual perception between Internet users who communicate and share objects within a 3D virtual space. The product developed by I-Maginer (http://www.i-maginer.fr) makes available to the general public a 3D environment where everyone can choose his avatar and develop his virtual space with a library of 3D objects. Since the user's perception through a virtual environment is limited, the animations of the avatars do not reflect exactly the user actions and emotions. MyBlog3D aims to strengthen the mutual perception of Internet communicators by real time vision and multimodal perception integrating the image and sound. To achieve the second objective, the project relies, firstly, on recent progress in spontaneous speech recognition with large vocabulary and constrained to real-time. Secondly, it requires a suitable dialogue management according to a defined task. The latter is chosen to be a job interview between an embodied conversational agent and a candidate who is the system user and is represented by his avatar. Moreover, the project uses two other research fields: face and gesture processing and embodied conversational agent. The face and gesture processing are related to the avatar animation which is driven by the user behaviour. This one is captured and detected by a webcam and then reproduced in real-time onto the avatar. On the other hand, the embodied conversational agent is controlled by the multimodal dialogue system. The project is in an early stage of development; the various modules work independently and are under validation before the integration step.

8.1   Wizard-of-Oz Experiments

A WoZ processing is a simulation of human-machine interaction during which the user is ignoring that some dialogue system functionalities are manually controlled by a human called the Wizard [17], [61], [58]. These experiments allow us to:

- Gather natural language corpus data to train and develop the dialogue systems.
- Assess the dialogue system performance in order to improve the initial dialogue modeling.

In MyBlog3D project we use a WoZ as a first dialogue model to especially collect a natural corpus dialogue database in order to improve real time speech recognition. The WoZ is designed using the Rapid Application Developer of the CSLU

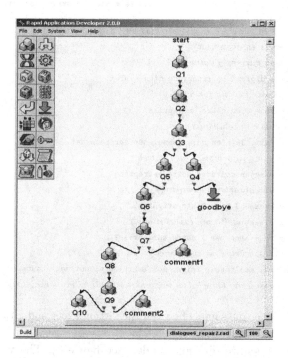

Fig. 3. WoZ system to simulate a job interview using RAD

Q1: Bonjour, Marie Jahhad du DRH, installez-vous!

  (*Hello, Marie Jahhad from HRD, have a seat please!*)

Q2: Je suis chargée de vous poser quelques questions pour le poste à pourvoir.

  (*I'm in charge of the interview for the position.*)

Q3: Avez-vous apportez un CV?

  (*Did you have a CV?*)

R1: oui, tout à fait.

  (*Yes, absolutely*)

Q4: Dites-moi, quel cursus avez-vous suivi?

  (*Tell me about your studies.*)

R2: J'ai au une licence en informatique, puis un DEA en télécommunications et ensuite un doctorat en traitement du signal et télécommunications.

  (*I have a BA degree in computer sciences, and a MS in Telecommunications and then a Ph.D. in signal processing and telecommunications*)

Q5: Pouvez-vous me décrire votre formation?

  (*tell me more about your training.*)

R3: J'ai suivi une formation à la fois théorique et pratique.

  (*My training has theoretical and practical aspects.*)

Q6: D'accord, et au niveau de la formation avec le recul, qu'est ce que vous en pensez ?

  (*Ok. With the experience that you have, what do you think of your training?*)

R4: Ma formation est très intéressante et polyvalente.
    elle m'ouvre des horizons à la fois dans le monde industriel que dans la recherche.

  (*My academic and professional background is very interesting and versatile. It gives me opportunities to get a job in industrie as well as in research.*)

Q7: Que faites-vous en ce moment?

  (*What are you currently doing?*)

R5: Je suis jeune diplomé en recherche d'un emploi.

  (*I am a graduate looking for a job.*)

Q8: Connaissez-vous bien notre entreprise?

  (*Do you know our company?*)

R6: Oui tout à fait. Je m'en suis renseignée sur internet.

  (*Yes. I got some information in the web.*)

Q9: Pourquoi avez-vous contacté notre entreprise?

  (*Why did you contact our company?*)

R6: Le poste correspond bien à mes attentes.

  (*The job corresponds to my expectations.*)

Q10: Que pensez-vous apporter à notre entreprise?

  (*What could you bring as experience to our company?*)

R7: Mon dynamisme, mon savoir faire, mon ambition seront mes atouts.

  (*My enthusiasm, my knowledge, my ambition will be my strengths.*)

Fig. 3. Dialogue sample between the virtual agent and a candidate

[65] using the finite-state dialogue model (see figure 3). The virtual conversational agent questions are pre-recorded which means that we use natural speech prompts with synchronized facial animation. At this stage of WoZ processing,

the speech recognition consists at recognizing words from a list of choices. The speech recognition system, constrained to real time and based on Julius is not yet integrated to the dialogue system.

In order to avoid finite state-based system limitations, we provide additional questions and transitions to cope with the range of possible user responses. We call this additional questions or comments *systems exceptions* triggered off according to user unforeseen response.

The figure 3 shows some dialogue sample according to the job interview application. User response are designed by means of keywords which if recognized will give rise to the next system action.

9   Conclusions and Perspectives

This paper gives a general overview on various aspects concerning the human-machine dialogue systems. The dialogue manager strategy adopted determines the degree of flexibility and fixes the requirements on the several technologies that are at stake. Since the interest in spoken dialogue systems is in growing with the spreading of virtual reality applications, to overcome the various limitations is as consequence a real challenge. Time-consuming, errors that are propagated between modules, unmatched training and testing condition environments, are the most encountered problems. The use of multimodality has greatly improved the performance and has offered more natural and flexible human-machine dialogue with more transparency. However it has elevated other kind of difficulties and challenge related to inputs information integration and synchronization between different modules.

Acknowledgment

This work is conducted within the ANR-MyBlog3D[1] project and the CompanionAble[2] Project.

References

1. Abe, M.: A segment-based approach to voice conversion, Acoustics, Speech, and Signal Processing. In: IEEE International Conference on ICASSP, pp. 765–768 (1991)
2. Ailomaa, M., Melichar, M., Rajman, M., Lisowska, A.: Archivus, a multimodal system for multimedia meeting browsing and retrieval. In: Proceedings of the COLING/ACL on Interactive presentation sessions, Morristown, NJ, USA, pp. 49–52 (2006)
3. Arnaldi, B., Fuchs, P., Tisseau, J.: Chapitre 1 du volume 1 du traité de la réalité virtuelle, Les presses de l'école de Mines de Paris (2003)
4. Béchet, F.: Processing spontaneous speech in deployed spoken language understanding systems: a survey, SLT (December 2008)

---

[1] https://picoforge.int-evry.fr/cgi-bin/twiki/view/Myblog3d/Web/
[2] http://www.companionable.net/

5. Bimbot, F., Chollet, G., Deleglise, P., Montacie, C.: Temporal decomposition and acoustic-phonetic decoding of speech. In: ICASSP, pp. 445–448 (1988)
6. Boda, P.P.: From stochastic speech recognition to understanding: an hmm based approach. In: Proc. IEEE ASRU, pp. 57–64 (1997)
7. Bonneau-Maynard, H., Ayache, C., Béchet, F., Denis, A., Kuhn, A., Lefevre1, F., Mostefa, D., Quignard, M., Rosset1, S., Servan, C., Villaneau, J.: Results of the french evalda-media evaluation campaign for literal understanding. In: Proceedings of the 5th international Conference on Language Resources and Evaluation (LREC), Genoa, Italy, pp. 2054–2059 (2002)
8. Bremer, D., Johnson, J., Jones, H., Liu, Y., May, D., Meredith, J., Veydia, S.: Application kernels on graphics processing units. In: Workshop on High Performance Embedded Computing (2005)
9. Camelin, N.: Stratégies robustes de compréhension de la parole basées sur des méthodes de classification automatique, Ph.D thesis, Université d'avignon (2007)
10. Cardinal, P., Dumouchel, P., Boulianne, G., Comeau, M.: Gpu accelerated acoustic likelihood computations. In: InterSpeech (2008)
11. Childers, D.G.: Glottal source modeling for voice conversion. Speech Communication, 127–138 (1995)
12. Chollet, G., Cernocký, J., Constantinescu, A., Deligne, S., Bimbot, F.: Toward alisp: Automatic language independent speech processing. Springer, Heidelberg (1998)
13. Chomsky, N.: Syntactic structures. Mouton, The Hague (1957)
14. Chong, J., Yi, Y., Faria, A., Satish, N., Keutzer, K.: Data-parallel large vocabulary continuous speech recognition on graphics processors, Technical report, University of California at Berkeley (2008)
15. Chu, S., Neill, I., Hanna, P., McTear, M.: An approach to multi-strategy dialogue management. In: INTERSPEECH, pp. 865–868 (2005)
16. Corradini, A., Mehta, M., Bernsen, N.O., Martin, J., Abrilian, S.: Multimodal input fusion in human-computer interactio. In: Proceedings of the NATO ASI 2003 Conference, NAREK center of Yerevan University, Tsakhkadzor, Armenia (2003)
17. Dahlback, N., Jönsson, A., Ahrenberg, L.: Wizard of oz studies: why and how. Knowl.-Based Syst., 258–266 (1993)
18. Damasio, A.R.: Descartes' error: emotion, reason, and the human brain. Grosset/Putnam, New York (1994)
19. Dixon, P.R., Caseiro, D.A., Oonishi, T., Furui, S.: The titech large vocabulary wfst speech recognition system. In: ASRU, pp. 443–448 (2007)
20. Dixon, P.R., Oonishi, T., Furui, S.: Harnessing graphics processors for the fast computation of acoustic likelihoods in speech recognition. Comp. Speech and Language 23, 510–526 (2009)
21. Dowding, J., Moore, R., Andry, F., Moran, D.: Interleaving syntax and semantics in an efficient bottom-up parser. In: 32nd Annual Meeting of the Association for Computational Linguistics, New Maxico (June 1994)
22. Dybkjaer, L., Bernsen, N.O.: The disc approach to spoken language system development and evaluation. In: LREC (1998)
23. Fang, X.W., Zheng, F., Xu, M.: Topic forest: A plan-based dialog management structure. In: Proceedings of ICASSP 2001, Salt Lake City (2001)
24. Fleury, M., Downton, A.C., Clark, A.F.: Parallel structure in an integrated speech-recognition network. In: Amestoy, P.R., Berger, P., Daydé, M., Duff, I.S., Fraysse, V., Giraud, L., Ruiz, D. (eds.) Euro-Par 1999. LNCS, vol. 1685, pp. 995–1004. Springer, Heidelberg (1999)

25. Foster, M.E., White, M., Setzer, A., Catizone, R.: Multimodal generation in the comic dialogue system. In: ACL 2005: Proceedings of the ACL 2005 on Interactive poster and demonstration sessions, pp. 45–48 (2005)
26. Fuchs, P., Nashashibi, F., Lourdeaux, D.: A theoretical approach of the design and evaluation of a virtual reality device. In: Virtual reality and prototyping, Laval, France, pp. 11–20 (1999)
27. Goddeau, D., Meng, H., Polifroni, J., Seneff, S., Busayapongchaiy, S.: A form-based dialogue manager for spoken language applications. In: Proc. ICSLP, pp. 701–704 (1996)
28. Gorniak, P., Roy, D.: Situated language understanding as filtering perceived affordances. Cognitive Science, 197–231 (2007)
29. Guedj, R.: Human-machine interaction and digital signal processing. In: IEEE International Conference on Acoustics, Speech, and Signal Processing, ICASSP, vol. 7, pp. 17–19 (1982)
30. He, Y., Young, S.: A data driven spoken language understanding system. In: IEEE Automatic Speech Recognition and Understanding Workshop, St. Thomas, U.S. Virgin Islands (December 2003)
31. He, Y., Young, S.: Hidden vector state hierarchical semantic parsing. In: IEEE ICASSP, Hong Kong, pp. 555–558 (2003)
32. Kain, A., Maccon, M.W.: Spectral voice conversion for text to speech synthesis. In: ICASSP, pp. 285–288 (1998)
33. Karam, W., Bredin, H., Greige, H., Chollet, G., Mokbel, C.: Talking-face identity verification, audiovisual forgery and robustness issues. EURASIP Journal on Advances in Signal Processing, Special Issue on Recent Advances in Biometric Systems: A Signal Processing Perspective (2009)
34. Kawamoto, S., Shimodaira, H., Nitta, T., Nishimoto, T., Nakamura, S., Itou, K., Morishima, S., Yotsukura, T., Kai, A., Lee, A., Yamashita, Y., Kobayashi, T., Tokuda, K., Hirose, K., Minematsu, N., Yamada, A., Den, Y., Utsuro, T., Sagayama, S.: Glatea: Open-source software for developing anthropomorphic spoken dialog agents incorporating voice dialogs in a multi-user virtual environment. In: Prendinger, H., Ishizuka, M. (eds.) Life-Like Characters, pp. 187–212. Springer, Berlin (2004)
35. Kim, K., Lee, C., Jung, S., Lee, G.G.: A frame-based probabilistic framework for spoken dialog management using dialog examples. In: Proceedings of the 9th SIGdial Workshop on Discourse and Dialogue, pp. 120–127 (2008)
36. Lamere, P., et al.: Design of the cmu sphinx-4 decoder. In: Proc. EUROSPEECH, pp. 1181–1184 (2003)
37. Landragin, F.: Physical, semantic and pragmatic levels for multimodal fusion and fission. In: Proceedings of the Seventh International Workshop on Computational Semantics (IWCS 2007), pp. 346–350. Universitätsverlag Tilburg (January 2007)
38. Lane, I., Ueno, S., Kawahara, T.: Cooperative dialogue planning with user and situation models via example-based training. In: Proc. Workshop on Man-Machine Symbiotic Systems, Kyoto, Japan, pp. 93–102 (2004)
39. Lee, A., Kawahara, T., Shikano, K.: Julius - an open source real-time large vocabulary recognition engine. In: Proc. EUROSPEECH, Aalborg, pp. 1691–1694 (2001)
40. Lee, C., Jung, S., Kim, S., Lee, G.G.: Example-based dialog modeling for practical multi-domain dialog system. Speech Commun. 51(5), 466–484 (2009)
41. Levin, E., Pieraccini, R.: CHRONUS, the next generation. In: DARPA Speech and Natural Language Workshop, January 1995, pp. 269–271 (1995)

42. Levin, E., Pieraccini, R.: Concept-based spontaneous speech understanding system. In: Eurospeech, pp. 555–558 (1995)
43. Levin, E., Pieraccini, R., Eckert, W.: Learning dialogue strategies within the markov decision process framework. In: Proc. IEEE ASRU, pp. 72–79 (1997)
44. Lin, E., Yu, K., Rutenbar, R.A., Chen, T.: Moving speech recognition from software to silicon: the in silico vox project. In: Interspeech (2006)
45. Lin, E., Yu, K., Rutenbar, R.A., Chen, T.: A 1000-word vocabulary, speaker independent, continuous live-mode speech recognizer implemented in a single fpga. In: Int. Symposium on Field-Programmable Gate Arrays, FPGA (2007)
46. Litman, D.J., Allen, J.F.: A plan recognition model for subdialogues in conversations. Cognitive Science 11(2), 163–200 (1987)
47. Madcow: Multi-site data collection for a spoken language corpus. In: DARPA Speech and Natural Language Workshop (1992)
48. Maynard, H., McTait, K., Mostefa, D., Devillers, L., Rosset, S., Paroubek, P., Bousquet, C., Choukri, K., Goulian, J., Antoine, J.-Y., Béchet, F., Bontron, O., Charnay, L., Romary, L., Vergnes, M.: Constitution d'un corpus de dialogue oral pour l'évaluation automatique de la compréhension hors et en contexte du dialogue. In: JEP (2004)
49. Miller, S., Bates, M., Bobrow, R., Ingria, R., Makhoul, J., Schwartz, R.: Recent progress in hidden understanding models. In: DARPA Speech and Natural Language Workshop, Austin, January 1995, pp. 276–280. Morgan Kaufman, San Francisco (1995)
50. MITRE, ARPA communicator homepage (2003)
51. Mohamed El Hadj, Y.O., Revol, N., Meziane, A.: Parallelization of automatic speech recognition, Research report 4110, INRIA (2001)
52. De Mori, R.: Spoken dialogues with computers. Academic Press, London (1998)
53. Nguyen, A., Wayne, W.: An agent-based approach to dialogue management in personal assistants. In: IUI 2005: Intelligent User Interfaces, pp. 137–144 (2005)
54. Noda, H., Shirazi, M.N., Zhang, B.: A parallel processing algorithm for speech recognition using markov random fields. Communication Research Laboratory 41(2), 87–100 (1994)
55. Orkin, J., Roy, D.: The restaurant game: Learning social behavior and language from thousands of players online. Journal of Game Development, 39–60 (December 2007)
56. Perrot, P., Morel, M., Razik, J., Chollet, G.: Vocal forgery in forensic sciences. In: International Conference on Forensic Applications and Techniques in Telecommunications. Information and Multimedia, e-Forensics 2009, 7p. (2009)
57. Phillips, S., Rogers, A.: Parallel speech recognition. In: InterSpeech 1997, pp. 135–138 (1997)
58. Rajman, M., Ailomaa, M., Lisowska, A., Melichar, M., Armstrong, S.: Extending the wizard of oz methodology for language-enabled multimodal systems. In: Proceedings of the 5th International Conference on Language Resources and Evaluation (LREC), Genoa, Italy, May 22-28, pp. 2539–2543 (2006)
59. Raymond, C., Bechet, F., Camelin, N., de Mori, R., Damnati, G.: Semantic interpretation with error correction. In: IEEE ICASSP, Montreal (2005)
60. Lee, C., Lee, S., Lee, G.: Example-based dialog modeling for english conversation tutoring. In: Proceedings of the 2nd International Conference on Next Generation Computing (2007)
61. Salber, D., Coutaz, J.: Applying the wizard of oz technique to the study of multimodal systems. In: Human-Computer Interaction Selected Papers. LNCS, pp. 219–230. Springer, Heidelberg (1993)

62. Seneff, S.: Robust parsing for spoken language systems. In: IEEE International Confrence on Acoustics, Speech and Signal Processing, San Francisco (1992)

63. Singh, S., Kearns, M., Litman, D., Walker, M.: Reinforcement learning for spoken dialogue systems. In: Proc. NIPS (1999)

64. Stallard, D.: Evaluation results for the talk'n'travel system. In: Human Language Technology Conference, San Diego, California (Mars 2001)

65. Sutton, S., et al.: Universal speech tools: The cslu toolkit. In: Proceedings of the International Conference on Spoken Language Processing (ICSLP), pp. 3221–3224 (1998)

66. Tokuda, K., Zen, H., Black, A.W.: An hmm-based speech synthesis system applied to english. In: Proceedings of IEEE Speech Synthesis Workshop, pp. 227–230 (2002)

67. Wahlster, W., Reithinger, N., Blocher, A.: Smartkom: Towards multimodal dialogues with anthropomorphic interface agents. In: MTI Status Conference, Saarbrücken, Germany, October 26-27 (2001)

68. Walker, M., Passonneau, R., Boland, J.: Quantitative and qualitative evaluation of darpa communicator spoken dialog systems. In: ACL/EACL Workshop (2002)

69. Ward, W., Issar, S.: Recent improvements in the CMU spoken language understanding system. In: ARPA Human Language Technology Workshop, pp. 213–216. Morgan Kaufman, San Francisco (1996)

70. Williams, J.D., Young., S.J.: Partially observable markov decision process for spoken dialog systems. Computer Speech and Language 21, 231–422 (2007)

71. Young, S.: The htk hidden markov model toolkit: Design and philosophy, Technical report, Cambridge University Engineering Department, UK (1994)

72. Zeigler, B., Mazor, B.: Dialog design for a speech-interactive automation system. In: Proc. EUROSPEECH 1995, Madrid, Spain, pp. 113–116 (1995)

Author Index

Albornoz, Enrique M.   242
Amehraye, Asmaa   423
Atassi, Hicham   255

Bauer, Dominik   346
Beskow, Jonas   157
Bevacqua, Elisabetta   113
Birkholz, Peter   337

Cambria, Erik   148
Cao, Yujia   134
Čereković, Aleksandra   80
Cerva, Petr   225
Chollet, Gérard   423

Delić, Vlado   354
Demeter, Peter   113

Eckl, Chris   148
Edlund, Jens   157
Esposito, Anna   255, 406

Fàbregas, Joan   197
Fagel, Sascha   294
Faundez-Zanuy, Marcos   197
Ferrer-Ballester, Miguel Ángel   197

Garrido, Javier   197
Gaussier, Philippe   50
Gonzalez de Rivera, Guillermo   197
Granström, Björn   157
Grinberg, Maurice   122
Gustafson, Joakim   157

Hakulinen, Jaakko   66
Hansen, Mervi   66
Havasi, Catherine   148
Heimonen, Tomi   66
Hella, Juho   66
Heylen, Dirk   92
Hoffmann, Rüdiger   337
Hoole, Phil   346
House, David   157
Hussain, Amir   148, 255

Jokinen, Kristiina   33
Juhár, Jozef   113

Kane, Bridget   314
Kannampuzha, Jim   346
Kendon, Adam   1
Khemiri, Houssemeddine   423
Kiryazov, Kiril   122
Koutsombogera, Maria   327
Kröger, Bernd J.   337, 346

Laivo, Tuuli   66
Laukkanen, Anne-Maria   286
Luz, Saturnino   314

Mäkinen, Erno   66
Maskeliunas, Rytis   217
Mata, Ana Isabel   382
Melto, Aleksi   66
Meng, Helen   337
Miettinen, Toni   66
Milone, Diego H.   242
Mokbel, Chafic   423
Moniz, Helena   382
Morales, Aythami   197
Murphy, Peter J.   286

Nagy, Katalin   397
Neubarth, Friedrich   207
Niculescu, Andreea   134
Nijholt, Anton   134
Nouza, Jan   225

Ondáš, Stanislav   113
Ortega-Garcia, Javier   197

Pakarinen, Santtu   66
Pandžić, Igor S.   80
Papageorgiou, Harris   327
Pejša, Tomislav   80
Prepin, Ken   50
Přibil, Jiří   268
Přibilová, Anna   268
Pucher, Michael   207

Raine, Roxanne B.   102
Raisamo, Roope   66
Rajaniemi, Juha-Pekka   66

Ramseyer, Fabian   182
Rantala, Jussi   66
Razik, Joseph   423
Riviello, Maria Teresa   255, 406
Rudzionis, Algimantas   217
Rudzionis, Vytautas   217
Rufiner, Hugo L.   242, 364

Schlotthauer, Gastón   364
Silovsky, Jan   225
Skowron, Marcin   169
Smékal, Zdeněk   255
Soronen, Hannu   66
Strom, Volker   207
Su, Jing   314
Sztaho, David   397

ter Maat, Mark   92
Torres, María E.   364
Trancoso, Isabel   382
Trojano, Luigi   304
Tschacher, Wolfgang   182
Turunen, Markku   66

Valkama, Pellervo   66
Vích, Robert   280
Vicsi, Klara   397
Vogel, Carl   16
Vondra, Martin   280
Vujnović Sedlar, Nataša   354

Zdansky, Jindrich   225
Zouari, Leila   423